MUD GAME PROGRAMMING

Ron Penton

PREMIER PRESS

GAME DEVELOPMENT

Premier

Press

SVP, Professional, Trade, Reference Group: Andy Shafran
Publisher: Stacy L. Hiquet
Senior Marketing Manager: Sarah O'Donnell
Marketing Manager: Heather Hurley
Manager of Editorial Services: Heather Talbot
Senior Acquisitions Editor: Emi Smith
Associate Marketing Manager: Kristin Eisenzopf
Project Editor: Betsey Henkels
Technical Reviewer: André LaMothe
Retail Market Coordinator: Sarah Dubois
Interior Layout: Danielle Foster
Cover Designer: Mike Tanamachi
CD-ROM Producer: Brandon Penticuff
Indexer: Kelly Talbot
Proofreader: Karen Gill

ISBN: 1-59200-090-8
Library of Congress Catalog Card Number: 2003094424
Printed in the United States of America
04 05 06 07 08 BH 10 9 8 7 6 5 4 3 2 1

Premier Press, a division of Course Technology
25 Thomson Place
Boston, MA 02210

For all of my friends.

Acknowledgments

I would first like to thank my family for putting up with me for the past few months... again. It's been an ordeal, but it was certainly worth it!

I would like to thank all of my friends for their encouragement and friendship, especially Jim, James, Dan, Scott, Andrew, Tracy, Jenny, Josephina, Brett, Kevin, Brian, Kristy, and Marla.

I would like to thank everyone at work for supporting me through this endeavor, and putting up with me being half asleep most of the time (and sometimes fully asleep!).

I want to thank the pioneers of Gamedev.net, Kevin Hawkins and Dave Astle, for paving the road for me and making a book such as this possible.

I would like to thank all of you in the #gamedev crew, specifically (in no particular order) Trent Polack, Evan Pipho, April Gould, Joseph Fernald, Andrew Vehlies, Andrew Nguyen, John Hattan, Ken Kinnison, Seth Robinson, Ernest Pazera, Denis Lukianov, Sean Kent, Nicholas Cooper, Ian Overgard, Greg Rosenblatt, Yannick Loitière, Henrik Stuart, Chris Hargrove, Richard Benson, Mat Noguchi, Richard Fine, Anthony Casteel, and everyone else!

I would like to thank the people of the non-existent *Tiberian Adventure* as well, for providing one of the most entertaining (yet non-existent) MUDs in the world. If you don't get this, then chances are you shouldn't be getting it!

And finally I would like to thank the crew of the old Buffalo DoomBBS for opening the door to MUDs for me. You know who you are!

About the Author

It has always been the lifelong dream of **Ron Penton** to be a game programmer. From the age of 11, when his parents bought him his first game programming book on how to make adventure games, he has always striven to learn as much as possible about how games work and how to create them.

MUDs have also been a particular fascination of his, ever since his favorite BBS installed *Swords Of Chaos* and *MajorMUD* in the early 1990s—games that wasted a good deal of his high school days.

Ron has a bachelor's degree in computer science and a minor in mathematics from the State University of New York at Buffalo, and has written one other book, *Data Structures for Game Programmers,* and has contributed to Bruno Sousa's book *Game Programming All in One.*

Contents at a Glance

Part Three
Creating a BetterMUD 355

Contents

Chapter 2
Winsock/Berkeley Sockets Programming 27

Chapter 3
Introduction to Multithreading........................ 71

Chapter 4
The Basic Library 101

Chapter 5
The Socket Library 127

Chapter 6
Telnet Protocol and a
Simple Chat Server 163

Part Two
Creating a SimpleMUD 189

Chapter 7
Designing the SimpleMUD 191

Chapter 8
Items and Players 211

Chapter 9
Maps, Stores, and Training Rooms 297

Chapter 10
Enemies, Combat, and the Game Loop 327

Part Three
Creating a BetterMUD 355

Chapter 11
The BetterMUD 357

Chapter 12
Entities, Accessors, and Databases 375

Chapter 13
Entities and Databases Continued 401

Chapter 18
Making the Game 577

Conclusion 633

LETTER FROM THE SERIES EDITOR

Welcome to *MUD Game Programming*—the first comprehensive book on the art of developing text-only Multi-User Dungeon games. Although everywhere you look you see the latest 3D rendering and graphical simulations, MUDs and text-only games are still going strong and indeed are experiencing a retro-resurgence with more and more developers creating games of this nature. There are a number of reasons for this. First, anyone with a terminal and Telnet can play these games, so that's always cool. But more importantly I think, game developers all over the world have a strong desire to learn network-programming skills, and MUDs are a great place to start. Unlike their real-time big brother with complex predictive algorithms, compression schemes, and mind numbing optimizations, MUDs don't take much in the way of network mastery. If you can send packets with sockets or Dplay, you are over-qualified.

With that in mind, the author, Ron Penton, has created the quintessential book on MUD game programming. He starts with network basics, teaching you everything you need to know to create a socket class on a Windows- or UNIX-based machine along with creating C++ classes to wrap all the details of making connections and transmitting data. Then based on this communication class, he builds a MUD, aptly named "SimpleMUD," to illustrate each concept of MUD programming until you have attacked each problem that arises when developing such games. By the end of the book you have a complete, fairly robust MUD called "BetterMUD" that contains all the major features of a contemporary MUD game. In fact, it's probably better than most and with a little work can be the starting point for a professional MUD, if you want to go that route.

In conclusion, if you missed the 70s and 80s, but are fascinated with Dungeons and Dragons, MUDs, and using your imagination rather than an nVidia accelerator, *MUD Game Programming* is definitely for you. Even if you never see yourself making a MUD, I still highly recommend this book to *everyone* in the game biz. It should be required reading for those interested in game-related topics such as large-scale network programming, database management, and synchronization techniques. Good luck, and when exploring your favorite MUD, do what I do when you see someone in the room:

ATTACK, ATTACK, ATTACK, RUN.

Sincerely,

André LaMothe
Premier Press *Game Development* Series Editor

Introduction

I f you've opened this book, you must already have some idea of what a MUD is and why you would program one, but I'll give you my ideas on MUDs anyway.

What the heck are MUDs? Any game programmer who's lived within the past 20 years should be familiar with them. You probably think of MUDs as text-based hack-and-slash games, in which you run around killing as many people as you can.

In a way, that's correct—but MUDs don't have to be limited to hack-and-slash. Some MUDs are communities of people who gather in their virtual worlds just to communicate with each other. MUDs don't have to be text-based either. In fact, almost all virtual-world style games have similar structures under the hood. It's really not all that difficult to adapt a graphical client program to interpret what is happening in the MUD.

History

In the very beginning of text adventure games, there were three games you've probably heard of: *Zork*, *Advent*, and *Dungen*. The last two have funny names because they were developed on old Digital Equipment Corporation (DEC) computers that only supported files with six characters in their names. *Advent* was really short for *Adventure*, and *Dungen* was short for *Dungeon*.

When Roy Trubshaw started working on making a multi-player game, he used the game *Dungen* as an inspiration, and ended up calling it, *Multi-User Dungeon*, or *MUD* for short.

So the fact that games in this genre are called *Multi-User Dungeons* is just an historical accident; the name of the original game became the name of the entire genre!

Nowadays, some people refer to MUDs as *Multi-User Dimensions*, but not too many people really care about what MUD stands for.

To make things more complicated, various derivatives of the original MUD have also used acronyms for their names, such as MOO, *MUD*, *Object Oriented*, MUSH, and *Multi-User Shared Hallucination*. These terms have also come into the common vocabulary of MUD-like games, as well as a few oddball terms that don't even have meanings, such as *MUCK* and *MUX*.

You may come across people who vehemently argue that there are fundamental differences between all the genres, but quite honestly it really doesn't matter. MUD-like games have become complex since the early days, and more often than not share many of the same features of the original games in all those genres, so there's little point in differentiating them. It's not uncommon for people to refer to all MUD-like games as *MU**s. Here the term *MU**s means all multiuser games. The asterisk symbol (*) is a computer symbol that means "any string of characters", which is a reference to regular expressions, but that's a complicated topic in computer science, so don't worry about it.

To sum up, most people call the games MUDs.

MUD Design

Aside from all the communications work, there are generally three parts to a MUD game engine. Some people say two and some say four, but I've found that the three-part system makes the most sense.

The *physical level* of a MUD is the level of the game that controls the physical aspects, such as the existence and movement of items, characters, rooms, and so on. Basically, anything that can be represented as a physical object is defined at the physical layer of the MUD. Objects defined at this level are typically referred to as *entities*.

The *logical level* of a MUD controls what happens to the physical level. Characters need to make decisions, items perform tasks when acted upon, and so forth. This is the part of the MUD that controls what a character does when attacked, or when given an item, for example.

The *data level* of a MUD is closely related to the physical level. This is the level of the MUD that *defines* all the physical entities in the game (as opposed to the physical level, which merely controls them). For example, whenever you load up a map into the physical layer, the map is loaded from the data layer.

Different MUDs implement these layers in different ways. In the very first MUDs, way back in the bad old days when every computer language was a *compiled language*, all these layers were stored in the MUD code itself. Everything (and I mean *everything*) was inside of the compiled code, and you couldn't change anything until you went into the code, modified it, recompiled, restarted the MUD, and then re-ran it.

Obviously having such interruptions is bothersome to the players of your MUD. There's not much sense in having a simulation of a world that needs to be shut down all the time. After all, the real world doesn't shut down (at least you had better hope not... makes you wonder what happens when you sleep...).

The first layer that was promoted to the idea of being *flexible* was the data layer. Why the heck should you put your game data inside the actual code? Isn't it a better idea to separate out that data and put it into a file, and then when the MUD runs, you can load that data from the file, or reload the data when it changes? The idea of coding data right into your game is so ancient that I honestly can't remember if I've ever seen a MUD-like game that does that.

Then came the idea that you could have a flexible logic system. Most MUDs today don't have a flexible logic system, but they're gaining popularity quickly. The basic idea is to separate out what controls objects into a scripting language, such as Python, LUA, or even something like LISP.

Of course, you could take this idea even further and create the physical level of the MUD in a flexible *interpreted language,* which would allow you to make a flexible world with new types of entities that could be added any time you wanted. This is the least common kind of MUD. Almost always, the need for a flexible physical layer just doesn't exist. Once you've got all the basic entities sorted out, you almost never need new kinds.

There are a few MUDs out there that implement this level in a flexible manner, however. Most people consider them to be MOOs or MUSHs, but as I said earlier, that really doesn't matter much.

The SimpleMUD

In this book, I'm going to take you through the construction of two MUDs—the first is called the *SimpleMUD*. This is a very simple MUD (the name doesn't lie!), but it's a good start for understanding how you can combine a simple data system with a networking reaction system. In the SimpleMUD, I use C++ exclusively to code the physical and logical aspects of the game, and simple ASCII data files to store the data level of the game.

The source for this MUD can be found on the CD in the directory /SimpleMUD, and sections of it are presented in the Demos for Chapters 8, 9 and 10. If you're interested in jumping in right away and know what a Telnet client is and how to use it, take a look at the version running on my Linux shell at telnet://dune.net:5100. It's likely to be deserted however, since there's not much you can do in that MUD. Everyone will probably be more interested in the second MUD.

BetterMUD

The BetterMUD is much more complicated and builds on the concepts learned in the SimpleMUD. It implements a flexible logic layer using the Python scripting language. If you don't know any Python, don't worry. Not only is the language very easy to pick up, but I have a whole chapter dedicated to teaching it to you (Chapter 17).

The BetterMUD version on the CD is actually very sparse, and doesn't do much "out of the box." This is because the BetterMUD is a very flexible MUD engine that supports reloadable logic. You can essentially change how the entire game functions while it is running, and because of this I don't want to force you into any single type of game. In the SimpleMUD I force you to use a specific economy, a specific battle system, and so on, but those aspects of the BetterMUD are completely flexible. For example, if you don't like the classic time-based style, you may decide to implement some sort of turn-based combat system; and that's just one example of what can be accomplished.

I'll have my own personal version of BetterMUD running on my Linux shell as well: telnet://dune.net:5110. Feel free to drop in.

All the scripts I add on to my own version will be freely available to download from my website, http://ronpenton.net/MUDBook/. If, for some unforeseen reason, I don't have my MUDs running at Dune.net anymore when you read this, be sure to check my website for information on where I've moved them.

Expectations

There are a few things you should know to comprehend this book. First of all, a basic knowledge of C++ is required, as well as knowing how to work with STL (especially the concepts of iterators and functors).

Templates are also used in a few places, so you should know about those as well. All the code in this book compiles under at least three compilers that I know of:

- Microsoft Visual C++ 6.0
- Microsoft Visual C++ 7.0
- GCC 2.95 and above

I don't have access to MSVC7.1, but theoretically the code should work with it as well. Appendix A contains the information on how to set up the compilers for the projects and demos.

Everything else, such as networking and threading, you learn within Part One of the book.

Book Layout

This book contains four major sections:

- Part One—The Basics
- Part Two—Creating a SimpleMUD
- Part Three—Creating a BetterMUD
- Appendixes (on the CD)

Part One—The Basics

The six chapters in the first part of the book deal with all the topics you need to understand to program the two MUDs in the book.

Chapter 1—Introduction to Network Programming

This chapter teaches you most of what you need to know about computer networks, how they work, and how they are used.

Chapter 2—Winsock/Berkeley Sockets Programming

This chapter covers the Winsock/Berkeley Sockets API, which is the defacto standard when programming network applications in C++. It's a relatively old API, however, and you may find yourself annoyed at how many simple little tasks require lots of code. That's why Chapter 5 exists.

Chapter 3—Introduction to Multithreading

Multithreading is a very important part of network programming, since you can never be sure when networks are going to work reliably.

Chapter 4—The Basic Library

This chapter shows you all the classes and functions that are within the BasicLib library that I made for the book.

Chapter 5—The Socket Library

Because programming in the original Sockets API is incredibly frustrating, I decided to make your life easier and create a socket library that wraps up most of the functionality into simple-to-use classes. The SocketLib uses the TCP Internet protocol exclusively, but that's fine, since MUDs almost always use TCP anyway.

Chapter 6—Telnet Protocol and a Simple Chat Server

This chapter teaches you about the Telnet protocol, which is the most often used in MUDs, as well as how to create a simple Telnet-based chat server using the SocketLib from Chapter 5.

Part Two—Creating a SimpleMUD

These four chapters explore the creation of the SimpleMUD in detail.

Chapter 7—Designing the SimpleMUD

This chapter takes you through all the design issues of SimpleMUD, showing you what the MUD can and cannot do.

Chapter 8—Items and Players

This chapter steps you through the creation of the basic physics layer as well as some logic layer stuff, mostly dealing with the item and player entity types. This chapter also goes over the creation of the basic networking module for the SimpleMUD built on top of the SocketLib.

Chapter 9—Maps, Stores, and Training Rooms

This chapter builds on what you learned in Chapter 8, adding a map system to the SimpleMUD, as well as the special room types that represent stores and training rooms.

Chapter 10—Enemies, Combat, and the Game Loop

This final SimpleMUD chapter and ties everything up into a full game. Enemies are added to the game, as well as combat, and the game loop which takes care of all timed events in the game.

Part Three—Creating a BetterMUD

This part of the book describes the creation of the BetterMUD, an extremely flexible MUD that is built around a flexible logic level built in Python.

Chapter 11—The BetterMUD

This chapter covers all the design issues related to the BetterMUD.

Chapter 12—Entities, Accessors, and Databases

This chapter goes over all the base entity classes, the concept of database accessors, and the base database classes as well. None of the classes discussed in this chapter are classes that can be instantiated, but rather base classes that will be used to build the final entity and database classes in the next chapter.

Chapter 13—Entities and Databases Continued

This chapter builds on what you learned from the previous chapter, to create the final entity and database classes that will be used within the game.

Chapter 14—Scripts, Actions, Logic, and Commands

This chapter goes over all the flexible concepts in BetterMUD. Everything discussed in this chapter provides the foundation for the flexible logic system, which is the main feature of BetterMUD.

Chapter 15—Game Logic

This chapter describes the physical engine of the BetterMUD, which includes entity management and the timer system.

Chapter 16—The Networking System

This is a relatively short chapter that describes the networking system of the BetterMUD. I don't spend much time on this chapter because there have already been five chapters in this book dealing with network programming, so most of this part of the BetterMUD is just replicating what you've seen before.

Chapter 17—Python

This chapter is an introduction to the Python programming language and describes how to integrate the Python interpreter into your game.

Chapter 18—Making the Game

This is the final chapter dealing with the BetterMUD, and it focuses mainly on making Python scripts used to mold the BetterMUD's logic system into something that resembles a game. I go over the main concepts of creating Python command objects and logic scripts to control item management, encumbrance, simple spells, arming weapons, initialization scripts, currency, merchants, and finally simple time-based combat.

Appendixes

The appendixes contain all the auxiliary information you might need to know. They are on the CD but not printed in the book.

Appendix A—Setting Up Your Compilers

Setting up the compilers for the code in the book was a difficult task for me, since I had to make sure the code ran on three different compilers at the same time. Because of the complexity of this task, compilation information and instructions are gathered into this appendix instead of being covered in separate chapters.

Appendix B—Socket Error Codes

There are so many things that can go wrong when you're dealing with socket programming, and there are a ton of error codes detailing what went wrong. This appendix lists all the common error codes and what they mean in plain English.

Appendix C—C++ Primer

C++ and STL are requirements for this book, but no one can possibly be required to remember every little quirk and detail about them. Because of this, I've included this simple primer that enables you to refresh your memory on the features you may have forgotten.

Appendix D—Template Primer

This is a bonus chapter from my Data Structures book on how to use templates.

Glossary

This is a glossary of all the fancy terms and acronyms used throughout the book.

Let's Get Ready to Rumble

This book focuses mainly on *how* to implement a MUD, but not so much on the various gameplay issues that will confront you. The basic reason behind this is that people don't like to be told how they should make their gameplay work. The great thing about MUDs is that no two MUDs are the same—every single one is customized to the likings of the person running it.

Because of this, I don't really want to tell you what kind of features and issues you need to have in your game. Chances are you already know what you want, and it's probably not what I have in mind.

Don't forget to drop me a line at MUDBook@ronpenton.net if you have any questions about the book. I'll try to respond to your mail as soon as possible.

With this in mind, you can start *MUD Game Programming*! Enjoy!

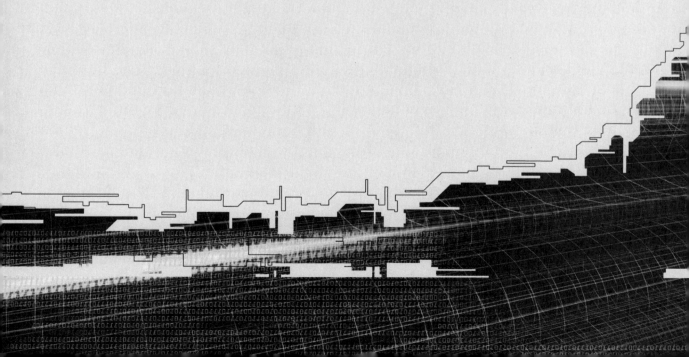

PART ONE

The Basics

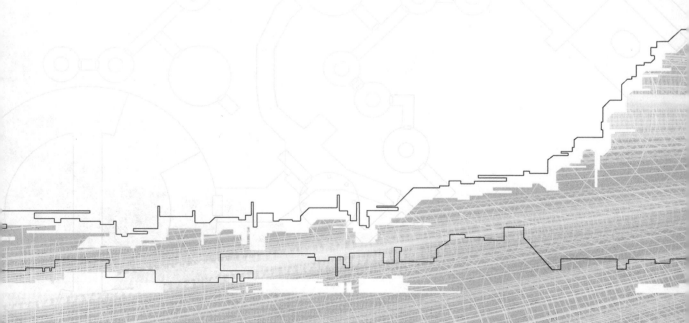

CHAPTER 1

INTRODUCTION TO NETWORK PROGRAMMING

Unless you've been living under a rock for the past 20 years, you've probably heard about something called the *Internet*. To most people, that word is associated with ominous things like e-mail, the *World Wide Web* (*WWW*), and naughty pictures. To you, the game programmer, the Internet is so much more—a universe of its own where you can create games to play with people who live across town as well as those who live thousands of miles away.

The Internet is a grand thing for game programmers. It adds community interaction to games and allows players to match wits and reflexes with anyone, instead of being required to play against typically dumb and repetitive artificial intelligences. To learn how to efficiently program MUDs, however, you must first have a solid understanding of network programming. This chapter supplies that foundation. If you already have a good grasp of network programming, you may safely skip this chapter.

In this chapter, you will learn to:

- Relate the history of communication networks to game programming
- Understand the philosophy and layered hierarchy of Internet Protocols (IPs)
- Understand the basics of common transport protocols
- Find additional information on networking protocols

Why Learn the Basics?

I have found that it is always a good idea to know the mechanics of anything I intend to work on. I disagree with computer professors and gurus who rant for hours about the beauty of abstracting the interface of a mechanism from its mechanics (how it works, in essence) to justify the concept that you shouldn't need to know how something works to use it.

Indeed, few people who drive actually know the physics of acceleration and energy usage or even how an internal combustion engine works. At first, this can seem like a good thing; anyone can jump into a car without knowing how the engine works. You press the gas, and the car goes; you press the brake, and the car stops.

It's not always that simple however. I can't count the number of times I've been at a stoplight and watched the car next to me

> **NOTE**
>
> *Throughput* is a communications term that describes how much data can go through the network per unit of time. For example, the throughput of a 56 kilobits modem is roughly around 56 kbps (kilobits per second), and the upstream throughput of my cable modem is around 128 kbps.

accelerate as fast as possible only to stop in a few hundred feet at the next stoplight. Whenever that happens, I know the person has no idea of how energy and acceleration work.

The person who accelerates to 50 MPH and then immediately brakes to a halt wastes far more energy than the person who accelerates to 30 MPH, coasts, and then brakes to a halt. The first car wasted energy accelerating 20 MPH faster, only to have that energy drained away as heat energy in the brakes.

So you can see that knowing how something works may not be necessary for operating a mechanism but is useful for operating it *efficiently*. And as you may know, game programming is all about using things efficiently and taking them to the limit.

History of Communication Networks in a Nutshell

From the beginning of history, communication has been an important part of human society. As important as communication has been, the mass distribution of communication through networks is only a recent development. Most early communication was accomplished through horseback riders carrying written messages.

The invention of railroads brought a major advancement in communications networks by facilitating the transfer of massive amounts of mail across the world. But communication was still inadequate. While the *throughput* of these railroad networks was large, the *latency* was also large.

> **NOTE**
>
> *Latency* is a communications term that describes how long it takes for one piece of data to reach its destination. For example, it takes less than one millisecond (msec) for data to go from one computer to another on my home network, and around 15 msec for data to reach my Internet Service Provider's (ISP's) routers.

While masses of mail could be sent through railroad networks, it still took weeks for some pieces to reach their destinations, and this was unacceptable to many people.

Electric Communication— Telegraphs to Telephones

In 1835, something amazing happened: The telegraph was invented.

The telegraph was essentially a long wire with a speaker on one end and a battery at the other. Figure 1.1 shows a simple telegraph "network." Whenever the battery was engaged, it sent an electrical signal down the wire that would power the speaker and cause a small tone to be heard. Since there were only two states of the communication—the presence or absence of sound—a special messaging system called *Morse code* was invented, which varied the number and length of tones to represent different characters. Short tones were called dots, and long tones were dashes.

Even though communication in this manner had a low latency (tones were transmitted almost instantly), you can imagine that the throughput of this method of communication was very low. There were no machines back then to convert signals from Morse code to English, so people had to do it by hand.

The next major innovation in communications occurred in 1876 with the invention of the telephone.

NOTE

It is a commonly held "fact" that Samuel Morse invented the telegraph, but there are conflicting reports about a person named C.M. Renfrew inventing it as well. You can read about this more on the Internet if you wish; there's good information about telegraphs at this site: http://www.worldwideschool.org/library/books/tech/engineering/HeroesoftheTelegraph/chap1.html.

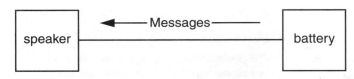

Figure 1.1

This simple telegraph network transmits electrical signals from one end to the other.

The telephone allowed people to encode sound data into an analog electrical pulse, which would then be sent down a wire, to the speaker on the other end (Figure 1.2). This method of communication was an incredible innovation, since with the direct interpretation of voice, communication could be accomplished without people encoding and decoding Morse code. This greatly improved the throughput of the communications, because voice data could now be transmitted in real time.

NOTE

Alexander Graham Bell is generally credited with inventing the telephone, but he was only lucky enough to get his patent approved first. Elisha Gray, working independently of Bell, simultaneously invented the telephone, but he didn't file his patent application fast enough. What have we learned today, class? Always file your patents immediately.

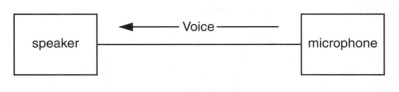

Figure 1.2

In this simple telephone network, voice data is turned into electricity by the microphone, and turned into sound on the other end by a speaker.

This method of communication only increased people's desire for faster and better communications, since only one person could use one telephone line at a time.

Switched Communication

Peer-to-peer networking connected many telephones to many other telephones. Alexander Graham Bell was a major proponent of this kind of network, and it worked well for small networks. Basically, every node in a peer-to-peer network is physically connected to every other node in the network through wires. This gets to be a major problem as the number of nodes grows, because, as you can probably see, the number of wires needed in this kind of network follows a geometric progression based on the number of nodes in the network. To add a third node to a network, you need two extra wires, making a total of three in the network. Table 1.1 shows a listing of the number of wires needed for networks with different numbers of nodes.

Table 1.1 Wires Needed for Peer-to-Peer Networks

Nodes	Wires
2	1
3	3
4	6
5	10
10	45
15	105
500	1,225

The number of wires needed in a peer-to-peer network follows this formula: $(n * (n-1))/2$. So you can see that any network that gets past a certain size is in the realm of being completely unmanageable.

Because of this, the concept of a centralized communications network was invented, and its implementation was called a *circuit-switched network*. This kind of network contains any number of *nodes* and one central *switching station*, arranged as shown in Figure 1.3.

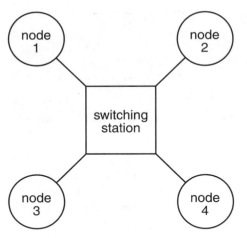

Figure 1.3

This simple switched communications network connects four nodes to a switching station.

Since only one conversation could be conducted at any given time on a telephone wire, the original networks had to use switching to enable multiple conversations to occur at the same time. Essentially, this is how it worked.

There was a human *operator* at the switching station, who monitored all the nodes for incoming activity. Whenever one of the nodes wanted to talk to any of the other nodes, a person called the operator from his node, and the operator asked whom he wanted to talk to. When the operator determined whom the caller wanted to talk to, he physically connected a wire from the caller's circuit to the destination circuit. For example, Figure 1.4 shows node 1 connected to node 4. When node 1 wants to talk to node 4, an operator physically connects the circuits with a wire.

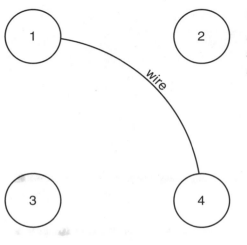

Figure 1.4

Four circuits at the circuit switching station from Figure 1.3.

So, with this network, a total of two conversations can be held at the same time, and any single node can talk to any other node, as long as the line is open. This spawned a major breakthrough in communications, but its service was still inadequate. Eventually these switching stations became too large for human operators to manage, so methods were developed to spread out the communications into many switches, as shown in Figure 1.5.

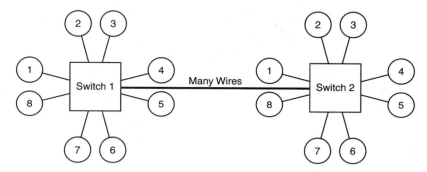

Figure 1.5

In this configuration, two switches are connected with many wires, allowing nodes from each local switch to connect to nodes on another switch.

When a person wanted to call someone at his local switch, the same procedure was followed. When a person wanted to call someone on another switch, the operator connected the person to the operator on the desired switch, and that operator connected the person to the right destination. Each switch had only a certain number of wires connecting it to other switches, and that limited the number of connections that could be made from switch to switch. For example, a switch may have 16 nodes, which

NOTE

The terms *intra* and *inter* refer to "internal" and "external" respectively. So *inter-switch* refers to connections between two nodes on one switch, but *intra-switch* refers to connections of nodes that are on different switches.

allows up to eight *intra-switch* connections at once, but it may have only four wires connecting to an adjacent switch, which means that only four *inter-switch* connections can be made.

Eventually, each switch in the United States was numbered with its own area code, and this led to our current area code system.

It didn't take long for these networks to become such huge messes of wires that it was difficult to make connections. Therefore, an even more centralized system was created. The switches were given centralized switches, sometimes called *hubs*. Figure 1.6 shows one of these networks.

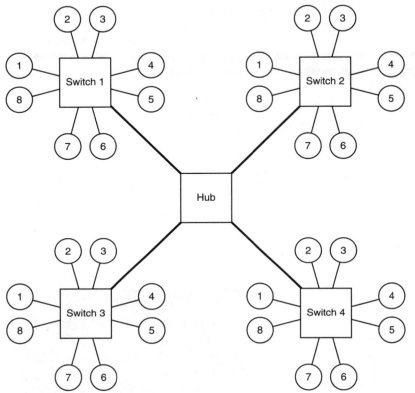

Figure 1.6

In this large switched network, the central switch controls connections among the intermediate switches.

Packet-Switched Networks

Traditional circuit switching was great, but it had too many limitations for our growing communications needs. Since traditional circuit-switched networks were so centralized, the main hubs could go down, and half of the communications in the country would instantly be halted. Only one line could be in use at any given time, limiting the number of concurrent connections drastically. There also came a time when it took about seven to eight minutes just to go through all the operators to connect to someone else on the network.

In the 1960s, the United States *Advanced Research Projects Agency* (*ARPA*) invented the first *packet-switched* network. The idea of such a network is to separate data into tiny chunks, called *packets*.

In this type of network, instead of only one connection per wire, special machines at the end of each wire accept discrete chunks of data (packets) and send each chunk one at a time down the wire, with the chucks arriving first sent first. These machines are called *switches*, but they are much more commonly known as *routers*. Figure 1.7 shows a simple network with two routers.

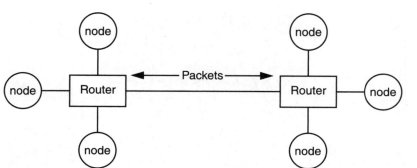

Figure 1.7

In a simple packet-switched network, the routers send packets of data down the single wire that connects them.

Whenever a node has data to send, it puts that data into a discrete-sized packet and then sends it to the router. The router decides where it goes and sends it to the right place. If the wire between the routers is busy, the router puts the packet in a queue and keeps it there until the wire opens up and is available for transmissions.

This kind of network is a great improvement, because it drastically reduces the number of wires needed to connect two switches. One of the downsides, however, is that since many more communications are now occurring on the same line at the same time, each connection has less bandwidth. The original *Defense Advanced Research Projects Agency Network* (*DARPANet*) didn't have enough bandwidth to transmit a single voice communication, unless it was the *only* communication going on at the time.

Since data packets had to be in a form that the routers could understand, and the routers were *digital* computers, it made sense that they would send digital data. Unfortunately, data sent over a wire is *analog* by nature, so the digital data needed to be turned into an analog signal using a device called a *modulator-demodulator* (*modem* for short). Early modems didn't do a great job of converting data efficiently, and were limited to a bandwidth of about 300 *baud.*

> **NOTE**
>
> **Bandwidth** is a networking term that generally describes how much data can be sent through a network. In the traditional sense, bandwidth refers to the size of a signal. For example, telephones have 3,000 Hz of bandwidth, from 400 Hz to 3.4 KHz. Telephone wires are not rated to send data above or below those thresholds. AM Radio broadcasts use about 10 KHz of bandwidth each, FM Radio broadcasts use about 200 KHz, and VHF/UHF TV broadcasts use 6 MHz of bandwidth. Most people, when dealing with packet-switched networks, refer to their throughput as bandwidth as well.

NOTE

Baud is an old term, dating back to the days of telegraphs. The term comes from the name of one of the engineers who first worked with telegraphs, Jean Maurice Emile Baudot. The speed at which an electronic circuit changed states was measured in *bauds*, and a baud was roughly equivalent to the number of bits per second that could be transmitted. So 300 baud is about 300 bits per second. Modems stopped using the term baud at around the time the 14,400 bps modem was invented. Does this sound like ancient history?

Over the years, significant improvements have been made to methods of data transmission over traditional copper wires. New inventions such as fiber-optic wires and even wireless *radio-frequency* (*RF*) communication allow data to be transferred in a much more efficient manner. Eventually, everything will be transferred over packet-switched networks, since they are far more cost-efficient and useful than the circuit-switched or broadcast networks that your telephone and cable companies use. You won't need a specific cable line, phone line, or Internet line; everything will connect into one standard interface.

NOTE

Eventually, all land-based copper wires will be replaced with *fiber optics*. Fiber-optic communication is an incredible breakthrough in the realm of wired communications. Every electrical circuit has resistance, which slowly saps out the signal strength and causes the wires to become hot. Therefore, to maintain signal strength on copper wires, repeaters must be placed on the wire to boost the signal and send it further. Not only do these boosters require lots of energy, but they slow down transmission speed as well. Fiber-optic wires directly transmit light impulses with much less signal drop-off, and since they transmit light directly, they are faster than traditional electrical signals as well. In addition, fiber-optic wires require fewer repeaters.

Communications

Broadband communications originally referred to cables that carried more than one type of data at the same time. The first types of broadband included Digital Subscriber Line (DSL) and cable modem technologies. However, the term now generally applies to any Internet communications that are faster than traditional modems, which are limited to 56 kilobits per second.

DSL lines are essentially an extension of the standard telephone lines to your house. While telephone wires are not *officially* supposed to handle data above 3.4 KHz bandwidth, most new telephone wires actually can handle that kind of data. Therefore, digital data can be encoded into an analog electrical signal above 4 KHz and transmitted to the phone company without disrupting the normal phone conversation. The most popular DSL variant is *ADSL* (the "A" stands for *asynchronous*, because it allocates more bandwidth for downloading than uploading), which uses the band of 25 KHz to 160 KHz for its upstream, and 240 KHz to 1,500 KHz for its downstream.

Unfortunately for me, DSL technology came too late. The year before DSL was standardized, my telephone company installed a digital switch in my neighborhood that encoded the telephone data into a digital stream of data and sent it to the phone company via a fiber-optic cable, ignoring any data outside of the standard telephone range of 400 Hz to 3.4 KHz. Therefore, DSL cannot be used in my neighborhood because the phone technology is too advanced for DSL. Talk about irony!

Cable modems work in a similar way to DSL, except they use the unused bands of the coaxial cable that goes into your house, instead of your telephone line. Cable modems typically use the band of 5 MHz to 65 MHz for upstream data and 850 MHz to 1000 MHz for downstream data. Cable modems use much more bandwidth for their signals, because coaxial cables are typically a lot longer than telephone cables, and signals on them are weaker.

Mechanics of Packets and the Internet Wonderland

The Internet is a very cool thing, but I'm sure you already knew that. I want to show you how packets actually work, so you can appreciate even more how wonderful the Internet is. The basis of the Internet lies in the *Internet Protocol* (*IP*). This protocol was invented in 1981, which really wasn't that long ago in the grand scheme of things.

The whole idea of the IP protocol was to define a standard method of communication among routers, switches, and nodes on a network. Basically, every chunk of data that is sent is prefixed with a *header*, also known as the *IP header*. Two versions of IP exist today: IPv4 and IPv6.

All About IPv4

Figure 1.8 shows the standard layout of an IPv4 header.

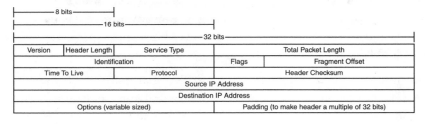

Figure 1.8

This is a standard IPv4 header.

The v4 means *version 4*. IPv4 is the current IP standard across the world, but there is a newer version called *IPv6*. (What happened to IPv5? Who knows? It's probably having a party along with DirectX 4.) I'll get into IPv6 later on, since it's not used too much—yet.

You don't have to understand all the little details of the header; they're really important only to network engineers. I'll go over the important points, though.

The first thing you should know is that the length of the header is variable. Everything up to the Options parameter (bottom row of the figure) is set in stone, but the Options parameter is variable. That is why there is a parameter that holds the length of the header (the Header Length parameter); any data past the header is the data stored in the packet.

The Total Packet Length parameter describes the entire length of the packet, in bytes, including the header. Since it's 16 bits long, an IP packet can be at most 65,535 bytes long.

The Time To Live (TTL) parameter is particularly interesting; it determines how long, in jumps, the packet lives. This prevents packets from accidentally being routed around in circles forever. Every time a packet passes through a new router, the TTL field is reduced by 1, and when it reaches 0, the router completely discards the packet. The field is 8 bits, so there can be at most 255 hops between routers before a packet is completely discarded. The 255 hops is an incredibly large number, so it is reasonable protection.

The Protocol parameter determines which protocol is being used on top of the IP header. Only a few kinds of protocols operate on top of IP. As a games programmer, you should mainly pay attention to two:

- Transmission Control Protocol (TCP)
- User Datagram Protocol (UDP)

I describe these protocols in more detail later on. The Header Checksum parameter is an important data integrity measure in IPv4. A *checksum* is a value that represents the data and is computed by a checksum algorithm. The checksum is a simple measure that verifies if data has been changed in the transmission. Whenever a router receives an IP packet, the packet's checksum is calculated and compared to the existing checksum value in the packet. If the numbers match, you can be reasonably certain that the data has not changed; if the numbers don't match, you know the data was somehow changed by an error or interference in the communication path. Whenever the checksums don't match, the router immediately discards the packet. You'll see why this is a good idea later on. Also, since the TTL parameter is changed at every router, the checksum is recalculated whenever a router passes a packet on.

Finally, the two most interesting parts of an IP packet are the source IP address and the destination IP address. Every node on an IPv4 network is given a 32-bit IP address, typically represented as four numbers, separated by periods, like this: 192.168.100.5.

The original Internet addressing scheme classified all addresses into three groups: large, medium, and small networks. This system was wasteful and isn't used much anymore, so I won't waste time describing it.

Using 32-bit addresses limits the number of total nodes on a network to a little more than 4 billion, which used to seem like a large number, but it seems smaller and smaller every day. There are already many more than 4 billion people on this planet, so giving every person his own IP address is not even possible anymore. This was the major concern for upgrading the system to IPv6, which I will touch on next.

> **NOTE**
>
> Under the old addressing system, organizations such as the University of California At Berkeley were given more IP addresses than the entire country of China. You can see how the old system just isn't going to work anymore, especially when you consider that Berkeley only has a few thousand people, and China has 1.2 billion.

IPv6: Bigger and Better

IPv6 was created in 1995, when the Internet community realized that IPv4 was too constrained. The biggest problem, by far, was the small address space allocated to IPv4. As I've said before, 4 billion addresses is simply not enough to identify all the computers on the planet now or in the future. Most large ISPs dynamically assign an IP address to a customer when he logs on and reuse that number for another customer once he logs off. This method isn't useful anymore, as most people are starting to realize the importance of permanent Internet addresses. How would you like a phone number that changed every day? In addition, as broadband connections are becoming the standard, more and more people are staying online longer and longer, making dynamic IP allocation less workable.

And finally, there are going to be thousands of devices in the future that will need their own IP addresses. IBM has even promised refrigerators that can connect to the Internet, and gosh darn it, I want them now!

Besides the larger address space, IPv6 has a host of new features making it more streamlined and functional, and even better security features have been added. However, if you're interested in those features, you should get a networking book, because this stuff isn't that important to game programming.

Figure 1.9 shows a diagram of an IPv6 header.

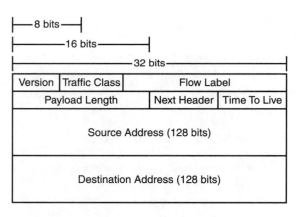

Figure 1.9

Notice that there are fewer fields in this IPv6 header than in an IPv4 header.

IPv6 has been simplified, and the rarely used portions of the IPv4 header have been removed. The other big change is the huge addresses; IPv6 addresses are 128 bits long. That means that there are a total of 3.4×10^{38} addresses available. That's 340 undecillion addresses, and when you haven't even heard of a number before, that means you've got enough addresses. But to further illustrate my point, I'm going to show you some more pointless calculations that illustrate the sheer size of the IPv6 address space.

At any rate, there should be enough addresses for at least the next few hundred

> **NOTE**
>
> The surface area of the earth, water included, is 5.1×10^{14} meters squared. If you divide 3.4×10^{38} by 5.1×10^{14}, you get 6.6×10^{23}. That means that there are around 660 sextillion IPv6 addresses available for *every square meter of space on the planet.* That ought to be enough for anybody— until we decide to give IP addresses to every molecule on the planet. Or until we provide free Internet to the multiverse.

years, so we'll let programmers find more addresses when the time comes. For now, there are places on the Internet where you can obtain a block of a few million—or even billion—IPv6 addresses.

The rest of the fields of an IPv6 header are pretty much the same as the important fields in IPv4, with updated names. They're not really important.

IP Philosophy and Layered Hierarchy

IP packets are not guaranteed. When you send an IP packet, you have absolutely no idea if it will be received. Even worse, you can't tell if a packet has reached its destination.

Doesn't that sound like an incredibly stupid way to design a network? Maybe so, but think about it for a moment. Imagine how much more complex the routing hardware would have to be to ensure that every IP packet arrived intact at its proper destination. Right now, the routers don't care; they take the data and keep relaying it on until it either gets to its destination, or they discard the packet as junk. Simple hardware is cheaper to build, and faster as well.

So, what is the point of unreliable communications? With digital data, even one byte missing out of a file can make the entire thing useless, so unreliable communications seems like the opposite of what you'd really want!

Instead of letting hardware control integrity and validation, the IP model puts software in charge. Before going into this topic, I want to explain the layered hierarchy of Internet communications.

Internet protocols are actually designed into four distinct layers:

- Network layer
- Internet layer
- Transport layer
- Application layer

Each time you send a packet of data over the Internet, it is encapsulated by a new header at each layer. For example, if you are sending *Hyper Text Transfer Protocol* (*HTTP*) data, which is basically web-page data, the data you send is first enclosed into an HTTP header at the Application layer. Then, the HTTP application sends the packet to the operating system, which adds a Transport layer packet header as well as an IP packet header for the Internet layer. (HTTP uses TCP as the Transport Layer Protocol. And I will get to TCP in a bit.) Finally, depending on what device you use for Internet access, a Network layer packet header is added to the packet, and finally it is sent on its way. Figure 1.10 is a pictorial representation of the layered hierarchy of Internet packets. This particular example demonstrates browsing the WWW with an Ethernet connection.

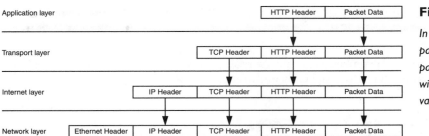

Figure 1.10

In this standard four-layer packet structure, each packet of data is prefixed with the header of the various protocols it uses.

Previously, I told you all about the IP protocol. This protocol makes its home in the second layer, the Internet layer. I started there first, because it is really the most important layer when dealing with Internet communications. Now I will go into more depth on the layers themselves.

Network Layer

The lowest layer is called both the *Network layer* and the *Physical layer*, because it is the layer that is added to a packet whenever a physical device sends the data. Examples of this include an Ethernet card (Ethernet Protocol), a modem (PPP Protocol), a wireless Internet card (802.11b protocol), or a cable modem (DOCSIS protocol). Each of these devices operates in a different way and has its own header format depending on its needs.

The great thing about the layered protocol system is that the physical devices *don't care* what kind of data you are sending over them, so you can send any kind of data, as long as the recipient of the data expects it and knows how to decode it.

Internet Layer

The *Internet layer* is perhaps the most important layer, since every device in a single network must understand and recognize it. The primary purpose of the Internet layer is to provide routing and addressing services, so the routers know where to send packets. A network can use many different kinds of devices, such as modems and Ethernet cards, and as long as they all understand the Internet layer protocol in use, the network should operate perfectly.

Of the three major Internet layer protocols, I have described the two most commonly used: IPv4 and IPv6. In the past, a third protocol, called *IPX* or *Internetwork Packet Exchange,* was widely used as well. IPX is superior to IP in a few ways, but it never really caught on and is pretty much dead today. One of IPX's notable characteristics was that it had a segmented address space. It had 32-bit network addresses, and each network also had a 48-bit node address, essentially using 80-bit addresses.

Transport Layer

I haven't talked much about this layer yet, but it is important. The *Transport layer* accommodates protocols such as TCP, UDP (explained in a section that follows) and Internet Control

Message Protocol (ICMP). These protocols are primarily designed to handle connections, rate of data transmission, and data integrity verification.

For example, as I mentioned before, if you use the IP protocol, you have absolutely no idea if the packet you sent reached its destination. To solve this problem, you need to have the Transport layer protocol handle the transmission.

For example, when you wrap your data into a *TCP* (*Transmission Control Protocol*) packet, TCP calculates the checksum of all of the data, and then your operating system wraps the entire TCP packet into an IP header and sends that out.

When the recipient of your packet gets the data you sent, it sends an *acknowledgement* (ACK) packet over TCP, saying that it got the packet. It may, however, fail to receive your message for a variety of reasons. If the original TCP packet gets lost, for example, the ACK packet would never have been sent, or the ACK packet itself may have gotten lost. If the sender doesn't receive the ACK packet, the sender sends the data again, and keeps sending the data until he receives a confirmation that the data has been sent. Here's a simple listing of the process:

1. Send packet.
2. Wait for ACK.
3. If no ACK in given amount of time, go back to 1.
4. Send next packet.

The hardware costs for this method of data verification are far lower than making the IP protocol itself check the integrity of data and respond to the sender that there was an error. The routing hardware doesn't really care much about acknowledgements; instead, it just assumes the communications succeeded, and it lets the end computers figure out if something went wrong. The reason this works is because the number of times data transmission fails is far fewer than the number of times that the transmission is successful, so there's really no point in making *every node* along the transmission path check that it is successful, and send errors backward along the path.

There is a slight chance of data transmission error, and that slows things down a little bit, because the sender keeps trying to send the data; but, in the end, that is a far more desirable solution than having incredibly expensive routing hardware.

The *User Datagram Protocol (UDP)* elects to forego the data integrity issues and opts instead for speed over integrity; in other words, delivery is not guaranteed. For this reason, UDP is quite often preferred over TCP for very fast games, such as first person shooters. I won't cover UDP in detail in this book because it is not an important protocol for low-speed MUDs. I'll be sticking with TCP, which is a little slower but more robust and has guaranteed delivery.

Application Layer

The *Application layer* is theoretically the highest layer of a packet header, and it contains information about the specific application you are using with the packet. Examples of popular Application layer protocols include HTTP, File Transfer Protocol (FTP), Telnet,

Simple Mail Transfer Protocol (SMTP), and so on. The topics in this book focus almost entirely on creating and using application layer protocols for MUDs.

Other Layers

The four-layer model is really just a recommendation for networking; it's not a necessity. In the past, some crazy people have demonstrated this fact using completely useless technologies. For example, there is an IP over SMTP protocol, which defines how to send IP packets over SMTP. Of course, SMTP is built on top of TCP, which in turn is built on top of IP, so what is the point? Who knows? Never underestimate what a nerd and some free time can accomplish. After all, as game programmers, who are we to judge?

It is usually accepted to use the slash notation (/) to show protocol layering. For example, you may have heard of TCP/IP. This means that you are using TCP over the IP protocol. It is literally pronounced "TCP over IP." Slash notation, however, is not common for other combinations, because the entire idea of networked communications is to keep the layers as independent as possible. That way, you can easily use higher protocols over different lower protocols. This is why you don't see people saying "HTTP over TCP over IP." Not only is it a mouthful to say, but you aren't really required to send HTTP over TCP anyway (though I've really never seen anyone who doesn't).

Common Transport Protocols

As a game programmer, you usually won't pay attention to the IP protocol; the operating system should take care of that for you automatically. You'll only be slightly more interested in the TCP and UDP protocols, since most compilers have built-in libraries to handle these protocols. I'll start with UDP first, since it's simpler.

UDP

UDP, as I've said before, is the User Datagram Protocol. A datagram is basically just a single packet of data. The UDP protocol is simple and doesn't offer the reliability of more complex protocols, such as TCP. Essentially, you just send the packet out and hope it gets there. This is a "fire and forget" protocol. Figure 1.11 shows the UDP header format.

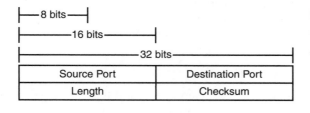

Figure 1.11

The header format for a UDP packet.

NOTE

The port fields for UDP (and as you'll see shortly, TCP as well) are 16 bits long. This means that a total of 65,536 ports are available for use. Ports below 1,024 are reserved for specific application-level protocols assigned by the *Internet Assigned Numbers Authority (IANA)*. To see a list of these ports, you can visit their Web site at http://www.iana.org. IANA covers things such as HTTP (80), FTP (21), Telnet (23), SMTP (25), as well as hundreds of other protocols that no one has ever heard of. You should generally try to keep your programs' port numbers above 1,024. If you are not running as root, UNIX-based systems won't even allow you to open ports below 1,024 (for servers). Table 1.2 shows a listing of common port numbers.

The first thing you should notice in Figure 1.11 is that the header is only 64 bits long, or 8 bytes. That's pretty small for a packet header, at least compared to other protocols.

Next, notice the two *port* fields. You see, once a packet gets to its destination, there really is no way for the receiving machine to figure out what program the packet is trying to get to. Therefore, the idea of ports was invented. When a port receives a packet, the operating system is supposed to read the port number off the packet and send the packet to the appropriate program. This way, you can have many different programs on the same machine, all using the network connection at the same time.

In Figure 1.11, you should also notice the length and the checksum fields. The length tells you the length of the packet data, including the header. The checksum field contains the checksum of the data in the packet, so that the receiving machine can figure out if the data is intact. If it isn't, the receiver just discards the packet altogether and acts as if it never got it.

UDP is a *connectionless* protocol. This means that UDP programs don't connect to each other; they just send the packet, and the server is supposed to accept it. Other protocols, especially TCP, will not accept incoming packets unless you explicitly connect to the other end first.

The fact that UDP does not guarantee delivery of packets can lead to problems. In a fast-paced game in which the server constantly sends the clients updates on the positions of other players, guaranteed delivery is not a great problem. If, for example, a position update packet is sent but never delivered, a reliable protocol like TCP will keep trying to send the packet; but by the time the protocol finally sends the original packet, the player's position may have changed. So in this case, UDP is a useful protocol.

Table 1.2 Common Ports

Port	Service	Purpose
17	QOTD	Quote of the day; sends a quote in text form
20	FTP Data	FTP data port
21	FTP Control	FTP control port
22	SSH	Secure Shell Terminal (a secure version of Telnet)
23	Telnet	Allows terminal control
25	SMTP	Simple Mail Transfer Protocol
37	Time	Sends the server time
53	DNS	DNS lookups
80	HTTP	World Wide Web pages
110	POP3	Post Office Protocol; more mail stuff
113	Ident	Identifies the name of a computer
119	NNTP	Newsgroups
143	IMAP	Another old mail protocol
6666	IRC	Internet Relay Chat
31415	PIE	Pieserver; it serves digits of pi*

* See my website at http://ronpenton.net/projects for more information on Pieserver.

But what happens with important data? What if something happens in a game, and the game is set up so that it won't retransmit that data later on? You could end up with your clients completely missing an important game event such as a gunshot and then getting out of sync. In this case, UDP isn't a very useful choice.

For MUDs and MMOGs, using UDP usually isn't a good idea, since most things that happen in these kinds of games are *event based*—that is, events occur once and the client absolutely needs to know they happened.

TCP to the Rescue!

TCP is probably the most highly used transport protocol, since it guarantees data delivery. If you tell your TCP library to send data, it *will* get there, barring any unusual events such as a nonexistent destination. Without TCP, file transfers and reliable communication over the Internet would be virtually impossible.

In contrast to UDP, TCP is a *connection-oriented* protocol. This means that the client must tell the server that he wants to connect, before the server will even listen to incoming data.

TCP is also a *streaming* protocol. This means that the protocol attempts to send streams of data, separated into packets for delivery over a packet-switched network. This is an important part of TCP, since it ensures not only that the data actually reaches its destination, but also that the data arrives there in the same order in which it was sent.

I've told you about TCP and the acknowledgement packet that it uses. Since this is important, here's a quick recap. Whenever a TCP port receives data, it sends an acknowledgement packet saying that the data was received. If the original sender never gets an acknowledgement, then the TCP port attempts to send the data again. Of course, this process is inefficient if the sender sends one packet and then waits for the acknowledgement before sending anything else.

> **NOTE**
>
> Because of the decentralized nature of the Internet, two packets you send from one place to another may follow two completely different paths, which means that you can't be sure that sending one packet first will mean it will arrive first. This makes TCP a great way to make sure that the connections receive their data in order.

That isn't how TCP actually works, though. TCP starts off sending all the packets it needs to in order, and just continues sending until there is nothing left to send. If TCP realizes that an acknowledgement packet hasn't come back for a packet it sent, it stops what it is doing and attempts to retransmit the packet that wasn't acknowledged.

On the receiving end, if the receiver detects that it is getting a packet out of order, it buffers the data in that packet until the packet or packets that are supposed to precede it arrive.

At the application level, all of these operations are transparent. Your TCP library handles all of this for you and makes sure you get the data in its intended order.

Unfortunately, all of these safeguards come with a price, as you see when you examine the TCP header shown in Figure 1.12. Note that the TCP packet header is much larger than a UDP header.

TCP is a feature-rich protocol. It includes not only the kitchen sink but the disposal too. The *minimum* size of a TCP header is 20 bytes, much larger than the 8 byte UDP header.

TCP uses the same port numbering scheme as UDP, 16-bit ports, which adds up to 65,536 ports. Like UDP, TCP has a checksum field, which is used for data integrity.

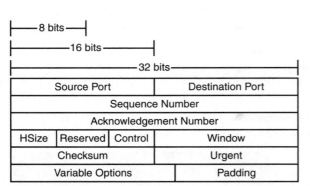

Figure 1.12

The standard for TCP packets.

The other fields you should at least note are the sequence, acknowledgement, window, and urgent fields. The *sequence field* denotes the position of the packet in the current stream at its transmission point; this is used so that the receiving end can piece together the packets if they arrive out of order. The acknowledgement field tells the receiver the acknowledgement number that the sender is expecting.

The window field is somewhat interesting. TCP implements flow-control mechanisms, which means that each side of a TCP connection can tell the other side how much data it is willing to accept. This is useful for preventing a connection from accidentally sending more information than the other side can handle.

Notifying the other side on acceptance limits is also particularly useful whenever there are dropped packets. Since TCP buffers data that is out of order, it may be useful for the receiver to tell the sender to stop sending data until it catches up. Buffered data can take up lots of room, since the TCP library can't do anything with that data until it gets all previous packets.

Finally, you should be aware that TCP supports a concept called urgent data, which the urgent field handles. *Urgent data* should not be used inside the data stream, but contains important connection and control information. The TCP library you are using should seamlessly strip this data out of the stream and take care of it automatically.

That sums up all the important things you as a programmer need to know about TCP. If you're interested in learning more about either UDP or TCP, networking books can do the trick. I just wanted you to know the basic mechanics of how these technologies work as they affect game programming.

Information on Networking Protocols

There is one important part of networking that I have neglected to mention: the standard documentation for all published networking protocols. Early on in the development of

> **NOTE**
>
> I'll let you in on an inside joke. There are many funny RFCs in the general RFC database. It is kind of an Internet tradition to submit one of these every April Fools' Day. For example, RFC 1149 is officially entitled "A Standard for the Transmission of IP Datagrams on Avian Carriers," which basically documents a method of transmitting IP packets using carrier pigeons. RFC 2324 is entitled "Hyper Text Coffee Pot Control Protocol (HTCPCP/1.0)" and defines a method of controlling coffee pots over HTTP. More recent is RFC 2795, "The Infinite Monkey Protocol Suite (IMPS)." I don't even want to know what that's about. We programmers have a strange sense of humor.

ARPANet, engineers recognized the need for a formal way to publish the standards and specifications of protocols. They eventually called the documents they created *RFCs*, which stands for *Request For Comments*.

You can easily look up RFCs by using their published identification numbers. For example, the current RFC describing IPv4 is RFC 791. You can search for that with any Internet search engine, and you'll get hundreds of links. RFCs are public documentation, and they're free to be published anywhere.

Once RFCs are submitted to the world, they can never be changed. If a protocol needs to be changed, the old RFC is *deprecated*, which means that it is no longer current, and a new RFC with updated information is published.

My favorite place for getting RFC information is at a website entitled *Connected: An Internet Encyclopedia,* which is located at http://www.freesoft.org/CIE/. If that site is down, you can probably find a mirror, as it is very popular. The site is fairly well updated with all the RFCs, and it's even got useful courses and background material for most of the networking topics I haven't covered here.

Summary

I hope you found this chapter interesting. I have a passion for history, and I feel that knowing your history is a good way of understanding why things are the way they are, what has succeeded and failed in the past, and where we can go in the future. Packet networking is a new development in the grand scheme of things, and we're still pioneering the field, so I think it is appropriate to know this material.

As I've said at the start of the chapter, you don't have to be an expert in something to use it, but it helps a lot if you at least know some of the mechanics. I hope you now understand the basics of how the IP, TCP, and UDP protocols work, and how networks work in general. This knowledge should pave the way to the next chapter, "Winsock/Berkely Sockets Programming."

CHAPTER 2

WINSOCK/ BERKELEY SOCKETS PROGRAMMING

A fter reading Chapter 1, "Introduction to Network Programming," you know the basics of Internet operations and networking in general for game programming. However, I have not yet shown you how to actually use network communications in your programming adventures.

Most people fear learning about network programming because it seems like such an advanced topic. I put off network programming for years because of this, and that was a mistake. I had absolutely no idea how easy networked communications were.

Many years ago, researchers at the University at Berkeley created an *Application Programming Interface* (API) to make it easy for the C programming language to use Internet communications. This API eventually became known as the *Berkeley Sockets API*. Nearly every UNIX-based operating system supports it, as does MacOS and Windows. Microsoft created its own version of Berkeley Sockets and called it *Winsock*. Very little is changed in the Winsock library, so it is entirely possible to use the two libraries interchangeably.

In this chapter, you will learn to:

- Understand the fundamentals of byte ordering
- Understand socket basics
- Work with the API for sockets
- Find IP addresses using the Domain Name System (DNS)
- Use demos that illustrate the concepts of the chapter

Byte Ordering

Before I delve into the socket theory, I want to discuss a nasty aspect of network programming—*byte ordering*. Almost everyone I know grumbles when this topic is mentioned.

A long, long time ago in a galaxy not so far away, computers had small amounts of memory and small data busses. The size of the data bus in a computer is typically called the *word size*. For example, some of the first computers had a bus size of 4 bits, and thus their word sizes were 4 bits.

> **NOTE**
>
> This is an inside joke in the computer world: Groups of 4-bit data are referred to as *nibbles*, which fits into the whole *bit* and *byte* theme.

Obviously, there was only so much a 4-bit CPU could do, so larger machines were invented that used 8-bit data. These machines became the standard for awhile, and the 8-bit data size became the standard *atomic* data structure, which meant that the smallest single piece of data you could store was 8 bits, also called a byte.

I don't want to dive too far into a discussion of binary math, so I'll briefly cover only what you need to know.

In any number system, the digit furthest to the right has the least significance (assuming the number is written left to right). In decimal, the digit furthest to the right is the ones column, the next is the tens column, then the hundreds, and so on. The same goes for binary, except the columns are ones, twos, and fours, each doubling the value of the previous as shown in Figure 2.1.

Decimal

10^7	10^6	10^5	10^4	10^3	10^2	10^1	10^0	
1	7	6	4	0	8	7	6	
1·10000000	7·1000000	6·100000	4·10000	0·1000	8·100	7·10	6·1	= 17640876

Binary

2^7	2^6	2^5	2^4	2^3	2^2	2^1	2^0	
1	1	0	1	0	0	1	1	
1·128	1·64	0·32	1·16	0·8	0·4	1·2	1·1	= 211

Figure 2.1

The juxtaposition of columns contrasts the arrangement of the digits of base 10 and base 2 numbers.

So when you increase the size of the data from 8 to 16 bits, you would naturally assume that the new 8 bits, representing the higher-order bits of the number, would appear to the left of the lower-order bits, as shown in Figure 2.2.

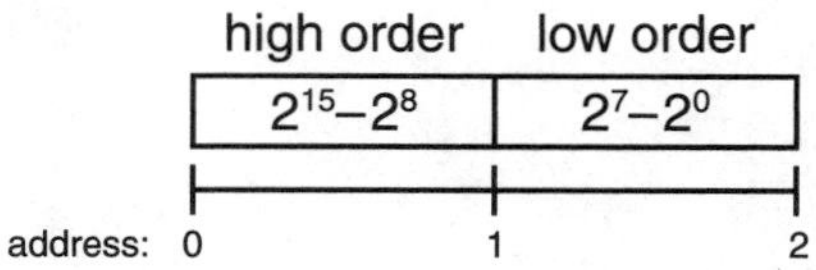

high order	low order
$2^{15}-2^8$	2^7-2^0

address: 0   1   2

Figure 2.2

A mathematical representation of a 16-bit number in a computer.

Unfortunately, things aren't that simple. When computers started switching over to 16 bits, people realized that they had a heck of a lot of code still running on 8-bit systems; the chip designers thought it would be a great idea to have a 16-bit processor and also be able to run 8-bit code. Backward compatibility is a wonderful thing, after all.

Well, due to the limitations of computer architectures, 16-bit processors also needed their memory aligned to 16-bit boundaries and stored in 16-bit areas of memory, even if the data was just 8 bits. Therefore, if you put an 8-bit piece of data into memory (without clever byte manipulations, of course), the compiler converts it to 16 bits and stores it aligned on a 16-bit boundary. Looking back at Figure 2.2 may help you picture this concept. In Figure 2.2, the data is being stored at address 0, but the actual data is placed at address 1, and a value of 0 is placed at address 0.

So, imagine what would happen if later on you wanted to retrieve that 8-bit value by using a pointer. You would load up address 0 and treat that as a byte and load that. But... oops! The data is actually at byte 1!

You could certainly have the processor auto-translate addresses, but that would make the processor much more complicated, and more complicated processors are slower and more expensive.

So, the solution that most chipmakers adopted was swapping the byte ordering, as shown in Figure 2.3. That way, both 8-bit and 16-bit programs know where their data is. The data in Figure 2.2 is said to be stored in *big-endian* format, and the data in Figure 2.3 is called *little-endian*.

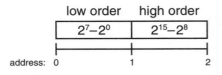

low order	high order
2^7–2^0	2^{15}–2^8

address: 0   1   2

Figure 2.3

Compare Figures 2.2 and 2.3 to see how the byte order was swapped.

Unfortunately, this made a huge mess for us all, because some chips use little-endian, and some chips use big-endian. When these computers attempt to communicate with each other with data larger than a byte, problems ensue.

Obviously, this is a huge problem for networking, since there must be a standard byte ordering for data over a network. Therefore, when the Internet was first created, the creators decided to use big-endian for the *network byte order*. Everything in every packet header is supposed to be in big-endian, the proper mathematical ordering. How the data is organized outside of the protocol headers is really up to you and how you design your Application layer protocols, but it is usually recommended that you keep data in big-endian for consistency's sake.

NOTE

The big-little-endian reference is actually an inside joke from the classic novel *Gulliver's Travels*, by Jonathan Swift (which is a scathing political commentary, not a children's tale, but that's a story for another day). In the book, two clans constantly argue over which side of a hard-boiled egg should be eaten first—the little end or the big end. They are called, respectively, the little-endians and the big-endians. You learn something new every day.

Now, the important question is this: How do I convert data from my *host byte order* (which may or may not be big-endian, depending on the system) to the network byte order? The Sockets API was nice enough to include four functions for just this purpose:

```
// host to network long:
unsigned long htonl( unsinged long );

// network to host long:
unsigned long ntohl( unsinged long );

// host to network short:
```

```
unsigned short htons( unsigned short );

// network to host short:
unsigned short ntohs( unsigned short );
```

Now that we've got that out of the way, on to the beef!

What Is a Socket?

You've probably heard the term many times before in many contexts, but what is a *socket*? Probably the first thing that springs to mind is an electrical socket, like that shown in Figure 2.4.

CAUTION

If you know that your system is in big-endian order, you should still use the `htonl` and `ntohl` functions, in the interest of portability. You never know when you'll want to convert the program to a different platform, and you can save yourself lots of headaches by using the functions. Besides, if your system is already in big-endian, calling these functions won't incur overhead, since any decent compiler will just ignore the function call. So omitting the functions doesn't speed things up.

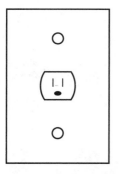

Figure 2.4

A typical electrical socket used in North America.

The electrical socket may look unfamiliar to you if you do not live in North America, but I'm sure you have your own equivalent. You plug an electrical device into the socket to make a connection and can then use all of its services, such as electricity.

There are literally thousands of other kinds of sockets, such as phone sockets (also known as RJ-11 *jacks*), Ethernet sockets (RJ-45), and so on.

Network sockets are similar in concept, but they aren't actual physical objects like electrical sockets are. With network programming, each machine in a two-machine connection creates a socket, and then one machine connects to the other. Figure 2.5 shows three computers in a simple socket network.

Before I let you dive down into some actual socket coding, I'll explain the different "kinds" of sockets. I put that word in quotation marks for a reason, which you will understand later on, when I get into the code examples.

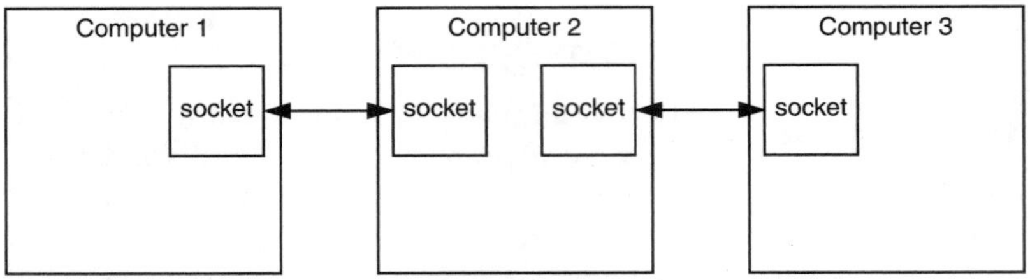

Figure 2.5

This simple network connects three computers (1 to 2, and 3 to 2).

Listening Sockets

The most important kind of socket is the *listening socket*. This is a socket that the server creates with a specific port number. Once the socket is created, it sits there and listens. Think of a person sitting by a telephone waiting for a call.

This kind of socket is used only with TCP connections, since TCP is a connection-oriented protocol. UDP does not use listening sockets.

Once a listening socket receives a TCP connection, it creates a new socket of a different type so that you can "talk" to the socket.

Data Sockets

The other kind of socket is a *data socket*. These sockets don't do any listening; instead, they "call" a server and, once connected to a server, data sockets can send or receive data (hence the name data sockets).

Connection Diagrams

Figure 2.6 shows a connection diagram for TCP. When the server starts up, it creates a listening socket and assigns it a port number. When the client wants to connect to the listening socket, it creates a data socket and tells it to connect to the listening socket. When the listening socket gets the connection request, it creates a new data socket, and then the server and the client can communicate through their data sockets.

UDP is even simpler, as shown in Figure 2.7.

Remember, UDP is a connectionless protocol, so there is no connecting needed, ever.

> ### NOTE
> Because UDP is connectionless and doesn't implement flow controls as TCP does, it is a popular protocol for Internet viruses and *Distributed Denial Of Service* (DDOS) attacks. UDP is one of the most abused protocols, but that doesn't mean you shouldn't use it.

You just create the socket on a specific port and send or receive packets.

Whether or not the data is actually received, the timing of the transmission is up to the Application layer protocol, instead of the Transport protocol.

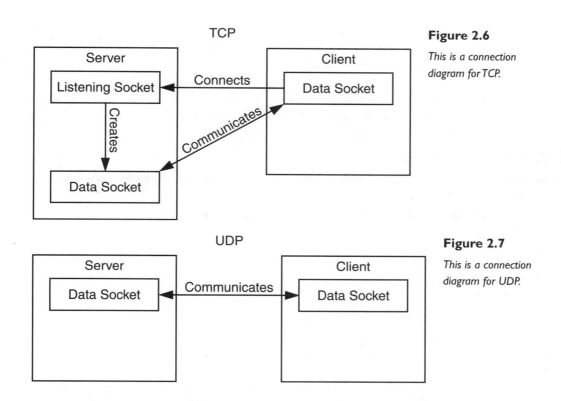

Figure 2.6

This is a connection diagram for TCP.

Figure 2.7

This is a connection diagram for UDP.

Sockets API

I'm going to be brutal here for a second; the Sockets API is *ugly*. It's versatile, it works, and it's stable, but it's ugly. The Sockets API was created when C was king, and C++ didn't even exist, so clean object-oriented interfaces were unknown.

Because of this, the entire API is built with all kinds of messy structs and unions, as well as badly named functions. Of course, the Sockets API is also the most popular networking API in the world, which means you usually have no choice but to bite the bullet and use it. The trick is to create a thin layer of sane software above it.

I'm not going to spend a great deal of time on the actual API; after all, this book is about MUDs, not network programming in

> **NOTE**
>
> The Microsoft Winsock API is an implementation of the Berkeley Sockets API, but they are not completely compatible. I will notify you about the differences when I get to them. Don't worry—there aren't many. A few `#ifdefs` here and there are enough to ensure that your networking programs are compatible with both UNIX and Windows. Platform independence is a wonderful thing.

general. There are literally hundreds of books that cover this material better than I can, since they are purely about networking. This chapter is an introduction to the API that teaches you its use in relation to MUDs; therefore, I won't get into the juicy details of multicasting and other things you may never use.

Two good books that cover this material are *Multiplayer Game Programming* by Todd Barron, and *Network Programming for Microsoft Windows*, by Anthony Jones and Jim Ohlund.

Header Files

The main difference between the Sockets API and Winsock is that they require different header files to access the APIs.

Winsock is easy in this regard; everything you need is in two files:

```
#include "winsock.h"
#include "ws2tcpip.h"
```

On UNIX systems, the Sockets API is spread among many different header files, thus making things more difficult. What a surprise, huh?

Table 2.1 lists the file names and their contents.

Don't worry if you don't know what some of that stuff means for now; I will eventually get to it all.

NOTE

The file winsock.h contains the header information for Version 1 of Winsock. The newer version of Winsock, Winsock 2, adds a whole slew of new networking features, but alas, they are for Windows only. The header for Winsock 2 is (surprise!) winsock2.h. It really makes no difference which header you use; however, stick to the base Sockets API, since Winsock 2 is completely backward compatible. In fact, it may even be better to use Winsock 2 (pretty much every Microsoft operating system since Windows 95 has had Winsock 2 built in) since the implementation is better optimized than in the old version. Just be sure to include the same version library file with your project. See Appendix A, "Setting Up Your Compilers" (found on the CD), for more information.

Unix

Table 2.1   Sockets API Header Files

File	Contents
sys/types.h	All the needed basic types
sys/socket.h	All the socket data structures
netinet/in.h	All the functions needed for IPv4 and IPv6
unistd.h	The `gethostname()` function needed to find the name of the local machine
netdb.h	All the needed DNS functions
arpa/inet.h	All the functions that start with `inet_`
errno.h	All the error handling stuff
fcntl.h	All the file control stuff

Socket API Errors

In UNIX, all sockets are files. The operating system doesn't differentiate between sockets and files, so you can use the same reading and writing functions with both. Because of this, whenever a socket error occurs, the global variable `errno` is set with the error value.

Unfortunately, Windows took an entirely different approach to the system, so sockets and files are treated as separate entities. To make matters worse, they've also made Winsock incompatible with the `errno` error reporting system. So, whenever an error occurs, you must retrieve the error by using the `WSAGetLastError()` function. Don't worry, though—they both return the same error values.

You can solve this conflict by using `#defines`, and I show you how to do this in Chapter 4, "The Basic Library," where I explain how to abstract the Socket APIs into a wrapper.

Appendix B, "Socket Error Codes" (found on the CD), has a complete listing of all the error codes and their meanings. I have attempted to list every error that is possible for each socket function in this chapter, but you should note that other socket errors might occur in the underlying network subsystem as well.

Initializing the API

This is another area in which Winsock strays from the pure Sockets API. The Sockets API doesn't need to be initialized; you can just jump right in and start using it. Winsock, however, needs to be initialized first. It also needs to be shut down when you are finished using it. The initialization and shutdown functions are listed here:

```
int WSAStartup( WORD wVersionRequested, LPWSADATA lpWSAData );
int WSACleanup( void );
```

The first function takes two parameters: the number of the Winsock version you want to use, and a pointer to a WSADATA structure that will contain data about Winsock. As of this writing, the most current Winsock version is 2.2, so you initialize Winsock like this:

```
WSADATA winsockdata;
WSAStartup( MAKEWORD( 2, 2 ), &winsockdata );
```

It is usually best to keep track of the WSADATA structure, even though you're probably not going to use it. The MAKEWORD function is a handy macro that creates a 16-bit value using the two-byte values you pass into it.

When initializing the API, either a zero is returned to indicate no errors, or an error value is returned. Table 2.2 lists all possible error values.

Table 2.2   WSAStartup() Error Codes

Error	Meaning
WSAENOTREADY	The network is not ready to be initialized.
WSAVERNOTSUPPORTED	The supplied Winsock version is not supported.
WSAEINPROGRESS	A blocking Winsock call is already in progress.
WSAEPROCLIM	There are too many programs running Winsock at the moment.
WSAEFAULT	The pointer to the WSADATA structure was invalid.

When you want to shut down Winsock, just call the WSACleanup function.

Creating a TCP Listening Socket

I will begin by showing you how to create a listening socket for TCP.

I've already described the different types of sockets, and unfortunately, the Sockets API doesn't really distinguish among them. All sockets are identified by a common datatype: int. Yep; every socket is just an integer. The Sockets API keeps track of everything for you internally.

> ## CAUTION
>
> In general, it is always safer to use the typedefs that the API provides. In Winsock, even though a SOCKET is an int when you use it, it may not always be. The Winsock API functions specifically use SOCKETs, and if Microsoft decides to change a socket into type foobar someday, then you'll be out of luck if you assumed you were using ints. While it would be inconvenient for Microsoft to do so, things like this have happened before. The bottom line is this: It's safer to use typedefs than to assume that you're using a specific datatype.

As an alternative, Winsock gives you the option of using the SOCKET typedef. If you trace all the way down through the header files, you eventually find that the SOCKET typedef is an int!

For now, I am going to assume that a socket is an integer; in Chapter 4, I will show you how to seamlessly abstract the two APIs into a single wrapper.

Creating the Socket

Here's the code to create a socket:

```
int sock = socket( AF_INET, SOCK_STREAM, IPPROTO_TCP );
```

This code calls the socket function, which attempts to create a socket for you. The first parameter is the *Address Family*, which determines what network your socket will use.

The second parameter is the *Socket Type*. The example uses a type called SOCK_STREAM, which means it will be a TCP socket. If you want to make this a UDP socket, you would use SOCK_DGRAM instead. (DGRAM means datagram.)

Finally, the last parameter is *Protocol*. Different socket types may have several associated protocols. For example, the most popular SOCK_STREAM protocol is IPPROTO_TCP, which is used in the example. The popular SOCK_DGRAM protocols are IPPROTO_UDP and IPPROTO_ICMP. As I said earlier, you're going to be concerned mainly with TCP and UDP.

> ## NOTE
>
> The Sockets API has the capability to use many types of networks, other than IP networks. However, in practice, you will almost never need to use any of these other networks, since most of them are either outdated or reserved for private companies. Therefore, you will almost always be using the AF_INET address family.

If the function fails, it returns -1. If the function succeeds, a socket descriptor is returned. Table 2.3 lists the various error values that errno/WSAGetLastError() will contain if it fails.

Table 2.3   socket() Error Values

Error	Meaning
ENETDOWN	The network has failed and is down.
EAFNOSUPPORT	The specified address family is not supported.
EINPROGRESS	A call to this function is still in progress, so the new call could not be completed.
EMFILE	No more socket descriptors are available.
ENOBUFS	There isn't enough memory available.
EPROTONOSUPPORT	The specified protocol is not supported.
EPROTOTYPE	The specified protocol is not supported by the socket type.
ESOCKTNOSUPPORT	The specified socket type is not supported by the address family.
WSAENOTINITIALIZED*	The Socket Library isn't initialized.

*Winsock only

Binding the Socket

So now you have a socket. Next you want to *bind* the socket to a port number. Unfortunately, it's not as easy as it sounds; first you need to fill out a messy data structure.

Before you do that, though, I will show you the function definition:

```
int bind( int socket, struct sockaddr *name, int namelen );
```

The first parameter is the socket descriptor that you created with the socket function.

The second parameter is a sockaddr structure, which describes all types of things about the socket—most importantly the port number. But there are other things as well, which I'll get to in a bit.

The final parameter is the size of the sockaddr structure. Why is this needed? The sockaddr structure really isn't that important in the grand scheme of things; it's a flexible structure that has no solid definition. Depending on the socket type and protocol you use, this structure varies in size, so it is important for the function to know this.

Here is the standard definition of the sockaddr structure:

```
struct sockaddr {
    unsigned short      sa_family;
    char                sa_data[14];
};
```

The first piece of data is the sa_family variable. This is set to the address family that your socket is using, which is almost always AF_INET, the Internet address family. The rest of the structure is just padding to fill out the 16 bytes.

Obviously, this doesn't contain a heck of a lot of information about a socket connection, so it's not that useful. Instead, you'll be using a more specific version, called sockaddr_in, where the in stands for Internet. You can think of this as an ancient form of inheritance, before inheritance was actually invented. The base structure is sockaddr, and a more specific version that is designed for IP networks is the sockaddr_in structure.

The new structure looks like this:

```
struct sockaddr_in {
    unsigned short   sin_family;
    unsigned short   sin_port;
    struct in_addr   sin_addr;
    char             sin_zero[8];
};
```

The first variable, sin_family, is the same as the sa_family from the sockaddr structure. The sin_port variable is simply the port number on which the socket will be open.

The third variable, sin_addr, is the IP address, which has two functions: First, if it's a listening socket, the socket uses this address for listening; second, if it's a client-side data socket, the socket uses this as the IP address for connecting. (I'll explain this in more detail in the section entitled "Creating a TCP Data Socket.")

Both the port and the address are supposed to be in network byte order.

The last variable, sin_zero, is just padding to fill the structure to 16 bytes. Some implementations of the Sockets API require that the padding must be filled in to zero, so you *must* do this.

So, now to actually bind a socket, you first create the sockaddr_in structure and fill it out:

```
struct sockaddr_in socketaddress;                       // create struct
socketaddress.sin_family = AF_INET;                     // set it for Internet
socketaddress.sin_port = htons( 1000 );                 // use port 1000
socketaddress.sin_addr.s_addr = htonl( INADDR_ANY );    // bind to any address
memset( &(socketaddress.sin_zero), 0, 8 );              // clear padding
```

This binds a socket to port 1000 and to address INADDR_ANY. Basically, this means that the socket will accept any incoming connections. You will almost always use that value, but you can use other values instead. For example, if you use the address 127.0.0.1 (the loopback

TIP

If you are running a Network Address Translation (NAT) on your own personal network, each computer on your local area network (LAN) has its own IP address (usually in the 192.168.0.* range of addresses), but from outside your LAN, the Internet sees all your computers as a single IP address. By specifying your LAN IP address, you can prevent people from accessing your network programs if they aren't on your LAN. That way, the socket will only accept connections from computers that are trying to reach your LAN address, which isn't visible on the Internet. Figure 2.8 shows a simple NAT/LAN setup, in which the Internet sees the attached computers as one IP address. All the computers behind the NAT are assigned internal IP addresses and are accessed by the Internet using the IP address of the NAT itself. The Internet doesn't know or care about the internal addresses.

address that references your own computer), the socket accepts only connections that are trying to connect to the IP address 127.0.0.1. Since packets that are sent to your computer from other computers won't be trying to access that address, the socket won't accept connections from outside your computer.

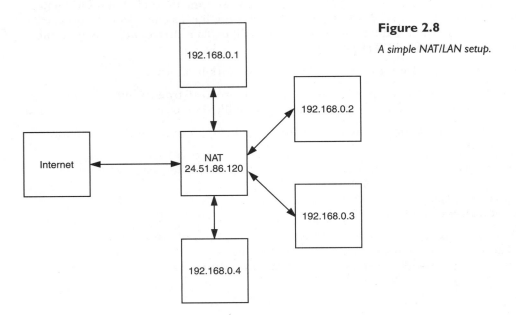

Figure 2.8

A simple NAT/LAN setup.

The Sockets API provides a handy function for converting an IP address in string form to an integer in network byte order. For example, if you want to use the IP address 127.0.0.1 in the sockaddr_in structure, you type this:

```
socketaddress.sin_addr.s_addr = inet_addr( "127.0.0.1" );
```

Finally, you want to bind the socket with the address structure, so you type this:

```
bind( sock, (struct sockaddr*)&socketaddress, sizeof(struct sockaddr));
```

If the function doesn't succeed, it returns -1. If it succeeds, it returns 0. Table 2.4 shows the possible error codes.

Table 2.4   bind() Error Codes

Error	Meaning
ENETDOWN	The network has failed and is down.
EINPROGRESS	A call to this function is still in progress, so the new call could not be completed.
ENOBUFS	There isn't enough memory available.
ENOTSOCK	The socket descriptor passed in is not a real socket.
EACCES	Access was denied.
EADDRINUSE	The address is already in use.
EADDRNOTAVAIL	The address is not valid for this machine.
EFAULT	One or more of the parameters were invalid.
WSAENOTINITIALIZED*	The Socket Library isn't initialized.

*Winsock only

Now your socket is bound and ready to accept connections!

Listening

Now that you've bound your socket to an address and port, you need to make it listen for connections. Luckily for us, this function is incredibly simple:

```
int listen( int socket, int backlog );
```

The function accepts a socket descriptor and a backlog parameter. The backlog essentially tells the socket how many connections to keep in its queue before it starts refusing them. A connection stays in the socket's queue until you use the `accept()` function to remove it.

Here is an example of calling the function:

```
listen( sock, 16 );
```

This tells the Sockets API that you want to listen on the socket, and you want it to queue 16 connections. If 17 machines try to connect to this socket before you are able to accept the connections, the seventeenth connection is refused, and the first 16 remain in the queue until you accept them. Whenever you accept a connection, it is removed from the queue, and more connections can then be queued up.

If no error occurs, 0 is returned; if an error occurs, -1 is returned. Table 2.5 lists the error codes for this function.

Table 2.5   listen() Error Codes

Error	Meaning
ENETDOWN	The network has failed and is down.
EADDRINUSE	The address is already in use.
EINPROGRESS	A call to this function is still in progress, so the new call could not be completed.
EINVAL	The socket is not valid.
EISCONN	The socket is already connected.
EMFILE	No more socket descriptors are available.
ENOBUFS	There isn't enough memory available.
ENOTSOCK	The socket descriptor passed in is not a real socket.
EOPNOTSUPP	The socket doesn't support this function.
WSAENOTINITIALIZED*	The Socket Library isn't initialized.

*Winsock only

Now your socket is listening, and you're ready to accept connections!

Accepting Connections

At last, you are at the final part of the listening socket cycle—accepting connections. It's taken quite a while to get this far, hasn't it? This is how you would call the function:

```
int accept( int socket, struct sockaddr *addr, socklen_t *addrlen );
```

The function has three parameters: the listening socket descriptor, a pointer to a `sockaddr`, and a pointer to an `int`.

The `sockaddr` structure is filled out by the function; you can think of it as a caller-id box; it indicates who is connecting to you. The `addrlen` pointer is supposed to contain the length of the `addr` structure. Why is it a pointer? Well, presumably, it is possible for the `accept` function to modify this value, but I've never seen it happen. It's just one of those quirks of the API. Here is how you would accept the function:

```
int datasock;
struct sockaddr_in socketaddress;
socklen_t sa_size = sizeof( struct sockaddr_in );
datasock = accept( sock, &socketaddress, &sa_size );
```

Now the `datasock` variable should be a data socket, and you can use it to communicate with the caller. If the function fails, it returns -1. Table 2.6 lists the possible error codes.

Table 2.6   accept() Error Codes

Error	Meaning
ENETDOWN	The network has failed and is down.
EINPROGRESS	A call to this function is still in progress, so the new call cannot be completed.
EINVAL	The socket is not valid.
EMFILE	No more socket descriptors are available.
ENOBUFS	There isn't enough memory available.
ENOTSOCK	The socket descriptor passed in is not a real socket.
EOPNOTSUPP	The socket doesn't support this function.
EFAULT	One or more of the parameters were invalid.
EWOULDBLOCK	The function exited because it would block.
WSAENOTINITIALIZED*	The Socket Library isn't initialized.

* Winsock only

One important aspect of this call differs significantly from any other calls I've shown you so far—it *blocks*. See the following sidebar for an explanation about blocking.

Blocking Functions

If you are unfamiliar with the term *blocking*, that's okay. If you've ever used the `cin` or `scanf` functions before, you've encountered blocking.

A blocking function depends on external input (keyboard or network) and cannot complete until that input is received. Unfortunately, these input sources are not reliable; keyboard input can take a long time if the user isn't there to type anything in, and network communications take time. However, a blocking function stops your entire program and just waits for that external data to arrive.

In the bad old days, this was desirable behavior. There were many programs running on a system, and whenever a program needed input from a potentially slow source, it could stop the program and switch to something else while waiting for input.

This isn't such a great idea for games, though. No one wants the entire game to stop just to wait for network or keyboard data—that's just annoying. Fortunately, there are ways around this. You can make sockets *nonblocking*, which means that any blocking function will fail and return an `EWOULDBLOCK` error if there is no data already queued up for it to use. I won't go into this method much; it is generally wasteful of CPU usage, since the CPU is wasting time by constantly polling every socket.

Another method uses the `select()` function to poll many sockets at once to check if any of them has activity. This is the desired method for *single-threaded* programs. I cover this method later on in this chapter.

A third popular option is to use *multithreading* and have each blocking call occur in its own thread, so that none disrupts the other threads of the program. I cover threading in detail in Chapter 3, "Introduction to Multithreading."

Creating a TCP Data Socket

You've just learned how to create a listening socket for TCP, which is great for servers. However, a listing socket is pretty useless if you don't have a method for connecting to it. This is where the data socket comes in.

Luckily, creating a data socket is nice and easy and takes only two function calls. The first one should be familiar to you.

Creating the Socket

Actually, creating the socket uses the same function as a listening socket: the `socket()` function. I bet you didn't see that one coming, right?

Basically, you'll use the same parameters as last time:

```
int datasock;
datasock = socket( AF_INET, SOCK_STREAM, IPPROTO_TCP );
```

Ta-da! You now have a socket!

Connecting the Socket

Connecting a data socket to a listening socket takes one function call. Can you guess the function name? If you said `connect()`, you get a star!

The function definition looks like this:

```
int connect( int socket, const struct sockaddr *name, int namelen );
```

The first thing you should notice is that it looks exactly like the `bind` function.

You need to fill out a `sockaddr`-type structure, which is going to be the `sockaddr_in` structure, since we're using TCP. This time, you're going to fill it out with the address you want to connect to. For example, if you want to connect to 192.168.0.2 on port 4000, you fill out the structure like this:

```
struct sockaddr_in socketaddress;
socketaddress.sin_family = AF_INET;
socketaddress.sin_port = htons( 4000 );
socketaddress.sin_addr.s_addr = inet_addr( "192.168.0.2" );
memset( &(socketaddress.sin_zero), 0, 8 );
```

After you fill that out, you can connect:

```
connect( datasock, &socketaddress, sizeof( struct sockaddr ) );
```

If there are no errors, 0 is returned; if there are errors, -1 is returned. Table 2.7 lists the error codes possible with this function.

If the function call succeeds, you are connected to a server and ready to send and receive data!

Table 2.7   connect() Error Codes

Error	Meaning
ENETDOWN	The network has failed and is down.
EINPROGRESS	A call to this function is still in progress, so the new call could not be completed.
EADDRINUSE	The address is already in use.
EINVAL	The socket is not valid.
EADDRNOTAVAIL	The remote address is not valid.
EAFNOSUPPORT	The specified address family is not supported.
ENOBUFS	There isn't enough memory available.
ENOTSOCK	The socket descriptor passed in is not a real socket.
EWOULDBLOCK	The function exited because it would block.
ECONNREFUSED	The server refused the connection.
EFAULT	One or more of the parameters were invalid.
EISCONN	The socket is already connected.
ENETUNREACH	The destination address is unreachable.
ENOTSOCK	The socket descriptor passed in is not a real socket.
ETIMEDOUT	The operation failed to complete in the time-out period.
WSAENOTINITIALIZED*	The Socket Library isn't initialized.

*Winsock only

Sending Data

Now that you've got a data socket, you can send data. This is an amazingly simple operation to accomplish, using the send function:

```
int send( int socket, const char *buffer, int len, int flags );
```

The first parameter is obviously the socket you want to use for sending the data, and the second parameter is a pointer to a buffer. The buffer is in *chars*, which is just a big chunk of bytes in memory. The next parameter is the length of the data in the buffer, and finally there is a Flags parameter. You'll probably never use any of the flags, since they're only useful to low-level network programmers, so I won't bother explaining them here. If you're really interested, networking books cover the details.

So, to send data, you would do something like this:

```
char* string = "hello, Internet!";
int sent;
sent = send( datasock, string, strlen( string ), 0 );
```

The function returns the number of bytes that send actually sent. Beware that the function may not send all the bytes you requested. In this case, you should attempt to resend what wasn't sent.

If the call fails, the value of -1 is returned. Table 2.8 lists the error codes for this function.

Pretty easy, don't you think?

Receiving Data

Receiving data is just as easy as sending data. Here is the function definition for the recv() function:

```
int recv( int socket, char *buffer, int len, int flags );
```

As you can see, the parameters are the same as the send() function. So you call it like this:

```
char buffer[128];
int received;
received = recv( datasock, buffer, 128, 0 );
```

This creates a buffer large enough for 128 bytes of data and then waits for incoming data. Note that this function probably returns before it gets a full 128 bytes of data, and it receives only a maximum of 128 bytes of memory, so you don't have to worry about the buffer overflowing.

As usual, the function returns -1 on failure. Table 2.9 lists the error codes.

Note also that recv() is a blocking function; it stops everything in the current thread and waits for the next TCP packet to arrive.

That's pretty much it.

Table 2.8   send() Error Codes

Error	Meaning
ENETDOWN	The network has failed and is down.
EINPROGRESS	A call to this function is still in progress, so the new call could not be completed.
EACCES	Access was denied.
EFAULT	One or more of the parameters were invalid.
ENETRESET	The network has been reset and the connection broken.
ENOBUFS	There isn't enough memory available.
ENOTCONN	The socket is not connected.
ENOTSOCK .	The socket descriptor passed in is not a real socket.
EOPNOTSUPP	The socket doesn't support this function or option.
ESHUTDOWN	The socket has been shut down.
EWOULDBLOCK	The function exited because it would block.
EHOSTUNREACH	The host is unreachable.
EINVAL	The socket is not valid.
ECONNABORTED	The connection was aborted and the socket is no longer usable.
ECONNRESET	The connection was closed by the other side.
ETIMEDOUT	The connection was closed unexpectedly.
WSAENOTINITIALIZED*	The Socket Library isn't initialized.

*Winsock only

Table 2.9   recv() Error Codes

Error	Meaning
ENETDOWN	The network has failed and is down.
EFAULT	One or more of the parameters were invalid.
ENOTCONN	The socket is not connected.
EINPROGRESS	A call to this function is still in progress, so the new call could not be completed.
ENETRESET	The network has been reset and the connection broken.
ENOTSOCK	The socket descriptor passed in is not a real socket.
EOPNOTSUPP	The socket doesn't support this function or option.
ESHUTDOWN	The socket has been shut down.
EWOULDBLOCK	The function exited because it would block.
EINVAL	The socket is not valid.
ECONNABORTED	The connection was aborted, and the socket is no longer usable.
ETIMEDOUT	The connection was closed unexpectedly.
ECONNRESET	The connection was closed by the other side.
WSAENOTINITIALIZED*	The Socket Library isn't initialized.

*Winsock only

Closing a Socket

Once you've finished using a socket, you close it by calling two functions: the `shutdown()` function and the `close()` function.

First, you call the `shutdown()` function. Here is the function definition:

```
int shutdown( int socket, int how );
```

The first parameter is the socket you are shutting down, and the second parameter is the method you are using to shut it down. In almost all cases, you use the value 2, which shuts down both sending and receiving. The other two possible options are 0 and 1, which shut down receiving and sending, respectively.

As usual, the function returns 0 on success and -1 on failure. Table 2.10 lists the possible error codes.

Table 2.10   shutdown() Error Codes

Error	Meaning
ENETDOWN	The network has failed and is down.
EINVAL	The socket is not valid.
EINPROGRESS	A call to this function is still in progress, so the new call could not be completed.
ENOTCONN	The socket is not connected.
ENOTSOCK	The socket descriptor passed in is not a real socket.
WSAENOTINITIALIZED*	The Socket Library isn't initialized.

*Winsock only

After you shut down a socket, it still exists in the system. The socket takes care of any pending data that is sent or received and *gracefully* shuts down, but the socket isn't yet closed. You need to make one more call to close it.

In UNIX sockets are files. Because of this, you can use the standard UNIX close() function to close a socket.

However, Windows sockets are *not* files, so calling the close() function on them won't work. For this reason, Microsoft changed the function's name to closesocket(). The parameters and the return values are the same. Here is the definition:

```
int close( int socket );
```

Pretty simple function, don't you think?

As usual, the function returns 0 on success and -1 on failure. This function has the same error codes as the shutdown() function, which are listed in Table 2.10.

Miscellaneous Functions

There are several other miscellaneous functions associated with the Sockets API.

Converting IP Addresses to Strings and Back

The first of these miscellaneous functions is the inet_addr() function, which takes an IP address in a string and converts it into an unsigned long:

```
unsigned long inet_addr( const char *string );
```

The string must be in *.*.*.* format, where each number between the periods is a number from 0 to 255. If you used an invalid string, the function returns the value INADDR_NONE. Also remember that the address is returned in network-byte-order (NBO), so there is no need to convert it when using it with the Sockets functions.

The next function does the opposite; it takes a numeric address and converts it to a string:

```
char* inet_ntoa( struct in_addr in );
```

This is one ugly function; I hate it with a passion. Okay, you know that Internet addresses are stored in unsigned longs, right? So why the heck does the function take a structure called in_addr? Who knows? The designers decided to make things difficult for us.

So you must convert your Internet address into an in_addr first, which requires code that looks like this:

```
unsigned long address = inet_addr( "192.168.0.1" );
struct in_addr addr;
addr.S_un.S_addr = address;     // ugh, UGLY!
char* addrstr = inet_ntoa( addr );
```

Isn't that ugly? The in_addr structure is a *union*, which is an ancient C concept that is rarely used nowadays, but it allows you to store many different types of data in the same amount of memory, as long as the different types don't exist at the same time. Make sense? If not, don't worry about it. It's not important.

So anyway, addrstr in the example will now be a pointer to a string. But you shouldn't do anything to it, except copy it immediately and store the result for your own use. The function actually has a static (or global, in some implementations) string buffer that it keeps for itself, and whenever the function is called, it overwrites the buffer contents. This means that you shouldn't try deleting the buffer either, which is another reason why this function is just plain ugly. Anyway, when it's done, the string should contain 192.168.0.1. If an error occurs (though I've never seen this happen), NULL is returned.

Getting Socket Information

The next function is used to get information about a socket:

```
int getsockname( int socket, struct sockaddr* name, socklen_t* namelen );
```

Essentially, this gets the port and address of a socket and stuffs it into a sockaddr_in structure. Here is an example:

```
struct sockaddr_in addr;
socklen_t sa_size = sizeof( struct sockaddr_in );// fill out the size
```

```
getsockname( sock, (struct sockaddr*)&addr, &sa_size );
unsigned short port = ntohs( addr.sin_port );    // get the port number
unsigned long address = ntohl( addr.sin_addr );  // get the address number
```

You can see why I dislike this function; it requires an inordinate amount of work to accomplish a simple task. You need to have an address structure, and you need to fill in an integer with its size as well. Then you can call the function and retrieve the data you want. Pain in the butt!

The other function in this category gets the information of the *peer*, which is the computer on the other side of the connection:

```
int getpeername( int socket, struct sockaddr* name, socklen_t* namelen );
```

This function is virtually identical to the previous one. Note that you may get ENOTCONN errors with the peer function, if it's not connected yet.

Domain Name System

IP addresses are like phone numbers. However, IP addresses are longer than phone numbers most of the time, and it is virtually impossible to remember them. Humans are typically bad at remembering long strings of numbers; words are much easier to remember.

Therefore, the designers of the Internet figured out a way to reference IP addresses by names. They decided to create a hierarchical system called the *Domain Name System (DNS)*.

DNS is hierarchical, which makes lookups easy to do. For example, in the beginning, the Internet had seven *Top-Level Domains (TLDs);* most should be familiar to you. They are listed in Table 2.11.

Table 2.11   Original Top-Level Domains

Domain	Meaning
.com	Commercial use
.net	Network providers, mostly ISPs
.org	Nonprofit organizations
.edu	Educational institutions
.mil	United States military sites
.gov	United States government sites
.int	International sites

As you can see, the domains were largely U.S.-centric, which led to many problems once the Internet became a worldwide construct. Because of this, each country has been assigned its own two-letter TLD, which it should use. Using the old domains is discouraged, although that's not stopping anyone. Some examples of these TLDs are .us (USA), .uk (United Kingdom), .fr (France), .de (Germany), .au (Australia), and even .ax (Antarctica—don't ask).

You can imagine that all of these addresses are at the top level of a tree. Figure 2.9 shows this. The next part of the DNS hierarchy is the domain level. For google.com, this would be "google." Essentially, each root DNS server keeps track of the IP address of every domain.

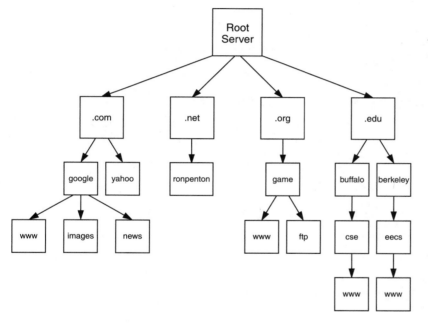

Figure 2.9

A partial hierarchy of the DNS system.

So when you ask your DNS server for the address of google.com, it goes to the .com server, looks up "google," and then returns the result. At the time of writing, google.com could be found at 216.239.33.100, but that might change by the time you read this.

That's not all a DNS server can do, however. For example, you're probably used to seeing addresses like "www.google.com." That "www" at the front is the name of a specific machine on Google's network. So when your DNS server looks up "google.com," it then contacts the DNS server on Google's main machine (216.239.33.100) and asks it for the address of the machine named "www." At the time of writing, that is returning 216.239.33.99. Again, that might change by the time you read this.

To further illustrate my point, "news" resolves to 216.239.51.104, and "images" resolves to 216.239.37.104. All three of those services—"www," "news," and "images"—are running on different machines in the Google network. The root .com DNS server doesn't know about the different machines (it doesn't *need* to know about them); the server only knows about the root google.com DNS server. Pretty cool, right?

As you look at Figure 2.9, you can see that it's possible to chain on servers if you want. Look at the two .edu entries on the right. You can construct an address using that tree going to www.cse.buffalo.edu, or www.eecs.berkeley.edu.

So that's my tiny intro to DNS. DNS is a huge subject, and if you're interested, I suggest a good networking book.

Now, how do you use DNS in the Sockets API? You might think it's possible to do something like this:

```
unsigned long google = inet_addr( "www.google.com" );
```

But you'd be wrong. The inet_addr function converts only standard format IP addresses to a number; it doesn't look up DNSs.

Performing a DNS Lookup

As with everything in the Sockets API, the function of getting an IP address from a DNS lookup is just plain weird and ugly. Once again, the function introduces another strange structure: hostent. Here is what hostent looks like:

```
struct hostent {
  char*    h_name;
  char**   h_aliases;
  short    h_addrtype;
  short    h_length;
  char**   h_addr_list;
};
```

ARGH! Almost makes you want to throw a brick at something, doesn't it? Honestly, since I'm not going to be using this structure for anything other than looking up IP addresses, I really don't care to know what all those things mean.

Here is the gethostbyname function, which performs a DNS lookup:

```
struct hostent* gethostbyname( const char* name );
```

gethostbyname accepts a string for the name and returns a pointer to the hostent structure. So how the heck do you get an IP address out of that? Well, the IP address is stored as the first four bytes of the two-dimensional array h_addr_list. Here is one way to get the address:

```
struct hostent* host;
host = gethostbyname( "www.google.com" );
unsigned long addr = *((unsigned long*)host->h_addr_list[0]);
```

The code is maddeningly ugly, but it's a necessary evil. The last line gets the address of the first character in the 2D array, h_addr_list, converts that into an unsigned long pointer, and finally, dereferences it. If you have no idea what I just said, it doesn't matter. Just know that it works, and you'll be fine.

The helpful folks who designed the Sockets API decided to make things a tad easier for us. Before you celebrate, though, you should be warned that it's not that much of an improvement. They created a macro, named h_addr, which is really just h_addr_list[0]. So, instead of that huge ugly line I showed you previously, you can now have a slightly smaller ugly line:

```
unsigned long addr = *((unsigned long*)host->h_addr);
```

Well, I'll give them an "A" for effort—or maybe not.

If there was an error, the function returns NULL instead of a pointer to the hostent. However, you can't look up the error using errno or WSAGetLastError(). Why would the designers make things easy for you?

Instead, you must retrieve errors through a variable called h_errno. There is one saving grace to this horrible mess of an API, however: h_errno works on both the Sockets API and Winsock. Hooray!

Table 2.12 lists the error codes that are returned by h_errno if gethostbyname fails.

Table 2.12   gethostbyname() Error Codes

Error	Meaning
HOST_NOT_FOUND	The address didn't resolve to anything.
TRY_AGAIN	The DNS server failed, but the address still might be resolvable. Try again.
NO_RECOVERY	An unrecoverable error has occurred.
NO_DATA	There is no data available about the address.

There is one other thing you should know: The function cannot resolve addresses if they are already in IP form. For example, trying to resolve "192.168.0.1" fails, since it is already an IP address. Just something to remember.

Now, the cool thing about DNS is that you can do *reverse* lookups, too; you give DNS an IP address, and the system tries to find the DNS entry that matches. This is accomplished by using the gethostbyaddr() function:

```
struct hostent* gethostbyaddr( const char* addr, int len, int type );
```

Again with the hostent structure—sigh. The first parameter is a pointer to the address that you want to resolve, in NBO. Note that you'll need to do some casting, since NBO wants a char pointer, instead of a pointer to an unsigned long. This is to ensure flexibility, so that the function isn't bound to any specific type of address. The second parameter is the length of the address, and since we're using IPv4, this will be 4. Finally, the type of the address is the last parameter; since you're using IPv4, this is going to be AF_INET. For example, this is how you would call the function:

```
unsigned long address = inet_addr( "216.239.33.100" );
struct hostent* host;
host = gethostbyaddr( (char*)&address, 4, AF_INET );
```

If the function succeeds, you can retrieve the string result of the lookup by accessing the h_name variable inside your hostent structure. If the function fails, 0 is returned, and you can access the error code through h_errno. This function uses the same error codes that are listed in Table 2.12.

By the way, you should not attempt to modify or delete the hostent structures returned by either function; the Sockets API owns and manages them. Unfortunately, that means the structures might be overwritten without notice, so you should copy the data you need from them immediately.

That's pretty much all you need to know about DNS, so on to the fun stuff!

Demo 2.1 Hello Internet Server

Now that you've learned the basics of network programming, you are ready to start your own network program. In this demo, I show you how to create a server that listens for a string of data, prints it out, and quits. You can find the code for this demo on the CD in the directory / Demos/Chapter02/Demo01-HelloInternetServer/, in the file Demo01.cpp. Appendix A (found on the CD) contains instructions for compiling this demo with various compilers.

Basically, the aim of this demo is to create a listening socket and wait for an incoming connection; the demo then reads 128 bytes of data, prints it out to the screen, closes the sockets, and quits.

Include Files

The first piece of code I am going to show you is what I call Code Block 2.1. This block of code appears in all the demos in this chapter, and I want to show it to you only once. Here it is:

```
// Code Block 2.1 - Header Includes
// This code block includes all of the standard Sockets API/Winsock headers
#ifdef WIN32                    // Windows 95 and above
    #include "winsock2.h"
    #include "Ws2tcpip.h"
#else                           // UNIX/Linux
    #include <sys/types.h>
    #include <sys/socket.h>
    #include <netinet/in.h>
    #include <unistd.h>
    #include <netdb.h>
    #include <arpa/inet.h>
#endif
// End Code Block 2.1 - Header Includes
```

This block of code essentially relies on the definition of the preprocessor macro `WIN32` to tell if it's running on Windows or UNIX/Linux. If you're running Windows, the code just includes Winsock2.h and ws2tcpip.h; if you're running something else, it includes all the official Sockets API header files.

Platform-Independent Defines

Since the base Sockets API and the Winsock libraries differ in some respects, you need to create a way to make your code work no matter which implementation you are using. Since the APIs are almost equivalent, this is easy.

You have several options in this regard; for example, you could do this whenever you want to close a socket:

```
#ifdef WIN32
    closesocket( sock );
#else
    close( sock );
#endif
```

This method tends to be a little messy unless, of course, you isolate the socket-closing code into one area, as I do in Chapter 4 when creating a socket wrapper. But for now, this is an awkward and somewhat ugly method. Instead, let me show you Code Block 2.2:

```
// Code Block 2.2 - Redefinitions and globals for cross-compatibility
#ifdef WIN32                 // Windows 95 and above
    WSADATA g_wsadata;       // Winsock data holder
    #define CloseSocket closesocket
    #define GetSocketError WSAGetLastError
    #define StartSocketLib WSAStartup( MAKEWORD( 2, 2 ), &g_wsadata );
    #define CloseSocketLib WSACleanup();
    #ifndef socklen_t
        typedef int socklen_t;
    #endif
#else                        // UNIX/Linux
    #define CloseSocket close
    #define GetSocketError errno
    #define StartSocketLib {}
    #define CloseSocketLib {}
#endif
// End Code Block 2.2 - Redefinitions and globals for cross-compatibility
```

Because Winsock needs a `WSADATA` structure, one is defined in the WIN32 branch of the code. The next four lines address the four differences between Winsock and the Sockets API. For the Windows branch, the macro `CloseSocket` is just another name for `closesocket` (note the capitalization differences), and for the Linux branch, it is another name for `close`. The same thing is done for `GetSocketError`, which calls either `WSAGetLastError` or `errno`, depending on the system.

Finally, the last two lines define the socket library initialization and shutdown stages, which exist in Winsock, but not in the Sockets API. Therefore, the Windows version of `StartSocketLib` calls `WSAStartup`, and the UNIX version does absolutely nothing (empty brackets).

The Windows block has an extra three lines in it. It turns out that in some older versions of Winsock, the datatype `socklen_t` is not defined; so whenever the function detects that it doesn't exist, I simply define it as an `int`. You'll need `socklen_t` for many socket functions.

The Rest of the Code

This demo follows the basic life cycle of a standard server:

1. Create socket.
2. Bind socket.
3. Listen on socket.
4. Accept connection.
5. Receive/send data.
6. Close socket.

Here's the code for starting up the program:

```
#include <iostream>
using namespace std;
int main() {
    int err;
    StartSocketLib;
```

The program uses the Standard C++ `iostream` library; if you're not familiar with the library and namespaces, you should check out "C++ Primer" Appendix C (found on the CD).

The `err` variable is used for error reporting, as you will see in a minute. After that, the `StartSocketLib` macro is invoked, and depending on what system you are using for compilation, starts up Winsock (Windows) or does nothing (Linux).

Here's the next code segment that creates a socket. (Note that this begins Code Block 2.3.)

```
// BEGIN CODE BLOCK 2.3 - Create a Listening Socket on port 4000
int sock = socket( AF_INET, SOCK_STREAM, IPPROTO_TCP );
if( sock == -1 ) {
    cout << "Socket creation error!" << endl;
    return 0;
}
cout << "Socket created!" << endl;
```

After the call to `socket()`, I check to see if an error occurred, and if so, print out a message and return, quitting the program. If no error occurred, I print out a success message. All of the other functions have similar error message blocks, so in the interests of brevity, I will not print them here.

Here's the rest of the program:

```
// create a sockaddr_in for binding, listening on port 4000
struct sockaddr_in socketaddress;
socklen_t sa_size = sizeof( struct sockaddr_in );
socketaddress.sin_family = AF_INET;
socketaddress.sin_port = htons( 4000 );
socketaddress.sin_addr.s_addr = htonl( INADDR_ANY );
memset( &(socketaddress.sin_zero), 0, 8 );

// bind the socket
err = bind( sock, (struct sockaddr*)&socketaddress, sa_size );
```

The first block of code fills out a sockaddr_in structure. The second block binds the socket to port 4000 on every IP address available. Here's the listening and accepting code. (Note that Code Block 2.3 ends after the socket is told to listen.)

```
// listen on the socket
err = listen( sock, 16 );
// END CODE BLOCK 2.3 - Create a Listening Socket on port 4000

// wait for an incomming connection now
int datasock;
datasock = accept( sock, (struct sockaddr*)&socketaddress, &sa_size );
```

It creates a new socket when a connection is received. The datasock is used for communicating with the client. And here is the code for receiving the message from a client and printing it:

```
// receive data
char buffer[128];
err = recv( datasock, buffer, 128, 0 );

cout << "Data received:" << endl;
cout << buffer << endl;
```

Finally, here is the code for closing the sockets and shutting down the system:

```
shutdown( datasock, 2 );
CloseSocket( datasock );

shutdown( sock, 2 );
CloseSocket( sock );

CloseSocketLib;
}
```

At this point, you could compile and run the program, but it's pretty pointless without the existence of anything that could send data to the program. That is what the next section is for.

Demo 2.2 Hello Internet Client

This demo is the counterpart to Demo 2.1. It actually sends the data to the server, so the server can print it.

The demo is located on the CD in the directory /Demos/Chapter02/Demo02-HelloInternetClient/, in the file Demo02.cpp. As usual, this is a regular console app, and you can compile it using the instructions found in Appendix A (found on the CD).

The demo starts off with Code Blocks 2.1 and 2.2, which have been printed earlier, so there is no need to show them again here. This code introduces a new block, Code Block 2.4, which basically creates a socket for connection. The code looks like this:

```
#include <iostream>
#include <string.h>
using namespace std;
int main() {
    // BEGIN CODE BLOCK 2.4 - Creat a connecting data socket
    int err;
    char message[128] = "Hello Internet!";
    char ip[16] = "";
    unsigned long ipaddr;

    // start the socket library
    StartSocketLib;
```

This example uses the err variable again and three new variables as well. The message string contains the message to be sent, the ip string that contains the IP address of the server in string form, and the ipaddr variable that holds the IP address in network byte order.

After the library is started, the program asks the user for an IP address for connection:

```
    cout << "Enter the IP address to connect to: ";
    cin >> ip;

    // convert the IP address.
    ipaddr = inet_addr( ip );
    if( ipaddr == -1 ) {
        cout << "Error: invalid IP address" << endl;
        return 0;
    }
```

If the program doesn't work, it converts the string IP address into binary form and returns an error. As with the Demo 2.1 listing, I will remove the error blocks from now on, to show you the "beef" of the code.

This next block of code creates a socket, fills out another `sockaddr_in` structure (oy!), and then attempts to connect the socket:

```
// create a socket
int sock = socket( AF_INET, SOCK_STREAM, IPPROTO_TCP );

// create a sockaddr_in for connection, on port 4000
struct sockaddr_in socketaddress;
socklen_t sa_size = sizeof( struct sockaddr_in );
socketaddress.sin_family = AF_INET;
socketaddress.sin_port = htons( 4000 );
socketaddress.sin_addr.s_addr = ipaddr;
memset( &(socketaddress.sin_zero), 0, 8 );

// connect the socket
err = connect( sock, (struct sockaddr*)&socketaddress, sa_size );
// END CODE BLOCK 2.4 - creating a connecting data socket
```

Note that Code Block 2.4 ended in the previous code section. By this point, the socket should be connected and ready to send data, so that's what we do next:

```
cout << "sending message: " << message << "..." << endl;

// send data
err = send( sock, message, strlen( message ) + 1, 0 );
```

This sends the message through the socket. Pretty simple, eh? Finally, the socket is shut down, and the connection is closed:

```
shutdown( sock, 2 );
CloseSocket( sock );

CloseSocketLib;
}
```

Now that this is finished, you can fire up the server in a console window, fire up Demo 2.2, and watch the results. If you have a friend who is willing to help you test it over the Internet, you can send him either the server or the client and ask him to run it, while you run the other part. Figure 2.10 shows a screenshot of the two programs running at the same time.

From the demo, you can see that I ran both demos on one computer and used the standard 127.0.0.1 "loopback" address to connect to my own computer.

So, as you can see, sending and receiving data is pretty easy.

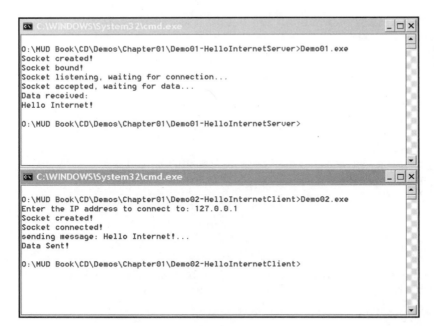

Figure 2.10

Demos 2.1 and 2.2 are running simultaneously.

Using select() to Avoid Multithreading

I have one more topic to cover in this chapter: using the `select()` function to avoid using multithreading in your programs. As you will see in Chapter 3, multithreading can sometimes be a pain in the butt; and you should consider yourself lucky that there is a way around it.

The `select()` function essentially checks a *set* of sockets, to see if any of them has activity. This helps greatly, because you do not need to waste time checking every socket to see if it has activity (like the non-blocking method), or creating a thread for every socket, which consumes memory.

The `select()` can handle a number of functions in the Sockets API block including the `accept`, `send`, and `recv` functions as well as the lesser-used DNS functions `gethostbyname` and `gethostbyaddr`. Unfortunately, you can't prevent the DNS functions from blocking, unless you specifically use multithreading, since DNS functions don't actually have anything to do with sockets. The `connect` function also blocks, but there is no way to prevent it from lagging up your program unless you use multithreading.

Here is the `select()` function definition:

```
int select( int numfds,
            fd_set *readfds,
```

```
fd_set *writefds,
fd_set *exceptfds,
struct timeval *timeout);
```

The first parameter is the number of the highest possible socket descriptor. Winsock just ignores this parameter, but UNIX doesn't. You can handle this in two ways. The first method is to keep track of your sockets and which one has the highest value. As you can imagine, this method is cumbersome; it's easier to just pass in the maximum value of an int, which is logically the highest value a socket descriptor can have. For a 32-bit system, you can pretty much assume that this is below the hexadecimal value 0x7FFFFFFF, which is the highest value for an int. Whether this changes on 64-bit systems remains to be seen.

> ## CAUTION
>
> You shouldn't really pass in 0x7FFFFFFF to the function, because that wastes a lot of time on UNIX-based systems. Since this is just a simple demo, I'm not terribly concerned about it, but when I get to the SocketLib in Chapters 4 and 5, you'll see me implement a better method.

The next three parameters of the select() function are all fd_sets, which are structures that keep track of a set of sockets. (fd means *file descriptor*, because in UNIX, sockets are files.)

You can use four helpful functions that relate to fd_sets: FD_ZERO, FD_SET, FD_CLR, and FD_ISSET. They clear an entire set, put a descriptor in a set, remove a descriptor from a set, and check to see if a descriptor is in a set, respectively. This example uses the four functions. The example assumes that sock is already defined elsewhere:

```
struct fd_set set;      // declare the set
FD_ZERO( &set );        // clear everything from the set
FD_SET( sock, &set );   // add sock to the set
FD_CLR( sock, &set );   // remove the socket from the set
bool b = FD_ISSET( sock, &set );      // this will return false
```

Pretty simple, isn't it?

Now, whenever you want to use the select() function, you need to fill out a set containing all of the sockets you wish to test using those functions. However, the function accepts three sets of sockets, so which set does what?

Check the first set of sockets, readfds, to see if you can read from them. For listening sockets, you can use this set of sockets to check if there are any incoming connections. For data sockets, this set of sockets tells you if any data has been received.

Check the second set of sockets, writefds, to be sure you can write to them. You can use this set of sockets to check if you can send data to the socket. (Sending data can block the system if you are trying to send too much at once.)

Check the final set of sockets, exceptfds, for errors. This set of sockets isn't used as often as the other two sets, because if an error occurs during the other operations, they return an error immediately anyway.

The final parameter to the function is a pointer to a timeval structure:

```
struct timeval {
    int tv_sec;      // seconds
    int tv_usec;     // microseconds
};
```

This structure essentially holds a number of seconds and microseconds, which the select function is supposed to wait for. If you set both values to 0, the function essentially returns immediately. If you pass NULL, the function waits forever, essentially blocking until something happens.

Instead of always creating a new structure whenever I call select, I like to create a global 0-time timeval structure and use that to pass into the function.

> **NOTE**
>
> Even though the timeval structure has a microsecond value, it's no-where near as accurate as that. You may find yourself waiting several thousand microseconds for the function to return, even if you specified 1!

So, finally, take a look at the function in action (assuming lsock and dsock are listening/data sockets that have been created previously):

```
struct fd_set set;
FD_SET( lsock, &set );
FD_SET( dsock, &set );
struct timeval zerotime;
zerotime.tv_usec = 0;
zerotime.tv_sec = 0;
int err = select( 0x7FFFFFFF, &set, NULL, NULL, &zerotime );
```

The function has a few different return values. If the function times out without finding sockets with activity, it returns 0. If there is an error, the function returns -1. If there are sockets with activity, the function returns the number of sockets that have activity.

So how do you know what sockets had activity? The function physically changes the three sets that were passed into it and removes every socket from the set that had no activity. Therefore, you need to go through each set, find out which sockets are still in them, and take care of them.

In the previous code example, the set variable contains lsock if there are any incoming connections, and dsock if the socket receives any data.

Easy, isn't it?

Demo 2.3 Hello Internet Server v2

Now that you know how to use the `select()` function, I want to show you how to actually use it to create an enhanced version of the "Hello Internet Server" program, Demo 2.1.

Instead of accepting just one packet, this program goes through a perpetual loop, using the `select()` function to poll the open sockets to see which have activity on them. Sounds easy, doesn't it?

This demo can be found in the directory /Demos/Chapter02/Demo03-HelloInternetServerV2/, in the file Demo03.cpp. As with the other demos in this chapter, this one also begins with Code Blocks 2.1 and 2.2, so I do not show them.

This time, a socket management system is needed to keep track of all of the open data sockets. To store them, I am using a `vector`, which is essentially an array. (See Appendix C on the CD if you are unfamiliar with vectors.) This is how the main routine of the demo starts:

```
int main() {
    int err;                   // for getting errors
    int lsock;                 // listening socket
    vector<int> socketlist;    // list of sockets

    // start the socket library
    StartSocketLib;
```

There is an error variable, a listening socket, and a vector of data sockets that is currently empty.

After this, Code Block 2.3 is inserted (see Demo 2.1), and that basically takes care of creating `lsock` as a listening socket.

The following code comes after the listening socket has been created. It basically creates all of the variables you need for the demo:

> **NOTE**
>
> I call the vector a "list of sockets," but don't confuse that with the **STL** container called `list`.

```
    fd_set rset;               // the read-set
    int i;                     // a generic iterating variable

    struct timeval zerotime;   // the zero-time timeval structure
    zerotime.tv_usec = 0;
    zerotime.tv_sec = 0;

    char buffer[128];          // used for getting messages
    bool done = false;         // used for quitting
    vector<int>::iterator itr; // a vector iterator
```

This should be self-explanatory. In the next part, the loop is begun, and the socket set is cleared out and filled with the listening and data sockets:

```
while( !done ) {
    // clear the set
    FD_ZERO( &rset );
    // add the listening socket
    FD_SET( lsock, &rset );
    // add all of the data sockets
    for( itr = socketlist.begin(); itr != socketlist.end(); itr++ )
        FD_SET( *itr, &rset );
```

After the set is filled with all the sockets you want to check, you can call the select function to find out which sockets have activity:

```
i = select( 0x7FFFFFFF, &rset, NULL, NULL, &zerotime );
```

After that, I check to see if i is more than 0, which indicates that there were sockets with activity. If there was activity, I check to see if there are any incoming connections on the listening socket:

```
if( i > 0 ) {
    if( FD_ISSET( lsock, &rset ) ) {
        // incoming connection
        int dsock = accept( lsock,
                            (struct sockaddr*)&socketaddress,
                            &sa_size );

        // add the socket to the list
        socketlist.push_back( dsock );
    }
```

After that, I loop through every data socket in the vector and check to see if there is activity on any of them. If there is activity on any of them, the function attempts to receive the data:

```
// loop through each socket and see if it has any activity
for( itr = socketlist.begin(); itr != socketlist.end(); itr++ ) {
    if( FD_ISSET( *itr, &rset ) ) {
        // incoming data
        err = recv( *itr, buffer, 128, 0 );
```

At this point, err should contain the number of bytes received: 0 if the socket was closed, or -1 if there was an error. Here is the code that handles that:

```
// quit if there's an error:
if( err == -1 ) {
    cout << "Socket receiving error!" << endl;
    return 0;
```

```
                }

                // just shut down and close sockets that have been disconnected
                if( err == 0 ) {
                    shutdown( *itr, 2 );
                    CloseSocket( *itr );
                    socketlist.erase( itr );    // erase socket from list

                    // move iterator back because we removed an item:
                    itr--;
                }

                // write out the data to the server window:
                else {
                    cout << "Data: " << buffer << endl;
                    if( strcmp( buffer, "servquit" ) == 0 )
                        done = true;
                }
            }
        }
    }
}
```

Most notable is the code that checks to see if the socket was disconnected. If it was disconnected, the function calls the shutdown and CloseSocket functions, and then the socket is removed from the vector. The iterator is decremented at the end of that block, because you've deleted an item, and the iterator skips over the next item in the vector if it isn't decremented.

The last block prints out the data it has received and checks to see if the text was servquit, which means a message was sent by the client telling the server to shut down.

Finally, here is the code that closes all sockets that are still open and shuts down:

```
    shutdown( lsock, 2 );
    CloseSocket( lsock );

    for( i = 0; i < socketlist.size(); i++ ) {
        shutdown( socketlist[i], 2 );
        CloseSocket( socketlist[i] );
    }

    CloseSocketLib;
}
```

Well, that's all there is to it. So now you can try compiling and running it. You can use Demo 2.2 to connect to this server, but it only prints the same message over and over; the server never quits. That's okay though; you can press Ctrl+C on your keyboard to halt the program.

Demo 2.4 Hello Internet Client v2

Now that you've got a more flexible server running, you'll probably want a more flexible client as well. Luckily, only a few more changes are needed to enable the client to send any message you want. I've also decided to add the ability to send more than one message before quitting.

The demo can be found in the directory /Demos/Chapter02/Demo04-HelloInternetClientV2/, in the file Demo04.cpp. As with all the other demos in this chapter, it is a console app, and can be compiled using the instructions from Appendix A (on the CD).

The demo starts off with Code Blocks 2.1 and 2.2 and also uses Code Block 2.4 (from Demo 2.2, shown previously). So at this point in time, you have a connected data socket called sock, and you're ready to start sending data!

This first section of code starts a loop that loops until the user tells it to stop, and gets user input from the console, separated by line:

```
bool done = false;
cout << "Type data to send now:" << endl;

while( !done ) {
    // get data to send
    cin.getline( message, 128 );
```

The getline() function of cin basically tells it to get data and store it into the message buffer until the user presses Enter, or 128 characters are reached. Once you've done that, you can send the data:

```
    // send data
    err = send( sock, message, strlen( message ) + 1, 0 );
    if( err == -1 ) {
        cout << "Socket sending error!" << endl;
        return 0;
    }
    if( strcmp( message, "servquit" ) == 0 ||
        strcmp( message, "quit" ) == 0 ) {
        done = true;
    }
}
shutdown( sock, 2 );
CloseSocket( sock );
CloseSocketLib;
}
```

If the message is equal to servquit or quit, the demo quits and closes its sockets. That's pretty much it.

You can now run the program in conjunction with Demo 2.3. Figure 2.11 shows the programs in action.

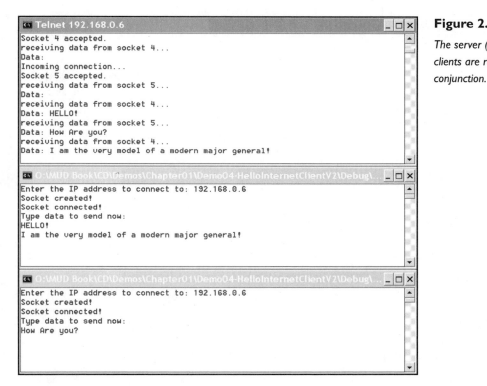

Figure 2.11

The server (top) and two clients are running in conjunction.

Essentially, what you've created is a one-way chat server; people can send messages to the server, but the server doesn't send anything back! It's not too useful, but it's still cool.

Summary

This is a big chapter, and I've thrown a lot of material at you. Fully covering the substantial subject of sockets programming would require an entire book. (Indeed, I've got several socket books of more than 500 pages sitting next to me right now.) I hope I've given you a full enough picture of using sockets. As a MUD programmer, the actual network programming aspect is only going to take up a little of your time, so I want to try to get on to the more interesting topics in the chapters that follow.

CHAPTER 3

INTRODUCTION TO MULTITHREADING

Multithreading is a subject that people love to hate, but it is pretty much a requirement for modern computing. The way things are happening in the computing world, it looks as if multiprocessing is the wave of the future. If you look at a modern video card, you can see that it's practically a general-purpose CPU on its own, and one day the entire concept of a chip specifically dedicated to video processing may be outdated; instead, you'll have many chips in every system, much like today's top-of-the-line four-processor workstations.

Multithreading harnesses the power of multiple processors, and it is also a virtual necessity when dealing with networked programming (even on a single processor machine). In the previous chapter, I showed you ways to poll the network system to see if there is any data available, but this method is wasteful. Wouldn't you rather have the network system tell your program, "Hey! I've got some data here!" instead of your program saying, "Anything yet? Anything yet? Anything yet?" like an annoying kid. Multithreading allows you to do this. It is an essential part of modern network programming, especially for MMOGs, which can have many thousands of open sockets at any given time.

In this chapter, you will learn to:

- Understand the advantages and disadvantages of multithreading
- Understand the multithreading library used in this book
- Implement ThreadLib mutexes
- Use demos that illustrate the concepts of the chapter

What Is Multithreading?

To be sure you know what multithreading is, let me give you a quick rundown.

Multithreading is the ability of a computer to run more than one thread of execution at the same time. (These threads can be part of the same program or separate programs entirely.) Back in the bad old days, only one program could be running at any given

> **NOTE**
> Pocket PCs and PalmPCs are already faster than some of the first super-computers. Isn't that nice to know?

time. You loaded the program and had to wait until it completed before you went on to anything else. Computers back then were expensive investments; people would pay millions of dollars for a computer that ran as fast as your average graphing calculator. To increase the return on the investment, people were allowed to use the computers for specified tasks, and users were charged by the amount of time they used.

Unfortunately, this system was inadequate. Imagine this situation: You've got a brand new computer capable of doing a million calculations per second, and someone loads a program and tries to run it. During the program's execution, it needs to stop and ask the operator for input. How fast can the operator respond? How many millions of CPU cycles are wasted waiting for the operator to type an entry? Obviously, when computing power was rare, this was seen as an obscene waste, so something had to be done.

The first time-sharing systems were invented to solve this problem; they were referred to as *round-robin*. In case you don't already know, every computer program consists of many instructions that the processor goes through and executes one by one. This process is called *serial execution*, because it executes instructions in a series, as shown in Figure 3.1.

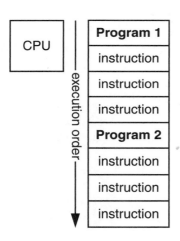

Figure 3.1

The execution order of instructions of two programs is in a serial system. The first program must complete before the second program starts.

For *round-robin* execution, however, the CPU switches to the first program, executes a few instructions, switches to the next one, executes a few instructions, and continues on through all open programs before returning to the first program. Whenever the CPU switches from one thread to another, the action is known as a *context switch*. Round-robin execution is shown in Figure 3.2.

Multithreading did wonders for enhancing the efficiency of computers.

As computer chips became cheaper, the *Personal Computer* (PC) concept became popular. Instead of logging into a public

NOTE

Modern systems no longer use simple round-robin processing because more efficient methods for handling tasks have been discovered. These days, most multithreaded systems assign priority values to threads and use priority queues to spend more cycles on the higher-priority threads. Additionally, programs can be interrupted by important events, and a context switch can be forced out of order; this is called *pre-emption*.

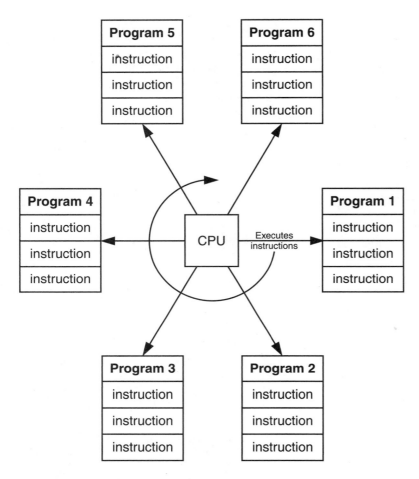

Figure 3.2

In this round-robin multithreaded system, a few instructions for each program are executed before the CPU moves on to the next program.

supercomputer to execute your programs, you can now use a PC any time you want. Since PCs were designed mainly for single users, they once again devolved into the world of serial execution. If you remember old operating systems such as DOS, you can remember being able to run only a single program at any given time. If you were running a word processor and needed to perform a quick math calculation, you needed to save your work, quit, open a calculator program, then quit that, and go back to your document. Incredible pain in the butt!

NOTE

It is important to note that single processors do not execute multiple threads at the same time. They work on one thread for a bit, and then stop working on that thread completely when it switches to another thread. This gives the appearance that the computer is running many programs at the same time, but it's really just switching between them really quickly.

Fortunately, within the past few years, multithreading has come back into favor, and our modern operating systems have supremely efficient threading capabilities. For example, as I write this, Windows XP reports that I have a total of 329 threads running at the same time. Every single thread is doing something different, such as running my calculator, my word processor, my paint program, Internet Explorer, downloads, and so on. It's just amazing what the systems can accomplish now. You probably think nothing of being able to just press Alt-Tab and move instantly to another program. I barely remember what it was like before we had systems like this, and I shudder when I think about the possibility of ever going back.

Multithreading is here to stay.

> **NOTE**
>
> There are some pretty cool processor technologies on the road ahead. Intel recently released its *hyperthreading* processor, which can actually run more than one thread at the same time on a single processor. AMD has its own solution in the works for the future, which actually has more than one execution core on the same chip.

What Is a Thread?

A *thread* is basically just a small independent section of code that the processor runs concurrently with other threads. A thread isn't necessarily a whole program (programs are commonly referred to as *processes* when dealing with multithreading), since a process can create as many threads as necessary. Figure 3.3 shows the relationship between a process and its threads.

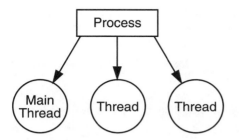

Figure 3.3

Every process has at least one thread: the main thread.

When you begin a process, it spawns one thread, which is the main thread. This *main thread* is really just the main() function in a program. You can elect not to spawn more threads (for single-threaded applications), or you can spawn as many threads as memory allows.

This is where things get sticky, however. At the level of the operating system (which manages all the threads), threading is rather easy. If every program is single threaded, you can pretty much assume that these programs will not be sharing memory, so you can set them off on their own threads and execute them as you see fit.

However, it's not so easy once you have multiple threads within one program. For example, say you have a program with two threads: the main game loop of your program, and a thread that receives data from an open socket.

Most of the time, the socket thread is going to be sitting there waiting for data to arrive, and not wasting CPU cycles by being constantly polled by the main thread. However, how does the main thread ever find out when data arrives? You need some way to tell the main thread about data arrival, at which time the main thread can do something with the data. This is usually accomplished using a shared variable or even a global variable. (This isn't recommended, though.) I'll get into the specifics later.

Synchronization

The main problem with multithreading, however, is *synchronization*. For example, in the same system, whenever you receive data, you shove it into a 128-byte buffer, and then tell the main thread that data has arrived. What happens if you start receiving more data while the main thread is still reading the old data? You might accidentally overwrite the data while it's being read! Areas in your code where these kinds of problems can occur are usually referred to as *critical sections*.

This is the biggest frustration when dealing with multithreaded applications. It is almost impossible to keep track of when data is going to be modified by each thread, so you need to enlist the help of objects that can help you synchronize your threads, without worrying about reading data that is being written to, or writing to data that is being read.

Mutexes

A *mutex* (which stands for **mutual exclusion**) is the simplest synchronization structure available. It's also the most useful. Essentially, a mutex is a Boolean variable associated with an object, and it determines if the object is *locked*. If an object is locked, it is being used by a thread, and any other threads that try to use the object must wait until it is unlocked.

Figure 3.4 shows an example of two threads using a mutex to prevent stepping on each others' toes when trying to process a single object. The first thread locks the mutex, and then goes on to process the object. After the mutex is locked, the second thread gets to a point where it wants to process the object as well, so it checks to see if the mutex is locked. When the second thread sees that the lock is in place, so it decides to wait for the mutex to unlock. Meanwhile, the first thread completes its processing and unlocks the mutex. Then the second thread locks the mutex and starts processing the object. Finally, when the second thread is done, it unlocks the mutex as well.

> **NOTE**
>
> In Figure 3.4, I show five different states relating to the mutex: check, wait, lock, process, and unlock. In reality, almost every mutex implementation out there implements the first three states (check, wait, lock) in one function and calls that "lock." I separated them in the figure to show you exactly what is happening behind the scenes.

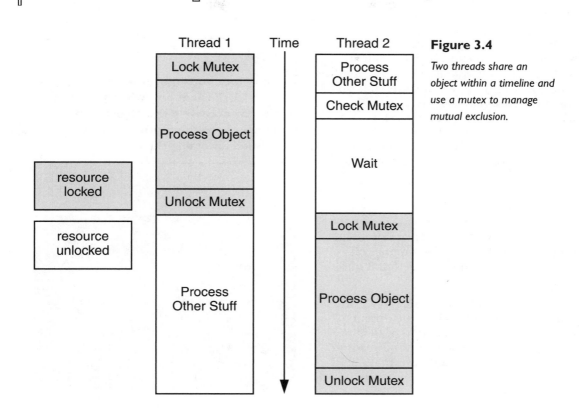

Figure 3.4

Two threads share an object within a timeline and use a mutex to manage mutual exclusion.

Essentially, a mutex allows only one thread to lock it, so that whenever other threads try to lock the same mutex, they must wait until it is unlocked. In an efficient system, the thread that is waiting for the mutex to unlock should usually be *sleeping*, which means that the operating system doesn't waste time processing that thread until the mutex is unlocked. This makes multithreading efficient, because you don't have to keep polling a variable to see if it is available for use.

Unfortunately, mutexes have some drawbacks. For example, suppose you forget to unlock a mutex? If so, any threads that attempt to lock the mutex when it is already locked wait forever. They become *zombie threads* (yes, that's a technical term)—threads that exist, but cannot be used for anything. Obviously, you don't want this to happen.

> **TIP**
>
> *Always* unlock your mutexes when you're done with them.

There's also another problem. What happens if you've got two threads that depend on a single object, and one of the threads needs to be constantly accessing the object (say, the state of a player in a game, accessed once per frame, which is about 30 to 60 times a second in a normal game). At the same time, another thread needs to do a lot of processing on the state. (This processing could take up to 30 seconds if the function is programmed inefficiently, and assumes that it can lock the mutex as long as it wants to, even if it isn't using the locked object.) What would happen? The thread that needs lots of updates would essentially be halted for a long time, waiting for the hog thread to finish, and your game would appear laggy.

> **TIP**
>
> Don't lock your mutexes for a long time. Lock them *only* when you are directly accessing the object, and unlock them the moment you are finished accessing the object.

Semaphores

A *semaphore* object is pretty easy to understand as well. Basically, a semaphore is an object that allows a certain number of threads to access an object before it starts blocking.

If you think about it, a mutex is really a semaphore that allows just one thread to access an object. A semaphore with a value of two would allow the first two threads to access the object, but any after that would have to wait until one of the first two threads unlocks itself.

> **NOTE**
>
> Semaphores are the flags that were waved by sailors to communicate with other ships on the sea, before wireless radio communication became popular. In essence, semaphore objects in computers do the same thing: They act as signals to other threads.

Figure 3.5 shows a thread diagram for three threads that want to access a semaphore that only allows two threads to access it.

Semaphores, while more flexible than mutexes, really aren't as useful as mutexes. Semaphores are most useful when used in conjunction with mutexes, so that you can create a system that allows many threads to read an object and only one to write to it when nothing is reading it.

This situation doesn't come up too often; indeed, some threading libraries don't even have semaphores, so I think that's about as much as I want to say about them.

Condition Objects

The third and final synchronization object I want to show you (don't worry, there are many more if you're interested) is called a *condition object*. These things are pretty cool and give you lots of control over the timing of thread execution.

Basically, a condition object has two main commands: wait and signal.

Say you have a bunch of threads that control the Artificial Intelligence (AI) of a group of bad guys. They're all lounging in the Bad Guy Headquarters Recreation Room, waiting for

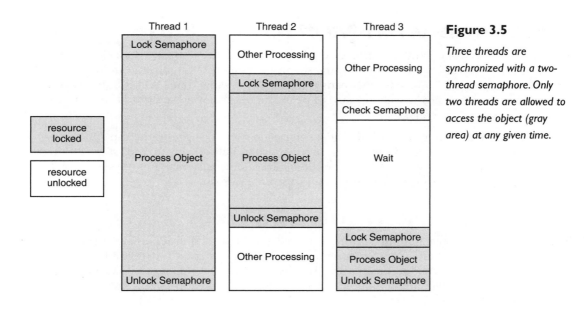

Figure 3.5

Three threads are synchronized with a two-thread semaphore. Only two threads are allowed to access the object (gray area) at any given time.

someone to break in. There's no need to continuously process their AIs, so you want to put them to sleep. But, you want an easy way to wake them up when the alarm is pulled, right?

So, you have a condition object representing the alarm, and then tell all the threads of the bad guy to wait on the alarm condition. When the alarm is tripped, the alarm condition is *signaled*, and all of the threads waiting on the *condition* are woken up.

Figure 3.6 shows this process with four threads.

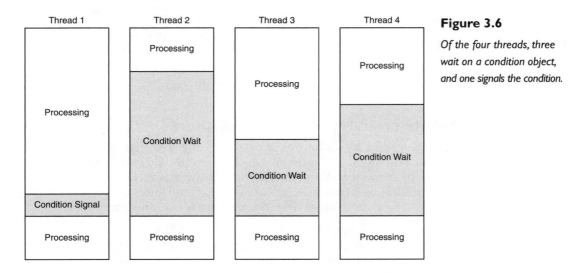

Figure 3.6

Of the four threads, three wait on a condition object, and one signals the condition.

Problems with Multithreading

Multithreading is wonderful! Multithreading is great! Multithreading is a *pain in the a***. When you first start using it, multithreading seems like a Holy Grail to programmers. Who wouldn't want to have hundreds of threads running at the same time? Who wouldn't want to have programs seamlessly scale upward in performance when moved onto two-, four-, or even eight-processor servers?

Then you start experimenting with threads. You create some test programs and run them— and then slam your keyboard against your monitor when half of your threads stop working for no reason at all. Ah yes, threads can be the bane of your existence. Let me show you a few ways in which threads can turn you into a frustrated person.

Threads Use More Memory

If you know how modern computers work, you are aware that each program has a data structure called a *stack* that it uses to keep track of local data for every function it is executing. If you don't know much about stacks, it's no big deal; all you need to know is that your program has a stack. Depending on how many functions are called, program stacks usually take up a fair amount of memory. Some systems use resizable stacks, and some use fixed size. Either way, the operating system tries to make absolutely certain that the stack is big enough to prevent overflowing when many layers of functions are being called at the same time.

When you get into multithreading and many threads are acting like little programs of their own, you suddenly realize that every thread needs its own stack. This can be a significant hindrance, if you planned on having threads for every little task in the entire program, because even the smallest of threads needs its own stack.

> **NOTE**
> Each thread keeps track of other things as well, such as the exact state of the CPU. However, in relation to everything else, the stack is by far the largest piece of a thread's overhead.

Depending on the implementation, stack sizes can range from a few kilobytes to multiple megabytes. So you always need to keep that in mind before you go crazy creating thousands of threads.

Threads Require More Processing

On a single-processor system, threads require additional processing overhead, because the operating system performs calculations to figure out which thread should run when and how long each thread should run. If you have thousands of threads, this takes a fair amount of processing power and may slow down your program in the long run. However, for systems that use blocking IO calls, threading is an absolute necessity, so there is really no way around it.

An important consolation exists, however. The great thing about multithreading is that theoretically, if you run your program on a two-processor machine, most (not all) of the processing overhead disappears, and your program runs faster than it would on a one-processor machine.

CAUTION

It is a common mistake to think that if you run a program on a two-processor machine, it will be twice as fast. However, this is definitely not the case. The same goes with four- or eight- processor machines as well. This is caused by *the law of diminishing returns*. Every time you introduce a new processor on a machine, you introduce more overhead as well. By far, the largest problem for *n*-processor machines is *memory bandwidth*. Only a certain amount of memory can be transmitted from main memory to each of the processors in a given amount of time, so when you start adding processors, they often want more memory than the memory bus can handle. In those cases, you'll end up with a system in which most of the processors will be waiting to read from or write to memory most of the time, instead of actually performing processing tasks.

Deadlock

Deadlock is an extremely nasty issue, and just mentioning it is enough to cause most programmers to run away screaming hysterically. If you do not think about every single way your threads will interact with other threads, I guarantee you will run into deadlock.

So what is deadlock? Imagine you have two resources, A and B. You also have two threads, 1 and 2. Thread 1, using a mutex, locks resource A and uses it. At the same time, thread 2 needs resource B, so B is locked by thread 2. A little bit later, thread 1 decides it needs to use resource B, so it tries to lock B as well. Because a mutex waits until the resource is available, thread 1 starts to wait. Then, a little bit later, thread 2 decides it needs resource A, so it tries to lock resource A and enters a mutex-waiting loop as well.

So what happens? Thread 1 is waiting for B, which 2 owns, but since 2 is waiting for A, which 1 owns, it cannot unlock B. Therefore, both threads wait for the other to release its resources, which never happens. This is *deadlock*.

Figure 3.7 shows this.

There are many ways deadlock can occur, and they may not all be immediately apparent. This is one of the most difficult problems you will face when developing multithreaded programs.

The programs in this book, however, won't be incredibly complex (in regards to threading) so deadlock shouldn't be a serious concern.

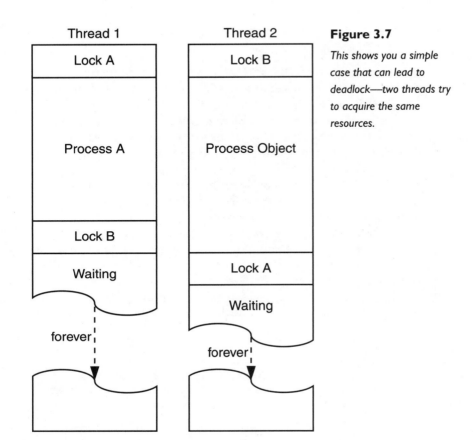

Thread 1 | Thread 2

Figure 3.7

This shows you a simple case that can lead to deadlock—two threads try to acquire the same resources.

Corruption

I have mentioned data corruption before, but it is such a serious concern with multithreading that I feel I must mention it again. Data corruption is a huge problem with multithreading if you do not use proper synchronization structures such as mutexes to control exclusive access to your data. You must be absolutely certain at all times that data is modified *only* when the thread modifying the data knows that nothing else is trying to read or write from it at the same time. Data contention can be the source of many unexplainable bugs.

Debugging

Debugging a multithreaded program is hell. It is extremely difficult to step through a multithreaded program because most debuggers don't support multithreading.

To make things worse, some debuggers that do support multithreading let other threads execute normally, while the thread you are debugging is essentially stopped. This makes it extremely difficult to time things correctly in a normal program.

Finally, multithreaded programs are *nondeterministic*. This means that the operating system controls when threads are started and stopped, and you have absolutely no control over it. In a singlethreaded program, you can simulate circumstances that led to a crash in your game by repeating the same inputs and using the same seed for the random number generator, but you can't simulate the execution order of threads. Because of this, your program may crash one time out of a hundred, but you cannot track down the cause of the crash easily because the circumstances that led to the crash will rarely repeat themselves!

Feel free to whack your head against the table when things like this happen.

Don't Let the Bedbugs Bite

It's always amusing to watch a game programmer write his first nongame application. You see, as game programmers, we're accustomed to having—actually, we *demand* having—complete control of the computer. We need to squeeze every last bit of processing power out of the machine, and if the player is dumb enough to be running Word or Excel in the background, well, that's *his* fault!

So when a game programmer starts working on nongame applications, he usually takes the same approach to the program and assumes that he has complete control over the machine. Usually we have a loop-based program that endlessly runs, waiting for something to happen or updating the screen at a blazing 60 frames per second.

Well, regular applications don't need this kind of power; and more often than not, we're wasting cycles when we program like this. Nothing is funnier than seeing a game programmer's first Telnet client application eat up 100% of the CPU cycles because it was programmed like a game.

To see an example of what I am talking about, go back to Chapter 2, "Winsock/Berkeley Sockets Programming," for a minute. I want you to run Demo 2.1. Once it is running, go about your regular computing tasks, such as opening up a word processor, or something like that. Nice and fast, eh? Now close the demo, and run Demo 2.3 instead. Now try doing your regular computing tasks. Not so fast, is it? In fact, even on a top-of-the-line computer system, your entire computer will chug along as if it's 10-years-old already! This, ladies and gentlemen, is not a good thing.

What was going on with these demos? Demo 2.1 uses blocking functions, which I've explained earlier. When a blocking function is called, the operating system puts that thread to *sleep* until something important happens, and then wakes it up.

Demo 2.3, however, doesn't play nicely with the operating system. Instead, it just endlessly loops, asking the Socket Library, "Did anything happen yet? Did anything happen yet?" until something actually happens. The application doesn't take into consideration that it's just running along, wasting everyone's time.

Sometimes, you've got to play along nicely with the operating system, even if you don't want to. Enter the concept of *manual sleeping*; almost every threading library comes with the ability to manually sleep. At the end of your game loop, you should tell the operating system that you want the thread to sleep. You're almost always allowed to specify the *minimum* amount of time you want a thread to sleep, which guarantees that the thread will sleep for at least that long, but possibly longer. Whenever you manually tell the operating system to put a thread to sleep, you're handing control over to the OS.

ThreadLib

Almost every operating system (at least those that support multithreading) have built-in multithreading libraries. Unlike the Sockets API, however, the libraries aren't very compatible.

Therefore, you need to select a library according to the platform you're developing on. Win32 has threading built in, so that is a great help. Linux usually depends on the *POSIX Threads* library, more commonly known as *pthreads*. I will be using both of these libraries to create our own ThreadLib library.

Since threading libraries usually differ, I want to take you through the design of the ThreadLib library that I use for the book before I go on to show you how to use threads.

To start off, I'll show you the main functions:

- Creating a thread
- Killing a thread
- Waiting for a thread to finish
- Getting the thread's ID
- Yielding a thread to the operating system

The entire library is enclosed within the ThreadLib namespace, by the way. Namespaces are a very handy way of avoiding naming conflicts with other pieces of code, and I explain them in much more detail in Appendix C, "C++ Primer" (found on the CD).

Headers and Typedefs

For starters, different thread libraries use the headers that are in different files. Depending on which compiler you are using, you'll want to include either windows.h (Win32) or pthread.h (Linux):

```
#ifdef WIN32             // Windows 95 and above
    #include <windows.h>
#else                    // Linux
    #include <pthread.h>
#endif
```

After that, I've got several typedefs, intended to make the library look cleaner. For example, I've got a function pointer typedef. (Again, see Appendix C on the CD if you are unfamiliar with function pointer typedefs.)

```
typedef void (*ThreadFunc)(void*);
```

This line defines a function pointer type that returns nothing (the first void) and takes a void pointer as its parameter. The type is named ThreadFunc. So what's the purpose of this? Whenever you create a new thread, you also need to tell it to execute a function. This typedef describes the kinds of functions that are to be executed as new threads.

The parameter void* allows you to pass in any single object as a parameter to the function. This is handy, because you can pass in a pointer to a number or a class, or you can even create your own collection class that has multiple data members, representing multiple arguments to a function. This will be demonstrated later on, when I show you how to create new threads.

Next on the agenda is the ThreadID typedef/class. Whenever you create a new thread, you need some way to reference it later on, in case you want to kill it, or wait for it to finish.

Let me start off by saying that Linux has taken the easy route and uses a single datatype to refer to threads—pthread_t. Nice and easy.

Windows, on the other hand, is a pain in the butt. You see, a thread in Windows has two values associated with it. The first is a HANDLE to the thread object, which is the WIN32 API's funky version of a pointer. The only difference is that you can have many handles all with different values referring to the same object. Therefore, there is really no way to compare two different handles to see if they point to the same object. And, it gets better. It turns out that Windows keeps track of every handle it passes out, and if you don't close every handle you have open, Windows never deletes the object that the handle refers to. (ugh!) Not only that, but sometimes when you request a handle to a thread, it gives you a *pseudo-handle*, which, as far as I can tell, is good for nothing!

Because of this crazy behavior of Windows threads and the fact that you cannot get the original handle to a thread once you're in a thread, I've made a hack of sorts to make the library easier to use. Here are the typedefs for the ThreadID:

```
#ifdef WIN32                    // Windows 95 and above
    typedef DWORD ThreadID;
    std::map< DWORD, HANDLE > g_handlemap;
#else                           // Linux
    typedef pthread_t ThreadID;
#endif
```

On the WIN32 side of things, there are two lines of code: The ThreadID type is defined to be a DWORD, and a global std::map is created as well. WIN32 uses DWORDS to hold thread ID numbers, so that's what I'm going to use as well. The map may not be as obvious, though. If you're unfamiliar with maps, I cover them in more detail in Appendix C (on the CD), but let me just give you a quick rundown here. A *map* is a data structure that stores *key-data pairs*. A map assumes that whenever you have a piece of data you want to store, you also have a unique key that is related to the data. For example, if you live in the USA, a social security number could be a key referring to a person.

So, in this case, I have a unique key (thread ID number) referring to data that I want to store (the handle to the thread). Whenever the ThreadLib needs to find the handle of a thread, it looks it up in the table. That way, the user's program only needs to know about the thread ID number and never needs to mess with the handle. This implementation hides the ugly Win32 implementation from the user.

The Linux version is much simpler; it just uses the `pthread_t` datatype.

From here on, you can use the `ThreadID` datatype to manage the threads within your programs.

Creating a New Thread

I mentioned previously that whenever you create a new thread, it needs a function pointer to execute. In this section, however, I'm discussing the function signatures of the functions needed by the two threading APIs, and these are different.

For example, the WIN32 threading library requires thread functions to be of the form

```
DWORD WINAPI Function( void* )
```

This means that the function returns a `DWORD` (a typedef that represents a 32-bit integer), has the `WINAPI` function calling style, and takes a `void*` as its parameter. This is an advanced topic that I don't get to, so don't worry about it; all you need to know is that the keyword `WINAPI` is required in front of the function name.

> **NOTE**
>
> A *function signature* (sometimes referred to as footprint) is just a formal phrase that describes the parameters and the return type of a function. For example, the signature of `int foo()` means that it returns an integer and takes no parameters. The function `int bar()` has the same signature, but `int baz( float blah )` has a different signature, since it has different parameters.

On the other hand, pthreads requires functions that look like this:

```
void* Function( void* )
```

This version returns a `void*`, has no function calling style, and takes a `void*` as its parameter. You may recall that I defined the `ThreadFunc` typedef to refer to functions of the form

```
void Function( void* )
```

This means that the `ThreadFunc` typedef is almost the same as the pthread style, except it has no return value.

Ultimately, I want you to use functions of the last form with the threading library. This made my job a little harder, because I needed to come up with a clever way to make the library convert `ThreadFunc` functions into the native platform signature, which is not an easy task. I considered making a few `#define` macros to handle the differences between the return values and the calling style, but that method is messy. Instead, I've opted for a dummy function system (sometimes called a *proxy* system).

Figure 3.8 shows this dummy system. When a thread is created, it is told to call the appropriate dummy function for the current platform, which in turn calls the intended function.

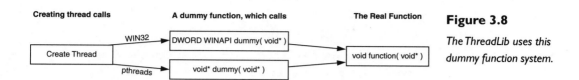

Figure 3.8

The ThreadLib uses this dummy function system.

So whenever you want to create a thread, you pass in both the function you want to execute (in ThreadFunc form) and the parameters. In turn, the function packages the function and parameters into a dummy data structure, and passes it to the dummy function, which then executes the function you wanted.

ThreadLib::DummyData Structure

The dummy thread functions need to know two things: the function the dummy thread needs to call, and the data to pass into it. Since the dummy function can only accept a single void* as a parameter, you need to package these two things into a class of their own. Here is the DummyData class:

```
class DummyData {
public:
    ThreadFunc m_func;
    void* m_data;
};
```

ThreadLib::DummyRun Function

Here is the dummy function that will run the function you want it to run:

```
#ifdef WIN32
DWORD WINAPI DummyRun( void* p_data )
#else
void* DummyRun( void* p_data )
#endif
{
    // convert the dummy data
    DummyData* data = (DummyData*)p_data;

    // run the function with the given data
    data->m_func( data->m_data );

    // now delete the data
    delete data;

    // and return 0.
    return 0;
}
```

> **CAUTION**
>
> Passing parameters into threads is a sticky business. You should always have a well-defined process to handle what happens to the parameters once the thread has executed. If you don't, you'll end up with memory leaks, and that's always a bad thing. This is also a reason to avoid killing threads prematurely—if the thread is supposed to delete its own parameters when it's finished with them, the thread won't get a chance to delete the parameters if you kill the thread manually.

The most interesting part of the code is the first five lines. The function signature defined depends on the system you are using. The rest of the function, however, is platform independent.

First the code casts the `void*` parameter into a `DummyData*`. The next command executes the `m_func` function pointer contained within the dummy data class, also passing it the `m_data` data.

Note that since a pointer is passed into the function, I need to allocate the `DummyData` class outside this function, and if I don't delete it, I'll have a memory leak. That works well for this purpose, because every call to the thread creation function creates a new dummy data class, and I can safely delete the class when I no longer need it.

ThreadLib::Create Function

After all this discussion, this section describes the part of the library that actually creates a new thread. For each operating system, you'll be calling a different function to create a thread (`CreateThread` for Windows, `pthread_create` for Linux).

First, let's look at the function signature:

```
inline ThreadID Create(ThreadFunc p_func, void* p_param )
```

The function returns a `ThreadID`, and its parameters are a `ThreadFunc` pointer and a `void` pointer. The function will create a new thread that will execute `p_func` using `p_param` as its argument.

Here's the first block of code from the function:

```
ThreadID t;
// create a new dummy data block
DummyData* data = new DummyData;
data->m_func = p_func;
data->m_data = p_param;
```

Basically, a new `DummyData` structure is created and set up.

```
#ifdef WIN32     // create a WIN32 thread
    HANDLE h;
    h = CreateThread( NULL, 0, DummyRun, data, 0, &t );
    if( h != 0 ) {
        // insert the handle into the handlemap
        g_handlemap[t] = h;
    }
#else                // create a Linux thread
    pthread_create( &t, 0, DummyRun, data );
#endif
```

On the WIN32 side, a new HANDLE is created. This will store the handle of the thread after the CreateThread( ) function returns. CreateThread uses the parameters described in the following paragraph.

The first parameter is a pointer to a structure that describes security attributes for the thread. Since I'm not using any of these features, I just pass NULL into it, which tells the function to use the default attributes. The next parameter is the initial stack size of the thread in bytes. Since the operating system automatically resizes this anyway, I just pass 0 in. This tells the operating system to use the default size, which can vary with the system setup, but that doesn't really matter much. After that, I pass in a pointer to the DummyRun function and the dummy data structure as well. The fifth parameter is a collection of flags to the operating system, none of which are interesting enough to mention, and a value of 0 is sufficient. The final parameter is a pointer to the ThreadID type, and the function will put the thread ID number into it.

After the new thread is created, this function checks to see if the handle is valid (not zero). If the handle is valid, it needs to be inserted into the handle map. As you can see from the code, this is an easy task to accomplish. You can insert a key/data pair into a map just as you would use an array, where t is the key (you can think of it as an index of an array, but it isn't actually an array), and h is the data to store in the table.

On the pthreads side of things, the function is similar, but simpler as well. The first parameter is a pointer to the thread ID so that it can be filled out when the function is complete, and the second parameter accepts creation flags, which are of little interest to us. The final two parameters are the function pointer and the dummy data structure.

Here's the final block of code:

```
    if( t == 0 ) {
        // delete the data first
        delete data;
         // throw an error
        throw Exception( CreationFailure );
    }
    return t;
}
```

This code checks to see if the thread ID is valid (any number except 0). If the ID is 0, the thread creation failed, so steps need to be taken to report the error and prevent memory leaks. As you can see, this block of code deletes the dummy data that was created earlier and throws a ThreadLib::Exception of type CreationFailure. I prefer exceptions because they greatly simplify code and don't usually clutter it up as traditional error checking code does. If you're not familiar with exceptions, see Appendix C, found on the CD.

Finally, the ID of the thread is returned, and you now have a new thread!

Getting the ID of a Thread

When you're in a thread executing code, you may need to find out which thread you are in by using the simple functions for obtaining the ID that are shown here:

```
inline ThreadID GetID() {
    #ifdef WIN32
        return GetCurrentThreadId();
    #else
        return pthread_self();
    #endif
}
```

On the WIN32 side of things, you can call the GetCurrentThreadID() function to get the thread ID. The Linux version uses the pthread_self() function.

Waiting for a Thread to Finish

Sometimes you'll want to be able to stop and wait for a thread to finish. This is usually helpful if you want to run parallel threads and have the main thread wait until the parallel threads are finished. This is a relatively easy thing to do.

In Windows, all you need to do is call the WaitForSingleObject() function with the threads handle, and the function will wait until the thread is done. Linux has a similar function, called pthread_join(), which joins the thread you want to finish with the current one. The two functions do the same thing, really.

```
inline void WaitForFinish( ThreadID p_thread ) {
    #ifdef WIN32
        // look up the handle and wait for the thread to finish
        WaitForSingleObject( g_handlemap[p_thread], INFINITE );
        // close the handle of the thread
        CloseHandle( g_handlemap[p_thread] );
        // remove the handle from the map
        g_handlemap.erase( p_thread );
    #else
        // "join" the thread. This essentially transfers control over to
        // the thread and waits for it to finish.
```

```
        pthread_join( p_thread, NULL );
    #endif
}
```

For the WIN32 code, the WaitForSingleObject() function needs a handle to the thread you want to wait for. Since the function accepts a ThreadID as its parameter, and not a handle, you'll need to consult the global handle map to look up the handle for the thread. Since maps are nice and easy to use, you can access a handle just as you would an array, using this code: g_handlemap[p_thread]. The code returns the handle of the thread. Pretty simple, don't you think? The second parameter of the function is how long you want to wait; you could wait for only a specified time, but I rarely need that kind of flexibility, so I just enter INFINITE as the time parameter. Of course, if the thread never finishes, you could run into some zombie-thread problems, but if you design things well, you shouldn't.

> **NOTE**
>
> Since WIN32 threads aren't actually removed from the system until you close the handle, you should try to call the WaitForFinish() functions on your threads, even if you know they are finished, just so the functions can close the handle. It's good programming practice, since you really shouldn't just launch a new thread and hope that it will finish correctly.

After you've waited for the thread, you can be certain that the thread is completed, so you should close the handle of the thread, and delete the handle from the handle map.

The Linux version is easy. It accepts the thread number and a pointer to some attributes that I'm not really concerned about, so I just pass NULL instead.

Killing a Thread

Sometimes, although rarely, you'll need to kill a thread outright. It's not recommended that you do so, however, because killing threads tends to lead to all sorts of problems, most notably memory leaks. However, you're still allowed to do so. Here's the code to kill a thread:

```
inline void Kill( ThreadID& p_thread ) {
    #ifdef WIN32
        // terminate the thread
        TerminateThread( g_handlemap[p_thread], 0 );
        // close the handle of the thread
        CloseHandle( g_handlemap[p_thread] );
        // remove the handle from the map
        g_handlemap.erase( p_thread );
    #else
        // cancel the thread.
        pthread_cancel( p_thread );
    #endif
}
```

As with the WaitForFinish() function, the WIN32 TerminateThread() function also requires a handle, so it is looked up in the handle map and passed into the function. The second parameter specifies the return value of the function. It's not very useful for what I'm doing here, so I just use 0.

After the thread is terminated, the function works the same way as the WaitForFinish() function: It closes the handle and erases it from the handle map.

The Linux version simply calls the pthread_cancel() function to cancel the thread.

Yielding a Thread

Earlier, I told you about putting a thread to sleep. This is a useful function for a threading library, so that you can play nicely with the operating system.

I use the Sleep function of Windows, and Linux's usleep function to tell the threading system to put the current thread to sleep.

There's one little "gotcha," though; usleep accepts the sleep time in *microseconds*, rather than the usual *milliseconds*. Don't ask me why the creators of the function decided they needed that kind of resolution, but that's just how it is. I use a default of 1 millisecond for my function, but you can pass in anything you like:

```
inline void YieldThread( int p_milliseconds = 1 ) {
    #ifdef WIN32
        Sleep( p_milliseconds );
    #else
        usleep( p_milliseconds * 1000 );
    #endif
}
```

Demo 3.1—Basic Threading

Now that I've shown you the basics of the ThreadLib, I want to show you how to create a program to demonstrate threading. For this demonstration, I'll show you three threads: The main thread will spawn two child threads, and each child thread will print out 10,000 letters. I'll call these the "a" and "b" threads, since the first one prints out "a"s and the second "b"s.

The demo is located on the CD in the directory /demos/Chapter03/Demo03-01/. The source is contained within Demo03-01.cpp. Instructions for compiling this demo can be found in Appendix A, "Setting Up Your Compilers" (found on the CD).

First, the thread library header file is included:

```
#include "ThreadLib/ThreadLib.h"
```

After that, the PrintThread function is defined. This function takes a single character as its parameter and prints that 10,000 times:

```
void PrintThread( void* data ) {
    // convert the data passed in into a character.
    char c = (char)data;

    for( int i = 0; i < 10000; i++ ) {
        cout << c;
        cout.flush();
    }
}
```

Since this function is meant to be passed into the ThreadLib::Create() function, the parameter must be of type void*. Since C++ allows you to cast anything into a void*, I exploit this and assume that the void* is actually just a char and not a pointer to anything. So on the fourth line of code, the data is cast into a character.

After that is the loop that runs for 10,000 iterations, printing out one character at a time, and flushing the buffer after each character is printed, so that the character is actually printed to the screen immediately. (If you don't manually flush it, cout tends to buffer a bunch of characters before it actually prints them to screen.)

Now, the main thread:

```
int main() {
    ThreadLib::ThreadID a, b;
    a = ThreadLib::Create( PrintThread, (void*)'a' );
    b = ThreadLib::Create( PrintThread, (void*)'b' );

    ThreadLib::WaitForFinish( b );
    ThreadLib::WaitForFinish( a );

    char c;
    cin >> c;
    return 0;
}
```

Two thread IDs are created: a and b. Then two new threads are created, both pointing to the PrintThread() function, one with the letter "a" as its parameter, and the other with the letter "b" (both casted into void*s). Once those threads are created, the main thread calls the WaitForFinish() function to wait until both threads finish executing.

Finally, the last three lines of code are input from the user and return 0. Windows NT has a bad habit of closing a console program window when it finishes, so this procedure prevents that from happening.

Figure 3.9 shows the results of the program when I ran it on my Windows XP computer.

As you can see from the figure, the two printing threads flip-flop back and forth, each printing a run of around 18 characters before the other thread kicks in.

Figure 3.9

Your results probably won't be the same as this screenshot from Demo 3.1, because all operating systems handle threading differently depending on what you have running at the time.

Demo 3.2—Yielding

Now that you have experienced creating threads and waiting for them to finish, I want to show you how to have more control over your threads. For this example, I'm going to make a simple change to Demo 3.2, so that the PrintThread function will add a YieldThread() function call after every letter it prints:

```cpp
void PrintThread( void* data ) {
    // convert the data passed in into a character.
    char c = (char)data;

    for( int i = 0; i < 10000; i++ ) {
        cout << c;
        cout.flush();
        ThreadLib::YieldThread();
    }
}
```

Ta-da! That's it. The demo can be found on the CD in the directory /demos/chapter03/demo03-02/ in the file demo03-02.cpp.

Now, what do you think will happen when you run this demo? Will the threads print out characters in alternating runs? Probably not. Whenever a character is printed, the function tells the operating system to yield and let another thread take a swing. Will this mean that we'll see nothing but an "abababab" pattern? Maybe not. Even though the threads may be queued alternately, that doesn't mean the operating system will run them in that order. We'll see what happens, though.

Figure 3.10 shows a screenshot of the program running on my Windows XP machine.

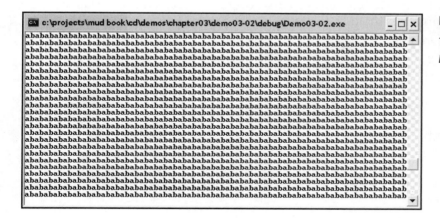

Figure 3.10

This is a screenshot from Demo 3.2.

No matter how hard I tried, I couldn't get the program to display something other than repeating "ab"s. But even so, you're still not guaranteed to get that pattern, so just be aware of that fact.

ThreadLib Mutexes

I've been playing around with threading, and I feel that the only synchronization structures that the ThreadLib really needs are mutexes, so that's all it has. There really was no reason to implement semaphores or conditions, because I don't use them. Anyway, the code for the mutex is located in the file /Libraries/ThreadLib/ThreadLibMutex.h on the CD. It's a pretty easy class to implement, because it requires only four functions.

There is one important thing I would like to mention before going on to show you the code. WIN32 has a structure called a mutex, and you might think I would use it in the ThreadLib, but it turns out that WIN32 mutexes are completely unnecessary for my purposes. You see, a WIN32 mutex is a *heavyweight* threading object, which means it can be used across processes, between different programs. Implementing this capability requires extra overhead though, and we only need *lightweight* mutex objects—objects that can be used across different threads, but always within the same process. The pthreads library for Linux is lightweight in nature; it deals only with threads within a single process. So what about WIN32? Well, WIN32 has an object known as a *critical section*, which is just a lightweight mutex. So, for the thread library, I'll use critical sections instead of heavyweight mutexes.

Data

I always like to show the class without functions first, just to give you an idea of what data the class is going to store. So without further ado, here it is:

```
class Mutex {
protected:
// define the base mutex types
#ifdef WIN32
    CRITICAL_SECTION m_mutex;
#else
    pthread_mutex_t m_mutex;
#endif
};  // end class Mutex
```

In WIN32, the class has a `CRITICAL_SECTION` object, and in Linux, the class has a `pthread_mutex_t` object.

Constructor

Both APIs require that mutex objects be initialized before they are used, and it's logical to do so within the constructor:

```
Mutex() {
    #ifdef WIN32
        // use critical sections in Windows; much faster
        InitializeCriticalSection( &m_mutex );
    #else
        pthread_mutex_init( &m_mutex, 0 );
    #endif
}
```

The only important point to note is the second parameter for the Linux function; it's supposed to be a pointer to an attributes structure, but that's not really needed. I pass in 0, meaning that the default attributes of a mutex are applied.

Destroying a Mutex

When you're finished with mutexes, they need to be destroyed. The destructor does this automatically for you:

```
~Mutex() {
    #ifdef WIN32
        DeleteCriticalSection( &m_mutex );
    #else
        pthread_mutex_destroy( &m_mutex );
    #endif
}
```

Locking a Mutex

As with destroying mutexes, locking mutexes is a simple task:

```
inline void Lock() {
    #ifdef WIN32
        EnterCriticalSection( &m_mutex );
    #else
        pthread_mutex_lock( &m_mutex );
    #endif
}
```

Unlocking a Mutex

Unlocking a mutex is also a simple task:

```
inline void Unlock() {
    #ifdef WIN32
        LeaveCriticalSection( &m_mutex );
    #else
        pthread_mutex_unlock( &m_mutex );
    #endif
}
```

See, I told you this would be easy! That's it for the code.

Demo 3.3—Mutexes

Now I want to show you how to use mutexes to lock resources in a demo. Basically, I'm going to use the same format that was used in Demo 3.1 and 3.2 and just change the PrintThread() function again. This demo is located on the CD at /Demos/Chapter03/Demo03-03/Demo03-03.cpp. The same compilation instructions apply.

This time, I want the threads to print 50 characters without being interrupted by the other printing thread. So, for every 50 characters, a global mutex will be locked to prevent the other thread from being called.

First, the mutex is defined:

```
ThreadLib::Mutex m;
```

Here's the new PrintThread() function:

```
void PrintThread( void* data ) {
    // convert the data passed in into a character.
    char c = (char)data;

    for( int i = 0; i < 200; i++ ) {
```

```
        m.Lock();
        for( int j = 0; j < 50; j++ ) {
            cout << c;
            cout.flush();
        }
        m.Unlock();
    }
}
```

Now the printing loop is separated into two loops; the outer loop prints 200 groups of 50 characters. Inside the outer loop, the mutex is locked, and then the 50 characters are printed. Once that is complete, the mutex is unlocked.

So what will you see when you run this program? Theoretically, you should see alternating blocks of 50 "a"s and then 50 "b"s. However, I'm again reminding you that this may not be the case. When the mutex is unlocked, it is entirely possible that execution may not switch to the other thread right away. In this case, the same thread might lock the same mutex and end up printing 100 characters in a row. While this is unlikely, it is still a possibility.

Figure 3.11 shows a screenshot of the demo in action.

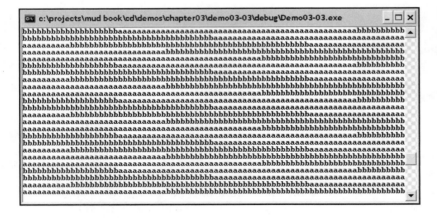

Figure 3.11

This is a screenshot of the mutex Demo 3.3.

As you can see, the characters were printed in blocks of 50, as predicted. So now you know how mutexes help you lock access to resources.

Summary

Threading is a difficult concept to get a handle on (no pun intended). I know many hardened veterans of the game industry who still shudder with fear whenever they hear threading mentioned. If you manage everything intelligently and don't go overboard with threading, you shouldn't have much of a problem.

Now you're ready to tackle the Socket Library that I'm going to use for this book. Good luck with the next chapter!

CHAPTER 4

THE BASIC LIBRARY

On the one hand, C++ is great because it's so flexible; on the other hand, since it is so flexible, it doesn't have much built into the basic libraries. C++ is sorely lacking in the areas of both string processing and precision timing. (The base C++ timer uses a resolution of one second, which is almost useless for game programmers.) Sure, C++ has come a long way from standard C strings (I'm sure you just shuddered—I did), but it still has a long way to go before it is even half as useful as some of the more robust string-based languages, such as Perl.

In this chapter, you will learn to:

- Create multiplatform 64-bit integers
- Create multiplatform time functions
- Create flexible timer objects
- Use C++ strings
- Extend the functionality of C++ strings
- Log errors and other events

Big Numbers

I'm going to come right out and say this: 32-bit integers are getting too small. Being able to store from -2 billion to +2 billion numbers, 32-bit numbers seemed big a long time ago, but that's just not enough storage space for numbers anymore.

Consider this: The standard C++ second-timer uses a signed 32-bit integer to store the number of seconds that has passed since 1970. What happens when you get past 2 billion seconds? Simple: Integers wrap around and become -2 billion instead. Obviously, this is a problem, but how long is 2 billion seconds anyway? It's 35 million minutes, or 596 thousand hours, which is 24 thousand days. That's 68 years. In 2038, all of our C++ second-timers will wrap around. That's a big problem.

As game programmers, we may not have to be concerned with wrapping second-timers; instead, we'll probably be using wrapping millisecond-timers. So how many milliseconds can 32 bits represent? About 24 days. Since this book is about programming persistent worlds with huge uptimes, 24 days just won't cut it for us.

So, why don't we use 64-bit numbers instead? A signed 64-bit number can hold from -9 quintillion to +9 quintillion. That's a huge number; in fact it's so large that you probably can't conceive how big it actually is. To put things is perspective, when used to store milliseconds, 64-bit integers can represent 292 million years. I think 64 bits ought to be enough for a timer.

So, the first thing you need to do is create a uniform 64-bit integer format. I'm going to do this within the BasicLib library package, which you can find on the CD in the directory /Libraries/BasicLib/. The file that will hold the 64-bit datatype is called BasicLibTypes.h. Everything within this file is also within the BasicLib namespace.

In the C99 standard, C is supposed to have a long long datatype (two longs), which is 64 bits. For example:

```
long long foo;          // signed 64 bits
unsigned long long bar; // unsigned 64 bits
```

Unfortunately, not all compilers are up-to-date. The Linux compiler, GCC, has no problems with 64-bit integers, but Microsoft Visual C++.NET and prior versions don't support it (VS.NET 2003 should support it, though); therefore, you need to use the Microsoft-specific 64-bit integer format:

```
__int64 foo;           // signed 64 bits
unsigned __int64 bar;  // unsigned 64 bits
```

In front of the int64 are two underscores, not just one. As far as I can tell, __int64 acts just like a long long, with just one exception: it doesn't support bitshifting. I'm not sure why this is, but it's one limitation you must keep in mind when using __int64 .

> **NOTE**
>
> Personally, I never use bitshifts anymore anyway. I put my trust into the compiler to make the best decision about optimizing my code, since it can do a much better job than I can.

So, finally, here's the code that seamlessly uses __int64's or long longs based on the system you are using:

```
#ifdef __GNUC__   // Linux
    typedef long long int sint64;
    typedef unsigned long long int uint64;
#endif

#ifdef WIN32      // Windows
    typedef __int64 sint64;
    typedef unsigned __int64 uint64;
#endif
```

I've typedefed the 64-bit integers into new types: sint64 and uint64. Now, whenever you need to use a 64-bit number, you can just include the BasicLib.h file, and use it:

```
#include "BasicLib/BasicLib.h"
sint64 foo;
uint64 bar;
```

Voilá! Platform-independent 64-bit integers!

64-Bit Integers and Streams

Visual C++ 6 has a major problem streaming 64-bit integers to and from streams. I think it's actually a bug somewhere in the template code, but regardless, you just can't do it. Since Microsoft has already created a newer and better compiler, I can't imagine it cares much about fixing the old version. You're going to have to live with this limitation.

I worked around the limitation and created a *hack*. Yes, hacks are an ugly thing, but sometimes they are just plain neccessary.

To cut a long story short, I had to create some way of determining if you're using VC6, and I did so using macros:

```
#ifdef WIN32
    #if _MSC_VER >= 1300
        #define GOODCOMPILER
    #else
        #define CRAPPYCOMPILER
    #endif
#endif


#ifdef __GNUC__
    #define GOODCOMPILER
#endif
```

If you have VC7 or above, or GCC, you have a good compiler. If you have VC6 or below, you have a crappy compiler. To work around the streaming problem, I created a few stream helper functions:

```
template< typename type >
inline void insert( std::ostream& s, const type& t );
template< typename type >
inline type& extract( std::istream& s, type& t );
```

These functions essentially perform the same task as the common `operator<<` and `operator>>` (see Appendix C, "C++ Primer," on the CD if you are unfamiliar with them), but since those operators are broken in VC6, you need to use these instead whenever you stream a `sint64` or `uint64`. For example:

```
sint64 bigint = 12345677889467365;
// cout << bigint << endl;    <-- WILL NOT COMPILE ON VC6
BasicLib::insert( cout, bigint );
BasicLib::extract( cin, bigint );
```

You can find these functions in the BasicLibString.h file on the CD; I had to create a *template specialization* for the 64-bit integer types, which wraps around the VC6 `_i64toa`, `_ui64toa`, and `_atoi64` functions. A template specialization is a function that works on a specific kind of datatype. It's a rather large and complex topic, so I won't be covering it here. All you really need to know is that you need to use `insert` and `extract` when streaming 64-bit integers.

What Time Is It?

Time is a tricky subject, because you need different ways of getting the time on every system out there. I'll only cover the methods for Windows and Linux.

Windows

On Windows, you can use the `timeGetTime()` API function, but this practice is usually frowned upon. While the function theoretically is a millisecond-timer, in actual use, it isn't nearly as accurate. Sometimes the function can be off by dozens of milliseconds, and it just doesn't cut the mustard when you need precision.

Luckily, there is an alternative Windows practice—the performance counter. All x86 CPUs since the original Pentium have had a performance counter timer built into them, that is incredibly precise. This means that you can't use the performance counter on machines older than a Pentium, but seriously, who still has those around?

Here's the catch though: The precision, while extremely accurate, varies based on the system. The performance counter has a value called the *frequency*, which represents how many times per second the performance counter is updated. A value of 1,000 means that the counter updates 1,000 times a second, and therefore every millisecond.

On my Athlon 1600, for example, this value is 3,579,545. In other words, the performance counter updates 3.5 million times a second, which means that my timer updates once every 279 nanoseconds. That's precise.

So, you can pretty much use the performance counter as a microsecond timer if you want, but I don't have a need for that much precision. I just want a decent millisecond timer.

Getting the Frequency

To use the performance counter functions, the windows.h file needs to be included in your source files. Here is the function definition for the frequency function:

```
BOOL QueryPerformanceFrequency( LARGE_INTEGER *lpFrequency );
```

LARGE_INTEGER is a type of data that is close to being an __int64, but isn't quite the same. This data is actually just a combination of two 32-bit integers to form a struct, which means you can't pass a sint64 pointer into the function; you need to cast it first:

```
sint64 freq;
QueryPerformanceFrequency( (LARGE_INTEGER*)(&freq) );
```

Theoretically, the function returns 0 if it doesn't succeed, and non-zero if it does; but we know that it can only fail on machines older than Pentiums, so I find it safe to ignore the return value.

The frequency value never changes, so you should retrieve it once, and store it. I'll show you how I do that further into the chapter.

Getting the Time

Getting the current time from the performance counter is similar. (Time in this case means the number of ticks since the computer was started.)

```
sint64 t;
QueryPerformanceCounter( (LARGE_INTEGER*)(&t) );
```

Now t will hold the number of ticks since the system was started; of course, this value is meaningless to you unless you have a frequency value. So, how do you use this time value? Dividing the time by the frequency should give you the number of seconds that has passed since the system was started:

```
t = t / freq;
```

But that's only seconds, and I wanted milliseconds. So, instead, I'll convert the frequency value from ticks per second into ticks per millisecond:

```
freq = freq / 1000;
QueryPerformanceCounter( (LARGE_INTEGER*)(&t) );
t = t / freq;
```

And now t holds the number of milliseconds passed since the system was started.

Linux

With Linux, it is somewhat easier to get the time. It has a nice function called gettimeofday, which uses a timeval structure. You've seen this before, when dealing with the select() socket function. It has two fields: one for seconds, and one for microseconds.

These fields are located within the Linux file sys/time.h, so you need to include that file to use the time features:

```
#include <sys/time.h>
struct timeval t;
gettimeofday( &t, 0 );
```

The first parameter of the function is a pointer to the timeval structure, and the second parameter is a pointer to a structure describing the time zone. The second parameter is not required, so I'm not going to bother with it.

The t_sec value of the timeval structure will have the number of seconds since 1970, and the t_usec value will have the number of microseconds past the current second, which means that it will lie somewhere from 0 to 1,000,000.

Milliseconds

Since the two different time retrieval methods get different times (Windows gets the time since the system was started, and Linux gets the time since 1970), you're obviously only going to be able to use these as *relative* timers—comparing them to see how much time has passed since the timer was last called that is. But don't worry—they're still useful.

So, the base of my entire time library is a millisecond timer, in a function entitled GetTimeMS(), which gets an arbitrary time in milliseconds. As I said before, this value is relative, so the only thing you're guaranteed about a call to this function is that it will accurately return a number that can be subtracted from any previous number, and it can be subtracted to find out the number of milliseconds that have passed.

Here's the Windows portion of the code:

```
sint64 GetTimeMS() {
    #ifdef WIN32
        sint64 t;
        QueryPerformanceCounter( (LARGE_INTEGER*)(&t) );
        return t / g_win32counter.m_frequency;
```

I'll get to the g_win32counter.m_frequency part in a little bit; for now, it's safe to assume that it holds the performance counter frequency.

And here is the Linux portion:

```
    #else
        struct timeval t;
        sint64 s;
        gettimeofday( &t, 0 );
        s = t.tv_sec;
        s *= 1000;
        s += (t.tv_usec / 1000);
        return s;
    #endif
}
```

The s variable will hold the end result of the calculations. Once the time is retrieved into t,

NOTE

The reason I split up the assignment of the tv_sec field and multiplied it by 1,000 is subtle. Since tv_sec is a signed 32-bit integer, multiplying anything above 2.14 million by 1,000 causes an overflow; 2.14 million seconds is less than a year. That means that any time after 1971 multiplied by 1,000 causes a 32-bit overflow. Therefore, the time is copied over into the 64-bit value and then multiplied by 1,000, thus ensuring that the numbers won't overflow.

the number of seconds is extracted and put into s and then multiplied by 1000 (remember, 1 second = 1,000 milliseconds).

Finally, the number of microseconds is divided by 1,000 (there are 1,000 microseconds in a millisecond), added to the sum, and the sum is returned. Ta-da! You now have a millisecond timer—sort of. There's one more thing you need to take care of.

What's the Frequency, Kenneth?

The easiest way to initialize the performance counter frequency is to make a function that initializes a global value, and remember to call that function whenever you start your program. I've done this before, and it gets tedious; I'd rather not waste my time trying to remember to initialize a timer, especially if it's only needed on Windows, and nowhere else.

So, I'm going to explain how I exploit a neat feature of C++: Global classes are constructed automatically when a program is first started. So what does this mean? I'm going to create a Windows performance counter frequency class and have its constructor automatically get the frequency value whenever your program is first run.

The class is inside the BasicLibTime.h file:

```
#ifdef WIN32
    class Win32PerformanceCounter {
    public:
        Win32PerformanceCounter() {
            QueryPerformanceFrequency( (LARGE_INTEGER*)(&m_frequency) );
            m_frequency = m_frequency / 1000;
        }
        sint64 m_frequency;
    };
    Win32PerformanceCounter g_win32counter;
#endif
```

Notice that this class exists only within WIN32; Linux has no idea about this file, and neither should users of the library. For all intents and purposes, this class shouldn't exist for anything but the WIN32 branch of the GetTimeMS() function. The class has one variable: m_frequency, which is the frequency of the performance counter divided by 1,000, so it represents ticks per millisecond. On the next-to-last line, a single instance of this class, g_win32counter, is created; you shouldn't try accessing this outside the BasiclLibTime.cpp file, because it literally doesn't exist outside this file. Basically, all you need to know is that this class is automatically constructed when you run your program, so you don't have to worry about initializing anything. I pull basically the same trick with the SocketLib in the next chapter.

Other Times

I included three other relative time functions in the library, each to get seconds, minutes, and hours. I don't think there is any need for a relative day or year function, but feel free to build one yourself. These time functions are called `GetTimeS`, `GetTimeM`, and `GetTimeH` respectively. Each of these functions relies on the result of `GetTimeMS` and divides the time by the appropriate value. For example:

```
sint64 GetTimeS() {
    return GetTimeMS() / 1000;
}
```

And so on.

Timestamps

You'll often want to get a text string representing the current time and date of the system. Luckily, C++ has built-in features. First, we'll need to get the current time as a `tm` structure, which is an interesting process, to say the least:

```
time_t a = time( 0 );
struct tm* b = localtime( &a );
```

First, the current time in seconds is retrieved using the standard C `time()` function; then a pointer to a `tm` structure is retrieved from the `localtime()` function. To work, the function requires a pointer to the current time. There's a similar function called `gmtime()`, which gets a `tm` structure using Greenwich Mean Time (GMT); the local time function gets the time according to your computer's time zone.

Now that you have a `tm` structure, you can use the `strftime()` function to get a string based on the time structure. This function is similar to the `sprintf()` C function, except it prints time values instead of variable values. The time values we'll be interested in are %H, %M, %S, %Y, %m, and %d, which represent hours, minutes, seconds, years, months, and days.

First, you'll need a buffer:

```
char str[9];
```

And then you'll fill the buffer with the function:

```
strftime( str, 9, "%H:%M:%S", b );
```

The first parameter to be filled is the char* buffer, the second parameter is the maximum length of the buffer, the third parameter is a string describing the output format, and the final parameter is a pointer to the `tm` structure. From the preceding example, you can see that I requested the time in `HH:MM:SS` format, which can have a maximum of eight characters, the ninth being the `NULL` character (used to terminate C-strings). For example, 8:00 A.M. should look like this: `08:00:00`.

Here's the `TimeStamp()` function:

```
std::string TimeStamp() {
    char str[9];
    time_t a = time(0);
    struct tm* b = gmtime( &a );
```

```
    strftime( str, 9, "%H:%M:%S", b );
    return str;
}
```

The `TimeStamp()` function returns a C++ `string`. In case you've never used C++ strings, I explain them later in this chapter.

The `DateStamp()` function is similar, except it returns times in `YYYY.MM.DD` format. (Yes! It's unorthodox, but as a mathematician and a programmer, *the most significant digits always go first!* It just makes more sense that way!)

```
std::string DateStamp() {
    char str[11];
    time_t a = time(0);
    struct tm* b = gmtime( &a );
    strftime( str, 11, "%Y.%m.%d", b );
    return str;
}
```

So the date May 30, 2010 would be represented as `2010.05.30`.

Timers

Up until now, you have only had functions to get relative times, but you don't really have any reliable way of creating a timer that will track the amount of time that has passed since you created or reset the timer. Enter the `Timer` class. I want to make a class that will start counting time from 0 whenever it is created, or when it is manually reset. This class should also be capable of being given a default time. Say you save a time to disk, close the program, and then run it again; you might want to resume the timer from when it was saved to disk.

To do this, a timer object must have two variables: the system time at which it was initialized or reset, and the official starting time of the timer. Usually, you'll start the timer off at 0, so for now, let's just assume the starting time is 0.

Here's the class with its functions and data:

```
class Timer {
public:
    Timer( sint64 p_timepassed = 0 );
    void Reset( sint64 p_timepassed = 0 );
    sint64 GetMS();
    sint64 GetS();
    sint64 GetM();
    sint64 GetH();
    sint64 GetD();
    sint64 GetY();
protected:
    sint64 m_inittime;
    sint64 m_starttime;
};
```

As you can see, there's a constructor (which basically calls Reset()), a Reset() function, and six functions that get the number of milliseconds, seconds, minutes, hours, days, or years that have passed since the timer was last reset or initialized.

Since the constructor of the timer just calls reset, let's look at the Reset() function:

```
void Timer::Reset( sint64 p_timepassed ) {
    m_starttime = p_timepassed;
    m_inittime = GetTimeMS();
}
```

In the class definition, the = 0 in the parameter means that the parameter can be omitted, and if omitted, it is assumed to be 0. For now, let's just assume that the parameter is 0; so the m_starttime value is reset to 0, and the m_inittime value is set to the current time of the system.

Now look at the GetMS() function:

```
sint64 Timer::GetMS() {
    return (GetTimeMS() - m_inittime) + m_starttime;
}
```

GetMS() basically subtracts the init time from the current time, adds the starting time (which is zero for this example), and results in exactly the number of milliseconds that has occurred since the timer was last reset.

Now, if you initialized the timer with a value of 10,000 milliseconds:

```
timer t( 10000 );
```

the timer will start off with a default value of 10 seconds. From then on, the timer will start counting from 10,000, instead of 0. This is very helpful for saving the value of the timer and then restarting it later, keeping the same amount of time.

For example (assume the comments represent a large amount of processing that you don't see here):

```
sint64 x;
timer t;
// code block 1
x = t.GetMS();
// code block 2
t.reset( x );
// code block 3
x = t.GetMS();
```

After code block 1 has finished executing, x should hold the number of milliseconds required for the processing. Code block 2 is then executed, and after that, the timer is reset to the value recorded before block 2 executed. That means that the timer essentially wasn't counting during the execution of block 2, but it is again counting after block 2. Finally, at the end of block 3, the value of x is again updated, and x should hold the number of milliseconds it took to execute blocks 1 and 3, but not 2.

All of the other time functions within the class are based on the GetMS() function; for example, here is the GetH() function:

```
sint64 Timer::GetH() {
    return GetMS() / 3600000;
}
```

There are 3,600,000 milliseconds in an hour (60 min/hr * 60 sec/min * 1000 ms/sec). All the other functions are similar, and there is no need to show them here.

This about concludes my section on time, but I will brush on the topic again in later chapters, to show you efficient ways of implementing a system that automatically executes functions after a specified amount of time. Specifically, I deal with a simple timer system in Chapter 10, "Enemies, Combat, and the Game Loop," and a more complicated queue-based timer system in Chapter 15, "Game Logic."

Strings

This book is about MUDs; therefore, it wouldn't be complete if I didn't include the information about strings that you need.

Strings in C are a messy issue. Almost every other language in the world has better string abilities. Standard C-strings are ugly to use, inflexible, prone to errors, and cause lots of security problems. When you create a C-string, you can't change its size—ever. Your only option is to completely destroy the string and create a new one. Rather than show you examples of C-strings, I'm just going to pretend that they don't exist. Believe me—it's better that way. You'll be saner without them.

So, what should you use instead of C-strings? I had considered writing my own string class for the book, with cool reference-counting features and optimizations. On doing more

---

TIP

C-strings are a security issue due to something called a *buffer-overflow* attack. There will be times when the users of your server will send lots of data, and with C-strings, you'll inevitably forget to check to see if you're writing past the end of the string in one place or another. Attackers use this situation to overwrite memory they shouldn't have access to, and many times this happens to be places in memory where the computer stores the instructions of your program. This means that hackers can actually overwrite the assembly code of your program, and execute anything they want!

research, I found that reference-counting optimizations aren't really such a great optimization after all. *Reference-counting* means that the string actually keeps track of how many things are pointing at the same string object, and only creates new strings when one of the strings is modified from the original. This sounds great in theory, but in reality it has tons of problems; I decided I didn't want to waste space by devoting an entire chapter to creating a string class. This is a book about MUDs after all, not strings!

C++ to the rescue! The designers of the C++ standard library were smart; they realized that people were just plain sick of C-strings. So, when creating the C++ standard template library (STL), they decided to add a string class, called `basic_string`. The absolutely best thing about this class is that it is flexible; it doesn't assume that you are using 8-bit ASCII characters. Instead, `basic_string` uses a template parameter, so you can use characters of any type:

```
#include <string>
std::basic_string<char> str1;        // ASCII 8-bit string
std::basic_string<wchar_t> str2;     // unicode 16-bit string
std::basic_string<int> str3;         // string of integers
```

Okay, so that notation looks a little ugly. Luckily, the designers of STL put in a couple typedefs:

```
typedef basic_string<char> string;
typedef basic_string<wchar_t> wstring;
```

By the way, the `wchar_t` type is a built-in C++ type that represents a wide character. So, to create an 8-bit ASCII string—the most common type of string there is—all you need to do is this:

```
std::string str1;
```

NOTE

For a primer on templates, see Appendix D, "Template Primer," on the CD.

Creating Strings

Strings are easy to use. Here are a few ways to create them:

```
std::string str1 = "Hello!";         // "Hello!"
std::string str2( "How are you?" );  // "How are you?"
std::string str3( 8, 'C' );          // "CCCCCCCC"
std::string str4 = str1;             // "Hello!"
std::string str5( str4 );            // "Hello!"
```

And here are a few ways to create strings from plain C-strings:

```
char cstring[] = "Hello!";           // "Hello!"
std::string str6 = cstring;          // "Hello!"
std::string str7( cstring );         // "Hello!"
std::string str8( cstring, 2 );      // "He"
```

I think it's a great idea to be able to do these kinds of things. In fact, whenever you have a string literal such as "Hello!" inside your program, the compiler sees that as a plain C-string (a char*). So the lines

```
std::string str1 = "Hello!"
std::string str6 = cstring;
```

from earlier are almost identical; they both create an std::string using a C-string.

Using Strings

C-strings are notoriously difficult to work with. You need to call functions on them to do anything useful, such as concatenating, comparing, or even just finding out the length of them. BLEH! However, C++ strings take care of all those little things for you. For example:

```
std::string str1 = "Hello!";
std::string str2 = "How are you?"
std::string str3;
str3 = str1 + " " + str2;          // "Hello! How are you?"
```

Isn't that cool? Using C-strings, you'd have to first check to see if str3 had enough room, which would mean that you'd need to find out the length of str1 and str2, and possibly resize a buffer, before calling a concatenate function.

Catch my drift? *Pain in the butt!* C++ strings take care of all of that junk for you.

Or how about comparing strings? Using C-strings, it looks like this:

```
char cstr1[] = "Hello!";
char cstr2[] = "Hello!";
if( cstr1 == cstr2 )
    // write some code here
```

A beginner would think that the code inside the if-statement would be executed; after all, the strings are equal, right? Not quite. C-strings are just pointers, and when you compare them like that, you're comparing the pointer values, not the actual strings. D'oh!

Now look at C++ strings:

```
std::string str1 = "Hello!";
std::string str2 = "Hello!";
if( str1 == str2 )
    // do some code here
```

This code works all of a sudden. The != operator and the less-than and greater-than operators work as well:

```
std::string str1 = "ABC";
std::string str2 = "BCD";
bool b;
b = ( str1 != str2 );        // true
```

```
b = ( str1 < str2 );            // true
b = ( str1 > str2 );            // false
```

The less-than and greater-than operators compare the strings alphabetically. ABC is less than BCD because it would come first in the dictionary.

And finally, you can find the size of a string:

```
std::string str1 = "Hello!";
int size = str1.size();         // 6
```

Pretty easy, isn't it?

> **NOTE**
>
> To use other terminology, you can also say that you compare strings *lexographically*. Impress your friends by using this big word that almost no one knows the meaning of! "Oh, today I lexographically compared two strings!"... nevermind.

Other String Functions

There are lots of string functions, so I'm only going to go over the important ones. Most string functions are based on searching, which is great, because that's how I use strings most often.

For example:

```
std::string str1 = "Hello Mr. Anderson.";
size_t pos;
pos = str1.find( "Mr" );          // 6
pos = str1.find( "He" );          // 0
pos = str1.find( "der" );         // 12
pos = str1.find( "narf" );        // string::npos
pos = str1.find( "o" );           // 4
pos = str1.find( "o", 5 );        // 16
```

There are two interesting cases in this code. When I try searching for narf, which doesn't exist within str1, the value string::npos is returned. This is a value for the string that cannot be valid, and whenever it is returned from a search function, it means that the search string was not found. The second interesting case is the last line of code. The second parameter of the function says, "Start searching for the search string at index 5," which means it will start searching for o after the first o was found at index 4.

There's also a reverse-find function:

```
pos = str1.rfind( "o" );        // 16
```

The function to find *any* character within a given set of characters is also useful. For example:

```
std::string vowels = "aeiou";
std::string str1 = "That is the sound of inevitability.";
size_t pos;
pos = str1.find_first_of( vowels );        // 2
pos = str1.find_first_of( vowels, 3 );     // 5
```

```
pos = str1.find_first_not_of( vowels );    // 0
pos = str1.find_last_of( vowels );         // 31
pos = str1.find_last_of( vowels, 30 );     // 29
pos = str1.find_last_not_of( vowels );     // 34
```

The functions with a second parameter tell the function to start searching at that index; first functions start at that index and go up, and last functions start at that index and go down.

There are more functions, of course, but I use them rarely if at all, so I don't want to spend any extra time explaining them. A good STL reference should explain all the functions in depth.

My Own String Functions

For a MUD, you're going to need to do a bit of string parsing on your own, since the C++ string library doesn't include those kinds of functions. That's not a big deal, though. Basically, I feel the extra string functions you're going to need in this book are functions to convert strings to uppercase/lowercase, trim whitespace off the ends of strings, get individual words from strings, and remove individual words from strings. And since the C++ string library doesn't have string->datatype or vice-versa functions, I'll create some of those, too.

Changing Cases

If you look at the standard C++ string class, you see that the equivalence operator is handy; but it has a problem. Look at the following example:

```
std::string str1 = "HELLO";
std::string str2 = "hello";
boolean b = (str1 == str2)    // false
```

Even though the strings contain the same word, they are not equal because they are different characters. This is sometimes particularly troublesome. So how would you go about trying to see if the words are the same?

The logical answer is to convert both strings to the same case, and then compare them. Unfortunately, there is no standard C++ method to convert a string to a particular case. Who knows whether this was an oversight or the developers felt it wasn't needed? Many compilers implement this function on their own, but it's not part of the standard.

So let's build our own! C++ *does* include a function for converting individual characters to upper- or lowercase, however. These functions are located in the standard C++ header <cctype>. These functions will be in the BasicLib files: BasicLibString.h and BasicLibString.cpp.

First, an uppercase function:

```
std::string UpperCase( const std::string& p_string ) {
    std::string str = p_string;
    for( int i = 0; i < str.size(); i++ ) {
```

```
        str[i] = std::toupper( str[i] );
    }
    return str;
}
```

The function essentially goes through every character in the string, converts it to uppercase, and then returns the new string. The LowerCase() function is identical, except the call to toupper is replaced with tolower. Therefore, there is no need to show it here.

Trimming Whitespace

Whitespace is a term used for space in text that is blank. Spaces, tabs, newline characters— they're all whitespace. Many times you're going to want to be able to trim the whitespace off the front and the back of a string. For example, you've got a string

```
"    hello    "
```

that has four blank spaces both in front of and behind the word "hello". You just want to get the word in there and ignore all that extra junk. Luckily, this is pretty easy using the string's search functions.

First, you need to define what whitespace actually is:

```
const std::string WHITESPACE = " \t\n\r";
```

This is a global const string that defines the four common whitespace characters. The first is a space; the second is \t, which is the C++ escape sequence that means tab; then \n, which is newline; and finally \r, which is a carriage-return. Here's the actual function:

```
std::string TrimWhitespace( const std::string& p_string ) {
    int wsf, wsb;
    wsf = p_string.find_first_not_of( WHITESPACE );
    wsb = p_string.find_last_not_of( WHITESPACE );
    if( wsf == std::string::npos ) {
        wsf = 0;
        wsb = -1;
    }
    return p_string.substr( wsf, wsb - wsf + 1 );
}
```

There are two locals: wsf and wsb. These stand for "white space front" and "white space back." The function uses the find functions to find the first and last characters in the string that aren't whitespace. For the example string I showed you before, wsf would be 4 and wsb would be 8, pointing at h and o. The if-statement in there checks to see if the string was entirely whitespace (meaning that no non-whitespace characters were found); if whitespace is found, the entire string needs to be cleared, so wsf is set to 0, and wsb is set to -1. Next you'll see why.

Finally, the substr function is called, chopping off the front and back whitespace portions. The first parameter to substr is the position from which the substring starts, and the second parameter is the length of the substring. So, in the example, the substring starts at index 4 ("h"), and is 8 - 4 + 1 (5) characters long. This results in `hello`. For the case of a string of only whitespace, the length calculation would result in 0 - -1 + 1, which is 0. So the result of `TrimWhitespace( "               " );` is a string that is 0 characters long.

Parsing

Parsing words out of a string is a somewhat simple task, once again utilizing the string class's search features. Basically, the idea is to count the number of *runs* of whitespace contained in a string (a run of whitespace is basically just one continuous chunk of characters that are all whitespace), until you find the word you want.

To show you how the function works in detail, I'll be referring to this string:

`"This is a string"`

The first thing the function does is find the first character in the string that isn't whitespace. This will be the beginning of the first word:

```
std::string ParseWord( const std::string& p_string, int p_index )
{
    int wss = p_string.find_first_not_of( WHITESPACE );
```

After that executes, `wss` has the index of the first word (word index 0) in the string. For the example, `wss` would be 0, because index 0, "T" is a non-whitespace character.

Now, in order to find the correct word, you must loop through the string `p_index` times, finding the end of the current word, and then the beginning of the next word:

```
    while( p_index > 0 ) {
        p_index--;
        wss = p_string.find_first_of( WHITESPACE, wss );
        wss = p_string.find_first_not_of( WHITESPACE, wss );
    }
```

As you can see, the loop runs until `p_index` is zero; if `p-index` is zero to begin with, the loop never executes. So it searches for the index of the first whitespace character after the current word. With the example string, this would be 4, since index 4 is the first whitespace character after the word "This." Then the loop searches for the next non-whitespace character; in the example, that character is index 5, "i."

Depending on which word you want, this loop can repeat over and over, until the desired word is found. At the end of the loop, the `wss` variable should be pointing to the first letter of the word you want to extract.

Now that you have the index of the first letter of the word you want, you need to find out how long the word is, by finding the end of the word:

```
    int wse = p_string.find_first_of( WHITESPACE, wss );
```

Now, if there was a problem finding the appropriate word (for example, you wanted the fifth word when there were only four words), wss should be std::string::npos. So you need to check that:

```
if( wss == std::string::npos ) {
    wss = 0;
    wse = 0;
}
```

If you couldn't find the word, set both indexes to 0, to signify that you want to return an empty string. Finally, you return the substring:

```
    return p_string.substr( wss, wse - wss );
}
```

Since wse is pointing to the first whitespace character *after* the word you want, you don't need to add a whitespace character to the length this time (as opposed to the TrimWhitespace() function). So, here it is in action:

```
std::string str1 = "This is a string";
std::string str2;
str2 = BasicLib::ParseWord( str1, 0 ); // "This"
str2 = BasicLib::ParseWord( str1, 1 ); // "is"
str2 = BasicLib::ParseWord( str1, 2 ); // "a"
str2 = BasicLib::ParseWord( str1, 3 ); // "string"
str2 = BasicLib::ParseWord( str1, 4 ); // ""
```

This kind of a function becomes incredibly useful when dealing with a MUD.

There is a similar function, RemoveWord(), but instead of returning the requested word, it returns the original string *without* the word. The function is identical to ParseWord() except for two aspects. The idea of removing a word is somewhat odd. Imagine the string "This is a string". If you wanted to remove word one ("is"), and only the word, you'd end up with "This a string", with two spaces between "This" and "a". That would look weird, wouldn't it? Basically, the best way to remove a word from a string is to not only remove the word, but the whitespace after the word as well. So you want to remove "is " and not "is". Therefore, you need to add another line of code to the function. After finding the first whitespace after the word to be removed, you need to find the beginning of the next word after that:

```
    int wse = p_string.find_first_of( WHITESPACE, wss );
    wse = p_string.find_first_not_of( WHITESPACE, wse );
```

Notice that the first line is the same as it was in the ParseWord() function. Now, wse should be the index of the first letter of the word *after* the word you want to remove.

The next difference is that you're not returning a substring. This time, you're going to call the string's erase function to remove the word:

```
    std::string str = p_string;
    str.erase( wss, wse - wss );
    return str;
}
```

Ta-da! Here are some examples:

```
std::string str1 = "This is a string";
std::string str2;
str2 = BasicLib::RemoveWord( str1, 0 );    // "is a string"
str2 = BasicLib::RemoveWord( str1, 1 );    // "This a string"
str2 = BasicLib::RemoveWord( str1, 2 );    // "This is string"
str2 = BasicLib::RemoveWord( str1, 3 );    // "This is a "
str2 = BasicLib::RemoveWord( str1, 4 );    // "This is a string"
```

Notice that when trying to remove word index 3, there is a space at the end of the string. This is the only anomaly in the algorithm, but it actually makes sense if you think about it. The RemoveWord() function treats the whitespace after the word as part of that word.

Conversions

Unfortunately, there is no direct way in C++ to convert a string to another datatype, or vice-versa. But it still is an easy process.

C++ has a stream class called stringstream, which acts like an input/output buffer, much like cin and cout. Luckily, C++ has built-in functions that allow you to convert basic datatypes to and from strings, via streams. For example, you can use cout to print ints, floats, strings, and so on:

```
std::cout << 10 << 3.1415 << "hello!";
```

You can do the same with stringstreams:

```
#include <sstream>
std::stringstream str;
str << 10 << 3.1415 << "hello!";    // "103.1415hello!"
```

You can also do it the other way around:

```
int i;
str >> i;                    // 103
```

Why is 103 in the integer? Because it picked out every digit it could find before it got to the period. If you streamed it into a float instead, it would be "103.1415".

That's how you can convert datatypes. In an effort to make the datatype easy to work with, I've created two functions to convert to and from strings. The first function converts a datatype into a string:

```
template< class type >
inline std::string tostring( const type& p_type ) {
    std::stringstream str;
    str << p_type;
    return str.str();
}
```

The first thing you should notice is that this is a template function. Templates make life much easier, so if you're not familiar with them, you should probably try to catch up. Since this function is templated, it will work with *any* datatype that can be streamed into a stringstream. If you create a custom class and have it support an operator<< into a basic ostream class, your class can automatically be converted into a string class using this function.

So, the function takes a parameter of any datatype, creates a stringstream buffer, and then streams the parameter into the buffer. Finally, the stream is converted into a string using the buffer's str() function, and returned. Voilá!

Here's how you use the lines of code:

```
std::string str1;
str1 = BasicLib::tostring( 42 );                 // "42"
str1 += " " + BasicLib::tostring( 3.1415 );   // "42 3.1415"
```

It even works with the sint64 type.

Now, the other way around is the totype() function, which converts a string into any datatype that has a defined stream-extraction operator.

```
template< class type >
inline type totype( const std::string& p_string ) {
    std::stringstream str;
    str << p_string;
    type t;
    str >> t;
    return t;
}
```

The totype() function is also a template function, which takes a string as a parameter and returns whatever you want. This function streams the string into the stringstream, creates a value of type type named t, and streams the buffer into it. Finally, t is returned.

Using this function is a little odd, however. For example, try doing this:

```
int i = BasicLib::totype( "42" );        // COMPILER ERROR!
```

Template datatypes can only be determined by the types of the function parameters, and this function only takes a std::string as its parameter; it can't tell that you want to return an int. So you need to tell the function yourself:

```
using namespace BasicLib;
int i = totype<int>( "42" );
float f = totype<float>( "3.1415" );
sint64 s = totype<sint64>( "1152921504606846976" );
```

Now you've got functions to convert datatypes' to and from strings.

Searching and Replacing

MUDs need another common function—the ability to search for a substring inside of a string and replace it.

To do this, I've created the SearchAndReplace helper function:

```
std::string SearchAndReplace(
    const std::string& p_target,
    const std::string& p_search,
    const std::string& p_replace );
```

SearchAndReplace is really just a simple function that uses the string's find and replace functions, so I'm not going to bother showing you the code. The code is on the CD in the file BasicLibString.cpp if you want to see it, though.

Basically, the function goes through a string and replaces all instances of p_search with p_replace, and returns the result. Here's some code:

```
string s = "This string has been read once, and only once.";
s = BasicLib::SearchAndReplace( s, "once", "twice" );
```

After that code runs, s will hold "This string has been read twice, and only twice."

Logging

As a MUD programmer, logging errors and other types of events is somewhat important. Because of this, I've created a simple log class, which is small and elegant.

The first concept you should be aware of is the *decorator* class. A decorator is a simple class that is designed to decorate the log entries you send to it. For example, you can make an HTML decorator, which will take log entries and add HTML codes to them.

> **TIP**
>
> In a game, whenever you have an error, you can log the message as "**ERROR**: blah blah blah"; and if your decorator class supports a colored format like HTML, it can search for that string and add red coloring to it, indicating that the string should stand out in the log file. Or if you're boring, you can just use a plain text decorator, such as the one I've provided for you.

Decorators

The decorator classes should have four functions: FileHeader(), Decorate(), SessionOpen(), and SessionClose(). All functions should return an std::string. The FileHeader() function returns a string representing the header of the file, such as an HTML header with the title, and so on. The Decorate() function takes a piece of text and decorates it according to the decorator rules. The SessionOpen() and SessionClose() functions return strings representing the beginning and ending of a single session. This would be great for keeping each session in a HTML table, or something similar.

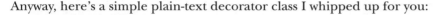

Anyway, here's a simple plain-text decorator class I whipped up for you:

```cpp
class TextDecorator {
public:
    static std::string FileHeader( const std::string& p_title ) {
        return "===============================================\n" +
               p_title + "\n" +
               "===============================================\n\n";
    }
    static std::string SessionOpen() {
        return "\n";
    }
    static std::string SessionClose() {
        return "\n";
    }
    static std::string Decorate( const std::string& p_string ) {
        return p_string + "\n";
    }
};
```

As you can see, this decorator class is simple. It prints out a simple header, and then prints out newlines for the session openings and closings.

Furthermore, a newline character is added to each entry you want to decorate, because it is assumed that you didn't put those in yourself. As I said, it's pretty simple.

The Logger

The logger is also pretty simple; it has only three functions: a constructor, a destructor, and a Log() function. It also has three data members: a file stream and two Booleans, which determine if the log should be time- and date-stamped. Here's the class definition:

```cpp
template<class decorator>
class Logger {
public:
    Logger( const std::string& p_filename,
            const std::string& p_logtitle,
            bool p_timestamp = false,
            bool p_datestamp = false );
    ~Logger();
    void Log( const std::string& p_entry );
protected:
    std::fstream m_logfile;
    bool m_timestamp;
    bool m_datestamp;
};
```

The Constructor

The constructor tries to create the file if it doesn't exist, or just open it if it does exist. You set the file name, the title of the log, and the two stamp Booleans as well. Those last two are optional parameters, and they default to false. Here's the function:

```
template<class decorator>
Logger<decorator>::Logger( const std::string& p_filename,
                           const std::string& p_logtitle,
                           bool p_timestamp,
                           bool p_datestamp ) {
    fstream filetester( p_filename.c_str(), std::ios::in );
    if( filetester.is_open() ) {
        filetester.close();
        m_logfile.open( p_filename.c_str(), std::ios::out | std::ios::app );
    }
    else {
        m_logfile.open( p_filename.c_str(), std::ios::out );
        m_logfile << decorator::FileHeader( p_logtitle );
    }
    m_timestamp = true;
    m_datestamp = true;
    m_logfile << decorator::SessionOpen();
    Log( "Session opened." );
    m_timestamp = p_timestamp;
    m_datestamp = p_datestamp;
}
```

Since C++ has no easy way to tell if a file exists (sigh), I created a temporary file stream named filetester. This is opened in read-only mode, which means that opening it fails if the file doesn't exist. So the line after that checks to see if the file's open, and if so, the temporary file is closed, and the log file is opened in append mode. That means that the contents of the file remain the same, and all new data is added to the end of the file.

If the file doesn't exist, the log file is still opened, and the decorator class is consulted to get a file header, which is then put into the log file.

The time- and date-stamp Booleans are both set to true, because the session's opening message should always be time- and date-stamped. The decorator class is once again consulted to get text to be written representing an open session, and then the entry Session opened. is logged. Finally, the time- and date-stamp Booleans passed in as parameters are copied from the parameter values.

The Destructor

Whenever a logger is destroyed, the appropriate session-closing text should be written to the file, and the file should be closed:

```
template< class decorator >
Logger< decorator >::~Logger() {
    m_timestamp = true;
    m_datestamp = true;
    Log( "Session closed." );
    m_logfile << decorator::SessionClose();
}
```

Once again, the session-closing text should also be time- and date-stamped.

It's Log, Log—It's Big, It's Heavy, It's Wood!

No one remembers that song? Bah!

Anyway, here's the Log function, which sends a string of text to your logfile.

> **TIP**
>
> **Watch more *Ren & Stimpy*.**

```
template< class decorator >
void Logger< decorator >::Log( const std::string& p_entry ) {
    std::string message;
    if( m_datestamp ) {
        message += "[" + DateStamp() + "] ";
    }
    if( m_timestamp ) {
        message += "[" + TimeStamp() + "] ";
    }
    message += p_entry;
    m_logfile << decorator::Decorate( message );
}
```

A string containing the message is created; if the user wants time- or date-stamps, they are added to the message, and the entry is added at the end as well. Finally, the message is sent through the decorator and then added to the file.

Using the Logger

To make things easier for you, I've included a typedef in the logger files:

```
typedef Logger<TextDecorator> TextLog;
```

Therefore, you don't have to do all kinds of ugly stuff just to use a text decorator with a logger. Here's how you would create one:

```
#include "BasicLib/BasicLib.h"
BasicLib::TextLog SystemLog( "syslog.txt", "System Log" );
SystemLog.Log( "Log Entry" );
```

After executing this code, I had a file named syslog.txt that looked like this:

```
=======================================================
System Log
=======================================================
```

```
[2003.05.19] [02:55:03] Session opened.
Log Entry
[2003.05.19] [02:55:03] Session closed.
```

Don't ask why I'm running code demonstrations at 3 A.M.—blah. Feel free to create your own decorator classes to make your log files prettier. HTML is a popular format nowadays for logs, so you might want to make an HTML decorator.

Summary

And there you have it. This chapter taught you all about the basic library functions that I'll be using throughout this book to make your life easier. So, to summarize, you've learned how to create large 64-bit integers, get platform-independent millisecond timers and timestamps, learned how to use strings and add functions to utilize strings better, and create an elegant and flexible log class. That's a lot of material to cover, but it's all mostly simple. Believe me—this stuff will make your life so much easier later on.

CHAPTER 5

THE SOCKET LIBRARY

B ack in Chapter 2, "Winsock/Berkeley Sockets Programming," I introduced you to the API for plain vanilla-flavored BSD sockets. Throughout that chapter, you may have noticed my distaste for the API, which is decades old and has clearly started to show its age lately. I particularly dislike how much code it takes to actually get something done. Think about it. It takes at least 12 lines of code to get a single listening socket created, and that doesn't even count error-handling code. I look at many MUDs out there, and I see socket code thrown in every which way. Most MUDs are a maintenance disaster because of this. If you want to do something correctly, you're going to have to design for it up front.

So that's the approach I'm taking with this chapter. I've created a comprehensive and flexible Socket Library for you (located on the CD in the directory /Libraries/SocketLib/). This library has two levels: classes that directly interface with the Sockets API ("wrapper" classes), and classes that build on top of those wrappers.

In this chapter, you will learn to:

- Create a flexible object-oriented socket hierarchy
- Abstract the Sockets API `select` function into a class
- Create an advanced policy-based connection class
- Create a class to manage listening sockets
- Create a class to manage connections

Sockets API Wrapper Classes and Functions

There are basically four classes that know about the implementation of the underlying Sockets API. Since I've shown you in Chapter 2 how to use the API, I'm going to focus in this chapter on showing you how to design the classes, and not the code behind them. In addition, I'll dig deeper into subjects I outlined in Chapter 2. After all, this book is about MUDs, not a super-awesome Socket Library!

Socket Wrapper

My main problem with the Sockets API is that it handles listening sockets and data sockets the same way; you can't tell them apart. This is an awkward design, and it can lead to many types of problems. For example, you can inadvertently call `send` on a listening socket; obviously, you should only be doing that on data sockets, but it's so easy to accidentally do something like that.

Using a proper class hierarchy can prevent stupid things such as that from happening. You can make sure that a call to send or recv is never made on a listening socket. With good design, you can completely remove some of the errors you had to check for in the past. Figure 5.1 shows the design I'll be using for the sockets. All three of the classes shown in the figure can be found on the CD in the files /Libraries/SocketLib/SocketLibSocket.h and /Libraries/SocketLib/SocketLibSocket.cpp.

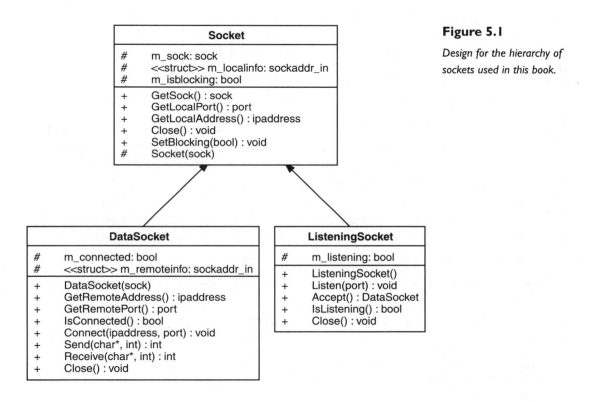

Figure 5.1

Design for the hierarchy of sockets used in this book.

Sockets

The base class is Socket. You'll notice it has a variable of type sock, which is just my typedef for a socket descriptor. I like typedefing things like that, because it makes programs more readable. When you see a function that takes a sock as a parameter, instead of just an int, you know that it wants a socket descriptor, and not some other type of data. The class also holds a sockaddr_in structure, which, if you remember from Chapter 2, holds information about a socket. For this class, it holds the *local* information about the socket (port number and address). All sockets have local information.

The last variable is a Boolean, m_blocking. This determines if the socket is blocking. Think back to Chapter 2, when you learned that sockets block by default. There are many exploits that are possible on blocking sockets.

UML

Figure 5.1 is drawn in a diagram style known as a *Unified Modeling Language (UML) Class Diagram*. UML is a pretty standard method of designing classes in object-oriented languages, so you should at least be familiar with it if you plan on doing some serious programming. It's not too difficult to understand. For example, you can see that the class name is in the top box, the datatypes are in the middle box, and the functions are in the third box.

- The hash (#) symbol means that the item is *protected*.
- The plus (+) means that it's *public*.
- The minus (-) means that it's *private*.

One aspect may look weird to you—the type of variable, or the return type of a function, is listed *after* the function/variable name, after the colon (:). There are also several types of arrows used in UML class diagrams; you only see the open-head *inheritance* arrows in this diagram. The other common arrow type is a plain arrowhead, which is the *uses* arrow. For a more comprehensive look at UML, there's a great chapter about it in *Game Programming Tricks of the Trade*, by Lorenzo Phillips (Editor).

In particular, there's an "exploit" that allows you to connect to a listening socket and then disconnect immediately; in the server, the select() function will detect the new connection, but by the time it gets to the accept() call, the connection no longer exists. If you've got the listening sockets in the same thread as everything else, this can cause your entire game to hang, because the call to accept() will block until someone tries to connect again. Therefore, you need the ability to set a socket to nonblocking mode.

Unfortunately, the method of setting the blocking mode of a socket is different with both Winsock and BSD Sockets. (Typical!) The SetBlocking() function takes a Boolean as its parameter: true if you want the socket to block, false if you don't want it to block.

The Winsock method is pretty easy:

```
void Socket::SetBlocking( bool p_blockmode ) {
    int err;
    #ifdef WIN32
        unsigned long mode = !p_blockmode;
        err = ioctlsocket( m_sock, FIONBIO, &mode );
```

Just one call to the ioctlsocket function is required; however, the blocking Boolean needs to be reversed for this function, because you're setting whether or not you want to enable nonblocking mode. It's just a minor difference in semantics, that's all.

The Linux method is a little trickier, because the function to set the blocking mode sets a whole bunch of other modes as well. Therefore, you need to retrieve the current flags of the socket, set or clear the nonblocking bit, and then set the new flags. It's a bit of a pain:

```
#else
    int flags = fcntl( m_sock, F_GETFL, 0 );
    if( p_blockmode == false ) {
        flags |= O_NONBLOCK;
    }
    else {
        flags &= ~O_NONBLOCK;
    }
    err = fcntl( m_sock, F_SETFL, flags );
#endif
```

So the flags are retrieved, and depending on what mode you want, the nonblocking flag is either set (using logical-or), or cleared (using logical-and). Finally, the new flags are sent back to the socket. Here's the conclusion:

```
if( err == -1 ) {
    throw( Exception( GetError() ) );
}
m_isblocking = p_blockmode;
}
```

The SocketLib library has some auxiliary functions and classes built into it, such as the Exception class and the GetError() function. I'll go over these in more detail when I get to the parts that use them more, but for now, you should just know that the SocketLib throws exceptions when errors occur, and GetError() is a wrapper that gets error codes from the Sockets API.

I won't show you the code for the other functions in this class, since I've already covered the basics in Chapter 2. If you're really interested, you can take a look at the source, but, as I've said, these socket classes are just a wrapper around the Sockets API that clean up the interface for you.

I need to make one other important point: The constructor for the Socket class is protected. This was done so that you could not create plain Socket classes on your own; they are pointless. The class only provides useful functions for the ListeningSocket and DataSocket classes.

Listening Sockets

As a subclass of the Socket class, the ListeningSocket class inherits all of the functions and data of Socket and adds a few new functions of its own. I don't introduce much that is new in the code, so I won't show you any of the internals, but I'll show you how to use a listening socket in a bit.

NOTE

I've put one important concept into listening sockets that I haven't told you about before. Whenever you tell a listening socket to listen on a port, the function turns on the socket's SO_REUSEADDR option. Whenever you start up a program and make it listen on a port, then close the program, and try to run it again, you probably receive an "address already in use" error if this option isn't turned on. For some odd reason, the operating system still thinks the address is in use, but turning on this option makes it work correctly, so that you receive only the address already in use error when you try opening two active listening sockets on the same port.

Data Sockets

Data sockets are the other subclass. They also inherit from the plain sockets, but they need more data and have more complex functions. For example, data sockets add another sockaddr_in structure; in this case, it represents the *remote* address, which the socket is connected to. Because listening sockets can't be connected to anything, they don't have remote addresses, but data sockets do. Also, data sockets need information on how to connect to remote addresses and send and receive data. Once again, the class is basically just a wrapper around what I showed you in Chapter 2, so I'm not going to show you the internal code; that would be redundant.

Using Sockets

Because of the way my Socket Library is set up, it's incredibly easy to use. Observe:

```
using namespace SocketLib;
ListeningSocket lsock;
DataSocket dsock;
lsock.Listen( 5000 );          // start listening on port 5000
dsock = lsock.Accept();        // wait for an incomming connection
```

Ta-da! Five lines of code for something that would take around 30-40 in the Sockets API. After this code has executed, dsock will contain a socket (if a client connects to you, of course) that you can send and receive data from:

```
char buffer[128] = "Hello there!";
dsock.Send( buffer, strlen( buffer ) );
dsock.Receive( buffer, 128 );
```

This simple program sends a bunch of text—"Hello there!"—and then waits for the client to send something back. Here again, stuff like this makes your life so much easier.

Socket Sets

The select() function is the other main feature of the Sockets API that I will frequently use. The select() function polls a set of sockets activity. For this, I've created the SocketSet class, which will keep track of an fd_set of sockets. It will essentially allow you to add sockets, remove sockets, "poll" the sockets (call select()), and check if a socket has activity. Figure 5.2 shows the class diagram for this class.

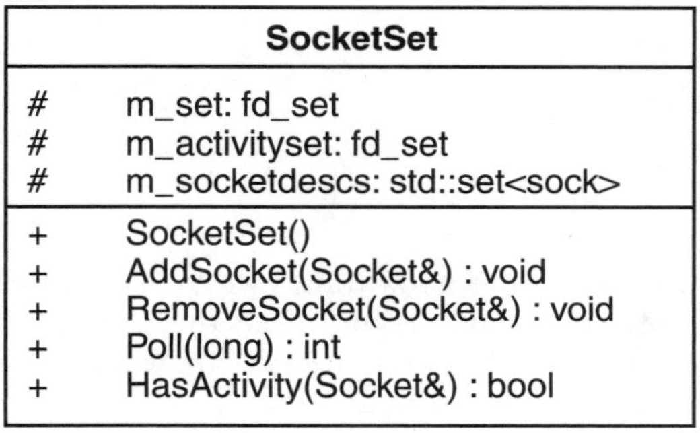

SocketSet
m_set: fd_set #   m_activityset: fd_set #   m_socketdescs: std::set<sock>
+   SocketSet() +   AddSocket(Socket&) : void +   RemoveSocket(Socket&) : void +   Poll(long) : int +   HasActivity(Socket&) : bool

Figure 5.2

Class diagram for the SocketSet *class, which tracks an* fd_set *of sockets.*

The SocketSet class is fairly simple, but it does have one extra optimization that I did not discuss in Chapter 2. Remember the first parameter of the select() function? It is supposed to be the value of the highest socket descriptor within the set, plus 1. Windows ignores this value and does its own thing, but if you don't put in a valid value for Linux, you're going to have problems.

In Chapter 2, I told you that you could just put 0x7FFFFFFF into it. That's a really dumb thing to do if you're looking for speed, however, and I did that just for simplicity's sake. If you put a huge number such as 0x7FFFFFFF into the function, it's going to take a long time to check the sockets (because it's basically a for-loop underneath in Linux). If you use too small a value, you might end up ignoring some sockets. As much as I hate doing extra work for tedious things such as this, I was forced to add the capability to detect the largest socket descriptor into the Linux branch of the code.

Note the last variable within the class diagram in Figure 5.2: m_socketdescs. I made the code so that variable doesn't exist in Windows, but it exists in Linux. It's basically an std::set that keeps track of all the descriptors that have been added to the fd_set.

The internal implementation of storing sockets inside an fd_set isn't standard, so there really is no way to check the largest value in a set without calling FD_ISSET() on every possible socket descriptor, and as you can probably imagine, that would take forever. I just keep an std::set of socket descriptors handy, so I can search through them whenever a socket is removed. If you know how `std::set`s work, you'll realize that the highest value is always at the end of the container if you're using regular numeric types, so to get the value of the largest descriptor, you simply need to get an iterator to the last item and dereference it. The code is simple, so I won't bother showing it to you here.

Here's an example of its use:

```
using namespace SocketLib;
DataSocket socks[3];
SocketSet sset;
// assume the sockets are connected here somewhere
sset.AddSocket( socks[0] );
sset.AddSocket( socks[1] );
sset.AddSocket( socks[2] );
int active = sset.Poll( 1000 );    // wait 1 second for activity
if( sset.HasActivity( socks[0] ) );// check if there is activity
    // handle activity
// later on:
sset.RemoveSocket( socks[0] );
```

And so on. It's pretty easy to use. However, you must remember a few things when using this class. First of all, different operating systems have different numbers of sockets that you can store inside an fd_set. For example, Windows is set at 64 sockets, while Red Hat 8, which I am running, is set at 1024. Other implementations differ as well, I imagine.

To handle this, I've included a handy `define` inside of the Socket Library, the MAX constant. `SocketLib::MAX` will hold the maximum number of sockets you can store in an fd_set.

So, you should remember to check the `SocketLib::MAX` variable to see how many sockets you can fit in a set. Also, the `SocketSet` class doesn't actually count how many sockets it contains; it's really up to whomever uses it to keep track.

Function Wrappers

I've included four functions within the SocketLib namespace to help you with network programming. They are located within the SocketLibSystem.h and .cpp files. Here are the functions:

```
ipaddress GetIPAddress( const std::string p_address );
std::string GetIPString( ipaddress p_address );
std::string GetHostNameString( ipaddress p_address );
bool IsIPAddress( const std::string p_address );
```

The `ipaddress` type is just a typedef for an `unsigned long int`, but, as I've told you before, turning items into typedefs makes your programs much more readable. Also, there's one little qualification I've made: ipaddresses *must* be in Network-Byte-Order (NBO). All socket functions assume that ipaddresses are in NBO, and if you play it right, you'll never have to convert addresses to and from host-byte-order.

So, you can use the GetIPAddress() function to convert string addresses into a binary IP address like this:

```
ipaddress addr = SocketLib::GetIPAddress( "www.google.com" );
addr = SocketLib::GetIPAddress( "127.0.0.1" );
```

Note that this function is smart. It can convert either DNS-capable addresses such as www.google.com, or numeric addresses such as 127.0.0.1. However, you'll have to be careful when converting a DNS-capable address; this function may block. (Remember from Chapter 2 that this function needs to contact your DNS server.) So it's usually wise to call this function in a thread separate from your main game, unless you know for sure that you're converting a plain numeric address.

The next function takes an IP address and converts it into its numeric string:

```
std::string str = SocketLib::GetIPString( addr );
```

After the code has executed, that string should contain "127.0.0.1" (assuming addr still contains the same address from the previous code example).

The other string conversion function does a reverse-DNS lookup:

```
addr = SocketLib::GetIPAddress( "www.google.com" );
str = SocketLib::GetHostNameString( addr );  // "www.google.com"
```

And finally, we come to a function that detects whether a string contains a numeric IP address, or an address that you should try to look up through DNS. This can help you determine if the GetIPAddress function might block or not:

```
bool b;
b = SocketLib::IsIPAddress( "www.google.com" );  // false
b = SocketLib::IsIPAddress( "127.0.0.1" );       // true
```

So if the function returns false, GetIPAddress will probably block.

Errors

A Socket Library wouldn't be complete without an error reporting system, because many things can go wrong with sockets, even when you prevent most errors with proper design.

Error Codes

The first thing I did was to create an enumerated type representing all the possible error codes:

```
enum Error {
    // errors that shouldn't happen; if they do, something is wrong:
    ESeriousError,

    // these errors are common
    ENetworkDown,
```

```
        ENoSocketsAvailable,
        ENoMemory,
        EAddressNotAvailable,
        EAlreadyConnected,
        ENotConnected,
        EConnectionRefused,
        ENetworkUnreachable,
        ENetworkReset,
        EShutDown,
        EHostUnreachable,
        EHostDown,
        EConnectionAborted,
        EConnectionReset,
        EOperationWouldBlock,

        // DNS errors
        EDNSNotFound,
        EDNSError,
        ENoDNSData,

        // These errors are specific errors that should never or rarely occur.
        EInProgress,
        EInterrupted,
        EAccessDenied,
        EInvalidParameter,
        EAddressFamilyNotSupported,
        EProtocolFamilyNotSupported,
        EProtocolNotSupported,
        EProtocolNotSupportedBySocket,
        EOperationNotSupported,
        EInvalidSocketType,
        EInvalidSocket,
        EAddressRequired,
        EMessageTooLong,
        EBadProtocolOption,
        EOptionNotSupported,
        EAddressInUse,
        ETimedOut,
        EShutDown,


        // auxiliary socketlib errors
        ESocketLimitReached,
        ENotAvailable,
        EConnectionClosed
};
```

As you can see, there are a plethora of possibilities, possibly even a cornucopia? In either case, there are a lot of them! I'm not going to take the time to explain them here, because most are equivalent to the errors I've shown you in Chapter 2 and are detailed in Appendix B, "Socket Error Codes" on the CD. Notice the third grouping of errors. Most of those errors have been eliminated through the design of the socket library. Theoretically, those errors should *never* occur. Theoretically, of course. Things might not work out that way in real life, so if those errors occur, something is seriously wrong with your program.

> **TIP**
>
> If you ever plan to make a better error-handling system, you might want to think about implementing a *severity* system, in which errors are assigned values that indicate how severe they are. For example, you can make certain errors have a severity level that tells your game that the connection needs to be closed, and others that tell your system that the entire network just isn't working, and the game must be shut down.

Translating Errors

Like all things in life, there are problems with the native error codes in the Sockets API. Windows is actually helpful here by giving each error its own specific value that you can retrieve using its `WSAGetLastError()` function. On the other hand, Linux muddles its system by using two different error-reporting mechanisms: `errno` and `h_errno`, which retrieve regular errors and host-lookup errors respectively. The problem is that both variables use different error-numbering systems, and some error codes conflict with each other on some systems.

To get around this problem, I've created a function to get errors that takes a Boolean parameter and determines which error source it should get errors from:

```
Error GetError( bool p_errno = true );
```

If the parameter is `true` (the default value), the function gets errors from `errno`; if `false`, it gets errors from `h_errno`. The WIN32 version of this function just ignores the parameter.

Then there is a function that actually does the translating:

```
Error TranslateError( int p_error, bool p_errno );
```

This function really shouldn't be used anywhere except by the `GetError()` function, so it's mainly just a helper function that takes an integer error code and translates it into an actual `Error` type. It's a huge and ugly function, so I recommend looking at the source only if you like seeing huge, ugly functions.

The SocketLib::Exception Class

And finally, here's the `SocketLib::Exception` class:

```
class Exception : public std::exception {
public:
    Exception( Error p_code );
```

```
    Error ErrorCode();
    std::string PrintError();
protected:
    Error m_code;
};
```

This class is very simple; it contains just a single error code and has functions to get the error code, as well as print the error message to a string. You can throw exceptions like this:

```
throw SocketLib::Exception( SocketLib::GetError() );
```

And then catch them like this:

```
try {
    // write socket code here
}
catch( SocketLib::Exception& e ) {
    // handle error here
}
```

If you don't know how to use exceptions, see Appendix C, "C++ Primer," on the CD for more information.

The Winsock Initializer

In Chapter 2, you learned that Winsock must be initialized and shut down whenever you use it. I'm going to use a clever trick to make the program automatically initialize the Winsock library by creating a global object, and initializing the library in that object's constructor.

In addition, I will shut down Winsock in the destructor of this object. The class is located in SocketLibSystem.cpp and is called System. The class has a member variable of type WSADATA, which, as you learned in Chapter 2, stores information about Winsock. Here's the class definition:

```
class System {
public:
    System()  { WSAStartup( MAKEWORD( 2, 2 ), &m_WSAData ); }
    ~System() { WSACleanup(); }
protected:
    WSADATA m_WSAData;
};
```

The constructor automatically initializes Winsock, and the destructor shuts it down. Error checking is not performed on either function, because it is dangerous. Throwing exceptions in constructors and destructors is generally a bad idea, and it doesn't help you notify the user about what is wrong (because there's nothing to catch the exceptions). If you threw an exception in the constructor, the program would immediately exit, and it wouldn't be able to notify the person running the program that there was a problem with Winsock. So, it's better to let it be, and detect the Winsock error when you try using the network system.

Also, if you throw an exception in the destructor, there is a very possibility that many things in your program may not shut down correctly. So, if shutting down Winsock fails, we really don't care, because the program is exiting anyway.

Finally, the global instance of the system object is declared:

```
System g_system;
```

This name appears only within the SocketLibSystem module, so it shouldn't cause name conflicts anywhere else in the program.

And that about sums up the portion of the library that wraps the Sockets API/Winsock.

Connections, Managers, and Policies, Oh My!

So now you've got a decent networking framework set up. You can connect to servers, listen for clients, send and receive data, and so on. But all that doesn't help you organize your game in a sensible manner. In an effort to make organizing a network module for this game easier, I've developed a large library of modular classes for you to use.

I want to launch into a discussion about the reasoning for this library before I get down to the nitty-gritty details. Over the years, I've been studying all the popular open-source MUDs, and I'm disappointed. Most of them began their lives 10 to 20 years ago, long before C++ was standardized.

So I understand why most MUDs that have been reworked, improved on, and expanded are extremely ugly today. Try adding a feature to a MUD, and you'll end up running around 100 files looking for bugs, or even worse, one huge multimegabyte source file. Count me out, thank you.

Another reason some MUDs are ugly is because people use them to start learning C and C++. It's a noble cause—but misguided. Because many older MUDs teach concepts that are out-of-date and no longer used, they teach people the wrong lessons.

So, I want to teach you how to program the proper way. As much as everyone hates templates, they are an integral part of C++, and when used correctly, they can add much flexibility to your programs. I hope you saw from Chapter 4, "The Basic Library," how useful templates can be for adding simple decorator features to a class.

In my extended Socket Library, I want to introduce you to the idea of a *policy* class. You're going to have sockets that send and receive data using a specific protocol. (I covered the concept of protocols in Chapter 2.) Now, a socket has no idea about the protocol; its job is to be dumb and just send and receive raw streams of bytes. That's a good way to think of it, because you can take the socket class and easily move it to some other type of application with no problems.

So now you have a socket class that doesn't care about what protocol it uses, but you want to expand it. You want to create some sort of flexible architecture in which you can say, "I want to create a socket that uses this protocol!" This is where the idea of a policy comes in. A socket will just receive raw data from the network and then send it off to its policy class, which will actually interpret that data. This can be done using templates. For this behavior, I've created a new kind of DataSocket, known as a Connection:

```
template< class protocol >
class Connection : public DataSocket
```

That's just the class declaration, for now. I'll get to the guts of the class later on. So, as you can see, it inherits from DataSocket, and it will be able to do everything a regular data socket does. It also has a template parameter that determines which protocol policy class to use. I'm jumping the gun a little bit here, but just for the purposes of explanation, you can assume that you've got classes called Telnet, FTP, and HTTP.

> **NOTE**
>
> I don't actually create FTP and HTTP classes anywhere in this book; they are imaginary classes used only for the sake of demonstrating the connection concept.

Those classes represent various Application layer protocols. So, if you've got those classes, this connection class allows you to do stuff like this:

```
Connection<Telnet> tcon;    // Telnet connection
Connection<FTP> fcon;       // FTP connection
Connection<HTTP> hcon;      // HTTP connection
```

That is the idea behind a policy class; those three protocol classes are policies that govern how data is interpreted.

Protocol Policies

The protocol policy classes you will be using in conjunction with the SocketLib are pretty simple. They're only required to have one function, which is the function that the Connection class calls whenever it receives raw data:

```
void Translate( Connection<protocol>& p_conn, char* p_buffer, int p_size );
```

The function takes as a reference the connection that is sending it data (for reasons illustrated in Figure 5.3), a pointer to the raw data buffer, and the size of the data in the buffer.

A protocol class must have one more item—a *typedef* (or an inner class, but I prefer a typedef)—that defines the *abstract* class (meaning that it defines only an interface) that will handle "complete" messages that the protocol object receives. This class is called protocol::handler (in the case of the Telnet protocol, you would refer to its abstract handler base class as Telnet::handler).

Imagine this scenario: You've got a protocol that sends discrete commands, but due to the unreliability of TCP network transmissions, each packet received by the connection may contain only a portion of the command, or even multiple commands. So, this raw data is sent to the protocol object, and when the protocol object detects that it has received one

full command, it shoots that command off to the connections' current protocol handler. Figure 5.3 demonstrates this process.

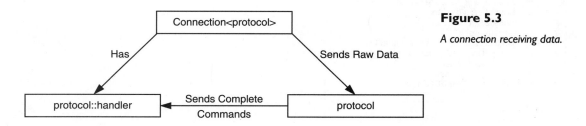

Figure 5.3

A connection receiving data.

I designed the system like this for a reason: The protocol class—and *only* the protocol class—should know the format for sending complete commands to the handler. The connection class doesn't know how to send data to its current handler, because it doesn't know what format the handler expects for data. The connection class simply hands raw data to its protocol, which then translates it and sends it to the handler.

Every connection handler is required to have a constructor that takes `Connection<protocol>&` as its parameter (where *protocol* is whichever protocol policy you are currently using), so that the handler can keep track of the connection it is linked to. You'll see more of this when I get into the specifics in Chapter 6, "Telnet Protocol and Simple Chat Server."

Protocol handler classes must also have the following functions, which are called whenever certain events occur to a connection:

```
void Enter();        // connection enters state
void Leave();        // connection leaves state
void Hungup();       // connection hangs up
void Flooded();      // connection floods
```

Additionally, you should always have at least one protocol handler class that has this function:

```
static void NoRoom( Connection<protocol>& p_connection );
```

This function is called whenever a connection manager receives a new connection, but there isn't enough room for it, and the connection must be told so. I will show you much more about the handler classes in Chapter 6, when I teach you about Telnet. For now, this is all you need to know about the protocol and protocol handlers.

Connections

As I mentioned before, I wanted to create a more specialized socket class, one that would communicate with a protocol class, and have other features as well. For this purpose, I've created the `Connection` class, located in the file /Libraries/SocketLib/Connection.h. Figure 5.4 shows the UML diagram of the `Connection` class.

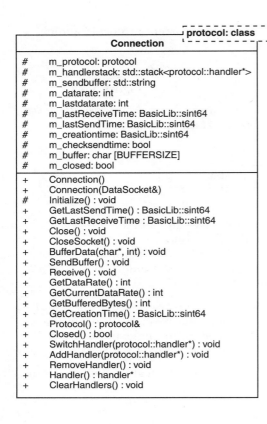

protocol: class

Connection
m_protocol: protocol
m_handlerstack: std::stack<protocol::handler*>
m_sendbuffer: std::string
m_datarate: int
m_lastdatarate: int
m_lastReceiveTime: BasicLib::sint64
m_lastSendTime: BasicLib::sint64
m_creationtime: BasicLib::sint64
m_checksendtime: bool
m_buffer: char [BUFFERSIZE]
m_closed: bool
+ Connection()
+ Connection(DataSocket&)
# Initialize() : void
+ GetLastSendTime() : BasicLib::sint64
+ GetLastReceiveTime : BasicLib::sint64
+ Close() : void
+ CloseSocket() : void
+ BufferData(char*, int) : void
+ SendBuffer() : void
+ Receive() : void
+ GetDataRate() : int
+ GetCurrentDataRate() : int
+ GetBufferedBytes() : int
+ GetCreationTime() : BasicLib::sint64
+ Protocol() : protocol&
+ Closed() : bool
+ SwitchHandler(protocol::handler*) : void
+ AddHandler(protocol::handler*) : void
+ RemoveHandler() : void
+ Handler() : handler*
+ ClearHandlers() : void

Figure 5.4

UML diagram of the
Connection *class.*

You can see that the class adds a bunch of new features on top of the regular data socket class, which I will go over in the next few sections.

New Variables

There are several new variables.

Protocol Object

First and foremost is the m_protocol member variable. You could theoretically make the protocol class *static,* which would mean that the class would exist without data, but that method has a problem. For example, it is entirely possible that you'll receive partial commands when receiving data from the connection; therefore, *something* needs to buffer that data. I've decided to let the protocol class handle the command buffering.

For the protocol class to handle the command buffering, the protocol class actually needs to be instantiated. Therefore, the Connection class will always keep an instance of its own protocol object. This method works really well if you ever plan to introduce multithreading into your engine.

NOTE

The dotted box at the top of the diagram represents a template parameter.

NOTE

Handler classes have one special characteristic you must be aware of—handler classes are *lightweight* classes, meaning that every connection has its own instances of its handler classes. Because the handler classes are also *Polymorphic* (which means they inherit from a common base class), each handler can behave differently. Using polymorphic inheritance, however, requires the use of pointers, which is why the stack holds pointers to handlers, instead of actual handler objects. This introduces yet another problem: Using individualized lightweight classes means that every connection needs a handler created by new. (Since handler classes are polymorphic, you need to use pointers.) This effectively makes the Connection class *own* all of its handlers. New handlers are passed into it, but from that point on, the Connection manages the handler, and deletes it when it is no longer needed. This is essential to avoid memory leaks.

The Stack of Handlers

The next variable is the m_handlerstack, which holds protocol::handler pointers. In a traditional network application, it is common to see connections maintaining a current *state*. For example, a connection could be "logging in" or "playing the game." These specific states are represented by individual protocol::handler objects. You'll have a handler class for connections that are logging in, a handler class for connections that are in the game, and a handler class for any other state you can think of. I show you a great deal about handlers in Chapter 6.

So why not just have a single handler pointer to represent the current handler? Well, there may be times when you're going to want *recursive* states. Say the user is in state 1 and then switches to state 2. When the user in state 2 is finished, you might want the connection to go back to the previous state. This is why I'm using a stack. When state 1 is on the top of the stack, you're in state 1, but when you switch to state 2, the new handler is pushed onto the top of the stack. Later on, when you exit the state, it is popped off the stack, and state 1 is back at the top. Basically, this system gives you flexibility. Figure 5.5 shows this process.

A Sending Buffer

The next variable is m_sendbuffer, which is an std::string. This buffer is used to store data that you want to send, until it can actually be sent. Why a string? Well, strings are good at storing plain bytes. You can easily make your job easier by adding large chunks of bytes to the end of strings, and the strings can also be turned into plain char* arrays by calling their data() function. Whenever you buffer data into a connection, it is put into this string, and then sent out later (when a connection manager deems it appropriate).

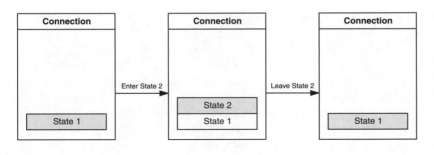

Figure 5.5

With the handler stack process, you can add new states on top of earlier states and go back to the earlier states later on, without the new states knowing which state to return to.

Rates and Times

The m_datarate variable keeps track of how many bytes-per-second the socket is receiving during the current "time chunk." (I'll explain this in a bit.) Likewise, m_lastdatarate stores the amount of data that was received during the previous time chunk. I calculate these values in chunks of time because computers are *discrete* machines; there's really no way to get an exact instantaneous value of data-per-time; instead, the best that can be done is to count the number of bytes received over a certain period. That's what these variables store.

Other related variables are m_lastReceiveTime and m_lastSendTime. As you can probably guess, these related variables store the last time data was received and sent. The m_checksendtime Boolean is used to check client deadlock. This is an issue I will discuss a little later on.

> **NOTE**
> These time variables are stored as second values, not millisecond values.

The m_creationtime variable holds the system time (in seconds) at which the connection was created, so you can tell how long the connection has been open.

Other Data

BUFFERSIZE is a const integer that determines how large a Connections receive buffer is, and then m_buffer is the actual buffer. I've hard-coded BUFFERSIZE at 1024 bytes, and I can't see much use in making it configurable, but you can change it if you want.

The last variable is a Boolean named m_closed that determines if the connection has been "closed." You'll see this in action later on when dealing with connection managers. The idea is that within the execution of a game, you may decide to close a connection, but you won't be able to inform the connection manager; instead, you will end up setting this Boolean to true, and the connection manager will go through every connection at a later point in time, to check if something wants the connection closed. At this point, the connection manager forcibly closes the connection and deletes it.

This is done because there are lots of problems with being able to close a socket immediately in many different parts of the code. For example, you may be in the middle of a loop going through all of the connections, and you receive data that makes the game want to close the connection (maybe a "quit" command). If you allow the game to shut down the connection immediately, the connection manager is going to run into problems later when it comes back to the iteration.

New Functions

There are a bunch of new functions in the class—functions that will help you buffer sends, get statistics, and receive data.

The Constructors

There are two constructors. The plain constructor simply constructs the connection and clears all the data members in it; the other constructor takes a reference to a DataSocket.

DataSockets and ListeningSockets don't do anything in their destructors, so you're free to pass them around between functions. It would be a real nightmare if you had sockets automatically close when they were destroyed. Why? Examine the following code:

```
void Function( DataSocket p_sock ) {
    // blah
}
// later on:
DataSocket s;
// connect the socket here somewhere
Function( s );
```

If sockets auto-close on destruction, what's wrong with that code? When you passed the socket into the function by-value into p_sock, you copied the socket, but when the function ended, it *automatically* destructed that socket object, which will tell the operating system to close whatever socket it is pointing to. So the next time you try using s, it won't be open. Believe me—you'll spend hours tracking down these kinds of bugs.

So, that's why I made sockets able to freely copy themselves. This becomes important when you look at the constructor of the connection class: It can take a data socket as a parameter and copy all the DataSocket information into itself. Then whoever created the original data socket can safely discard it and use the Connection. You'll see me do this later on, when I show you the ConnectionManager class. Here's the code for the two constructors:

> **TIP**
>
> If you're feeling really ambitious, you may want to consider *reference-counted* sockets. These are sockets that keep track of how many times they are referenced in your program, and whenever they drop down to a count of 0, they automatically close themselves.

```
template< class protocol >
Connection<protocol>::Connection() {
    Initialize();
```

```
}
template< class protocol >
Connection<protocol>::Connection( DataSocket& p_socket )
    : DataSocket( p_socket ) {
    Initialize();
}
```

The first constructor just calls the `Initialize()` function; the second takes a `DataSocket` as a parameter and then uses the standard base-class constructor notation to construct the `DataSocket` portion of the `Connection`. (See Appendix C on the CD for more information on base-class constructors.)

Both functions call `Initialize`:

```
template< class protocol > void Connection<protocol>::Initialize() {
    m_datarate = 0;
    m_lastdatarate = 0;
    m_lastReceiveTime = 0;
    m_lastSendTime = 0;
    m_checksendtime = false;
    m_creationtime = BasicLib::GetTimeMS();
    m_closed = false;
}
```

As you can see, the code just resets all members to their default values.

Receiving Data

The connection class has its own overloaded `Receive` function. The class has its own receive buffer and also keeps track of the incoming datarate, so this function doesn't take parameters or return anything.

Instead, the `Receive` function attempts to receive data into its buffer; then it shoots that buffer off to the protocol policy. Here's the function (split up into logical blocks):

```
template<class protocol>
void Connection<protocol>::Receive() {
    int bytes = DataSocket::Receive( m_buffer, BUFFERSIZE );
```

The function first tries to receive as much data as it can. The `DataSocket::Receive` function either blocks, or throws an exception if it's in nonblocking mode and there is no data to receive. (This latter method assumes you've used a `select`-based method to poll the socket.)

```
    BasicLib::sint64 t = BasicLib::GetTimeS();
    if( (m_lastReceiveTime / TIMECHUNK) != (t / TIMECHUNK) ) {
        m_lastdatarate = m_datarate / TIMECHUNK;
        m_datarate = 0;
        m_lastReceiveTime = t;
    }
```

The previous code fragment gets the current system time (in seconds), and then makes a few calculations on it. Let me explain this segment. Data is sent in discrete chunks and is rarely continuous. For example, one second you might get data in a huge burst, and then the next second, you might get nothing. For MUDs, this could be a problem. For example, the particular client a person is using may store a large command and then send it all at once. The server will see this burst of activity, think that it's being flooded during that one second, and disconnect the user. Meanwhile, the user was just typing one command and was probably going to take a few seconds to type the next command.

Disconnecting your users like that is bound to annoy them to no end, so you need a better system. Instead of keeping track of bytes per second, the class keeps track of bytes per 16 seconds. Why 16? I like to use 16 seconds because it's a nice power-of-two that is close to 1/4 of a minute. Since it's a power-of-two, the compiler will almost certainly optimize the division so that it doesn't take much time. If you feel that 16 is inappropriate, you can change the value of the TIMECHUNK variable at the top of the file to whatever you wish.

Whenever the function has detected that a new 16-second block has begun, it records the datarate for the previous 16 seconds and resets the datarate to 0.

Here's the next part of the function:

```
    m_datarate += bytes;
    m_protocol.Translate( *this, m_buffer, bytes );
}
```

The number of bytes received is added to the datarate, and the buffer is sent to the protocol to be translated.

Sending Functions

On many systems, it is *expensive* in terms of processing power to repeatedly call socket functions such as send and recv. For a typical MUD game loop, you'll end up sending multiple lines of text to a single connection during one loop, but you don't actually want to make a call to the send function every time you send a line, right? So, the smart method is to buffer all the data you want to send, and then, at the end of the game loop, make just one call to send, trying to send the entire buffer. In practice, this usually works well.

```
template<class protocol>
void Connection<protocol>::BufferData( const char* p_buffer, int p_size ) {
    m_sendbuffer.append( p_buffer, p_size );
}
```

The function takes a char* buffer and its size; then it appends the buffer to the end of the m_sendbuffer string, using the append function.

Now, when you want to send it all, you do this:

```
template<class protocol>
void Connection<protocol>::SendBuffer() {
    if( m_sendbuffer.size() > 0 ) {
```

```
int sent = Send( m_sendbuffer.data(), (int)m_sendbuffer.size() );
m_sendbuffer.erase( 0, sent );
```

All right, the first part of the function is no-nonsense. The function tries to send what's in the buffer, counts how many bytes are sent (nonblocking sockets return 0 when nothing is sent), and then erases all those bytes from the front of the buffer.

```
if( sent > 0 ) {
    m_lastSendTime = BasicLib::GetTimeS();
    m_checksendtime = false;
}
```

The previous code fragment checks to see if any data was sent. If so, the time is recorded, and the m_checksendtime Boolean is cleared to false. When this Boolean is false, it is assumed that there are no problems sending data; you'll see how this works in the next segment:

```
    else {
        if( !m_checksendtime ) {
            m_checksendtime = true;
            m_lastSendTime = BasicLib::GetTimeS();
        }
    }   // end no-data-sent check
}   // end buffersize check
}
```

The final code segment occurs when no data was sent. If that happens, you know there is a problem sending data. (Either the client is under deadlock and it's not accepting data, or you're flooding it with too much data.) If the m_checksendtime flag has not been previously set, this is the first time you've noticed a sending problem, so you mark down the current time in m_lastSendTime. Although technically you didn't send anything, it is important to mark down the time you noticed sending problems. If the flag is already set, that means you've noticed there have been sending problems before, so don't update the time.

> **NOTE**
>
> This isn't an entirely accurate method of discovering when a client stops accepting data. For example, if the client hasn't been sent anything in a long time, you'll notice that the client has stopped receiving only when you try sending data to it. Because of this, it is often useful to send a *ping* to clients occasionally, so that if they do end up disconnecting without notifying you, you'll notice within a minute or so.

Closing Functions

Connections are designed to be used in conjunction with a connection manager, which, as the name implies, will manage connections. You'll learn about connections later on, but for now, you should know that whenever you manually close a connection, the connection manager must know about the connection closing, so it knows not to manage that connec-

tion any longer. There are a number of possible solutions to this problem:

1. You could require the programmer to manually tell the connection manager.
2. You could make every connection be aware of its manager, and make the connection tell the manager it has been closed.
3. You could simply store a Boolean, and have the connection manager check that later on.

Method 1 is a bad idea. Whenever you make code that's going to be difficult to use, it will anger people who use it (including yourself!), and generally make the project much more difficult to work on. Method 2 is also somewhat bad; it introduces *cyclic dependencies* (see Appendix C on the CD for more information about these), and generally uses more memory and management. (That is, you have to tell every connection about its manager in the first place.)

I have chosen method 3, as you may have already noticed when I showed you the data stored within the class. There are three functions concerned with closing:

```
inline void Close()        { m_closed = true; }
inline bool Closed()       { return m_closed; }

inline void CloseSocket()  {
    DataSocket::Close();
    if( Handler() )  Handler()->Leave();
    while( Handler() ) {
        delete Handler();
        m_handlerstack.pop();
    }
}
```

The Close function simply sets the m_closed Boolean to true, so that when the connection manager checks the Boolean later using Closed, it can then really close the socket, using the CloseSocket function.

Whenever the program physically shuts down a connection using CloseSocket, it calls the underlying DataSocket::Close function to close the socket. After the socket is closed, the function checks to see if the connection is active inside a state; if so, then the handler's Leave function is called, to notify the current state that this connection has left it.

Once that has been done, the function goes through every state in the stack and deletes them (without re-entering them).

Handler Functions

There are five functions in the class concerning protocol handlers, which make working with them somewhat easier than manipulating the handler stack directly. Here are the functions:

```
void AddHandler( typename protocol::handler* p_handler );
void RemoveHandler();
typename protocol::handler* Handler();
```

```
void SwitchHandler( typename protocol::handler* p_handler );
void ClearHandlers();
```

The code for those functions is really quite simple, so I won't bother to go over it here. For example, adding a handler involves pushing a new handler on top of the handler stack, and then calling its Enter function. The RemoveHandler does the opposite; it calls its Leave function and pops it from the stack.

Switching handlers involves these actions: leaving and popping the current handler, and then pushing and entering the new handler (completely bypassing any handler that may have been below the first one). Clearing handlers involves leaving the top handler and deleting all of them.

The first function pushes a new handler onto the top of the handler stack. This is important: Whenever you pass a handler at the top, you *must* pass in one that has just been created using new. For example, if you have a handler named logon, you'd pass it in to a connection like this:

```
conn->AddHandler( new logon( *conn ) );
```

It is also important never to delete that handler; the RemoveHandler function takes care of that for you. So whenever you pass in a new handler to the connection, it's pushed on top of the handler stack, and then the handler's NewConnection function is called, telling it that the connection has entered that state.

The RemoveHandler function deletes the handler at the top of the stack, since it's no longer needed, and then the pointer to that handler (which is no longer needed) is popped off the stack.

Finally, the Handler function is a simple way of retrieving a pointer to the handler on top of the stack.

Other Functions

All the rest of the functions are pretty simple; most are just accessor functions that return a value. One is more interesting than the rest: GetLastSendTime().

```
template< class protocol >
BasicLib::sint64 Connection<protocol>::GetLastSendTime() const {
    if( m_checksendtime ) {
        return BasicLib::GetTimeS() - m_lastSendTime;
    }
    return 0;
}
```

When the m_checksendtime flag isn't set, the function always returns 0. This function is meant to return the amount of time that has passed since a connection has noticed sending problems, so it returns 0 if there aren't problems. Otherwise, if there *are* problems, the function returns the difference between the current time and the time when the connec-

Table 5.1   Accessor Functions for Connection's

Function	Purpose
GetLastReceiveTime	Is the system time (in seconds) at which data was last received on the socket
GetCreationTime	Is the system time at which the connection was created
GetDataRate	Is the number of bytes per second received by the connection over the previous time chunk
GetCurrentDataRate	Is the number of bytes per second received by the connection during the current time chunk
GetBufferedBytes	Returns the number of bytes of data currently buffered on the connection
Protocol	Returns a reference to the connection's protocol object

tion noticed sending problems.

Table 5.1 lists the other functions.

All these functions are just simple accessors with nothing substantial in the code, so there is no need to show you the source for them.

Listening Manager

For the Socket Library, I've developed two manager classes—classes that will manage sockets and connections for you. The first of these is the ListeningManager class. As the name suggests, this manager takes care of listening sockets.

Altogether, the ListeningManager is really a simple manager. It allows you to add ports, listen on the listening sockets, and set a ConnectionManager. Whenever a ListeningManager detects a new connection, it sends the connection off to its current connection manager. Figure 5.6 shows the class diagram for the ListeningManager class.

The first thing you should take note of is the fact that this class has two template parameters: protocol and defaulthandler. Obviously, the protocol is the protocol policy class that

> **NOTE**
>
> Some ISPs block outgoing connections on certain ports, so you may find that users might not be able to connect to your server because of their ISP. In this situation, it's very useful to be able to listen on more than one port.

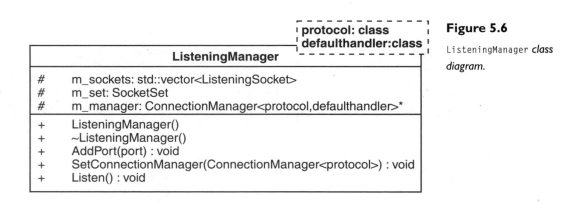

Figure 5.6

`ListeningManager` *class diagram.*

connections in this manager will use (like Telnet, which I cover in Chapter 6). The second template parameter is the default handler of a connection. Whenever a new connection is created, it obviously must be given a default handler, right? So that's what this template parameter represents.

You can see that the `ListeningManager` maintains a vector of listening sockets; this means that the `ListeningManager` class maintains multiple listening sockets. This is a neat feature if you want your programs to listen on more than one port for the same purpose, which can be helpful in certain situations.

Constructor and Destructor

The constructor for this class is simple; it just clears the connection manager pointer to 0, meaning that it hasn't been given a connection manager yet:

```
template<typename protocol, typename defaulthandler>
ListeningManager<protocol, defaulthandler>::ListeningManager() {
    m_manager = 0;
}
```

And the destructor:

```
template<typename protocol, typename defaulthandler>
ListeningManager<protocol, defaulthandler>::~ListeningManager() {
    for( size_t i = 0; i < m_sockets.size(); i++ ) {
        m_sockets[i].Close();
    }
}
```

This goes through every listening socket and closes them, so that whenever a listening manager is destructed, all of the sockets are automatically closed.

Adding New Sockets

Here's the function to add new listening sockets:

```
template<typename protocol, typename defaulthandler>
void ListeningManager<protocol, defaulthandler>::AddPort( port p_port ) {
    if( m_sockets.size() == MAX ) {
        Exception e( ESocketLimitReached );
        throw( e );
    }
    ListeningSocket lsock;
    lsock.Listen( p_port );
    lsock.SetBlocking( false );
    m_sockets.push_back( lsock );
    m_set.AddSocket( lsock );
}
```

You may have noticed from the class diagram in Figure 5.5 that the class contains a SocketSet. It uses the set to poll all the sockets it contains, to see if there are any new connections. Therefore, the number of listening sockets you're allowed to have is limited to the number of sockets a SocketSet can contain. If there isn't enough room, the function throws

Nonblocking Listening Sockets

Unless you dedicate an entire thread to each socket, it is important that you make listening sockets nonblocking. There is a certain exploit when listening sockets are used in conjunction with the select() system call. Imagine a client that sends a connection request and then quickly shuts down. The select() call will detect that there's a connection, but by the time you call accept(), there's no more connection available, and your thread starts blocking. If this thread is responsible for more than just listening for new connections, your program is going to stop until another person actually connects to it. This is bad. Therefore, you should usually try to make listening sockets nonblocking.

an exception of type ESocketLimitReached.

Then, the function creates a listening socket, tells it to start listening, sets it to nonblocking mode, adds the socket to the socket vector, and finally adds the socket to the socket set as well.

Listening for New Connections

For now, the model of the ListeningManager is pretty simple. Once you've got all the ports added that you want to listen to, you must manually call the Listen() function whenever you want to listen for new connections.

Here's the function:

```
template<typename protocol, typename defaulthandler >
void ListeningManager<protocol, defaulthandler>::Listen() {
    DataSocket datasock;
    if( m_set.Poll() > 0 ) {      // check if there are active sockets
        for( size_t s = 0; s < m_sockets.size(); s++ ) {
            if( m_set.HasActivity( m_sockets[s] ) ) {
                try {              // accept socket and tell the connection manager
                    datasock = m_sockets[s].Accept();
                    m_manager->NewConnection( datasock );
                }
                catch( Exception& e ) {
                    if( e.ErrorCode() != EOperationWouldBlock ) {
                        throw; // rethrow on any exception but a blocking one
                    }
                }
            }   // end activity check
        }   // end socket loop
    }   // end check for number of active sockets
}
```

The function first polls the socket set, to see if any of the listening sockets have action. If they do, a for-loop goes through every listening socket and checks to see if it has activity.

The try-block tries to accept a data socket from any listening sockets that have activity, and then sends the socket to the m_manager, which is the ConnectionManager class I mentioned before. The catch-block after that catches any socket exceptions, and checks to see if they are EOperationWouldBlock errors. The existence of a would-block error means that someone may be trying to exploit your server, but you detected it. So, that error is just ignored. Any other kind of error, which will almost definitely be a fatal network system error, is rethrown.

NOTE

Using the threading knowledge you learned from Chapter 3, "Introduction to Multithreading," you should know enough about threading now to be able to create a threaded system, in which you have three threads. The first thread would simply listen for any connections, and then pass them off to your connection manager. Your connection manager would be running in a thread of its own as well, and would ship data off to the final thread—the game thread. I have not implemented this kind of system in this book due to space constraints, but I may in the future. Check my website for updates: http://ronpenton.net/MUDBook.

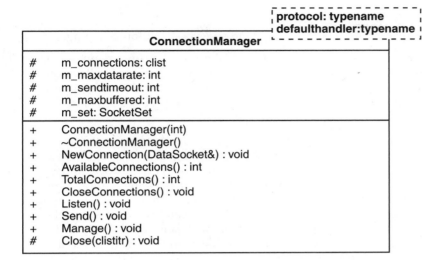

Figure 5.7

Class diagram for the `ConnectionManager` *class.*

Connection Manager

The `ConnectionManager` class is the most complex class within the SocketLib. This class manages connections of a certain type. Like the `ListeningManager` class, `ConnectionManager` is also templated with a protocol and a default handler. Figure 5.7 shows the class diagram.

Variables

The first variable is a `std::list` that stores connections. The most common complaint about templates I hear is that they are ugly. The people who say that are absolutely right. Templates *are* ugly. Unfortunately, they are also very handy.

The good news, however, is that typedefs can be good friends and remove a lot of the ugliness when you are dealing with templates. For example, every time you want to refer to this kind of list, you'd need this code:

```
std::list< Connection<protocol> >
```

But with a typedef, you can do something like this instead:

```
typedef std::list< Connection<protocol> > clist;
typedef std::list< Connection<protocol> >::iterator clistitr;
clist m_connections;
```

Believe me—it makes your life so much easier. Imagine that later you want to create an iterator for that kind of list:

```
// without typedef:
std::list< Connection<protocol> >::iterator itr;
// with typedef:
```

```
clistitr itr;
```

Typedefs make your code cleaner and easier to read, and save you from lots of typing.

The class has three integers that represent three different limits of the connection manager. m_maxdatarate is the maximum datarate (in bytes per second) that the manager allows on a socket. As soon as that socket goes over that datarate, it is kicked for flooding. If the socket cannot send data, the m_sendtimeout variable determines how much time (in seconds) before a connection is kicked. This prevents deadlocked clients.

The third variable, m_maxbuffered, protects against attackers. Imagine that you set the send timeout value to 60, so that if data cannot be sent for 60 seconds, the connection is kicked out. The attacker might know this, and so he sets his connection to accept one byte of data per minute from your server, thus keeping it from detecting that he is having sending problems. Now this attacker is in your game, and data is continually sent to him. Data is buffered up, and only one byte of data is removed from the buffer each minute. Since the string class in the connection will theoretically keep expanding to fit all the data it's buffering, you'll eventually run out of memory. Therefore, it is logical to impose a limit on the amount of data that can be buffered. So, once the buffer reaches the given size, you can assume that there are major problems with the connection, and the connection manager will close it. As with the listening manager, this class has its own SocketSet, named m_set.

Functions

The connection manager has quite a few functions, and not many of them are accessors, so I will be showing you most of the code for the class.

Constructor and Destructor

The constructor for the connection manager has three optional parameters. More than likely, you're not going to use the default values of the parameters, as they are only guidelines. The three parameters are:

- Maximum data reception rate, which defaults to 1024 bytes per second
- Send timeout period, which defaults to 60 seconds
- Maximum buffer size per connection, which defaults to 8192 bytes

The maximum data reception rate determines how many bytes per second you can receive before the connection handler kicks a connection for flooding. The send time period determines how long the connection manager waits for a connection to respond after it first notices a sending problem. The maximum buffer size per connection determines how much data can be buffered to send before it assumes there's a sending problem and terminates the connection.

```
template<typename protocol, typename defaulthandler>
ConnectionManager<protocol, defaulthandler>::
ConnectionManager( int p_maxdatarate, int p_sentimeout, int p_maxbuffered ) {
    m_maxdatarate = p_maxdatarate;
    m_sendtimeout = p_sentimeout;
```

```
    m_maxbuffered = p_maxbuffered;
}
```

As for the destructor, it simply closes every connection:

```
template<typename protocol, typename defaulthandler>
ConnectionManager<protocol, defaulthandler>::~ConnectionManager() {
    clistitr itr;
    for( itr = m_connections.begin(); itr != m_connections.end(); ++itr )
        itr->CloseSocket();
}
```

Because the connections do not throw exceptions when they are closed, you don't need to catch any if something goes wrong.

Adding New Connections

The NewConnection() function adds new connections to the manager. The function takes a reference to a DataSocket as its parameter and then turns that into a Connection. Here's the code listing:

```
template<typename protocol, typename defaulthandler>
void ConnectionManager<protocol, defaulthandler>::
NewConnection( DataSocket& p_socket ) {
    Connection<protocol> conn( p_socket );   // create new connection
    if( AvailableConnections() == 0 ) {
        defaulthandler::NoRoom( conn );       // ack! no room!
        conn.CloseSocket();                   // just close it then
    }
    else {
        m_connections.push_back( conn );      // add the connection
        Connection<Telnet>& c = *m_connections.rbegin();
        c.SetBlocking( false );               // nonblocking
        m_set.AddSocket( c );                 // add to set
        c.AddHandler( new defaulthandler( c ) );
    }
}
```

The function first creates a Connection out of the socket (conn). Then it checks to see if there is any more room for the connection within the manager.

Remember when I first showed you the concept of the protocol::handler classes? I said that some of them must have a static NoRoom function. Whatever class you decide to use as a default handler for a connection manager, it *must* have this function. Because the connection manager is essentially clueless about what protocol it's actually using, it doesn't know how to tell a connecting client that there is no more room for it. You *could* leave the job to the protocol class, but that's not really customizable. A protocol implementation is supposed to be general, not specific to the server you're going to be running, so it's not wise to give that responsibility to it. If you delegate the responsibility to the default protocol::handler, however, you gain flexibility and you can customize messages sent back to the client about how full the server is, or whatever else you might want to do. You'll see this implemented in Chapter 6, when I show you how to implement a Telnet handler. So, once the "no room" message has been sent, you need to close the socket; it's assumed that anyone sending sockets to this class is in "fire and forget" mode, which means that they shoot sockets off to the handler and then assume that the manager takes complete control of that socket.

On the other hand, if there is room for the connection, you need to do a little more work. First, the connection is added to the back of the list via the push_back function, and then a reference to the connection inside the list is created, named c. Remember, STL containers use *copy-by-value*, so conn is not the same connection as what is actually stored in the list; it's now a different connection. After that, it puts the socket into nonblocking mode, adds the connection into the connection managers' SocketSet, and finally adds a new defaulthandler to the connection's handler stack.

The connection is placed into nonblocking mode due to the buffering system; you don't want your connections blocking when you are trying to send data that might not get sent.

Closing Connections

There are two functions associated with closing connections: Close() and CloseConnections(). The first function is used to immediately close a connection, and the second is used to go through all of the connections to check if they need to be closed. Here's the first function:

```
template<typename protocol, typename defaulthandler>
void ConnectionManager<protocol, defaulthandler>::
Close( clistitr p_itr ) {
    m_set.RemoveSocket( *p_itr );
    p_itr->CloseSocket();
    m_connections.erase( p_itr );
}
```

The connection is removed from the socket set so that it is no longer polled for activity (because it will be closed in a moment!); then it's physically closed, and finally erased from the list of connections. Note that this function requires an iterator into the connection list, and because there's no way to get an iterator outside of the manager class, this function can only be called internally.

Here's the other function:

```
template<typename protocol, typename defaulthandler>
void ConnectionManager<protocol, defaulthandler>::
CloseConnections() {
    clistitr itr = m_connections.begin();
    clistitr c;
    while( itr != m_connections.end() ) {
        c = itr++;
        if( c->Closed() )  Close( c );
```

```
  }
}
```

This essentially loops through every connection that it is managing and checks to see if the connection should be closed. If so, then the function calls the Close helper function that I showed you previously.

You should notice that the function uses two iterators: itr, and c. At the beginning of the loop, c is set to the position pointed at by itr, and then itr is incremented to the next position. If you close a connection, the position pointed to by c disappears, and that iterator

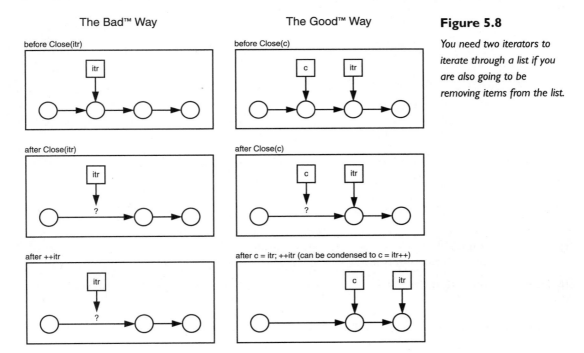

The Bad™ Way   The Good™ Way

Figure 5.8

You need two iterators to iterate through a list if you are also going to be removing items from the list.

is completely invalid. You can't increment it or do anything else; your only viable option is to discard it. Luckily, because you have already saved the next position into itr, you can simply assign itr to c, and then move itr to the next position.

This process is shown in Figure 5.8. The method using only one iterator is on the left, and the method using two iterators is on the right.

Listening for Data

The Listen() function is quite long and complex, so I'm going to break it up into sections and explain them piece by piece. Here's the function:

```
template<typename protocol, typename defaulthandler>
void ConnectionManager<protocol, defaulthandler>::Listen() {
    int socks = 0;
    if( TotalConnections() > 0 ) {
        socks = m_set.Poll();
    }
```

The previous segment checks to see if there are any connections in the manager, and if so, polls them. There's really no sense in polling an empty socket set, especially considering that you know it will eventually call select(), which is a system call, and will probably have more overhead than a simple if-statement at this level.

```
    if( socks > 0 ) {
        clistitr itr = m_connections.begin();
        clistitr c;
        while( itr != m_connections.end() ) {
            c = itr++;          // set itr to the next, and use c as current
            if( m_set.HasActivity( *c ) ) {    // check activity
                try {
                    c->Receive();              // try to receive data
                    if( c->GetDataRate() > m_maxdatarate ) {
                        c->Handler()->Flooded();   // connection flooded
                        Close( c );                // close em!
                    }
                }
```

The previous code segment is executed whenever sockets have activity. It loops through every connection within the manager using two iterators—itr and c—just as you saw before with the CloseConnections function.

If the m_set reports that connections have activity, it tries to receive data from the connection. If it receives the data, it then checks to see if the datarate of the connection exceeds the m_maxdatarate variable. If it does, the connections' handler is notified that it was flooding, and then the connection is forcibly closed.

```
                catch( ... ) {
                    c->Close();              // tell connection it's closed
                    c->Handler()->Hungup();// tell handler it hung up
                    Close( c );              // actually close connection
                }
            }   // end activity check
        }   // end socket loop
    }   // end check for number of sockets returned by the poll
}
```

The catch-block catches exceptions that occurred when data was being received; it is assumed that if there was an exception, it was a fatal error. Even a would-block error is fatal in this case; it would be a signal that something was seriously messed up with the connection, since the socket set said there was something to receive on it. Therefore, the connection is told that it has been closed, the connection's current handler is notified that the connection hung up, and it is closed.

Sending Data

Because of the buffering system that all connections employ, to minimize the system calls, it is most efficient to buffer all the data you want to send and then send it all at once at a later time. The Send function does this by going through every connection and attempting to send the contents of each sending buffer. Here it is:

```
template<typename protocol, typename defaulthandler>
void ConnectionManager<protocol, defaulthandler>::Send() {
    clistitr itr = m_connections.begin();
    clistitr c;
    while( itr != m_connections.end() ) {
        c = itr++;      // move itr forward, keep c as current
        try {
            c->SendBuffer();    // try sending
            if( c->GetBufferedBytes() > m_maxbuffered ||   // too much data
                c->GetLastSendTime() > m_sendtimeout ) {   // or send timeout
                c->Close();                 // tell connection it has closed
                c->Handler()->Hungup();     // tell handler it hung up
                Close( c );                 // close connection
            }
        }
        catch( ... ) {          // catch all exceptions and hang up on them
            c->Close();
            c->Handler()->Hungup();
            Close( c );
        }
    }   // end while-loop
}
```

Inside the try-block, the buffer for every connection is sent. Assuming the transmission succeeds, the next if-statement checks to see if there were any sending problems. It checks the buffer size and the amount of time that has passed since the connection started having sending problems (if any at all; see the Connection class from earlier in this chapter). If either problem exists, the connection's handler is told that the connection hung up, and then it is closed.

If an exception was thrown when sending the buffer, it is caught in the catch-block. In this case, any exception thrown will be a fatal error, so the connection's handler is told that it has hung up, and the connection is closed.

Summary

This was a large chapter, and you may find it lacking because it didn't include a code demo. For that, I apologize, but the Socket Library is unusable until you have a working protocol and its associated handler class(es) written as well. Don't despair. The next chapter is going to make up for the lack of a demonstration in this chapter by containing a large demo.

In this chapter, you learned how to abstract the base Sockets API into an easy-to-use collection of classes, as well as how to expand the library into a nice collection of classes used to manage sockets and connections.

I hope you can see the usefulness of having the modular protocol class I've shown you; it's really amazing to see how flexible this sort of design can be. And without further ado, here's the chapter on Telnet!

CHAPTER 6

Telnet Protocol and a Simple Chat Server

In the previous chapter, I showed you the base `SocketLib` library and the protocol policy system I've set up. Unfortunately, I couldn't actually show you any demonstrations, since the library needs a complete protocol policy to work and I haven't shown you any protocols yet!

So, in this chapter, I'm going to introduce you to the Telnet protocol, which is bar-none the most common protocol used for text MUDs. The great thing about the protocol is that it is so simple, and almost every operating system has built-in Telnet clients. Because of this, there's no need to dig too far into learning how to create clients. This is good, because it gives me more room to go over the real meat of MUDs—the servers.

In this chapter, you will learn to:

- Understand the basics of the Telnet protocol
- Work with the standard VT100 control codes
- Create a Telnet protocol policy class
- Create Telnet handlers
- Create a simple chat server using Telnet
- Use demos that illustrate the concepts of the chapter

Telnet

Way back in the bad old days before the Internet even existed, all computer-human interaction was done on something called a *terminal*. Essentially, a terminal is just a screen that prints characters as a display and is connected to a keyboard on which the user types the characters. Terminals are usually connected to a mainframe or a server via a phone line or some other means.

When the Internet came along, it was possible to connect computers over TCP/IP, but there was no standard way of emulating the relationship between a terminal and a server. Then along came Telnet. The latest Telnet protocol is defined in RFC 854, and it's not likely to change.

Essentially, the Telnet protocol says that a stream of 7-bit characters is going to be transmitted in *duplex mode* (both ways); this stream of characters can contain occasional *control codes* that define the behavior of the terminal device.

You won't be concerned with the majority of the control codes available, so I won't explain them in depth.

Simple Telnet Example

I want to show you a simple example of a Telnet server. This server simply accepts characters that are sent to it, buffers them, and then prints them back out to the terminal when an end of line is reached. In Telnet, the end of a line is always signaled with a carriage-return, line-feed combination, also known as CRLF. A CRLF in C++ is represented by the escape codes "\r\n".

At this point, I want to begin Demo 6.1, which can be found on the CD in the \Demos\Chapter06\Demo06-01\ directory. It uses the SocketLib, and you can find compilation instructions for the demo in Appendix A, which is on the CD.

> **NOTE**
> If you're running either VC6 or VC7, you can just open up the project files and click Compile, assuming you've set up your compiler as specified in Appendix A, "Setting Up Your Compilers," which is on the CD. In Linux, all you need to do is type "make" and the demo compiles.

Demo 6.1—Very Simple Telnet Server

```cpp
#include "SocketLib/SocketLib.h"
using namespace SocketLib;
int main() {
    ListeningSocket lsock;
    DataSocket dsock;
    char buffer[128];
    int size = 0;
    int received;
    lsock.Listen( 5098 );      // listen on port 5098
    dsock = lsock.Accept();    // wait for a connection
```

The previous code sets up two sockets (one listening, one data), a buffer, and two integers. The listening socket is told to listen on port 5098. Then the listening socket is told to wait for a data connection using the Accept function.

```cpp
    dsock.Send( "Hello!\r\n", 8 );   // send "Hello!" to client when connected
    while( true ) {                   // run for eternity
        received = dsock.Receive( buffer + size, 128 - size );
        size += received;
        if( buffer[size - 1] == '\n' ) {    // when you get an "\n",
            std::cout << size << std::endl; // print size of string
            dsock.Send( buffer, size );     // send it back to client
            size = 0;                       // reset the size
        }
    }
    return 0;
}
```

The last code segment first sends a welcome message—"Hello!"—and then it loops infinitely, trying to receive data from the data socket. Whenever data is received, the size is updated, and the last character is checked to see if it is '\n', a linefeed character. If so, the buffer is sent out, and the size is reset. That's it.

> **NOTE**
>
> The default Telnet port is 23, but Linux does not allow you to open ports below 1024 unless you are root. Because of this, I've chosen to run on an arbitrary port.

Here are a few caveats about the program. If you reach 128 characters without pressing Enter, the server crashes, since it's trying to receive 0 bytes (128 - 128 = 0), and that's not allowed by the Socket Library. (Think about it; why would you try to receieve 0 bytes?) The server *must* receive at least 1 byte. So don't type more than 128 characters. This process is illustrated in Figure 6.1.

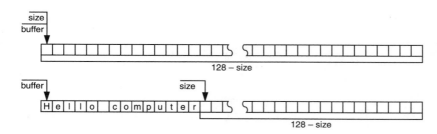

Figure 6.1

One string of text, "Hello computer" being received from a client. At the start, a full buffer of 128 bytes can be received, but after receiving "Hello computer", the size becomes 14, and only 114 more bytes can be received before the buffer is full.

Also, when the client is closed, the server automatically terminates, because an exception is thrown whenever the server tries to receive data from the socket after it has been closed. This program does not catch it, and allows the exception to propogate upward until the program terminates. This is a little messy, but you get the idea. Eventually, you'll see more robust programs, instead of this little hack.

Running Demo 6.1

After you've compiled the program, you can run it on the operating system you compiled it for. Once the server is running, you can connect to it using your favorite Telnet program. Windows and Linux have Telnet programs built in, so you can open a Telnet program simply by typing "Telnet localhost 5098" on a command line, or by replacing 'localhost' with the address of the machine you're running it on, if it's not the same machine. There are other popular Telnet clients out there as well; the most popular is probably PuTTY. (TTY is an acronym that typically stands for *TeleTYpewriter*.) You can find the newest version at http://www.chiark.greenend.org.uk/~sgtatham/putty/, but I've also included a version on the CD in the directory /goodies/ Clients/PuTTY/. (It even comes with source code, if you're devious enough to want to see it.)

Once you're connected, you can type various strings of text. Try typing "testing". The string "testing" is printed out while you're typing it. (Systems may vary.) Then you can press Enter, and "testing" should appear on the next line as well. If you look at the console window on which the server is running, it should have printed out the number "9", which means that it received 9 characters: the 7 characters in "testing", and the CRLF 2-character combination representing the end of the line.

Processing Codes

The Telnet standard uses 7-bit ASCII as its method of data transmission. 7-bit ASCII actually takes up 8 bits of space; it defines the first 128 values in each byte and leaves the last bit undefined. There is an 8-bit ASCII format as well, which puts the total number of defined characters at 256. But Telnet doesn't officially support them, and there's no guarantee that any Telnet clients or servers will be able to support characters with codes larger than 127.

If you look at the values of the first 32 ASCII characters, you can see that they are not actual characters, but are control codes. Here are the most common ones:

> 10 means "newline"
>
> 13 means "carriage-return"
>
> 8 means "backspace"
>
> 9 means "tab"
>
> 7 means "bell"

Most of the other codes are no longer used, so they aren't that important.

> **NOTE**
>
> PuTTY is a really great Telnet program that wonderfully supports all Telnet options (I will explain these to you a little bit later), unlike certain other Telnet programs out there. However, because the servers in this book won't support Telnet options, you can simply set PuTTY to "raw" mode. It will still interpret VT100 codes, but it won't process or send Telnet option packets.

> **NOTE**
>
> Way back in the bad-old days, before there were even computer monitors, computer output was displayed on mechanical typewriters. These typewriters understood ASCII codes and used them to format output. For example, the "carriage return" code told the printer head on the typewriter to move all the way back to the left, and the "newline" code would move the paper up one line. The "bell" code would make a little bell on the printer ring. Incidentally, many Telnet programs still support the bell code, and you can use it annoy people.

So, when a Telnet server or client is receiving characters, it needs to actually process the meanings of some of these codes.

Load up Demo 6.1 again. This time, type in "aaabbbccc", and press Enter. The server should say it received 11 characters. Now, type "aaabbbccc", and then press Backspace three times. Then type "ddd" and press Enter. What is printed? It's "aaabbbddd". But, how many characters did the server get and then send out again? It should now say 17, even though 11 characters are printed to the Telnet client (9 letters, 1 CR, 1 LF). The truth is that you sent "aaabbbccc<backspace><backspace><backspace>ddd<CR><LF>" back to the client. The client erased those three c's when it found the backspace codes and replaced them with the d's.

So, both sides on a Telnet connection should expect to receive and process control characters. I'll show you how to do this later on when I create the Telnet protocol class.

Telnet Options

Telnet has a system that enables you to configure a server or client by using specific *options*. A Telnet option can either be on or off on either the client or the server.

For example, there is an option named "echo", and when it is on within the server, the server echoes every character it receives from the client back to the client. If echo is off in the server, it does not immediately send back whatever it receives. On the client side, if echo is on, the client echoes every character it receives to the screen, and so on. Different clients support different default modes, but you'll find that most of them use local-echo by default. If you couldn't see what you were typing in Demo 6.1, you're probably using a client that has disabled local-echo by default.

> **NOTE**
>
> There's a certain built-in Telnet client out there that millions of people have on their operating systems, which shall remain nameless! (Okay, I confess, it's Windows XP's Telnet client.) This client doesn't support echo options properly. You can tell the client to stop echoing, and it gladly obliges, but if you tell it to turn echo back on, it ignores you. I have no idea why it does this, but this is one of the reasons I decided not to bother too much with Telnet options.

Telnet options are represented as 3-byte codes within a stream of text. The first character of an option is always 0xFF, or 255 in decimal. The next character can be one of the four codes listed in Table 6.1.

This seems like a good way to negotiate which options are available, and then customize server output based on what you know the client can handle, but alas, it doesn't quite work out that way.

You see, in a network environment, you don't have control over the client. You can tell the client to do things, but it doesn't have to listen. Even worse, you can tell the client to do things, and it can reply, "Okay, I'm doing it." But in actuality, it may just be ignoring you.

Table 6.1 Telnet Option Operation Types

Value	Name	Meaning
251 (0xFB)	WILL	The sender of the command enabled an option.
252 (0xFC)	DO	The sender of the command wants the receiver to enable an option.
253 (0xFD)	WONT	The sender of the command disables or refuses to enable an option.
254 (0xFE)	DONT	The sender of the command wants the receiver to disable an option.

I've been playing around with several Telnet clients for a while, and I'm sick of options. It's amazing how many clients out there just outright ignore options altogether, and other clients gleefully turn off echoing, but absolutely refuse to turn echoing back on.

It's madness, and you're much better off ignoring options completely. Yeah, it's not proper, but for MUDs, the options really aren't useful anyway. It's useful to know that the options exist, however.

VT100 Terminal Codes

I previously told you about terminals that were used to access servers and mainframes. Most terminals supported the base ASCII codes, but they wanted to add new things to the terminals—things that weren't supported by ASCII. Of course, the emergence of many new terminals at about the same time with no standard for extended features resulted in a huge mess of incompatible terminal types.

Years down the road, the ANSI group decided to settle on the DEC VT100 standard for extended terminal control codes. VT100 is pretty much supported by every Telnet client in existence, so you can assume that Telnet clients support the control codes.

Among other things, the VT100 has codes for color, cursor control, and clearing text from the screen. All VT100 control codes start with the ASCII "escape" character, 0x1B, or 27 in decimal, and after that most of them have the left-square-bracket "[". Table 6.2 lists the most common codes.

Load Demo 6.1 again, and log into the demo by using your favorite Telnet client. This time, I want you to play around with the VT100 codes (by pressing the Esc key), and then the rest of the code. For example, "<ESC>[31m" will make your text turn red, and it will stay red until you reset it or change the color.

Table 6.2   Common VT100 Control Codes

Code	Meaning
<ESC>[0m	Reset all color and text attributes
<ESC>[1m	Bright/bold color
<ESC>[2m	Dim/unbold color
<ESC>[4m	Underline text
<ESC>[5m	Blinking text
<ESC>[7m	Reversed color text (foreground and background colors are swapped)
<ESC>[8m	Hidden text (characters not displayed)
<ESC>[30m	Black foreground color
<ESC>[31m	Red foreground color
<ESC>[32m	Green foreground color
<ESC>[33m	Yellow foreground color
<ESC>[34m	Blue foreground color
<ESC>[35m	Magenta foreground color
<ESC>[36m	Cyan foreground color
<ESC>[37m	White foreground color
<ESC>[40m	Black background color
<ESC>[41m	Red background color
<ESC>[42m	Green background color
<ESC>[43m	Yellow background color
<ESC>[44m	Blue background color
<ESC>[45m	Magenta background color
<ESC>[46m	Cyan background color
<ESC>[47m	White background color
<ESC>[<R>;<C>H	Move the cursor to row <R> and column <C>, or to the "Home" position if both <R> and <C> are omitted*
<ESC>[<C>A	Move the cursor up <C> lines, or one line if <C> is omitted.*
<ESC>[<C>B	Move the cursor down <C> lines, or one line if <C> is omitted.*
<ESC>[<C>C	Move the cursor forward <C> spaces, or just one if <C> is omitted.*
<ESC>[K	Erases everything after the cursor on the current line
<ESC>[1K	Erases everything before the cursor on the current line
<ESC>[2K	Erases the current line
<ESC>[J	Erases every line below the current line
<ESC>[1J	Erases every line above the current line
<ESC>[2J	Erases the entire screen

*The values <R> and <C> are meant to be replaced by actual numbers.

The codes listed in the table are pretty much all you're going to need. There are other codes available, but they aren't as useful for MUDs; they're mostly obscure commands that don't do anything useful.

ConnectionHandler Class

I've created a special generic class for the Socket Library called `ConnectionHandler` (found in SocketLib/ConnectionHandler.h). It defines all the standard handler functions.

```
template<typename protocol, typename command>
class ConnectionHandler {
public:
    typedef Connection<protocol> conn;
    ConnectionHandler( conn& p_conn ) : m_connection( &p_conn ) {}
    virtual void Handle( command p_data ) = 0;
    virtual void Enter() = 0;
    virtual void Leave() = 0;
    virtual void Hungup() = 0;
    virtual void Flooded() = 0;
protected:
    conn* m_connection;
};
```

If you look back at Figure 5.3 in Chapter 5, you understand that the `ConnectionHandler` is essentially an abstract version of the `protocol::handler` class shown in that figure, which defines only the constructor.

The class has two template parameters: the protocol used with the handler, and the class that defines a *command*. For example, for a simple Telnet protocol, you would most likely choose something such as `std::string` to represent a complete Telnet command. Whenever the protocol object for a connection receieves enough data to make a complete command, it packages the data up into a `command` class and sends it off to the `command` class's `Handle` function.

Also note that the class automatically keeps track of a pointer to its connection; it's usually a good idea for each handler to know which connection it is attached to.

If you're not quite sure what the point of this class is, just continue reading; all will become clear in the next section.

Creating a Telnet Protocol Class

At last, I can show you how to implement a class that interprets Telnet input. In this case, you're going to be accepting input from a client and processing it so that you can use it within your game. This class is located in the files \Libraries\SocketLib\Telnet.h and \Libraries\SocketLib\Telnet.cpp.

It may seem like a cool feature to be able to accept command codes from the client, but I usually advise against it. There are many possible *exploits* if you allow that kind of stuff. Whenever I make a Telnet server, I strip out all nonprintable characters from the stream, and process the basic command codes: CR/LF/BS. This usually makes things much easier in the long run.

For example, imagine a new player logging into the game and deciding to be "cool" by using colors in his name, so that it looks like "<ESC>[31mJohnSmith". What a mess!

> **NOTE**
>
> An *exploit* is the common term used to describe a part of a network program that can be used to perform behaviors (usually devious) that it wasn't meant to perform. Some people may call this being *hacked*, even though true geeks don't really use that term.

Whenever your program searches for user "JohnSmith", it won't match the real name, since it's got a huge, ugly command code structure in front.

So the best bet is to strip out all nonprinting characters. It makes your life much easier. Officially, Telnet doesn't support the 8-bit ASCII set, but it does support the 7-bit version. Therefore, you should generally strip out characters above 127 as well. If you know your clients will support the extended ASCII codes, by all means, use them, but it's generally not a good idea.

Data

Remember that Chapter 5 explained that each `Connection` maintains its own protocol object. Since you *cannot* be assured that you will get complete commands in one receive call, you need someplace to buffer the data. The `Connection` class doesn't do this for you; it just sends off the raw data stream to the protocol and assumes the protocol object handles it.

In our case, the `Telnet` protocol object accepts the raw data, strips out bad characters and process command codes, and then stores the results in its own buffer. For now, I've decided to use a static buffer of 1 kilobyte. (I use the same `BUFFERSIZE` constant integer defined in the Connection.h file from Chapter 5.)

```
class Telnet {
public:
    typedef ConnectionHandler<Telnet, string> handler;
protected:
    char m_buffer[BUFFERSIZE];
    int m_buffersize;
};
```

Note the typedef at the beginning of the class. This is essentially saying that the `Telnet` class uses the `ConnectionHandler` class as its base handler class. Remember: the `ConnectionHandler` is abstract and declares functions for you to define later on. Declaring it with the template parameters Telnet and string means that it works on Telnet connections, and sends complete messages in the form of a string. (Telnet is naturally just text commands.)

So, whenever you use Telnet::handler, you're actually referring to the ConnectionHandler<Telnet, string> class, which declares all of the functions for you. Now, whenever you want to implement a real handler for your program, all you need to do is inherit from Telnet::handler, and define the functions.

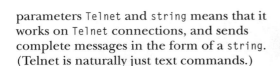

NOTE

If you were defining your own custom protocol, you might decide to create a structure that represents your commands instead of using just a string.

The m_buffer is the array that holds the processed data, and m_buffersize remembers the amount of data in the buffer.

Functions

There are four functions in the Telnet class: the constructor, the Handle function, the SendString function, and the Buffered function.

The first just clears the size of the buffer to zero:

```
inline Telnet() { m_buffersize = 0; }
```

The next function accepts a buffer of raw data and translates the data into its own buffer until a full command can be found:

```
void Translate( Connection<Telnet>& p_conn, char* p_buffer, int p_size ) {
    for( int i = 0; i < p_size; i++ ) {
        char c = p_buffer[i];      // pick out a character
        if( c >= 32 && c != 127 && m_buffersize < BUFFERSIZE ) {
            m_buffer[m_buffersize] = c;  // insert it into buffer if good
            m_buffersize++;              // increase buffer size
        }
```

The previous code segment starts a loop through every character in the raw data buffer. The character is added to the buffer and the buffersize is incremented if the following conditions are met: The character is greater than or equal to 32 (meaning it's a printable character); the character is not 127 (for some reason, 127 is the only oddball character above 32 that isn't printable); and the buffer isn't full.

```
        else if( c == 8 && m_buffersize > 0 ) {
            m_buffersize--;
        }
```

If the character is value 8 (backspace), and the buffer isn't empty, the size of the buffer is decreased by 1, meaning that the last character is erased.

```
        else if( c == '\n' || c == '\r' ) {
            if( m_buffersize > 0 ) {
                p_conn.Handler()->Handle( string( m_buffer, m_buffersize ) );
                m_buffersize = 0;
            }
        }
    }
}
```

And finally, if the character is either a CR or an LF, and the buffer isn't empty, the current handler of the connection is notified about the new command, and the buffer size is reset to 0.

The third function is the SendString function. I have not discussed this function before for a good reason: Not all protocols support sending strings of text to a client, but Telnet does. You should give whatever protocol you're using functions that allow you to send data back to the connection. For example, if you have a protocol that supports three different kinds of responses, you can give your protocol class three different functions—one to send each kind of response. The protocol object would then assemble the raw data and ship it off to the connection. Figure 6.2 shows this system.

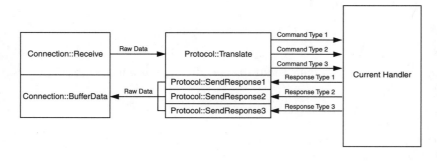

Figure 6.2

This shows the interaction between a connection and a connection handler being mediated by a protocol object. There can be many types of commands inside the program, and it's the protocol object's job to translate to and from raw byte data.

As you'll notice, the protocol stands as a mediator between connections and their handlers. Whenever data is received from a connection, it is sent to the protocol and translated into something that a handler understands.

I've refined the figure and made it apply to only the Telnet protocol class, which you can see in Figure 6.3. This figure is a specialized version of Figure 6.2, applied to the Telnet protocol class. As you can see, the class has only one type of command: string. Connections send raw data to Telnet, which then performs the calculations you saw earlier to extract one full command. Then it shoots that command off to the current handler on the connection. The handler can do whatever it wants; then it shoots a string back to the Telnet class, and then back to the connection.

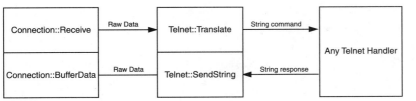

Figure 6.3

The class has only one type of command: string

When you are sending data from a handler to a connection using SendString, you have the option to just buffer raw Telnet data on the connection. I don't find that method to be very good, however.

For example: VT100 only supports 8 colors, or 16 if you count both the bold and dim versions of each color. This is obviously very limited for modern day computing, in which computers can support millions of colors. So, what if, later on, you decide to make your own protocol—one that supports all kinds of new features, such as font control?

Even more ambitious: What if you decide to make your server handle both Telnet and your extended protocol, so that users can log in using regular Telnet clients, or your own custom client if they want to? You certainly don't want every one of your handlers to make a distinction every place you send data to a connection, right?

So, instead, you can make your protocol object able to tell what kind of connection the client is using, and then translate the data.

TIP

It's generally a bad idea to tie your game code in with a specific protocol. For example, if you want to send the string "Hello" in red text over ANSI Telnet, you'd send "\x1B[31mHello". (\x is a control code in C++ that inserts a character into a string using the two hexadecimal numbers following the character. So \x1B means you're inserting ASCII character 0x1B, or 27, the escape character.) Down the road, you might decide to use a different protocol, but you've limited yourself to VT100 codes within your game engine. Now you'll have to search out and change every occurrence of those codes. Believe me—that's a pointless waste of time. Instead, you can have your own control code format that is independent of the protocol. In that case, you can send something such as "<red>Hello!" to the protocol, and the protocol finds the "<red>", strips it out, and puts whatever the current protocol uses in its place. This is an incredibly flexible way of programming.

For now, I don't do any translation, because I'm leaving it for later chapter (Chapter 16, "The Networking System"). So the function just passes the string straight to the connection's buffer:

```
void Telnet::SendString( Connection<Telnet>& p_conn, std::string& p_string ) {
    p_conn.BufferData( p_string.data(), p_string.size() );
}
```

Codes

Also included within the Telnet.h file are static `std::string`s that represent some of the more popular VT100 codes. Here they are:

```
const std::string reset = "\x1B[0m";
const std::string bold = "\x1B[1m";
const std::string dim = "\x1B[2m";
const std::string under = "\x1B[4m";
const std::string reverse = "\x1B[7m";
const std::string hide = "\x1B[8m";
const std::string clearscreen = "\x1B[2J";
const std::string clearline = "\x1B[2K";
const std::string black = "\x1B[30m";
const std::string red = "\x1B[31m";
const std::string green = "\x1B[32m";
const std::string yellow = "\x1B[33m";
const std::string blue = "\x1B[34m";
const std::string magenta = "\x1B[35m";
const std::string cyan = "\x1B[36m";
const std::string white = "\x1B[37m";
const std::string bblack = "\x1B[40m";
const std::string bred = "\x1B[41m";
const std::string bgreen = "\x1B[42m";
const std::string byellow = "\x1B[43m";
const std::string bblue = "\x1B[44m";
const std::string bmagenta = "\x1B[45m";
const std::string bcyan = "\x1B[46m";
const std::string bwhite = "\x1B[47m";
const std::string newline = "\r\n\x1B[0m";
```

The only thing to note is `newline`, which is a combination of a CRLF and a reset command. It's almost always a good idea to reset the colors to normal on every line; you don't want to accidentally leave the color codes the same on each new line.

Demo 6.2—SimpleChat

In an attempt to tie together the concepts of Telnet, protocol policies, and protocol handlers, I'm going to show you how to implement a simple Telnet chat server, known as SimpleChat.

The chat server is going to have two handlers: one to handle logging in, and one to handle chatting.

As well as these two handlers, the chat server is going to need a database structure, which will keep track of every user in the chat server. Figure 6.4 shows these classes.

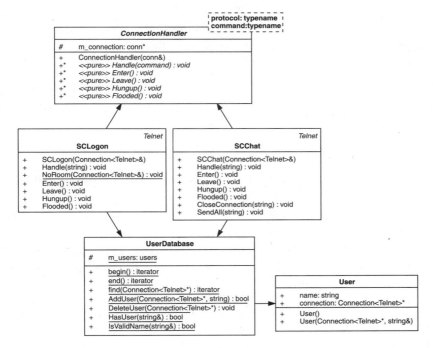

Figure 6.4

Class diagrams for the two handlers and the user database class with functions that are underlined representing static functions.

The SimpleChat is going to need all three classes. The SimpleChat is Demo 6.2, and the directory \Demos\Chapter06\Demo06-02\ on the CD contains the source files needed for the program (SCUserDB.h/.cpp, SCLogon.h/.cpp, SCChat.h/.cpp, and Demo06-02.cpp).

Database

The most important part of the chat is the user database. The database stores simple User objects in a list that represents all the users who are currently connected. The database and User class are located within the files SCUserDB.h and SCUserDB.cpp.

Users

First let's look at the concept of a user. This chat isn't a *persistent world* program, because it doesn't save data on users anywhere. A user can log in with one name and then quit, and any other user can subsequently log in with that same name.

So users are simple objects; in fact, all that needs to be stored is the user's name and a pointer to his connection, as you saw from Figure 6.4. A constructor initializes a user using a connection pointer and a name as well.

Database Data

As you can see in Figure 6.4, the UserDatabase class has one data member: m_users, which is of type users. The users type is really just a typedef for a list of User objects:

```
typedef std::list<User> users;
typedef std::list<User>::iterator iterator;
```

I've also taken the liberty to typedef the list<User>::iterator class as just plain iterator. As I have mentioned many times before, typedefs make programming easier.

Iterator Functions

There are three iterator functions inside the DB class, which are designed to make the DB class act somewhat like a regular STL container. Here are the first two functions:

```
static iterator begin() { return m_users.begin(); }
static iterator end()   { return m_users.end(); }
```

The functions return iterators pointing to the beginning of the database and the end of the database. Just like STL, the end function returns an invalid iterator, one that you can use to test whether you've reached the end of the map.

Here's an example of using the iterator:

```
UserDatabase::iterator itr = UserDatabase::begin();
string name = itr->name;        // get the name of the first user
++itr;                          // move to the next user
bool b = ( itr == UserDatabase::end() )   // if true, iterator is invalid.
```

You can see that the UserDatabase::iterator class acts just like a regular STL unidirectional iterator.

The other iterator function performs a search on the database for a given connection pointer:

```
static iterator find( Connection<Telnet>* p_connection ) {
    iterator itr = m_users.begin();          // start at front
    while( itr != m_users.end() ) {          // loop while valid
        if( itr->connection == p_connection ) // compare pointers
            return itr;                      // match found, return itr
        ++itr;                               // no match, keep looking
    }
    return itr;                              // no match, return itr
}
```

The function essentially loops through the entire database, looking for a connection that matches the pointer that was passed in. If a connection is found, an iterator pointing to that user is returned. By the time the function gets to the second-to-last line of code, the iterator should be equal to m_users.end(), so it is just returned. Remember: Whenever you use a function that returns an iterator, if it is equal to the end iterator, that means that the function didn't find what it was looking for.

Database Functions

There are a number of database functions that can add, remove, or check the existence of IDs or usernames. Here's the function to add users:

```
bool UserDatabase::
AddUser( Connection<Telnet>* p_connection, string p_name ) {
    if( !HasUser( p_name ) && IsValidName(p_name ) ) {
        m_users.push_back( User( p_connection, p_name ) );
        return true;
    }
    return false;
}
```

The function checks that the username doesn't exist in the DB and checks that the name is valid. If the username passes both of those checks, a new User object is created and pushed onto the back of the user list. true is returned on success, and false is returned on failure.

Next up is the user deletion function, which deletes a user based on his connection pointer:

```
void UserDatabase::DeleteUser( Connection<Telnet>* p_connection ) {
    iterator itr = find( p_connection ); // find the user
    if( itr != m_users.end() )            // make sure user is valid
        m_users.erase( itr );             // then delete the user
}
```

The function finds the User class associated with the connection, and then deletes it from the list. (Assuming it exists. If it doesn't, nothing happens.)

Now the function checks whether a username is being used within the DB:

```
bool UserDatabase::HasUser( string& p_name ) {
    iterator itr = m_users.begin();
    while( itr != m_users.end() ) {
        it( itr->name == p_name )  return true;
        ++itr;
    }
    return false;
}
```

This is similar to the find function that searched based on connection pointers, but this compares names instead.

Valid Usernames

It's always a good idea to place restrictions on usernames. Otherwise, you'll end up having people with confusing names like "__()><?`%", and that's just madness. For this reason, I've included a function within the database that checks the validity of usernames. There are three stipulations. The user name must

Not contain any of the predetermined invalid characters

Not be longer than 16 characters, or shorter than 3 characters

Start with an alphabetic character

You don't want huge or tiny names; those just annoy everyone. It's also a personal preference of mine to force usernames to start with an alphabetic character, but it's not strictly necessary. Here's the function:

```
bool UserDatabase::IsValidName( const string& p_name ) {
    static string inv = " \"'~!@#$%^&*+/\\[]{}<>()=.,?;:";
    if( p_name.find_first_of( inv ) != string::npos ) {
        return false;    // has invalid characters
    }
    if( p_name.size() > 16 || p_name.size() < 3 ) {
        return false;    // too long or too short
    }
    if( !std::isalpha( p_name[0] ) ) {
        return false;    // doesn't start with letter
    }
    return true;
}
```

The function maintains a static string named `inv`. This string contains all the characters that are invalid in usernames. The function first tries to find invalid characters within the string, and if it does, it returns `false`. Next the function checks the size of the name, and finally it checks to see if the first character is alphabetic.

If the string passes all those tests, you've got a valid name.

Logon Handler

Now I get to show you the two handlers that are used within the program. The first one the chat uses is a handler to manage the logon process. Overall, it's going to be a fairly simple handler, because all it needs to do is verify usernames and send them over to the chat handler.

This class is located within the SCLogon.h and SCLogon.cpp files. It inherits from the `Telnet::handler` class, which you should remember from earlier descriptions is just another name for a `ConnectionHandler<Telnet, string>`. This means that the `SCLogon` class needs to implement a constructor that takes a `Connection<Telnet>*` as its parameter, as well as the `Handle`, `Enter`, `Leave`, `Hungup`, and `Flooded` functions.

Last but not least, the class also has a NoRoom function, because it is going to be the default handler in the SimpleChat, so it needs to know how to tell connections when there's no more room.

No Room

When the connection manager has no more room for a new connection, it leaves it up to the default protocol handler to send an error to the connection, notifying the connection that there is no more room. For SimpleChat, the SCLogon handler is the default handler, so it must know how to send these messages. Here is the code:

```
static void NoRoom( Connection<Telnet>& p_connection ) {
    static string msg = "Sorry, there is no more room on this server.\r\n";
    try {
        p_connection.Send( msg.c_str(), (int)msg.size() );
    }
    catch( SocketLib::Exception ) {
        // do nothing here; probably an exploiter if sending that data
        // causes an exception.
    }
}
```

Because the connection isn't added to the connection manager (there is no room!), the function tries to send the data directly to the connection, instead of buffering it. This is the important part: The data is enclosed within a try/catch block because the Send() function may throw exceptions if it cannot send data properly. You want to catch any exceptions before they crash your program. In this case, if an exception is thrown, it will probably be in the very rare circumstance that the person connecting to you is trying to crash your server. There's really no logical reason for the client to be unable to accept sends right after the client connects to the server, but you should always be on the safe side, and you shouldn't assume that the send will work.

New Connections

Whenever a new connection arrives, the connection manager automatically invokes the Enter function of a connection's handler.

Whenever the logon handler gets a new connection, it simply sends a welcoming string to the new connection:

```
void SCLogon::Enter() {
    m_connection->Protocol().SendString( *m_connection, green + bold +
        "Welcome To SimpleChat!\r\n" +
        "Please enter your username: " + reset + bold );
}
```

Whenever the SDLogon class is constructed by the connection manager, it is automatically given a pointer to its connection, so you don't have to worry about the m_connection variable being invalid.

Basically, the function just uses the connection's protocol object to send a string. Note the usage of the VT100 color codes.

I showed you the Telnet::SendString() function earlier in this chapter, which buffers data on the connections buffer. This is generally the best behavior, because the connection manager handles all the sending details later (as long as you remember to tell it to), so you don't have to worry about timeouts and sending errors here.

Handling Commands

Whenever the Telnet protocol handler detects that a full command has been entered (anything ending in "\r" or "\n"), it sends the message to the handler. The logon handler treats any command as a person's desired username and tries to validate it.

```
void SCLogon::Handle( connectionid p_connection, string p_data ) {
    Connection<Telnet>* conn = m_connection;
    if( !UserDatabase::IsValidName( p_data ) ) {
        conn->Protocol().SendString( *conn, red + bold +
            "Sorry, that is an invalid username.\r\n" +
            "Please enter another username: " + reset + bold );
        return;
    }
```

This first batch of code checks to see if the username is valid. If the username is not valid, the user is told so, and the function immediately returns.

```
    if( UserDatabase::HasUser( p_data ) ) {
        conn->Protocol().SendString( *conn, red + bold +
            "Sorry, that name is already in use.\r\n" +
            "Please enter another username: " + reset );
        return;
    }
```

The previous code segment then checks to see if the username has already been taken, and if so, it again tells the client that the name was rejected, and returns. Here's the final code segment:

```
    UserDatabase::AddUser( conn, p_data );
    conn->Protocol().SendString( *conn, "Thank you for joining us, " +
                                  p_data + newline );
    conn->RemoveHandler();
    conn->AddHandler( new SCChat( *conn ) );
}
```

NOTE

There is one important thing I would like to mention: the RemoveHandler function. This function, when called from inside a handler, actually deletes the handler that is calling it. This is a tricky situation, but it's not all that bad if you pay attention to what you are doing. Whenever you call this function, *all* of the current handler's class data is deleted. For this simple handler, that means that the m_connection pointer no longer exists, and using its value causes some bad things to happen. *Local* variables, on the other hand, are still perfectly valid, which is why the pointer to m_connection is stored into conn at the beginning of the function. When you think about it, it's not really a huge problem. Whenever you are calling the RemoveHandler function, you're essentially leaving the state of that handler, so the next and only thing that should be done is either going back to a previous state, or entering a new state. In this case, the connection is entering the SCChat state. After that, the function should quit.

At this point, the username is acceptable, so the function simply adds the connection and the name to the user database and tells the user that he's entered the chat. After that, the logon handler is removed using the RemoveHandler function, and the connection is moved into the SCChat state, using AddHandler.

Other Functions

The other three handler functions—Flooded, Hungup, and Leave—are empty for the logon class:

```
void Hungup() {};
void Flooded() {};
void Leave() {};
```

The handler functions are empty because the handler doesn't actually keep track of connections until a valid nickname is entered, at which time connections are automatically transferred over to the chat handler. So, essentially the logon handler doesn't care if the connections hang up, flood, or quit before it enters a valid username.

NOTE

You may one day want a logon handler to care about flooding. If you catch a user continually flooding your server, you should usually try banning that user. Some systems can do this automatically if you code for it.

Chat Handler

The chat handler is a little more complex than the logon handler, and it even adds two new functions to help you along. It is located in the SCChat.h and SCChat.cpp files.

New Connections

Handling new connections is a simple task for the chat handler. Since the logon handler has already added the user to the database, all you need to do here is announce that a new user has arrived:

```
void SCChat::Enter() {
    SendAll( bold + yellow + UserDatabase::find( m_connection )->name +
            " has entered the room." );
}
```

The function uses the SendAll() function, which I will examine later on. For now, all you need to know is that this function sends a string to every connection in the user database.

Exiting Connections

Whenever a connection leaves the SCChat state, you need to make sure that user is deleted from the user database:

```
void SCChat::Leave() {
    UserDatabase::DeleteUser( m_connection );
}
```

Take note that this function is called whenever a connection moves to a different state, or simply leaves this state (for example, when a connection is being deleted), so you should never call this function on your own. This function basically exists to perform some house-cleaning whenever it's needed.

Handling Commands

There are two types of commands that the handler knows about: regular chatting and instructional commands. Whatever you type with a '/' character in front of it is interpreted as an instructional command; everything else is assumed to be regular chatting.

At this time, there are only two instructional commands supported: /who and /quit. The first command compiles a list of everyone on the server and sends it back to you. The second disconnects you from the server.

The function first gets the name of the user who is sending the text and determines if the text is a command:

```
void SCChat::Handle( string p_data ) {
    string name = UserDatabase::find( m_connection )->name;
```

```
if( p_data[0] == '/' ) {
    string command = BasicLib::ParseWord( p_data, 0 );
    string data = BasicLib::RemoveWord( p_data, 0 );
```

If the text is a command, the function creates two new strings: one represents the command (command); the other represents the rest of the string (data). The next part of the function handles /who commands:

```
if( command == "/who" ) {
    string wholist = magenta + bold + "Who is in the room: ";
    UserDatabase::iterator itr = UserDatabase::begin();
    while( itr != UserDatabase::end() ) {
        wholist += (*itr).name;    // add user's name to end
        ++itr;                     // go to next user
        if( itr != UserDatabase::end() ) {
            wholist += ", ";       // add comma if not last user
        }
    }
    wholist += newline;
    m_connection->Protocol().SendString( *m_connection, wholist );
}
```

If the command is a /who command, the function creates a new string, named wholist, as well as an iterator for the database. Then the function iterates through every user in the database and appends each user's name to the end of the list. For every user except the last, a comma and a space are added to the list as well. So you'll end up with, "Who is in the room: Bob, Sue, Zach", for example. Finally, the who-list string is sent back to the connection using the Telnet::SendString function.

Here's the code that handles quitting:

```
else if( command == "/quit" ) {
    CloseConnection( "has quit. Message: " + data );
    m_connection->Close();
}
}
```

If the command were to quit, the CloseConnection() function would be called. The function is a helper function that basically tells everyone in the room that the user has quit, and it even allows you to add a quit message at the end. /quit goodbye! would result in "Bob has quit. Message: goodbye!" being printed to everyone.

After that, the connection is told to close. (But remember, it won't actually be closed until the connection manager gets around to it.)

The next section of code deals with anything that isn't a command:

```
else {
    if( BasicLib::TrimWhitespace( p_data ).size() > 0 ) {
```

```
            SendAll( green + bold + "<" + name + "> " + reset + p_data );
        }
    }
}
```

First, it checks the size of the string to ensure that all whitespace has been trimmed. If the check returns 0, nothing happens. This prevents people from typing things like "   " into the chatter, which would be extremely annoying.

So basically the code encases your nickname in angle brackets, puts it in green, and then adds your message at the end after resetting the colors. If your name is "Bob" and you typed "Hello", it would print out "<Bob> Hello" to everyone.

The SendAll Function

I've included a function here, which you've seen used earlier, that sends data to every connection in the database.

```
void SCChat::SendAll( const string& p_message ) {
    UserDatabase::iterator itr = UserDatabase::begin();
    while( itr != UserDatabase::end() ) {
        itr->connection->Protocol().SendString( *itr->connection,
            p_message + newline );
        ++itr;
    }
}
```

The function simply performs a loop through the database using the iterator class, and sends the string in the parameter to every user, with a newline tacked onto the end.

Closing Function

The next important function in the chat manager is the CloseConnection function. This is essentially a helper function that makes it easier for you to close connections.

```
void SCChat::CloseConnection( const string& p_reason ) {
    SendAll( bold + red + UserDatabase::find( m_connection )->name +
        " " + p_reason );
}
```

In this case, the function simply sends a message to everyone saying that the user has quit. As I said, it's just a simple helper.

Other Functions

There are two other simple functions within the handler, all very simple. They are Flooded() and
Hungup(), which are called when connections are forcibly closed by the connection manager:

```
void SCChat::Hungup()  { CloseConnection( "has hung up!" ); }
void SCChat::Flooded() { CloseConnection( "has been kicked for flooding!" );
```

These two functions simply utilize the CloseConnection helper function to notify everyone in
the chatroom that the user has left.

Tying It All Together

Finally, you can integrate all the pieces together to form the chat server. This is done within
the Demo06-01.cpp file.

```
int main() {
    SocketLib::ListeningManager<Telnet> lm;
    SocketLib::ConnectionManager<Telnet> cm( 128 );
```

First, the two managers are created with the names lm and cm. The next step is to make the
listening manager know about its connection manager, and then tell it to start listening on a
port:

```
    lm.SetConnectionManager( &cm );
    lm.AddPort( 5099 );
```

Here's the final part of the code:

```
    while( 1 ) {
        lm.Listen();
        cm.Manage();
        ThreadLib::YieldThread();
    }
}
```

The listening manager is told to listen on port 5099, and then the loop starts. The loop
listens for incoming connections, and tells the connection manager to listen/send/close
connections. Finally, it calls the thread library's yield function, so that the program doesn't
consume 100% of your computer's resources.

That's pretty much it. Pretty easy, isn't it? You can compile this program using the instructions found in Appendix A, which is on the CD; the program uses the SocketLib,
ThreadLib, and BasicLib.

Figure 6.5 shows a screenshot from the chat.

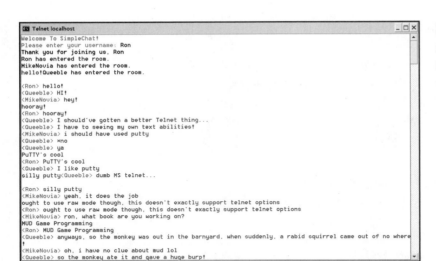

Figure 6.5

Screenshot from the SimpleChat.

Summary

This chapter introduced you to the Telnet protocol and showed you how to use it. While Telnet is not a complex protocol, it has its quirks. This chapter also showed you how to use and create protocol policies as well as protocol handlers to manage your connections.

You may have seen Telnet programs that involve far less design and coding, and you may even be saying that this design was overkill for a simple chat program. Well, you're correct if your end result is only a chat program. However, my goal goes above and beyond. The biggest problem with most MUDs is that they are too difficult to build on and expand.

If you've ever worked on a MUD, you know that 90% of the fun is building on it and expanding it. Unfortunately, most MUDs I see are just huge messes of unorganized code, and every time someone adds something, the whole thing gets a little more ugly and unmaintainable.

So, with this design, I hope you will find the entire networking subsystem to be nice and flexible. This allows you to add cool features to your games later on, if you decide you want them.

This chapter concludes the introduction section of the book; now I will delve into the depths of MUD mechanics.

PART TWO

CREATING A SIMPLE MUD

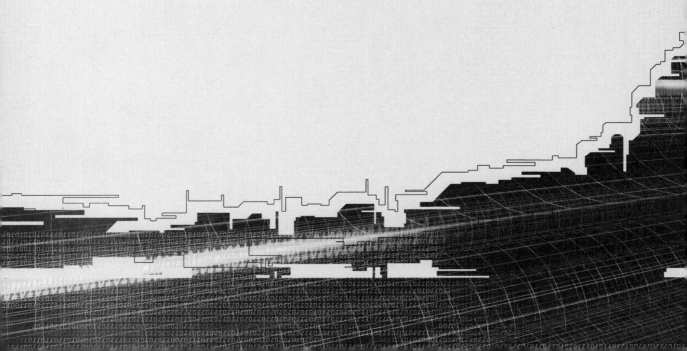

CHAPTER 7

DESIGNING THE SIMPLEMUD

U ntil now, this book has focused on teaching networking and building the three main libraries that are used throughout the book. Little about actual MUDs has been discussed. You must be bored to death! Unfortunately, those things are essential to the groundwork of a MUD, so they were necessary. As they say, work comes before play.

Have no fear. This is where things get interesting! In this part of the book, I introduce you to the basics of MUD programming concepts, in an attempt to show you how they are structured.

The culmination of Part Two is creating a complete MUD, dubbed "SimpleMUD." Obviously, this MUD is going to be fairly straightforward to demonstrate the fundamentals of MUD programming.

This chapter is dedicated to designing the MUD and doing so before a single line of code is written. This is an important part of programming, because you need to understand exactly what you want to do before you start doing it. Many programmers fail to design things up front and adopt a "shoot from the hip" attitude about game programming. Most of their projects fail miserably, because by the time they are months into coding, they realize that they should have allowed for more flexibility. By the time they get to that point, the project is a disaster.

In this chapter, you will learn:

- Choose game attributes
- Choose a setting
- Determine player attributes
- Determine attributes for items
- Determine enemy attributes
- Select a map system
- Select special rooms
- Track store items
- Develop the combat system
- Select commands

Choosing Game Characteristics

As you know if you've been playing for a significant amount of time, MUDs come in all shapes and sizes. The first thing you need to decide when creating a MUD is what kind of MUD it should be.

MUD guru, Dr. Richard Bartle, in his famous article "*Hearts, Clubs, Diamonds, Spades: Players Who Suit MUDs,*" categorizes four types of MUD players: killers, socializers, achievers, and explorers. Because of the diversity of MUD plays, it's impossible to tailor a MUD to suit one specific category of player.

I've seen MUDs in which people don't take time to talk; they do nothing but compete to be number one on the ranking list. I've also seen MUDs in which no one uses any of the MUD features; they use the game essentially as a chat room.

Obviously, when creating your own MUD, you've got to consider which of these characteristics you want to emphasize. Do you want people to socialize? Fight against each other? Explore new areas? Try to win?

I prefer a healthy mix of all these characteristics. Obviously socializing is a must; without it, what's the point of having a multiuser game? But, of course, you'll want some aspect of exploration in your game as well; it keeps your game fresh in the minds of players. Competition is good to have, whether direct through killing other players, or indirect through gaining more points than everyone else. Competition compels people to play the game and to continue playing to beat everyone else.

So with this in mind, the SimpleMUD will be designed to combine an equal distribution of four characteristics: socializing, participating in a multiuser game, exploring, and competing.

So what kinds of things should you plan for? The game will be the classic type with nothing fancy—this is a simple MUD, after all. A setting needs to be chosen first, and that partly determines the attributes and features of players, as well as the enemies. Items and the map structure will also be considered.

Setting

When designing your MUD, take time to carefully consider the setting you want. Classically, MUDs are in a medieval, fantasy setting, but this is only a tradition. Realistically, your MUD can be whatever genre you want it to be, whether it be medieval, futuristic, modern, or something else entirely. Keep in mind that the setting you choose is likely to influence game design considerations, so it's best to think of the setting up front. Most modern-day games don't work too well, for example, because guns enable an inexperienced player to kill someone who's been playing the game for months, and that will hardly seem fair to your high-level players, so you probably won't keep players around long that way.

I've always been a fan of medieval genres; call it clichéd, I don't care. I just love the idea of a glorified version of history. Face it—there really wasn't anything glorious about wearing 200 pounds of metal and trying to whack someone's head off with a sword that weighed another 50 pounds! Alas, our ideas about the time period are based on fictional epics. That's part of the allure; modern culture has already imbued medieval stories with glory and chivalry; therefore, the Middle Ages holds a certain draw.

Another asset of medieval settings is that they seem more game-like. I can't imagine anything duller than a shootout between people randomly aiming machineguns or laser cannons at each other; but with old-fashioned combat, you have a sense of physical and competitive skill, and that's alluring. So, a fantasy medieval world will be the setting for the SimpleMUD.

Players

Once you've nailed down the setting, you need to figure out how the players will be represented. There are many aspects of a player you should be concerned with.

Attributes

When you describe a human being in the real world, you can use many words. He can be strong, fast, agile, intelligent, and so on.

If you've ever played paper-and-pencil role playing games (RPGs), you know that most systems quantify these attributes using numbers. It's not a coincidence that most MUDs use a similar system, since MUDs are the digital equivalent of RPGs. Even modern graphical games, such as the *Diablo* series, and MMORPGs, such as *Dark Age of Camelot* and *Everquest,* use collections of numbers to represent player attributes.

So which attributes should you represent? Some complex MUDs have dozens of attributes; but for SimpleMUD, I'll only use the few listed in Table 7.1.

That's 12 attributes—for a simple game! You can see that attributes for more complex games can become numerous.

Core Attributes

The first three attributes listed in Table 7.1 are *core attributes* (strength, health, and agility); they define actual physical abilities. Pretty much everything else is gained within the game, changed frequently, or based on the core attributes.

In any game system, you've got to create attributes that reflect the abilities your players are going to have in the game. The calculations for these attributes must be tuned and balanced perfectly. I'll go into more depth on this subject later on, so it's okay to just fudge the meanings of these attributes and their calculations for now.

> **NOTE**
>
> You should keep in mind that the attribute system of the SimpleMUD is really *arbitrary.* You really shouldn't feel obligated to copy it or emulate it if you don't want to. I'm sure if you've played RPGs, MUDs, and MMORPGs, you have an idea what kind of attribute system you want to implement already, so don't think that what I show you here is set in stone.

It is a general practice in many MUDs and RPGs to assign random values (or let the user choose them) to the core attributes, and then calculate everything else based on those.

The most popular system, *Dungeons and Dragons (D&D),* uses three rolls of a six-sided die to give each player's attributes a value from 3–18, but for now, I'm just going to use a simple one-to-infinity scale for all three of the core attributes. All players are going to start off with 1 for each core attribute and are awarded 18 attribute points, which they can allocate to any of the attributes they want. So when a new player joins, he can configure a character the way

Table 7.1   SimpleMUD Player Attributes

Attribute	Purpose
Strength	This determines how strong you are and directly affects play within the game, such as how much damage you deal out to other people when attacking.
Health	This attribute determines the overall well-being of your character. This affects things such as how many hitpoints you gain and heal over time.
Agility	This attribute determines how agile you are and affects how accurate you are with weapons and how adeptly you dodge attacks.
Experience points	These tabulate your experience in the game. Experience points are like scores; whenever you kill someone, you get experience points.
Level	This is an artificial ranking that allows you to compare players within the game. Generally, players with the same level should be equal in capabilities and power.
Money	This is the amount of money you have.
Hitpoints	What would a MUD be without some way to gauge how much life a player still has in him? Basically, these points work as they do in any game; if they drop to zero, you die. Hitpoints are affected by your health.
Regen amount	This determines how many hitpoints you regenerate per minute and is affected by your health.
Accuracy	This determines how accurate your strikes are and is affected by your agility.
Dodging	This determines how well you can dodge attacks—also affected by agility.
Strike damage	When added to your weapons attributes, this determines how much damage your attacks inflict on enemies. This is affected by your strength.
Damage absorption	This determines how much damage you suffer whenever you're hit. This is also affected by your strength.

NOTE

You need to figure out if your attributes should be open-ended or closed. For example, in *D&D*, you can range from 3–18, and that's a closed system. You can't go lower than 3 or higher than 18, and you can't change your attributes in the game. This works well on paper because it's so difficult to recalculate everything whenever your attributes change, but MUDs run on computers, which are designed to do tons of calculations quickly. As a result of this, you'll see that many MUDs tend to prefer open systems, because they give you opportunities to extend the gameplay. Any time you offer the player an extra chance to improve his skills, you're adding more gameplay and probably making the game more flexible and enjoyable to your players. Of course, the downside to open-ended systems is that it's possible for people to advance an attribute further than a reasonable level. Because of this, open-ended systems tend to become *unbalanced* quickly, when certain players figure out which attributes give them super powers past a certain number. (It happens.)

he wants; he can even everything out and put everything at 7 points, or give a completely uneven spread with strength being 19, and health and agility being 1. It's up to the user.

Furthermore, whenever a player advances a level, he is given two extra attribute points, which he can put toward any of his three core attributes.

Life Attributes

The hitpoints (HP) attribute has two associated variables: Maximum Hitpoints (MHP) and Current Hitpoints (CHP). Your MHP is calculated using your health and level attributes. When you start off, you are at Level 1, and you are given 10 HP, plus your health divided by 1.5 (with the result truncated using integer division). Since your

NOTE

Regenerating hitpoints is a concept that you won't find in every MUD. Many MUDs refuse to give you any free hitpoints (even though human bodies regenerate naturally), and instead force you to gain your hitpoints by manually healing yourself at something like a temple, or with magical spells and potions. I tend to prefer a regeneration system, however, simply because it makes the game more playable. Makes it a little easier too; I *hate* difficult games. Maybe you're tougher on your players, though, and don't want to give them free hitpoints.

> **TIP**
>
> To take the idea further, think about how humans regenerate. If you scratch or lightly cut yourself, you stop bleeding in a minute, and the scar is gone a few days later. But it's kind of difficult to imagine a person slowly regenerating his health after suffering a rendezvous with a sharp sword to the neck. If you want a realistic system, maybe you should consider making people regenerate health more quickly when they are healthy, and more slowly when they are at their deathbeds. Maybe you can even take it further, and have players *degenerate* after they have gone below a certain point; i.e., your bleeding is slowly draining your health and you can't stop it on your own.

health core attribute can vary from 1 to 19 at Level 1, your MHP can range from 10 to 22. (1/1.5 is 0.6666, but that turns into 0 when truncated into an integer; 19/1.5 is 12.6666, which is 12 when truncated.) Whenever you gain a level, your MHP increase by (Health/1.5) + PreviousLevel. So if you're Level 1, and you increase to Level 2, and your health is 19, you get an extra 13 HP (19/1.5 + 1 = 12 + 1 = 13).

The number of hitpoints you regenerate per minute (HPR) is calculated by your health attribute. It is simply your health divided by 5. So if your health is 15, you regenerate 3 hitpoints per minute.

Accuracy and Dodging Attributes

Both accuracy (ACC) and dodging (DG) are based on your agility attribute. These values are percentage based, but they don't strictly fall into the 0–100% range. When I get to the combat section, you'll see how these work out, but for now, you should know that both accuracy and dodging are calculated as Agility*3, so an Agility of 1 gives you accuracy and dodging values of 3, while an Agility of 19 gives you 57.

Damage Attributes

Like the accuracy and dodging attributes, Strike Damage (SD) and Damage Absorption (DA) have base and current values.

> **TIP**
>
> For a more complex MUD, you might consider keeping an array of strike-damage values, based on the type of weapon you are using. For example, an assassin would be adept at using a knife and would get a special bonus when using knives, but he would be absolutely awful when yielding a two-handed sword that a person like *Conan The Barbarian Governor* could handle with ease.

These values are raw-point based, so that a 1 for damage absorption means that you absorb 1 point of damage every time you are hit, and a 1 for strike damage adds 1 point of damage to all strikes you deal out to enemies.

Your SD and DA values are calculated by dividing your strength by 5, meaning that for every 5 strength points you gain, both your SD and DA will go up by 1.

Bases

In the previous four sections, I told you about nine different player attributes. Every player within the game will have two values for each of those nine attributes: a dynamic value and a base value. The dynamic value of each attribute is calculated based on the player's current level, attributes, and inventory; these values aren't going to be saved to disk anywhere, since they are completely calculated at run-time.

On the other hand, all nine attributes will also have *base* values—values that are permanent to a player. The base values will be modified by items that give permanent effects (such as magic potions or other such stuff). These base values are the ones that will be saved to disk.

Within the game, the *true* value of any given attribute is calculated by adding the base and the dynamic values of each attribute.

> **NOTE**
>
> The base/temporary value system is fairly common in MUDs. This system allows you to apply both temporary and permanent attribute modifications to players. This in turn gives you more flexibility and expandability in the game, by adding more effects. For example, you could have cheap potions that increase your strike damage for a few minutes, or go for the real deal and buy a permanent strike damage potion (only costs an arm and a leg!).

Experience and Leveling

To keep people in your MUD interested in playing, you need a system by which the players can see a noticeable progression in their characters. If players don't see improvements, they tend to get bored and leave. Some games do this very well, and have even earned reputations for how well they present progress (if you've ever heard the term *Evercrack*, then you know what I'm talking about).

The classic way of representing a player's progression is through levels. Every time a user gains a level, he also gains power, and this power is the reward for playing the game.

So how do you determine how the player increases in levels? The classic method is to use an experience system. Every player has a certain number of Experience Points (EXP), and these points are awarded to the player for doing various things throughout the game (though most games just hand these out only when you kill, which is the case for SimpleMUD).

So, whenever you reach a predetermined number of EXP points, their level can be increased by 1.

What kind of system should you use? A *linear* system, in which you increase in level every x points, tends to unbalance games quickly. What happens is that some people get far too powerful far too quickly, and then the game isn't really fun for them anymore, since after a month of serious playing, they can become virtual gods.

I've always preferred *exponential* experience curves. Take a look at Figure 7.1.

In the example, I've used two different formulas to calculate the curves. For the linear curve, I've used the formula *experience = (level - 1) * 100.* That means that for every 100 points, you can advance to another level. At 100 points, you go to level 2, and at 200 points, you go to level 3, and so on.

> **NOTE**
>
> **You might want to think about a system that awards points for things other than killing. In a truly community-oriented game, you're going to have characters who aren't great at killing but provide some other valuable services (such as healing foolish heroes who think that they can take on a diamond-skinned dragon to impress a damsel in distress). Awarding points only for killing can lead to players never wanting to play other parts in the game. This can eventually make your MUD completely combat based.**

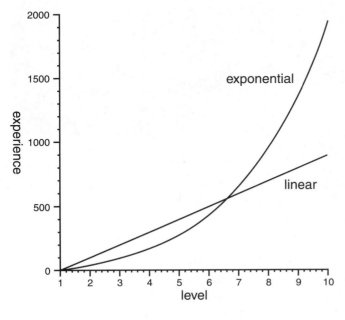

Figure 7.1

If players advance with exponential curves, games are more interesting than with linear curves.

The exponential approach takes a bit more to get to the higher levels. I used the formula *experience = 100 * (1.4$^{(level-1)}$-1)*. If you're not sure what exponentials are, let me give you a quick rundown. An exponential curve follows a basic formula n^x, in which n is a constant, and x is a variable. Basically, n^{x+1} is equal to $n*n^x$, so you know that if n is 2, increasing x by 1 doubles the result. In the case of the formula I showed earlier, every level requires 1.4× as many experience points as the level before it. Table 7.2 shows the number of experience points needed to attain levels 1–10 with both formulas.

You'll notice that for levels 1 through 6, the amount of experience needed for each level on the exponential curve falls below the linear curve. This shows that the exponential curve gives an easy start to players. Beyond level 6 though, the exponential curve takes off way past the linear curve, and it takes more and more experience to reach each new level.

For example, it takes 100 experience points to go from level 8 to 9 on the linear model, but it takes 421 points on the exponential model. Even worse, 9 to 10 takes 591 on the exponential model, but still only 100 on the linear. Notice that each number in the difference column is approximately 1.4 times larger than the number before it.

> ### NOTE
>
> There is an extra *-1* thrown into the exponential formula for good reason. Mathematical rules state that no matter what n is, n^0 is always 1. So at level 1, if you don't have the extra *-1*, you're calculating $1.4^0 * 100$, giving you 100. This means that you need 100 EXP just to reach level 1. In reality, we want 0 instead of 100, so we take 1.4^0-1 instead, which is 0. This way, the graph starts off at 0 when your level is 1.

> ### NOTE
>
> Some MUDs I've played on use a precalculated method, which follows no real formula, but has a general trend of increasing experience requirements. As you'll see from playing the SimpleMUD, the experience requirements get extremely high at higher levels, so even the exponential method has its drawbacks.

With this kind of a curve built in to your game, you can ensure that people don't rapidly outpace your game and beat it within a month. You must be careful, however, because using an exponential curve eventually makes it virtually impossible for the players to advance.

Inventory

Every player in your game has an inventory—a place where he keeps all the items he is carrying. Many complex games use complicated systems for this, but for our purposes, each player simply has an array of 16 objects he can carry at any given time.

As well as having an inventory, players have two different types of items *equipped*: a weapon and a piece of armor. When a weapon is equipped, all its bonuses are added to the player's

Table 7.2   Linear Versus Exponential Levels

Level	Linear	Exponential	Exponential Difference
1	0	0	-
2	100	40	40
3	200	96	56
4	300	174	78
5	400	284	110
6	500	437	153
7	600	652	188
8	700	954	302
9	800	1375	421
10	900	1966	591

attributes, and the player uses that weapon to attack enemies. The armor similarly adds bonuses to the player's attributes to help him in combat.

Other Data

Other than the attributes and the inventory, SimpleMUD players don't have much else. Many complicated MUDs have more data per player, but that's really not needed for this MUD. The only other pieces of data SimpleMUD players have are their names, passwords, and user classes.

User classes determine the abilities of players. When players first sign on, they are class "REGULAR", which means they are just regular users. People who keep order within the game will be given the "GOD" class, in which they can kick unruly users if they need to. You, the operator of the MUD, will be in the "ADMIN" class, however. This means that you have access to the special commands that allow you to control the game.

Items

Throughout the game, there are items that the player can pick up and use. Previously, I've mentioned weapons and armor, and these are the majority of items found throughout the MUD. However, there are other items as well—items that heal players and give them attribute bonuses.

There are three main item types:

- Weapons
- Armor
- Healing Items

Every item will have a number of variables, some of which have meanings for some types of items, some of which don't. They are all listed in Table 7.3.

Table 7.3   Item Attributes

Attribute	Weapon	Armor	Healing
Min	Min damage applied	No meaning	Min healing applied
Max	Max damage applied	No meaning	Max healing applied
Speed	Seconds between swings	No meaning	No meaning
Price	Cost of item	Cost of item	Cost of item
9 attributes	Temporary bonuses	Temporary bonuses	Permanent bonuses

I'll go more into detail about these in the next few sections.

Weapons of Mass Destruction

Weapons are used to harm enemies in the game. As such, they require two damage attributes: a minimum amount of damage, and a maximum amount of damage (thus using the min and max values). This is a pretty typical system, but I'm sure you've got one of your own designs already.

For example, if you have a weapon, such as a knife, and its values are 1 and 5, using a random number generator, the knife could inflict 1, 2, 3, 4, or 5 damage points on your attacker.

Weapons can also be slower or faster than one another. Obviously, with small weapons such as knives, you can attack faster, as opposed to large weapons, such as clubs. Therefore, all weapons have a value that determines the number of seconds between swings.

All values within the set of nine standard attributes are *temporary*, meaning that you gain those bonuses when you have the weapon armed, but you lose them when you disarm the weapon. It's usually typical to give weapons varying values of the accuracy attribute because some weapons are more accurate than others. Items can also have negative values for any of the attributes, making the game a little bit more interesting. Imagine a tradeoff in which

> **NOTE**
>
> The SimpleMUD uses a simple linear random number generator to calculate the damage done by a weapon. This means that if you have a weapon that does 1, 2, or 3 damage points, all three values have an equal chance of being generated. You may want to experiment with other random number-generating methods, however. For example, a *simulated normal generator* would generate numbers so that the middle values occur most often, and the lowest and highest values are generated least often. This gives you a more realistic approach, because really high and really low strikes aren't very common. I've included a special normal random number generator in the BasicLib (BasicLibRandom.h) that you can call like this: `int n = BasicLib::RandomIntNormal( 1, 3 );`. How it works isn't important, however, and would require a whole book on mathematical theory to show you.

you can make a really huge sword do lots of damage, but you can make it lower the player's accuracy because it's so huge and difficult to manage.

Your Knight in Shining Armor

In any MUD, you're going to need some way to clothe and protect your characters. For SimpleMUD, I provide just one type of item, called *Armor*. The main purpose of this kind of item is simply to be put on the player, so he can wear it for the bonuses it gives him.

Armor is a lot simpler than weapons because the only attributes that are valid for armor are the cost and the set of nine standard attributes. Basically, a piece of armor adds its attributes to a player's character when you arm it, and removes those attribute bonuses when you remove it.

> **NOTE**
>
> Armor in the game naturally focuses mainly on the damage absorption and dodging attributes. Armor naturally absorbs shocks, which is where the DA comes from, but you can also make armor lightweight and give it higher dodging values. For example, a piece of chainmail armor would obviously have a higher dodging attribute than a full suit of platemail. Don't feel obligated to stick to these two attributes, though. It's perfectly reasonable to create magical items that increase other attributes, such as your strength or strike damage.

Heal, Brother!

Healing items serve a dual purpose in the SimpleMUD. Their main use is as simple hitpoint healers; they calculate a random number between min and max, and add that number to the player.

On the other hand, healing items cannot be equipped, although they still have a set of the nine player attributes, and it would be a shame to waste all that storage space. When healing items are used, they permanently add their attribute values to your player's character. If a healing item has a value of 1 for accuracy, your player's accuracy is permanently increased by 1 whenever the item is used.

> **TIP**
> This can work both ways, by the way. You can give healing items negative values, for substances that work like a poison to destroy your health if you use them.

To prevent rampant abuse of them, though, the game is set up so that they disappear from your inventory the moment they are used.

Here There Be Dragons!

Since this is a combat-oriented MUD, you need enemies. For the SimpleMUD, these enemies are going to be (you guessed it) simple. Since you're going to be fighting them, they obviously need some combat attributes: hitpoints, accuracy, dodging, strike damage, and damage absorption.

In addition to those combat attributes, enemies have a default weapon, from which their damage range will be taken.

Whenever you end up defeating an enemy, you gain a number of experience points; so enemies also have a set number of experience points, which are added to your points whenever you kill them.

MUDs would be boring if all you got when you killed enemies was points; so enemies also have *loot*! Whenever you kill an enemy, there's a chance it will drop some money. This is represented by two values: a min and a max. The game generates a random number between the min and the max, and that's the amount of money a monster drops when he dies.

Money is fun on its own, but it's awfully impersonal. If everyone just dropped money, it would get too boring. If enemies can drop special items when they die, however, that makes the game more interesting. You can make certain enemies drop items that can't be found anywhere else in the game, and so on. Each item in an enemy's loot list has two values associated with it: the item number, and the percent chance that the item will be dropped.

That's about it for the enemies.

It's a Small World, After All

The world is going to be simple. I'm going to use a room-based system (I can't think of a single MUD that doesn't use a similar system). The world will basically have just a vector of rooms. Each room is a separate entity in the game, a unit that encapsulates a number of things.

Give Me Some Room Here

Rooms in the game are relatively simple. They mainly act as a way of separating the various parts of the game from each other, so that everything doesn't happen in the same place. Because of this, rooms need to know who and what is in them, as well as where the exits are.

Each room has four possible adjacent room indexes, representing indexes of the rooms to the north, east, south, and west. So if a room's north variable is 10, that means room 10 is to the north. If an exit does not exist, the value is 0. Figure 7.2 shows an example of how the rooms are designed. This figure is a visual representation of the rooms. You can see that every room has four connectors, pointing toward another room, and that when its connector value is 0, there is no exit from the room in that direction. Furthermore, each room has strings representing the room name and a description of the room.

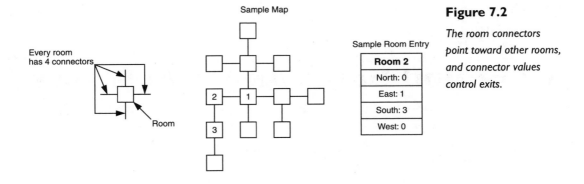

Figure 7.2

The room connectors point toward other rooms, and connector values control exits.

During the game, the map also uses two lists to track which players and enemies are in the room. This information isn't stored on disk, and I'll go into far more detail on these issues in Chapter 9, "Maps, Stores, and Training Rooms."

Items are also stored in lists, which means that theoretically each room can store an infinite number of items. This may seem like a good idea at first, but it doesn't work out in the real world. Most of the time, every room in the realm ends up getting packed full of worthless items that people can't be bothered to pick up and use. Therefore, I've put a limit on the number of items that can be in a room at any given moment, and that number is 32. Whenever someone drops something, and there are already 32 items on the floor, the oldest item just vanishes forever.

Each room also stores the amount of money lying on the floor.

Rooms have a type value. There are different kinds of rooms with special features. The first room type is a normal room and contains nothing special.

Another type of room is a *storeroom*. In these rooms, you can buy and sell items. Each storeroom has an extra associated value, which is the store number. Since the realm may contain several different stores, a storeroom needs to be able to tell which type of store it is. I'll cover stores in the next section.

The other kind of room is a training room, where you can train for the next level when you have gained enough experience.

Rooms also have information about what kinds of enemies they spawn. In MUDs, if your players go around killing everything, eventually they're going to run out of enemies, and your players won't appreciate that. Therefore, you need some way of creating more enemies. I've elected to take a simple approach and make the rooms determine what kind of enemies should respawn. To work, this requires two values: the ID of the enemy you want to spawn, and the maximum number of those enemies you want in the room at any given time.

The game works on a respawn cycle: Every 2 minutes, the game goes through every room and tries respawning enemies. If there are too many enemies in a room, additional enemies are not spawned. If you want, you can use this method to make sure that rooms have only one enemy, or up to 16 if nothing is killed in the room for 32 minutes.

That's all the data that is stored in each room.

Come and See What's in Store

Stores are simple—each store has a list of items that it will buy and sell. SimpleMUD doesn't track the number of each item in stock; that's an advanced feature for more advanced MUDs.

Instead, SimpleMUD assumes that the stores have an infinite amount of items available to sell, so they never run out.

Whenever you buy an item, that item is placed in your inventory, and the amount it costs is subtracted from your money.

Mortal Combat

Combat within the MUD is also pretty simple. There are a few things that must be considered. First of all, you're only allowed to attack enemies. Player Versus Player (PvP) combat is a somewhat more complex subject, so I'll tackle that in the more advanced MUD.

There are two parts to the attack phase: First, you need to see if you actually hit the enemy, and second, you need to calculate how much damage you did.

Both players and enemies have accuracy and dodging attributes. When a player is attacking, a random number from 0 to 99 is generated. The enemy's dodging attribute is subtracted from the player's accuracy attribute, and the result is compared to the random number. If the random number is below the calculated value, the enemy is hit.

Here is the basic formula:

```
if random(0,99) < (player.accuracy - enemy.dodging) then hit
```

For example, if the player's accuracy is 80%, and the enemy's dodging is 10%, the calculated value is 70, which means that the player hits the enemy about 70% of the time. The random number would need to be 0–69 to get a successful hit.

Note that by using this system, it's possible to have accuracies higher than 100%, which means that you'll have extraordinary accuracy against enemies with very low dodging attributes.

The next part is the damage calculation. Assuming you get a successful hit, you need to calculate how much damage it does. The first part of this is to calculate a random number within the range of your current weapon. If you are not using a weapon, it is assumed you are attacking with your fists, and a range of 1–3 is used automatically. Once a value has been calculated, the value of your strike damage attribute is added to it. Then, the value of the enemy's damage absorption attribute is subtracted from the result, and that value is compared to 1. If it is less than 1 (which is possible if the enemy has really tough armor), the value is reset to 1. Finally, the calculated value is subtracted from the enemy's hitpoints. Here's the formula:

```
damage = random( weapon.min, weapon.max ) + player.SD - enemy.DA
if damage < 1 then damage = 1
```

Now, obviously, this is just psuedocode; I'll show you the real code in Chapter 10, "Enemies, Combat, and the Game Loop," when I get to coding these algorithms.

Now, what happens when you kill an enemy? The game goes through all the enemy's possible droppable items and figures out if it drops any, as well as how much money it drops.

Enemies return your attacks by using the same formulas, so it's possible for you to die. What happens when you die? Some games give you a certain number of lives, which represent the number of times you can die before your character is permanently deleted. I don't like this method; it tends to make people freak out when they are running low on lives, or get system operators to cheat and give them more.

I like an approach that penalizes you by subtracting 10% of your experience points. This doesn't change your level, but it makes you further away from gaining another level. But that's not enough punishment. So in addition, you lose 10% of the money you're carrying and one item randomly chosen. I don't like players to lose everything when they die because it makes it far too easy for scavengers to steal all their hard-earned stuff. I tend to be generous, though; in your own MUDs, you're allowed to be devious bastards if you like. So after you've lost an item and your money, you're automatically transported back to the starting room in the world, and you're hoping you didn't lose an important item.

Some MUDs have a combat state, in which the game automatically attacks for you. This feature is somewhat advanced, and thus SimpleMUD doesn't have it. Every time you want to attack someone, you must manually enter the attack command. The game will notify the user if he has attacked, or if he still needs to wait for the next time he can attack, since it might be a few seconds before the user can attack again.

I Command Thee

Obviously, SimpleMUD uses a simple text interface through Telnet to interact with the players. Therefore, I need to make a list of all commands that a player can use within the game.

There are three groups of commands: player commands, god commands, and administration commands.

> **NOTE**
>
> Many MUDs like to add "interaction" commands that help the players show their current state of mind. Stuff like "cry," "laugh," and "smile" are quite common. While these commands seem somewhat pointless to the overall design of the game, you'd actually be surprised at how much *immersion* these things add to the game.

Player Commands

Players have certain commands available to them at all times, as listed in Table 7.4.

The additional commands that are available if you are in stores or training rooms are listed in Table 7.5.

God and Admin Commands

If you're a god or admin in the game (you lucky dog, you), you have access to all the normal player commands, as well as some extra commands to control things within the realm. Table 7.6 lists these commands.

You should never underestimate how valuable it is to have these kinds of commands in the game. If any of your players start acting unruly, it's a good idea to have a god kick him, so that the player clearly knows that someone more powerful is nearby, and is not afraid to kick some insubordinate butt.

Summary

Let me finish by saying that this has been a very difficult chapter for me to write, and a difficult game for me to design. If you're anything like me, you'll know what I'm talking about. I'm a person who aspires to make the most perfect game possible at all times, and if you're like me, you were probably saying things like "Only 16 items per player! That's too limiting!"

Table 7.4   Regular Player Commands

Command	Alternate	Use
attack <enemy>	a <enemy>	Initiates an attack on the indicated enemy.
	get <item>	Attempts to pick an item off the ground. If a number is used in place of the item name, it assumes you want to pick up that much money.
drop <item>	-	Drops an item or money in the room.
help	-	Shows a listing of the commands available to you.
north	n	Moves north.
east	e	Moves east.
south	s	Moves south.
west	w	Moves west.
quit	-	Quits the game.
who	-	Lists who is online.
use <item>	-	Arms or uses an item in your inventory.
remove <weapon/armor>	-	Disarms your weapon or your armor.
chat <text>	-	Sends text to everyone in the realm.
whisper <player> <text>	-	Sends text to a single person.
say <text>	-	Sends text to everyone in the room you are in.
inventory	inv	Shows you all the items in your inventory.
stats	st	Shows you all your statistics.
experience	exp	Shows you how much experience you have, and how much you need for the next level.
/	-	Repeats the previous command you made.
time	-	Shows you the system time.
look	l	Shows you the description of the room that you are in.

Table 7.5 Store and Training Room Commands

Command	Room	Use
list	Store	Lists all the items available to buy or sell.
buy <item>	Store	Player tries to buy an item in stock.
sell <item>	Store	Player tries to sell an item.
train	Trainer	Trains you to the next level if you have enough experience.
editstats	Trainer	Takes you to the stats editing mode so you can allocate your statpoints.

Table 7.6 God Commands

Command	Rank/Class	Use
kick <user>	God	Kicks a user out of the game.
announce <msg>	Admin	Makes a system announcement to everyone.
changerank <user> <rank>	Admin	Changes the rank/class of a user.
reload <database>	Admin	Reloads the specified database (items, enemies, stores, rooms, or individual players).
shutdown	Admin	Shuts down the MUD and saves all data to disk.

I love to go with the best features available when I'm designing my games, and it was incredibly difficult for me to decide which simple features to keep, and which advanced features to put off until later. There's an advantage in this method, however. If you constantly plan for the best, you're going to be in a perpetual state of planning, and you'll never get anything coded. For the SimpleMUD, I've chosen a bunch of very simple features to put into the game, and I decided to go no further.

Once I have the simple design completed and fully coded, *then* I'll go on to more complex things.

The next few chapters show you how to assemble the SimpleMUD and administer it. Once that is complete, you go on to the next part of the book, in which I design a more advanced MUD, using dozens of new features.

CHAPTER 8

1TEMS AND PLAYERS

In the previous chapter, I showed you what capabilities I wanted to put into the SimpleMUD. It's generally a good practice to spell out game capabilities even before you begin coding, so that you're not surprised when you think of something new that you want to put into the game. Now that I know what I want within the SimpleMUD, I can begin to design the software and code it.

This chapter is fairly large, but it covers a large part of the SimpleMUD. Most of the base classes shown in this chapter are reused throughout the game. The chapter also introduces you to the concepts of items and players within the game.

In this chapter, you will learn to:

- Create entities that are matchable using partial strings
- Create a map-based database
- Create a vector-based database for game entities that need better lookup speed
- Create "Smart database pointers" that allow you to access the databases transparently
- Create logging classes
- Create a class that represents the common attributes of players and items
- Create the class representing items, as well as a database for them
- Create the class representing players, as well as a database for them
- Store items and players to disk
- Create the connection handler that handles players logging in
- Create the connection handler that handles editing player statistics
- Create the connection handler that manages all game commands
- Code the basic commands related to players, interaction, and items

Groundwork

The first thing I want to do is lay the groundwork for the *entity* classes, which are the classes that represent physical objects within the game, such as players, items, and enemies. Within the game, all these entities will have names and unique ID numbers that identify the entities. The ID is important, because it is used to reference entities throughout the game. Instead of having a huge mess of pointers all over the place, you'll track entity IDs instead. This way, you can easily tell the game, "Hey, I want to access item number 403."

Within this chapter, all the code that I create for SimpleMUD is placed within the Demos\Chapter08\Demo08-01\SimpleMUD directory on the CD. Since I'm building the entire MUD incrementally throughout the next few chapters, I don't want you to look at the full codebase, so I've separated out just the parts that are needed for this chapter. At the end of the chapter, I show you a demo that gets what I've coded up and running for you.

Table 8.1 shows a listing of all the files introduced within this chapter and their purpose.

Table 8.1 Chapter 8 Files

File	Purpose
Attributes.h	Stores all the enumerations needed, as well as the `Attributes` class
DatabasePointer.h/.cpp	Special pointers used to access databases
Entity.h	Stores the `Entity` class
EntityDatabase.h	Stores both the map- and vector-based database classes
Game.h/.cpp	The connection handler that handles game commands from players
Item.h	The class that represents items
ItemDatabase.h/.cpp	The database that stores items
Logon.h/.cpp	The connection handler that handles players trying to log on
Player.h/.cpp	The class that represents players
PlayerDatabase.h/.cpp	The database that stores players
SimpleMUDLogs.h/.cpp	The files that hold the MUD logging classes
Train.h/.cpp	The connection handler that handles players editing their stats

Entities

As I mentioned before, entities in the game are composed of two things: their names and their ID numbers. I could create separate player, item, and monster classes, and give each of these classes those variables individually, but that's unorganized and prone to error.

I prefer to create classes that minimize the amount of coding you need to do. Using this philosophy, I've decided to create an `Entity` class to take care of this responsibility. This class is located in the Entity.h file. Here's a listing of the class's data and function declarations:

```
typedef unsigned int entityid;
class Entity {
public:
    inline Entity();                    // constructor
```

```
    inline string& Name();           // name reference
    inline entityid& ID();           // ID reference
    inline string CompName();        // name in lowercase
    bool FullMatch( const string& p_name ); // full match
    bool Match( const string& p_name ) ;    // partial match
protected:
    string m_name;
    entityid m_id;
};
```

Look at the data first. The name is a simple std::string (although I removed the std:: from the code just so it looks better), and IDs are just unsigned integers. (The entityid typedef is at the top of the code segment.) I like to use typedefs because they make your code cleaner. In the game, 0 is considered the invalid value, and every other value is valid, giving you about 4 billion valid IDs for each entity type. It is assumed that each entity type is independent of all the rest, so item 1 is a different entity than enemy 1 or player 1. Theoretically, memory considerations aside, SimpleMUD supports up to 4 billion items, 4 billion players, and 4 billion enemies.

Accessors

There are several functions included along with the Entity class. Two of the functions, Name and ID, are just simple accessor functions that return a reference to the variable they point to:

```
inline entityid& ID()           { return m_id; }
inline string& Name()           { return m_name; }
```

Because these variables return references, you can modify the variables through the functions, like this:

```
n.Name() = "John";
```

The constructor (which I do not show) simply initializes the name to "UNDEFINED", and the ID to 0, indicating that the object hasn't been constructed.

Full Matching

The other functions perform useful tasks on the class. For example, the CompName function returns the name of the string in lowercase form (using the BasicLib::LowerCase function from Chapter 4). This is mainly used for name comparisons. The fact that strings don't recognize "ABC" as being equal to "abc" can be annoying. Imagine being in the game and wanting to refer to an inconsiderate person named "JoHn". If you use a plain string comparison, the computer won't recognize who you're talking to unless you exactly match the case of each letter of the string. In other words, the computer will think that "john" is a different player than "JoHn." The CompName function solves this problem by converting both names into lowercase, when making comparisons.

There are two ways of determining if two names match. The first method, called full matching, only returns a positive match if the names are identical (ignoring case as I just mentioned). This functionality is stored within the MatchFull function:

```
inline bool FullMatch( const string& p_str ) {
    return CompName() == LowerCase( p_str );
}
```

Figure 8.1 shows two examples of full matching.

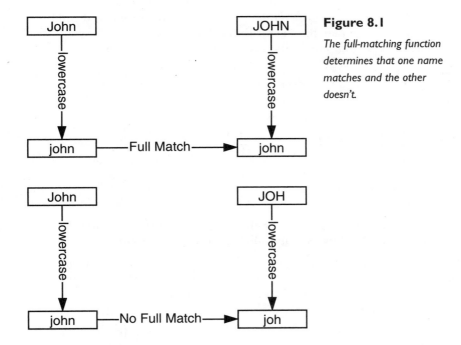

Figure 8.1

The full-matching function determines that one name matches and the other doesn't.

Partial Matching

The other method is called partial matching, and it returns a positive match if the search string matches the beginning of an entity's name.

For example, in a game in which partial matching isn't available, if a guy has a really long name, such as "ReallySuperAwesomeDude," whenever you want to refer to him, you'd have to type his full name. With partial matching, however, you can type "reall" or "rea" or any other partial string that matches the front of the entity's name, and the computer returns a match. The partial matching capability is found within the Match function.

Furthermore, after you've played a lot of MUDs, you'll find that the ability to partially match any word within a string is useful. For example, when you see a "Jeweled Sword" sitting in a room, the word "Jeweled" is eye candy, and your mind interprets that simply as a "sword." So you quickly type "get sword" without thinking about it. The partial matching function accommodates your greed and recognizes "get sword" as "Jeweled Sword" by performing partial matching on any word within a string.

Here's the function:

```
inline bool Match( const string& p_str ) const {
    if( p_str.size() == 0 )
        return true;
```

This first segment of code returns true if the size of the search string is 0. The reason for this is convenience; many times, there's just one enemy or one item in a room, and you can just type attack or get, and the partial matching algorithm will match on that item (or if there are more, it will match on the first one in the room). It's a convenience issue.

```
    string name = CompName();
    string search = BasicLib::LowerCase( p_str );
    size_t pos = name.find( search );
    while( pos != string::npos ) {
        if( pos == 0 || m_name[pos-1] == ' ' )
            return true;
        pos = name.find( search, pos + 1 );
    }
    return false;
}
```

The previous code segment performs the partial matching. It first records the lowercased versions of the name and the search string (because they are used more than once).

Then the code performs a search on the name, and records the position into pos. If no match was found, the find function returns std::string::npos, which is a value representing the "invalid" string index. If that happens, there was obviously no partial match, so the function skips the loop, and false is returned.

If the position isn't npos, however, the body of the loop is executed. If pos is 0, that means that a match was found at the beginning of the name. For example, the string "rus" would return 0 when searched for within "rusty stake". The function would then return true, because the beginning of the string matched.

The partial matching function also checks to see if the character before pos is a space. This would happen if you searched for "sta" inside "rusty stake". The find function would return 6 (the index of the substring), and because the previous character is a space, true is returned.

So why is there a loop in the function? Imagine for a moment that you're searching for "st" within "rusty stake". Use Figure 8.2 as a guide for this example.

The first match for "st" is in the middle of "rusty", and that obviously doesn't count as a valid partial match. But you haven't searched the entire string yet, so you need to keep looking. Therefore, the find function is called again, this time starting at pos + 1. Now the function finds another match for "st", this time at position 6. Because this is the beginning of a word, the function matches, and true is returned. The function loops through the entire string looking for any partial match. If no matches are found, when find reaches the end, it returns std::string::npos, the loop terminates, and false is returned.

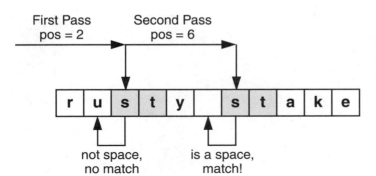

Figure 8.2

A loop is needed when the partial matching function searches for partial matches within a name.

Entity Function Listing

Table 8.2 shows a listing of all the functions within the Entity class.

Table 8.2   Entity Functions

Function	Purpose
Entity()	Constructs the entity with "invalid" values
string Name()	Returns the name of the object
string CompName()	Returns a lowercase version of the name, used for comparisons
bool Match(string str)	Determines if str partially matches the name of the entity
bool MatchFull(string str)	Determines if str fully matches the name of the entity
entityid& ID()	Returns a reference to the entity's ID

Entity Functors

Throughout the game, you're going to need to perform searches on groupings of entities, using full or partial matching. Obviously, you can't rely on your grouping classes such as the EntityDatabase, or any STL container to perform searching for you. STL relies on algorithms for searching, so I'll do the same.

STL searching algorithms typically rely on the operator== of a datatype for comparisons, but this is a problem for Entity's, since there are two ways to compare entities with strings. So that's not going to work. Luckily for us, STL searching algorithms also have some backups that allow you to use *functors* to check if an object meets a specific criterion.

A functor is somewhat like a function pointer in the guise of a class/struct. The advantages this method has over function pointers are numerous. The most useful benefit is that a functor is allowed to have variables that represent its state. It's true that functions can have static local variables, but *everything* that calls that function will use the same variables. Using classes allows you to have many different functors in various states. There are other benefits as well, but I won't go over them; it's time to move on.

Functors are usually simple in nature and always overload an operator(). That's a weird operator to overload, but just bear with me for a moment.

> **NOTE**
>
> Functors are really nothing more than the C++ equivalent to function pointers—classes that act like functions. The examples I use here should be pretty simple to understand, but if they still confuse you, there are many great books on STL that can help (such as *The C++ Standard Library, a Tutorial and Reference*, by N. Josuttis). I'll try to do my best, though!

I'm going to show you the basic layout of my matchentityfull functor, without function bodies:

```
struct matchentityfull {
    string m_str;
    matchentityfull( const string& p_str );
    bool operator() ( const Entity& p_entity );
    bool operator() ( Entity* p_entity );
};
```

You should note that the functor contains a string that you will be searching for within entities. The constructor takes a constant reference to a string, which will copy that into the m_str variable. This means that a string matching functor keeps track of the string that you are searching for. Before I show you the functions, let me show you a simple example of how this functor works:

```
matchentityfull matcher( "john" );     // functor that searches for "john"
Entity a;
Entity* b;
// assume that 'a' and 'b' are initialized somewhere before the next line:
bool t = matcher( a );                 // see if 'a' matches "john"
t = matcher( b );                      // see if 'b' matches "john"
```

So you can see that this class simply performs a full entity-name match on Entity's and Entity pointers.

Here's the code for the constructor:

```
matchentityfull( const string& p_str )
    : m_str( p_str ) { /* do nothing */ }
```

All the constructor does is record the string and keep track of it for future use. Note that I use the *initializer-list* syntax to construct the string, and do nothing within the function body.

Initializing variables in this manner is faster, as described in Appendix C, "C++ Primer," which is on the CD.

Here's the code for the two other functions:

```
bool operator() ( const Entity& p_entity ) {
    return p_entity.MatchFull( m_str );
}
bool operator() ( Entity* p_entity ) {
    return p_entity != 0 && p_entity->MatchFull( m_str );
}
```

The first version just calls the `Entity::MatchFull` function and returns the result. The pointer version first checks to make sure the pointer is nonzero and then calls the matching function. This way, if a `NULL` pointer is ever passed in, it always returns `false`. Otherwise, trying to dereference a `NULL` pointer may end up crashing it.

There is another functor, called `matchentity`, which is almost identical to `matchentityfull`; the only difference is that it calls the `Entity::Match` function instead of `Entity::MatchFull`, so there's no need to paste the code here.

So, now that you know what functors are, and what they can do, let me show you a more complicated way to use them. Say, for example, you have a vector of entities, and another vector of entity pointers, and you'd like to search them for a name.

```
vector<Entity> evec;
vector<Entity*> epvec;
// pretend we fill up both vectors somewhere before this line:
vector<Entity>::iterator itr1 = find_if( evec.begin(),
        evec.end(), matchentityfull( "john" ) );
vector<Entity*>::iterator itr2 = find_if( epvec.begin(),
        epvec.end(), matchentity( "john" ) );
```

See Appendix C on the CD for a short intro to STL if you're not familiar with its inner workings. Essentially, the previous code segment automatically searches a vector of `Entitys` for the first full match on the name "john", and searches a vector of `Entity` pointers for the first partial match of the name "john". The cool thing is that you can use this algorithm on any STL container that supports forward iterators. You'll see that the `EntityDatabase` class I show you next works quite well with STL algorithms.

For future reference, both of these functors are modeled around the concept of *predicate* functors, which are functors that evaluate a piece of data and return a Boolean, determining if the data satisfies a criterion. In this case, `matchentity` returns `true` if a player partially matches a string, and `matchentityfull` does so with full matches.

Entity Database Classes

Now you need a class to manage all the entities while they are in the game. In larger MUDs and in the bad old days, memory was not cheap, and it was hard to come by. But nowadays you can get memory for almost nothing, so I'm not going to spend any time in the

SimpleMUD concentrating on memory optimization.

The game has two kinds of databases: map-based, and vector-based. If you know much about data structures, you know that STL maps have an O(log n) access complexity, which means that the map performs *log n* comparisons when searching for an item in a database of size *n*. A database of 255 items would need at most 8 comparisons to find any item, and a database of 65,535 items would require at most 16 comparisons.

Although this seems like a great database to use for everything, it's not optimal for some cases. There will be times when 16 comparisons are too long, so a database with faster access is required. That's where the vector comes in: an STL vector is basically just an array, and because of that, it has O(1) complexity. Accessing any given index with the STL vector takes just one calculation.

For the SimpleMUD, the entity databases will simply be static classes that enclose either `std::map`'s or `std::vector`'s, called `EntityDatabase` and `EntityDatabaseVector`. The base classes will be stored in the file EntityDatabase.h.

Because the classes are static, you should be able to access a single database within the game globally, without worrying about instantiating it. I'm sure people have told you before that globals are bad, and they're right; but honestly, for database-type stuff, globals really aren't *that* bad. How many different user/item/enemy databases do you need in a single game? I'm comfortable with having just one.

Map-Based Database

As I mentioned previously, the map-based database simply wraps around an `std::map`.

Class Definition and Data

First of all, every entity database is a template class. It is assumed that you are going to be storing `Entity` objects within the database, but each database should store only one type of entity. Therefore, runtime polymorphism (virtual inheritance) is inappropriate to use in this case, and compile-time polymorphism (a fancy term describing templates) will be used instead:

```
template< class datatype >
class EntityDatabase {
protected:
    static std::map<entityid, datatype> m_map;
};
```

I've stripped out all the functions and the iterator class, which I will get to in a bit. For now, all you need to know is that each entity database stores a specific datatype by ID within an `std::map`. I prefer maps because they are easy to iterate through, and offer relatively quick search times. In an ideal world, if you had completely contiguous IDs for an entity type, you might prefer to store them in a `std::vector`, but I find maps easier to use. Maps are helpful in case you forget to assign a specific ID to any entity, and they prevent your MUD from unexpectedly crashing when you try accessing an entity that doesn't exist.

Iterator Inner Class

As I explain in Appendix C, which is on the CD, std::maps are awkward to iterate through when compared to the other container iterator types. This is because they don't actually store a single type of data within them, but rather a pair of data. So whenever you access an iterator into a map, the iterator doesn't return a single piece of data, but rather an std::pair structure that holds both the key and the data. This make things a little ugly to use, however. If you make the map-based database return iterators pointing directly into the std::map<entityid, datatype>, you must always use the iterators like this:

```
// this code assumes you have an EntityDatabase that stores players named
// PlayerDatabase
PlayerDatabase::iterator itr = PlayerDatabase::begin();
// now access the player that the iterator points to:
itr->second.Name() = "Ron";
```

You'll need to constantly use the second variable of the iterator, which gets plain annoying; wouldn't you rather just code like this:

```
itr->Name() = "Ron";
```

With the EntityDatabase class, I've created an *inner iterator* class, which inherits from std::map::iterator, and redefines the operator* and operator-> functions, so that they return a reference to the second value directly. The code isn't that complex, so I won't be presenting it here. This is what is known as an *iterator proxy* class.

Figure 8.3 shows the basic concept of a database iterator and illustrates its relationship to a database. Iterators point directly to entities; therefore, accessing entities is an instantaneous operation.

Like the PlayerDatabase class from Chapter 6, "Telnet Protocol and a Simple Chat Server," the EntityDatabase class has the standard begin and end iterator functions.

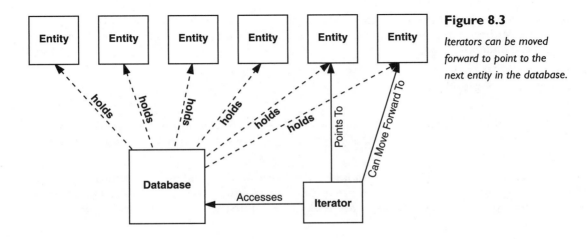

Figure 8.3

Iterators can be moved forward to point to the next entity in the database.

> **NOTE**
>
> You may have noticed the odd change in the way I name functions for this class. I usually like my function names to be named as "Capitalize all important words," making functions like `Begin`, and `FindFull`. However, this class ignores that naming convention and makes everything lowercase. I do this for a simple reason: I want the database class to look more in tune with the STL. Because a database is really just another data structure, it makes sense to use the same nomenclature.

While the `PlayerDatabase` class from SimpleChat could simply return iterators to its internal list, I can't quite do that here, since I'm using an iterator proxy class. That means that I must construct them first, using the contents of a map iterator:

```
inline static iterator begin() { return iterator( m_map.begin() ); }
inline static iterator end() {   return iterator( m_map.end() );   }
```

As you can see, the database class simply mimics the `std::map` `begin` and `end` functions by passing their results into the constructor of the inner `iterator` class.

Searching the Database

There are numerous ways to search for and retrieve entities from the database, aside from using the iterator class.

ID-Based Lookups

ID-based lookups are the easiest; they involve looking up an entity based on its ID. There are three of these functions: `has`, `find`, and `get`. The first lookup determines if an ID exists within the database:

```
inline static bool has( entityid p_id ) {
    return ( m_map.find( p_id ) != m_map.end() );
}
```

Remember that the `map::find` function returns the same iterator as the `map::end` function if the key doesn't exist within the map, so if the two iterators are different, the key *does* exist, and `true` is returned.

The `EntityDatabase::find` function looks for an ID within the database, and returns an iterator pointing to the entity with that ID (or an invalid iterator if not found). This is done mainly for optimization purposes; if you look up an ID first to see if it even exists, and then look it up again to retrieve it, you're doing twice the necessary work. Instead, it's easier to get an iterator to the object, and then see if the iterator is valid. If you use this method, you can immediately use the value you looked up instead of doing it twice. Here's the code:

```
inline static iterator find( entityid p_id ) {
    return iterator( m_map.find( p_id ) );
}
```

As you can see, the code simply wraps around the map::find function, because the map already knows how to search by ID.

The final function is the get function, which simply returns a reference to the data attached to the given ID.

```
inline static datatype& get( entityid p_id ) {
    return m_map[p_id];
}
```

The function just returns a reference to the item with the ID you were looking for, but beware: If the ID you look up does not exist within the database, it will be created for you automatically. This means that a new entity is inserted into the database with only the default values (since you didn't fill it in). This could produce some interesting side effects.

Name-Based Lookups

You'll also want to look up entities based on their names. This becomes particularly useful when someone types in "attack Joe" in the game, and the game wants to find out who Joe is. In an effort to make the game easier on players, the game can also perform partial name lookups.

There are four name-based lookup functions: has, hasfull, find, and findfull. You'll notice that two of those functions (has and find) are also used for ID-based lookups, but I've overloaded the functions to take different parameters.

Because you're doing string-based lookups now, you can't just use a simple lookup in a map. Sure, you could store all the names within a map and have them retrieve the entities, but there's a serious problem with that method: You can't do partial matches using that method.

> **NOTE**
>
> There is a special data structure, called a *trie*, which is short for *retrieval-tree* (and there are holy wars fought over whether it's pronounced "try" or "tree"). The *trie* data structure is specifically designed for rapid string-based lookups using a special kind of tree. A special feature of tries is that they can also perform partial-matching quickly. Unfortunately, I don't have the time or space required to go into tries in more detail, so I'll leave that up to you to explore on your own.

To perform a partial name lookup, you need to perform a comparison on every entity in the database. Here's the has function, the simplest of them all:

```
inline static bool has( std::string p_name ) {
    return find( p_name ) != end();
}
```

The function simply calls the find function to find a partial match to the given name, and then returns true if the iterator returned is not equal to end (meaning that the player exists), or false if they are equal.

The hasfull function is similar, replacing find with findfull:

```
inline static bool hasfull( std::string p_name ) {
    return findfull( p_name ) != end();
}
```

find functions are interesting. Here's the first one, which searches for partial matches:

```
static iterator find( const std::string& p_name ) {
    return BasicLib::double_find_if( begin(), end(),
        matchentityfull( p_name ),
        matchentity( p_name ) );
}
```

NOTE

To make the database classes more useful, they have been given two different name-based lookup methods. You can search for an exact name match (ignoring case, of course) using the hasfull and findfull functions. But an Entity also supports partial matching. I considered making the database respond to requests to perform a straight partial match, but this leads to complications. Because of the method for searching the database, if you have two players in your database named "Johnny" and "John" (in that order within the database), whenever you do a partial search for "john", the database would always think you're talking about "Johnny", because that's the first person the database finds that partially matches "John". As simple as this sounds, it can be a nuisance to your users by making the real "John" totally impossible to reference. Therefore, I've decided to make the database's partial matching find and has functions first try to find an exact name match, and if none is found, then perform a partial match. This makes your life much easier. To do this, I've created a new STL-like algorithm function named double_find_if, and you can find that in the Libraries/BasicLib/BasicLibFunctions.h file. I'm not going to show you the code because it's just a simple helper function, but you should be aware that it acts just like std::find_if, except it has a fourth parameter: a functor that is used for a second pass, if nothing was found on the first pass.

The function makes use of my custom `double_find_if` function to perform a two-pass search on the database. First it tries to find a full match using the `matchentityfull` functor I showed you earlier; then it uses a partial match using the `matchentity` functor.

The `findfull` function is similar, but because it only needs one pass, it uses the standard `find_if` function:

```
static iterator findfull( const std::string& p_name ) {
    return std::find_if( begin(), end(), matchentityfull( p_name ) );
}
```

This function just does a single-pass full match using `std::find_if`.

EntityDatabase Function Listing

Table 8.3 shows a listing of all the functions within the `EntityDatabase` class.

Table 8.3   EntityDatabase Functions

Function	Purpose
iterator begin()	Returns an iterator pointing to the beginning of the database
iterator end()	Returns the "invalid" iterator, pointing past the previous entity
bool has(entityid id)	Determines if an entity with id exists within the database
bool has(string str)	Determines if an entity with partial name str exists
bool hasfull(string str)	Determines if an entity with the exact name str exists
iterator find(entityid id)	Returns an iterator pointing to the entity with id
iterator find(string str)	Returns iterator pointing to entity with partial name str
iterator findfull(string str)	Returns iterator pointing to entity with exact name str
datatype& get(entityid id)	Returns reference to entity with given id
size_t size()	Returns number of items within database

Vector-Based Database

The vector-based database class is pretty simple compared to the map-based database. Let me show you the class definition and data first.

Class Definition and Data

Here's the class definition for the `EntityDatabaseVector` class:

```
template< typename datatype >
class EntityDatabaseVector {
    typedef std::vector<datatype>::iterator iterator;
protected:
    static std::vector<datatype> m_vector;
};
```

As usual, I've removed the function declarations, so you can see the data more easily. As you can see, it simply wraps around a vector.

The other interesting thing to note is that the class typedefs an `std::vector<datatype>::iterator` as its own `iterator` class. Remember how map iterators work and that they don't actually return the data stored in the map; instead, they return an `std::pair<key,data>`, which means that for iterators of maps, you'll have to use `itr->second` to access the data, and that's really annoying. Because of that, I created my own iterator class that would take care of that for you within the `EntityDatabase` class.

However, `vectors` are much easier to use, and because their iterators directly return the data, there's absolutely no need to create my own iterator class. Instead, an iterator for the `EntityDatabaseVector` class is really just a `std::vector<datatype>::iterator`. That makes things easier.

Functions

The vector-based database has a different purpose from the map-based database. A map-based database is often used to search for entities with *sparse* ID numbers (the IDs aren't continuous, and you could have IDs 1–10 and 91–100 defined, but then have nothing defined for 11–90), but the vector-based database is used more for storing data that needs to be quickly accessible, and won't change much. This means that things in vector databases are rarely added or deleted. There are just four simple functions in the database:

```
inline static iterator begin()  { return m_vector.begin() + 1; }
inline static iterator end()    { return m_vector.end(); }
inline static size_t size()     { return m_vector.size() - 1; }
inline static datatype& get( entityid p_id ) {
    if( p_id >= m_vector.size() || p_id == 0 )
        throw std::exception();
    return m_vector[p_id];
}
```

When introducing `entityids`, I mentioned that the value 0 is always considered invalid. Unfortunately, vectors always begin with index 0, so you're going to have one "dummy" index, where there isn't valid data.

NOTE

If you're *really* concerned about wasting that one index, you could make the `get` function simply subtract 1 from the index whenever it is called, thus treating the real index 0 as index 1, and so on.

The first two functions are iterator functions, which return iterators pointing to the first and one-after-last indexes in the array. Because index 0 is assumed to be invalid, the Begin function actually returns an iterator pointing to index 1.

Also, because one index is always invalid, whenever the `size` function is called, 1 is subtracted from the size.

> **NOTE**
>
> I could have used the `vector::at` function instead of my own version, but unfortunately, that was a late addition to the STL standard, and not all compilers support it.

The last function is the `get` function, which returns data at a given index. The function uses bounds checking, so if you try accessing an invalid index, an exception is thrown.

That's pretty much it for the actual database classes.

Database Pointers

Throughout the game, you're going to want to access entities within the databases. One easy way to do this would be to use pointers, but I usually recommend against this method. Many more advanced MUDs keep data on disk as much as possible, and only keep a few entities in memory at any given time. In such systems, when entities haven't been accessed for a while, they are automatically written back to disk and reloaded when they are needed again. As you can imagine, in such a system, entities are constantly at different addresses and are a pain in the butt to keep track of.

So pointers are out of the question. Because each entity has a unique ID number, it would make sense to store those throughout the game. Unfortunately, this is annoying in its own way; whenever you want to use the entity that the ID points you to, you'll have to manually look it up in the database class. Assuming there's an item database named `ItemDatabase`, this is how you'd do it:

```
Item& i = ItemDatabase::get( id );
```

That can tend to get quite tiresome after a while, so I've decided to create a `databasepointer` class. For all intents and purposes, this class will act just like an `entityid`, but will also have some overloads to make it act like a pointer to an entity as well. You'll see how this works in just a bit.

The relationship between a database pointer and an entity database is shown in Figure 8.4.

Database pointers are slower than iterators, because you must look up the entity in the database when you want to use it. This may seem like a bad thing at first, but it's very safe this way. Iterators can be invalidated if the database moves around too much (maps rearrange their structure when things are added and deleted), but a database pointer is *always* valid, as long as the database knows how to get it.

Unfortunately, C++ is a language that has inherited a lot of ancient quirks from C. One problem in particular is *circular dependencies*. If you are unfamiliar with C++, you can learn the details of the C/C++ compiler in Appendix C, which is on the CD.

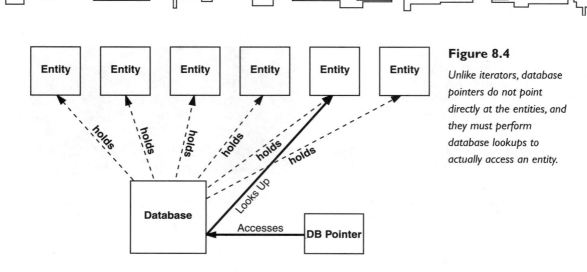

Figure 8.4

Unlike iterators, database pointers do not point directly at the entities, and they must perform database lookups to actually access an entity.

The problem is that there are lots of circular dependencies connected with the database classes. Take, for example, players and rooms.

The player database needs access to the Player class. The player database pointer class needs access to the player database. Examine Figure 8.5 for a moment.

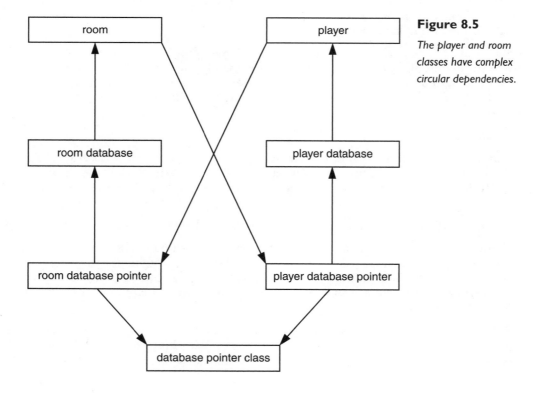

Figure 8.5

The player and room classes have complex circular dependencies.

The relationship among rooms, players, their databases, and a database pointer class is quite complicated, and you might not even see the problem at first. Database pointers are extremely generic concepts, and as such, I would really like to implement them as a generic template class. Because of this, I've created the generic `databasepointer` class, which I will show you in a little bit. First I want to show you how I organized the files so that there are no circular dependencies. These are shown within Figure 8.6.

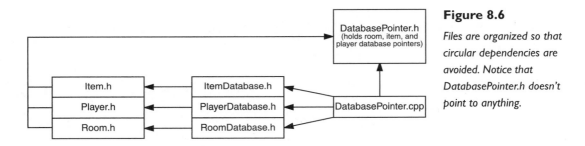

Figure 8.6

Files are organized so that circular dependencies are avoided. Notice that DatabasePointer.h doesn't point to anything.

The important thing to note is that the DatabasePointer.h file doesn't have any links to other files; it doesn't include any of the other files shown in Figure 8.6. You'll see how this all works out.

Before Templates, There Were Macros

Unfortunately, despite the best laid plans of mice and men, templates just won't work for database pointers. The problem is that you can't mix cyclic dependencies with templates— it's not going to happen in C++. Sure, you may get some compilers to do it for you, but those compilers aren't following the standard, and you really shouldn't count on that behavior.

Before we had templates and all of the great things they added, programmers had to rely on macros. If you've been properly taught C++, you might be feeling some shivers right now, but let me tell you; there is a time for ideals, and there is a time for reality. You could spend weeks and weeks trying to figure out how to get this done "the proper way," or you could put together a quick macro in a few minutes and watch it work immediately. It's up to you to determine which way is more "proper." I would wager that sometimes it's more proper to make a little hack to save yourself tons of wasted effort.

So the MUD has a macro named DATABASEPOINTER, which declares the functions of a database pointer (some of which are inlined), and another macro named DATABASEPOINTERIMPL, which contains the implementations of the functions.

Here is the declaration macro:

```
#define DATABASEPOINTER( pt, t )                    \
class t;                                            \
class pt {                                          \
```

```
public:                                                  \
    pt( entityid p_id = 0 )                              \
        : m_id( p_id ) {}                                \
                                                         \
    pt& operator=( entityid p_id ) {                     \
        m_id = p_id;                                     \
        return *this;                                    \
    }                                                    \
                                                         \
    operator entityid() {                                \
        return m_id;                                     \
    }                                                    \
    operator t*();                                       \
                                                         \
    t& operator*();                                      \
    t* operator->();                                     \
                                                         \
    entityid m_id;                                       \
};                                                       \
                                                         \
inline ostream& operator<<( ostream& s, const pt& p ) { \
    s << p.m_id;                                         \
    return s;                                            \
}                                                        \
                                                         \
inline istream& operator>>( istream& s, pt& p ) {        \
    s >> p.m_id;                                         \
    return s;                                            \
}
```

The declaration macro will take two parameters: the name of the pointer (pt) class, and the name of the entity class (t). For example, to create a database pointer class named player that retrieves Player entities (note the capitalization of the "p"), you would create it like this:

```
DATABASEPOINTER( player, Player );
```

The classes created by the macro are essentially just wrappers around a 32-bit entityid, which makes it lightweight, yet powerful.

You may notice that some functions are inline, yet others are not. There is a good reason for this: The inline functions don't need to access the database in any form—they simply operate on the m_id variable. The functions that aren't inline *do* access the database. This proves to be a problem, however. Because the database pointer header file can't include the database header files (circular dependency errors!), it can't know about the database classes. Because this file doesn't know about the database classes, you can't make inline functions access database functions; therefore, they must be placed within the .cpp file instead.

The first two functions—the constructor and the assignment operator—are simple and just assign the parameter to the m_id variable of the classes, so I don't need to show you their code.

Conversion Operators

There are two *conversion operators*: operator entityid and operator t*. Conversion operators are an interesting feature of C++ that allows the compiler to treat a datatype as another type when needed.

The first conversion operator allows you to use database pointers just as if they were entityids. Here's an example of using a database pointer as an entityid:

```
// this code assumes the existence of an "item" database pointer class:
item ptr = 10;
entityid i = ptr;      // i is now 10.
ptr = ptr + 10;        // ptr.m_id is now 20.
```

See, isn't that cool? For (almost) all intents and purposes, database pointers are entityids with added functions.

There's a reason I've included the operator t* function, which is the other conversion operator. This operator would allow you to treat a database pointer like a pointer to the entity you want to access. For example, you can treat an item database pointer as a pointer to the actual entity type, Item*.

I did this because of the two entity functors I showed you earlier: matchentityfull and matchentity. To save you lots of effort, these two functors can operate on containers holding just pointers to entities. But database pointers aren't exactly pointers; they're classes. If you didn't have this conversion operator, and you had a vector of items, you couldn't use it in conjunction with the matchentity or matchentityfull functors, because they expect an Entity*, and this container holds items.

CAUTION

I said "almost" because there are times when database pointers don't act like entityids. That's my fault; I'm lazy. You see, database pointers don't support the operators +=, -=, *=, /=, and so forth. To support those operators, you'd need to actually write them into the macro manually. The other option, of course, is to write things such as : ptr - ptr + 10;. The compiler accepts that, because it tries adding ptr with 10, and to do so, it converts ptr into an entityid automatically using the conversion operator, and then assigns the new value to ptr using the assignment operator. So just watch out for that.

This is where the conversion operator comes in. (This is actually within the `DATABASEPOINTERIMPL` macro.)

```
pt::operator t*() {                                        \
    if( m_id == 0 )                                        \
        return 0;                                          \
    return &( db::get( m_id ) );                           \
}
```

This looks up the ID within the database and returns the address of the `Entity` that it found. If the ID is 0, the value 0 is returned. This is done because performing lookup on a nonexistent ID can cause the program to crash—a bad thing.

Now you can freely use any STL container of database pointers with any of the functors.

Dereference Operators

There are two operators within the macro that dereference the database pointer classes the macro creates, and allow you to use them just like pointers to entities (kind of like STL iterators). Sound cool? I think so, too.

The two functions are also declared inside of the `DATABASEPOINTERIMPL` macro:

```
t& pt::operator*() {                                       \
    return db::get( m_id );                                \
}                                                          \
                                                           \
t* pt::operator->() {                                      \
    return &( db::get( m_id ) );                           \
}                                                          \
```

CAUTION

Remember that database pointers have a hidden overhead that regular pointers don't have. In this case, every call to the pointer conversion operator is an O(log n) algorithm on the map-based databases, as opposed to O(1) for regular pointers, so any O(n) STL algorithm you call on an array of database pointers automatically converts into an O(n log n) algorithm. For this reason, it is advisable to only use STL algorithms on relatively small containers of database pointers.

These functions perform a lookup of the entity in the database and return references or pointers to that item. You can use these functions just as you would access any iterator within the game:

```
// this uses the "item" class again; I haven't shown it to you yet
// but it's just a regular database pointer
item iptr = 10;          // make it point to item 10
iptr->Name() = "Sword";  // change item 10's name to "Sword"
Item& i = *iptr;         // make it a reference to item 10.
```

This way, you are not required to make your code look really ugly by performing manual database lookups; you let the pointer class take care of it instead.

Stream Operators

This isn't a huge topic, but I just want to mention it. Each of the database pointer classes has two stream operators (operator<< and operator>>), which simply stream the ID of the pointer to and from iostreams.

Defining the Macros

I showed you earlier how to declare a DATABASEPOINTER macro, but let me show you an example again:

```
DATABASEPOINTER( player, Player )
```

These definitions must be placed within the DatabasePointer.h file.

On the other hand, you declare the DATABASEPOINTERIMPL macros in the .cpp file, like this:

```
DATABASEPOINTERIMPL( player, Player, PlayerDatabase )
```

This macro takes three parameters: the name of the database pointer class, the name of the entity class, and the name of the database that holds those items.

Logs

Right now I'm going to sidestep the main path of this chapter to tell you about the log classes. SimpleMUD has two text logs: the user log, and the error log. I showed you the logging capabilities in Chapter 4, "The Basic Library," using the BasicLib::Logger class, and the text-file version named BasicLib::TextLog. SimpleMUD uses global text logs. The definitions for them can be found in the files Demos\Chapter08\Demo08-01\SimpleMUD\SimpleMUDLogs.h and .cpp.

Because the logs are meant to be globals, I need to declare them as extern in the header file like this:

```
extern TextLog ERRORLOG;
extern TextLog USERLOG;
```

Any part of your program that uses these files can include the .h file, and you can use either of the logs that you like.

However, you still need to construct the logs somewhere, so this is done in the .cpp file:

```
TextLog ERRORLOG( "logs/errors.log", "Error Log", true, true );
TextLog USERLOG( "logs/users.log", "User Log", true, true );
```

Remember the parameters for the constructor. The first parameter is the file name of the log, the second is the name of the log, and the two Booleans determine if you want to datestamp and timestamp every entry in the log. As you can see from the previous code segment, the logs are stored in a subdirectory named "logs", and the files are named "errors.log" and "users.log".

Whenever errors occur in the game, it is advisable to log them to the error log, and user actions such as logging on and off should be logged into the user log.

Attributes

As I mentioned in Chapter 7, "Designing the SimpleMUD," players and items will have groupings of attributes. In a simple MUD such as this, you could make an individual variable for each attribute within a player or item, but that gets to be unmanageable at a certain level. Whenever you add stuff, your code becomes more and more messy. You can find all the attribute-related stuff in the Attributes.h file.

Attribute Class

Instead of making an individual variable for each attribute within a player or an item, I've decided that it's easier to create an enumeration:

```
enum Attribute {
    STRENGTH       = 0,
    HEALTH         = 1,
    AGILITY        = 2,
    MAXHITPOINTS   = 3,
    ACCURACY       = 4,
    DODGING        = 5,
    STRIKEDAMAGE   = 6,
    DAMAGEABSORB   = 7,
    HPREGEN        = 8
};
const int NUMATTRIBUTES = 9;
```

Those are all nine of the attributes of players and items, including the first three base attributes, as I showed you in Chapter 7. There's also an array of strings called ATTRIBUTESTRINGS, which contains the names of all the attributes; I don't show them here.

There are also these two functions:

```
Attribute GetAttribute( string p_attr );
string GetAttributeString( Attribute p_attr );
```

I'm not going to bother showing you the code, because it's pretty boring; it only converts a string to an Attribute, and vice versa.

Attribute Sets

When creating the item and player classes, it would make sense to give them an array of attributes. However, it would make even more sense to create a custom class whose only purpose is to group a collection of attributes together. For this purpose, I've created the AttributeSet class, which will act like an array, and provide other basic features as well:

```
class AttributeSet {
public:
    AttributeSet();
    int& operator[]( int p_attr );
    friend ostream& operator<<( ostream& p_stream, const AttributeSet& a );
    friend istream& operator>>( istream& p_stream, AttributeSet& a );
protected:
    int m_attributes[NUMATTRIBUTES];
};
```

Simply put, the constructor loops through all the attributes in the m_attributes array, and clears them to zero. You can use the operator[] to treat an attribute set just like an array:

```
AttributeSet s;
s[HEALTH] = 10;
s[STRENGTH] = 9;
```

It's the little things like that which make your code so much easier to read and understand.

You may have noticed that attribute sets can also be inserted into and extracted from streams using the standard operators << and >>. The main reason for this is that, for file storage, all the file formats I'm using for SimpleMUD are going to be plain text ASCII files. I'll touch on the reasons more when I show you the Item and Player classes. Here's the code for the first stream function:

```
ostream& operator<<( ostream& p_stream, const AttributeSet& a ) {
    for( int i = 0; i < NUMATTRIBUTES; i++ ) {
        p_stream << "[" << GetAttributeString( (Attribute)i ) <<
                    "] " << a.m_attributes[i] << "\n";
    }
    return p_stream;
}
```

The function loops through all the attributes within the set, and prints within square brackets first the name, and then the value. The output of this function looks something like this:

```
[STRENGTH] 10
<snip>
[HPREGEN] 5
```

And so on. I didn't paste all nine attributes, just the first and last ones to save on space. Likewise, here's the stream extraction function:

```
istream& operator>>( istream& p_stream, AttributeSet& a ) {
    std::string temp;
    for( int i = 0; i < NUMATTRIBUTES; i++ ) {
        p_stream >> temp >> a.m_attributes[i];
    }
    return p_stream;
}
```

As you can see from the function, there is a temporary string named `temp`. This is used to "eat" the labels of each attribute. Whenever the line [STRENGTH] 10 is read in, the [STRENGTH] part is read into `temp` and discarded, and the value 10 is read into the current attribute. Because this function ignores line labels, the order of the attributes within a stream *must* remain in the same order as they were originally printed. The line labels are there primarily to help users of the system figure out the meanings of the values.

Items

Between the `Entity`, `EntityDatabase`, `EntityDatabaseVector`, `databasepointer`, `Attribute`, and `AttributeSet` classes, there was quite a bit of code. The good news is that because I spent so much time developing the groundwork, the job of developing the rest of the game suddenly becomes easier. You'll see how this works throughout the rest of this chapter.

Now that the groundwork is done, it's time to move on to the first type of entity that will be used within the game—items.

Item Class

Items, as I described in Chapter 7, are simply physical objects that you can pick up and carry around in the game. Since items will have names and IDs, they are inherited from the `Entity` class.

Item Types

As I also mentioned in Chapter 7, items come in three flavors: weapons, armor, and healing items. Because of this, I created an enumerated type (found in Attributes.h):

```
enum ItemType {
    WEAPON,
    ARMOR,
    HEALING
};
```

In addition to this enumeration, I've created two functions to help convert types to strings and vice versa. First is the `GetItemType` function, which gets a type from a string, and the second is the `GetItemTypeString` function, which does the opposite. These functions make reading and writing enumerations to streams easier and make your output files more legible. However, since the way they work isn't that important to MUD programming in general, I hope you'll forgive me if I move along without showing you the code. Don't worry though; you can see it if you're still interested in the Attributes.h file on the CD.

Money: It's What I Want

For SimpleMUD, I use a simple typedef to represent the money type:

```
typedef unsigned long int money;
```

This uses an unsigned 32-bit integer, so that means that the money type can represent anything from 0 to 4 billion dollars. This can be changed at any later date if you wish.

Item Attributes

Items have two types of attributes: the attributes of the item itself, and the attribute modifiers, which will be added to a player's attributes when that particular item is used.

Here's a skeleton of the Item class, with the function declarations removed:

```
class Item : public Entity {
    ItemType m_type;
    int m_min;
    int m_max;
    int m_speed;
    money m_price;
    AttributeSet m_attributes;
};
```

Obviously, each item has its own type to identify to the game what kind of item it is. Based on the item type, the three variables m_min, m_max, and m_speed have different meanings. Table 8.4 lists the uses for each of those attributes for each item type.

Table 8.4   Item Attribute Uses

Type	m_min	m_max	m_speed
Weapon	min damage caused	max damage caused	pause between swings in seconds
Armor	not used	not used	not used
Healing	min damage healed	max damage healed	not used

In addition to those three attributes, every item also has a money type, representing how much money the item is worth, and an AttributeSet, corresponding to the nine attributes that players have. This attribute set contains *deltas*, which determine how much of each attribute to add or subtract to a player whenever that item is used.

For example, a weapon with an accuracy attribute of 10 would add 10 to the player's accuracy whenever that weapon was armed and remove 10 whenever it was disarmed.

Writing and Reading Items from Disk

I haven't really discussed how items are read and written to disk yet.

When designing a MUD, you have many options. Many older MUDs store their data in binary format, since in binary form data is packed tightly, and thus uses less memory. (For example, a 32-bit integer in binary always takes up 4 bytes, but a 32-bit integer in ASCII may take up to 10 bytes.) More complex MUDs may even offload the disk storage capabilities into a dedicated database server, such as a SQL server of some sort.

For SimpleMUD, you don't need anything fancy. It's going to stay nice and simple. Since I don't have room to introduce editor tools to you, I'm going to use the simplest and most editable format available—plain ASCII text files.

There's a lot of hype going around about XML data storage, but XML is far too complex for what I need; instead, I'm just going to use a simple line-by-line approach to store data. Each item will be defined as a seven-line string of ASCII text, in which each line contains a single attribute. Each line is composed of two things: the name of the attribute, contained within square brackets, and the value of the attribute.

Here's an example of an item string:

```
[ID]            1
[NAME]          Knife
[TYPE]          WEAPON
[MIN]           2
[MAX]           4
[SPEED]         2
[PRICE]         10
[STRENGTH]      0
[HEALTH]        0
[AGILITY]       0
[MAXHITPOINTS]  0
[ACCURACY]      10
[DODGING]       0
[STRIKEDAMAGE]  0
[DAMAGEABSORB]  0
[HPREGEN]       0
```

Since most of the writing capabilities of C++ files depend on using iostreams, I've decided to keep the tradition, and let items use iostreams as well. Because of this, items have the standard stream extraction operator, but not stream insertion, since there is no need to write items back to disk:

```
friend istream& operator>>( istream& p_stream, Item& i );
```

There is no stream insertion operator, simply because there is no need for one. Items are never changed in the game; therefore, they never need to be written to disk.

Here's the function:

```
inline istream& operator>>( istream& p_stream, Item& i ) {
    std::string temp;
    p_stream >> temp >> std::ws;    std::getline( p_stream, i.m_name );
    p_stream >> temp >> temp;       i.m_type = GetItemType( temp );
    p_stream >> temp >> i.m_min;
    p_stream >> temp >> i.m_max;
    p_stream >> temp >> i.m_speed;
    p_stream >> temp >> i.m_price;
    p_stream >> i.m_attributes;
    return p_stream;
}
```

As you can see, the code is mostly straightforward. For each attribute, the line label is read into temp and ignored; then the real attribute is read into the appropriate variable.

There are two things to pay attention to, however: When reading in an item name, instead of streaming the name using operator>>, I use the std::getline function. This is important, because item names may have spaces in them, such as "Chainmail Armor". If you used the standard operator>>, it would just read the first word, which isn't what I want. Luckily, the std::getline function exists and reads in everything in the stream up until a newline character. Also note that the previous line pipes the stream into the std::ws object, which simply "eats" all the whitespace leading up to the next word. This is essential because the std::getline function doesn't do that automatically for you.

> **NOTE**
>
> There is one limitation you should know about when extracting items: the attribute labels in the stream mean absolutely nothing to the computer; they are there only for you, so that when you open the file in a text editor, you know which attribute means what. The computer, when loading in items, ignores the labels within the brackets, and assumes that the items within the stream are in the appropriate order.

You should notice the two lines that read in the type of the item. Within the text file, as you saw when I listed a sample item printout, the item type is an actual word, like "weapon" or "armor". Because of this, I need to make use of the GetItemType function to convert a string into an ItemType enumeration.

Finally, you may have noticed that the function doesn't load in the ID of the item; instead, the item database class is relied on to do that, which you will see a little later on.

Item Function Listing

Table 8.5 lits all the functions in the Item class, omitting those inherited from the Entity class.

Table 8.5   Item Functions

Function	Purpose
Item()	Constructs an item with "invalid" values
ItemType& Type()	Returns the type of the item
int& Min()	Returns the min attribute
int& Max()	Returns the max attribute
int& Speed()	Returns the speed attribute
money& Price()	Returns the price of the item
int& GetAttr(int attr)	Returns a reference to player attribute 'attr'

As you can see, all the functions are simply accessor functions; items have little need for anything else. The GetAttr function works with the standard Attribute labels, like so:

```
Item i;
i.GetAttr( HEALTH ) = 10;
int s = i.GetAttr( STRENGTH );
```

And so it continues. This saves you the trouble of writing different accessors for each attribute.

Item Database

The item database is an incredibly simple class, because most of the work has already been accomplished with the EntityDatabase class. There are only a few things I need to do to make a fully functional item database class. You can find the class within the ItemDatabase.h and .cpp files on the CD.

File Storage

The first issue you need to tackle is the question of file storage: How will you store items to disk? Previously, I deemed it optimal for a simple MUD like this to use ASCII text to store data, since you can open text files in any text editor, without expending significant time making a custom editor for items.

So now you need to figure out how items will actually be stored. When analyzing the game, you may notice that items are just static objects and really should not be modified. Therefore, you can assume that the MUD won't be modifying items, and there's really no need to be able to write them back out to disk while the MUD is running.

Because of this, I've decided to store all the items in one large text file: /items/items.itm. When the database starts up, it loads all the items from this file.

Class Definition

Here's the definition for the ItemDatabase class, which is located within the ItemDatabase.h file:

```
class ItemDatabase : public EntityDatabase<Item> {
public:
    static bool Load();
};
```

As you can see, an ItemDatabase is simply an EntityDatabase that stores Items. Additionally, it has one new function: the Load function, which loads the database from the /items/ items.itm file.

Since all the database classes are meant to be static, the Load function is static as well. This means you can call it like this within the game:

```
ItemDatabase::Load();
```

Also, there's one more note I should make: Since the m_map member inside the EntityDatabase class is static, it *must* be defined in a .cpp file somewhere, or else you'll end up with linker errors when you compile. So here's the definition:

```
std::map<entityid, Item> ItemDatabase::m_map;
```

You must do this for every class you create that inherits from EntityDatabase.

Loading the Database

Finally, here's the function to load the database from the /items/items.itm file:

```
bool ItemDatabase::Load() {
    std::ifstream file( "items/items.itm" );
    entityid id;
    std::string temp;
    while( file.good() )  {
        file >> temp >> id;
        m_map[id].ID() = id;
        file >> m_map[id] >> std::ws;
        USERLOG.Log( "Loaded Item: " + m_map[id].Name() );
    }
    return true;
}
```

The function basically opens up the item file, and tries to read in item after item until there is nothing more to read. The first thing the function does within the loop is read in the ID of the item.

Once I have the ID, I use the `std::map::operator[]` function to look up the item with that ID. At this point, one of two things can happen: If an item with the ID already exists, its ID is simply overwritten with the same value that I just read in from disk (essentially accomplishing nothing). If the item doesn't exist, `operator[]` has a little side effect that I rely on: A new item with the given ID is created and inserted into the map automatically, and its ID is set to what was just loaded in. Then, the rest of the item is loaded in from the file, and all the whitespace after the item entry in the file is eaten up using the `std::ws` stream modifier.

The final act is to notify the userlog that an item was loaded.

Item Database Pointers

Finally, when accessing items within the item database, it's usually a good idea to use a database pointer, modeled around the database pointer macros I showed you earlier.

This simply requires a macro definition (which is located in the DatabasePointer.h file):

```
DATABASEPOINTER( item, Item )
```

Now you can use `item` throughout the game (notice that "i" is lowercase) just like a pointer into the `ItemDatabase`, as I described earlier. You can use it like this:

```
item i = 10;
i->Dodge() = 20;
```

And so on.

Populating Your Realm with Players

Now that you've got all the classes dealing with items in the game, it's time to move on to a more complicated topic: the classes dealing with players. Players represent any person in the game who actually connects to it, as opposed to computer-controlled entities, which are a separate concept.

Player Class

Before I figure out how I'm going to store the player data to disk, I first need to know *what* data I need to store to disk. All this data is, of course, going to be stored within the `Player` class, which is found within Player.h and .cpp.

Player Variables

The class contains all the attributes I discussed in Chapter 7 and will be a child of the Entity class. In addition to having the nine standard attributes, players have variables representing non-savable session info, as well as other information. Here's a listing of the data:

```
const int PLAYERITEMS = 16;
class Player : public Entity {
    // Player information
    string m_pass;
    PlayerRank m_rank;

    // Player attributes
    int m_statpoints;
    int m_experience;
    int m_level;
    room m_room;
    money m_money;
    int m_hitpoints;
    AttributeSet m_baseattributes;
    AttributeSet m_attributes;
    BasicLib::sint64 m_nextattacktime;

    // Player inventory
    item m_inventory[PLAYERITEMS];
    int m_items;
    int m_weapon;
    int m_armor;

    // Non-savable info
    Connection<Telnet>* m_connection;
    bool m_loggedin;
    bool m_active;
    bool m_newbie;
};
```

In addition to a name and ID inherited from the Entity class, players have a password and a rank. The ranks correspond to the same ranks defined in Chapter 7, and the next section shows you the enumeration used to define the ranks.

There are seven extra player attributes in addition to the nine defined within the AttributeSet class. Those seven attributes represent a player's statpoints, level, experience, room number, money, current hitpoints, and the next time he may attack. (This last one won't be used until Chapter 10, "Enemies, Combat, and the Game Loop.") You may note that these attributes are not included within the AttributeSet class. There's a reason for this: Items have attribute sets, and whenever you use an item, all the attributes in the item class are added to the player's attributes. However, there are certain stats that should never be modified by an item, and those attributes are kept outside of the attribute set.

The class has two player sets: m_baseattributes and m_attributes. The first set contains all the "base" attributes, or permanent values. Whenever you use an item, these are the stats that are modified and saved to disk. The other set is the "dynamic" values—values that are calculated by the game, based on your level. A player's real values are calculated by adding the values within the two sets. Figure 8.7 shows the representation of the two attribute sets. To get a player's actual attributes, the values within the base and dynamic sets are added to form the final result.

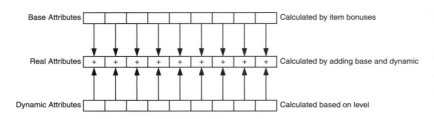

Figure 8.7

The relationship between the two sets of attribute data, and the third "virtual" attribute set.

There is one datatype in there that you may not be familiar with—room. A room is basically a database pointer pointing to a Room class. Because I haven't covered the map system for the MUD yet, you have no idea what a Room or a room is yet, so this is going to cause a minor problem. However, I'm going to stipulate right here that all rooms within the game also use entityids to be uniquely identified, and that the room class acts like a databasepointer. So for now, I temporarily inserted this line near the top of the Player.h file:

```
typedef entityid room; // REMOVE THIS LATER
```

I'll remove this in the next chapter, when I cover the map system.

The player's inventory is managed by four variables: an array of item database pointers, the number of items within that array, and the indexes of the player's current weapon and armor. Whenever an index in the array contains a zero, that means there's no item in that slot; any other value is the ID of the item the player is carrying in that slot. Weapon and armor index values of -1 mean that you don't have a weapon or armor armed.

Each player has four variables that are temporary and are only valid per "session"; therefore, those variables won't be saved to disk. They are Connection<Telnet>*, which represents the player's connection, and three bools that indicate if the player is logged in, active, or a newbie.

"Activity" isn't something that I've discussed before. Throughout the game, players may temporarily "leave the realm" to accomplish a task such as editing their preferences or statistics, but they are still connected. When they are in these states, the players are said to be "inactive," meaning that the game won't send the players chat messages, and so on. I'll show you more about this later on in the chapter.

The "newbie" Boolean tells the game that the player is new to the game, and will be taken to the character-training screen when he logs in. You'll see how this works when I show you the login process.

Player Ranks

The `PlayerRank` type is defined as an enumerated type like this:

```
enum PlayerRank {
    Regular,
    God,
    Admin
};
```

If you'll recall from Chapter 7, regular, god, and admin are the three player ranks. Like the `ItemType` and `Attribute` enumerations I covered before, `PlayerRank` also has two helper functions that allow you to convert ranks to and from strings (`PlayerRank GetRank( string )` and `string( GetRankString( PlayerRank )`. Like before, their code isn't important, so I won't bother pasting it here.

Directly Modifiable Attributes

Throughout the game, you're going to need ways of modifying certain attributes. However, you don't want to just give access to all the attributes to anyone who feels free to change them; this could rapidly destabilize your game. For example, if some function were to randomly add 10 levels to a player (purely by accident, of course *wink*), you could get into some serious problems, since the player will not have all the stat points he should have earned by gaining those levels. Therefore, you need to restrict access to only those attributes that should be changed without side effects.

All directly modifiable attributes use a single function as their accessor. All these functions are inline and return a reference to the attribute, like this:

```
inline money& Money() { return m_money; }
```

As shown, you can either read or change variables using the function, like this:

```
Player p;
p.Money() = 100;          // modify
int m = p.Money();        // read
```

The directly modifiable attributes are as follows: `m_pass`, `m_rank`, `m_connection`, `m_loggedin`, `m_active`, `m_newbie`, `m_statpoints`, `m_experience`, `m_room`, `m_money`, and `m_nextattacktime`.

Level Functions

Several functions deal with players' levels. These functions are mainly used for informational purposes, but there's one function that performs the task of "training" a player to the next level if he has enough experience to merit the training.

Informational Level Functions

First and foremost is the NeedForLevel() function. This simply determines how many experience points a player needs for a specific level:

```
inline int Player::NeedForLevel( int p_level ) {
    return (int)(100 * ( pow( 1.4, p_level - 1 ) - 1 ));
}
```

This uses the formula I showed you from Chapter 7. You should note that this function is static, which means that you don't need a specific player instance to call it. You can simply use Player::NeedForLevel(5) to find out how many experience points are needed for level 5.

The next function determines how many more experience points a player needs to advance to the next level:

```
int Player::NeedForNextLevel() {
    return NeedForLevel( m_level + 1 ) - m_experience;
}
```

The function simply subtracts the experience you have from the experience you need for the next level. Because of this, the result may be positive (you need more experience) or negative (you have enough experience for the next level).

The final informational function is the Level function, which returns a player's current level:

```
inline int Level() { return m_level; }
```

Training

The last level function is the Train function, which is executed whenever your player trains inside a training room. It returns a Boolean, which tells you if the player trained to the next level successfully. Whenever you train, you gain more stat points and your attributes are recalculated. Here's the function:

```
bool Player::Train() {
    if( NeedForNextLevel() <= 0 ) {
        m_statpoints += 2;
        m_baseattributes[MAXHITPOINTS] += m_level;
        m_level++;
        RecalculateStats();
        return true;
    }
    return false;
}
```

If you don't need more experience to go to the next level, you're awarded two stat points, your base maximum hitpoints are increased by the value of your current level, your level is increased by one, and your stats are recalculated.

If you don't have enough experience to go to the next level, false is returned, and nothing is changed.

Attribute Functions

Attribute functions can be separated into four groups: the recalculation function, hitpoint functions, attribute set functions, and general accessors. These function groups deal with all the attributes that the modifiable-attribute accessor functions didn't take care of already.

Recalculating Stats

You've already seen the function to recalculate stats used before, inside the Train function. Essentially, the function goes through all the dynamic attributes (m_attributes) and recalculates them based on your level or other attributes that may have changed.

```
void Player::RecalculateStats() {
    m_attributes[MAXHITPOINTS] = (int)
        10 + ( m_level * ( GetAttr( HEALTH ) / 1.5 ) );
    m_attributes[HPREGEN] =
        ( GetAttr( HEALTH ) / 5 ) + m_level;
    m_attributes[ACCURACY] = GetAttr( AGILITY ) * 3;
    m_attributes[DODGING] = GetAttr( AGILITY ) * 3;
    m_attributes[DAMAGEABSORB] = GetAttr( STRENGTH ) / 5;
    m_attributes[STRIKEDAMAGE] = GetAttr( STRENGTH ) / 5;
    // make sure the hitpoints don't overflow if your max goes down:
    if( m_hitpoints > GetAttr( MAXHITPOINTS ) )
        m_hitpoints = GetAttr( MAXHITPOINTS );

    if( Weapon() != 0 )
        AddDynamicBonuses( Weapon() );
    if( Armor() != 0 )
        AddDynamicBonuses( Armor() );
}
```

Essentially the Train function uses the formulas I showed you in Chapter 7 to calculate the values of six of your attributes. Pay attention to the last four lines of code, which call a helper called AddDynamicBonuses; essentially this takes the bonuses of a player's current weapon and armor and adds them to his stats. I haven't gone over player item functions yet, but this is simple enough to understand.

This functionality is contained within a single function for a good reason. MUDs were designed to be tinkered with, and as such, they should be designed with the utmost flexibility. Whenever you change your strength, it's not a good practice to manually change the DAMAGEABSORB and STRIKEDAMAGE attributes within the function that changed the strength; this can lead to errors. It is always better to keep your formulas in one place throughout the entire game.

Also, you could end up later on making a certain core attribute affect another attribute, so it's good to have one place in the code that can take care of all changes.

It is important to note that the three core attributes (strength, health, and agility) aren't affected by any of the other six attributes, and don't have dynamic values. It is also important to note that six non-core attributes do not affect other attributes either. If you *do* end up making the attributes affect each other, you may end up introducing bugs into your code, depending on the order that your stats are recalculated.

Hitpoint Functions

There are two functions dealing with hitpoints:

```
inline int HitPoints() { return m_hitpoints; }

void Player::AddHitpoints( int p_hitpoints ) {
    m_hitpoints += p_hitpoints;
    if( m_hitpoints < 0 )
        m_hitpoints = 0;
    if( m_hitpoints > GetAttr( MAXHITPOINTS ) )
        m_hitpoints = GetAttr( MAXHITPOINTS );
}
```

The HitPoints function is a simple nonmodifiable accessor, which simply returns the player's current hitpoints.

The AddHitpoints function is an "adding" function. I decided that instead of a direct "Set value" function, it would be easier to "add" to the value. For example, throughout the game, you're much more likely to be adding deltas to a player's hitpoints. The following code depicts the "set" versus "add" methods when adding 10 hitpoints to a player:

```
player.SetHitpoints( player.Hitpoints() + 10 ); // function doesn't exist
player.AddHitpoints( 10 );  // much easier to use
```

Obviously, the "add" method is far more usable. By the way, if you want to subtract, you can easily use a negative number in the parameters.

The modification function handles some extra work in addition to modifying the hitpoints. To keep the game consistent, the modification function makes sure that your hitpoints never go below 0 or above your maximum amount.

Attribute Functions

Four attribute functions operate on the nine attributes, which exist within AttributeSets. You've already seen one attribute used in a few functions: GetAttr.

```
inline int Player::GetAttr( int p_attr ) {
    int val = m_attributes[p_attr] + m_baseattributes[p_attr];
    if( p_attr == STRENGTH || p_attr == AGILITY || p_attr == HEALTH ) {
        if( val < 1 )     return 1;
    }
    return val;
}
```

As you saw earlier in Figure 8.7, this function generally adds the dynamic and the base values of an attribute together to obtain the final result. There is one special case that the

function needs to look out for, however. Officially, a character's core attributes should never fall below 1; the game has undefined behavior if that happens. The problem is that some people may accidentally use a bunch of "cursed" items that lower their base attributes below 1. So, to fix that, the "reported" value of any negative core attribute will be 1, no matter what its "real" value is.

You can also obtain the value of just a base attribute:

```
inline int Player::GetBaseAttr( int p_attr ) {
    return m_baseattributes[p_attr];
}
```

I haven't found a pressing need to have a function that retrieves the dynamic attribute values alone, but if a need ever arises, you can simply subtract the base value from the total value.

The final two functions are called SetBaseAttr and AddToBaseAttr, which, as you can imagine, set and add to any of your base attributes:

```
void Player::SetBaseAttr( int p_attr, int p_val ) {
    m_baseattributes[p_attr] = p_val;
    RecalculateStats();
}
void Player::AddToBaseAttr( int p_attr, int p_val ) {
    m_baseattributes[p_attr] += p_val;
    RecalculateStats();
}
```

Whenever one of your attributes is changed, these functions also automatically call RecalculateStats, to update the dynamically calculated stats of your player.

Other Attribute Functions

The remaining four attribute functions are the StatPoints, Experience, CurrentRoom, and Money functions. They return references so you can modify their values however you please.

Item Functions

There are several player functions that deal with items in your inventory. They range from simple accessors to helper functions, and to functions that physically modify your inventory.

Accessors

There are five item accessor functions. The first three of those are simple:

```
inline item GetItem( int p_index )    { return m_inventory[p_index]; }
inline int Items()                     { return m_items; }
inline int MaxItems()                  { return PLAYERITEMS; }
```

These functions return an item representing an item within your inventory, the number of items in your inventory, and the maximum number of items you can have in your inventory.

The other two accessors retrieve items representing your current weapon and armor:

```
inline item Player::Weapon() {
    if( m_weapon == -1 )              // if no weapon armed
        return 0;                     // return 0
    else
        return m_inventory[m_weapon]; // return item id
}
inline item Player::Armor() {
    if( m_armor == -1 )               // if no armor armed
        return 0;                     // return 0
    else
        return m_inventory[m_armor];  // return item id
}
```

The Weapon and Armor functions actually return an item (a database pointer object), pointing to the item that those variables represent. Obviously, if either of those variables is -1 (meaning that you don't have a weapon or an armor equipped), the item returned is equivalent to 0, which is the invalid ID for all entities.

Helpers

There are two item helper functions: one to add temporary item bonuses to a player, and one to add permanent item bonuses to your base attributes. You've already seen the first one used:

```
void Player::AddDynamicBonuses( item p_item ) {
    if( p_item == 0 )           // make sure item is valid
        return;
    Item& i = *p_item;          // get reference
    for( int x = 0; x < NUMATTRIBUTES; x++ )
        m_attributes[x] += i.GetAttr( x );  // add each attr
}
```

The first function loops through every index in your m_attributes attribute set (the temporary set, not the base set), and adds each attribute from the item. This function is only meant to be called from within RecalculateStats.

The other function adds permanent bonuses:

```
void Player::AddBonuses( item p_item ) {
    if( p_item == 0 )               // make sure item is valid first
        return;
    Item& itm = *p_item;            // get ref to actual Item object
    for( int i = 0; i < NUMATTRIBUTES; i++ ) {
        m_baseattributes[i] += itm.GetAttr( i ); // add each attribute
    }
    RecalculateStats();
}
```

This function calls RecalculateStats at the end, because you want to update everything after you've modified the attributes.

Inventory Modification

Two functions deal with modifying a player's inventory by physically adding or removing items to or from it. Since it's easier to add items than remove them, I'll show you the add function first:

```
bool Player::PickUpItem( item p_item ) {
    if( m_items < MaxItems() ) {
        item* itr = m_inventory;
        while( *itr != 0 )
            ++itr;
```

The previous code segment finds the first place in the inventory with an open slot. Since the function checks to make sure that you are carrying less than the maximum number of items, this loop *should* always find an open slot. (If it doesn't, you're in deep trouble as it is, so this function wouldn't be able to fix it anyway.) Here's the second half:

```
        *itr = p_item;
        m_items++;
        return true;
    }
    return false;
}
```

The item is inserted into your inventory, your item count goes up, and the function returns true. If there is no room, then nothing is inserted, and false is returned.

The next function removes an item from your inventory; the difference is that instead of passing in an item ID as the parameter, you're now passing the index of the item within your inventory array. So if you want to remove the item at index 0 (no matter what item ID it has), you'd pass in 0.

```
bool Player::DropItem( int p_index ) {
    if( m_inventory[p_index] != 0 ) {
        if( m_weapon == p_index )
            RemoveWeapon();
        if( m_armor == p_index )
            RemoveArmor();
        m_inventory[p_index] = 0;
        m_items--;
        return true;
    }
    return false;
}
```

This function first checks to see if 0 exists at the index you want to remove. If it does, you obviously cannot remove it (since it doesn't exist!), so false is returned. If a valid item exists at that index, however, the function continues.

If the item is either your current weapon or your current armor, it is removed from your person by calling the RemoveWeapon() or RemoveArmor() functions. Then a 0 is inserted into your inventory, and the number of items you are carrying is reduced.

Weapon and Armor Modification

You may recall from Chapter 7 that players can have a single weapon and a single piece of armor that is *armed*, which means that the player is holding a specific weapon or wearing a specific piece of armor. To deal with this, there are four functions; two of them *disarm* something, and two of them *arm* something. Since it's easier to remove stuff, I'll show you one of the removal functions first:

```
void Player::RemoveWeapon() {
    m_weapon = -1;
    RecalculateStats();
}
```

The RecalculateStats helper function is called after a weapon has been removed, so that the player's stats can be updated.

Arming an item is a little more difficult, because if an item is already armed, it must first be disarmed:

```
void Player::UseWeapon( int p_index ) {
    RemoveWeapon();
    m_weapon = p_index;
    RecalculateStats();
}
```

Again, the armor function is virtually identical, so I'm not going to paste it here.

Item Searching

At times within the game, you're going to need to search for items within a player's inventory based on a string name. Instead of forcing you to manually perform this kind of lookup, I've included a function that returns the index of an item that matches a name:

```
int Player::GetItemIndex( const std::string& p_name ) {
    item* i = double_find_if( m_inventory,
                              m_inventory + MaxItems(),
                              matchentityfull( p_name ),
                              matchentity( p_name ) );
    if( i == m_inventory + MaxItems() )
        return -1;
    return i - m_inventory;
}
```

You know, I really love this piece of code. It is incredibly beautiful. As you can see, m_inventory is just a regular array of items (which are databasepointers), but the double_find_if algorithm still works on it!

In any STL algorithm, a pointer to an array acts just like an iterator, so you can pass m_inventory as the starting iterator, and m_inventory + MaxItems() (which points to the address just past the end of the array) as the ending iterator.

The function performs a double-pass search on your inventory array, first trying to fully match the name, and then to partially match it. If there was no match, the function returns a pointer to the item inside the array that matches the name, or m_inventory + MaxItems(). If there was no match, -1 is returned, indicating that nothing was found inside the inventory.

Finally, if an item *was* found, a little bit of pointer math is used: i - m_inventory. Since both values are pointers, the difference between those two pointers is the number of indexes between them. So the function returns the index of an item within the inventory, matching your string.

Constructor

Like all good classes, the Player class has a constructor. This clears the variables inside of the class to values that represent a brand new player. Here's the code:

```
Player::Player() {
    m_pass = "UNDEFINED";
    m_rank = REGULAR;
    m_connection = 0;
    m_loggedin = false;
    m_active = false;
    m_newbie = true;
    m_experience = 0;
    m_level = 1;
    m_room = 0;
    m_money = 0;
    m_baseattributes[STRENGTH] = 1;
    m_baseattributes[HEALTH]   = 1;
    m_baseattributes[AGILITY]  = 1;
    m_statpoints = 18;
    m_items = 0;
    m_weapon = -1;
    m_armor = -1;
    RecalculateStats();
    m_hitpoints = GetAttr( MAXHITPOINTS );
}
```

As per Chapter 7, all three of your core stats start at 1, and the number of stat points you have is set to 18. Once all the core and base stats are set, all your other stats are set using the RecalculateStats() helper function.

The final step is to set your current hitpoints equal to your maximum hitpoints.

Communication

Obviously, since every connection in the game is tied to a player, and every player has a connection pointer, the Player class is going to be in charge of how the game communicates information back to the clients. For the Player class to be in charge, every player has a function named SendString, which sends a string of text to the player:

```
void Player::SendString( const std::string& p_string ) {
    // make sure the player is connected:
    if( Conn() == 0 ) {
        ERRORLOG.Log( "Trying to send string to player " +
                      Name() + " but player is not connected." );
        return;
    }
    // send the string plus a newline:
    Conn()->Protocol().SendString( *Conn(), p_string + newline );
    // send the statbar if the player is active:
    if( Active() ) { PrintStatbar(); }
}
```

This is just a simple function that helps manage what is sent to a player's connection. If a string is accidentally sent to a player who isn't connected, that event logs an error in the error log and returns without doing anything. Stuff like that shouldn't happen, but if it does, you don't want your program to unexpectedly crash and potentially lose data.

If the connection is active, the function uses its current Telnet protocol object to send the string to the user. It also tacks on a newline at the end.

Finally, if the player is active within the game, his status bar is also printed out to the connection, so that the player can see his vital stats whenever something happens in the game.

The status bar function is simple, but it is somewhat long; for that reason, I am going to refrain from showing it here. All you need to know is that the status bar function prints out the status of the player in a [current hitpoints/max hitpoints] format.

Functors

There are three player functors. Two of these are *predicates*, just like the matchentity and matchentityfull functors you saw earlier, and one is a *unary function*.

The two predicate player functors determine if a player is active or logged in. Here's the active functor:

```
struct playeractive {
    inline bool operator() ( Player& p_player ) {
        return p_player.Active();
    }
    inline bool operator() ( Player* p_player ) {
```

```
        return p_player != 0 && p_player->Active();
    }
};
```

As you can see, the active functor is structurally similar to the previous two, so I'm not going to spend any more time explaining it. The other predicate functor is playerloggedin, which simply checks if a player is logged in.

Designed to be used in STL algorithms such as std::for_each, the third functor performs an operation on every object in a collection:

```
struct playersend {
    const string& m_msg;
    playersend( const string& p_msg )
        : m_msg( p_msg ) { /* do nothing */ }

    void operator() ( Player& p ) {
        p.SendString( m_msg );
    }
    void operator() ( Player* p ) {
        if( p != 0 )  { p->SendString( m_msg ); }
    }
};
```

This functor simply sends a string to a player. Assuming you had an array of 16 players named parray, you could use it like this:

```
std::for_each( parray, parray + 16, playersend( "Hello!" ) );
```

File Functions

The final two functions load and save players to a specific file. Like the Item class, the Player class knows how to read and write to streams.

```
friend ostream& operator<<( ostream& p_stream, const Player& p );
friend istream& operator>>( istream& p_stream, Player& p );
```

The functions are structurally similar to the Item functions performing the same task: The stream insertion routine (operator<<) goes through every attribute, writes out its name in square brackets, and then writes out its value. The stream extraction routine assumes that all the variables are in a specific order, and ignores the attribute labels on each line.

Here's a sample of the insertion function:

```
inline ostream& operator<<( ostream& p_stream, const Player& p ) {
    p_stream << "[NAME] " << p.m_name << "\n";
    p_stream << "[PASS] " << p.m_pass << "\n";
```

The function continues in the same manner for these variables, in this order: m_name, m_pass, m_rank, m_statpoints, m_experience, m_level, m_room, m_money, m_hitpoints, m_nextattacktime, and m_baseattributes. The attack time variable deserves special mention, because VC6 doesn't support streaming 64-bit integers, so I need to use the BasicLib::insert function to insert the value:

```
p_stream << "[NEXTATTACKTIME] "; insert( p_stream, p.m_nextattacktime );
```

After that, the inventory is written out, and this is a special exception:

```
p_stream << "[INVENTORY] ";
for( int i = 0; i < p.MaxItems(); i++ ) {
    p_stream << p.m_inventory[i].m_id << " ";
}
p_stream << "\n";
```

For the inventory, all 16 items are written on the same line, with a single space separating each one. Remember: item database pointers know how to write themselves to streams. They write their ID number. Once those are written, the final two attributes are written: m_weapon, and m_armor.

The stream extraction routine is similar. Here are a few lines to give you a taste:

```
inline istream& operator>>( istream& p_stream, Player& p ) {
    std::string temp;
    p_stream >> temp >> std::ws;     std::getline( p_stream, p.m_name );
    p_stream >> temp >> p.m_pass;
    p_stream >> temp >> temp;        p.m_rank = GetRank( temp );
<SNIP>
    p_stream >> temp; extract( p_stream, p.m_nextattacktime );
    p_stream >> p.m_baseattributes;
    p_stream >> temp;
    p.m_items = 0;
    for( int i = 0; i < p.MaxItems(); i++ ) {
        p_stream >> p.m_inventory[i].m_id;
        if( p.m_inventory[i] != 0 )  { p.m_items++; }
    }
<SNIP>
    return p_stream;
}
```

I snipped out most of the uninteresting code and left the important parts. This code should remind you of the Item class extraction code, but there's one important addition. When a player's items are loaded, the function automatically counts how many items are in his inventory and updates its m_items variable. This saves you the trouble of writing the value out to disk and possibly introducing bugs into your program.

Player Function Listing

Table 8.6 shows a listing of all the Player class functions for easy reference.

Table 8.6   Player Functions

Function	Purpose
Player()	Constructs a new player.
int NeedForLevel(int level)	Calculates the experience total needed for 'level'.
int NeedForNextLevel()	Calculates how much more experience a player needs for the next level.
bool Train()	If a player has enough experience, this takes him to the next level and recalculates his stats. If not, `false` is returned.
int Level()	Returns a player's level.
void RecalculateStats()	Recalculates a player's stats.
void AddHitpoints(int h)	Adds 'h' to a player's hitpoints, but doesn't exceed the player's max hitpoints, or below 0.
int HitPoints()	Returns a player's current hitpoints.
int GetAttr(int attr)	Returns the full value of a player's attribute 'attr'.
int GetBaseAttr(int attr)	Returns the base value of a player's attribute 'attr'.
void SetBaseAttr(int attr, int val)	Sets the base value of 'attr' and recalculates stats.
void AddToBaseAttr(int attr, int val)	Adds 'val' to base value of 'attr' and recalculates stats.
int& StatPoints()	Returns the number of statpoints a player has.
int& Experience()	Returns the experience of a player.
room& CurrentRoom()	Returns a player's room number.
money& Money()	Returns a player's money.
sint64& NextAttackTime()	Returns the game time at which a player can next attack.
item GetItem(int index)	Returns the ID of the item at 'index' in inventory.
int Items()	Returns the number of items in inventory.
int MaxItems()	Returns the number of items a player can hold at max.

continues on next page

Table 8.6   Player Functions (continued)

Function	Purpose
item Weapon()	Returns the ID of current weapon.
item Armor()	Returns the ID of current armor.
void AddBonuses(item i)	Adds item i's bonuses to a player's base attributes.
void RemoveBonuses(item i)	Removes item i's bonuses from a player's base attributes.
bool PickUpItem(item i)	Makes the player attempt to add an item to his inventory. Returns `false` on failure (not enough room).
bool DropItem(int index)	Makes the player attempt to remove an item from his inventory. Returns `false` on failure (item doesn't exist).
void RemoveWeapon()	Removes the player's current weapon. (The weapon stays in inventory.)
void RemoveArmor()	Removes the player's current armor. (The armor stays in inventory.)
void UseWeapon(int index)	Attempts to use a weapon in a player's inventory.
void UseArmor(int index)	Attempts to use armor in a player's inventory.
int GetItemIndex(string name)	Attempts to find the index of the item with 'name'; returns -1 if not found.
string& Password()	Returns a player's password.
playerRank& Rank()	Returns a player's rank.
connection<Telnet>*& Conn()	Returns a player's connection pointer.
bool& LoggedIn()	Returns whether a player is logged in.
bool& Active()	Returns whether a player is active.
bool& Newbie()	Returns whether a player is a newbie.
void SendString(string str)	Sends 'str' to a player's connection.
void PrintStatBar()	Prints a player's statbar to a player's connection.

Disk Storage

Using text files to store data is a tricky task. The problem arises when you come across the fact that text data is constantly changing in size. For example, let's assume that you have 500 players in your game, all stored within one file, just as items are stored. One of the players who started at the beginning of the game, number 10 or so, had a health of 8 when the file was saved. Then he went into the game, played around a while, and gained three more health points, giving him 11. At that point, the player wanted to quit, and his character was saved back to disk.

But you have a problem. The player's health is now 2 characters long instead of just 1, so you need more room for that data. You're going to have to move everything after the player's position down one byte, and doing that within a file is a ridiculously slow and awkward operation.

With binary files, you usually don't have that problem; you know exactly how much space each number takes up, and you usually limit your strings to a certain length.

The most common solution for this problem is to use separate files for each player. That way, whenever a player is saved to disk, the program can safely overwrite the entire file, without worrying about affecting other files. This is the approach I'm taking. Players are stored within a subdirectory named /players/, and every player file is named "name.plr". So, JohnDoe's file would be stored in "/players/JohnDoe.plr".

Of course, it wouldn't be life without a little snag thrown in for good measure. The C++ standard doesn't define a method to retrieve file names from a specific directory; it actually just assumes you know what files you'll need. So you can't sort through the /players/ directory and pick out all .plr files and load them. Instead, you need another file, which contains the names of the player files within the directory. This file is also within the / players/ directory, and is called "players.txt". This file simply contains a list of all player files to be loaded when the game starts up, like so:

```
JohnDoe.plr
RonPenton.plr
```

And so on. Figure 8.8 shows this in action, as well as the organization of the files within the /player/ directory of the SimpleMUD. Players' names are stored within a file named "players.txt", and the files that store the players are named "player.plr", where "player" is the player's actual name.

Whenever a new player is added within the game, the software automatically appends the filename to the end of the players.txt file. The only downside is that if you create your own players, you must remember to add their file names to the text file, otherwise, the MUD has no idea that the players exist. Creating your own players isn't recommended, but as the runner of the MUD, you're certainly entitled to do so.

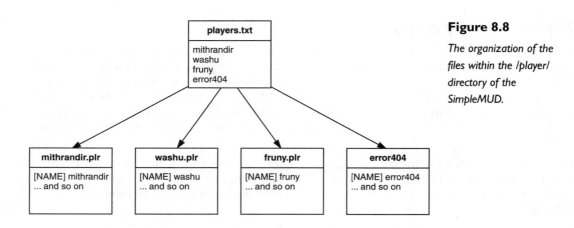

Figure 8.8

The organization of the files within the /player/ directory of the SimpleMUD.

PlayerDatabase

The database that stores players is just like the database that stores items. The `PlayerDatabase` is a child class of the `EntityDatabase` class and is stored in the PlayerDatabase.h and PlayerDatabase.cpp files.

In addition to loading players, the `PlayerDatabase` must know how to save the players back to disk.

Class Declaration

Here's the class declaration:

```
class PlayerDatabase : public EntityDatabase<Player> {
public:
    static bool Load();
    static bool Save();
    static bool AddPlayer( Player& p_player );
    static inline string PlayerFileName( const string& p_name );
    static void LoadPlayer( string p_name );
    static void SavePlayer( entityid p_player );
    static entityid LastID();
    static iterator findactive( const std::string& p_name );
    static iterator findloggedin( const std::string& p_name );
    static void Logout( entityid p_player );
};
```

As you can see, the class adds no new data and has functions to load/save the entire database, and to load/save individual players. Additionally, there's a function to add new players to the database, and a whole bunch of helper functions as well.

Loading the Database

The LoadDatabase function basically loads the player's players.txt file and attempts to load every player listed in the file. If the player already exists within the database, he is essentially overwritten. Here's the code:

```
bool PlayerDatabase::Load() {
    ifstream file( "players/players.txt" );
    string name;
    while( file.good() ) {              // while there are players
        file >> name >> std::ws;       // load in the player name
        LoadPlayer( name );            // call the LoadPlayer helper function
    }
    return true;
}
```

The players.txt file is read in. Then the player file names are read into name one by one (with whitespace "eaten" using std::ws), and loaded from disk into the database. This function uses the LoadPlayer helper function, which takes a player's name and loads that player from disk.

It may seem awkward to need a helper function for that, but it has to do with the way I've set up player file names. Examine the source code for the helper:

```
void PlayerDatabase::LoadPlayer( string p_name ) {
    entityid id;
    string temp;
    p_name = PlayerFileName( p_name );     // create the proper file name
    ifstream file( p_name.c_str() );       // open the file
    file >> temp >> id;                    // load the ID
    m_map[id].ID() = id;
    file >> m_map[id] >> std::ws;          // load the player from the file
    USERLOG.Log( "Loaded Player: " + m_map[id].Name() );
}
```

The C++ file stream classes cannot be constructed with an std::string as the file name. This is probably because file streams were created before the string class was standardized, but that doesn't matter: It creates a problem. File streams expect char*s for the file names, and you can't pass strings into the constructors. In addition, strings cannot be automatically converted into char*s using conversion operators. (Believe me—that's a whole other can of worms.) You have two options: You can use the antiquated C-style methods to create the proper file name, or you can accept this limitation and create a helper function to handle the loading for you. I'll get to that in a bit.

Like the ItemDatabase class, the database is responsible for loading the IDs and then loading in the actual player.

I'm a huge fan of code flexibility, and the player file name helper-function helps quite a bit. Some people may complain, "Ah, but there are 100 functions all over the place," but they've probably never worked on projects requiring constant change. I'll show you exactly what I mean in a bit. This loader function takes a player's name and loads that player in from disk into a `Player` object. You can spot the flexibility in the code by looking at the `PlayerFileName` function, which is another helper:

```
inline string PlayerFileName( string& p_name ) {
    return string( "players/" + p_name + ".plr" );
}
```

It's just a simple one-line function. "What the heck does that need a whole function for?" you may ask. Consider this: Throughout the database class, you may need to construct the file name of a player from his name. You could take the easy way out and put `"players/"` + `name` + `".plr"` in about 20 places in your code, or you could leave all the code that creates a file name in one central location. Imagine your embarrassment if you accidentally spell the directory name "player/", leaving the 's' out. How long would it take you to track that down or even to notice it in the first place? And what if, later on, you want to change the directory name to something else? You'd need to search for every instance in which you create a file name and change it. Blah! Too many bugs are created that way. Programming is the art of trying to avoid doing work. Trust me.

At this point, you might be saying, "But too many function calls make the game slow!" That's possible but unlikely. The function is *inlined*, which means that you're telling the compiler to optimize it sort of like a macro. If you're not familiar with this stuff, I explain it in Appendix C, which is on the CD. The bottom line is this: Your compiler is really smart, and will probably optimize the function better than you could manually. Trust in your compiler!

Saving the Database

Saving the database is simple as well. The process opens up and destroys players.txt and then rewrites all the names of the players into the database (just for safety's sake; you can never tell when your files might get corrupted by accident). The process also saves every player to his own file.

> **CAUTION**
>
> The function that saves the database always returns `true`, because I didn't take the time to do proper error checking here, in case you run out of disk space, or if any other unexpected error occurs. In a more robust system, it's advisable to check if there were any errors, and take appropriate action based on

```
bool PlayerDatabase::Save() {
    ofstream file( "players/players.txt" );
    iterator itr = begin();
    while( itr != end() ) {              // loop through every player
        file << itr->Name() << "\n";     // write the player's name
        SavePlayer( itr->ID() );         // save the player
        ++itr;                           // go to the next player
    }
    return true;
}
```

There's nothing too special about the function; it simply uses the internal iterator class to loop through every player in the database.

Saving a Single Player

Saving a single player to disk requires only an ID:

```
void PlayerDatabase::SavePlayer( entityid p_player ) {
    std::map<entityid, Player>::iterator itr = m_map.find( p_player );
    if( itr == m_map.end() )    return;
    std::string name = PlayerFileName( itr->second.Name() );
    ofstream file( name.c_str() );
    file << "[ID]          " << p_player << "\n";
    file << itr->second;
}
```

If you're trying to save a player who doesn't exist to disk, the function can fail. Other than that, you're pretty much homefree. The function makes sure to write out the ID of a player before writing out the actual player.

Adding New Players

Whenever a new player logs into the MUD, the game needs to be able to add new players to the database. Since the player database is very closely linked with the representation of players on your hard drive, the function to add new players should take steps to ensure that all relevant information about the player is written to disk immediately.

So whenever a new player is added to the database, his file name is added to players.txt, and the initial state of the player is written out to disk. The function also has a few precautionary measures to make sure players aren't duplicated. Here's the code:

```
bool PlayerDatabase::AddPlayer( Player& p_player ) {
    if( Has( p_player.ID() ) )                  // make sure ID doesn't exist
        return false;
    if( HasFullName( p_player.Name() ) )        // make sure name doesn't exist
        return false;
    m_map[p_player.ID()] = p_player;            // insert player into database
    std::ofstream file( "players/players.txt", std::ios::app );
    file << p_player.Name() << "\n";            // add player's name to file
    SavePlayer( p_player.Name(), p_player );    // write player to disk
    return true;
}
```

As you can see from the code, the game checks to see if a player's ID or name already exists within the database. If either of them already exists, the function fails, and the player isn't added.

If both of the tests succeed, the player is added into the database, and players.txt is opened in "append" mode, which preserves the contents and allows you to write to the end of the file. The name of the player's datafile is written to the player's .txt file, and finally the player is saved to his own .plr file.

Searching the Database

Two functions search the database for a player—the `findactive` and `findloggedin` functions— which search the database for players who are active or logged in. These functions are pretty simple, actually, because of the functors I defined earlier in conjunction with the `double_find_if` algorithm I defined in the `BasicLib`. Here's the code:

```
static iterator findactive( const std::string& p_name ) {
    return BasicLib::double_find_if(
        begin(), end(), matchentityfull( p_name ),
        matchentity( p_name ), playeractive() );
}
static iterator findloggedin( const std::string& p_name ) {
    return BasicLib::double_find_if(
        begin(), end(), matchentityfull( p_name ),
        matchentity( p_name ), playerloggedin() );
}
```

These two functions utilize the 5-parameter version of `double_find_if`, which takes 2 iterators and 3 *predicate* functors. In the 4-parameter version, only 2 functors are used— one for the first pass and one for the second pass. The 5-parameter version uses the first functor (`matchentityfull`) on the first pass in conjunction with the third functor (`playeractive` or `playerloggedin`), and then uses the second functor for the second pass, again in conjunction with the third functor.

When the `findactive` function performs the first pass, it checks to see if the name matches fully *and* if the player is active. If neither of those conditions is true, the algorithm keeps searching. The end result is that the `findactive` function finds a player who matches the given name and is also active. The `findloggedin` function does the same for logged in players.

Logging Out

The player database class also has a function that performs all the operations that are needed to successfully log a player out of the game:

```
void PlayerDatabase::Logout( entityid p_player ) {
    Player& p = get( p_player );
    USERLOG.Log(
        SocketLib::GetIPString( p.Conn()->GetRemoteAddress() ) +
```

```
            " - User " + p.Name() + " logged off." );
        p.Conn() = 0;
        p.LoggedIn() = false;
        p.Active() = false;
        SavePlayer( p_player );
}
```

The user log is told that the player is logging out, the connection is cleared, and both the logged in and active Booleans are cleared. The final act is to save the player to disk. It's always a good idea to frequently save players to disk in case of disaster.

Database Pointers

There is one final aspect of the player database that I have not yet covered: the database pointers. Since I covered the concepts of such structures earlier, there is no need to go into detail about them again. Here are the player macro definitions:

```
// in DatabasePointer.h:
DATABASEPOINTER( player, Player )
// in DatabasePointer.cpp:
DATABASEPOINTERIMPL( player, Player, PlayerDatabase )
```

This code simply allows you to use the player datatype like a pointer into the player database. As with the item and Item classes, pay attention to the capitalization.

Handler Design

The SimpleMUD has several connection handlers. Almost all of them are going to be related to using the player and the player database classes, so you'll need to have a firm understanding of the general design. Within this chapter, there is a section on each handler that will be used. Some of the handlers are outlined in this chapter and then fleshed out later in the book.

There are three handlers within the game: a logon handler, a game handler, and a training handler.

Logon Handler

First, when you log into the game, you'll be prompted with the logon handler, which is similar in purpose to the logon handler found in SimpleChat from Chapter 6. This time the handler has more responsibility, since it needs to support more options.

First and foremost, the logon handler has to accept two types of users: new users and existing users. For existing users, it needs to check passwords and check to see if the user is already logged in before it can let a connection into the game. For new users, it needs to validate usernames and passwords and add them to the database.

It's always a good idea to be able to picture a process, so I've drawn a flowchart of the logon handler functions in Figure 8.9.

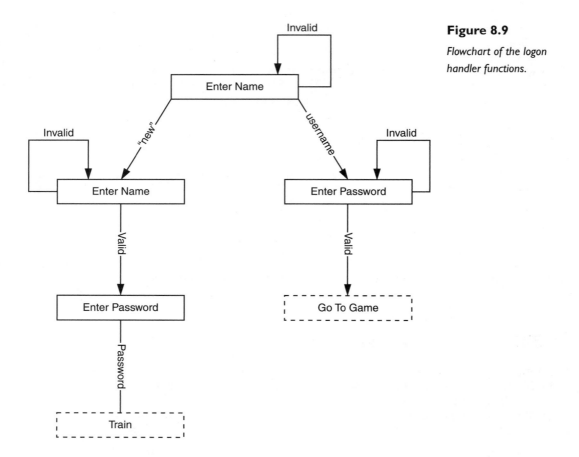

Figure 8.9

Flowchart of the logon handler functions.

From Figure 8.9, you can see that the logon handler starts off by asking the player his name. At that point, the player has two options: entering "new" to indicate that he's a new player, or entering his existing username. If the player enters anything but "new", and what he entered into the handler doesn't exist within the player database as an existing name, that is considered an *invalid* response, and the state remains the same.

New users are prompted to enter their desired names and are notified if those names already exist. If the names don't exist, the users are prompted for their desired passwords; when the users enter their passwords, they are taken to the training handler, where they modify their stats.

Existing users are prompted for their passwords; when they enter the appropriate password, they are taken to the game.

Note that whenever five invalid responses are received by the logon handler, it automatically disconnects the player.

Logon States

A connection that is logging on can be in four different states at any given time. These four states are represented by the four solid boxes within Figure 8.9:

```
enum LogonState {
    NEWCONNECTION,          // first state
    NEWUSER,                // new user; enter desired name
    ENTERNEWPASS,           // new user; enter desired password
    ENTERPASS               // existing user; enter password
};
```

Logon Data

The SimpleMUD: Logon class has several pieces of data attached to it:

```
class Logon : public Telnet::handler {
protected:
    LogonState m_state;
    int m_errors;      // how many times has an invalid answer been entered?
    string m_name;     // name
    string m_pass;     // password
};
```

Every logon handler stores the state, the number of errors a connection has made, and the name and password that the connection has entered.

Logon Functions

Here is a listing of all the functions that a logon handler has:

```
void Enter();
void Leave();
void Hungup();
void Flooded();
static void NoRoom( Connection<Telnet>& p_connection );
void Handle( string p_data );
void GotoGame( bool p_newbie = false );
static bool AcceptableName( const string& p_name );
Logon( Connection<Telnet>& p_conn );
```

The first six function names should be familiar to you, because they are the standard handler functions inherited from the Telnet::handler class to handle events from a ConnectionManager.

The GotoGame function converts a connection from the logon handler to the SimpleMUD::Game handler, and the AcceptableName function determines if a username is acceptable. The last function is a constructor.

Hanging Up, Flooding, and No Room

I'd like to cover the simpler functions first, if I may. Essentially, the logon handler does not care too much if a connection floods or hangs up; the connection manager automatically disconnects that connection when those situations occur, and the logon handler doesn't really need to do anything special.

Nevertheless, it always helps to keep a log of what is happening on your server, so those two functions record the events in the user log:

```
void Hungup() {
    USERLOG.Log(
        SocketLib::GetIPString( m_connection->GetRemoteAddress() ) +
        " - hung up in login state." );
};
void Flooded() {
    USERLOG.Log(
        SocketLib::GetIPString( m_connection->GetRemoteAddress() ) +
        " - flooded in login state." );
};
```

These functions retrieve the IP address of the offending connection and write that information to the user log.

When there's no more room left, a message needs to be sent to the connection trying to join:

```
static void NoRoom( Connection<Telnet>& p_connection ) {
    static string msg = "Sorry, there is no more room on this server.\r\n";
    try {
        p_connection.Send( msg.c_str(), (int)msg.size() );
    }
    catch( SocketLib::Exception ) {
        // do nothing here; probably an exploiter if sending that data
        // causes an exception.
    }
}
```

The function must physically send the data to the socket using the Connection::Send function instead of queuing it up using Connection::BufferData, since I can't rely on the ConnectionManager to send queued data. (The connection isn't managed by the connection manager; it is immediately discarded and closed.)

Since I am calling Connection::Send here, there is a remote possibility of an exception being thrown, so I need to be ready for that, too. Because the connection is closing anyway, the catch block simply catches the exception and ignores it.

Leaving and Entering

Whenever connections leave or enter this state, the Leave and Enter functions are called. Luckily, the logon handler doesn't have to clean up after any connections when they leave (since they haven't been added to the game yet), so you can leave it as an empty function:

```
void Leave() {};
```

On the other hand, when connections enter the game, the logon handler needs to send it a welcoming message:

```
void Enter() {
    USERLOG.Log(
        GetIPString( p_connection.GetRemoteAddress() ) +
        " - new connection in login state." );

    p_connection.Protocol().SendString( p_connection,
        red + bold + "Welcome To SimpleMUD v1.0\r\n" +
        "Please enter your name, or \"new\" if you are new: " + reset );
}
```

It's not an imaginative welcome message, but it works. A more flexible method of displaying a welcome message is to load a message from a text file on the server, and print that, but that's just a special feature that's not essential to the game. Feel free to implement it if you wish.

> **TIP**
>
> A more advanced MUD would put IP-address detection into the connection process, so one person couldn't flood your MUD with connections.

Handling Commands

Remember what I showed you in Chapters 5 and 6: whenever a full command is received by a protocol policy object, it passes the command onto the connection's current handler. The Logon::Handle function is called whenever a connection is using the Logon class as its current handler.

Essentially, this function performs the actions that I described earlier and illustrated within Figure 8.9. Since it's a relatively large function, I'm going to break it up into a few chunks, to describe it better. Here's the first part (p_data is the string that the user typed in):

```
void Logon::Handle( string p_data ) {
    if( m_errors == 5 ) {
        m_connection->Protocol().SendString( *m_connection, red + bold +
            "Too many incorrect responses, closing connection..." +
            newline );
        m_connection->Close();
        return;
    }
```

The previous section of code detects if five errors have occurred in the login process, and if so, the connection is informed of this and closed. This prevents people from endlessly trying passwords, trying to break into an account.

The next part of the code handles brand new connections:

```
if( m_state == NEWCONNECTION ) {
    if( BasicLib::LowerCase( p_data ) == "new" ) {
        m_state = NEWUSER;
        m_connection->Protocol().SendString( *m_connection, yellow +
            "Please enter your desired name: " + reset );
    }
```

If the user enters "new" as the name, the state of the logon immediately moves to the NEWUSER state, and the user is asked to enter his desired username. If the user enters anything other than "new", this next piece of code is executed:

```
    else {
        PlayerDatabase::iterator itr = PlayerDatabase::findfull( p_data );
        if( itr == PlayerDatabase::end() ) ) {
            m_errors++;
            m_connection->Protocol().SendString( *m_connection,
                red + bold + "Sorry, the user \"" + white + p_data + red +
                "\" does not exist.\r\n" +
                "Please enter your name, or \"new\" if you are new: " +
                reset );
        }
```

The player database is checked to see if any full names match the name the new user wants. I used a full-name match so that people could have names that partially matched each other. If the name doesn't exist, the user is told that he chose an invalid name, and the connection's error count goes up. If the name already exists, however, the next piece of code is executed:

```
        else {
            m_state = ENTERPASS;
            m_name = p_data;
            m_pass = itr->Password();
            m_connection->Protocol().SendString( *m_connection,
                green + bold + "Welcome, " + white + p_data + red +
                newline + green + "Please enter your password: " +
                reset );
        }
    }
    return;
}
```

The state changes to the state in which an existing user is prompted for his password, and the user's name is recorded into the m_name string. Next, the player's password is retrieved and stored into the m_pass string, and the user is prompted to enter his password.

The previous three code fragments should take care of every possible outcome whenever a new connection makes an entry. Once the segment is complete, the function simply returns, because the user's command has been handled.

The next segment takes care of new users:

```
if( m_state == NEWUSER ) {
    if( PlayerDatabase::hasfull( p_data ) ) {
        m_errors++;
        m_connection->Protocol().SendString( *m_connection,
            red + bold + "Sorry, the name \"" + white + p_data + red +
            "\" has already been taken." + newline + yellow +
            "Please enter your desired name: " + reset );
    }
```

First, the function checks to see if the database has the name that the player wants to use. If the name is already in use, the player is told that the name has already been taken, and the error count is increased again. If the name isn't taken, the function goes on to check if the name is acceptable:

```
else {
    if( !AcceptibleName( p_data ) ) {
        m_errors++;
        m_connection->Protocol().SendString( *m_connection,
            red + bold + "Sorry, the name \"" + white + p_data + red +
            "\" is unacceptable." + newline + yellow +
            "Please enter your desired name: " + reset );
    }
```

If the name isn't acceptable, the error count is again increased, and the user is told that the name isn't acceptable. (I haven't covered that function, but it is almost identical to the UserDatabase::IsValidName function found in the SimpleChat demo, Demo 6.2 section in Chapter 6.)

Here is the final segment of code for the NEWUSER state:

```
else {
    m_state = ENTERNEWPASS;
    m_name = p_data;
    m_connection->Protocol().SendString( *m_connection,
            green + "Please enter your desired password: " +
            reset );
        }
    }
    return;
}
```

At this point, the user has entered a name that is both acceptable and new to the game, so the name is recorded into the m_name string, and the user is asked to enter his desired password. After all of this, the code block returns.

The next block of code handles new password commands:

```
if( m_state == ENTERNEWPASS ) {
    if( p_data.find_first_of( BasicLib::WHITESPACE ) != string::npos ) {
        m_errors++;
        m_connection->Protocol().SendString( *m_connection,
                red + bold + "INVALID PASSWORD!" +
                green + "Please enter your desired password: " +
                reset );
        return;
    }
}
```

The function performs a search on the desired password; if the function finds whitespace, the password is rejected. This has to do with the fact that when passwords are read in by the player database, the database assumes the password won't contain whitespace.

If the password is acceptable, the function continues:

```
    m_connection->Protocol().SendString( *m_connection,
            green + "Thank you! You are now entering the realm..." +
            newline );
    Player p;
    p.Name() = m_name;
    p.Password() = p_data;
```

The user is told that he is now entering the game, and a new Player object is created. The player's name and password are recorded. And this is where the going gets a little tricky. First, before you can insert the user into the database, you need to find him a valid ID. I've decided to use a simple method to calculate the next available ID: find the highest ID in the database, and add 1. Of course, this opens up a whole new can of worms, because the database might be empty.

To solve this problem, I first check to see if the database is empty, and if so, I assume that the first user logging in has an ID of 1 and becomes the administrator of the MUD:

```
    if( PlayerDatabase::size() == 0 ) {
        p.Rank() = ADMIN;
        p.ID() = 1;
    }
    else {
        p.ID() = PlayerDatabase::LastID() + 1;
    }
    PlayerDatabase::AddPlayer( p );
    GotoGame( true );
    return;
}
```

I haven't shown you the PlayerDatabase::LastID function at all, but it's so simple it doesn't really need to be shown. This function retrieves an iterator to the last player in the database and returns its ID.

Once the ID of the player is set, the player is added to the database, and the GotoGame function is invoked with a parameter of true. The parameter signifies that this is a new character, and the handler should set up the next state accordingly. I'll show you what this means when I cover the GotoGame function.

The last block of code for this function checks an existing user's password. Remember that when the player entered an existing username, the function looked up that user's password and stored it in the m_pass string. Here's the code:

```
if( m_state == ENTERPASS ) {
    if( m_pass == p_data ) {
        m_connection->Protocol().SendString( *m_connection,
                green + "Thank you! You are now entering the realm..." +
                newline );
        GotoGame();
    }
```

The code checks to see if the player's entry matches the password of the player he's trying to log in as. If so, the player is told that he's entering, and the GotoGame function is called.

Here's the last part of the code that rejects an incorrect password:

```
    else {
        m_errors++;
        m_connection->Protocol().SendString( *m_connection,
                red + bold + "INVALID PASSWORD!" + newline +
                yellow + "Please enter your password: " +
                reset );
    }
    return;
    }
}
```

That pretty much sums up the logon command handler code.

GotoGame Function

There's only one more piece of code I want to show you before moving on to the training handler. The GotoGame function prepares a connection to connect to the Game handler.

I told you earlier that the function takes a Boolean as a parameter, but it's optional. If you don't pass anything in, the Boolean is assumed to be false. The parameter, when true, indicates that the connection is a "newbie" to the game, and that this is the player's first time connecting. Here's the function:

```
void Logon::GotoGame( bool p_newbie ) {
{
    Player& p = *PlayerDatabase::findfull( m_name );

    if( p.LoggedIn() ) {
```

```
        p.Conn()->Close();
        p.Conn()->Handler()->Hungup();
        p.Conn()->ClearHandlers();
    }
```

First, the connection retrieves a reference to the player. (It assumes that the lookup works, considering that any code that calls this function should have already verified that the player exists.) Next, the code checks to see if the player is already logged in. If so, it's probably because the connection died, and the server didn't detect it yet; therefore, the server is told to close the connect and then notify its current handler that the connection hung up. The code continues:

```
        p.Newbie() = p_newbie;
        p.Conn() = m_connection;
        p.Conn()->SwitchHandler( new Game( *p.Conn(), p.ID() ) );
    }
```

The "newbie" state of the player is recorded from the parameter, the new connection is recorded into the player's connection pointer, and the Logon handler is removed and swapped with a new Game handler using the SwitchHandler function. This is a tricky thing to do, though, because when you remove the handler from a connection, it is physically deleted, along with any member variables within the handler. Why is this a concern? Because the function being executed belongs to the handler that *you just deleted!* Therefore, if you access any member variables from this point on, you crash the program. Because of this, whenever you change states, you need to make sure that the function immediately exits and does *not* access members.

> **NOTE**
>
> Note that since GotoGame is called by another member function, the functions also need to make sure they exit without accessing members. You should notice that in the Handle function, the function returns after every call to GotoGame.

Finally, the Game handler is set as the connection's new handler, and it's notified about the connection's ID.

Training Handler

The next handler I'm going to cover is the simplest of the three SimpleMUD handlers—the handler that allows a player to assign his statpoints to his three core attributes (strength, health, and agility).

Class Skeleton

First, let me show you the class skeleton:

```
class Train : public Telnet::handler {
public:
```

```
    void Handle( string p_data );
    void Enter();
    void Leave();
    void Hungup();
    void Flooded();
    void PrintStats( bool p_clear = true );
    Train( Connection<Telnet>& p_conn, player p_player );
protected:
    player m_player;
};
```

Once again, you can see that the class inherits from the `Telnet::handler` class, which I showed you back in Chapter 6, and the first four functions in this class are the same handler functions you've seen several times before. The new function (besides the constructor) that this class defines is a helper function. `PrintStats` prints out a players stats to the player's connection.

The constructor simply takes a reference to a connection, and a `player` database pointer object, which it records into `m_player`, so I'm not going to show that function to you.

Leaving and Entering

Like the `Logon` handler, the `Training` handler doesn't need to clean up after connections when they leave, so the `Leave` function is empty:

```
void Leave() {};
```

Whenever a connection enters the traning state, the handler needs to perform a little housekeeping. Here's the code:

```
void Enter() {
    Player& p = *m_player;              // retrieve the Player object
    p.Active() = false;                 // make the player "inactive"
    if( p.Newbie() ) {
        p.SendString( magenta + bold +
            "Welcome to SimpleMUD, " + p.Name() + "!\r\n" +
            "You must train your character with your desired stats,\r\n" +
            "before you enter the realm.\r\n\r\n" );
        p.Newbie() = false;
    }
    PrintStats( false );
}
```

The function retrieves the actual `Player` object and makes it inactive. Once that is done, the connection checks to see if the player is a newbie, in which case it prints out a simple welcome message, notifying the user that he needs to assign his 18 statpoints to the various core attributes, and the newbie flag is cleared.

Finally, the function displays the player's stats, using `false` as the parameter for the `PrintStats` function. (This means that it shouldn't clear the screen and wipe out the welcome message that was just displayed to the player.)

Closing Connections

Of course, the handler also needs to be able to handle connections that accidentally close (due to flooding, or hanging up). Both the Flooded and Hungup functions call the PlayerDatabase::Logout function:

```
void Train::Hungup() {
    PlayerDatabase::Logout( m_player );
}
void Train::Flooded() {
    PlayerDatabase::Logout( m_player );
}
```

Handling Training Commands

Four commands are accepted when a character is in the training state: 1, 2, 3, and quit. The three numbers represent three core attributes, with 1 being strength, 2 health, and 3 agility. Whenever a player types quit, the handler removes itself from the connection's handler stack, and the connection should return to the state in which it existed previously (the game state).

```
void Train::Handle( string p_data ) {
    p_data = BasicLib::LowerCase( ParseWord( p_data, 0 ) );
    Player& p = *m_player;                  // load the player object
    if( p_data == "quit" ) {
        PlayerDatabase::Save( p.ID() );  // save player
        p.Conn()->RemoveHandler();        // remove the Training handler
        // tell the previous handler that it now has control again:
        p.Conn()->Handler()->NewConnection( *p.Conn() );
        return;
    }
```

The previous code block is just the first half of the function. The string that the player typed in, p_data, is first lowercased, and then the Player object representing the current player is retrieved. If the player types quit, the player wants to exit the training mode, and go back to the game. Therefore, the newly modified character is saved to disk, the training handler is removed, and the game handler (or whatever handler was below the training handler on the connection's handler stack) is notified that the connection has re-entered that state. Notice how the function immediately returns, since the handler has been changed. I described the reasoning for this with the Logon handler previously.

```
    char n = p_data[0];
    if( n >= '1' && n <= '3' ) {             // make sure number is 1, 2, or 3
        if( p.StatPoints() > 0 ) {           // make sure user has points
            p.StatPoints()--;                // subtract a point
            p.AddToBaseAttr( n - '1', 1 ); // add the point to a base attribute
        }
    }
```

```
    PrintStats( true );                    // print stats and clear screen
}
```

The last half of the code extracts the first letter of the player's command. If it's a valid command, the letter should be 1, 2, or 3. The function checks to make sure that the first letter is 1, 2, or 3, and also makes sure the user has some extra statpoints. If neither of those conditions occurs, the input is ignored.

If the player entered a valid number and has extra statpoints left, the base attribute corresponding to that number is incremented. The line that does this may be a little confusing however, so let me explain it. In the Attribute enumeration I showed you earlier in this chapter, the strength, health, and agility enumerations are given values of 0, 1, and 2. So when the user enters the character 1, and the character 1 is subtracted from that value, you get the actual integer value 0, which is the value of the strength enumeration. Likewise, 2 - 1 yields the actual integer 1, and 3 - 1 yields 2. That's it for this function.

Printing Stats

The final function I want to show you is the PrintStats function:

```
void Train::PrintStats( bool p_clear ) {
    Player& p = *m_player;            // get player object
    if( p_clear ) {
        p.SendString( clearscreen ); // clear screen if needed
    }
    p.SendString( white + bold +     // send stats
        "--------------------- Your Stats ---------------------\r\n" +
        dim +
        "Player:            " + p.Name() + "\r\n" +
        "Level:             " + tostring( p.Level() ) + "\r\n" +
        "Stat Points Left: " + tostring( p.StatPoints() ) + "\r\n" +
        "1) Strength:       " + tostring( p.GetAttr( STRENGTH ) ) + "\r\n" +
        "2) Health:         " + tostring( p.GetAttr( HEALTH ) ) + "\r\n" +
        "3) Agility:        " + tostring( p.GetAttr( AGILITY ) ) + "\r\n" +
        bold +
        "------------------------------------------------------\r\n" +
        "Enter 1, 2, or 3 to add a stat point, or \"quit\" to go back: " );
}
```

The function retrieves a player from the database, clears the screen if requested to do so, and then prints out the player's statistics, consisting of name, level, stat points remaining, and the three core attributes.

Game Handler

The third and final handler, the Game handler, is the largest and most complex handler in the game. This is the handler that reacts to every command that the user types.

The previous two handlers—the logon handler and the training handler—are complete. They don't need features added later on in the game. The Game handler, however, will obviously be incomplete when this chapter is finished. I haven't defined enemies, shops, or the entire map system yet, so things like combat, commerce, and movement cannot be implemented.

Instead, the current incarnation of this handler implements all the features of the game that don't require rooms, enemies, or shops.

Here is a list of all the user commands that will be implemented in this version of the game handler:

```
chat
experience
help
inventory
quit
remove
stats
time
use
whisper
who
kick
announce
changerank
reload items
shutdown
```

If you'll remember back from Chapter 7, everything above kick is available to everyone, everything above announce is available to gods and higher, and every command is available to admins.

Game Data

Several pieces of data are associated to the game handlers. (I've removed the functions.)

```
class Game : public Telnet::handler {
protected:
    player m_player;
    string m_lastcommand;
    static BasicLib::Timer s_timer;
    static bool s_running;
};
```

The handler keeps a `player` database pointer so that it can look up a player's data whenever it needs to. It also keeps a `string`, which tracks the last command the user entered. It's usually a good "user interface" issue to allow a player to repeat his last command, so this helps.

The handler also has two *static* variables, which means they act like global variables inside of the `Game` class. The `s_timer` keeps track of how long the game has been running, and the `s_running` Boolean keeps track of whether the game is actually running. Setting the Boolean to `false` tells the game that it has been shut down, and causes the program to exit.

Game Functions

The `Game` handler has quite a few functions dealing with all sorts of stuff, so I'm going to list them in related categories. The first category is, of course, the standard handler functions:

```
void Handle( string p_data );
void Enter();
void Leave();
void Hungup();
void Flooded();
```

You've seen them all a few times before, so there's really no need to explain their purposes yet again. The next group of functions sends text to different groups of players:

```
static void SendGlobal( const string& p_str );
static void SendGame( const string& p_str );
static void Announce( const string& p_announcement );
static void LogoutMessage( const string& p_reason );
void Whisper( string p_str, string p_player );
```

Four out of the five functions are static, which means that they can be called within any part of the game without needing a `Game` object. `SendGlobal` is a function that sends a single string to *any* player who is logged on, no matter what state he is in.

The `SendGame` function is similar, but instead of sending a string to every player who is logged in, it limits the scope a little and sends a string to every player who is active within the game. `Announce` and `LogoutMessage` are simple wrappers around `SendGlobal` and `SendGame`. They attach standard coloring schemes and text to game announcements and logoff announcements, so that the game keeps a consistent look and feel.

> **NOTE**
>
> When a connection is still in the `Logon` state, it hasn't actually logged on to a player yet, so the `SendGlobal` function does not send text to connections within that state.

Finally, the `Whisper` function attempts to "whisper" some text from the current player to a player named within the `p_player` parameter string.

The next functions deal with generating informational strings:

```
static string WhoList( const string& p_who );
static string PrintHelp( PlayerRank p_rank = REGULAR );
string PrintStats();
string PrintExperience();
string PrintInventory();
```

The first two strings are static, since they require no specific player information to be generated. The who-list is a listing of everyone in the game, and the help-list generates a list of all the functions available to any person who has been given a rank.

The stats, experience, and inventory listings all depend on a single player in the game, so those obviously cannot be static.

And finally, here's the rest of the functions:

```
bool UseItem( const string& p_item );
bool RemoveItem( string p_item );
inline static BasicLib::Timer& GetTimer()          { return s_timer; }
inline static bool& Running()                      { return s_running; }
Game( Connection<Telnet>& p_conn, player p_player );
inline static void Logout( player p_player );
void GotoTrain();
```

Those are functions to use an item ("arm" an item), remove an item ("disarm"), get the timer object, get the running Boolean, construct the game handler, log a player out (this is a helper function), and move a player into the training state (another helper function).

Handler Functions

Three out of the four handler functions are pretty simple; the only exception is the Handle function, which is pretty large. I'll cover the simple handler functions first.

·New Connections

If you'll recall the Logon handler, whenever a player successfully logs on in that handler, it switches the state of the connection to the Game handler. When that happens, this function is called:

```
void Game::Enter( ) {
    USERLOG.Log(  GetIPString( p_connection.GetRemoteAddress() ) +
                  " - User " + m_player->Name() +
                  " entering Game state." );
    m_lastcommand = "";
    Player& p = *m_player;
    p.Active() = true;
    p.LoggedIn() = true;
    SendGame( bold + green + p.Name() + " has entered the realm." );
    if( p.Newbie() )
        GotoTrain();
}
```

The function is fairly straightforward. The player log is updated to show that a player entered the game state, the connection is recorded, and the last command string is cleared.

You should remember the "newbie" status from the Logon handler section of this chapter. If a player logs in for the first time, that player has his "newbie" flag set, but it isn't set for a pre-existing player who logs in. If a player is a newbie, he hasn't changed his stats and must be taken to the Train handler. New players also have their room ID set to 1, which is the "main room" of the game.

If the player isn't a newbie, he's activated, and everyone in the game is told that he's joined.

Leaving the Handler

Of course, whenever the player leaves the game state, he needs to tell the game about it, so that's what the Leave function takes care of:

```
void Game::Leave() {
    m_player->Active() = false;
    if( m_connection->Closed() )
        PlayerDatabase::Logout( m_player );
}
```

This code deactivates the player, and checks to see if the connection has been closed. If it has been, the player database is told to log the player out. Otherwise, it is assumed that the player is still logged into the game (probably switching to the training state), and you don't want to log him off if that happens. You should log a player off when the connection closes.

Closed Connections

Whenever a connection is unexpectedly closed, the game handler needs to take care of this occurrence:

```
void Game::Hungup() {
    Player& p = *m_player;
    LogoutMessage( p.Name() + " has suddenly disappeared from the realm." );
}
void Game::Flooded() {
    Player& p = *m_player;
    LogoutMessage( p.Name() + " has been kicked out for flooding!" );
}
```

Instead of just logging players off as the training handler does, the players within the game handler notify everyone else within the game when they log out. Both of these functions utilize the LogoutMessage helper function to notify everyone.

Handling Commands

By far, the largest function within the game handler is the Handle command. In a more complex MUD, this kind of function would be more segmented, but this MUD is simple enough so that's not necessary.

I'm splitting up the function so that I can show you each command in detail, starting with the repeating command:

```
void Game::Handle( string p_data ) {
    Player& p = *m_player;
    if( p_data == "/" ) {
        p_data = m_lastcommand;
    }
    else {
        m_lastcommand = p_data;
    }
    string firstword = BasicLib::LowerCase( ParseWord( p_data, 0 ) );
```

As usual, p_data is the string that contains the command that the player typed in.

The command to repeat the player's last command is simply a slash (/). If the command is a slash, p_data is reassigned with the value of the m_lastcommand string. If the user typed in anything other than a slash, the m_lastcommand is updated with the value of p_data.

The last part of the code fragment strips out the first word the player typed, makes the word lowercased, and then stores it in a local variable named firstword. Now the function starts trying to find out what command the player typed in:

```
    if( firstword == "chat" || firstword == ":" ) {
        string text = RemoveWord( p_data, 0 );
        SendGame( white + bold + p.Name() + " chats: " + text );
        return;
    }
```

I've added a shortcut for players to use when they chat. Instead of being required to type "chat hello everyone!", players can type a single colon instead of the whole word "chat". For example, a player would type ": hello everyone!" instead. The function removes the command ("chat" or ":") from the string and stores the rest of the string in text, and then sends that text out to everyone who is active in the game, in the form of "Ron chats: hello everyone!". Since the command was successfully handled, the function returns; there is no need to continue checking to see if the command needs to be handled.

The next four commands simply display status reports for the current player:

```
    if( firstword == "experience" || firstword == "exp" ) {
        p.SendString( PrintExperience() );
        return;
    }
    if( firstword == "help" || firstword == "commands" ) {
        p.SendString( PrintHelp( p.Rank() ) );
        return;
    }
    if( firstword == "inventory" || firstword == "i" ) {
        p.SendString( PrintInventory() );
        return;
```

```
    }
    if( firstword == "stats" || firstword == "st" ) {
        p.SendString( PrintStats() );
        return;
    }
```

I'm pretty sure those commands are self-explanatory, so we'll move on:

```
    if( firstword == "quit" ) {
        m_connection->Close();
        LogoutMessage( p.Name() + " has left the realm." );
        Logout( p.ID() );
        return;
    }
```

Closing connections is always a tricky business, simply because it's so difficult to keep track of connections if they suddenly disappear. Remember that the Connection class simply sets a Boolean to true whenever you close a connection, so that a ConnectionManager can later check and close the connection when it does its housekeeping.

The realm is told that the player left, and the player is logged out, so there's nothing more for this function to do.

Here are the two item functions:

```
    if( firstword == "remove" ) {
        RemoveItem( ParseWord( p_data, 1 ) );
        return;
    }
    if( firstword == "use" ) {
        UseItem( RemoveWord( p_data, 0 ) );
        return;
    }
```

The syntax for the remove command is relatively simple. You don't tell the game the name of the item you want to disarm; instead, you tell the game remove armor or remove weapon. That makes life simpler, really. That's why the function parses out word 1 (remember, remove is word 0), and passes that into the RemoveItem helper function.

When a player uses an item, however, you need to type the name of the item you want to use, such as use giant sword or whatever. That's why the use command strips out the word remove and passes the rest of your string into the UseItem helper.

While not completely necessary for the game, I always find it extremely useful to have a time function:

```
    if( firstword == "time" ) {
        p.SendString( bold + cyan +
                    "The current system time is: " + BasicLib::TimeStamp() +
                    " on " + BasicLib::DateStamp() +
                    "\r\nThe system has been up for: "
```

```
                              + s_timer.GetString() + "." );
        return;
    }
```

This function displays the current system time, and then it shows how long the server has been running. I like to have functions like this so I can tell how long the server has been running. Admit it, as a nerd, it's always fun to brag about how long your system has been online. Linux geeks especially like to brag about this stuff, and frequently use this information to win arguments with Windows nerds. As much as I love the newest versions of Windows, you have to admit, Linux stays up and running much longer.

Next up is the "whisper" command, which allows a player to privately message another person in the game, without everyone else hearing what he has to say. This can help when a player is planning some nefarious scheme or another; here's the code:

```
if( firstword == "whisper" ) {
    string name = ParseWord( p_data, 1 );
    string message = RemoveWord( RemoveWord( p_data, 0 ), 0 );
    Whisper( message, name );
    return;
}
```

You use the command like this: "whisper ron Hello there!" The function strips out word 1 ("ron"), which is the name of the player you are whispering to, and then it strips off the first two words ("whisper ron") and uses the rest of the string ("Hello there!") as the message. Finally, it calls the Whisper helper function.

The final regular-user command is the "who" command:

```
if( firstword == "who" ) {
    p.SendString( WhoList( BasicLib::LowerCase(
        ParseWord( p_data, 1 ) ) ) );
    return;
}
```

This function follows a process similar to other commands, by stripping off word 1. Then it lowercases the second word, and sends it off to the WhoList function, which displays a list of people in the realm to the player.

There's a reason why this command has a parameter: You can choose which people are included in the list. By default, if there is no parameter, the result of WhoList is just the return of a list of everyone who is currently logged in. If you use the parameter of all, however, such as who all, the function returns a list of *everyone* in the entire game, even those who aren't logged in.

Now, here is the "kick" god-command, which physically kicks people out of the game:

```
if( firstword == "kick" && p.Rank() >= GOD ) {
    PlayerDatabase::iterator itr =
        PlayerDatabase::findloggedin( ParseWord( p_data, 1 ) );
```

```
        if( itr == PlayerDatabase::end() ) {
            p.SendString( red + bold + "Player could not be found." );
            return;
        }
        if( itr->Rank() > p.Rank() ) {
            p.SendString( red + bold + "You can't kick that player!" );
            return;
        }
        itr->Conn()->Close();
        LogoutMessage( itr->Name() + " has been kicked by " +
                        p.Name() + "!!!" );
        PlayerDatabase::Logout( itr->ID() );
        return;
    }
```

The function first searches for someone who is also logged in to kick. You can't kick people who aren't logged in, of course. If no person is found, the kicker is informed.

If a person *is* found, the game compares ranks; a person can only kick a person whose rank is lower. In SimpleMUD, this means that gods cannot kick admins, since the rank of admins is higher. It's "chain of command" type stuff.

Finally, the connection for the kickee is closed, the realm is notified that the player was kicked out, and the database is also told about it.

The last four commands are administrator-only commands, meaning that only people with a rank of ADMIN can execute them. The "announce" command sends an announcement to everyone in the game (even people in the Train handler):

```
    if( firstword == "announce" && p.Rank() >= ADMIN ) {
        Announce( RemoveWord( p_data, 0 ) );
        return;
    }
```

This simply removes the first word "announce" from the string, and sends it off to the Announce helper function.

Here is the command to change a player's rank:

```
    if( firstword == "changerank" && p.Rank() >= ADMIN ) {
        string name = ParseWord( p_data, 1 );
        PlayerDatabase::iterator itr = PlayerDatabase::find( name );
        if( itr == PlayerDatabase::end() ) {
            p.SendString( red + bold + "Error: Could not find user " +
                            name );
            return;
        }
        PlayerRank rank = GetRank( ParseWord( p_data, 2 ) );
        itr->Rank() = rank;
        SendGame( green + bold + itr->Name() +
```

```
                    "'s rank has been changed to: " +
                    GetRankString( rank ) );
        return;
    }
```

This function finds a player with the name you requested and changes his rank; the player doesn't even have to be online. Everyone in the game is made aware of the rank changing as well.

The next command allows you to reload the item database:

```
if( firstword == "reload" && p.Rank() >= ADMIN ) {
    string db = BasicLib::LowerCase( ParseWord( p_data, 1 ) );
    if( db == "items" ) {
        ItemDatabase::Load();
        p.SendString( bold + cyan + "Item Database Reloaded!" );
    }
```

If the user wants the item database to be reloaded, he needs to type in "reload items", and this immediately causes the item database to be reloaded. Reloading the player database isn't currently possible with the version of the MUD described in this chapter, but this functionality will be added in the next chapter.

The last command allows an administrator to remotely shut the server down. Because of this command, it is wise to entrust administrator access only to responsible people, so that they don't end up shutting down the MUD as a prank:

```
if( firstword == "shutdown" && p.Rank() >= ADMIN ) {
    Announce( "SYSTEM IS SHUTTING DOWN" );
    Game::Running() = false;
    return;
}
```

All that needs to be done is setting the Game::s_running Boolean to false (through the Running() accessor function), and the main game loop detects that setting and shuts the game down.

And finally, if the game doesn't recognize your command, it sends the text as a chat message:

```
    SendGame( bold + p.Name() + " chats: " + p_data );
}
```

This line of code only exists for the time being. In the next chapter, when I develop the map system, all invalid commands are interpreted as "talking to everyone in the current room". Obviously, since there's no map system yet, I can't have that functionality.

Sending Functions

As you have seen before, five different "sending" functions are defined within the Game class. They are all pretty simple, so I'm not going to launch into a huge lecture about them; rather, I'll go over them somewhat quickly.

Sending to the Game and Sending Globally

The functions SendGame and SendGlobal send strings to every connection that is active or logged in, respectively. For example:

```
void Game::SendGlobal( const string& p_str ) {
    operate_on_if( PlayerDatabase::begin(),
                   PlayerDatabase::end(),
                   playersend( p_str ),
                   playerloggedin() );
}
```

This calls my special operate_on_if algorithm from the BasicLib. Essentially, operate_on_if acts like the std::for_each algorithm, except that instead of using the playersend functor on every value in the collection, it applies playersend only to players who pass the playerloggedin testing functor. (I showed this functor to you when I was showing you the Player class.) Essentially what this means is that it loops through every player in the database and sends the string to everyone who is logged on.

The SendGame function is virtually identical; the only difference is that instead of the playerloggedin functor, it uses the playeractive functor to send stuff only to active players, not to inactive players.

Helpers

There are two helper functions that help send strings; I've mentioned them before:

```
void Game::LogoutMessage( const string& p_reason ) {
    SendGame( SocketLib::red + SocketLib::bold + p_reason );
}
void Game::Announce( const string& p_announcement ) {
    SendGlobal( SocketLib::cyan + SocketLib::bold +
                "System Announcement: " + p_announcement );
}
```

As I've said before, these functions exist to provide a certain look and feel to the game, because many different places within the code may be making announcements or saying that someone has logged off, and you want these messages to look consistent throughout the game.

Whispering

Whispering from one person to another requires a little bit more work than the other communication methods. First, the game needs to find the person you're whispering to, and then tell that person what you said, as well as telling yourself what you said to that player:

```
void Game::Whisper( std::string p_str, std::string p_player ) {
    PlayerDatabase::iterator itr = PlayerDatabase::findactive( p_player );
    if( itr == PlayerDatabase::end() ) {
        m_player->SendString( red + bold + "Error, cannot find user." );
    }
```

```
    else {
        itr->SendString( yellow + m_player->Name() + " whispers to you: " +
                        reset + p_str );
        m_player->SendString( yellow + "You whisper to " + itr->Name() +
                        ": " + reset + p_str );
    }
}
```

If the player isn't found, an error string is printed. But if the player *is* found, the message is sent to both the player and yourself, albeit in slightly different forms for each. If you type whisper bob hello!, he'll see Ron whispers to you: hello!, and you'll see You whisper to bob: hello!.

Status Printers

I am really running short on space about now, and I'm sure you're getting tired of seeing all this code as well. Therefore, I'll skip showing you the status printing code, since it is essentially just a big mess of formatted text-printing functions.

There *is* one note I'd like to make however, which is about the WhoList printer. To get a configurable function that would optionally print only players who are online, or all players in the database, I decided to use the operate_on_if algorithm and create a wholist functor (notice the lack of capitals), which prints out the "wholist entry" line for a single player.

Here's part of the code for the WhoList function:

```
wholist who;
who = BasicLib::operate_on_if(
                PlayerDatabase::begin(),
                PlayerDatabase::end(),
                wholist(),
                playerloggedin() );
```

The operate_on_if algorithm returns the "operation functor" that you passed into it, because in this case, the wholist functor keeps track of a string of who-list entries. Every time wholist finds a player who is logged in, it creates an entry for that player and adds that string to the end of its str member variable, so when the function returns, you can get a string representing every entry in the list generated from the function. As you can see, the operation of the operate_on_if algorithm combined the wholist functor on a collection of players. The entry of every player who is online is calculated and added to the wholist's str, which is a string. Of course, the entries consist of more than just the player's name, but for simplicity's sake, that's all I show here.

Figure 8.10 shows a loose representation of what occurs.

Figure 8.11 shows a sample who-listing screenshot.

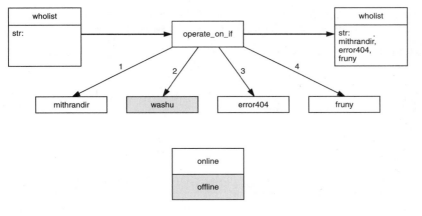

Figure 8.10

Every time wholist *finds a player who is logged in, it creates an entry for that player and adds that string to the end of its* str *member variable.*

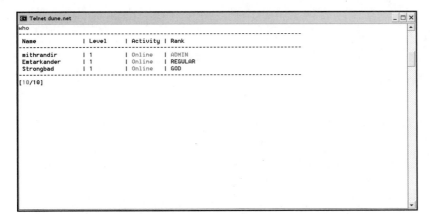

Figure 8.11

In this sample who-listing, each entry consists of a player's name, level, online activity, and ranking.

Item Functions

The final functions I'm going to cover here are the two item functions, which arm/use or disarm items in a player's inventory.

Using an Item

You can use the use command on all three types of items, and the behavior of the function differs depending on the type. Let me show you the code first:

```
bool Game::UseItem( const std::string& p_item ) {
    Player& p = *m_player;
    int i = p.GetItemIndex( p_item );
    if( i == -1 ) {
        p.SendString( red + bold + "Could not find that item!" );
        return false;
    }
```

The previous code segment attempts to retrieve the index of the item the player is requesting for use. If none is found, the function tells the player so and returns.

```
Item& itm = *p.GetItem( i );
switch( itm.Type() ) {
case WEAPON:
    p.UseWeapon( i );
    return true;
case ARMOR:
    p.UseArmor( i );
    return true;
```

Once the item is found, it is retrieved from the item database, and the function performs a switch on the type of the item. Armor and weapons are similar; they each call the player's UseWeapon or UseArmor functions. Nothing is printed out to the user at this time; this functionality is implemented in the next chapter.

```
case HEALING:
    p.AddBonuses( itm.ID() );
    p.AddHitpoints( BasicLib::RandomInt( itm.Min(), itm.Max() ) );
    p.DropItem( i );
    return true;
}
    return false;
}
```

In the case of a healing item, however, the bonuses of that item are added to the player's stats, the hitpoints that the item heals are calculated using the BasicLib::RandomInt function and added to the player, and then the function calls the Player::DropItem on the item you just used. If you remember, the DropItem removes an item from a player's inventory. Once you use a healing item, it simply disappears, to prevent you from using it over and over again.

Disarming an Item

And finally, a player can disarm his weapon or his armor:

```
bool Game::RemoveItem( std::string p_item ) {
    Player& p = *m_player;
    p_item = BasicLib::LowerCase( p_item );
    if( p_item == "weapon" && p.Weapon() != 0 ) {
        p.RemoveWeapon();
        return true;
    }
    if( p_item == "armor" && p.Armor() != 0 ) {
        p.RemoveArmor();
        return true;
    }
    p.SendString( red + bold + "Could not Remove item!" );
    return false;
}
```

Depending on whether the player types weapon or armor, the player's weapon or armor is removed, but only if the player has a weapon or piece of armor that is armed in the first place. If a player has nothing armed, an error is printed to the player.

Helpers

There is one helper function, whose main purpose is to put a player into the training state:

```
void Game::GotoTrain() {
    Player& p = *m_player;
    p.Active() = false;
    p.Conn()->AddHandler( new Train( p.ID() ) );
    LogoutMessage( p.Name() + " leaves to edit stats" );
}
```

It's a helpful function to use whenever a player needs to edit his stats.

Demo 8.1—The SimpleMUD Baseline: The Core, Players, and Items

Finally! At long last, you have reached (almost!) the end of this chapter. An incredible amount of code was put into everything you've seen so far, so let me tell you something that will make you feel a lot better.

The code for the Demo 8.1 main module is incredibly simple. Seriously. I've designed the rest of the game and the entire framework leading up to it to make the code for actually running the game incredibly simple.

You can find the code for the main module within the Demo08-01.cpp file in the /Demos/ Chapter08/Demo08-01/ directory on the CD.

Here goes nothing:

```
using namespace SocketLib;
using namespace SimpleMUD;
int main() {
    try {
    ItemDatabase::Load();
    PlayerDatabase::Load();
    ListeningManager<Telnet, Logon> lm;
    ConnectionManager<Telnet, Logon> cm( 128, 60, 65536 );

    lm.SetConnectionManager( &cm );
    lm.AddPort( 5100 );
    Game::GetTimer().Reset();
```

```
Game::Running() = true;

while( Game::Running() ) {
    lm.Listen();
    cm.Manage();
    ThreadLib::YieldThread();
}   // end while
}   // end try
```

The item and the player databases are loaded, and both a logon manager and a connection manager are created. The two managers are told to use the Logon class as their default handlers, and the connection manager is set up to allow a flood limit of 128 bytes per second, a sending timeout limit of 60 seconds, and a sending buffer limit of 65,536 bytes, or 64 kilobytes.

Once those have been created, the listening manager is told about the connection manager, the listening manager is told to listen on port 5100, the game timer is reset, and the game's running Boolean is set to true.

After that, the loop starts, and it runs while the Game::Running Boolean continues to return true. Inside the loop, the listening manager is told to listen for new connections, the connection manager is told to manage its sending and receiving tasks, and the thread library yields the thread so that the application doesn't suck up your entire CPU power.

That's it for the actual game logic.

Now, the entire thing is enclosed within a try block, so whenever an exception is thrown, you can catch it:

```
catch( SocketLib::Exception& e ) {   // catch socket exceptions
    ERRORLOG.Log( "Fatal Socket Error: " + e.PrintError() );
}
catch( ThreadLib::Exception& ) {     // catch thread exceptions
    ERRORLOG.Log( "Fatal Thread Error" );
}
catch( std::exception& e ) {         // catch standard exceptions
    ERRORLOG.Log( "Standard Error: " + std::string( e.what() ) );
}
catch( ... ) {                       // catch other exceptions
    ERRORLOG.Log( "Unspecified Error" );
}
SimpleMUD::PlayerDatabase::Save();   // save the player database
}
```

Four types of exceptions can be thrown: socket, thread, standard, and miscellaneous. Technically, miscellaneous exceptions should never be thrown, but when developing software on top of libraries, you should be prepared for the unexpected. If a simple line of code or two can prevent that, you want to prevent a random crash from wiping out minutes of changes to the database.

Each error type logs a message within the error log, so if the game crashes, you can get an idea of what caused the crash, and then the player database is saved back out to disk.

That's all folks. Seriously.

Now that you've got a very basic "talker" server up and running, which is barely a MUD, it's a good time to briefly discuss the overall design.

What you've got is a basic *reactionary* server. It doesn't do anything except listen for connections and act on new commands from the existing connections. Figure 8.12 shows an example of what happens when the listening manager is told to listen and a new connection logs on.

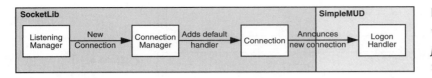

Figure 8.12

When a new connection joins the game, the SocketLib *library handles almost all the action.*

Once a connection is logged on, whenever the connection sends data, the connection manager picks up the data whenever its Manage command is invoked and follows a process somewhat like that shown in Figure 8.13. Again, as you can see from the figure, almost all the messy low-level networking stuff is handled by the SocketLib, so the SimpleMUD only really cares about actual game logic, which is the way things should be. I can't tell you how many MUDs I've seen with the game logic inextricably and directly entwined within the Sockets API, and those always end up as huge messes in the end.

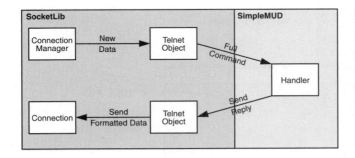

Figure 8.13

Notice the route the process takes as it sends data from a connection to the game and when the server responds.

And now for some screenshots! Once you've got the MUD up and running, just find your favorite Telnet client, and telnet into your IP address on port 5100.

Figure 8.14 shows a screenshot of a sample stats printout, inventory listing, and experience printout.

Figure 8.15 shows a few inventory commands.

And finally, Figure 8.16 shows some speaking commands.

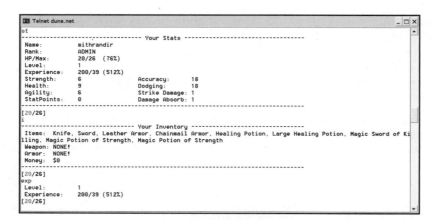

Figure 8.14

Three status-printing functions.

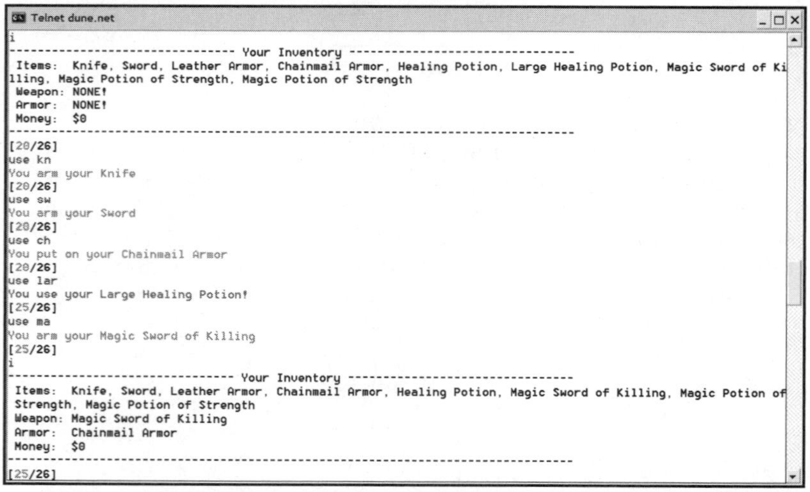

Figure 8.15

A person playing around with his inventory of items.

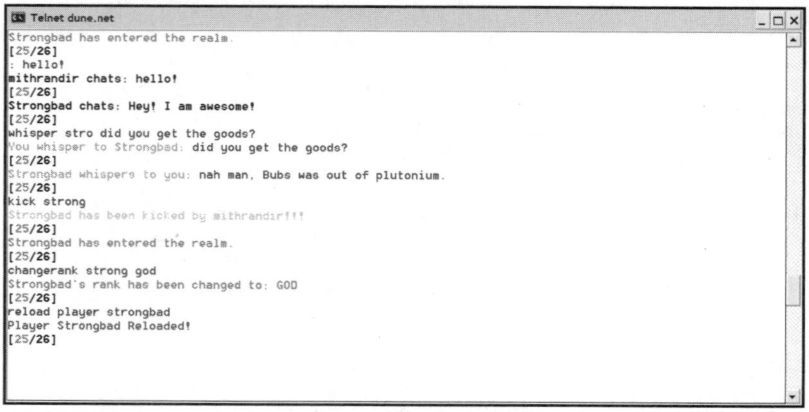

Figure 8.16

Various user-interaction commands in use.

Summary

I must apologize for the length of this chapter. The truth of the matter is that MUDs are extremely complex games internally, and the only way you're going to get anything done is with tons of designing, and tons of code.

Within this chapter, I've shown you some important concepts about entities within the game, and how they are stored to disk. I've also shown you the three main connection handlers used within SimpleMUD: the logon, training, and game handlers.

All these concepts will be built upon and improved within the next few chapters. For the next chapter, I'll be covering the map system and the store system of SimpleMUD.

CHAPTER 9

MAPS, STORES, AND TRAINING ROOMS

In the previous chapter, I showed you the complete baseline for the SimpleMUD, which included everything dealing with entities, databases, logs, items, players, and the three connection handlers. Unfortunately, with all that code, you still don't have anything more than a glorified chat program.

This chapter takes the game to the next level, by adding the mapping system, as well as stores and training rooms, which are special types of rooms.

In this chapter, you will learn how to:

- Add a simple map system to the game
- Add stores to the game
- Add training rooms to the game
- Implement the new commands dealing with maps, stores, and training rooms
- Implement the new item getting-and-dropping commands

Adding New Features to the Baseline

I've added a bunch of new things to the game in this chapter: rooms, room databases, room database pointers, stores, and store databases. Table 9.1 lists all the new components and where they are stored within the /Demos/Chapter09/Demo09-01/SimpleMUD directory on the CD.

Table 9.1   New Component Files

Component	Location
Room class	Room.h and .cpp
RoomDatabase class	RoomDatabase.h and .cpp
room database pointer class	DatabasePointers.h and .cpp
Store class	Store.h and .cpp
StoreDatabase class	StoreDatabase.h and .cpp

Rooms

The first order of business is the Room class. A Room, like almost every other object within the game, is derived from an Entity. This means, of course, that rooms have names and IDs, but you don't typically search through room names as you did in the previous chapter with players and items. Room names simply describe the room to the player, so he can navigate around the MUD easily, always having a general idea of where he is.

Room Data

Rooms have all the data described in Chapter 7, "Designing the SimpleMUD," and they store three different groups of data.

Template Data

First, there is the "template" data—data that is loaded from disk, but never changes within the game:

```
RoomType m_type;              // type of the room
int m_data;                   // storeid if it is a store
string m_description;         // description of the room
entityid m_rooms[NUMDIRECTIONS]; // exits
enemytemplate m_spawnwhich;   // which enemy to spawn
int m_maxenemies;             // how many enemies max
```

Three new features need to be described at this point:

- RoomType—enumeration describing room function
- NUMDIRECTIONS—constant. Number of exits per room
- enemytemplate—database pointer for enemy templates

RoomType is a simple enumeration, much like the ItemType and PlayerRank enumerations in the previous chapter. (They are found within the Attributes.h file.) The three values are PLAINROOM, TRAININGROOM, and STORE, and these values obviously represent the three types of rooms. This design means that rooms can serve only one purpose.

NUMDIRECTIONS can also be found in Attributes.h, and simply represents the number of directions a player can move in any room. (Remember: for the SimpleMUD this is four.)

> **NOTE**
>
> This is a classic method of representing *special* rooms, and it works well in the SimpleMUD. However, there may be a time when you need rooms to be more than one type (for example, a room that serves both as a training room *and* a store). For that kind of implementation, you should consider an alternative method of storing this information. One way would be to use bitmasks, in which the first bit would represent whether the room is a store, the second bit would represent whether it is a training room, and so on. The BetterMUD in this book takes a completely different approach, as you'll see in Chapter 11, "The Better MUD."

Finally, the `enemytemplate` type is a `databasepointer<EnemyTemplate, EnemyTemplateDatabase>`. Unfortunately, I don't go over those until the next chapter, so at the top of Room.h, I define it as a simple `entityid`:

```
typedef entityid enemytemplate;    // REMOVE THIS LATER
```

Volatile Data

Here's the next group of data:

```
list<item> m_items;             // items in the room
money m_money;                  // money on the floor
```

Basically, this data is *volatile*. (It changes.) Whenever the game needs to save all the current rooms to disk, there's no need to write all the template data I showed you previously, such as the room name and description (since it never changes), so instead of writing out all a room's data, it needs to write only the volatile data. I'll go into more detail on this when I cover room databases.

Because I mentioned in Chapter 7 that the capacity of a room is limited to 32 items, you may think that it would be logical to use an array-like structure, such as a vector, to store the items. However, vectors are problematic for two reasons. First, you'd need to keep one of these arrays per room, which means that every room would have the capacity to store all 32 items all the time. Obviously, you'll never even come close to having that many items lying around in the game, so this would waste space. The second problem is that the continuous adding and removing of items are expensive vector operations. In contrast, lists are quick for insertions and removals, so they actually work better in this situation.

Temporary Volatile Data

Here's the final group of data:

```
list<player> m_players;
list<enemy> m_enemies;
```

These two lists store players and enemies (in the form of `databasepointers`, of course). You won't see the `enemy` class until Chapter 10, "Enemies, Combat, and the Game Loop," but for now you can assume that it's a `databasepointer<Enemy, EnemyDatabase>`.

However, the lists are never saved to disk (as items and money are). Keeping this information on disk is redundant, since players and enemies already know the room they are in.

Imagine this scenario for a moment: You're editing the databases, and you change the room that a player is in. The map databases track which players are in which rooms, though, which means that you'll have to find the room within the room database and move that player's ID to the new room. This is an incredibly inconvenient way of editing the databases, and it also wastes space by storing redundant data.

Since players and enemies know which room they are in (on disk), when the players and enemies are loaded, the game finds what rooms they exist in and inserts the entities into the appropriate rooms. Then, depending on their identities, the players and enemies insert themselves into the `m_players` or `m_enemies` lists.

Room Functions

Next I want to cover the functions that you can use on rooms. Many functions are fairly simple, but a few are complex; I'll show you the simple functions first.

Accessors

As with most classes in this book, a bunch of simple accessor functions simply allow you to access and modify room attributes. Here's a listing of the accessors:

```
inline RoomType& Type()        { return m_type; }
inline int& Data()             { return m_data; }
inline string& Description()   { return m_description; }
inline entityid& Adjacent( int p_dir ) { return m_rooms[p_dir]; }
inline enemytemplate& SpawnWhich() { return m_spawnwhich; }
inline int& MaxEnemies()       { return m_maxenemies; }
inline list<item>& Items()     { return m_items; }
inline money& Money()          { return m_money; }
inline list<enemy>& Enemies()  { return m_enemies; }
inline list<player>& Players() { return m_players; }
```

I don't *really* need to explain all those to you, do I? Make a special note of the Adjacent function, however. The function returns the ID of the room adjacent to it in the given direction as an entityid. Basically, you can call it like this:

```
Room r;
// *** do init stuff somewhere here ***
entityid south = r.Adjacent( SOUTH );
```

Of course, as with all aspects of entity IDs, the value 0 is invalid, so the return of zero from the function means there is no exit in that direction. The enumeration values are defined in Attributes.h as part of the Direction enumeration, and there are four values representing the four directions: NORTH, EAST, SOUTH, and WEST.

Player Functions

The two player functions are somewhat simple. They allow you to add and remove players (based on ID) to and from a room:

```
void Room::AddPlayer( player p_player ) {
    m_players.push_back( p_player );
}

void Room::RemovePlayer( player p_player ) {
    m_players.erase( std::find( m_players.begin(),
                                m_players.end(),
                                (entityid)p_player ) );
}
```

As you can see, it's simply wrapping STL code into easy-to-use functions. A new player is always added to the back of the list. Players are removed using a combination of `std::list::erase` and `std::find`. The `find` function is used to find a player within the list, compared to `p_player`. You may have noticed, however, that `p_player` is explicitly converted to an `entityid` before it is used within the `find` function. This is because database pointers don't know how to compare themselves with other database pointers, but they *do* know how to compare themselves to `entityids`.

NOTE

I used lists to store the players in a room here, but you should feel free to use whatever you want. Lists are helpful because they are resizable, and keep things in order. In the BetterMUD, you'll see that I didn't have much use for keeping players in order, so I opted to use sets instead.

Ambiguity Errors

The lack of an `operator==` to compare two database pointers with each other is intentional. In addition, there is no `operator==` function that compares `entityids` either, but to the compiler, it looks as if there is one because all database pointers have an `operator entityid()` conversion operator function. If you have a database pointer named `dbp1` and an `entityid` named `id`, the line `dpb1 == id` would actually end up automatically calling the conversion operator of the pointer object, thus converting it into an `entityid`. This would then call `operator==` on the IDs. Since you know that IDs are just typedefs for integers, you should see that they already have a built-in `operator==`.

If, however, you wrote some code such as `dbp1 == dbp2`, you would get an *ambiguity error*, meaning that the compiler couldn't figure out which function to call. Since database pointers can be converted to actual pointers (for example, `Player*` in the case of class `player`), they can't figure out if you're trying to compare `Player*`s or `entityids` (even though you know they should be equivalent).

It gets even worse if you add an `operator==` to compare database pointers into the mix, because then the program can't figure out if you want to compare `Player*`s, `entityids`, or database pointers. That means that the new `operator==` you just added would never be called and would be pointless code. Because of this, it is *required* that you convert your database pointers into plain `entityids` before you compare them with other database pointers.

Item Functions

Three functions deal with items, and two of the functions are virtually identical to the two player functions I just showed you: AddItem and RemoveItem. Both functions take item database pointers as parameters.

Since the code is virtually identical, I'll show you only the third item function, which doesn't have a player equivalent:

```
item Room::FindItem( const string& p_item ) {
    std::list<item>::iterator itr =                // find an item that matches
            BasicLib::double_find_if(
                m_items.begin(), m_items.end(),
                matchentityfull( p_item ), matchentity( p_item ) );

    if( itr == m_items.end() )
        return 0;
    return *itr;
}
```

Using a full or partial name as a parameter, this function finds the ID of an item within the room. Basically, it's a wrapper around the double_find_if function, which you used in the previous chapter. If an item isn't found, the ID of zero is returned, and if an item *is* found, its ID is returned. For example, if you had items "Sword", "Axe", and "Club" in a room, and you run this function with input "sw", it returns the ID of the "Sword" object.

File Functions

Three functions deal with loading and saving rooms to and from disk. They are

```
void LoadTemplate( istream& p_stream );
void LoadData( istream& p_stream );
void SaveData( ostream& p_stream );
```

The first function loads all the template data from disk. There's no equivalent save function, simply because there doesn't need to be one; template data is loaded once from disk and shouldn't be modified.

> **NOTE**
>
> There is one tiny difference in the AddItem function: When the function detects that there are 32 or more items in the room, it automatically pops off the first item in the room. Since all new items in the room are added to the end of the list, the first item in the list is also the oldest item in the list. This means that whenever there are 32 items in a room, and you drop a 33rd, the oldest item in the room is destroyed, and you can't get it back. This prevents certain rooms from getting completely flooded with items that people don't seem to pick up.

On the other hand, the next two functions deal with loading and saving the volatile data—namely, the items and money within a room.

I don't want to spend much space showing you the contents of these functions; they closely resemble the player and item loading and saving functions described in the previous chapter. I'll show you sample entries, however.

Here's what a sample room template looks like:

```
[ID]             1
[NAME]           Town Square
[DESCRIPTION]    You are in the town square. This is the central meeting place for the
realm.
[TYPE]           PLAINROOM
[DATA]           0
[NORTH]          2
[EAST]           25
[SOUTH]          4
[WEST]           5
[ENEMY]          0
[MAXENEMIES]     0
```

This shows you that the ID of the room is 1, the name is "Town Square", and a brief description of the room follows. It's a plain room, meaning that it's not a store or a training room; thus, the [DATA] tag isn't meaningful for this room. For a store, however, this tag would be the ID of the store.

There are exits in all four directions; going north leads you to room 2, east to 25, south to 4, and west to 5. There are no enemies within the room, which means that the [MAXENEMIES] entry is meaningless, too.

Now here's an example of volatile data entry for a room:

```
[ROOMID] 1
[ITEMS] 10 5 6 3 1 11 0
[MONEY] 200
```

The entry contains the room ID, a list of all item IDs in the room (ending with a zero, commonly known as a *sentinel value*), and the amount of money in the room. From this entry, you can see that there are six items in the room (items 10, 5, 6, 3, 1, and 11, whatever they may be), and $200 on the floor.

I'm going to show you the LoadData function, because it contains the most interesting function code. Here it is:

```
void Room::LoadData( istream& p_stream ) {
    string temp;  p_stream >> temp;   // chew up "[ITEMS]" tag

    m_items.clear();                  // clear and load items
    entityid last;
    while( extract( p_stream, last ) != 0 )
```

```
            m_items.push_back( last );

    p_stream >> temp;    p_stream >> m_money;   // load money
}
```

The function uses the `BasicLib::extract` function to extract item IDs from the stream and scan until it reaches zero, the sentinel value.

I need to make one important point about the function. Whenever this function is called, the room clears its item list. The reasoning is that you may want to *reload* the room while in the game, and if you start appending data to the end of the item list, you may end up with duplicated data. Imagine that a room contains items 10, 11, and 12, and then in the middle of the game, you reload that room. If you don't clear the item list, you'll end up with two of each item: 10, 11, 12, 10, 11, 12.

Also, as with the item and player loading functions that were described in Chapter 8, "Items and Players," the database manages the loading in and setting of the entity ID; therefore, this code doesn't load in the [ROOMID] tag.

The Room Database

Like players and items, rooms have a database as well. If you guessed that the database is called `RoomDatabase`, you earned a cookie! No, I'm not mailing you a cookie; you'll have to come here and get it.

Anyway, the room database is very simple, and it inherits from the `EntityDatabaseVector` class I showed you in the previous chapter. Here's the class definition:

```
class RoomDatabase : public EntityDatabaseVector<Room> {
public:
    static void LoadTemplates();
    static void LoadData();
    static void SaveData();
}; // end class RoomDatabase
```

The room database class has functions for loading the templates for each room, loading the volatile data for each room, and saving the volatile data for each room.

All the room data is stored within two files: /maps/default.map, which holds all the template data, and /maps/default.data, which holds all the item and money data.

The maps are separated into two files for a reason; periodically in the game, all the item and money data must be written to disk. Unfortunately, since I'm using ASCII text files, there's really no way to go into the existing file and modify what has been changed. As I told you in Chapter 8, the only way to write out ASCII data to disk is to completely destroy the file and rewrite all the data. Obviously, since there is no reason to write the template data back to disk, it makes sense to keep the template data in one file, and the volatile data in another, so that just the volatile data can be written out when it needs to be.

Figure 9.1 shows a sample of the file setup for rooms. You can see that the template data is stored in one file, regular volatile data in another, and temporary volatile data isn't stored at all.

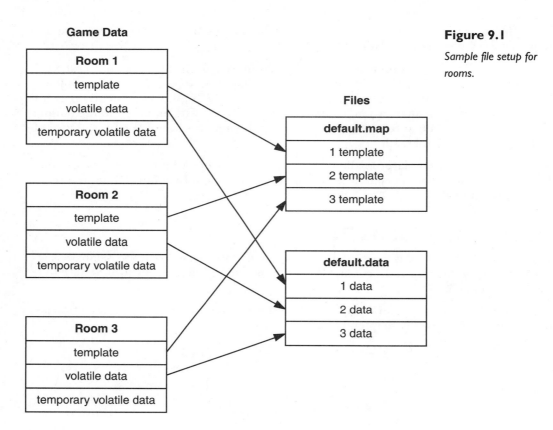

Figure 9.1

Sample file setup for rooms.

The code for the three file functions is pretty simple and similar to what you've seen before with the player and item databases, but since you haven't seen a vector-based database yet, I'll show you some of the code in action.

Loading Templates

The process for loading the templates from disk is fairly straightforward. For each room, the room ID is loaded in first, and then the vector is resized if there isn't enough room available. Once you know there's enough room in the vector for the room you're loading the template for, the ID for that room is set, and the template is loaded:

```
void RoomDatabase::LoadTemplates() {
    std::ifstream file( "maps/default.map" );
    entityid id;
```

```
        std::string temp;

        while( file.good() ) {
            file >> temp >> id;              // load ID
            if( m_vector.size() <= id )      // check if there's room
                m_vector.resize( id + 1 );   // resize if there isn't

            m_vector[id].ID() = id;          // set the ID
            m_vector[id].LoadTemplate( file ); // load template
            file >> std::ws;                 // eat whitespace after it
        }
    }
```

Basically, the only thing new here is the vector resizing. With an associative container such as a map, STL automatically creates and inserts items when you call its operator[] on a key that doesn't exist, but vectors aren't as easy to work with. Calling operator[] on a non-existent index is an error, and depending on your STL implementation, it may throw an exception. Don't worry, though; this behavior is actually a good thing. With a map, if you accidentally try inserting something with a large key (in the billions, say), you'll insert at most one new item. If a vector auto-resized on operator[], however, your program would try to resize the array to within the billions, which is obviously not a good thing.

Loading Data

The LoadData function is similar to LoadTemplates. Essentially, the only differences are that it calls Room::LoadData on each room, instead of Room::LoadTemplate, and it doesn't resize the vector either. LoadData doesn't resize the vector because it shouldn't need to. Whenever you load a room from disk, the template should have already been loaded; thus, the ID should already be valid.

> **TIP**
>
> In a more robust MUD, it would be a good idea to add some error checking. I've neglected to do so due to time and space constraints, but you should always put lots of error-checking code into your MUD projects.

Saving Data

Saving the temporary data, just as with every other saving function you've seen in this book so far, is a simple task:

```
void RoomDatabase::SaveData() {
    std::ofstream file( "maps/default.data" );
    iterator itr = begin();
    while( itr != end() ) {
        file << "[ROOMID] " << itr->ID() << "\n";  // write ID
        m_vector[itr->ID()].SaveData( file );      // write data
        file << "\n";
```

```
        ++itr;
    }
}
```

As I mentioned earlier, rooms don't know how to load or save their IDs to and from disk, so it is the responsibility of the database to do it instead. The function essentially loops through every room, writes out the ID, and then writes out the rest of the data.

Room Database Pointers

If you're beginning to notice a trend here, you're absolutely correct. Everything entity-based in the game has a similarly designed database and similar means of being accessed. Therefore, it shouldn't come as a surprise that the room database also has database pointers, just as players and items do. The definition of these pointers has been added to the /SimpleMUD/DatabasePointer.h and .cpp files:

```
// .h file:
DATABASEPOINTER( room, Room )
// .cpp file:
DATABASEPOINTERIMPL( room, Room, RoomDatabase )
```

Keeping with the standard naming scheme I've been using all along, pointers to rooms are called room (lowercase), while the actual room objects are Rooms (first letter capitalized).

Stores

The other major topic I cover in this chapter is stores. Stores are simple entities; their only purpose is to store a list of all the kinds of items that can be bought and sold there.

Because of this, the Store class is simple:

```
class Store : public Entity {
public:
    typedef std::list<item>::iterator iterator;
    iterator begin()    { return m_items.begin(); }
    iterator end()      { return m_items.end(); }
    size_t size()       { return m_items.size(); }
    item find( const string& p_item );
    bool has( entityid p_item );
    friend istream& operator>>( istream& p_stream, Store& s );
protected:
    list<item> m_items;
};
```

In terms of data storage, all a store needs is a list of the items that are bought and sold there.

Helper Functions

To make stores more usable, stores utilize some of the standard STL container functions, which basically wrap around existing algorithms and functions.

For example, you can see that stores have the standard begin, end, and size functions, in addition to two search functions: find and has.

The find function searches the store using a double full-then-partial name match, such as you saw used in Chapter 8, and it returns the ID of the item it found, or zero if nothing is found. The other searching function simply returns true or false if an item ID exists within the database.

Those two functions simply wrap around the BasicLib::double_find_if and std::find algorithms respectively, so let me just skip to the file streaming function.

Stream Extraction Function

Since stores don't change throughout the game, you need only one function to deal with files: a stream extraction function. Obviously, this function extracts a store from a stream.

First, let me begin by showing you a sample store entry in a file:

```
[ID]        1
[NAME]      Bobs Weapon Shop
[Items]     40 41 42 43 44 58 59 60 61 62 63 64 65 66 67 68 0
```

The ID and the name are inherited from Entity, so every store has them as well as a list of all items the store sells. This should remind you of the way that items are stored inside of rooms, and it should come as no surprise that these are loaded in the same manner:

```
inline istream& operator>>( istream& p_stream, Store& s ) {
    string temp;
    p_stream >> temp >> std::ws;            // chew whitespace
    std::getline( p_stream, s.Name() );     // read name
    s.m_items.clear();                      // clear existing items
    entityid last;
    p_stream >> temp;                       // chew up "[ITEMS]" tag
    while( extract( p_stream, last ) != 0 ) // loop while item ID is valid
        s.m_items.push_back( last );        // add item
    return p_stream;
}
```

As usual, the database manages the loading of the [ID] tag, and this function simply loads the name and every item until the sentinel value 0 is reached (using the BasicLib::extract function for help).

The Store Database

The store database is probably the simplest database class in the entire game. Take a look at the definition:

```
class StoreDatabase : public EntityDatabase<Store> {
public:
    static bool Load();
}; // end class StoreDatabase
```

As you can see, the store database inherits from the map-based `EntityDatabase` class. It contains a single function to load the database from disk.

All stores are kept in a text file named /stores/stores.str. The `Load` function is almost identical to the other `EntityDatabase` loading functions you saw from Chapter 8, so I'm not going to show you the code here; it's largely redundant and boring.

Also note that there is no associated database pointer for the `Store` class; there simply isn't a need for one in the game.

Ch-Ch-Ch-Changes

Now that you know about the major components of the game that have been added for this chapter, you can go on to the existing components that have been changed. There are many changes that need to be made to enable the new components to work, such as making sure players are properly added to and removed from rooms, adding the new room commands, and many other changes as well.

Entering and Leaving the Realm

Whenever a player is within the `Game` handler/state, that player's ID *must* be within a room's `m_players` list. The easiest way to make sure this happens is to add the player to the room list whenever he enters the state, and remove the player from his room list whenever he exits the state.

Luckily, we have two functions—`Game::Enter` and `Game::Leave`—that are called whenever a player enters or leaves the state!

Entering

So the first order of business is making sure that a player is always inside of a room whenever he is in the game state, by adding this line to the `Game::Enter` function. (I'm going to refrain from posting the whole function, since you've seen it earlier, and I need to conserve space for more interesting things.)

```
    p.CurrentRoom()->AddPlayer( p.ID() );
```

Within the function, p is a Player reference.

To make the game seem a little easier to play, the following is added to this function:

```
if( p.Newbie() )    GotoTrain();
else                p.SendString( PrintRoom( p.CurrentRoom() ) );
```

The first line of this code segment should be familiar to you—it is from Chapter 8. It hasn't changed. The addition is bolded (second line). If a player is not a newbie, the room's current description is printed out to the player. (It isn't printed for newbies. The new player is immediately going into the training state, so the player doesn't need a room description yet.) The bolded code uses the Game::PrintRoom function, which I will show you in a little bit. And the bolded code gives a player a sense of his bearings whenever he enters the game.

Leaving

On the other hand, whenever a player is leaving the game state, he needs to be removed from the room that he is in. This line of code is added to the Game::Leave function:

```
p.CurrentRoom()->RemovePlayer( p.ID() );
```

No other changes need to be made to this function.

New Room-Related Commands

There are a bunch of new room-related commands that have been added to the Game::Handler function:

> **look**—prints a description of the current room
>
> **north**—moves a player north
>
> **east**—moves a player east
>
> **south**—moves a player south
>
> **west**—moves a player west
>
> **get**—picks up an item from the ground
>
> **drop**—drops an item from a player's inventory

First, let's look at the *look* command:

```
if( firstword == "look" || firstword == "l" ) {
    p.SendString( PrintRoom( p.CurrentRoom() ) );
    return;
}
```

If the user types in either look or just l, the contents of the room are sent to his connection using the PrintRoom function that I mentioned before.

All four movement commands are structurally similar, so I'm only going to show you the first one, for moving north:

```
if( firstword == "north" || firstword == "n" ) {
    Move( NORTH );
    return;
}
```

If the user types north or just n, the Game::Move function is called to move a player in a specified direction. As you can probably imagine, south calls Move with a parameter of SOUTH, and so on.

Finally, there are the two item commands:

```
if( firstword == "get" || firstword == "take" ) {
    GetItem( RemoveWord( p_data, 0 ) );
    return;
}
if( firstword == "drop" ) {
    DropItem( RemoveWord( p_data, 0 ) );
    return;
}
```

Both commands strip off the first word (get, take or drop), and then call either the GetItem or DropItem functions with the name of the item, so get sword calls GetItem("sword"). I discuss these functions in the next section.

New Room Functions

In the preceding sections, you saw four functions that you haven't seen before: Game::PrintRoom, Game::Move, Game::GetItem, and Game::DropItem. Along with those, there is one more function dealing with rooms—Game::SendRoom—which sends a string of text to everyone within a given room.

Printing Room Descriptions

The PrintRoom function is a long and boring one; it just goes through the contents of a room, formatting and coloring things as it goes along. I'm going to show you bits and pieces of it, but on the whole, it's not an important function.

```
string Game::PrintRoom( room p_room ) {
    string desc = "\r\n" + bold + white + p_room->Name() + "\r\n";
    string temp;
    int count;
    desc += bold + magenta + p_room->Description() + "\r\n";
```

The function starts out by printing (to a string) the name of the room in white, and then the description of the room in magenta. The next part of the code prints out the exits from the room:

```
    desc += bold + green + "exits: ";
    for( int d = 0; d < NUMDIRECTIONS; d++ ) {
```

```
        if( p_room->Adjacent( d ) != 0 )
            desc += DIRECTIONSTRINGS[d] + "  ";
    }
    desc += "\r\n";
```

It checks to see if there is an exit in each direction, and if so, it prints out the name of the direction of the exit. The next part is item and money printing:

```
temp = bold + yellow + "You see: ";
count = 0;
if( p_room->Money() > 0 ) {
    count++;
    temp += "$" + tostring( p_room->Money() ) + ", ";  // print money
}

std::list<item>::iterator itemitr = p_room->Items().begin();
while( itemitr != p_room->Items().end() ) {
    count++;
    temp += (*itemitr)->Name() + ", ";                  // print item
    ++itemitr;
}
```

The function checks if there is money on the ground, and if so, it's printed. The code block after that loops through every item in the room, and prints each description.

The next block of code chops off the last two characters of the item string (if there are any items in the room at all) and appends the item string to desc:

```
if( count > 0 ) {
    temp.erase( temp.size() - 2, 2 );
    desc += temp + "\r\n";
}
```

Why are the last two characters chopped off? Well, if you had some items in a room, it would end up looking like this: You see: Sword, Knife, Axe, , with an extra comma and a space at the end. This is just a minor annoyance, but it is an annoyance nonetheless, so this code fixes it.

I'm not going to show you the rest of the function, since the next part of the function is essentially the same as the item printing, except that it prints the people in the room instead.

Here's an example of what a room listing looks like:

```
Town Square
You are in the town square. This is the central meeting place for the realm.
exits: NORTH  EAST  SOUTH  WEST
You see: Rusty Knife, Heavy Longsword, Jeweled Dagger
People: mithrandir, Washu, Tyraziel
```

In the next chapter, I revisit this function to add enemy printing as well.

Moving Between Rooms

There is a helper function as part of the Game handler that moves a player in one direction.
There are a number of things it needs to accomplish to successfully move a player in a
direction, as you'll see from the function:

```
void Game::Move( int p_direction ) {
    Player& p = *m_player;
    room next = p.CurrentRoom()->Adjacent( p_direction );
    room previous = p.CurrentRoom();
```

The first thing the helper function does is get a reference to the player (p) and then get the
room ID of the player's current room (previous) and the room to which the player is
moving (next).

```
    if( next == 0 ) {
        SendRoom( red + p.Name() + " bumps into the wall to the " +
                DIRECTIONSTRINGS[p_direction] + "!!!",
                p.CurrentRoom() );
        return;
    }
```

If there is no exit in the direction the player wants to go, everyone is told that the player
bumped into the wall (much to his embarrassment), and the function ends.

At this point, you know that there is a room in the direction the player wants to go, so you
need to remove the player from that room, and tell everyone he left:

```
    previous->RemovePlayer( p.ID() );
    SendRoom( green + p.Name() + " leaves to the " +
            DIRECTIONSTRINGS[p_direction] + ".",
            previous );
    SendRoom( green + p.Name() + " enters from the " +
            DIRECTIONSTRINGS[OppositeDirection(p_direction)] + ".",
            next );
    p.SendString( green + "You walk " + DIRECTIONSTRINGS[p_direction] + "." );
    p.CurrentRoom() = next;
    next->AddPlayer( p.ID() );
```

The previous code segment also tells everyone in the new room that the player has entered
it, and tells the player that he moved to a different room. The player's current room is reset
to next, and the player is added to the room's player list.

```
    p.SendString( PrintRoom( next ) );
}
```

The last bit of code shows the room's description to the player, so he can navigate easily
without constantly looking around. This approach is okay for small MUDs like this, but for a
larger MUD, you might consider having two different room descriptions, one long and one
short; when players move around, the short description displays, but when they explicitly
type look, the long description displays.

Getting Items

Picking up items from the floor is a complicated task; there are so many different things that you need to check.

The first part of the function checks to see if the player wants to pick up any money that's on the ground. This is done by checking if the player typed in the character '$' as the first letter of the parameter string:

```
void Game::GetItem( string p_item ) {
    Player& p = *m_player;                 // get player reference
    if( p_item[0] == '$' ) {               // check if player wants money
        p_item.erase( 0, 1 );              // chop off the '$'
        money m = BasicLib::totype<money>( p_item );  // get amount desired
```

If the player did indeed type '$', the '$' is erased from the string, and the amount of money the player wants to pick up is converted into m. Next, the program checks that there's enough money on the ground to satisfy the greedy player:

```
        if( m > p.CurrentRoom()->Money() ) {  // make sure enough money exists
            p.SendString( red + bold + "There isn't that much here!" );
        }
        else {
            p.Money() += m;                    // add money to player
            p.CurrentRoom()->Money() -= m;     // subtract money from floor
            SendRoom( cyan + bold + p.Name() + " picks up $" +
                      tostring( m ) + ".", p.CurrentRoom() );
        }
        return;
    }
```

If there isn't enough money, then obviously the player can't pick it up, and the player is told so. On the other hand, if there is enough money, the amount of money the player wants is added to his character, subtracted from the room, and the entire room is told about how much money the player took. Then the function returns.

> **NOTE**
>
> Because the game thinks that if you type in get $<whatever> you want money, it never thinks that an item starts with the character $. Therefore, you should never name items starting with the letter $, because the game will never detect them when you want to get or drop them. Why anyone would want to, I don't know.

NOTE

This method of keeping money separate from regular items is really just a hack. In real life, it's more logical to represent a pile of coins as a bunch of coins. Unfortunately there is no easy way to solve this kind of dual treatment of items and money, simply because the game would find it extremely difficult to treat a few thousand coins in a single room as separate objects. I explore a different way to tackle this problem in the BetterMUD.

On the other hand, if the first character isn't $, the game assumes that the player is trying to get an item:

```
item i = p.CurrentRoom()->FindItem( p_item );
if( i == 0 ) {                  // check if item exists in room
    p.SendString( red + bold + "You don't see that here!" );
    return;
}

if( !p.PickUpItem( i ) ) {    // try to pick up item
    p.SendString( red + bold + "You can't carry that much!" );
    return;
}

p.CurrentRoom()->RemoveItem( i );  // remove item from room
SendRoom( cyan + bold + p.Name() + " picks up " + i->Name() + ".",
        p.CurrentRoom() );
}
```

First the room is searched to see if it contains an item named p_item (a string), and the ID of that item is stored in i. If the search turns up dry, the room doesn't have an item matching the name. The player is told so, and the function returns.

Then, the player's PickUpItem function is called, attempting to pick up the item. If it returns false, that means that the player didn't have enough room for the item, and thus the item isn't picked up.

Finally, if the function passes both tests, the item is removed from the room, and the room is told that the player picked up the item.

Dropping Items

Dropping an item is essentially the opposite process from getting an item; if you're dropping money, the game code makes sure you have enough money, and then drops it. If you're dropping an item, the game code makes sure you have the item, and then drops it into the room using the Room::AddItem function (which makes sure that there are at most 32 items in a room at any given time). Because the code is similar, I don't want to waste precious space in this chapter. I hope you'll forgive me for moving on.

Sending Text to a Room

To send text to a room, you need to be able to find every player in that room and send text to their connections. This is where the m_players list inside every Room comes in handy. It would strain your MUD to have a function that searches every player in the database to see if he is in a specific room, and then sends text to him; so instead, I use the list of people already in a room:

```
void Game::SendRoom( string p_text, room p_room ) {
    std::for_each( p_room->Players().begin(),
                   p_room->Players().end(),
                   playersend( p_text ) );
}
```

Here, I utilize the std::for_each algorithm and the playersend functor (from Chapter 8) to send p_text to every player in room p_room. This works because the playersend functor was designed to work on both containers of Rooms, and containers of Room*s (or datatypes that work just like Room*s, such as the room database pointer class). See Chapter 8 for an in-depth discussion on this, if you haven't already.

Commands Related to New Store

In addition to the movement commands, there are three new store commands:

> **list**—lists everything a store sells and buys
>
> **buy <item>**—buys an item from the store
>
> **sell <item>**—sells an item to the store

These commands are added into the Game::Handle function. Here's the part that handles store listing:

```
    if( firstword == "list" ) {
        if( p.CurrentRoom()->Type() != STORE ) {
            p.SendString( red + bold + "You're not in a store!" );
            return;
        }
        p.SendString( StoreList( p.CurrentRoom()->Data() ) );
        return;
    }
```

This code makes sure you're in a store first, and then it calls the Game::StoreList function (which you haven't seen yet), passing in the ID of the store (contained within the current rooms' Data() variable), to get a list of the items in the store.

Buying items is similar:

```
if( firstword == "buy" ) {
    if( p.CurrentRoom()->Type() != STORE ) {
        p.SendString( red + bold + "You're not in a store!" );
        return;
    }
    Buy( RemoveWord( p_data, 0 ) );
    return;
}
```

This time the code calls the `Game::Buy` command with the name of the item you wish to purchase (by removing the "buy" from the string). The "sell" command is equivalent, except that it calls `Game::Sell` instead.

The StoreList Function

I don't know about you, but I think that code that prints information is boring. Unfortunately, MUDs are packed with them, and the `Game::StoreList` function is one of them. Here's the function declaration:

```
string Game::StoreList( entityid p_store );
```

Essentially the function takes the ID of a store, and prints out the items that are available to buy or sell. The function is a large loop inside, utilizing the `Store`'s iterator functions, and I don't want to take up space showing you the code. Instead, I'll show you just a sample listing of a store:

```
------------------------------------------------------------
Welcome to Bob's Weapon Shop!
------------------------------------------------------------
Item                     | Price
------------------------------------------------------------
Rusty Knife              | 5
Knife                    | 15
Dagger                   | 40
Shortsword               | 50
------------------------------------------------------------
```

Ta-da!

Buying Items

It requires roughly the same amount of checking to buy items as to pick them up. The function to buy items should check that the store has the item the player wants, check if the player has enough money to pay for the item, and check if the player has enough room to carry it. Here is the code:

```
void Game::Buy( const string& p_item ) {
    Player& p = *m_player;              // get player
    Store& s = StoreDatabase::get( p.CurrentRoom()->Data() );  // get store
    item i = s.find( p_item );          // find if store has item
    if( i == 0 ) {                      // store doesn't have item
        p.SendString( red + bold + "Sorry, we don't have that item!" );
        return;
    }
    if( p.Money() < i->Price() ) { // see if player has enough money
        p.SendString( red + bold + "Sorry, but you can't afford that!" );
        return;
    }
    if( !p.PickUpItem( i ) ) {      // see if player can carry it
        p.SendString( red + bold + "Sorry, but you can't carry that much!" );
        return;
    }
    p.Money() -= i->Price();          // subtract money
    SendRoom( cyan + bold + p.Name() + " buys a " + i->Name(),
            p.CurrentRoom() );
}
```

That wasn't so difficult, was it?

Selling Items

Selling an item in a store is a little different from buying an item. The selling process first finds the item the player wants to sell, and then finds out if the store wants to buy it, and finally sells it.

```
void Game::Sell( const string& p_item ) {
    Player& p = *m_player;                  // get player
    Store& s = StoreDatabase::get( p.CurrentRoom()->Data() );  // get store
    int index = p.GetItemIndex( p_item );   // get inventory index of item
    if( index == -1 ) {                     // make sure player has item
        p.SendString( red + bold + "Sorry, you don't have that!" );
        return;
    }
    item i = p.GetItem( index );            // get the ID of the item
    if( !s.has( i ) ) {                     // see if store sells it
        p.SendString( red + bold + "Sorry, we don't want that item!" );
        return;
    }
    p.DropItem( index );                    // remove item from inventory
    p.Money() += i->Price();                // add price
    SendRoom( cyan + bold + p.Name() + " sells a " + i->Name(),
            p.CurrentRoom() );
}
```

As you can see from this code and the buying code you examined previously, stores in SimpleMUD are, well, simple. In a more realistic game, stores would have limits to the amount of items they have to be bought and sold. I'll get to this kind of stuff when going into BetterMUD.

New Training Room Commands

Finally, the last two commands added to the game in this chapter are

train—trains a player to the next level when he has enough experience

editstats—edits a player's stats and allocates statpoints to his attributes

The good news is that these commands are pretty easy to implement. Here's the "train" command (added to Game::Handle):

```
if( firstword == "train" ) {
    if( p.CurrentRoom()->Type() != TRAININGROOM ) {
        p.SendString( red + bold + "You cannot train here!" );
        return;
    }

    if( p.Train() ) {
        p.SendString( green + bold + "You are now level " +
                    tostring( p.Level() ) );
    }
    else {
        p.SendString( red + bold +
                    "You don't have enough experience to train!" );
    }
    return;
}
```

Obviously, a player can only train inside of a training room, so the function makes sure the player can do that first. If the player is inside a training room, the Player::Train function is called, which returns a Boolean determining if the player has successfully trained. In either case, the player is told if he went to the next level. If the player trained successfully, the Player::Train function automatically adds his new bonuses to his character.

The editstats command simply takes you into the training state:

```
if( firstword == "editstats" ) {
    if( p.CurrentRoom()->Type() != TRAININGROOM ) {
        p.SendString( red + bold + "You cannot edit your stats here!" );
        return;
    }
    GotoTrain();
    return;
}
```

Once again, the command checks to see if the player is in a training room, and if the player is not, the command prints out an error to the player, and quits out of the function. Otherwise, the player is approved to move, and `Game::GotoTrain` is called, putting the player into the training state.

Database Reloading

In Chapter 8, I showed you how to reload the item database and the player database within the game. In this chapter, I'm going to continue, and show you how to add a room template and store reloading from within the game, so that you don't have to stop and re-run the game every time you change some datafiles.

This is the code that is added to the `Game::Handle` function (inside the block of code that handles the `reload` command):

```
else if( db == "rooms" ) {
    RoomDatabase::LoadTemplates();
    p.SendString( bold + cyan + "Room Template Database Reloaded!" );
}
else if( db == "stores" ) {
    StoreDatabase::Load();
    p.SendString( bold + cyan + "Store Database Reloaded!" );
}
```

Therefore, the two new reloading commands are

> `reload rooms`—reloads all the room template data from disk

> `reload stores`—reloads all the store data

I don't allow you to reload volatile room data, simply because editing that data is a very dangerous thing to do while the MUD is running. Imagine this scenario:

You take the /maps/default.data that the MUD saved previously (you'll see this in the next chapter), and start editing it. Meanwhile, someone comes into that room, and accidentally drops a valuable item. Then, you finish editing the file, and reload it. The poor player finds out that his precious item has been lost forever, because you just overwrote it by reloading the database.

NOTE

The "disappearing item" problem is only in SimpleMUD, and that's due to its limited design. You see, rooms keep track of items within them on disk, and that's not such a great idea in the grand scheme of things. In reality, items should keep track of where *they* are, but that kind of system was a bit complex for SimpleMUD. I use this kind of a system in the BetterMUD, however.

Miscellaneous Changes

This section describes a few minor changes.

Removing the Old Room Definition

For example, this line, created in Chapter 8 inside of /SimpleMUD/Player.h needs to be removed:

```
typedef entityid room;   // REMOVE THIS LATER
```

I just went ahead and deleted it.

Default Commands

In Chapter 8, SimpleMUD would interpret every unrecognized command a player typed in as a global chat. In that effect, just saying something like hello would cause your player to chat hello to everyone in the game. Now that the game supports room-based talking, however, the old line

```
SendGame( bold + p.Name() + " chats: " + p_data );
```

is changed to this instead

```
SendRoom( p.Name() + " says: " + p_data, p.CurrentRoom() );
```

Now, whenever you say something in a room, it is sent only to whomever is in that room, and the only way to send global messages is to use the chat or : commands now.

Using and Removing Items

Whenever a player uses or removes an item (this functionality was introduced in Chapter 8), he's obviously performing an action that everyone in the room can see, so why not make the game more realistic, and add code to the Game::UseItem and Game::RemoveItem functions to send messages to the room the player is in?

For example, here's the large switch statement from Game::UseItem with the newly added parts in bold:

```
switch( itm.Type() ) {
case WEAPON:
    p.UseWeapon( i );
    SendRoom( green + bold + p.Name() + " arms a " + itm.Name(),
            p.CurrentRoom() );
    return true;
case ARMOR:
    p.UseArmor( i );
    SendRoom( green + bold + p.Name() + " puts on a " + itm.Name(),
            p.CurrentRoom() );
```

```
            return true;
    case HEALING:
            p.AddBonuses( itm.ID() );
            p.AddHitpoints( BasicLib::RandomInt( itm.Min(), itm.Max() ) );
            p.DropItem( i );
            SendRoom( green + bold + p.Name() + " uses a " + itm.Name(),
                      p.CurrentRoom() );
            return true;
    }
```

It's little things like this that make the game more fun. People can watch a player as he arms his "Magic Sword Of Super Powers" and be in awe, or laugh at his "Rusty Knife."

Changes to the Main Module

Finally, now that you've got everything else programmed, you can make the final two changes. Demo09-01.cpp contains the same code as Demo08-01.cpp (from Chapter 8), with two minor additions (in bold):

```
int main() {
    try {
    ItemDatabase::Load();
    PlayerDatabase::Load();
    RoomDatabase::LoadTemplates();
    RoomDatabase::LoadData();
    StoreDatabase::Load();

<SNIP>

    PlayerDatabase::Save();
    RoomDatabase::SaveData();
}
```

Basically, all you need to do is load the room and store databases when the program begins, and save the room database back out when the program ends. That's it!

Running the Improved SimpleMUD

Compiling this version of SimpleMUD is done the same way as the SimpleMUD from Chapter 8, and you can find compilation instructions in Appendix A, "Setting Up Your Compilers," on the CD.

Once you've got SimpleMUD up and running, you can Telnet into it on port 5100 and play around. I've included some sample datafiles, so you can play it the way it is.

Figure 9.2 shows a screenshot of the movement and store listing in action.

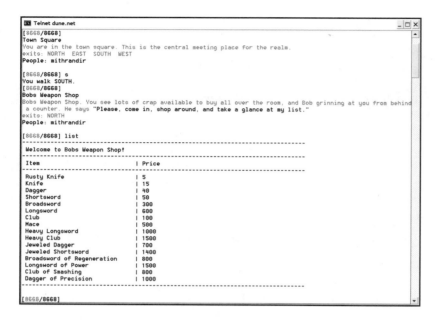

Figure 9.2

Examples of room listings, store listings, and movement in the new version of SimpleMUD.

There's not much going on here; the player logs in, walks south, and takes a look at the listing in a weapon shop. Yes, the character has over 8,000 hitpoints, but hey, I'm doing that for *testing purposes!* Yeah!

Figure 9.3 shows the item and room interaction features.

Pay attention to the first four lines in this figure. When a player types buy kn, he buys a rusty knife. The same thing happens if a player types buy knif or buy k or buy kni. However, the command buy knife buys the player a plain Knife instead of a Rusty Knife. Why does this happen?

Remember: All searching algorithms perform a dual-pass search, attempting to match the full name of an item first, and then performing a partial match. Therefore, when you type get knife, the algorithm detects the plain "Knife" because it fully

> **NOTE**
>
> You might have noticed that the text of Bob speaking appears brighter than the rest of the room's description. That's because it uses a different color. I managed to get this effect by manually placing the VT100 color code for white into the room's description in the /maps/default.map file. While this method is adequate for SimpleMUD, I wouldn't really recommend doing this for more advanced games. I explore a much better way of accomplishing this in Chapter 16, "The Networking System."

matches. Any other partial match of "knife" is instead detected as a "Rusty Knife", since "Rusty Knife" is the first in the list. It's just a minor issue you should watch out for, and if you design your stores correctly, people may never notice it.

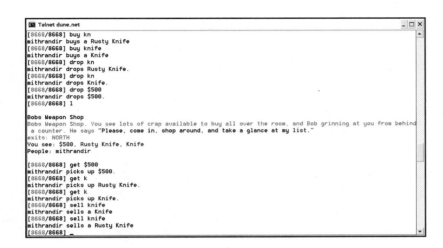

Figure 9.3

New item commands available to players in SimpleMUD.

Figure 9.3 also shows the player dropping, getting, and selling knives and using money.

Summary

This chapter has shown you how to create a simple map system that interacts with players and items. It's pretty simple, but then again, this is a SimpleMUD. Having only four directions of freedom is somewhat unrealistic and limiting, but it serves the

> **NOTE**
>
> When using a dual-pass search, it's usually a good idea to put objects with the simplest names first in the list. For example, it may be more *user friendly* to list "Knife" before "Rusty Knife", even if it costs more. It's up to you, though.

purpose. In Part Three of the book, I'll be showing you how to create a much more complex *portal* system that allows you to make your maps much more realistic and less limited. Of course, this also makes editing them more difficult, but the benefits in terms of flexibility far outweigh the minor inconveniences.

In this chapter, I also showed you the basics of an economy within your MUD. It's nothing glamorous, but as far as showing you how some basic things are accomplished, it does the job. Part Three of this book progresses to more complicated issues dealing with your economy.

Now, only enemies need to be added to the MUD, and it will be complete!

CHAPTER 10

ENEMIES, COMBAT, AND THE GAME LOOP

By now, you've seen how maps, stores, items, and players work within the SimpleMUD. It took quite a bit of code just to get them all working together, and in the end, you had nothing more than a simple online world where all you could do was to run around and talk. (And if you managed to hack in some money through the datafiles, you could play around with items, too.)

But where's the fun? The adventure? The *action*? In this chapter, I introduce you to the final part of SimpleMUD: enemies and combat, as well as the game loop.

In this chapter, you will learn to:

- Implement enemies
- Use enemy instances and enemy templates, using a simple system designed to minimize memory usage
- Create a simple game loop to manage timed events
- Handle play/enemy combat and death
- Make the changes needed to integrate combat into the SimpleMUD

Enemies and Enemy Templates

Enemies are set up a little differently from everything else in the game. There are actually two different enemy classes: enemies themselves, and enemy templates. This is a fairly standard way of representing things in a game that has a few volatile attributes (such as hitpoints) and many attributes that won't change at all (everything else).

> **NOTE**
>
> Please note that when I refer to *enemy templates*, I am referring to an actual class within the SimpleMUD, and not the C++ language feature known as *templates*.

The idea is to conserve memory. As Figure 10.1 shows, the templates store data that won't change about a particular type of enemy, and the enemy classes store volatile data about each individual enemy in the game. Whenever the game needs to access the nonvolatile data of an enemy, it looks at the template. But if the game needs to access an individual enemy's hitpoints, it looks into the regular enemy class.

So the Enemy class represents individual *instances* of enemies within the game, and the EnemyTemplate class represents data about individual *types* of enemies within the game. You'll have a template representing Thugs, a template representing Thieves, a template representing Evil Monkeys, or whatever else you decide to put into the game.

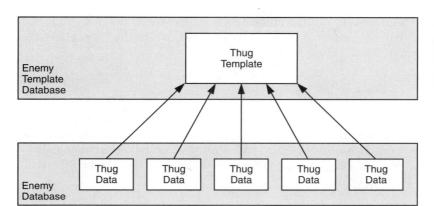

Figure 10.1

Relationship between enemies and enemy templates.

EnemyTemplate Class

Since enemy templates store all the base information about an enemy, I'll go over them first.

Data

Because an enemy's only purpose is to add combat into the game, all an enemy really needs are combat-based variables. You'll need hitpoints, obviously, as well as accuracy, dodging, strike damage, and damage absorption attributes. When a player dispatches an enemy within the game, he is rewarded with experience points, so templates must also know how much experience they are worth.

Enemies in the SimpleMUD get their minimum and maximum damage variables (as well as their swing time) from an item, which will serve as their weapon.

Enemy templates have three more elements: the min and max money variables (which determine how much money an enemy drops when he dies) and a list of loot, which I will get to in a moment. First, here's the class listing:

```
class EnemyTemplate : public Entity {
public:
    EnemyTemplate();
    int m_hitpoints;        // number of HP
    int m_accuracy;         // accuracy of enemy
    int m_dodging;          // dodging of enemy
    int m_strikedamage;     // strike damage
    int m_damageabsorb;     // damage absorption
    int m_experience;       // experience gained when killed
    item m_weapon;          // weapon enemy uses
    money m_moneymin;       // min $ enemy drops when it dies
    money m_moneymax;       // max $ enemy drops when it dies
    list<loot> m_loot;      // list of items that drop when it dies
};
```

The major thing to note about this class is that all its data is public; you'll see that this is because this class is never really directly manipulated by anything except the Enemy class, so you don't really have to worry about hiding its data.

The loot structure is simple:

```
typedef std::pair< item, int > loot;
```

I used the std::pair class (std::maps use pair objects to store pairs of keys and data) to define a piece of loot as being an item ID and an integer. The item ID is obviously the ID of the item you want the enemy to drop. The integer represents the percentage chance that the item will be dropped. So a loot entry containing a 10 and a 1 has a 1% chance that item 10 will be dropped when the enemy dies.

Functions

There are only two functions involved with the enemy templates; the constructor (which clears every variable to 0, so I'm not going to waste space with it here), and the stream extraction (operator>>) function.

Before I go into the latter function, let me show you the format of an enemy template on disk:

```
[ID]               1
[NAME]             Rabid Monkey
[HITPOINTS]        6
[ACCURACY]         40
[DODGING]          -30
[STRIKEDAMAGE]     0
[DAMAGEABSORB]     0
[EXPERIENCE]       4
[WEAPON]           40
[MONEYMIN]         0
[MONEYMAX]         2
[LOOT]             40   3
[LOOT]             35   2
[ENDLOOT]
```

The only really major thing you need to pay attention to is the loot listing; everything else is fairly straightforward.

Every loot entry contains two values: the item ID to drop, and the percent chance that it drops. After every loot entry (even if there are no entries), you absolutely *must* have an [ENDLOOT] tag.

Because of the way this is set up, enemies can drop any number of items that you want them to.

I'm going to forgo showing you most of the operator>> function, and just show you the little snippet that loads in the loot entries:

```
t.m_loot.clear();
while( extract( p_stream, temp ) != "[ENDLOOT]" ) {
    entityid id;
```

```
    int chance;
    p_stream >> id >> chance;
    t.m_loot.push_back( loot( id, chance ) );
}
```

In this code, t is an EnemyTemplate object, and p_stream is the stream the enemy template is being extracted from. At the top of the code, the loot list is cleared (in case there is anything already in it; see my note about reloading room databases in Chapter 9, "Maps, Stores, and Training Rooms").

Then, the code loops through the stream until the token "[ENDLOOT]" is found. For each entry, the ID and the chance that the item is dropped are loaded into temporary local variables, and then pushed onto the back of the m_loot list.

Enemy Class

The Enemy class is a *proxy* class. Basically, it looks like a full enemy, but it really holds only a small amount of information.

Class Data

Here's the class definition with all function definitions removed:

```
class Enemy : public Entity {
protected:
    enemytemplate m_template;
    int m_hitpoints;
    room m_room;
    BasicLib::sint64 m_nextattacktime;
};
```

There are four attributes:

- The corresponding template in the form of an enemytemplate class, which you haven't seen yet. You can see, however, from the naming scheme that it's a database pointer to an EnemyTemplate/.
- The enemy's hitpoints.
- The room the enemy is in.
- The next time the enemy may attack.

This last variable is explained more when I get around to the game loop later on in this chapter.

Class Functions

Since this class acts like a proxy into an enemy template, a number of functions enable you to completely hide the fact that this class accesses a template:

```
// regular functions:
Enemy();
```

```
void LoadTemplate( enemytemplate p_template );

// plain accessors:
int& HitPoints()              { return m_hitpoints; }
room& CurrentRoom()           { return m_room; }
sint64& NextAttackTime()      { return m_nextattacktime; }

// proxy accesors:
string& Name();
int Accuracy();
int Dodging();
int StrikeDamage();
int DamageAbsorb();
int Experience();
item Weapon();
money MoneyMin();
money MoneyMax();
list<loot>& LootList();
```

I've grouped the functions into three different categories: the regular functions, the plain accessors, and the proxy accessors.

The constructor puts 0s into every attribute, so there's no need to show it to you. The LoadTemplate function loads in an enemy's hitpoints from an enemy template:

```
void Enemy::LoadTemplate( enemytemplate p_template ) {
    m_template = p_template;
    m_hitpoints = p_template->m_hitpoints;
}
```

Even though Enemys are Entitys, their m_name variable is not used. Instead, the variable is left empty, to conserve memory (since enemy names are already stored in the corresponding enemy template).

You can see that the three plain accessors simply return the values of three of the data members (not including the template).

The rest of the functions, however, are *proxy* functions, which means that they actually look up the corresponding EnemyTemplate, and return the requested value. Here is the code for three of them:

```
std::string& Enemy::Name()    { return m_template->Name(); }
int Enemy::Accuracy()         { return m_template->m_accuracy; }
int Enemy::Dodging()          { return m_template->m_dodging; }
```

Since m_template is an enemytemplate database pointer, you can use it to look up the corresponding EnemyTemplate class, and return its values. Figure 10.2 shows a small example of how this works. Enemy instances hold a small amount of data, but when you request things like accuracy and names, they look up those values from an enemy template.

The rest of the functions are similar.

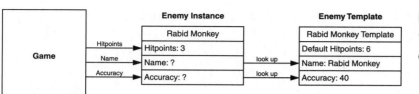

Figure 10.2

The system of enemies and enemy templates.

Stream Functions

Enemies can be streamed both into and out of C++ streams, utilizing the standard operator>> and operator<<. There is absolutely nothing special about the code, so let me show you the format of an Enemy class when written to disk:

```
[ID]              1
[TEMPLATEID]      1
[HITPOINTS]       6
[ROOM]            5
[NEXTATTACKTIME]  0
```

This shows that Enemy 1, which is an instance of enemy type 1 (as you saw earlier, "Rabid Monkey" is template 1), currently has 6 hitpoints, is in room 5, and the next time the enemy can attack is 0. You'll see later that the last value means that this enemy can attack the moment he sees a player.

Databases

I'm beginning to feel like a broken record here: "Here's the player database; here's the item database; here's the room database...". Guess what? Here are the enemy databases! (I bet you didn't see that one coming).

There are two enemy databases, as you saw earlier in Figure 10.1: one database to store enemy templates, and one database to store enemy instances.

It is crucial to determine what kind of database will be optimal to use for each of these different types. First you need to think about how they are used.

Enemy Template Database

Enemy templates are loaded one time, from disk, and then never modified. If you're careful when you create the enemy templates, they should have contiguous ID

> **CAUTION**
>
> Since you're storing the enemy templates inside of a vector array, the IDs of your templates *need* to be contiguous, or else you'll have holes in your database; you'll have enemy templates that just don't exist, but the database thinks they do.

numbers (meaning that if you have 50 enemies, they should occupy IDs 1 through 50). Because of these properties, a vector-based database sounds ideal, and that's what I use:

```
class EnemyTemplateDatabase : public EntityDatabaseVector<EnemyTemplate> {
public:
    static void Load();
};
```

The database simply uses one function to load the template data from disk. The file is /enemies/enemies.templates. The Load function is similar to all the other database loading functions you've seen in the past two chapters, so I'm not going to bother with it here.

Enemy Database

The enemy database stores all of the enemy instances within the game. These instances are far more volatile than the templates. The instances are created whenever the game needs more enemies, and they are deleted when the enemies die. It makes a lot more sense to use a map-based database for these:

```
class EnemyDatabase : public EntityDatabase<Enemy> {
public:
    static void Create( entityid p_template, room p_room );
    static void Delete( enemy p_enemy );
    static void Load();
    static void Save();
};
```

There are two functions that deal with creating and deleting instances, and two functions dealing with loading and saving. I'll skip the file functions (if you're interested, you can always look at the source, but they basically loop through the enemies/enemies.instances file and load in individual enemy instances) and go right into the creation and deletion functions.

Creating Enemy Instances

The game should be capable of quickly and painlessly creating new enemies. The EnemyDatabase class has a function designed just for that purpose. It's a *factory* function, which means that you just tell it what kind of enemy you want and where you want it, and the function creates the enemy for you.

NOTE

Factory generators are a popular method of generating actual instances of entities in MUDs. I like the method so much that the BetterMUD uses it almost exclusively.

Here's the code:

```
void EnemyDatabase::Create( entityid p_template, room p_room ) {
    entityid id = FindOpenID();      // find an open ID
    Enemy& e = m_map[id];            // get reference to enemy at ID

    e.ID() = id;                     // set its ID
    e.LoadTemplate( p_template );    // load its template
    e.CurrentRoom() = p_room;        // set its room

    p_room->AddEnemy( id );          // add the enemy to its room
}
```

The function uses the `EntityDatabaseVector::FindOpenID` function to find the first ID in the map that isn't being used. Once you have an ID, the function uses the map's `operator[]` to retrieve a reference to the `Enemy` object bundled with that ID. (It doesn't matter that it doesn't exist. I showed you previously that `std::map::operator[]` automatically creates entries that don't exist.)

After the ID of the enemy is set, the enemy's template is loaded, and the enemy's current room is set. The final step is to add the enemy to the room.

Within the game, you can simply call the function like this:

```
EnemyDatabase::Create( 1, 5 );
```

That creates an enemy of type 1 in room 5.

Deleting Enemy Instances

Deleting enemy instances is a simpler process—it must merely reverse the creation process:

```
void EnemyDatabase::Delete( enemy p_enemy ) {
    p_enemy->CurrentRoom()->RemoveEnemy( p_enemy );
    m_map.erase( p_enemy );
}
```

The enemy is removed from its room, and then erased from the `std::map` that stores all the instances. That's it!

Database Pointers

As with most of the previous entity types you've seen (players and items in Chapter 8, rooms in Chapter 9), both enemy classes have corresponding database pointers.

These two lines are added to the SimpleMUD/DatabasePointer.h file:

```
DATABASEPOINTER( enemy, Enemy )
DATABASEPOINTER( enemytemplate, EnemyTemplate )
```

And these two lines are added to the .cpp file for the implementation of the pointer functions:

```
DATABASEPOINTERIMPL( enemy, Enemy, EnemyDatabase)
DATABASEPOINTERIMPL( enemytemplate, EnemyTemplate, EnemyTemplateDatabase )
```

Now you have access to two database pointer classes: enemy and enemytemplate. They are used just like any other database pointer object within the SimpleMUD.

Game Loop

Entities are finally finished, so you can sigh in relief or have a party. Now, I'll show you the marvelous *game loop*.

The game loop is a concept in SimpleMUD that handles everything that depends on timers. For example, the databases need to be saved at particular time intervals, players need to heal, and enemies need to look for players to attack. The game loop manages all these functions.

Up until this point, the SimpleMUD was purely an *event-based* system; everything that happened in the game was triggered by something a connected player sent to the

> **NOTE**
>
> Event-based systems are really efficient, because they ensures that you do work only when events occur, rather than constantly checking to see if something happened. However, there's really no way you can ever go to a complete event based system, which is why a simple game-loop is needed.

game. The game loop adds some independent initiative to the game, so that it will actively perform actions when it needs to, instead of just responding to player input.

The game loop is stored in a class appropriately named GameLoop, which you can find in the files /SimpleMUD/GameLoop.h and .cpp. Here's a listing of the class:

```
class GameLoop {
public:
    GameLoop()      { LoadDatabases(); }
    ~GameLoop()     { SaveDatabases(); }

    void LoadDatabases();       // load all databases
    void SaveDatabases();       // save all databases
    void Load();                // load gameloop data
    void Save();                // save gameloop data
    void Loop();                // perform one loop iteration
    void PerformRound();        // perform combat round
    void PerformRegen();        // perform enemy regen round
    void PerformHeal();         // perform healing round

protected:
```

```
    BasicLib::sint64 m_savedatabases;
    BasicLib::sint64 m_nextround;
    BasicLib::sint64 m_nextregen;
    BasicLib::sint64 m_nextheal;
};
```

First, take a look at the constructor and destructor. They call the LoadDatabases and SaveDatabases functions respectively. So whenever you create a GameLoop object, all of the databases are automatically loaded from disk, and whenever a GameLoop object is destroyed, all the databases are saved to disk. You'll see this in action when I show you Demo10-01.cpp later on in this chapter.

Next look at the data: There are four 64-bit integers, representing four different times. These four times are in *system time* (which is kept by the Game::s_timer timer object), and indicate times when the following events should occur: the next time the databases save, the next combat round, the next monster regen, and the next player healing.

I'll get more into system timing in a little bit.

> **NOTE**
>
> System time is kept in milliseconds, starting from 0, inside the Game::s_timer object. For example, a system time of 10,000 ticks would mean that the system has been running for 10,000 ticks / 1000 ticks/second = 10 seconds. If GameLoop::m_savedatabases is 900,000 ticks (900 seconds, or 15 minutes), that means that the system will save the databases 15 minutes after the system has started.

Loading and Saving Databases

When the database loading/saving functions are called, they are designed to automatically load or save every database that needs to be loaded or saved to disk. For example, the GameLoop::LoadDatabase function is as follows:

```
void GameLoop::LoadDatabases() {
    Load();
    ItemDatabase::Load();
    PlayerDatabase::Load();
    RoomDatabase::LoadTemplates();
    RoomDatabase::LoadData();
    StoreDatabase::Load();
    EnemyTemplateDatabase::Load();
    EnemyDatabase::Load();
}
```

The Load function deals with loading the four system-time variables from disk.

Saving is similar, but since not all databases need to be saved back to disk, the function is simpler:

```
void GameLoop::SaveDatabases() {
    Save();
    PlayerDatabase::Save();
    RoomDatabase::SaveData();
    EnemyDatabase::Save();
}
```

In addition to the time variables saved with the `GameLoop::Save` function, only players, rooms, and enemies need to be saved to disk.

Loading and Saving Time Variables

The time variables are saved within a text file entitled game.data. When you start your MUD for the first time, the game time starts at 0 and increases based on how long it's running. When the game has been up for a period of time, and is then shut down, the MUD should save the time at which it was sent to disk, so you know what time it is when you turn the game back on.

Saving

The `GameLoop::Save` function saves the time variables to disk:

```
void GameLoop::Save() {
    std::ofstream file( "game.data" );
    file << "[GAMETIME]      ";
    insert( file, Game::GetTimer().GetMS() ); file << "\n";
    file << "[SAVEDATABASES] ";
    insert( file, m_savedatabases );          file << "\n";
    file << "[NEXTROUND]     ";
    insert( file, m_nextround );              file << "\n";
    file << "[NEXTREGEN]     ";
    insert( file, m_nextregen );              file << "\n";
    file << "[NEXTHEAL]      ";
    insert( file, m_nextheal );               file << "\n";
}
```

I've used the `BasicLib::insert` function to insert the times into the text file (due to the fact that VC6 does not stream 64-bit integers properly). As you can see, the function essentially writes the current system time, and then the four other time variables. Here's a sample listing of the datafile:

```
[GAMETIME]      3917661
[SAVEDATABASES] 4500000
[NEXTROUND]     3918000
[NEXTREGEN]     3970000
[NEXTHEAL]      3960000
```

Since the times are millisecond-based, you can tell that the server represented by this file has been up for about an hour, and that the next round will occur in less than one second from the current time (3918000 minus 3917661 = 339, so in 339 milliseconds, the next combat round for enemies will occur), and that the database is due to be saved in 9 minutes.

Loading

Loading the variables is slightly more complicated. In a "clean" installation of SimpleMUD, the game.data text file won't exist, so all five timers must be reset to the default values.

First, let me show you the default value definitions:

```
sint64 DBSAVETIME = minutes( 15 );
sint64 ROUNDTIME  = seconds( 1 );
sint64 REGENTIME  = minutes( 2 );
sint64 HEALTIME   = minutes( 1 );
```

These values determine how much time should pass between certain actions. For example, the databases should be saved every 15 minutes (the seconds and minutes helpers are in the BasicLib), combat rounds occur every second, monsters regen every two minutes, and players heal once a minute. I refer to these values as *delta* values. (Delta is a mathematical term commonly associated with change.)

Now the loading function:

```
void GameLoop::Load() {
    std::ifstream file( "game.data" );  // open file
    file >> std::ws;                    // eat whitespace
    if( file.good() ) {                 // detect if file is good
        std::string temp;
        sint64 time;
        file >> temp;   extract( file, time ); // read system time
        Game::GetTimer().Reset( time );        // reset timer to that time

        // read other variables:
        file >> temp;   extract( file, m_savedatabases );
        file >> temp;   extract( file, m_nextround );
        file >> temp;   extract( file, m_nextregen );
        file >> temp;   extract( file, m_nextheal );
    }
```

The previous code segment is executed when the game.data file exists. It loads in the current system time, and resets the Game's timer object to the current system time, and then proceeds to load the other variables.

If the file is corrupted, however, this code is executed:

```
    else {
        Game::GetTimer().Reset();
        m_savedatabases = DBSAVETIME;
```

```
        m_nextround = ROUNDTIME;
        m_nextregen = REGENTIME;
        m_nextheal = HEALTIME;
    }
    Game::Running() = true;
}
```

The game timer is reset to 0, and the four time values are set to their deltas, meaning that the first database saving will occur at 15 minutes, and so on.

Finally, the game is told to start running.

The Loop

In the SimpleMUD, the GameLoop::Loop is called once every cycle, and this function takes care of the various time-based activities:

```
void GameLoop::Loop() {
    if( Game::GetTimer().GetMS() >= m_nextround ) {
        PerformRound();
        m_nextround += ROUNDTIME;
    }

    if( Game::GetTimer().GetMS() >= m_nextregen ) {
        PerformRegen();
        m_nextregen += REGENTIME;
    }

    if( Game::GetTimer().GetMS() >= m_nextheal ) {
        PerformHeal();
        m_nextheal += HEALTIME;
    }

    if( Game::GetTimer().GetMS() >= m_savedatabases ) {
        SaveDatabases();
        m_savedatabases += DBSAVETIME;
    }
}
```

The function checks the four timer variables to see if their time has come. For example, if m_nextround is 4534000, and the timer is at 4534013 (13 milliseconds later), the PerformRound function is called, and ROUNDTIME (1 second, or 1000 milliseconds) is added to m_nextround, making it 45345000. Since the timer is not guaranteed to be called on 1-millisecond boundaries, you *must* check to see if the timer has gone past the time at which one of the actions was set to execute. The function does the same for the other three time variables.

NOTE

This is an inefficient method of timing, but it serves its purpose in SimpleMUD. Imagine if you had more than four different timed events. The function would become large and wasteful in terms of processing power. It gets even worse when you want enemies to have different attack times, instead of all enemies in the game attacking on the same game loop. I will be exploring much better methods of utilizing timers in the next part of the book.

Performing the Combat Round

Whenever the game decides to perform a combat round, the GameLoop::PerformRound function is called. This function simply goes through every enemy in the game, and if the enemy sees a player in the same room, it is told to attack:

```
void GameLoop::PerformRound() {
    EnemyDatabase::iterator itr = EnemyDatabase::begin();
    sint64 now = Game::GetTimer().GetMS();

    while( itr != EnemyDatabase::end() ) {
        if( now >= itr->NextAttackTime() &&     // make sure enemy can attack
            itr->CurrentRoom()->Players().size() > 0 ) // check players
            Game::EnemyAttack( itr->ID() );     // tell enemy to attack
        ++itr;
    }
}
```

For every enemy, two things are checked: Can the enemy attack, and are there any players in the room? Enemies keep track of the next time they are allowed to attack, which is based on which weapon they are using. You'll see how this works when I show you the Attack function.

If there are no players in the room, there's obviously no one for the enemy to attack, so the function doesn't do anything.

Regenerating Enemies

Every two minutes, the game performs an enemy regeneration cycle, in which it tries to put more enemies into the rooms that have too few. As you saw in Chapter 7, rooms can have one type of enemy, and each room can have a maximum number of enemies per room.

The process for this entails looping through every room, and determining if a new enemy should be spawned:

```
void GameLoop::PerformRegen() {
    RoomDatabase::iterator itr = RoomDatabase::begin();
    while( itr != RoomDatabase::end() ) {
        if( itr->SpawnWhich() != 0 &&     // make sure room can spawn enemies
            itr->Enemies().size() < itr->MaxEnemies() ) // don't overflow
        {
            // tell the database to create a new enemy in the room
            EnemyDatabase::Create( itr->SpawnWhich(), itr->ID() );
            Game::SendRoom( red + bold + itr->SpawnWhich()->Name() +
                            " enters the room!", itr->ID() );
        }
        ++itr;
    }
}
```

It's not a complex process; it uses the EnemyDatabase::Create function to create enemies in each room that needs them. The loop checks two conditions per room: First, it determines if enemies should be created (because rooms with a SpawnWhich ID of 0 shouldn't spawn any enemies), and second, it decides if more enemies can fit into the room.

If these conditions are met, a new enemy is created, and a message is sent to the room stating that the enemy has entered the room.

> **NOTE**
>
> This is also an inefficient process, but it works for SimpleMUD. In the next part of the book, I explore more efficient methods of filling your realm with enemies, as well as other things, such as the impact on the economy. If you think about it, an endless supply of enemies means an endless supply of loot, and therefore an endless cycle of inflation.

Regenerating Health

It is typical in MUD-like games for users to have regenerating health. Having to constantly buy healing potions can get annoying to your players after a while, so regenerating is usually used as a solution.

Once every minute, the game goes through all the players, and if they are logged in, the players' hitpoints are regenerated:

```
void GameLoop::PerformHeal() {
    PlayerDatabase::iterator itr = PlayerDatabase::begin();
    while( itr != PlayerDatabase::end() ) {
        if( itr->Active() ) {
            itr->AddHitpoints( itr->GetAttr( HPREGEN ) );
            itr->PrintStatbar( true );
```

```
        }
        ++itr;
    }
}
```

As you can see, the player's `HPREGEN` attribute is added to his hitpoints, and his statbar is updated.

Attacking and Dying

Finally, we reach the best part of the game—controlling what happens when enemies attack and when they kill players. Even though these functions are called by the

`GameLoop`, they reside within the `Game` class, so I can keep the logic in one central place.

Here are the declarations of the two functions that control this:

```
void EnemyAttack( enemy p_enemy );
void PlayerKilled( player p_player );
```

The `Attack` function tells the game that `p_enemy` should find a player and attack him. The `Killed` function tells the game that `p_player` has died.

When Enemies Attack!

The `Attack` function follows the basic combat rules I defined in Chapter 7. Before I get into that, however, the enemy first needs to figure out *who* he wants to attack. This is handled with the assistance of the `std::advance` function, which takes an iterator, and moves it forward however many places you specify:

```
void Game::EnemyAttack( enemy p_enemy ) {
    Enemy& e = *p_enemy;        // get enemy
    room r = e.CurrentRoom();   // get room
    std::list<player>::iterator itr = r->Players().begin();
    std::advance( itr, BasicLib::RandomInt( 0, r->Players().size() - 1 ) );
```

Basically, the previous code skips to a random player in the room, which means that the enemy attacks a random person every round. Although these random attacks are not realistic, I did this for "security" reasons: It prevents people from leaving the room, letting the enemy concentrate on someone else in the room, and then come back in.

The next part of the code calculates how much damage is done by the enemy's current weapon:

```
    Player& p = **itr;          // get player
    sint64 now = Game::GetTimer().GetMS();
```

```
int damage;
if( e.Weapon() == 0 ) {  // fists, 1-3 damage, 1 second swingtime
    damage = BasicLib::RandomInt( 1, 3 );
    e.NextAttackTime() = now + seconds( 1 );
}
else {   // weapon, damage, and swing time based on weapon attributes
    damage = BasicLib::RandomInt( e.Weapon()->Min(), e.Weapon()->Max() );
    e.NextAttackTime() = now + seconds( e.Weapon()->Speed() );
}
```

If the enemy doesn't have a weapon, it is assumed the enemy will damage things in the 1–3 range, with a swing time of one second. (This means that the enemy can attack again in one second.) If the enemy is using a weapon, the damage range and swing time are taken directly from that enemy's weapon object.

Next, the game figures out if the enemy hit the player.

```
if( BasicLib::RandomInt( 0, 99 ) >= e.Accuracy() -
    p.GetAttr( DODGING ) )
{
    Game::SendRoom( white + e.Name() + " swings at " + p.Name() +
                    " but misses!", e.CurrentRoom() );
    return;
}

damage += e.StrikeDamage();
damage -= p.GetAttr( DAMAGEABSORB );
if( damage < 1 )
    damage = 1;
```

The code generates a random number from 0 to 99, and if the accuracy of the enemy minus the dodging of the player is more than or equal to the random number, the enemy missed.

For example, an enemy has an accuracy of 80, and the player has a dodging level of 20. Since 80 – 20 = 60, if the random number is between 60 and 99, the enemy misses. That means that the enemy hits the player about 60% of the time. If the enemy misses, the function returns.

If the enemy *does* hit the player, the enemy's strike damage is added to the overall

NOTE

Calculating whether the enemy hit a player could have been accomplished earlier, but it turns out that waiting until this point saves code. No matter what, when an enemy swings, its next attack time should be increased. So while you're calculating the next attack time, why not calculate the damage as well?

damage value, and the player's damage absorption is subtracted. This means that if the damage was 5, the enemy's SD is 1, and the player's DA is 3, then the actual damage dealt is 5 + 1 – 3 = 3. Finally, the damage is checked to see if it is below 1, and if so, it's reset to 1.

You don't want enemies doing negative damage (that is, adding hitpoints), or 0 damage to players (which would mean that the enemy missed, but we've already determined that he hit the player).

Here's the final chunk of code:

```
    p.AddHitpoints( -damage );
    Game::SendRoom( red + e.Name() + " hits " + p.Name() + " for " +
                    tostring( damage ) + " damage!", e.CurrentRoom() );
    if( p.HitPoints() <= 0 )
        PlayerKilled( p.ID() );
}
```

The damage is removed from the player, and the room is told that the player got hit. Finally, if the player's hitpoints are 0 or lower, the game is notified that the player was killed.

Live and Let Die

As in real life, everyone dies someday. In a dangerous world such as the SimpleMUDs, death comes often if you're not careful.

Whenever a player is killed, the `Game::PlayerKilled` is called, and the unfortunate player is penalized. A bunch of things need to happen, so I'm splitting up the code into segments:

```
void Game::PlayerKilled( player p_player ) {
    Player& p = *p_player;          // get the player
    Game::SendRoom( red + bold + p.Name() + " has died!", p.CurrentRoom() );
    money m = p.Money() / 10;    // calclate how much money to drop
    if( m > 0 ) {
        p.CurrentRoom()->Money() += m;
        p.Money() -= m;
        Game::SendRoom( cyan + "$" + tostring( m ) +
                        " drops to the ground.", p.CurrentRoom() );
    }
```

The function in this code segment tells the room that a player has died, calculates how much money to drop, and then drops it.

The next part of code drops a random item:

```
    if( p.Items() > 0 ) {          // make sure the player has an item
        // loop through random indexes until you hit a valid item:
        int index = -1;
        while( p.GetItem( index = RandomInt( 0, PLAYERITEMS - 1 ) ) == 0 );

        item i = p.GetItem( index );     // get the item to drop
        p.CurrentRoom()->AddItem( i );   // add it to the room
        p.DropItem( index );             // remove it from the player

        Game::SendRoom( cyan + i->Name() + " drops to the ground.",
```

```
                    p.CurrentRoom() );
    }
```

The function essentially performs a "random bounce" to find an inventory item to drop. This is somewhat awkward, but it's simple and it works for the SimpleMUD. Just keep in mind that this could take a while to find an item, if the player isn't carrying much.

After an item is found, the item is added to the room and removed from the player's inventory, and the room is told that the item was dropped.

The final part of the code subtracts 10% experience, and moves the player to Town Square:

```
    int exp = p.Experience() / 10;
    p.Experience() -= exp;    // subtract 10% exp

    p.CurrentRoom()->RemovePlayer( p_player );
    p.CurrentRoom() = 1;      // move player to room 1
    p.CurrentRoom()->AddPlayer( p_player );

    // set player HP to 70%
    p.SetHitpoints( (int)(p.GetAttr( MAXHITPOINTS ) * 0.7) );

    // send messages:
    p.SendString( white + bold +
                "You have died, but have been ressurected in " +
                p.CurrentRoom()->Name() );
    p.SendString( red + bold + "You have lost " + tostring( exp ) +
                " experience!" );
    Game::SendRoom( white + bold + p.Name() +
                  " appears out of nowhere!!" , p.CurrentRoom() );
}
```

The player's hitpoints are reset to 70% of maximum. You obviously don't want the player to be ressurected with 0 (or less!) hitpoints, but you also don't want the player to start off with full hitpoints either, so 70% is a good tradeoff.

The last thing the function does is print out messages to the player and to the people in the room in which the player respawns, telling them about his entrance.

Game Additions

The two main additions to this version of the MUD are enemies and the game loop, but additions have been made to the old versions as well. You've already seen the EnemyAttack and PlayerKilled functions that were added to the Game class. Along with those additions, there are two more combat functions, and two new commands ("attack" and "reload enemies") added to the Game class. These constitute a bunch of tiny changes and additions.

Other Combat Functions

The other two combat functions are PlayerAttack (which is executed when a player attacks an enemy) and EnemyKilled (which runs when an enemy is killed).

The PlayerAttack function is similar to EnemyAttack, which is a result of the design of the game. Since *players* and *enemies* are two completely different entities within the game, you need specialized functions to perform attacks in both ways.

Attacking Enemies

The first part of the PlayerAttack function (where the function finds the target) is the only thing that differs from the EnemyAttack function. In the enemy version, the enemy picks a random player to attack, but whenever a player attacks an enemy, he has usually typed in the name of the enemy (for example attack goblin), so the function needs to take that text and figure out which enemy the player is trying to attack:

```
void Game::PlayerAttack( const string& p_enemy ) {
    Player& p = *m_player;
    sint64 now = Game::GetTimer().GetMS();

    // check if player can attack yet
    if( now < p.NextAttackTime() ) {
        p.SendString( red + bold + "You can't attack yet!" );
        return;
    }

    // find the enemy, and if it isn't found, tell player.
    enemy ptr = p.CurrentRoom()->FindEnemy( p_enemy );
    if( ptr == 0 ) {
        p.SendString( red + bold + "You don't see that here!" );
        return;
    }
```

Remember that since this function is within the Game handler, it knows which player is attacking (m_player). The parameter for the function contains the name of the enemy the player wishes to attack.

The rest of the function is essentially the same; it calculates the damage, swing time, whether the enemy is hit, and so on. When PlayerAttack detects that an enemy has died, it calls the EnemyKilled function.

Killing Enemies

The process that occurs when an enemy is killed is much different from the process that occurs when players die. The most obvious difference is that enemies don't have to be immediately respawned, since the game loop already takes care of that.

Another difference is that the function needs to go through the enemy's loot-list and figure out what to drop, as well as how much money to drop, and how much experience to add to the player who killed it.

Here's the first part of the code, which notifies a room about an enemy being killed and drops its money:

```
void Game::EnemyKilled( enemy p_enemy, player p_player ) {
    Enemy& e = *p_enemy;
    SendRoom( cyan + bold + e.Name() + " has died!", e.CurrentRoom() );

    // drop the money
    money m = BasicLib::RandomInt( e.MoneyMin(), e.MoneyMax() );
    if( m > 0 ) {
        e.CurrentRoom()->Money() += m;
        SendRoom( cyan + "$" + tostring( m ) +
                " drops to the ground.", e.CurrentRoom() );
    }
```

The parameters of the function are the instance ID (not template ID) of the enemy who has died, and the player ID of the player who killed him.

The code uses a random number generator to generate the amount of money that has dropped, and then drops it, and tells everyone about the new fortune on the floor.

The next piece of code drops all the loot:

```
    std::list<loot>::iterator itr = e.LootList().begin();
    while( itr != e.LootList().end() ) {
        if( BasicLib::RandomInt( 0, 99 ) < itr->second ) {
            e.CurrentRoom()->AddItem( itr->first );
            SendRoom( cyan + (itr->first)->Name() +
                    " drops to the ground.", e.CurrentRoom() );
        }
        ++itr;
    }
```

The code loops through every entry in the loot list and calculates if the item needs to be dropped. This is done by generating a random number from 0 to 99, and checking to see if the loot's percent chance is less than this number. For example, a loot entry with a probability of 20 would be dropped whenever the numbers 0–19 are generated (20 numbers out of 100, or 20%), and an entry with a probability of 0 would never be dropped (since the generator can never generate numbers lower than 0). Entries with a probability of 100 will always be dropped (because the generator always generates numbers below 100).

The last piece of code rewards the slayer and removes the enemy from the game:

```
Player& p = *p_player;
p.Experience() += e.Experience();
p.SendString( cyan + bold + "You gain " +
              tostring( e.Experience() ) + " experience." );
EnemyDatabase::Delete( p_enemy );
}
```

That's all there is to combat in SimpleMUD.

New Game Commands

The Game class must be augmented to handle the two new commands introduced in this version of the MUD: attack and reload enemies. As usual, these commands are added to the large Game::Handle function found within /SimpleMUD/Game.cpp.

Here's the first one:

```
if( firstword == "attack" || firstword == "a" ) {
    PlayerAttack( RemoveWord( p_data, 0 ) );
    return;
}
```

This simply calls the PlayerAttack function you saw earlier with the word attack removed from the string. (For example, attack goblin would pass goblin into the function.) You can also use the letter a as a shortcut for the whole word, as in a goblin.

Code for reloading enemies is added in the middle of the reload command you read about in the two previous chapters. The new code block is in bold and the code blocks above and below it are for reference.

```
else if( db == "stores" ) {
    StoreDatabase::Load();
    p.SendString( bold + cyan + "Store Database Reloaded!" );
}
else if( db == "enemies" ) {
    EnemyTemplateDatabase::Load();
    p.SendString( bold + cyan + "Enemy Database Reloaded!" );
}
else {
    p.SendString( bold + red + "Invalid Database Name" );
}
return;
```

Essentially, the code tells the enemy template database to load all its templates. The instance database cannot be reloaded for the same reasons I gave in the previous chapter about not being able to reload room data, only room templates.

Additional Code Changes

Many changes still need to be made to the code to support the addition of enemies into the SimpleMUD.

Database Pointer Placeholders

First and foremost, these two lines need to be removed from Room.h:

```
typedef entityid enemytemplate;     // REMOVE THIS LATER
typedef entityid enemy;             // REMOVE THIS LATER
```

This is because those two classes are now defined in DatabasePointer.h, and the lines would cause a compiler error.

New Room Functions

The next step is to add three functions to the Room class:

```
enemy FindEnemy( const string& p_enemy );
void AddEnemy( enemy p_enemy );
void RemoveEnemy( enemy p_enemy );
```

You saw the code presented earlier in this chapter using these three functions to find, add, and remove enemies in rooms. These three functions are similar to the FindItem, AddItem, and RemoveItem functions, so I'm not going to show you the code here.

> **NOTE**
>
> The AddEnemy function's logic is slightly different from AddItem. The item function automatically deletes items once it reaches the limit of 32 items, as you saw in Chapter 9, but the enemy version of the function doesn't do this. Instead, the maximum number of enemies in a room is determined by the MaxEnemies function of the Room class. Enemies are never deleted, because the spawning function makes sure the maximum is never exceeded.

Printing Enemies

The final addition is within the Game::Printroom function, where code is added to print a list of all the enemies within a room. The code for printing enemies is added after the code that prints players, but it's really not that interesting, so I'll show you the results of the code instead:

```
Alley
You're in a dark alley, where shadows obscure your view and hide
dangerous things...
exits: NORTH  SOUTH
People: mithrandir
Enemies: Rabid Monkey, Rabid Monkey, Rabid Monkey
```

Now players always know what enemies are in a room with them.

Main Module Changes

The main module for this version of SimpleMUD is contained within the Demo10-01.cpp file, and it is much different from the versions you saw in Chapters 8 and 9.

The main module in the two previous versions explicitly called the loading and saving functions of the various databases, but you don't need to do that anymore. The GameLoop class has functions to do that for you.

So instead of manually loading all the databases in the main module, you'll declare a GameLoop object instead. Later on, in the actual while-loop, the GameLoop objects' Loop function is called. Here's the main part of the main function, with the important sections bolded:

```
try {
    GameLoop gameloop;

    ListeningManager<Telnet, Logon> lm;
    ConnectionManager<Telnet, Logon> cm( 128, 60, 65536 );
    lm.SetConnectionManager( &cm );
    lm.AddPort( 5100 );

    while( Game::Running() ) {
        lm.Listen();
        cm.Manage();
        gameloop.Loop();
        ThreadLib::YieldThread();
    }
}
```

The loop object is created at the top of the previous code segment. The loop object automatically loads all databases when it is created, so you don't have to do that here anymore.

The next bolded line shows the function that calls GameLoop::Loop inside the main while-loop. This ensures that the loop object performs all the necessary timer-based actions (enemy attacking, spawning, player health regeneration, and database saving).

The final bolded element is the final bracket on the last line of the code. When your code exits this try-block, the GameLoop object goes out of scope, which means that its destructor is called. A GameLoop's destructor automatically saves all of the databases that need to be saved, so there's no need to manually call those earlier.

Running the Final Version

Now you're ready to run the final version of SimpleMUD. You would compile it just as you compiled the previous two MUDs. (Complete instructions are in Appendix A on the CD.) Once you have SimpleMUD compiled, you can run the MUD, then Telnet into it on port 5100 (just as with the previous versions), and play around!

Figure 10.3 shows an example of my ultra-powerful (cheating!) character beating the tar out of a poor monkey and a thug. It doesn't show up well in black-and-white, but the colors used by the server in a Telnet client make the output much clearer.

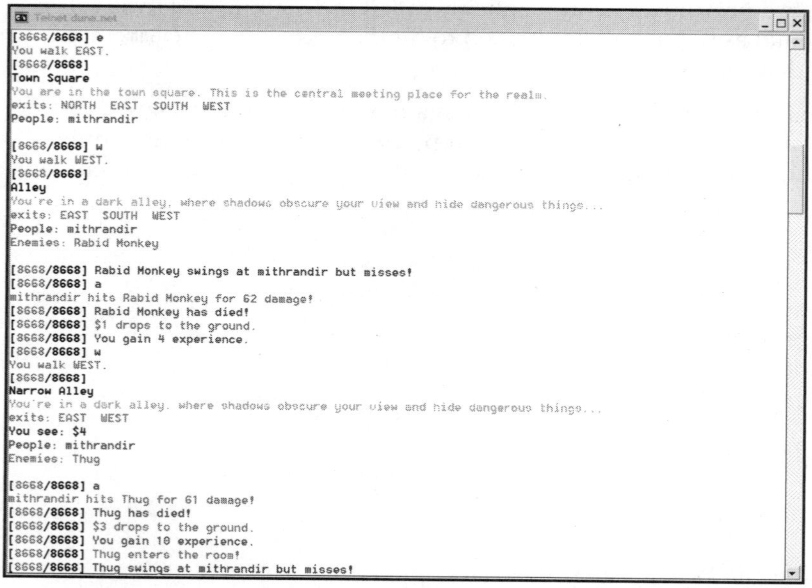

Figure 10.3

A player attacking and killing a rabid monkey and a thug within the SimpleMUD.

Figure 10.4 shows a more active battle, with a new player and the thug again. Woe is me. The player fought in vain and died. You can see the player drop money and an item when he dies.

You may notice that the figures show some text that looks a little strange. For example, you can see in Figure 10.4: [9/12] aThug swings at Gandalf but misses! The letter "a" before "Thug" seems out of place, but that's just the nature of Telnet.

I typed the letter a when I was trying to attack the thug. But before I could press Enter, the thug attacked me, and the message that he attacked me was added onto the end of whatever I had already typed in.

Depending on what kind of Telnet client you use, you may or may not see this behavior. I was using the Telnet program of Windows XP.

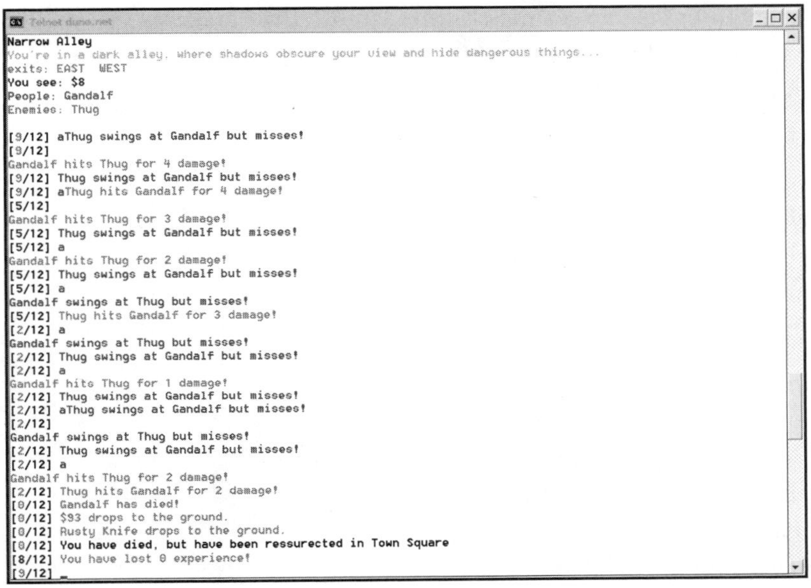

Figure 10.4

A player (who isn't cheating) valiantly fighting a dastardly thug.

Summary

Congratulations! You have now completed a full, albeit simple, MUD. That was a lot of work involved for a game concept that many consider "primitive." Writing stable server code is a daunting and difficult task, however.

Crashing simply is not an option for servers. You need to have these things run for days at a time, and this is much more difficult to do than a regular game.

Anyway, I hope you've learned a good deal about the basics of making a MUD. In the next part of the book, when I show you the BetterMUD, I'm not going to be nearly as "code oriented" as I was with SimpleMUD. Instead, I'm going to focus on general design issues instead of the nitty-gritty details. By this point, you should have a somewhat solid understanding of simple MUD-like server programs.

Let me go over everything you should have learned in this part of the book.

In Chapter 8, you learned how to:

- Design a handler system to act as an intermediary between the SimpleMUD and players
- Design a login system
- Design a simple alternate-state handler to handle player statistics editing
- Design a simple command parsing system
- Build simple template database classes to minimize the amount of code repetition required

- Build a simple smart-pointer class to seamlessly interact with the databases
- Design players for a simple combat-oriented MUD
- Design items and understand how they interact with players

In Chapter 9, you learned how to:

- Design a simple global map system
- Add stores and training rooms to the game
- Use simple economic interaction via stores
- Connect players, items, rooms, and stores

And in this chapter, you learned how to:

- Implement enemies
- Use a simple instance/template system for enemies
- Implement a simple game loop that takes care of timed events
- Handle player/enemy combat
- Handle player/enemy death
- Connect everything together, creating a full MUD

I would once again like to invite you to play on my version of SimpleMUD, running on telnet://dune.net:5100. It may not be too active, because most people would probably prefer playing around in BetterMUD, but if you're interested, I'll have it running.

Essentially, what you just learned how to make was a flexible-data MUD, with hard-coded physics and logic. If you ever decide to expand the codebase, you should be aware that expanding the logic for SimpleMUD (that is, controlling how enemies and items act), you might find it a difficult task. This is one of the things you will learn how to fix in the next section.

Now, off to BetterMUD!

PART THREE

CREATING A BETTER MUD

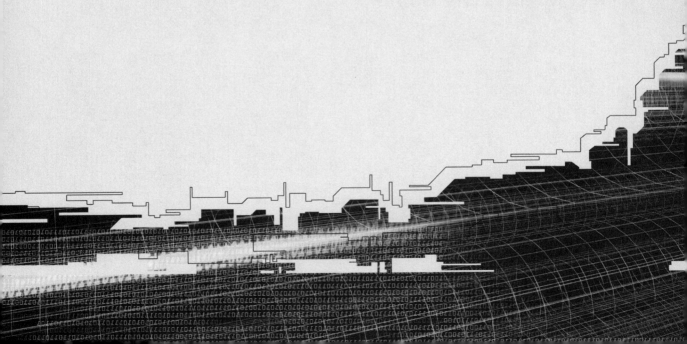

CHAPTER 11

THE
BETTERMUD

This is where the book starts to get exciting. If you didn't have your fill of fun with designing the SimpleChat and SimpleMUD, then I'm sure you'll enjoy creating the BetterMUD.

SimpleMUD was a basic MUD, which I'm sure is obvious from its name. Unfortunately, even though it was simple, it still took considerable work to make a stable and robust server application. The SimpleMUD, in its final form, was 5,500 lines of actual code (about 9,000 with comments and whitespace). That's a lot of code for a simple project, especially if you're one person.

In this section of the book, you will learn how to make a far more complex MUD—the BetterMUD.

In this chapter, you will learn to:

- Understand the limitations and flaws of the SimpleMUD
- Expand the SimpleMUD
- Give up the idea of expanding the SimpleMUD in favor of making a BetterMUD
- Appreciate the importance of abstracting the physics of a game from its logic
- Understand the major entities involved in the BetterMUD

Idea Behind the BetterMUD

In many ways, the BetterMUD is simpler than the SimpleMUD, but in other ways, it is more complex. That may sound like a contradiction, but as I explain, it should make more sense.

Flaws of SimpleMUD

If you've ever played an established MUD before, you know that the SimpleMUD is really dry. The most you can do is run around killing people and buying stuff. I got bored with it in a few days. As one of my friends affectionately told me, "The SimpleMUD is like a MUD with attention deficit/hyperactivity disorder (ADHD)."

As a learning experience, it was pretty cool, though. You learned to make a persistent world, and if you're new to MUD programming, you have probably never made a

> **TIP**
>
> As I write these words, SimpleMUD has consumed exactly 7 minutes and 59 seconds of CPU time over the past 33 days, and is using 0.1% of the system memory. The CPU time is kept really low through thread yielding, and the memory usage is kept low through the automatic management of STL containers. Believe me—knowing about those tools is valuable.

> ## CAUTION
>
> Your players become especially angry when you make a change, hit compile, and the compile fails. At that point, you spend another hour or two tracking down the new bugs you just created, while your players can't log on, and they constantly message you asking, "When will the MUD be back up!?" Believe me, this will happen; I know from experience. It gets even worse if your players have paid to play on your MUD, because they expect a certain quality of service for something they pay for. Your players don't have much leverage if the MUD is free, though.

program that remained active for longer than a few hours. As I'm writing this, my version of the SimpleMUD (on Dune.net) has been running for 33 days solid, and that's a long time for a program to run, so I hope the SimpleMUD was a valuable learning experience for you.

Another flaw of the SimpleMUD is its static nature. To change anything but the physical data, you have to stop the MUD, make the code changes, and then recompile it. This can become a significant problem if you continuously make changes, because it interrupts the community and angers your players.

So basically, all you can do to expand the SimpleMUD while it is running is to add new rooms, monsters, items, and stores, and that quickly becomes boring.

You can't do anything special with items, besides using them as weapons, armor, or healing potions. Monsters can't move around. There's no player versus player combat, and so on. I could make a list a mile long of the things that SimpleMUD is missing.

Example of Extending SimpleMUD

So, now you've just read that the SimpleMUD is too simple, but the BetterMUD is in some ways simpler than SimpleMUD. No, I'm not on drugs (though I may be crazy anyway). I'm being completely serious here.

Imagine this scenario for a generic MUD. There's a player who can create medical potions from herbs found in the ground in a forest. Since herbs are plants that grow abundantly in forests, you have a few options for implementation.

Thinking in SimpleMUD terms, the naive way of implementing this scenario is to hack a new check into the GameLoop module, and every 24 hours or so, it would fill up the room with 32 herbs (the maximum number of items allowed per room in the SimpleMUD). This method has several downsides:

- All items remaining in the room at the end of the day are destroyed, since the SimpleMUD destroys the oldest items first when you go over the limit of 32.

- Walking into the room will treat you to a description of "Herb, Herb". That looks annoying on this page, and that will certainly look annoying to your players.

Okay, so scratch the 24-hour refill method. Perhaps you could make a one-hour refill. Every hour, generate another herb? Or better yet, make a check to see if there is an herb in the room, every hour, and if not, *then* generate one?

As you can see, we're getting somewhere, but the process still doesn't correspond to how herbs grow. Obviously, new plants don't appear out of nowhere every hour, and even if this *is* just a game, it still looks cheesy. In reality, when you walk through a forest, there are hundreds of different plants, and that's the sense you'd like to convey in the game.

So an even better method would be to make this type of check on a room: "If player picks an herb, create a new one." Functionally, this is a good method in terms of what it accomplishes, until you start thinking about where you're going to put the code.

From my vantage point, it looks as if this code would go somewhere within the `Game::GetItem` function. (See Chapters 8, "Items and Players," 9, "Maps, Stores, and Training Rooms," and 10, "Enemies, Combat, and the Game Loop," if you are unfamiliar with the layout of the SimpleMUD.) I would like to *strongly* caution you against doing so, however.

What would the code look like? Perhaps something like this (in pseudo code):

```
if player.room == HERBROOM and item == HERB
    then insert new herb
```

That seems simple enough, at first. Then you realize: `HERBROOM` and `HERB` are *hard-coded* into the game now; and if you move the room, or change the herb to something else, your game still thinks that it needs to generate that item within that room. You may end up with some interesting side effects if you change your data around a lot.

At this point, you might be saying to yourself, "Well, it's only one item and one room; I can remember not to change them!" Sure, right now you remember. Next week you might remember as well—heck, maybe even next year. But what if you let someone else edit your files? Will he remember? What if you make more hacks like that in other rooms? Eventually you will have so many hacks that you won't remember which items and rooms should not be modified.

So you can see that hard-coding is a bad method after all. And you may have thought up a better alternative such as this: adding a piece of data to a room with this type of code— "room respawns item X when picked up".

Hey, that works! Then in the game, you can check:

```
if player.room.respawnitem == item_you_are_picking_up
    then insert new item_you_are_picking_up
```

Awesome! Well, not quite. Feel free to hit your head on a table right now. I know this must be frustrating to see me shoot down so many different ideas, but we're almost there.

TIP

If you look closely at Figure 11.1, you'll notice that its items are sorted by time. I did this for a good reason; you can reap significant optimization benefits by storing items in a sorted manner. When the items are sorted by time, you can make certain assumptions about the data. For example, if you know that the top item has the lowest time, you know that every item below it has a higher time. If you check the registry at time 9,000 and see that the top item has a spawn time of 10,000, you know that you don't have to spawn anything, and you don't have to bother checking anything else in the registry. This speeds up operations significantly. Sorting is an expensive operation, but luckily the STL has a `priority_queue` container that has relatively quick insertions and deletions (O(log n) times, for those of you who know about algorithmic analysis), and the container handles the sorting for you. I'll touch on this subject again when explaining the BetterMUD timer system in Chapter 15.

What is the problem with this method? For starters, it adds extra data to every room in the game. How many rooms are you going to have that respawn items in your game? Probably one or two, maybe a dozen or two at most. So if you have 1,000 rooms, roughly 980 of them will have this extra piece of data that is completely superfluous. The rooms don't care about respawning items, and yet here they are, every one of them with an extra integer (4 bytes) and an extra 4 KB of memory. Yeah, yeah, I know, 4 KB is nothing these days, but bear with me for a moment.

Later on, you decide to make a special herb—one that can cure only a special kind of illness (ignoring the fact that the SimpleMUD doesn't have illnesses), and due to its rarity, you need to make it respawn once a week or so. Frustrated yet? You should be.

So, you begin to figure out how to make this happen. Perhaps you could create a global registry of items that need to be respawned and a schedule for respawing. You could check this registry to see if things need to be spawned during the game loop, and if so, spawn them into the game. Figure 11.1 shows this process.

Item Respawn Registry

Item	Time	Room
Herb	10000	10
Super Herb	12000	20
Herb	14000	14
Herb	18000	32

After Time 10000 →

Item	Time	Room
Super Herb	12000	20
Herb	14000	14
Herb	18000	32

Figure 11.1

The operation of a theoretical item respawn registry, which manages which items the game respawns and when.

Now that you have a registry added, you need to figure out how items determine how much time they need to spawn. The best way to do this is to add yet another field to the room class—a "how much time does X take to respawn?" field. That's another 4 KB of memory for a MUD with 1,000 rooms, and most of that 4 KB is wasted. (It's another 8 KB if you decide to go with 64-bit integers to represent time!)

On top of all that, every time you change the physics of an entity class, you need to some-how go through all your data files and add the extra field, or else your loading functions won't know what to do.

Now, what if you want to...no, I'm kidding. I've taken this example far enough already, so there's no need to torture you with a thousand "what if's" and "should I's". I hope you see the point: The inherent flaw in the design of the SimpleMUD is that it cannot be extended without a significant amount of work.

Hey! Wouldn't It Be Cool If... ?

A MUD is unique in being the one kind of game you can expand at small intervals. There's none of this "one expansion pack a year" stuff that you see with some MMORPGs, or "one expansion pack, total" that you see in nonpersistent-world games. MUDs are small communi-ties in which people want to build their own virtual worlds and love jumping in and creating new areas or items whenever that meets their fancy.

Perhaps the best source of inspiration for MUD expansion occurs while you're playing the game, an idea randomly hits you, and you blurt out, "Hey! Wouldn't it be cool if... ?" and right then and there, you decide to start adding on.

This is the source of many problems in MUDs, however. So many of these "Hey! Wouldn't it be cool if...?" ideas are simple, little one-time deals. Maybe you want to add a simple little effect, but don't plan to use it anywhere else. I touched on this idea a little earlier; why would you add the capability to achieve one minor effect to *every* object in the game, when most of those objects never need it? When you design like that, you're wasting your time. You have to add these little of snippets of code all over the place, and that's just ridiculous.

Separating the Physical from the Logical

To make a flexible system, you need to separate the *physical* aspects of the game from the *logical* aspects of the game. What is the physical? The physical aspect of the game is basically the rule set that describes what can happen in the game.

For example:

> Items can be picked up and dropped by players.
>
> Players can move from room to room.
>
> The game produces "visual events" that players can see.
>
> Items and players are created or destroyed.
>
> Characters can see other characters moving around.

Those aspects are physical; they deal with what actually happens in the game. The logical side, on the other hand, controls the physical. You can think of the logical part of the game saying, "This is what happens when object X does Y." In the examples I showed you previously, the logical part of the game determines if and when herbs should be respawned, and the physical part of the game only cares about when the object is spawned. Figure 11.2 shows an example of abstraction for a normal room and for an herb-respawning room. This figure shows the benefits of having optional logic modules attached to the physical objects. Only items that require special behavior have logic modules attached to them. Note that logic modules may also need extra data. (Data is shaded in the figure.)

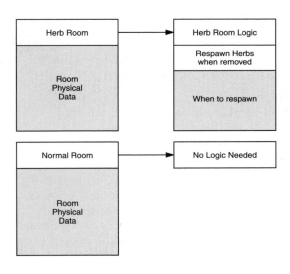

Figure 11.2

Abstraction for a normal room and for an herb-respawning room.

Because of the way normal rooms are designed, they are not involved with respawning and don't even know how to respawn. So, whenever an herb-room is told that someone picked up an herb, the logic module is consulted, and the module says, "I'm going to insert another herb into the room at time X".

When a normal room is told that someone picked an herb, the normal room recognizes that it doesn't have a logic module, and therefore doesn't care what happens. Not only that, but since a normal room doesn't have a logic module, it takes up less memory. The herb-room's logic module manages all the special data it needs to know, such as when to respawn a new herb. The actual room has no reason to know about that data.

> **NOTE**
>
> To implement the "at time X" section of the logic module, you need a global timer registry, similar to the one I showed you in Figure 11.1. I'll go into this more in Chapter 15.

Choosing an Implementation for Logic

Implementing the physics of the game is fairly easy. You can do that in C++, and there's really no need to change the physics of the game often. So that's not going to be a problem.

The logic modules, however, are a different story. If you're still using C++, this may pose a problem. Sure, logic modules can be written in C++, and doing so greatly increases the cleanliness of your code, which is a good thing. But you still have that nasty little problem of not being able to add logic dynamically. This means that to add new pieces of logic to the game, you must stop, recompile, and run the code again. Unfortunately, these are the very procedures that are not advisable for MUDs, as I mentioned previously.

Loading data dynamically is easy, as you saw with the SimpleMUD, and as you have probably experienced in different contexts. Loading logic, which is always in code form, is a much more difficult process, but fortunately, there are a bunch of ways around this.

If you're targeting the Windows operating system, one popular way to load logic is by using DLLs, which are like EXEs, but you can load them at runtime, and call functions from them. This is a fast and easy way to support extensibility, but the cost involved is nonportability. Linux has no DLL files, so using this method limits you to Windows, which typically isn't as good a server platform as Linux.

Linux has expansion modules as well (SO files) but these can be a royal pain in the butt. To use SO files in Linux, you need to have your root administrator add the dynamic library to the list of globally available modules, which can be a big problem; root administrators are cautious about adding code when they are not sure what the code does. They don't want to inadvertently add a virus or a backdoor to the system, so you'll find many administrators unwilling to add new modules for you.

NOTE

I mentioned earlier that the SimpleMUD has been running for 33 days. The longest my WindowsXP box ever ran was about 25 days. That's not to say that Windows is a bad server platform; it's actually pretty good. But Windows computers tend to be used for more than just server programs. For example, on the computer I am writing this on, I run lots of nonserver applications, like my word processor, audio player, compiler, IRC clients, instant messenger clients, and so on. All of these programs can have minor side effects that eventually destabilize the operating system. On a Linux server, you typically run only tried-and-true server applications, so they don't mess up the server. I would recommend looking into a cheap Linux box to run your MUD server, and if you're really serious about running one, look into a shell service. (I use dune.net, and it's pretty good.) I list a bunch more in the Conclusion of this book.

Scripting

Another option for loading logic is to use a scripting language. There are tons of scripting languages out there, each with its strengths and weaknesses. Some languages are nice and simple; others are huge and complex. If you're particularly devious, you may try embedding a full stack-machine language such as Java into your MUD, but that's going overboard in my opinion.

After playing around with a few languages, one jumped out at me—Python. Lately, Python seems to have gained quite a large following, and for a good reason—it's simple and powerful.

> **NOTE**
>
> Python was named after the British comedy troupe *Monty Python*. So, whenever you're working with Python, be sure to insert as many references to Monty Python as possible. Perhaps include some characters running around saying, *"Help, help, I'm being repressed!"* or *"This is supposed to be a happy occasion. Let's not bicker and argue about who killed who!"* Or even, perhaps, a riddle that involves knowing the air-speed of an unladen swallow.

The best thing about Python, however, is that it has a well-defined and documented C API, which means that it is incredibly easy to integrate with your application and easy as well to call Python scripts from your C/C++ program. Chapter 17 goes over everything you need to know about Python for this book. I'm not going to be able to include a comprehensive tutorial of the entire language, but believe me, you'll catch on quickly. The Python website (http://www.python.org) has a wonderful tutorial on the language, as well as a complete index of every built-in module. (There are tons of built-in modules—everything from math to sockets, and strings to threading.) You can check ahead if you like, but until I cover Python in Chapter 17, I focus mainly on implementing the physical side of BetterMUD.

Logic Modules

Logic modules in the BetterMUD are simply Python scripts that can be attached to any entity type. Every entity has the capability to be given any number of logic modules, which allows you to mix and match behaviors.

For example, in my version of the BetterMUD, I have character logic modules named "combat" and "encumbrance." Chapter 18, "Making the Game," shows you how to implement these, so for now all you need to know is that when characters have these modules, they have the ability to attack other characters, and they have the ability to weigh the number of items a character is carrying. Now, if I take away the "combat" module from any character, that character cannot be attacked or attack anyone else, because the logic module is what gives the character those abilities. Likewise, if I take away "encumbrance," the game happily allows your characters to carry an infinite number of items without weighing them to see how much they can carry.

A cool thing about logic modules is that they use a flexible set of attributes that you can access from within C++. This means that from C++, you can ask a logic module to get a 32-bit signed value based on its name. I'll show you how this works a bit later on when explaining character quests.

Overall Physical Design

As well as having a completely flexible logical design, the BetterMUD has a flexible network layer, because it is more abstracted from the game than the SimpleMUD's network layer.

Like the SimpleMUD, the BetterMUD focuses on the idea of *entities*, so I won't need to spend much time going over entity concepts. In the BetterMUD, however, there are different kinds of entities.

Regions

The first major change from the SimpleMUD to the BetterMUD is the addition of *regions*. Most MUDs have regional systems, which allow you to organize your game more easily. Figure 11.3 shows a simple three-region layout. Regions also make it easy to group logic, and they ease the strain on your auto-saving system.

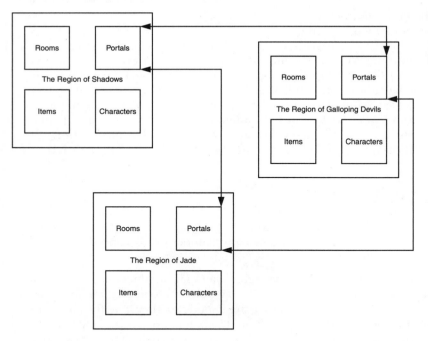

Figure 11.3

Regions make it easy to group entities.

Regions and Scripts

To understand regions, imagine a collection of rooms in the magical forest of the realm. Whenever evil monsters such as orcs and goblins enter the forest, they receive a curse that slightly lowers their stats. Without regions, there's really no easy way to do this. To make this work, you give a region the logical actions "character entered" and "character left," which are executed whenever characters enter or leave. So when an evil monster enters a magical forest, the magical forest's logic module curses the character, and when the character leaves the forest, the curse is removed. This is a nice, elegant system of implementing a large collection of scripts in just one area, instead of putting them in every room that is in the forest area.

Regions and Databases

Regions make things easier for the database, too. Imagine a large game, with thousands, or even tens of thousands of rooms. Whenever your game tries to do a complete database dump, it takes a long time, and the game is going to lag up for a second at least, or maybe much longer.

To prevent the lag, you may want your game to save one region at a time, splitting up the job over a long period of time, so that the game doesn't lag.

Regions and Data

Regions are simple entities. They need to know only the basics: their name, ID, and description, as well as a logic module, and lists of all entities contained within the region.

Rooms

In the BetterMUD, rooms are similar to and simpler than SimpleMUD rooms. In the BetterMUD, rooms are no longer involved with money on the ground, simply because money isn't a special case object. Neither do they deal with tracking who respawns in the room, because this functionality is provided in the logic modules you implement instead.

The physical aspect of a room in the BetterMUD deals only with a few things: room name, description, ID, associated region, exits from the room, characters in the room, and the items on the floor.

Portals

Portals are a new concept in the BetterMUD. In the SimpleMUD, each room simply had four exit IDs—those are the IDs of the rooms attached to that room. In the BetterMUD, it's not that simple—every room has a list of *portals*, which are basically structures that describe a path from one point to another. Every portal has one or more entries into it, as shown in Figure 11.4. Rooms are never explicitly linked; instead, they point to a portal, and the portal manages the entry of a player to different rooms depending on which room they entered the portal from.

Portals are complex, and I evaluated many designs before selecting one. You could easily go with simple one-way portals, but there are problems with that kind of a design.

For example, it would make sense that if a portal door is closed, both one-way portals would need to know that it is closed, which would mean that the portals need a communication system between their logic modules. Overall, that's a bad design because it can blow up in your face rather quickly.

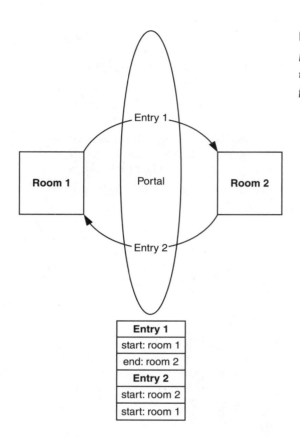

Figure 11.4

Rooms point to portals that control the entry of players.

Entry 1	
start: room 1	
end: room 2	
Entry 2	
start: room 2	
start: room 1	

Other designs had me thinking about a *segmented* approach, in which there were two types of portals: inter-regional (portals that connect rooms in two different regions), and intra-regional (portals that connect two rooms in the same region). This design is complicated as well, because each room must track whether its portals are inter- or intra-regional, which violently explodes the amount of code needed. (Trust me—I tried implementing it as a test to see how much code would actually be needed.) The best rule you can use is the *KISS* rule; *keep it simple, stupid.*

The current portal design is nice and robust and is not limited to one- or two-way designs, since it uses a list of variable entries. When a player enters a portal, the list of variable entries searches for the player's starting point, and then spits the player out at the ending point. If there is a logic module attached to a portal, it tells the module that someone is trying to enter the portal.

This is where portals are cool—portal logic modules have the option of *rejecting* an entrance. Let's say you create a magical portal that only admins can enter, and if a nonadmin tries entering, it says, "Nope, you're not getting in here, buddy!" Or even better, you could have magic force field logic scripts that not only reject entering, but also damage the players who try to enter. (That'll teach them!) The possibilities are endless, and I could go on for days listing what logic modules can accomplish.

Accounts

Accounts are another new concept in the BetterMUD. There are times when you're going to want to have more than one player in the game—maybe an extra player to hold your loot and booty, or someone to help you along in battles. Whatever the case, the ability exists. Therefore, your players can create new characters without changing usernames or passwords.

An account is simply an entity and needs only the following:

- ID
- Name
- Password
- Access level
- Number of characters allowed
- Indication of whether or not characters are banned
- List of all the players it owns

You'll see how this works in Chapter 16, when I go over the networking system.

Characters

In SimpleMUD, there were players and enemies; therefore. it was awkward for players to fight each other without copying large amounts of code, which is *always* a sign of a weak design. In the BetterMUD, I've unified the concepts of players and enemies into one entity type: *characters*.

Basically, a character is any living being in the game. Characters can hold stuff, move around, see things, and die.

Attributes

Characters have attributes, much like the attributes in the SimpleMUD, but instead of hard-coding these attributes, you're going to be able to access them via strings. This is because characters in the BetterMUD are somewhat flexible. You load the attributes from a text file on disk whenever the MUD starts, and the scripts and everything else have access to those variables.

Absolutely none of the attributes are hard-coded in the BetterMUD. This was designed to give you complete flexibility over what you want to do with the engine. I'm not going to say "players must have health and hitpoints!", because quite frankly, you may decide not to have those kinds of things in your MUD. When I get to Chapter 18, you'll see how this whole thing works out; believe me, it's cool.

Containers

Characters need containers for various things, such as for a list of items that the character is currently carrying.

Characters also have a collection of logic modules (in fact, all entites have these), and a special collection of logic modules named *command modules*. Command modules allow characters to interface with the game. Every character can have a personalized collection of commands, so you can do things like giving blacksmiths a "repair" command to repair broken items—an ability other characters won't have.

Conditions

Characters will have all sorts of logic modules, and you can use them for varying purposes. You could make logic modules represent *conditions*—stuff like "on fire" or "poisoned." With this kind of system, you can say, "If a character has the logic module *on fire*, that character is actually on fire!"

Conditions are usually time based, which means that they last for a certain duration, or that they have an event that repeats. (For example, the "on fire" condition logic would take off X hitpoints every second until it burned out.)

When a condition is activated, it should typically perform some operation on a player (usually just modifying an attribute). During the activation sequence, the module has several options. For example, it can set itself up to terminate after a minute or so, by adding an entry to the global timer registry. Or the module can remain resident in a

> **NOTE**
>
> I go over the timer registry and action events in detail in Chapters 14 and 15.

player and wait for another logic module in the game to remove it. (For example, a player could pay a witchdoctor to remove a curse.) The other option would be to set up an event in the global timer registry that would message the condition at a later time, telling it to perform its "repeating" action (that is, the burning of the fire). Every time the fire module receives a "burn" command, it will immediately add another "burn" command to the global timer registry.

Figure 11.5 shows three methods for using condition modules. The first method sets a condition and then waits for another module to deactivate the condition. The second method shows the activation telling the timer registry to remove the condition at a specific time. The final example shows a condition that has also registered a repeating condition, which repeats until the condition is deactivated.

Characters are by no means forced to use only those three methods with conditions. For example, a character could be poisoned with a special venom that doesn't leave his bloodstream, and the venom continues to call the repeating action of the condition until the character finds a cure. Due to the highly flexible nature of these script objects, anything can happen. Maybe you can implement a linked set of conditions, such as a cold. First, you can

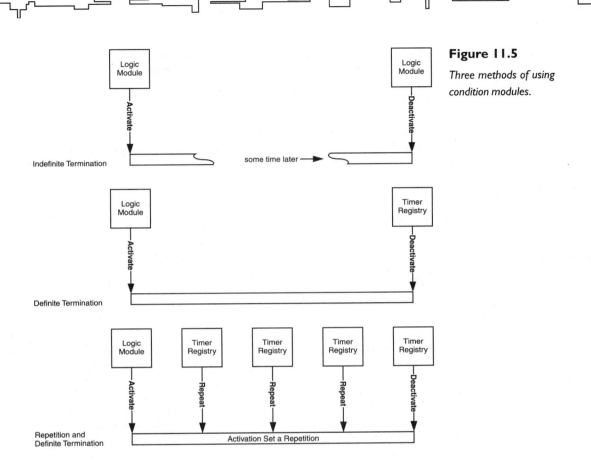

Figure 11.5

Three methods of using condition modules.

activate a symptomatic condition, which only slightly modifies the character. After a certain amount of time when that condition is deactivated, it automatically activates another condition, which makes the character even sicker. The chain can continue until the character is eventually incapacitated or finds help. The possibilities are endless.

Quests

You can also use logic modules to represent *quests*, which constitute a large part of expanding the gameplay in the BetterMUD. In the game, characters obviously want to do more than run around killing everything in their paths, as they do in so many hack-and-slash games. The BetterMUD is flexible, so why not put that flexibility to good use?

For example, let me use a common occurrence in RPG-type games: the Kill All Rats quest.

Newly arrived in the city, a player goes to the town employment office to get a job. The clerk examines his papers and says, "Hey, we've got a rat problem in the sewers. Why don't you go down there, kill 40 rats, and then come back for your pay?" The game then assigns the rat-quest to the character, and he starts killing rats.

Whenever an action involves a character, all of his logic modules are notified. For example, whenever a character kills a rat, the game checks all the character's logics and tells each one of them that he killed something. The rat-quest module then says something like, "Oh! He killed a rat! I'll add one to the tally now!"

Logic modules also have attributes, which allow other scripts to determine the state of a module, if it knows what kind of module it is. For example, the "kill all rats" quest would allow you to retrieve a variable named `ratskilled`, which would allow other logic modules in the game to figure out if you've killed the requisite 40 or not.

It's advisable to keep the number of logic modules active in a current player to a minimum, but that's up to you. Just keep in mind that the more script objects, the slower the game, since every logic module must be notified about everything that happens to a character.

Items

Items are the final entity type in the game, and they are basically anything inanimate. Items are always owned by a room or a character, and the items know who owns them.

Items have a listing of attributes, which corresponds to the attributes the players have. As with characters, there are no default item attributes; you customize everything. I show you some recommended values in Chapter 18.

There are two main types of items in the game; single items and collections of items. Single items are always single items; they typically represent large items such as weapons and armor, or even smaller stuff such as potions and scrolls.

Collections of items, on the other hand, are single items that have a count value, and thus act like many of the same item. Only certain types of items can be combined into collections—mostly things such as coins, jewels, diamonds, and maybe even weapon-type stuff such as stars that can be thrown, or arrows for a bow.

Collection objects can be split, but only by dropping them, giving them to other characters, or picking them up. Whenever a collection object enters a new domain (either a room or an inventory of a character), the object automatically merges with other collection objects of the same type. Strictly speaking, splitting doesn't have to work this way, but it's easier on the interfaces if it does.

For example, you enter a room with a pile of 23 gold coins. There is an enemy in the room, and when you kill him, he drops a pile of 10 gold coins. Instead of creating two piles—a pile of 23 gold coins and a pile of 10 gold coins—the game merges them to create one pile of 33 gold coins. It's not too realistic, but it really cuts down on the clutter. It would be really annoying to enter a room that has 20 piles of the same kind of object, because everyone is too lazy to pick them up.

Items also have logic modules, which are told about actions such as being dropped and picked up.

Summary

This chapter taught you about all of the basic ideas that are going to be implemented within the BetterMUD. I have not shown you a complete picture of things yet (for example, I barely mentioned databases, or the networking setup), but for now, I hope I've set your mind clicking so that you can understand how things work from a broad perspective.

The SimpleMUD was mainly concerned with specifics such as, "How do I make this work?" and "What data does this have?" I don't know about you, but I usually find that explaining every little nook and cranny of the code is extremely tedious. Honestly, how much did you care about the implementations of each SimpleMUD database class? Not much, eh?

I'm going to take an entirely different approach when showing you the BetterMUD. The SimpleMUD was all about learning how to actually code a MUD application; the BetterMUD is all about how to design a flexible and extensible MUD.

CHAPTER 12

ENTITIES, ACCESSORS, AND DATABASES

The basic layout of the data in the BetterMUD is similar to that of the SimpleMUD, but there are improvements all over the place—tools that reduce the amount of code you need to write, tools to automate usage, and so on. Overall, the basic entity classes and databases aren't complex, and since they have the same basic layout as SimpleMUD classes that serve the same purpose, this chapter is short. I focus on the better stuff later on. Hello scripting system! Aren't you excited?

In this chapter, you will learn to:

- Understand basic entities
- Use mixin classes to enhance entities
- Understand database accessors
- Comprehend the basic entity database classes

Basic Entity Concepts

All things in the BetterMUD, just as in the SimpleMUD, are entities. They are the physical objects within the game, which will be stored by the databases and operated on by the C++ physics core.

IDs

Entities are accessed by their entityid just as in the SimpleMUD. In the SimpleMUD, I chose to use 32-bit unsigned integers for these IDs, which gave you a range of around four billion available IDs for each entity type.

Due to some limitations in Python, however (the fact that it doesn't support unsigned integers, for one), I used signed integers as IDs in the BetterMUD. A signed integer can have roughly two billion positive values, so if you assume that negative IDs and 0 are invalid, you're left with two billion possible IDs.

Now, before you start saying "Oh no! Less is worse!" you should think about that for a moment. Two billion is an incredibly large number. If you assumed that you just stored

> **NOTE**
>
> Older bit MUDs that were built around 16-bit values frequently ran over their boundaries, and this was a serious problem in the past. However, 32-bit values are quite large and should be enough for what you need. If you don't think so, it's easy to convert the entities over to some 64-bit format, and with 18,446,744,073,709,551,616 total possible IDs, I think it's a safe bet that you'll never run out. I'm comfortable with my puny two billion entity limit, however.

the IDs for two billion objects in memory, at 4 bytes per ID, you're looking at requiring 8 GB of memory, just to store the ID numbers of two billion entities. I've never seen a MUD that required anywhere near that many entities.

At the heart of it all is the Entity.h file, which contains the `entityid` datatype and the `Entity` class. Here's the typedef for `entityid`:

```
typedef signed int entityid;
```

Now, whenever you refer to entities in the game, you refer to this typedef. If you need to change the typedef, all it takes is one simple change to this line, and suddenly all your entities are based on a different numbering scheme. It's that simple.

Entity Class

In the SimpleMUD, the base entity class had two things: an ID and a name. I've expanded that a bit, and entities in the BetterMUD have four things:

- ID
- Name
- Description
- Reference count

The actual entity class has these functions:

```
std::string Name() const;
std::string Description() const;
entityid ID() const;
void AddRef();
void DelRef();
int Ref() const;
void SetName( const std::string& p_name );
void SetDescription( const std::string& p_desc );
void SetID( entityid p_id );
```

As you can see, these are your standard get-and-set accessor functions. In the SimpleMUD, I used mainly functions that returned references, but that was only for brevity. Strictly speaking, that's bad engineering practice. Even though it's a little bit more work to create separate get- and set- functions for each variable, you'll be thanking me when you need to change the game so that modifying one variable makes something else happen within the game.

Auxiliary Classes

There are a few auxiliary classes you can use in conjunction with entities. Different types of entities may share traits in common with other entities, but not all entities share all traits.

Reference Counting and the Future

The reference count in the previous list is designed to facilitate future additions to the MUD. I haven't gone over this idea yet, but there are objects in the BetterMUD that act similar to the SimpleMUD's database pointers; I call them *accessors*. An accessor is a simple lightweight class that is used to access entities in the databases.

Whenever you create an accessor pointing to an entity, that entity's reference count is increased, and whenever you destroy the accessor, that entity's reference count is decreased. What this means is that if the game is currently using entities somewhere, the reference count will be more than 0. If you've got three different places in the code with accessors pointing to one entity, its reference count is 3.

The idea behind this is that someday you may want to move the BetterMUD into a true multithreading environment, so that the database and the game can operate on different threads, and so that the database knows when it's safe to write individual entities to disk. If the reference count is more than 0, the game is currently using that entity somewhere and may be modifying its data, so it's not safe to write it to disk.

Another benefit is that the accessors could be modified to use mutexes (remember them from Chapter 3?), so that if the database is writing an entity to disk, an accessor has to wait until the database is finished to access the entity. I may implement these ideas one day, if I get a chance to create a better database system for the BetterMUD. Check out the news on the BetterMUD (dune.net, port 5110) to see the latest improvements.

Basic Data Classes

For example, the character and item entity types both need to know which rooms and regions they are in. For other entities, such as portals, regions, and rooms, having this information would be useless; a room can't be in another room (at least in this design, it can't), and a region definitely can't be in a room, because it's supposed to be the other way around. Portals can be in rooms, but they are a special case, since they can be in many rooms at once.

So, what do you do? Do you give characters and items their own m_room variables? That's a lot of wasted work if you ask me. Do you create a new class, say, RoomEntity, and have characters and items inherit from that? That may work at first, but eventually you're going to end up with lots of multiple inheritance problems if you try sharing other variables across entities.

The method I chose is to use a simple *data class*. Here is the data class for a room tag:

```
class HasRoom {
public:
    HasRoom() : m_room( 0 ) {}
    entityid Room() const           { return m_room; }
    void SetRoom( entityid p_room ) { m_room = p_room; }
protected:
    entityid m_room;
};
```

The class has a piece of room data, named m_room, and it has three functions. Room returns the ID, SetRoom sets the ID, and the constructor auto-initializes the room variable to 0 whenever it is created. There are two other classes like this: HasRegion and HasTemplateID.

Container Classes

Following in the same tradition, there are several container classes that you can add to your entities. In the game, entities often need to know the IDs of objects that they contain; characters need to know what items they have, rooms need to know what items they contain (the characters and portals they have), and so on. As before, since different types of entities can share similar containers of items, it makes sense to make a special class that holds a container of that specific item, and inherit from that.

Here's an example of the HasCharacters class:

```
class HasCharacters {
public:
    typedef std::set<entityid> characters;
    typedef characters::iterator charitr;
    void AddCharacter( entityid p_id )      { m_characters.insert( p_id ); }
    void DelCharacter( entityid p_id )      { m_characters.erase( p_id ); }
    charitr CharactersBegin()               { return m_characters.begin(); }
    charitr CharactersEnd()                 { return m_characters.end(); }
    size_t Characters()                     { return m_characters.size(); }
protected:
    characters m_characters;
};
```

The class uses two typedefs to define a set of entityids and an iterator into that set.

I've decided to go with sets for storing data within entities. I could easily have gone with lists or vectors, but I feel that sets hold the best performance capabilities. Sets have O(log n) insertion and deletion time, which on average, works out better than the O(1) insertion and O(n) deletion time for lists and vectors.

> **TIP**
>
> I use typedefs quite often within the BetterMUD, espe-
> cially for containers. The reasoning for this is quite simple:
> In the future, you may need to change the way a container
> works by turning it into a list or something else. This way,
> whenever someone uses your room class, he can refer to
> its container of characters as: `Room::characters`, instead of
> needing to remember which container it actually is stored
> in. I've also typedefed the iterator, so you can refer to
> character iterators inside a room like this: `Room::charitr`.
> Trust me—typedefs make your life so much easier.

Sets also have an interesting property that will make your life much easier in the long run: They can't hold duplicate data. This means that the set data structure automatically makes sure that you never have more than one ID inside it. This can save you lots of pain in case you accidentally add an entity to a room more than once.

I have created four different container classes: `HasCharacters`, `HasItems`, `HasRooms`, and `HasPortals`.

> **NOTE**
>
> When an algorithm is classified as O(log n), that means
> that if there are *n* elements inside the container, you take
> the logarithm of that number, and that's approximately
> how many operations it will take to complete the algo-
> rithm at *most*—an upper bound, in other words. The base-2
> logarithm of 128 is 7, meaning that to insert and delete
> anything from a set of 128 items will take approximately
> 14 operations (7 for insertion, 7 for deletion). On the
> other hand, if you used a list of the same size, inserting
> would be instant (O(1). That means about 1 operation. To
> delete something from the list, you need to search
> through the whole thing to find what you want to delete.
> That would take on average 64 operations (1 at minimum,
> 128 at maximum). Lists are great for insertions, but bad
> for searching-deletions.

Complex Function Classes

There are two complex classes that entities inherit from as well: the DataEntity class and the LogicEntity class.

Data Entities

The DataEntity class stores a databank. In Chapter 11, "The BetterMUD," I told you that characters and items have access to a flexible system of attributes, so that you can add and remove attributes from characters and items at any time during the game. A databank implements this behavior; I will go over it in more detail a little later on. For now, all you need to know is what a data entity can do.

A data entity has five functions:

```
int GetAttribute( const std::string& p_name );
void SetAttribute( const std::string& p_name, int p_val );
bool HasAttribute( const std::string& p_name );
void AddAttribute( const std::string& p_name, int p_initialval );
void DelAttribute( const std::string& p_name )
```

For the BetterMUD, all attribute values are stored as ints. I've found that I rarely have a use for floats and I dislike their lack of precision, so using ints for attribute values is an acceptable compromise.

All these functions are string based, which means you can use entities that inherit from this class flexibly. Look at the following code, for example, which assumes that I have a data entity named d:

```
d.AddAttribute( "strength", 10 );     // insert an attribute into the object
int s = d.GetAttribute( "strength" );// get attribute
bool b = d.HasAttribute( "strength" );  // true
b = d.HasAttribute( "pies" );           // false
d.SetAttribute( "strength", 20 );       // stronger now!
d.DelAttribute( "strength" );           // no more strength
s = d.GetAttribute( "strength" );       // uh oh! Exception thrown!
```

Most scripting languages are built around the same ideas (especially Python, which acts the same with any datatype you use; see Chapter 17, "Python," for the nitty gritty details).

This should give you a really great opportunity to increase the flexibility of your MUD.

Logic Entities

On the other side of the spectrum are logic entities, which wrap around a LogicCollection. A logic collection is a cool object in the BetterMUD. It essentially wraps around a bunch of logic modules, so that entities can have more than one logic module attached to them, as Figure 12.1 shows.

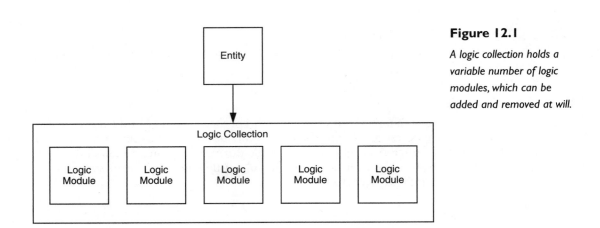

Figure 12.1

A logic collection holds a variable number of logic modules, which can be added and removed at will.

Basically, with a logic collection installed into an entity, you can add whichever logic module you want. If you have a special logic module that responds when someone tells it something, you can add that logic into it, without changing its responses to other actions within the game.

Here are the functions that a `LogicEntity` has. (I use some classes and concepts you haven't seen before, so bear with me for a moment.)

```
bool AddLogic( const std::string& p_logic );
bool AddExistingLogic( Logic* p_logic );
bool DelLogic( const std::string& p_logic );
Logic* GetLogic( const std::string& p_logic );
bool HasLogic( const std::string& p_logic );
int DoAction( const Action& p_action );
int DoAction(
    const std::string& p_act,
    entityid p_data1 = 0, entityid p_data2 = 0,
    entityid p_data3 = 0, entityid p_data4 = 0,
    const std::string& p_data = "" )
```

I'm jumping ahead a little here, since I explain the logic system in detail in a later chapter, but for now, it is important to know what your entity classes can do.

Within the game, all logic modules are referenced by name, so you can add door-logic to a portal as follows:

```
p.AddLogic( "portallogic_door" );
```

As long as the game knows about a logic module named `portallogic_door`, your portal now acts like a door, and refuses access to people when it is closed. The cool thing about this is that you can add other modules whenever you want:

```
p.AddLogic( "portallogic_onlyadmins" );
```

This kind of door acts like other doors and also blocks access to people who aren't admins.

> **NOTE**
>
> I mentioned that `LogicEntitys` **wrap around** `LogicCollections`. **Because of this, I'm not going to show you the code for this class, since it basically just passes the arguments on to the collection class. One thing you should be aware of, however, is that when collections have errors, they throw exceptions by default. However, it's not really a good idea to have your entity classes throwing exceptions around all over the place. The four functions that return Booleans catch exceptions and return** `false` **if an error occurred. This way, those functions are safe to call and won't cause your program to cascade out of control if they can't execute.**

Pretty cool, isn't it?

You can remove logic just as easily, and check to see if an object has a logic module of a specific type installed, and so on. It's all very flexible, and that's great.

Now, whenever an action happens to the entity, you just send the action event to the entity using `DoAction`, and every module is automatically told about the action.

I will go over logic modules, collections, and actions in much more detail in Chapter 15, "Game Logic." For now, you only need to have a general idea of what they can do.

Entity Requirements

Tables 12.1, 12.2, and 12.3 show listings of which entities need which auxiliary classes.

Using these classes, you can simply mix-and-match which parts you need for each entity. (It's like putting together a wardrobe.) These classes are typically called *mixins*. Figure 12.2 shows the inheritance hierarchy for two types of entities: characters and regions.

Note that `LogicEntity` inherits from the base `Entity` class. This is done because logic entities need to be able to tell their logic modules which ID they are attached to. So if a class inherits from a `LogicEntity`, the class doesn't have to inherit from an `Entity`. Here's a sample class declaration for characters, which multiple-inherits from all of its mixins:

```
class Character :
    public LogicEntity,
    public DataEntity,
    public HasRoom,
    public HasRegion,
    public HasTemplateID,
    public HasItems
```

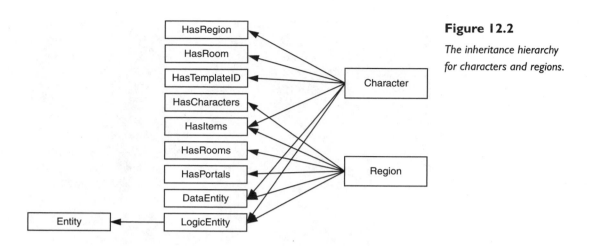

Figure 12.2

The inheritance hierarchy for characters and regions.

CAUTION

Using multiple inheritance (MI) is a controversial topic. Some people love it, and some people hate it. Some people never even need MI, but if it makes your life easier, why not use it? In the classes I use, MI is simple and easy to manage. This is because all the base classes are *mutually exclusive*, which means, that they don't share any bases, functions, or data in common. MI gets to be tricky if you use conflicting bases, though. For example, suppose you added another line to the inheritance list of the character class, `public Entity`. Now, since `LogicEntity` inherits from `Entity` as well, what the heck happens? It turns out, by default, C++ creates a class that has two instances of the `Entity` class, which you almost certainly didn't want. To solve this, you need to use *virtual inheritance*, which fixes the so-called *diamond-inheritance problem*. This issue is beyond the scope of this book, so feel free to explore it on your own. Just beware that MI is a tricky concept to implement correctly.

Accessors

In a major departure from the SimpleMUD, I decided against the use of *database pointer objects*. I have found that it's much easier to keep containers of IDs in memory, rather than pointer objects. All accessors in the BetterMUD can be found in the directory /BetterMUD/BetterMUD/accessors on the CD.

Comparing Database Pointers to Accessors

Instead of pointer objects, I use *accessor* objects.

Table 12.1 Auxiliary Data Needed by Entities

Entity	HasRoom	HasRegion	HasTemplateID
character	yes	yes	yes
item	yes	yes	yes
room	no	yes	no
portal	no	yes	no
region	no	no	no
account	no	no	no

Table 12.2 Containers Needed by Entities

Entity	HasCharacters	HasItems	HasRooms	HasPortals
character	no	yes	no	no
item	no	no	no	no
room	yes	yes	no	yes
portal	no	no	no	no
region	yes	yes	yes	yes
account	yes	no	no	no

Table 12.3 Complex Containers Needed by Entities

Entity	Data	Logic
character	yes	yes
item	yes	yes
room	yes	yes
portal	yes	yes
region	yes	yes
account	no	no

Figure 12.3 shows an example of the two different methods you can use to access entities in a database. The first method, used by the SimpleMUD, is slow and elementary. The second method, used by the BetterMUDs, has accessors that are quicker and more efficient because they perform the database lookup when they are created.

> **NOTE**
>
> Database accessors are basically smarter pointers than the database pointers of the SimpleMUD. To avoid confusing the two different methods, however, I refer to the new idea as accessors, rather than pointers.

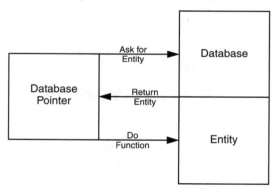

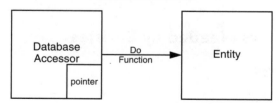

Figure 12.3

Two methods for performing functions on entities stored within databases.

Database pointers were a quick hack in the SimpleMUD; they were essentially a proxy class that would perform lookups from the database and then work on the object. Of course, that was all wasted effort if you did two operations in a row, like this:

```
player p = 10;
p.Name() = "RON";
p.Money() = 100000000;  // I wish
```

The operations perform two lookups in the database, even though the lookups are for the same object. So this represents wasted effort. To fix this in the SimpleMUD, I found myself using the following code quite often instead (assuming `dbp` is a `player` database pointer object):

```
Player& p = *dbp;
p.Name() = "RON";
p.Money() = 100000000;
```

I ended up asking the database pointer object to return a reference to the player, and then used the actual `Player` object to work on, which really defeated the whole idea of a database pointer in the first place.

Features of Accessors

To fix this, I created a database accessor concept.

Database accessors have several features:

- They perform lookups when they are created.
- They increment their entities' reference count when they are created.
- They are used from within Python to access needed parts of the game.
- They release their hold on an entity when they are destroyed, decreasing its reference count.

> **NOTE**
>
> In my opinion, the lack of a base class for database accessors or macro is the one big flaw of the BetterMUD. I had to make this choice for many reasons, however. First and foremost is the major problem of circular dependencies, which I highlighted with the SimpleMUD. C++ limits itself quite a bit sometimes, and it is annoying, but we have to live with it. Another problem is the way that I generate interfaces between Python and C++, which you'll see in Chapter 17. The code generators I use don't play well with templates and inheritance. (The generators were designed for C, after all.) So, basically, as you'll see later on, accessor classes basically need to be copied and pasted from the class you are accessing. This can be annoying, but since most of the game expansion can be done in Python anyway, it's not a big deal. You'll find that you won't need to be changing the accessor class definitions too often.

Here's an example of the `character` accessor, which performs lookups for `Character` entities:

```
character c( 100 );
c.SetName( "Ron" );
c.SetDescription( "He is an awesome dude, as Strongbad would say." );
```

When the accessor is created, it looks up a pointer to the `Character` object it needs to access, which it then keeps so that you can perform fast operations on it, without needing to look up the entity again. When the accessor goes out of scope, the accessor tells the entity that it's no longer referencing it, and its reference count is decreased, so that the database knows there is one less accessor pointing at that entity.

> **NOTE**
>
> I chose to use the same naming scheme as the SimpleMUD for entities and their accessor objects. For example, the class `Character` with a capital "C" represents the actual entity, and the class `character` with a lowercase "c" represents the accessor objects.

Accessor Iterators

Accessors typically have their own iterators built in, which means that an accessor acts like an iterator. Take the character entity, for example. Characters have container items that they are carrying, and because of this, you need a way to iterate over those items.

Of course, the easiest way to do this would be to make the accessor return an actual iterator to the item container, but alas, there is a problem with this method. The program I use to generate interfaces between C++ and Python doesn't fully support interaction between C++ and Python iterators. (There is limited support for vector iterators, but I'm not using vectors. D'oh!)

So instead, accessors sometimes wrap around a single iterator for each of their containers. Characters wrap around an item iterator, and you can use functions like this:

```
character c( 100 );
c.BeginItems();
while( c.IsValidItem() ) {
    entityid i = c.CurrentItem();
    c.NextItem();
}
```

It's fairly simple. If you ever need another iterator, you can easily create another accessor object.

That's as much as I want to tell you about entity accessors for the time being. I'll get back to them later on, after I've shown you the intermediate stuff.

Helpers

To help with matching names of entities, I've included a few helper functions and classes inside the `Entity.h` file. Since you're probably sick of all of the string-matching code I threw at you in the SimpleMUD, I'll spare you the details and just show you how to work with the helpers.

Manual Matching

Two functors deal with string matching: one matches full names, and one matches partial names. They are called `stringmatchfull` and `stringmatchpart`. (How original!) Anyway, they work like this:

1. Creates a matching functor with the name you are looking for
2. Loops through a list of names to see if any of them match

Here's an example of full matching:

```
stringmatchfull matcher( "the rain in spain" );
bool b = matcher( "The grain in spain" );   // false
b = matcher( "the RAIN in spain" );         // true
b = matcher( "the rain" );                  // false
```

Matchers automatically disregard case, for obvious reasons. Partial matchers work the same way:

```
stringmatchpart matcher( "the rain in spain" );
bool b = matcher( "the" );                  // true
b = matcher( "spain" );                     // true
b = matcher( "ain" );                       // false
b = matcher( "grain" );                     // false
```

The matchers use the same matching rules that the SimpleMUD used. Partial matching only returns true at the start of words; it won't match sequences of characters inside a word. That's why "ain" returns false, even though it appears twice in the statement.

Automatic Matching

I have three automatic matching functions that you can use on an STL container of `entityids` to either perform single or dual-pass matches, or a dual-pass partial name search.

However, the functions need to know what type of accessor you are using to look up the entities. Say you have a set of IDs, named s, which represents a bunch of characters. This is how you would perform a one-pass full match on the set:

```
set<entityid>::iterator itr;
itr = matchonepass<character>(
    s.begin(), s.end(),
    stringmatchfull( "Ron" ) );
```

One odd bit of syntax you may notice is the `<character>` after the function name. When calling template functions, C++ usually deduces the template types by the arguments you pass into it; however, since you're not passing in a `character` accessor, the function has no way of knowing that you're trying to search a container of characters. Instead, you must tell the function that you're looking for characters. If you were looking through a container of IDs that represented `Item` objects, you would call it like this: `matchonepass<item>`.

The function returns an iterator and takes two iterators and a functor as its parameters. The two iterator parameters are supposed to represent the range of items you want to search, so you have the option of searching only a particular range, or the whole container. The third argument is a functor that returns either `true` or `false`. When scanning through the container, an iterator is returned that points to the first object that returns `true`. So, after running this code, `itr` can be one of two things: an iterator pointing to a character entity whose name is "Ron", or `s.end()`, which means that "Ron" isn't within the container.

You can easily turn that into a one-pass partial matcher by replacing `stringmatchfull` with `stringmatchpart`.

Of course, there will be times when you need to perform a dual pass search on a container as well:

```
set<entityid>::iterator itr;
itr = matchtwopass<character>(
    s.begin(), s.end(),
    stringmatchfull( "Ron" ),
    stringmatchpart( "Ron" ) );
```

This code performs a two-pass search. First it searches for full matches, and then, it searches for partial matches if no full matches were found.

The final function is a helper that automatically performs a full/partial two-pass search on a container of `entityids`:

```
set<entityid>::iterator itr;
itr = match<character>( s.begin(), s.end(), "Ron" );
```

As you can see, it's a lot cleaner than the other two functions.

Databases

Now that you have a basic comprehension of entities, I can move on to the databases of the BetterMUD.

Designs

For the SimpleMUD, I threw a design at you and said, "This is what the SimpleMUD is using!" Well, there are many ways to implement databases, especially for a persistent-world game.

The SimpleMUD and the BetterMUD don't actually have databases but rather simple containers that hold entities and aren't nearly as complex as some of the *real* databases out there.

There are tons of technologies to choose from. SQL is a popular database format. (I've played around with the MySQL implementation of SQL, and I liked what I saw. It's free, too! You can download it at http://www.mysql.org.) Lots of computer languages have built-in APIs that talk to these databases.

There are database programs you can buy for lots of money, but you probably won't need the kind of performance that they provide. MUDs usually aren't nearly as ambitious (in terms of player and world size) as the latest MMORPGs, so most of the time having a dedicated database program is a waste of effort.

The key benefit of a dedicated database is the fact that they (usually) abstract the data and the logic of a game onto two separate machines. Look at Figure 12.4 for a moment.

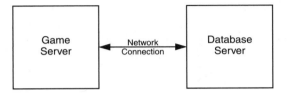

Figure 12.4

Typical database setup.

Usually, you have the database on one machine, and the game on the other. Whenever the game needs to access information, it asks the database to look it up and send it over the network connection. Although networks are much more unreliable than having everything in one machine, databases are typically installed on the same network as the game machine, so you probably have a fast Ethernet connection between the two. That eliminates any concerns about speed, and connection losses are also going to be rare (if not nonexistent).

The *really* great thing, however, is that the database machine can safely offload (store on to disk) the data, without slowing down the game. This is a flaw that the SimpleMUD and the BetterMUD both have; eventually, the world can get large enough so that just saving the database periodically ends up lagging the game.

I would have loved to have shown you how to implement a full "real" database for the MUD, but I only have so much room. So I chose to go light on databases and focus on the really cool parts of the scripting system of the BetterMUD.

Database Types

There are five major database types in the BetterMUD, four of which I present in this chapter. The fifth variation is the `PythonDatabase`, which is a class that manages Python scripts. I'll go over that in Chapter 16, "The Networking System," along with its offspring: the `CommandDatabase` and the `LogicDatabase`.

All of the database classes I discuss in this section can be found on the CD in the files BetterMUD/BetterMUD/databases/database.h and database.cpp, within the same directory.

Figure 12.5 shows the relationship hierarchy between all the databases I discuss in this chapter.

The base `Database` class implements a number of helper functions that all entity databases use, and the map- and vector-based databases are similar in design to the databases of the SimpleMUD.

Note that the Template/Instance database doesn't inherit from either the map or vector databases; instead, it contains a copy of each.

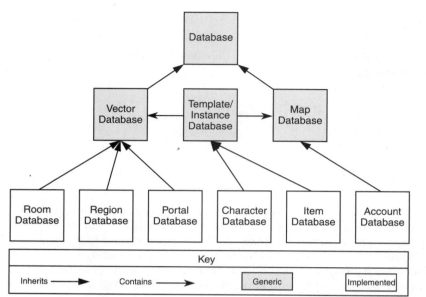

Figure 12.5

Relationships between all the entity databases in the BetterMUD.

Basic Database

The basic Database class is a generic class that uses a single container to store entities. The main reason for the existence of this class is the fact that even though maps and vectors store data in two completely different ways, there are operations that you'll need to perform on both types. Here is a listing of those functions:

```
container::iterator begin();
container::iterator end();
virtual entityid findname( const std::string& p_name ) = 0;
virtual entity& get( entityid p_id ) = 0;
virtual entity& create( entityid p_id ) = 0;
size_t size() { return m_container.size() - 1; }
void LoadEntity( std::istream& p_stream );
void SaveEntity( std::ostream& p_stream, entity& p_entity );
void LoadDirectory( const std::string& p_dir );
void LoadFile( const std::string& p_file );
void Purge();
```

The begin and end functions simply return iterators into the database, and findname does a full name match for entities within the database. The other functions need to be described in more detail, though.

Getting and Creating

Data retrieval is the most common function you perform with a database. The get function retrieves an existing entity from the database and returns a reference to that entity. However, you have to be really careful when performing this function; if you get an entity that doesn't exist, the database throws an exception at you.

On the other hand, if you want to create a new entity in the database, you should call the create function, which creates an entity at the ID you specify and returns a reference to the brand-new entity. If you call this function by the name of an entity that already exists, the function still works. It's designed so that if you call it, you are guaranteed to get an entity, unless you run out of memory or some other problem occurs. In addition, all entities returned from this function already have their m_id data filled out.

You should note that these two functions are purely virtual, meaning that the Database class doesn't implement them; it only says that the functions are available. This is because maps and vectors are fundamentally different data structures and require different methods to perform these functions.

Loading and Saving Entities

Loading and saving entities is more automated in the BetterMUD than in the SimpleMUD. All entities are required to have these two functions:

```
void Save( std::ostream& p_stream );
void Load( std::istream& p_stream );
```

They save and load an entity to or from a stream, which is a great thing to have, because you can use file streams with these functions and save them to disk.

The Database class counts on the fact that these functions are available, and because of this, it has automated its loading and saving functions. Here's an example of the loading function:

```
void LoadEntity( std::istream& p_stream ) {
    entityid id;
    std::string temp;
    p_stream >> temp >> id;     // load the ID

    entity& e = create( id );   // load/create entity
    e.Load( p_stream );         // load it from the stream
    p_stream >> std::ws;        // chew up extra whitespace
}
```

This function performs the following simple task, which is repeated quite often. For that reason, the function is built into the base database class:

1. Eat up the [ID] tag in the stream.
2. Load in the ID of the entity.
3. Create/load the entity from the database.
4. Load the data from the stream and put it into the entity.

Because of this process, the Load function of each entity should not load IDs from the stream It should always assume that the ID has already been loaded previously by the database. This also means that every entity in a file must start off with its ID tag, like this:

[ID]

And the rest of the data follows after that.

The saving process is simpler; it just writes out the tag, writes out the ID, and then writes out the entity using its Save function.

Loading a Directory or File

From working with the SimpleMUD, I learned that working with one file per entity type was an incredible pain in the butt. So, for the BetterMUD, I've decided that the ability to automatically load an entire directory of files is a powerful tool. Therefore, the BetterMUD expands on the same ideas used by the player database of the SimpleMUD.

In every directory that databases load files from, there is a manifest file, simply named "manifest". It's a simple text file, and on every line is the name of a file within that directory that you want the database to load. Figure 12.6 shows an example of a manifest file pointing to other files that a database is supposed to load.

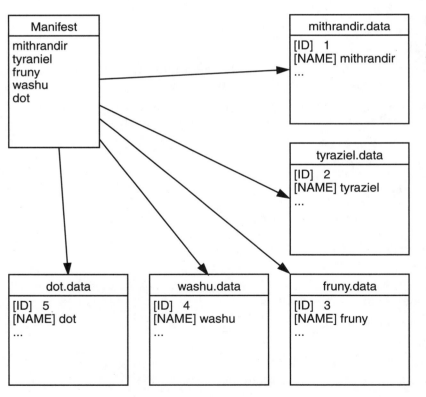

Figure 12.6

Files that aren't listed in the manifest aren't loaded.

> **TIP**
>
> Even though C++ doesn't have the ability to iterate over the files in a directory,
> the need for such an operation is so common that it's built into almost every
> operating system. Because every operating system has its own operating method
> and none of the implementations are similar, people have created their own
> libraries to wrap around operating systems. One library is the C++ Boost library,
> which you can download and use free at http://www.boost.org. It's a really cool
> library that has a component named boost::filesystem that implements iterators
> to iterate over files in a directory. Unfortunately, due to some issues with VC6,
> and the fact that boost is still a work-in-progress, I couldn't get it to work prop-
> erly (though it worked like a charm in VC7 and GCC for Linux). So, I don't use
> boost here. You should feel free to look into it on your own, however. I've included
> the most recent version on the CD for you to play around with if you want. It's in
> the directory /goodies/Libraries/boost.

So, like in the SimpleMUD's player database, the BetterMUD's general Database class can
load a directory of files using a manifest file. Here is the code to do it:

```cpp
void LoadDirectory( const std::string& p_dir ) {
    std::ifstream dir(
        std::string( p_dir + "manifest" ).c_str(),
        std::ios::binary );      // open the manifest file
    dir >> std::ws;              // chew up whitespace

    std::string filename;
    while( dir.good() ) {
        dir >> filename >> std::ws;
        LoadFile( p_dir + filename );
    }
}
```

The function loads up the manifest file and then reads in name after name. For each name,
it calls the LoadFile helper function. LoadFile simply loops through every entity in a file,
loading each one:

```cpp
void LoadFile( const std::string& p_file ) {
    std::string filename = p_file + ".data";
    std::ifstream f( filename.c_str(), std::ios::binary );
    f >> std::ws;

    while( f.good() )
        LoadEntity( f );
}
```

Purging

There may be times in the game when you want to purge the entire contents of a database (rare, but it happens). Because of this, all databases have a Purge function, which completely empties the database.

Map and Vector Databases

The map and vector databases are similar to the map and vector databases from the SimpleMUD, so I'm not even going to show you their implementations. The vector-based database class is called VectorDatabase, and it doesn't add anything to the functions of normal dataabases.

The map-based database, MapDatabase, has some extra functions: FindOpenID, which finds an open ID and returns it, and erase, which finds an entity and erases it from the database. Vectors can't delete entities, because they shouldn't contain open spaces, and deleting entities at any index leads to open holes in the vector. I haven't come across the need to delete portals, rooms, or regions while the game is running, so I didn't bother implementing that function.

Template/Instance Database

Now, in the game, the *dynamic* objects (rooms, portals, and regions are all *static* objects, which cannot be created or deleted at runtime, except by loading a new database) are the characters and the items. All these items are generated from a *template* and are essentially stored in a database similar to the enemy database of the SimpleMUD; whenever a new character or item is created, the entity is copied over from a template.

To do this, I created a special database, the TemplateInstanceDatabase, which actually contains two databases: one vector-based, and one map-based. Figure 12.7 shows this concept. Whenever a new instance is created, a template is copied into it to store the initial values.

Since the template database doesn't inherit from the other databases, it has to wrap over their functions and add new functions as well.

Functions

Here's a listing:

```
instances::iterator begin();
instances::iterator end();
templates::iterator begintemplates()      { return m_templates.begin(); }
templates::iterator endtemplates()        { return m_templates.end(); }

entity& get( entityid p_id );
size_t size();
size_t sizetemplates();
entityid findname( const std::string& p_name );
```

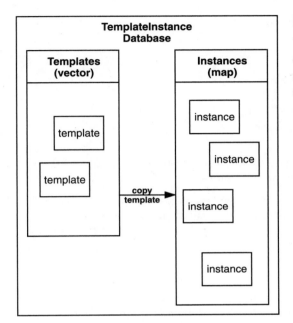

Figure 12.7

The template-instance database is a dual database that holds templates and instances.

```
void erase( entityid p_id )
bool isvalid( entityid p_id )

void LoadEntityTemplate( std::istream& p_stream );
void SaveEntityTemplate( std::ostream& p_stream, entity& p_entity );
void LoadEntity( std::istream& p_stream );
void SaveEntity( std::ostream& p_stream, entity& p_entity );
void Cleanup()
void Purge()
void LoadFile( const std::string& p_file )

templateentity& gettemplate( entityid p_id );
entityid generate( entityid p_template );
```

The begin, end, get, size, findname, erase, and all the Load/Save functions simply wrap around the template instance database that it contains. The only functions involved with templates at all are gettemplate, generate, begintemplates, and endtemplates. The generate function takes an ID of a template as its parameter, creates a new entity instance based on that template, and returns the ID of the new instance.

For example, if you had a human template character at ID 1, you could create a new human character like this:

```
entityid human = CharacterDB.generate( 1 );
```

And then human would hold the ID of the new character.

Here's the code for that function:

```
entityid generate( entityid p_template ) {
    entityid id = m_instances.FindOpenID();
    entity& e = m_instances.create(id);
    e.LoadTemplate( m_templates.get( p_template ) );
    return id;
}
```

It finds an open ID within the instances database, creates a new entity at that ID, and then calls that entity's LoadTemplate function to copy the template over.

The instance class entity and the template class entitytemplate don't have to be different, but I would make them different. I've found that templates usually need less data than instances (which you see when you look at the Character and CharacterTemplate classes), so it's a good idea to keep the data to a minimum.

Garbage Collection

Deleting instances of entities in the game is dangerous. Since you can never be completely sure who is hanging on to a reference of an entity when you delete it, a template/instance database keeps a set of all of the IDs that the game wants cleaned up. For example, here's what happens in the erase function:

```
void erase( entityid p_id ) {
    m_cleanup.insert( p_id );
}
```

When you want to remove an instance, instead of being blown away immediately, the instance's ID is inserted into the m_cleanup set, and the game eventually cleans up that entity at a later time, by calling the Cleanup function:

```
void Cleanup() {
    cleanup::iterator itr = m_cleanup.begin();
    while( itr != m_cleanup.end() ) {
        cleanup::iterator current = itr++;
        entity& e = m_instances.get( *current );
        m_instances.erase( *current );
        m_cleanup.erase( current );
    }
}
```

This essentially loops through the entire cleanup set, and erases the instances from the instance database.

Summary

This chapter gave you a brief glimpse of the underlying concepts of entity storage and management concepts, which should be familiar to you from learning the SimpleMUD.

I've expanded on and improved those concepts in a number of areas, making the system more reusable and flexible, and because of this, I was able to reduce the code at higher levels. Whenever I want to make a database load a directory of entities, all I need to do is issue a command like this: `DB.LoadDirectory( "data/blah/" )`.

In the next chapter, I'll show you the complete implementations of all of the entity classes, but I keep that simple as well. The actual entities are simple classes that don't have much to do with the actual game, except that they contain data. The main idea I'm trying to promote here is keeping the hard-coded stuff to a minimum, while making the actual game as flexible as possible, without making it *too* flexible.

CHAPTER 13

ENTITIES AND DATABASES CONTINUED

The previous chapter described the base entity and database classes and outlined the accessor classes, but didn't show you how to actually implement the final entity or database classes. This chapter does so. The good news is that since most of the work has already been accomplished in the base classes, the final entity and database classes are really quite simple.

In this chapter, you will learn to:

- Use databanks to make your entities flexible
- Work with the six entity classes: accounts, characters, items, rooms, portals, and regions
- Use entity databases to store files to disk
- Use entity accessors as iterators

Databanks

Before discussing entities, I'd like to show you a special class. In the previous chapter, I mentioned that there is a mixin class called DataEntity, which wraps around a *databank*.

A databank gives flexibility to the BetterMUD. I'm sure you're used to figuring out what kinds of data you need, programming the data, and then realizing that you might not need an attribute or two. If you create instead a flexible structure that can store an unlimited amount of data, you can easily add variables to your characters while the game is running. If you think this idea is cool, just wait until I show you Python.

The flexible structure I've described requires storing objects with arbitrary names, and what better structure to store them in than an std::map? If you don't know this already, you should learn that std::maps used with std::strings are practically the coolest thing you can ever do in C++. Examine this code segment:

```
std::map<std::string, int> intbank;
intbank["pie"] = 20;
intbank["cool"] = 30;
int a = intbank["pie"];    // 20
a = intbank["cool"];       // 30
```

Pretty cool, isn't it? You can insert as many items as you want, and since it's a map, you'll have some decent performance (O(log n) for those algorithm-obsessed folks) when inserting or retrieving items. Sure, it's not nearly as fast as accessing variables directly by a memory offset (which is the way that precompiled variables are accessed), but I believe that the time has finally come when the benefits of having such an extensible system far outweigh the need to squeeze every drop of speed out of your system.

Databank Class

The `Databank` class itself is fairly simple; it's a wrapper around an `std::map` that allows you to manage the attributes within it easily:

```cpp
template< typename type >
class Databank {
public:
    typedef std::map< std::string, type > container;
    typedef container::iterator iterator;
    iterator begin()     { return m_bank.begin(); }
    iterator end()       { return m_bank.end(); }

    bool Has( const std::string& p_name )
    void Set( const std::string& p_name, const type& p_val )
    type& Get( const std::string& p_name )
    void Add( const std::string& p_name, const type& p_val )
    void Del( const std::string& p_name )
    void Save( std::ostream& p_stream )
    void Load( std::istream& p_stream )
    void Clear()
    size_t size()

protected:
    container m_bank;
};
```

You can create databanks of any type you want, since this is a template class: for example, a `Databank<int>`, or `Databank<float>`. You can also iterate through databanks to see which variables they hold.

The second grouping of functions allows you to access and use the databank. To make databanks more "consistent," they throw exceptions when you try getting or changing attributes that don't exist, rather than accidentally creating them. Of course, to avoid throwing exceptions, you can first use the `Has` function to see if an attribute exists.

Since the functions simply wrap around the `std::map` functions and add exception throwing in the appropriate places, I'm not going to show you the code. You can find this class in /BetterMUD/entities/Attributes.h.

Using a Databank

Using a databank is pretty simple, as you can see from this example:

```cpp
Databank<int> bank;
bank.Add( "health", 10 );
bank.Add( "strength", 20 );
int i = bank.Get( "health" );     // 10
```

```
i = bank.Get( "strength" );      // 20
bank.Del( "health" );
i = bank.Get( "health" );        // *THROWS EXCEPTION*
bank.Set( "strength", 30 );
```

A databank is string-based, so you can easily add any variables to it that you want. Every entity (except accounts) in the BetterMUD has a databank that you can use and access through the scripts, which will allow you almost limitless freedom to add variables to characters in the game.

Databanks and Streams

Databanks also have stream loading and saving functions, which makes it easy to load and save databanks to disk. Here's an example of the saving code:

```
void Save( std::ostream& p_stream ) {
    p_stream << "[DATABANK]\n";

    iterator itr = m_bank.begin();
    while( itr != m_bank.end() ) {
        p_stream << BasicLib::tostring( itr->first, 24 ) <<
            itr->second << "\n";
        ++itr;
    }
    p_stream << "[/DATABANK]\n";
}
```

This will create files that look like this:

```
[DATABANK]
health              10
strength            20
hitpoints           100
[/DATABANK]
```

Nice, pretty, and readable. The call to the BasicLib::tostring makes sure there are 24 columns between the start of the attribute and the start of the variable. I could have used the setw function of streams to accomplish the same thing, but problems occur when compilers work in different ways (strange for a "standard" library, right? C++ still has a long way to go.).

A databank is loaded in a similar way:

```
void Load( std::istream& p_stream ) {
    std::string temp;
    p_stream >> temp;        // extract "[DATABANK]"

    while( BasicLib::extract( p_stream, temp ) != "[/DATABANK]" ) {
```

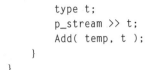

```
        type t;
        p_stream >> t;
        Add( temp, t );
    }
}
```

The loop extracts each data tag using the BasicLib::extract function; each pass compares the data tag to see if it is the [/DATABANK] tag. If it is, the loop ends.

If the databank doesn't have an attribute extracted from the stream, it is automatically loaded. This is a particularly useful feature, because it allows you to load a databank from a file without manually adding all the attributes first.

Entities

There are six entity classes in BetterMUD, representing accounts, characters, items, rooms, regions, and portals. Most of them share a good deal in common, which makes it easier on us, since all we need to do is make them inherit the features they need. Two of these entities are *volatile*, which means that they can be created and deleted at any time while the game is running. Accounts can be created, but not deleted, so they're not exactly volatile. The only way to create new rooms, portals, and regions is to reload their template files.

Accounts

The "oddball" of the group is the *account* entity. Accounts really aren't used within the game, and their main reason for existing is to manage the characters that your players can own. Here's the class definition:

```
class Account :
    public Entity,
    public HasCharacters
{
public:
    void Load( std::istream& p_stream );
    void Save( std::ostream& p_stream );

    // Accessors
    std::string Password()
    BasicLib::sint64 LoginTime()
    accesslevel AccessLevel()
    bool Banned()
    int AllowedCharacters()

    void SetPass( const std::string& p_pass )
    void SetLoginTime( BasicLib::sint64 p_time )
```

```
        void SetAccessLevel( accesslevel p_level )
        void SetBanned( bool p_banned )
        void SetAllowedCharacters( int p_num )

protected:
        std::string m_password;         // user's password
        BasicLib::sint64 m_logintime;   // time of first login
        accesslevel m_accesslevel;      // access level of player
        int m_allowedcharacters;        // number of characters player is allowed
        bool m_banned;                  // is user banned?

};  // end class Account
```

The first thing you should notice is that the class inherits from Entity and HasCharacters, so it automatically gets every piece of data and function from those classes. Consult the previous chapter to review information on the Entity and HasCharacters classes.

In addition to the standard entity datatypes and a collection of character IDs, the account entity has five variables, representing various data about itself including the following: a password, the time the account first logged in, the access level of the account, how many characters the account is allowed, and whether or not the account is banned.

NOTE

I put in the access-level ranking system for future expansion. Eventually, I would like to have an online editor capable of logging into the game and uploading new maps and items; this kind of capability would require a special implementation of the networking system, with its own protocol and handlers.

Most of this should be self-explanatory; the access level is about equivalent to the ranking system of the SimpleMUD, but it's not that important for the BetterMUD.

You can also ban people from the game, if they become too unruly; the logon process will not allow banned characters to log in.

Characters

There are actually two character entity classes in the game: character templates and the actual characters.

A character template is a simple structure that holds data about a character and copies that data into a new character every time the game generates one.

Character Template Class

The character template class is basically just a placeholder; it's meant to hold data loaded from a template file on disk, so that actual character instances in the game can copy this information into their characters. Here's the class skeleton:

```
class CharacterTemplate :
    public Entity,
    public DataEntity {
    friend class Character;
public:
    void Load( std::istream& p_stream );
protected:
    typedef std::list< std::string > names;
    names m_commands;
    names m_logics;
};
```

The character class is a simple template class that inherits from the Entity and DataEntity mixin classes. The line in bold declares that the Character class is a friend, and that it should have access to all the data held within it.

I typedefed a list of strings and called it names, and then gave the class two of these lists. These lists represent the names of the command modules and logic modules for characters. I'll discuss commands and logic modules when I get to the scripting and python chapters, so for now, all you need to know is that templates hold the names of scripts, rather than script objects themselves.

The template class can't do much. In fact, it only has one function: to load itself from a stream:

```
void CharacterTemplate::Load( std::istream& p_stream ) {
    std::string temp;
    p_stream >> temp >> std::ws; std::getline( p_stream, m_name );
    p_stream >> temp >> std::ws; std::getline( p_stream, m_description );

    m_attributes.Load( p_stream );

    p_stream >> temp;        // chew up the "[COMMANDS]" tag
    while( BasicLib::extract( p_stream, temp ) != "[/COMMANDS]" )
        m_commands.push_back( temp );

    p_stream >> temp;        // chew up the "[LOGICS]" tag
    while( BasicLib::extract( p_stream, temp ) != "[/LOGICS]" )
        m_logics.push_back( temp );
}
```

As you can see, it's not difficult. Both the name and the description of a character are loaded by line, because their names can have spaces. The databanks know how to load themselves automatically—you simply call m_databanks.Load(p_stream), and it loads.

Here's an example of a sample character template in a text file:

```
[ID]                   1
[NAME]                 Human
[DESCRIPTION]          This is a normal Human Being
```

```
[DATABANK]
health                 10
strength               10
[/DATABANK]
[COMMANDS]
go say chat get give drop look quit quiet
[/COMMANDS]
[LOGICS]
combatmodule encumbrancemodule humanmodule
[/LOGICS]
```

This defines a character template named Human, who has two attributes (health and strength), nine game commands, and three logic modules. It's not important what these modules and commands do right now, but keep this in the back of your mind.

Character Class

The Character class is a more complex version of the CharacterTemplate class. Instead of having names of commands and logic modules, it has the actual modules, as well as a slew of additional data that templates don't really care about (why would a template care if a character is logged in or not?).

Character Hard-Coded Data

Here's a condensed version of the Character class, with the functions removed so you can first see what data it has:

```
class Character :
    public LogicEntity,
    public DataEntity,
    public HasRoom,
    public HasRegion,
    public HasTemplateID,
    public HasItems {
public:
    typedef std::list<Command*> commands;
protected:
    entityid m_account;          // account number
    bool m_quiet;                // interpret typing as chat or command?
    bool m_verbose;              // print room descriptions?
    bool m_loggedin;             // are you logged in?
    std::string m_lastcommand;   // the last command the character entered
    commands m_commands;         // which commands the character has
};  // end class Character
```

Characters inherit a logic collection, a databank, a room, a region, a template ID, and a collection of item pointers from their mixin classes.

On top of those things, the class also has a pointer to its associated account, two *style modes*, a logged-in state, a string representing the last command typed in, and a list of command pointers.

The *quiet* mode of a character is only applicable to players, and it involves how commands are interpreted by the game module. The gist is that if a character is in quiet mode, misspelling a command doesn't result in his accidentally saying something in the current room he's in. See Chapter 15 for a complete description (in the commands section).

> **TIP**
>
> **You can reward and punish players by adding and removing commands. If a player continuously abuses the global chat command, you can delete his chat command object to teach him a lesson, and if players prove worthy to your MUD, you can give them commands that allow them to help you run the realm. It's a cool, flexible system.**

The *verbose* mode determines whether or not room descriptions are printed out to players when they enter a new room. Often, room descriptions are large and make the game run slow if you're moving around quickly, so you have the option of turning them off, and just seeing the name, people, items, and exits within a room.

The logged-in value should be self-explanatory, and the last command string serves the same purpose it did in the `SimpleMUD::Game::m_lastcommand` string from the SimpleMUD.

The final variable is a list of command pointers, which represents every command you can execute while in the game. If you have a command object named `go`, you can say `go north` while in the game, and the game searches for that command and executes it, or gives you an error if you don't have the `go` command.

Data Accessors

There are accessor functions for each of the hard-coded pieces of data (in addition to those inherited from the base mixin classes):

```
entityid GetAccount( )
bool Quiet( )
bool IsPlayer( )
bool Verbose( )
std::string LastCommand( )
bool IsLoggedIn( )

void SetAccount( entityid p_account )
void SetQuiet( bool p_quiet )
void SetVerbose( bool p_verbose )
void SetLastCommand( const std::string& p_command )
void SetLoggedIn( bool p_loggedin )
```

All simple accessors return a variable directly, set a variable directly, or perform a simple calculation. (IsPlayer checks to see if m_account != 0.) I don't think any of this code is important, so I'm going on to more interesting topics.

Other Functions

The Character class has more functions—functions that are more complex and interesting than the accessor classes:

```
Character();
~Character();

void Add();
void Remove();
void LoadTemplate( const CharacterTemplate& p_template );

void Load( std::istream& p_stream );
void Save( std::ostream& p_stream );

commands::iterator CommandsBegin()  { return m_commands.begin(); }
commands::iterator CommandsEnd()    { return m_commands.end(); }
commands::iterator FindCommand( const std::string& p_name );
bool AddCommand( const std::string& p_command )
bool DelCommand( const std::string& p_command )
bool HasCommand( const std::string& p_command )
```

Construction Time Again

The first two functions are the constructor and destructor.

The constructor simply initializes the variables with default values:

```
Character::Character() {
    m_account = 0;
    m_loggedin = false;
    m_quiet = false;
    m_verbose = true;
}
```

Obviously, a character doesn't have an account when first created, so it can't be logged in. The quiet mode is set to false, so that players entering the game can chat by default, and the verbose mode is set to true, so that players see the full room descriptions when they start off.

The destructor is important for characters because of the command system. Whenever a new command is retrieved from the command database, a new pointer to a Command object is returned, and the database assumes that the character who requested the command will manage it from then on. This means that you need to delete all commands when a character is destructed:

```
Character::~Character() {
    commands::iterator itr = m_commands.begin();
    while( itr != m_commands.end() ) {
        delete *itr;
        ++itr;
    }
}
```

Adding and Removing

The Add and Remove functions are helper functions that are used when loading a character from disk. These functions physically add and remove a character from the room and region he is in:

```
void Character::Add() {
    region reg( m_region );
    reg.AddCharacter( m_id );
    room r( m_room );
    r.AddCharacter( m_id );
}

void Character::Remove() {
    if( m_region != 0 && m_room != 0 )        {
        region reg( m_region );
        reg.DelCharacter( m_id );
        room r( m_room );
        r.DelCharacter( m_id );
    }
}
```

The code uses *accessor classes* to perform database lookups, a concept I've discussed before. Later on in this chapter, I'll show you the actual room and region classes used to do this.

The Remove function removes a character from a room and region if its room and region are valid.

The next section explains the reason for these functions.

Loading and Saving

Every entity in the game has the ability to load and save itself to disk. Furthermore, the Load function can *reload* an entity from a stream, overwriting whatever data already exists in the character with new data. Let me show you the loading function first:

```
void Character::Load( std::istream& p_stream ) {
    if( !IsPlayer() || IsLoggedIn() )
        Remove();
```

At this point, the code has checked to see if the character is a player and if he is logged in. If either of those conditions is not true, then the Remove function is called, essentially removing the character from his room and region in the game.

Imagine this scenario; you have a character in room 5, and you reload him from a stream. The only problem is that the stream moves him to room 6. If you haven't removed the character from room 5 yet, the character thinks he's in room 6, but room 5 still thinks the character is there! D'oh! So you need to remove the character before any data is loaded. Now you can load the hard-coded attributes:

```
std::string temp;
p_stream >> temp >> std::ws; std::getline( p_stream, m_name );
p_stream >> temp >> std::ws; std::getline( p_stream, m_description );
p_stream >> temp >> m_room;
p_stream >> temp >> m_region;
p_stream >> temp >> m_templateid;
p_stream >> temp >> m_account;
p_stream >> temp >> m_quiet;
p_stream >> temp >> m_verbose;
m_attributes.Load( p_stream );
```

And load the commands:

```
p_stream >> temp;        // chew up the "[COMMANDS]" tag
while( BasicLib::extract( p_stream, temp ) != "[/COMMANDS]" ) {
    if( AddCommand( temp ) ) {
        // command was added successfully, continue loading data
        commands::reverse_iterator itr = m_commands.rbegin();
        (*itr)->Load( p_stream );
    }
    else {
        throw Exception( "Cannot load command: " + temp );
    }
}
```

The function will first chew up a [COMMANDS] tag, which represents the start of a block of commands. Then it tries loading command names until it finds [/COMMANDS]. You'll see exactly how this works a bit later when I show you a sample of a character in text form. If a command fails to load, an exception is thrown, and the loading of the character is abandoned. It's up to whomever calls this code to safely reinsert the character into the realm.

When the new command has been loaded, the code obtains a *reverse iterator* that basically points to the end of the command list, which is the command that was just added; I then tell the new command to load itself from the stream.

Next, the logic module is loaded:

```
m_logic.Load( p_stream, m_id );
```

Character files hold more than just characters; they also hold a listing of all the items the character is currently holding. So the function starts a loop to do this:

```
    p_stream >> temp;            // chew up "[ITEMS]
    while( BasicLib::extract( p_stream, temp ) != "[/ITEMS]" ) {
        ItemDB.LoadEntity( p_stream );
        p_stream >> temp;        // chew up each "[/ITEM]" tag
    }
```

Any list of items in a character is surrounded by "[ITEMS]" and "[/ITEMS]" tags, and every item entry in the character is surrounded by "[ITEM]" and "[/ITEM]" tags. To actually load an item, the ItemDB, which is a global instance of the ItemDatabase class, is called and told to load an entity instance from the stream.

Here's the final act:

```
    if( !IsPlayer() || IsLoggedIn() )
        Add();
}
```

This code adds the character back into the game, but only if he's neither a player, nor is logged in. This stipulation exists because players who aren't logged in aren't actually in the game; they're off in some strange imaginary ether-world, and the game just ignores them when they're logged off, so you don't want to add logged-off players to rooms.

Here's a sample character file:

```
[ID]                    1
[NAME]                  Mithrandir
[DESCRIPTION]           You are a plain old boring human. Deal with it.
[ROOM]                  1
[REGION]                1
[TEMPLATEID]            1
[ACCOUNT]               1
[QUIETMODE]             0
[VERBOSEMODE]           1
[DATABANK]
strength                20
health                  30
[/DATABANK]

[COMMANDS]
get
[DATA]
[/DATA]
give
[DATA]
[/DATA]
drop
[DATA]
[/DATA]
```

> **NOTE**
>
> You can see from the listing that logic modules and command modules each have [DATA] and [/DATA] tags after the name of the module. This means that script modules, such as commands and logics, actually store data of their own. A command could keep track of the last time it was executed to ensure it is only executed once a day; or a logic module for a monster could track if it is hunting down a player or trying to get revenge for committing Goblin Genocide. The format is flexible enough for whatever you need to store.

```
[/COMMANDS]

[LOGICS]
humanlogic
[DATA]
[/DATA]
[/LOGICS]

[ITEMS]
[ITEM]
[ID]                2
[NAME]              Pie
[DESCRIPTION]       A BIG CUSTARD PIE
[ROOM]              1
[REGION]            0
[ISQUANTITY]        0
[QUANTITY]          1
[TEMPLATEID]        2
[DATABANK]
[/DATABANK]
[LOGICS]
[/LOGICS]
[/ITEM]
[/ITEMS]
```

NOTE

As you can see from the file listing, the data format for this game has become quite complex. The format I have will do for now, but maybe in the future, you could look into something designed to be even more flexible, like **XML**. The greatest thing about **XML** is that there are **XML** file editors out there that can edit the data for you, no matter what it stores.

As you can see, it's a pretty complicated data format. Character files can become pretty large if they contain many items, commands, and logic modules. Of course, the benefit of having so much data available is that this becomes a flexible format for storing characters.

Saving players to a stream is a similar process, so I'm not going to bother with the code here.

Loading Templates

Loading a character from a character template is a fairly easy process. For the most part, you just need to copy the data over. You also need to generate new commands and logic modules:

```
void Character::LoadTemplate( const CharacterTemplate& p_template ) {
    m_templateid = p_template.ID();
    m_name = p_template.Name();
    m_description = p_template.Description();
    m_attributes = p_template.m_attributes;
```

The previous chunk of code copies over the template ID (the normal ID of the current character should have already been set by the database when it was first created), the name, and the description. The last line copies over m_attributes, the databank. This is a really cool part of the databank class: You can copy it automatically (almost like magic!) into any other databank, because all the STL containers support copying. The downside is that any existing members of the databank are overwritten, but that's not such a big deal, since we're supposed to be loading the character template into a brand new character anyway.

The code continues, loading all the commands and logic modules:

```
CharacterTemplate::names::const_iterator itr =
    p_template.m_commands.begin();
while( itr != p_template.m_commands.end() ) {
    AddCommand( *itr );
    ++itr;
}

itr = p_template.m_logics.begin();
while( itr != p_template.m_logics.end() ) {
    AddLogic( *itr );
    ++itr;
}
}
```

These two loops circle through the m_commands and m_logics lists inside the template, extracting each name, and adding the command or logic module to the character, using the AddCommand or AddLogic helpers. AddLogic was inherited automatically from the LogicEntity class from the previous chapter.

> **NOTE**
>
> The implication of loading a logic module based only on name alone from a template means that you can't give that module any default data. Giving the module default data would be useful when you want to use a certain logic module that contains different data in many places, but honestly, that situation hasn't come up much for me. Still, if it bothers you, you might want to find a way to eventually make script objects clonable (right now they aren't), so that when you create a new character from a template, you can clone the template's scripts, rather than get names and generate new scripts.

Command Functions

The last major grouping of functions in the character entity class deals with the commands. There are six of these functions: two to retrieve iterators into the command list; one to search for a given command name; and functions to add, remove, and check the existence of commands in a character.

`CommandsEnd` and `CommandsBegin` are simply wrappers around `m_commands.end()` and `m_commands.begin()`, so I won't bother posting them here.

The function to find a command (`FindCommand`) is somewhat complicated, however. Whenever you're playing a text-based game, the ability to condense and shorten commands is a very common feature, because typing `attack goblin` every time you see a goblin is going to become frustrating.

Instead, you'd like the players to be able to type `att go` or maybe even `a g`. Sure, you could hard-code some shortcuts, just as in the SimpleMUD (`a` or `attack`, `n` or `north`, and so on), but that quickly begins to limit your engine.

Instead of providing shortcuts in the BetterMUD, I've decided to use a dual-linear search through the commands, trying to find complete and then partial command matches. For example, let's assume a character is given these commands:

```
go
attack
look
north
south
east
west
say
```

When a user wants to find a command named g, he first loops through all those commands finding one matching the complete name g. Obviously there's no command g, so the game then starts the second iteration, looking for a partial match. This time, go matches partially, so the game thinks the user wants to go somewhere.

This is the same process you've seen used before in the SimpleMUD, when matching item and monster names.

Here's the command matching function, which returns an iterator pointing to the matching function (or the end iterator if none was found):

```
iterator FindCommand( const std::string& p_name ) {
    stringmatchfull matchfull( p_name );    // match full
    commands::iterator itr = m_commands.begin();
    while( itr != m_commands.end() ) {
        if( matchfull( (*itr)->Name() ) )   // check match
            return itr;
        ++itr;
    }

    stringmatchpart matchpart( p_name );    // match part
    itr = m_commands.begin();
    while( itr != m_commands.end() ) {
        if( matchpart( (*itr)->Name() ) )    // check match
            return itr;
        ++itr;
    }

    return itr;
}
```

> **NOTE**
>
> Incidentally, this is the same reason why I don't use an std::map for the commands, but use an std::list instead. When you insert things into a map using strings as the key, the items are sorted by alphabetical order, since maps compare keys using the operator< of the key, and operator< on strings returns true when the items are in alphabetical order (apple < orange). For this reason, if you used maps, say would always come before south, so whenever the user types s, meaning to go south, the game will think he's trying to say something instead. This can become particularly annoying, so using a list is a better idea, because you can rearrange the order in which commands are inserted, and put the most frequently used commands first.

I couldn't use the `BetterMUD::match` function, since that only works on containers full of `entityids`, so I had to hack up my own dual-loop here, but it's not such a big deal.

The other three functions add, delete, or check the existence of command objects. These functions usually involve invoking the scripts in some way. For example, adding a command initializes a script that checks the existence of a command, and deleting a command retrieves its name. Executing scripts is prone to failure. You'll see this theme repeated throughout the last part of this book—scripts can fail at any time. These functions are *exception-safe*. They catch everything and return a Boolean based on success or failure:

```
bool Character::HasCommand( const std::string& p_command ) {
    commands::iterator itr = m_commands.begin();
    while( itr != m_commands.end() ) {
        try {
            if( (*itr)->Name() == p_command )  // compare name
                return true;
        }
        catch( ... ) {}      // just catch script errors
        ++itr;
    }
    return false;
}


bool Character::AddCommand( const std::string& p_command ) {
    if( HasCommand( p_command ) )        // can't add if it already has
        return false;
    try {
        m_commands.push_back( CommandDB.generate( p_command, m_id ) );
        return true;                     // command added successfully
    }
    catch( ... ) {}      // just catch errors
    return false;
}


bool Character::DelCommand( const std::string& p_command ) {
    try {
        commands::iterator itr = m_commands.begin();
        while( itr != m_commands.end() ) {        // find command
            if( (*itr)->Name() == p_command ) {
                delete (*itr);                     // delete command object
                m_commands.erase( itr );           // erase from list
                return true;                       // success!
            }
            ++itr;
        }
    }
```

```
    catch( ... ) {}      // just catch errors
    return false;
}
```

Since all the commands are stored as pointers within the list, you need to dereference them to get a pointer by calling (*itr), and then use the operator-> to access members of the actual command classes. You can see from the AddCommand function that it tells something called the CommandDatabase to generate a new command (the line is in bold). I will cover this database in Chapter 14. Essentially the database creates a brand new Command object when you give it a name, returns the Command object, and assumes that your character will manage that command from now on. When your character is destroyed, he must delete the command objects, or you will get a memory leak.

Items

Items are the other volatile entity in the game, but they're somewhat simpler than characters. Since items *are* volatile entities, they're stored within template/instance databases, and thus need template and instance classes. In the naming conventions for characters, items are named ItemTemplate, and Item.

It's good to be consistent, so the classes dealing with items resemble the character classes, and thus I won't need to show you too much about them.

Item Templates

The item template class inherits from the base mixin classes you saw from the previous chapter. Noticing a trend here? The mixin classes are quite helpful since they are used so often:

```
class ItemTemplate :
    public Entity,
    public DataEntity {
friend class Item;
public:
    typedef std::list< std::string > names;
    void Load( std::istream& p_stream );
protected:
    bool m_isquantity;        // is this a quantity object?
    int m_quantity;           // if so, what is the quantity?
    names m_logics;
};
```

In addition to variables inherited from the mixins, items come with only two hard-coded variables, Boolean and a quantity, which represent whether or not the item represents a *quantity item*. As I told you in Chapter 11, a quantity item is an item that represents a simple item type that can be grouped together, like coins and jewels.

Items have a databank and a collection of logic modules. Like character templates, the item templates store these logic modules as simple names, and load the actual scripts when the items are instantiated.

Here's a sample item template that can be loaded from a stream:

```
[ID]                    1
[NAME]                  Fountain
[DESCRIPTION]           This is a large granite fountain.
[ISQUANTITY]            0
[QUANTITY]              1
[DATABANK]
[/DATABANK]
[LOGICS]
cantget
[/LOGICS]
```

This is a simple item template; it doesn't have any data, and it holds one logic module, cantget. You'll see this module in Chapter 18. It prevents any character from picking it up.

That's really all there is to know about item templates.

Items

The actual Item class is somewhat simple too, as you can see from its definition:

```
class Item :
    public LogicEntity,
    public DataEntity,
    public HasRoom,
    public HasRegion,
    public HasTemplateID {
public:
    void Add();
    void Remove();
    void LoadTemplate( const ItemTemplate& p_template );
    void Load( std::istream& p_stream );
    void Save( std::ostream& p_stream );

    Item();
    std::string Name();
    bool IsQuantity()
    int GetQuantity()
    void SetQuantity( int p_quantity )
protected:
    bool m_isquantity;          // is this a quantity object?
    int m_quantity;             // if so, what is the quantity?
};  // end class Item
```

Items inherit logic collections, databanks, a room, a region, and a template ID. In addition items have the same Add and Remove functions as in the SimpleMUD so that they can be added and removed from a location (items are a bit more complex than characters, though, since they can either be in a room or on a character, whereas characters can only be in a room). Items also have a LoadTemplate function, which loads item template data from an ItemTemplate, and the standard Load and Save functions, which stream an item to and from iostreams.

One function in the Item class is of particular interest—the Name function. You should have noticed that this function has already been inherited from the Entity class, so why in the world would I redefine it in the Item class? The answer involves the fact that items can be quantities. What happens if a player sees an item lying on the ground that represents 27 gold coins? Should it say, "Pile of Coins?" Or how about, "27 Gold Coins?" Or maybe, "Pile of 27 Coins?" There are so many possibilities that you should avoid hard-coding such a thing. Instead, I've opted for a flexible method. Items that are quantities have names such as "Pile of <#> Coins" or "<#> Gold Doubloons". This special Name function finds any instances of "<#>" in the string and replaces it with the quantity of items. So "Pile of <#> Coins" turns into "Pile of 27 Coins". The code to do this is really simple:

```
std::string Item::Name() {
    using BasicLib::SearchAndReplace;
    using BasicLib::tostring;
    if( m_isquantity )
        return SearchAndReplace( m_name, "<#>", tostring( m_quantity ) );
    else
        return m_name;
}
```

This code uses my custom SearchAndReplace function from the BasicLib to search for and replace all instances of <#> with the string representation of the quantity.

The streaming functions and the template loading function are similar to the streaming and template loading functions from characters, so I don't think you'll be interested in seeing all that code.

Here's a sample listing of an item object instance:

```
[ID]                 11
[NAME]               Fountain
[DESCRIPTION]        This is a large granite fountain.
[ROOM]               1
[REGION]             1
[ISQUANTITY]         0
[QUANTITY]           1
[TEMPLATEID]         1
[DATABANK]
[/DATABANK]
[LOGICS]
cantget
```

```
[DATA]
[/DATA]
[/LOGICS]
```

As you can see, the layout is similar to that of a template item, with the addition of the room and region, as well as the existence of the data fields for logic modules. The `cantget` module doesn't need data; therefore, there's nothing within its `[DATA]` and `[/DATA]` tags.

Ownership of Items

I've mentioned before that items can be owned by two different kinds of entities—rooms and characters. I use a really simple method for defining how an item knows where it is. When an item exists within a room, its `m_room` variable represents the ID of that room, and `m_region` represents the region.

If the item is on a character, however, `m_room` is the ID of the character that the item belongs to, and `m_region` is 0.

Rooms

Rooms are a very simple entity types as well, and they don't add any extra data above and beyond the mixins they inherit:

```cpp
class Room :
    public LogicEntity,
    public DataEntity,
    public HasRegion,
    public HasCharacters,
    public HasItems,
    public HasPortals {
public:
    void Save( std::ostream& p_stream );
    void Load( std::istream& p_stream );
    void Add();
    void Remove();
}; // end class Room
```

Rooms have a listing of all characters, items, and portals that are within that room, and they know what region they exist within.

This section is the shortest in the chapter, since there isn't anything remarkable about rooms at all. The real power comes from the logic modules of the rooms, which allow them to react to any event that may occur inside of a room. You'll see this in much more detail in Chapter 15.

Regions

Regions are almost as simple as rooms. In fact regions within BetterMUD exist only for a few reasons. First, regions help with the organization of the datafiles. It is incredibly difficult to manage a huge realm in the SimpleMUD, because the map data is all stashed in one file, and that can get unbelievably unmanageable after a while.

The second reason is behavior; sometimes you want a specific event to occur in *every* room within a region, and it really doesn't make much sense to use 80 copies of a single logic module within 80 rooms, when all the rooms in a region should have it.

The final reason is efficiency; the game is going to save single regions to disk at different intervals throughout the game, so that you don't end up dumping the entire database to disk at once, and lag up the game. Without regions, you're bound to dump everything at once when your game becomes large.

Almost all the discussion about regions deals with loading and saving them to disk, which is done in the `RegionDatabase` class, later on in this chapter.

Here's the class listing:

```
class Region :
    public LogicEntity,
    public DataEntity,
    public HasCharacters,
    public HasItems,
    public HasRooms,
    public HasPortals {
public:
    void Save( std::ostream& p_stream );
    void Load( std::istream& p_stream );
    std::string& Diskname() { return m_diskname; }
    void SetDiskname( const std::string& p_name )  { m_diskname = p_name; }
protected:
    std::string m_diskname;
}; // end class Region
```

One variable has been added to the regions you were familiar with in the SimpleMUD, and that variable is their `diskname`. You'll see later on that regions frequently have names such as "The Elven Forest", or "The Dwarven Mines". There's nothing remarkable about that, except that those names have spaces in them, and on some operating systems, spaces in a file name are a huge no-no.

As you'll see later, I store regions inside their own directories, so "The Elven Forest" would ideally be located inside /data/regions/The Elven Forest/. That's also an illegal directory name on some operating systems, so most of the time you'll be making it look like this instead: data/regions/TheElvenForest/. Of course, it would look stupid in the game if a player saw: `Mithrandir enters TheElvenForest`. Instead of messing with that, I've added a new string that represents the name of the directory the entity is supposed to be located in. So a region with the name `The Elven Forest` would have a disk name of `TheElvenForest`.

Here's a sample of a region entity on disk:

```
[ID]                    1
[NAME]                  Betterton
[DESCRIPTION]           Betterton is a run down town.
[DATABANK]
[/DATABANK]
[LOGICS]
[/LOGICS]
```

This region entity has no data or logic yet.

Portals

Portals are a part of the physical world in BetterMUD that differ most from the physical structure of the SimpleMUD.

In the SimpleMUD, the rooms knew how players could exit from them and move into different rooms, but the BetterMUD doesn't use this concept. Instead, it has portals, which define how players move from one place to the next, by defining a starting and an ending point.

A large part of building any world-type game is the ability to deny a player's access to an area and force him to perform tasks to gain access. For example, there's the classic "find the key to this door" quest, which you can probably find in every MUD out there.

The SimpleMUD has no way of denying access to a room; anyone can go anywhere. That makes the game simple, but that was the point in the first place.

In the BetterMUD, on the other hand, such a solution is unacceptable. You could easily hard-code the requirement for rooms to have "key-locks" on the doors, but hard coding such a thing into the physical world is unnecessary and limiting. One day, you might want to come up with a special "double-locked" door (the kind you see in all those military movies) for which you need two keys turned at the same time to access the nuclear command system behind the door. Or maybe a magic door that denies entrance to people of a specified level of "evilness", or whatever else you may think of. Heck, you may even want portals that have traps that switch on when a player enters the door (watch out for those saw blades! Ouch!), or doors that magically bless a player who walks through. Anyway, I'm sure you can think of hundreds of ideas, which is why hard-coding *anything* into a portal is a bad idea.

The basic design of the portals is that they have innumerable "paths," and each is a one-way path starting at one room and ending at another.

Let's say you have a portal with one pathway, which leads from room 1 to room 2. When a player is in room 1 and tries entering that portal, the game asks the portal if he can enter that portal, and if he can, the game tells the portal that the player has entered it, and then moves him to room 2.

Of course, if the portal doesn't have a path from room 2 back to room 1, the player can't get back (unless of course, there's a different portal object somewhere with that pathway in it).

Figure 13.1 shows a sample of some of the many possible ways to use portals.

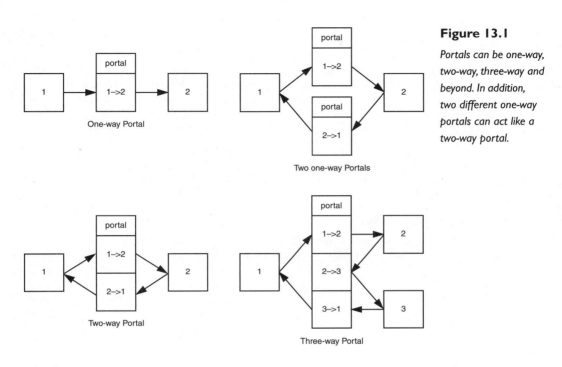

Figure 13.1

Portals can be one-way, two-way, three-way and beyond. In addition, two different one-way portals can act like a two-way portal.

Basically, portals are objects that connect rooms and allow characters to move throughout the game.

Portal Entries

When designing portals, you could take any route you want. You could easily make portals just one-way objects, but then you'll have problems linking together two portals that should share a single module of logic (a door closed on one side should be closed on the other side).

You could make portals two-way, but that's not really flexible. If you assume every portal has two ways, you couldn't easily make one-way paths, or other tricky maneuvers.

So, the best idea I could come up with was using an *n-way* portal, which can contain any number of paths. These paths are defined by a simple portalentry structure:

```
struct portalentry {
    entityid startroom;            // starting room
    std::string directionname;     // name of the direction
    entityid destinationroom;      // ending room

    void Load( std::istream& p_stream );
    void Save( std::ostream& p_stream );
};
```

An entry consists of three pieces of data: a starting room, a destination room, and the name of the exit that the path represents.

The SimpleMUD supported four directions in the game: north, east, south, and west. The BetterMUD doesn't support any directions; it only supports exits based on portal names. Any room can have an infinite number of exits from it, as long as each exit has a unique name. For example, if you want a portal to connect rooms 1 and 2, and going from 1 to 2 is considered "going north," the direction name of that exit should be north. You'll see how this works a little later on.

Entries know how to load and save themselves to disk too, which makes loading and saving portals easier. You'll also see this later.

Portal Entity Class

The actual portal entity class is pretty simple. The only thing it adds on top of the various mixins it inherits is a list of portal entries, representing all the paths in a portal:

```
class Portal :
    public LogicEntity,
    public DataEntity,
    public HasRegion {
public:
    typedef std::list<portalentry> portals;
    portals::iterator PortalsBegin()              { return m_portals.begin(); }
    portals::iterator PortalsEnd()                { return m_portals.end(); }

    void Load( std::istream& p_stream );
    void Save( std::ostream& p_stream );
    void Remove();
    void Add();
protected:
    portals m_portals;           // list of entries
};  // end class Portal
```

Very simply, every portal has a list of entries and functions to iterate through it. Also present should be the familiar Add and Remove commands (customized for portals, of course), as well as the Load and Save commands. These have, of course, been customized for the portal's needs, but they are very similar to the same functions found in other entities, so I won't show them to you here.

Here is a sample listing of a portal that can be loaded from disk:

```
[ID]                 1
[REGION]             1
[NAME]               Garden Path
[DESCRIPTION]        This is a plain garden pathway.
[ENTRY]
```

```
        [STARTROOM]             1
        [DIRECTION]             North
        [DESTROOM]              2
[/ENTRY]
[ENTRY]
        [STARTROOM]             2
        [DIRECTION]             South
        [DESTROOM]              1
[/ENTRY]
[/ENTRIES]
[DATABANK]
[/DATABANK]
[LOGICS]
[/LOGICS]
```

Note the entries. This particular portal contains two entries: one leading from room 1 to room 2, and the other going back the other way. The name of the first path is simply North, meaning that's the direction a player needs to type to enter it (that is, go north). You can change the name to whatever you want (flazzleblap?), as long as it makes sense for the room. You can use this feature to give your game a more "realistic" touch, since your rooms are not limited to 4 or 8 "specific" exits.

Adding and Removing Portals

The Add and Remove functions for portals are a bit more sophisticated than those for the other entity types. This is mostly because a single portal can exist within any number of rooms. So how does one determine if a portal exists within a room? If a portal has a one-way path from room 1 to room 2, should it exist in both rooms? What if it doesn't have a path back?

The best way to manage this is to insert portals only into rooms that are starting points. If you have a portal that goes from 1 to 2 and 2 to 3, it should only exist within rooms 1 and 2, but not 3, since there's no starting point in room 3.

Databases

In the last chapter, I went over the various database base classes: Database, VectorDatabase, MapDatabase, and TemplateInstanceDatabase. None of these databases actually stored any entities, however; they just provided the framework for the actual entity databases within the BetterMUD: CharacterDatabase, ItemDatabase, RoomDatabase, PortalDatabase, RegionDatabase, and AccountDatabase.

The beautiful part about all these classes is that they are simple. Heck, the RoomDatabase is so insanely simple that it doesn't add a single member variable or function to the VectorDatabase that it inherits from!

The two databases that hold volatile entities (characters and items) inherit from the `TemplateInstanceDatabase` class, which means that they have a vector of templates and a map of instances.

Accounts are stored in a map database; portals, rooms, and regions are all stored in vector databases.

This means that looking up item and character templates, portals, rooms, and regions is fast. It's a little bit slower to look up item and character instances and accounts, but it's not *that* slow. If you think about it, even with a completely full map database of 4-billion entities, it takes around 32 comparisons to find any item in the database.

I don't want to spend much more time going over the databases, simply because the database system for the BetterMUD is quick and dirty.

In reality, you can swap out all these classes with more professional versions, if the need ever arises. The problem with these "databases" is that they keep everything in memory, which means that your game is ultimately limited by how much memory you have on the system at any given time. While that's not such a big deal when you start out, multiple hundreds of megabytes eventually seems limiting, if your MUD gets large enough. That's when you should start considering adding in a real database.

Account Database

The database that stores accounts is mildly complex. The main purpose of this database is to manage accounts, and that's precisely what it does. Here's the class skeleton:

```
class AccountDatabase : public MapDatabase<Account> {
public:
    entityid Create( const string& p_name, const string& p_pass );
    bool AcceptibleName( const string& p_name );
    void Load();
    void Save();
};


extern AccountDatabase AccountDB;
```

You should also note that I've created a global instance of the database named `AccountDB`. Remember that the databases from the SimpleMUD were all static classes, but they're globals in the BetterMUD. It's really just semantics; after working with the SimpleMUD for a while, I found that I was constantly annoyed by typing `MonsterDatabase::blah()`. In the BetterMUD, you access the databases by calling the global instance instead, such as `AccountDB.Save()`.

The account database can do three things above and beyond what a `MapDatabase` provides: create new accounts, test if various names are acceptable names for an account, and provide operations for loading and saving all accounts from and to disk.

Creating New Accounts

The account creation function is simple:

```
entityid AccountDatabase::Create( const string& p_name,
    const string& p_pass ) {

    entityid id = FindOpenID();
    Account& a = m_container[id];
    a.SetID( id );
    a.SetName( p_name );
    a.SetPass( p_pass );
    a.SetLoginTime( g_game.GetTime() );
    return id;
}
```

This code gets an open ID from the map, creates the new account by retrieving it using the [] operator, and then sets all the information for it. Finally, the ID is returned.

Checking Name Validity

The account database's AcceptibleName function is the same as those of the SimpleChat and SimpleMUD, so I'm not going to bother showing the function here. The gist is that this function can't accept names with the following characteristics: weird characters such as " \"'~!@#$%^&*+/\\[]{}<>()=.,?;:"; fewer than 3 characters; longer than 16 characters, names that don't start with an alphabetic character; and names that are not equal to "new" (which screws up the login system).

Loading and Saving

Loading and saving the account database is a simple affair, especially loading:

```
void AccountDatabase::Load() {
    LoadDirectory( "data/accounts/" );
}
```

This code simply wraps around the Database::LoadDirectory function, which automatically loads up a manifest file in the directory, and proceeds to load as many entities as it can, automatically inserting them into the database as it goes.

Saving is a bit more complex, since there's no solid definition in the Database class that shows how datafiles are spread out:

```
void AccountDatabase::Save() {
    // load up the manifest file:
    static std::string dir = "data/accounts/";
    static std::string manifestname = dir + "manifest";
    std::ofstream manifest( manifestname.c_str(), std::ios::binary );
```

```
    container::iterator itr = m_container.begin();

    // loop while there are accounts, saving each one to its own file:
    while( itr != m_container.end() ) {
        std::string accountfilename = dir + itr->second.Name() + ".data";
        std::ofstream accountfile( accountfilename.c_str(),
                                   std::ios::binary );
        SaveEntity( accountfile, itr->second );

        // add an entry to the manifest:
        manifest << itr->second.Name() << "\n";
        ++itr;
    }
}
```

The function loads up the manifest (which clears its contents since you're overwriting the existing contents of the file). Then the function loops through all accounts and saves a file for each, and also adds the name of the account to the manifest file.

Character Database

The character database is a template/instance database that stores characters and character templates. Seems obvious in retrospect, doesn't it?

This database can be queried to find players (a special subset of characters, representing anyone who can log in and play the game), save players to disk, load individual players, load all templates, and load individual templates:

```
class CharacterDatabase :
    public TemplateInstanceDatabase<Character, CharacterTemplate> {
public:
    bool HasName();
    entityid FindPlayerFull( const std::string& p_name );
    entityid FindPlayerPart( const std::string& p_name );
    void SavePlayers();
    void LoadPlayers();
    void LoadTemplates();
    void LoadTemplates( const std::string& p_file );
    void LoadPlayer( const std::string& p_name );
};


extern CharacterDatabase CharacterDB;
```

Characters are a special type of entity in the BetterMUD; they can exist as computer-controlled objects, or they can exist as players, which are controlled by people who log into the MUD.

Because of this, it's often a good idea to store your players in a place separate from the rest of the characters in the game. I have opted to place them all in /data/players.

The database only allows you to save players, not every character. It's actually the region database, which you'll see later, that saves non-player characters to disk.

The SavePlayers and LoadPlayers functions are almost equivalent to the Save and Load functions from the account database; they just load character files instead of account files. Because of this, I'm not going to show you their code (how much stream code can a person take anyway?).

The other functions simply wrap around existing databases or functions, so I won't bother showing those to you either; you've seen similar code a hundred times already.

The two LoadTemplates functions are designed to load character templates from disk. The function that doesn't take any parameters loads up the manifest file found in /data/templates/characters, and loads character templates from every file located within the manifest.

The function that takes a string parameter loads a specific file; for example if you passed in playercharacters.data, the function would try to load all character templates from /data/templates/characters/playercharacters.data.

Item Database

The item database function is extremely simple as well:

```
class ItemDatabase : public TemplateInstanceDatabase<Item, ItemTemplate> {
public:
    void LoadTemplates();
    void LoadTemplates( const std::string& p_file );
};


extern ItemDatabase ItemDB;
```

Each of these functions simply wrap around the VectorDatabase functions, LoadDirectory and LoadFile functions, that are rerouted to load from the /data/templates/items directory. These two functions perform the same way as the LoadTemplates functions from the character database.

Room and Portal Databases

The room and portal databases are among the simplest database classes in the BetterMUD. Observe:

```
class RoomDatabase : public VectorDatabase<Room> {};
extern RoomDatabase RoomDB;
class PortalDatabase : public VectorDatabase<Portal> {};
extern PortalDatabase PortalDB;
```

They're empty classes! That's it! I don't need to add any extra functions at all. This is because all the work of loading and saving rooms and portals is done through the region database class.

Region Database

The region database is the most complex of all the databases in terms of what it adds to the base database classes. Here's the class skeleton:

```
class RegionDatabase : public VectorDatabase<Region> {
public:
    void LoadAll();
    void LoadRegion( const std::string& p_name );
    void SaveRegion( entityid p_region );
    void SaveAll();
};
extern RegionDatabase RegionDB;
```

Using this class, you can load every region in the game, load a specific region, save a specific region, or save every region in the game.

Every region in the game is stored within a directory of its own, and these directories contain five files: region.data, rooms.data, portals.data, characters.data, and items.data. As you might have guessed, these files store information about the region and all the rooms, portals, non-player characters, and items in the region.

Loading from a Manifest

In the game directory /data/regions, there is a manifest file, which should contain the names of every region in the game. For example, you might have a manifest file that looks like this:

```
Betterton
DwarvenMines
ElvenForest
```

With this manifest file, the game tries to load regions from the directories /data/regions/Betterton, /data/regions/DwarvenMines, and /data/regions/ElvenForest. This function loads each of those names from the manifest and loads each region independently:

```
void RegionDatabase::LoadAll() {
    static std::string dir = "data/regions/manifest";
    std::ifstream manifest( dir.c_str(), std::ios::binary );
    manifest >> std::ws;

    std::string regionname;
    while( manifest.good() ) {
        manifest >> regionname;
        LoadRegion( regionname );
    }
}
```

As you can see, the function simply invokes the LoadRegion helper function.

Loading a Specific Region

The database loads specific regions from disk using the LoadRegion function. You simply pass the name of the region you want to load, such as LoadRegion("Betterton"), and the function tries loading that region from /data/regions/Betterton.

Here's the code:

```
void RegionDatabase::LoadRegion( const std::string& p_name ) {
    std::string dir = "data/regions/" + p_name + "/";
    std::string regionfilename = dir + "region.data";
    std::ifstream regionfile( regionfilename.c_str(), std::ios::binary );
    Region &reg = LoadEntity( regionfile );     // load region from file
    reg.SetDiskname( p_name );                  // set its disk name

    // now load each individual component:
    RoomDB.LoadFile( dir + "rooms" );
    PortalDB.LoadFile( dir + "portals" );
    CharacterDB.LoadFile( dir + "characters" );
    ItemDB.LoadFile( dir + "items" );
}
```

The function first calculates the name of the directory you're loading, and then the name of the region's datafile. Once that is finished, the region is loaded using LoadEntity (inherited from the Database class—isn't that neat, and the disk name of the region is set, so that it knows how to save the region back to disk.

After that, the function manually invokes the LoadFile helper for the room, portal, character, and item databases for each file in the directory (for example rooms.data, portals.data). You don't need to add .data to the end of the filenames, because the Database::LoadFile function does that for you automatically.

That's all you need to load a region!

Saving a Specific Region

Saving a specific region to disk is slightly more complicated, mostly because the database classes don't have any kind of SaveFile function. Instead, you need to manually stream everything you need back to the files you need them in.

I'm going to split this function up to explain it better:

```
void RegionDatabase::SaveRegion( entityid p_region ) {
    Region& reg = get( p_region );
    std::string workingdir = "data/regions/" + reg.Diskname();
    std::string regionfilename = workingdir + "/region.data";
    std::ofstream regionfile( regionfilename.c_str(), std::ios::binary );
    SaveEntity( regionfile, reg );
```

The preceding code gets the region you want to save, and then constructs a working directory string, which is simply data/regions/ added to the disk name of a region.

Once the string is constructed, the function opens up the "region.data" file in that directory, and streams the region right into it, overwriting whatever was there.

The code continues and saves the rooms of a region to disk:

```cpp
std::string roomsfilename = workingdir + "/rooms.data";
std::ofstream roomsfile( roomsfilename.c_str(), std::ios::binary );
Region::rooms::iterator ritr = reg.RoomsBegin();
while( ritr != reg.RoomsEnd() ) {
    Room& r = RoomDB.get( *ritr );        // get room
    RoomDB.SaveEntity( roomsfile, r );    // save it
    roomsfile << "\n";                    // add newline
    ++ritr;                               // go to next
}
```

Saving the portals is a very similar process:

```cpp
std::string portalsfilename = workingdir + "/portals.data";
std::ofstream portalsfile( portalsfilename.c_str(), std::ios::binary );
Region::portals::iterator pitr = reg.PortalsBegin();
while( pitr != reg.PortalsEnd() ) {
    Portal& p = PortalDB.get( *pitr );
    PortalDB.SaveEntity( portalsfile, p );
    portalsfile << "\n";
    ++pitr;
}
```

However, saving characters is a little different. Remember that characters are saved to their own files inside of the /data/players directory, so this directory needs to store only non-player characters (NPCs), which requires an if-statement:

```cpp
std::string charactersfilename = workingdir + "/characters.data";
std::ofstream charactersfile( charactersfilename.c_str(),
                              std::ios::binary );
Region::characters::iterator citr = reg.CharactersBegin();
while( citr != reg.CharactersEnd() ) {
    Character& c = CharacterDB.get( *citr );
    if( !c.IsPlayer() ) {                 // only save non-players
        CharacterDB.SaveEntity( charactersfile, c );
        charactersfile << "\n";
    }
    ++citr;
}
```

And finally, items are saved by using a process similar to rooms and portals:

```cpp
std::string itemsfilename = workingdir + "/items.data";
std::ofstream itemsfile( itemsfilename.c_str(), std::ios::binary );
```

```
Region::items::iterator iitr = reg.ItemsBegin();
while( iitr != reg.ItemsEnd() )
{
    Item& i = ItemDB.get( *iitr );
    ItemDB.SaveEntity( itemsfile, i );
    itemsfile << "\n";
    ++iitr;
}
}
```

That's the function that takes up the most space.

> **NOTE**
>
> You can clearly see that the blocks to save entities are very similar, and this should be setting off a warning bell in your head. You may consider writing some sort of templated function to perform this kind of a task in the future, if you ever plan on expanding the game. I just want you to know that the whole database system is a quick and dirty system, and you should by no means spend all your time studying it. My main focus in the BetterMUD is the separation of logic and data. I may one day implement a *true* database engine in the BetterMUD, but this will have to do for now.

Saving the Whole Thing

The final function in the region database is saving all the databases to disk:

```
void RegionDatabase::SaveAll() {
    iterator itr = m_container.begin();
    while( itr != m_container.end() ) {
        if( itr->ID() != 0 ) {
            SaveRegion( itr->ID() );
            ++itr;
        }
    }
}
```

The function essentially loops through all the regions (checking to make sure none of them has an ID of 0), and calls the SaveRegion helper to save that region to disk.

Directory Structure

The directory structure for the data of the BetterMUD is hierarchical; I've put everything into directories that make sense. All the data for the game is stored within the directory /data, which has many subdirectories, as shown by Figure 13.2.

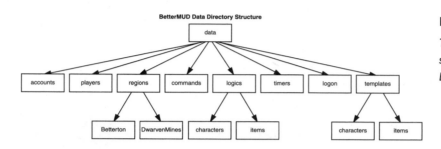

BetterMUD Data Directory Structure

Figure 13.2

The general directory structure of the BetterMUD.

Accounts and players are all stashed in the /data/accounts and /data/players directories. Regions, of course, are another level, in which each region has its own directory. The figure shows two regions, Betterton and the Dwarven Mines.

I haven't covered the /data/commands or /data/logics directories yet, but these two directories store scripts designed to be used within the game. Timers keep a listing of all timers in the game (see Chapter 15), logon keeps all the logon-related text files and scripts (see Chapter 16), and /data/templates stores all the item and character template files.

Accessors

The final topic I want to discuss in this chapter is the accessor classes. These classes are very similar to the database pointer classes of the SimpleMUD, except that they are a bit more abstracted; they don't actually allow direct access to the entities that they point to, but instead *wrap* around them. This is because the accessor classes are designed to be used as wrappers into the Python language, and also as lightweight pointer classes.

Accessors are simple; they all contain a pointer to the object they point to, and they all manage reference counts to the entities they point to. If you've got 10 accessors pointing to an object in the game, that object's reference count is also going to be 10; the game always knows when something is pointing to an entity.

Unfortunately, I ran into the same problem with accessors that I did with database pointers from the SimpleMUD: circular dependencies and templates *just don't mix*. It's an unfortunate side effect of the 1-pass nature of C++, but there's not much you can do to fix it.

Accessor Problems

Unfortunately, the problem with C++ circular dependencies and templates is much bigger for the BetterMUD, since accessors are wrapper (or *proxy*) classes. The accessor classes actually need to be given all the functions you want to use with them, and there are many. For example, an item accessor needs all the entity wrapper functions (accessors for ID, name, and description), the "has room" functions, "has templateid" functions, and so on. You could end up with an accessor looking like this (warning, do not attempt this at home!):

```
class item {
public:
    item( entityid p_id );
    item( const item& p_right );
    item& operator=( const item& p_right );
    ~item();
    entityid ID();
    std::string Name();
    std::string Description();
    void SetID( entityid p_id );
    void SetName( const std::string& p_name );
    void SetDescription( const std::string& p_desc );

... <SNIP> ...

protected:
    Item* m_item;
};
```

And then you could start on the `character` accessor class:

```
class character {
public:
    character ( entityid p_id );
    character ( const character& p_right );
    character& operator=( const character& p_right );
    ~character ();
    entityid ID();
    std::string Name();
    std::string Description();
    void SetID( entityid p_id );
    void SetName( const std::string& p_name );
    void SetDescription( const std::string& p_desc );

... <SNIP> ...

protected:
    Character* m_character;
};
```

Notice anything similar? Almost everything! Well, this is a predicament. It gets even worse when you implement the functions in the .cpp file; even *more* code duplication!

Solution

I solved this problem using macros. I know macro use is frowned upon by almost everyone, but sometimes you just have to choose the right tool for the job. Using macros in this case will save you hours and hours of trying to figure out how to implement accessors using templates instead (with circular dependencies, you can't), or wasting time copying the same code over and over.

In the /BetterMUD/accessors/AccessorMacros.h file, I've included a bunch of macros to be used in accessor classes. Here's a listing of the "header" macros—the macros that define the required function headers:

ENTITYHEADERS(AC)—constructor, destructor, copy constructor, ID, Name, Description accessors

ENTITYTEMPLATEHEADERS(AC)—accessors for template classes, like `ItemTemplate` and `CharacterTemplate`

HASREGIONHEADERS—region accessors

HASROOMHEADERS—room accessors

HASTEMPLATEIDHEADERS—template ID accessors

HASCHARACTERSHEADERS—character collection accessors

HASITEMSHEADERS—item collection accessors

HASROOMSHEADERS—room collection accessors

HASPORTALSHEADERS—portal collection accessors

HASDATABANKHEADERS—databank accessors

HASLOGICHEADERS—logic module accessors

HASCOMMANDSHEADERS—command accessors

I'll show you a listing of all the functions these macros define a little bit later on. All these macros have implementation equivalents, which contain implementation code. Instead of `HEADERS` at the end of the macro, you have `IMPLEMENTATIONS` instead.

Example

Let me show you how to use macros with a simple example. This is the `item` accessor class:

```
class item {
public:
    ENTITYHEADERS( item );
    HASROOMHEADERS;
    HASREGIONHEADERS;
    HASTEMPLATEIDHEADERS;
```

```
    HASDATABANKHEADERS;
    HASLOGICHEADERS;

    bool IsQuantity();
    int GetQuantity();
    void SetQuantity( int p_quantity );
protected:
    Item* m_item;
};  // end class item
```

The item accessor has entity headers, room headers, region headers, template ID headers, databank headers, and logic headers. I'll get to the parameters in a bit.

Once you have your accessor class defined, you can go ahead and shove the implementation macros into your .cpp files:

```
ENTITYIMPLEMENTATIONS( item, m_item, ItemDB );
HASROOMIMPLEMENTATIONS( item, m_item );
HASREGIONIMPLEMENTATIONS( item, m_item );
HASTEMPLATEIDIMPLEMENTATIONS( item, m_item );
HASLOGICIMPLEMENTATIONS( item, m_item );
HASDATABANKIMPLEMENTATIONS( item, m_item );
bool item::IsQuantity()                     { return m_item->IsQuantity(); }
int item::GetQuantity()                     { return m_item->GetQuantity(); }
void item::SetQuantity( int p_quantity ){ m_item->SetQuantity( p_quantity ); }
```

Note that the functions that are *unique* to items, such as the quantity functions, are actually defined and implemented normally; everything that's in a macro is repeatable, and used in other accessor classes.

A Macro

I bet you're a bit confused at the moment about the macros and their parameters, so to clear your head I'm going to show you two of the macros.

Here is the ENTITYHEADERS macro:

```
#define ENTITYHEADERS( AC )                                         \
    AC( entityid p_id );                                            \
    AC( const AC& p_right );                                        \
    AC& operator=( const AC& p_right );                             \
    ~AC();                                                          \
    entityid ID();                                                  \
    std::string Name();                                            \
    std::string Description();                                     \
    void SetID( entityid p_id );                                    \
    void SetName( const std::string& p_name );                     \
    void SetDescription( const std::string& p_desc );
```

This macro takes a single parameter, which is meant to be the name of the class. In the item class definition you can see that I passed in item. When expanding the macro, the compiler searches for any instances of AC, and replaces it with the parameter, which is item. So when processing this macro, the compiler actually sees this:

```
item( entityid p_id );
item( const item& p_right );
item& operator=( const item& p_right );
~item();
entityid ID();
std::string Name();
std::string Description();
void SetID( entityid p_id );
void SetName( const std::string& p_name );
void SetDescription( const std::string& p_desc );
```

Your item class automatically has all these functions declared.

Of course, function declarations aren't worth anything unless you define them, which is what the ENTITYIMPLEMENTATIONS macro does:

```
#define ENTITYIMPLEMENTATIONS( AC, PT, DB )                              \
AC::AC( entityid p_id )                                                  \
{                                                                        \
    PT = &(DB.get( p_id ) );                                            \
    PT->AddRef();                                                        \
}                                                                        \
AC::AC( const AC& p_right )                                              \
{                                                                        \
    PT->DelRef();                                                        \
    PT = p_right.PT;                                                     \
    PT->AddRef();                                                        \
}                                                                        \
AC& AC::operator=( const AC& p_right )                                   \
{                                                                        \
    PT = p_right.PT;                                                     \
    PT->AddRef();                                                        \
    return *this;                                                        \
}                                                                        \
AC::~AC()  { PT->DelRef(); }                                             \
entityid AC::ID()                      { return PT->ID(); }              \
std::string AC::Name()                 { return PT->Name(); }            \
std::string AC::Description()          { return PT->Description(); }     \
void AC::SetID( entityid p_id )        { PT->SetID( p_id ); }            \
void AC::SetName( const std::string& p_name )                           \
                                       { PT->SetName( p_name ); }        \
void AC::SetDescription( const std::string& p_desc )                    \
                                       { PT->SetDescription( p_desc ); }
```

For the implementation macro, you pass in three parameters: the name of the accessor class (item), the name of the pointer member variable that the class has (m_item), and the database used to look up entities (ItemDB). So for example, the constructor would turn from this:

```
AC::AC( entityid p_id )                                          \
{                                                                \
    PT = &(DB.get( p_id ) );                                     \
    PT->AddRef();                                                \
}                                                                \
```

into this:

```
item::item( entityid p_id )
{
    m_item = &(ItemDB.get( p_id ) );
    m_item->AddRef();
}
```

Isn't that cool? You can do this for all the entity types, and keep code duplication at a minimum.

Iterators

I have mentioned this before, but not really in depth. Accessors act like iterators to collections that they point to. For example, if you have a character accessor, you can use that accessor object as an iterator over the items the character has in his inventory.

While I haven't shown you the functions available to the accessors yet, I'm sure you'll have no problem picking up this example of a character accessor iterating over his items:

```
character c( 10 );
c.BeginItem();                       // reset to first item
while( c.IsValidItem() ) {           // loop while item is valid
    process( c.CurrentItem );        // some imaginary process function
    c.NextItem();                    // go to next item
}
```

Most of the accessors have *iterator seek* functions, which will seek the iterator to a specific position, like this:

```
c.SeekItem( "sword" );
```

If the character has a sword, c.CurrentItem returns the ID of it, or c.IsValidItem will be false.

Members of the Accessors and Macros

In this section, I'm giving you listings of the functions available in each of the accessor macros and accessor types, for easy reference.

Entity Functions

```
accessor( entityid p_id );
accessor( const accessor& p_right );
accessor& operator=( const accessor& p_right );
~accessor();
entityid ID();
std::string Name();
std::string Description();
void SetID( entityid p_id );
void SetName( const std::string& p_name );
void SetDescription( const std::string& p_desc );
```

For the previous listing, I've replaced the name of the actual accessor class with the string accessor.

Region Functions

```
entityid Region();
void SetRegion( entityid p_region );
```

Room Functions

```
entityid Room();
void SetRoom( entityid p_room );
```

TemplateID Functions

```
entityid TemplateID();
void SetTemplateID( entityid p_templateid );
```

Character Container Functions

```
void AddCharacter( entityid p_id );
void DelCharacter( entityid p_id );
size_t Characters();
void BeginCharacter();
entityid CurrentCharacter();
void NextCharacter();
bool IsValidCharacter();
void SeekCharacter( const std::string& p_name );
```

Item Container Functions

```
void AddItem( entityid p_id );
void DelItem( entityid p_id );
```

```
size_t Items();
void BeginItem();
entityid CurrentItem();
void NextItem();
bool IsValidItem();
void SeekItem( const std::string& p_name );
```

Room Container Functions

```
void AddRoom( entityid p_id );
void DelRoom( entityid p_id );
size_t Rooms();
void BeginRoom();
entityid CurrentRoom();
void NextRoom();
bool IsValidRoom();
void SeekRoom( const std::string& p_name );
```

Portal Container Functions

```
void AddPortal( entityid p_id );
void DelPortal( entityid p_id );
size_t Portals();
void BeginPortal();
entityid CurrentPortal();
void NextPortal();
bool IsValidPortal();
void SeekPortal( const std::string& p_name );
```

Databank Functions

```
int GetAttribute( const std::string& p_name );
void SetAttribute( const std::string& p_name, int p_val );
bool HasAttribute( const std::string& p_name );
void AddAttribute( const std::string& p_name, int p_initialval );
void DelAttribute( const std::string& p_name );
```

Logic Module Functions

```
bool AddLogic( const std::string& p_logic );
bool AddExistingLogic( Logic* p_logic );
bool DelLogic( const std::string& p_logic );
Logic* GetLogic( const std::string& p_logic );
bool HasLogic( const std::string& p_logic );
int DoAction( const Action& p_action );
```

```
int DoAction( const std::string& p_act,
              entityid p_data1 = 0,
              entityid p_data2 = 0,
              entityid p_data3 = 0,
              entityid p_data4 = 0,
              const std::string& p_data = "" );
int GetLogicAttribute( const std::string& p_logic,
                       const std::string& p_attr );
void AddHook( TimedAction* p_hook );
void DelHook( TimedAction* p_hook );
size_t Hooks();
void ClearHooks();
void ClearLogicHooks( const std::string& p_logic );
```

I get to logic modules in Chapters 14 and 15, so don't worry if you don't yet know what the previous listed functions do. The same goes for the command functions.

Command Functions

```
bool HasCommand( const std::string& p_command );
bool AddCommand( const std::string& p_command );
bool DelCommand( const std::string& p_command );
void BeginCommands();
std::string CurrentCommand();
std::string CurrentCommandUsage();
std::string CurrentCommandDescription();
void NextCommand();
bool IsValidCommand();
void SeekCommand( const std::string& p_name );
```

Those are all the functions defined by the macros; everything else that the accessors have is defined normally in the accessor classes.

Accessor Dependencies

Table 13.1 shows the accessor class used by each accessor macro.

Account Accessor Functions

Account accessors have these functions in addition to their macros (as listed in Table 13.1):

```
std::string Password();
BasicLib::sint64 LoginTime();
int AccessLevel();
bool Banned();
int AllowedCharacters();
```

```
void SetPass( const std::string& p_pass );
void SetLoginTime( BasicLib::sint64 p_time );
void SetAccessLevel( int p_level );
void SetBanned( bool p_banned );
void SetAllowedCharacters( int p_num );
```

Character Accessor Functions

Characters have these extra accessor functions:

```
bool Quiet();
bool IsPlayer();
bool Verbose();
void SetQuiet( bool p_quiet );
void SetAccount( entityid p_account );
bool IsLoggedIn();
void SetLoggedIn( bool p_loggedin );
std::string LastCommand();
```

Table 13.1   Accessor Classes and the Macros They Need

Macro	Account	Character	Item	Room	Region	Portal
Entity	yes	yes	yes	yes	yes	yes
Region	no	yes	yes	yes	no	yes
Room	no	yes	yes	no	no	no
TemplateID	no	yes	yes	no	no	no
Characters	yes	no	no	yes	yes	no
Items	no	yes	no	yes	yes	no
Rooms	no	no	no	no	yes	no
Portals	no	no	no	yes	yes	no
Databank	no	yes	yes	yes	yes	yes
Logic	no	yes	yes	yes	yes	yes
Commands	no	yes	no	no	no	no

Item Accessor Functions

Items have these extra accessor functions:

```
bool IsQuantity();
int GetQuantity();
void SetQuantity( int p_quantity );
```

Portal Accessor Functions

Portals add a bunch of iterator functions that iterate through their list of path entries:

```
void BeginPath();
entityid CurrentStart();        // get current starting room
std::string CurrentDirection(); // get current direction name
entityid CurrentEnd();          // get current ending room
void NextPath();
bool IsValidPath();
void SeekStartRoom( entityid p_room );
void SeekEndRoom( entityid p_room );
```

The path iterator is a bit different from previous iterators, since you're actually accessing a complex `portalentry` structure, rather than just an entity ID, as the other container iterators do. It's not that difficult though; for each path in a portal, `CurrentStart` returns the ID of the starting room, `CurrentDirection` returns the name of that path, and `CurrentEnd` returns the ending point of that path.

Likewise, there are two seek functions: one that seeks to the first path that has a starting room of `p_room`; and the other that seeks to the first path that has an ending room of `p_room`.

Summary

I hope I didn't bore you to death with all the mundane details about entities, their databases, and their accessor classes. I know you must be impatient to get to the real meat of the BetterMUD, so that you can start making your own cool MUD, instead of dealing with all this low-level management. Don't worry, it gets more interesting after this.

In the next chapter, I start getting into the interesting stuff, such as the basics of the scripting engine and how to abstract the logic and the data of the game away from each other.

In this chapter, you learned to make your life easier by combining many little "mixin" classes to form larger classes that share bits and pieces of functionality. The same concept was applied toward all the databases, and macros were used for the same purpose when dealing with the accessor classes.

In the introduction of the book, I told you about the different layers of MUDs, and how you can hard-code certain parts of a virtual world and leave other parts flexible. As you can see from this chapter, the physical layer of the world is entirely hard-coded, and it is very difficult to change (in terms of downtime of the MUD, that is). That's just one of the things you have to deal with when programming in a static language such as C++.

I want you to start thinking about the future of your MUD projects, however, and think about possibly implementing a dynamic physics system of your own. One thing that I've learned from using C++ is that when you build a static physical world like this, you need to be sure to include data and functions for *everything* you might need, whereas, as you'll see with the dynamic logic part of the game, you can simply add features whenever you like.

Off to logic!

CHAPTER 14

Scripts,
Actions,
Logic,
and Commands

T his chapter explains the following flexible concepts of the BetterMUD: actions, logic, and commands. I've briefly touched on all of these topics, but I never took the full plunge into what they are and how they are implemented. For that, I apologize. The BetterMUD is a complex beast, and there's no way I can split up the C++ core and gradually add features. On the Python side of things, that's easy to do, but unfortunately, the core is best viewed as a whole entity with many interlinked components. So, with this chapter, I explore the extendible concepts of the BetterMUD.

In this chapter, you will learn to:

- Understand the basic ideas behind script objects
- Learn what data actions contain
- Learn the three major kinds of actions
- Understand the parameters the actions require
- Learn the workings of logic modules
- Learn how commands work
- Implement simple commands in C++
- Implement a database that generates command objects

Scripts

I'll be explaining the specifics of implementing Python scripts in Chapters 17 and 18. That doesn't prevent me, however, from showing you the basic interfaces that Python objects use throughout the game.

The basic concept behind any piece of removable logic in the BetterMUD is the *script*. A script is, simply, any object that holds logic (computer code) and can hold internal data.

The basic function of generic script objects is to load and save themselves to disk, however, so that's just what the Script interface defines:

```
class Script {
public:
    virtual void Load( std::istream& p_stream );
    virtual void Save( std::ostream& p_stream );
    virtual std::string Name() = 0;
    virtual ~Script() {};
}; // end class Script
```

It should be noted that the Load and Save functions aren't *pure virtual*, but rather *standard virtual*. The Script class defines default implementations of these functions.

> **CAUTION**
>
> The Script class has a virtual destructor, which is *very important* to have due to a little-known quirk in C++. Imagine having a class that returns new Script* objects (such as a script database/factory), and relies on you to delete them. When you delete the script and the language has no virtual destructor, only the destructor of the Script object that is called. If you have a child class that inherited from the Script class, and it needs to delete data in its destructor that Scripts don't know about, you've just given yourself a memory leak, because that child class never properly deletes what it needs to delete. It's enough to make you crazy sometimes, isn't it? Supposedly the next standard of C++ will support automatic virtual destruction, but that may be a few years off. We'll see.

Since all script objects are capable of storing variable amounts of miscellaneous data, it makes sense that the scripts need to know how to write this data to disk. For example, you might give a special command to a player that can be executed only once a week. Obviously, this command's script object needs to store the last time the command was invoked, so that the next time a player tries to use it, it can check, and say, "Hey, it hasn't been a week yet!" In addition, if you had to shut down the MUD and then reload it without saving the data in the scripts, a player could use the command again, even if it hadn't been a week.

Or worse yet, imagine what would happen if a player who was on a week-long quest was just hours away from snapping up the Holy Grail, and all his quest data was wiped out because the script did not save its data to disk. D'oh!

So scripts must save their data to disk. To do so, they use this format:

```
scriptname
[DATA]
... data goes here ...
[/DATA]
```

Even if there is no data, the [DATA] and [/DATA] tags must be written to disk. The default implementation of the load and save functions does this for you automatically.

Actions

Everything that happens in the physical part of the world is considered an action and this includes characters moving, attributes changing, items moving around, and people speaking.

A naive design would give each entity in the game specific calls for each event to look something like this:

```
class Character {
    void SawCharacterLeave( entityid p_char, entityid p_portal );
```

```
    void SawCharacterEnter( entityid p_char, entityid p_portal );
    ...
    ...
    ...
};
```

Depending on the number of physical actions, this can end up making your codebase literally explode in size.

Instead, as mentioned previously, I use a special structure to represent actions, called the Action structure. (You can find this in /BetterMUD/Entities/Action.h.)

```
struct Action {
    std::string actiontype;
    entityid data1;
    entityid data2;
    entityid data3;
    entityid data4;
    std::string stringdata;
};
```

> **NOTE**
>
> There's a constructor that I didn't show in the previous code segment, but it simply takes parameters matching each one of the fields. It also uses default parameters for each of the arguments, so you don't have to use all the arguments all the time. You'll see this used in a bit.

An action contains six fields of data: two strings, and four entityids. These fields contain enough data to represent the details of every physical action within the game.

For example, if you want to tell the game that character 1 entered the realm, you could create an action like this:

```
Action a( "enterrealm", 1 );
```

Or when that character attempts to speak, you could create an action like this:

```
Action b( "attemptsay", 1, 0, 0, 0, "Hello Game!!!" );
```

The constructor uses default parameter values, but if you want to use the data string, you need to pass in all parameters, even if they aren't used.

> **NOTE**
>
> I show you the meanings of all of the action parameters in a bit.

There are three major types of actions within the BetterMUD: attempted actions, query actions, and completed actions.

Attempted Actions

Attempted actions are basically requests to the game. You have a script attached to a character, and the script wants to move the character through a portal. The script then tells the game, "Hey, I want this character to go through a portal!" Some attempted actions such as trying to go through portals may fail; others, such as entering the realm, always work.

Attempted actions are *always* registered with the game module, which I show you in the next chapter.

Here is a listing of player-related attempted actions:

> **enterrealm**—a player is entering the realm
>
> **leaverealm**—a player is leaving the realm
>
> **announce**—a system-wide announcement is being made
>
> **chat**—a player wants to globally chat
>
> **attemptsay**—a player wants to speak in a room
>
> **vision**—a room-wide vision event is occurring
>
> **command**—a player wants to execute a command

Then we have some physical event requests:

> **attemptportalenter**—a character wants to enter a portal
>
> **attempttransport**—a character wants to teleport to another room without using a portal
>
> **transport**—a character is forced to teleport to another room, without asking permission
>
> **spawncharacter**—a new character wants to be spawned in a room
>
> **spawnitem**—a new item wants to be spawned at a location
>
> **destroycharacter**—a character is told to die
>
> **destroyitem**—an item is destroyed
>
> **attemptdropitem**—a character tries to drop an item
>
> **attemptgetitem**—a character tries to get an item
>
> **attemptgiveitem**—one character gives an item to another

There are also events that deal with the databases:

> **cleanup**—tells the item and character databases to clean up all their deleted instances
>
> **savedatabases**—tells the game to save all databases to disk
>
> **saveregion**—tells the game to save a particular region to disk
>
> **saveplayers**—tells the game to save the players (not all characters) to disk
>
> **savetimers**—tells the game to save all timers to disk
>
> **reloaditems**—tells the game to reload the item template database
>
> **reloadcharacters**—tells the game to reload the character template database
>
> **reloadregion**—tells the game to reload a particular region
>
> **reloadcommandscript**—tells the game to reload a command script by name
>
> **reloadlogicscript**—tells the game to reload a logic script by name

And then there are the attribute modifiers:

> **modifyattribute**—modify an attribute of an entity

And finally, here are the other actions that don't fit into the other categories:

messagelogic—send a generic text message to any logic module in the game

addlogic—add a logic module to an entity

dellogic—delete a logic module from an entity

do—send a generic action event to an entity

Query Actions

Query actions are often supposed to return Booleans, and they govern things that can happen in the realm. For example, you may want to prohibit players of a specific type from picking up items of a specific type, or you may want items of a specific type to refuse to be picked up at all.

To figure out just what the heck can happen in the game, you need a bunch of *query actions*, which ask an item if an action is allowed.

Here is a list of query actions:

cansay—can a character say something?

canleaveregion—can a character leave a region?

canenterregion—can a character enter a region?

canleaveroom—can a character leave a room?

canenterportal—can a character enter a portal?

cangetitem—can a character get an item?

candropitem—can a character drop an item?

canreceiveitem—can a character receive an item given by another character?

query—generic query that asks custom questions.

All these actions (except query, which I go over in much more detail in Chapter 15) should return a value of zero if the action is acceptable, or one if unacceptable. I know this sounds strange, since zero usually means "no" or "false," but it involves the workings of the action reporting system.

A collection of logic modules governs the actions of every character. If several scripts are attached to a character, the character asks each script if the action can be accomplished. Whenever an action returns non-zero, it is assumed that it is important to return the information to whomever called the script, so the game engine stops sending the action to each module, and just returns the value. Figure 14.1 shows the chaining system of the BetterMUD logic modules.

So, if a character has a module (for example, a logic module for someone dedicated to a church) that prevents him from picking up certain items (such as an evil relic), that script returns a value of 1 whenever the script prevents the character from getting an item. The script returns 0 if the action is allowed.

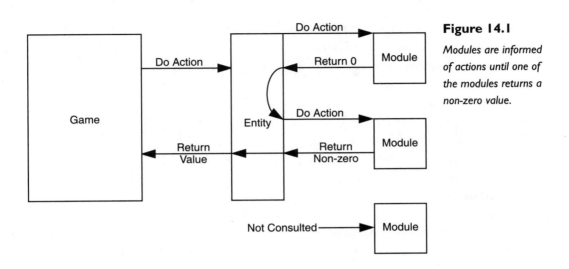

Figure 14.1

Modules are informed of actions until one of the modules returns a non-zero value.

In a similar way, items and rooms are asked if they will allow characters to pick things up; I go over the specifics of all this logic in the next chapter.

Completed Actions

Now that you've seen what actions can be requested by scripts, you need to know about the other side of the equation. When you tell the game about an action, it tries to accomplish that action, and if it succeeds, it must tell every actor in the equation about what happened.

For example, if a script requests that a player enter a portal, the game tries to move the player, and a number of things must be done to accomplish that move. First, the player must ask the portal for permission to enter, and if he receives permission, the room and everyone in it is told that the player left the room and moved into a portal, the portal is told that the player entered, and then the new room and everyone in it is told that the player entered.

Here are the completed actions that entities are informed of:

>**enterrealm**—A character entered the realm.
>
>**leaverealm**—A character left the realm.
>
>**leave**—The game tells a character to leave the game state.
>
>**hangup**—The game tells a character to hang up.
>
>**enterregion**—A character entered a region.
>
>**enterroom**—A character entered a room.
>
>**leaveroom**—A character left a room.
>
>**leaveregion**—A character left a region.
>
>**enterportal**—A character entered a portal.

getitem—A character got an item.

dropitem—A character dropped an item.

giveitem—A character gave an item to another character.

error—An error occurred.

announce—A system announcement was made.

say—Someone said something.

spawnitem—A new item was spawned.

spawncharacter—A new character was spawned.

destroyitem—An item was destroyed.

destroycharacter—A character was destroyed.

messagelogic—A message was sent to a logic module.

modifyattribute—An attribute was modified.

The preceding lists constitute all of the actions possible within the entire game. Table 15.1 shows which entities are notified about which events.

Action Parameters

Tables 15.2, 15.3, and 15.4 list the parameters for each action event type.

Most of the time you don't have to pass room numbers as arguments, since the logic modules can assume that the room in question is the room that currently contains the player.

A few of the actions are "routable" actions, in which the action is routed to a specific entity in the game. These actions have an entity type and an entity ID that determine where they go. Here is a listing of the entity types:

0—character

1—item

2—room

3—portal

4—region

So if you wanted to set attribute `foo` of item number 24 to the value 80, then you would construct an action like this:

```
Action a( "modifyattribute", 1, 24, 80, 0, "foo" );
```

Logic

Logic modules are modules that react to actions. When I showed you the entity classes in Chapter 12, I told you about the `Logic` and the `LogicCollection` classes, which are simple classes that wrap around scripts (or C++ implemented functions too, if you want).

Table 15.1   Entity Event Notifications

Event	Items	Characters	Rooms	Regions	Portals
enterrealm	no	yes	no	no	no
leaverealm	no	yes	no	no	no
leave	no	yes	no	no	no
hangup	no	yes	no	no	no
enterregion	no	yes	no	yes	no
enterroom	yes	yes	yes	no	no
leaveroom	yes	yes	yes	no	no
leaveregion	no	yes	no	yes	no
enterportal	no	yes	no	no	yes
getitem	yes	yes	yes	no	no
dropitem	yes	yes	yes	no	no
giveitem	yes	yes	no	no	no
error	no	yes	no	no	no
announce	no	yes	no	no	no
say	yes	yes	yes	no	no
spawnitem	yes	yes	yeso	no	no
spawncharacter	no	yes	yes	no	no
destroyitem	yes	yes	yes	yes	no
destroycharacter	no	yes	yes	yes	no
messagelogic	yes	yes	yes	yes	yes
modifyattributes	yes	yes	yes	yes	yes

Table 15.2   Attempted Action Parameters

Action	arg1	arg2	arg3	arg4	data
chat	player	-	-	-	text
announce	-	-	-	-	text
vision	room	-	-	-	text
enterrealm	player	-	-	-	-
leaverealm	player	-	-	-	-
attemptsay	character	-	-	-	text
command	character	-	-	-	text
attemptenterportal	character	portal	-	-	-
attempttransport	character	room	-	-	-
transport	character	room	-	-	-
attemptgetitem	character	item	quantity	-	-
attemptdropitem	character	item	quantity	-	-
attemptgiveitem	character	character	item	quantity	-
spawnitem	template	room/person	isroom/person?	quantity	-
spawncharacter	template	room	-	-	-
destroyitem	item	quantity	-	-	-
destroycharacter	character	-	-	-	-
cleanup	-	-	-	-	-
savedatabases	-	-	-	-	-
saveregion	region	-	-	-	-
saveplayers	-	-	-	-	-
savetimers	-	-	-	-	-
reloaditems	-	-	-	-	file
reloadcharacters	-	-	-	-	file
reloadregion	-	-	-	-	name
reloadcommandscript	-	-	-	-	name
reloadlogicscript	-	-	-	-	name
modifyattribute	entity type	entityid	value	-	name
messagelogic	entity type	entityid	-	-	name
addlogic	entity type	entityid	-	-	logic
dellogic	entity type	entityid	-	-	logic
do	entity type	entityid	-	-	text

Table 15.3   Query Action Parameters

Action	arg1	arg2	arg3	arg4	data
cansay	character	-	-	-	text
canleaveregion	character	region	-	-	-
canenterregion	character	region	-	-	-
canleaveroom	character	room	-	-	-
canenterroom	character	room	-	-	-
canenterportal	character	portal	-	-	-
cangetitem	character	item	quantity	-	-
candropitem	character	item	quantity	-	-
canreceiveitem	giver	receiver	item	quantity	-
query	optional	optional	optional	optional	optional

The Logic class is basically just an interface that wraps around a script. The class skeleton looks like this:

```
class Logic : public Script {
public:
    virtual bool CanSave();
    virtual int Attribute( const
std::string& p_attr );
    virtual int DoAction( const Action&
p_action );
}; // end class Logic
```

The first thing of interest in the listing is the CanSave function. The reason for this function is that some logic modules shouldn't be saved to disk when an entity is saved to disk. For example, you'll see in Chapter 16 that I implement player connection interaction classes as Logic modules (logic modules that dictate how to send data to a connection),

NOTE

The Logic class is abstract and doesn't define an implementation. Originally, I had planned on making both C++ and Python implementations of logic modules, but after playing around with it, I realized that C++ modules aren't even needed; you can do anything you want from within Python. The design is still there, however; so if you ever feel like implementing hard-coded logic modules in C++, feel free. Just beware that you'll have to stop and restart the MUD to make any changes, and that's not good.

Table 15.4   Happened Action Parameters

Action	arg1	arg2	arg3	arg4	data
enterrealm	player	-	-	-	-
leaverealm	player	-	-	-	-
leave	-	-	-	-	-
hangup	-	-	-	-	-
enterregion	character	region	-	-	-
enterroom	character	portal	-	-	-
leaveroom	character	portal	-	-	-
leaveregion	character	region	-	-	-
enterportal	character	portal	-	-	-
getitem	character	item	-	-	-
dropitem	character	item	-	-	-
giveitem	character	recipient	item	-	-
error	-	-	-	-	text
announce	-	-	-	-	text
say	character	-	-	-	text
spawnitem	item	-	-	-	-
spawncharacter	character	-	-	-	-
destroyitem	item	-	-	-	-
destroycharacter	character	-	-	-	-
messagelogic	entity type	entityid	-	-	name
modifyattribute	entity type	entityid	value	-	name

but obviously these modules aren't important when a character exits the game (because he is no longer connected), so he shouldn't be saved to disk.

Logic modules can have attributes that are accessible from outside the module, and this accessibility is implemented by using the Attribute function. This is especially useful for quests, since other logic modules in the game need to check the state of a quest in order to react to it.

> **NOTE**
>
> Even though this code doesn't show it (since it is an abstract class), all logic modules need to be initialized with the ID of the object that it is attached to. You'll see this when I show you the PythonLogic class in Chapter 17.

The final function is the DoAction function, which performs an action on the particular logic module.

The Python-implemented version of this class can be found in the directory /BetterMUD/ scripts/python. I go over the code in Chapter 17.

Commands

Previously, I explained the idea of commands, which are scriptable objects that can be given to players to enable them to communicate with other players and with the game.

Perhaps the best aspect of commands is that they can be given to people on a per-person basis, and this is probably a good place to have a rewards system. Imagine this scenario: A character spends a lot of time in woods and forests, so having the ability to find herbs and turn them into elixirs would be useful. But the character doesn't know how to do that; the BetterMUD has no way of saying "convert this object into that."

Perhaps, as a reward for completing a quest or by paying for schooling, the character can be given the ability to issue a makeelixer command. Then, whenever the character invoked that command on herb-items in his inventory, the command script would destroy the herbs and generate a new elixir in his inventory.

That's how commands work; they're simple scripts that can be executed by characters.

The Command class is very simple:

```
class Command : public Script {
public:
    virtual void Execute( const std::string& p_parameters ) = 0;
    virtual std::string Usage() = 0;
    virtual std::string Description() = 0;
};  // end class Command
```

The command class has three functions: a player can execute the command, obtain its "usage," and can get its description.

In the game, whenever a player types /blah blarg, the game interprets that as a command. The game tries to find a command named blah, and executes it with a parameter's value of blarg.

The usage and the description of a command are just strings that describe the syntax of the command and describe what it accomplishes. Usage and description help the player figure out what to do.

The Commands class can be found in the directory /BetterMUD/scripts in the files Command.h and .cpp. Like logic scripts, Commands is an abstract class that can be implemented in either Python or C++.

> **NOTE**
>
> It is important to note that all commands must be given the ID of the character that they belong to, so that when the commands are executed, they know who executed them. You will see how this is done when new command objects are created.

C++ Commands

Before I had the Python engine up and running, I had a few C++ commands running as a test case, which means I implemented the Command module class in C++. You can find this class in the same directory as the Command class, in the file CPPCommand.h.

Here is the implementation of the C++ version of the class:

```
class CPPCommand : public Command {
public:
    CPPCommand( entityid p_character, std::string p_name,
        const char* p_usage, const char* p_description );
    std::string Name()          { return m_name; }
    std::string Usage()         { return m_usage; }
    std::string Description()   { return m_description; }
protected:
    std::string m_name;
    const char* m_usage;
    const char* m_description;
    character m_character;
}; // end class CPPCommand
```

The class is a simple one; it contains one string and two const char* pointers. Since many instances of the individual command classes have the same nonchanging description and usage strings, it doesn't make sense to store the actual string data on a per-instance basis, so I'd rather have pointers to the strings instead.

This class doesn't implement the Execute command, but lets classes that inherit from this class implement it instead.

C++ Commands Implemented

I've implemented a few commands in C++. These commands are located in the file CPPCommands.h (note the "s" at the end of the file name and that the base CPPCommand class is in a different file, CPPCommand.h). For example, the first command I implemented was the Quit command:

```
class CPPCommandQuit : public CPPCommand {
public:
    CPPCommandQuit( entityid p_character ) :
        CPPCommand( p_character, "quit", "\"quit\"",
        "This removes your character from the game and takes you"
        " back to the Game Menu." ) {}

    void Execute( const std::string& p_parameters ) {
        m_character.DoAction( Action( "leave", m_character.ID() ) );
    }
}; // end class CPPCommandQuit
```

This defines the Quit command. When you give this command to a player, he can type /quit and the game logs him out. As you can see from the Execute function, this command simply tells the game that a player is leaving the realm. That's all there is to it!

Here's another example:

```
class CPPCommandChat : public CPPCommand {
public:
    CPPCommandChat( entityid p_character ) :
        CPPCommand( p_character, "chat", "\"chat <message>\"",
        "This sends a message to every player who is currently "
        "logged into the game." ) {}

    void Execute( const std::string& p_parameters ) {
        if( p_parameters.size() == 0 ) {
            m_character.DoAction( "error", 0, 0, 0, 0, "Usage: " + Usage() );
            return;
        }
        g_game.AddActionAbsolute(
            0, "chat", m_character.ID(), 0, 0, 0, p_parameters );
    }
}; // end class CPPCommandChat
```

This one is slightly more complex. It checks to see if the user supplied the appropriate parameters (that is, any text after "chat"), and if there is no parameter, the game prints an error to the character who tried to chat.

Otherwise, the game is told about the chat action, using the AddActionAbsolute command, which you'll learn about in the next chapter. For now, all you need to know is that the chat action adds a command to the game, and that the command is executed as soon as the game can get to it. (The first parameter is the time to execute the command, and zero means right away.)

There are other commands in the file—commands that make players say things, reload scripts, move around the map, look at a room, kick other players, and set quiet-mode, which is a feature I will get to in the next chapter when I show you how to execute commands.

I'm leaving these commands in the game as sort of a "legacy," so you can get an idea of how you can implement logic modules in C++. In Chapter 18, however, I'll show you how to create commands in Python, and I hope you'll agree that Python is preferable to C++. The primary reason, of course, is the fact that Python commands are reloadable at run-time, which means that you can add stuff to existing commands if you need to.

Command Database

I took the liberty of creating a class that will manage all commands for you. Since the database is closely linked with Python, you won't be able to understand *everything* that it does until Chapter 17, but it's easy enough to follow. Here is the class skeleton and the definition of the global instance of the database:

```
class CommandDatabase : public PythonDatabase {
public:
    CommandDatabase() : PythonDatabase( "data/commands/" ) {}
    Command* generate( const std::string& p_str, entityid p_character );
    void GiveCommands( entityid p_character, accesslevel p_level );
};


extern CommandDatabase CommandDB;
```

The database inherits from a `PythonDatabase` class, which you'll see in Chapter 17. All you need to know at this point is that the `PythonDatabase` class generates Python scripts, and that you can wrap those into a `PythonCommand` object (also in Chapter 17), which is the Python version of the `Command` class. Figure 14.2 shows this relationship.

The `CommandDatabase` returns new instances of any kind of command you give it.

Generating Commands

Whenever the database is asked for a command, this is the function it calls:

```
Command* CommandDatabase::generate(
    const std::string& p_str, entityid p_character ) {
    if( p_str == "quit" )
        return new CPPCommandQuit( p_character );
    else if( p_str == "go" )
        return new CPPCommandGo( p_character );
    else if( p_str == "chat" )
        return new CPPCommandChat( p_character );
    else if( p_str == "say" )
```

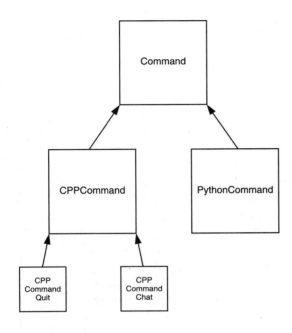

Figure 14.2

Commands have a partial inheritance hierarchy.

```
    return new CPPCommandSay( p_character );
else if( p_str == "kick" )
    return new CPPCommandKick( p_character );
else if( p_str == "quiet" )
    return new CPPCommandQuiet( p_character );
else if( p_str == "shutdown" )
    return new CPPCommandShutdown( p_character );
else if( p_str == "look" )
    return new CPPCommandLook( p_character );
else if( p_str == "commands" )
    return new CPPCommandCommands( p_character );
else if( p_str == "reloadscript" )
    return new CPPCommandReloadScript( p_character );
```

I'm going to split up the code right here, and I would like to note that this kind of code is generally considered ugly. Whenever you add a new command class to the BetterMUD in C++, you also need to come back to this class and make sure it knows how to create and return the new kind of class. That can get extremely annoying if you end up adding lots of C++ classes.

Here's the rest of the function, which executes when it can't find a C++ command with the name you requested:

```
else {
    try {
        // try to load a Python script
```

```
            PythonInstance* command = SpawnNew( p_str );
            return new PythonCommand( p_character, command );
        }
        catch( ... ) {
            PyErr_Print();
            // no script found
        }
    }
    throw Exception( "Unknown Command Script" );
}
```

This code uses classes you won't see until Chapter 17, but I hope makes some sense to you right now. The code calls the `PythonDatabase::SpawnNew` function to get an instance of a new Python class, and once it has that, it creates a new `PythonCommand` object that wraps around the Python class instance.

If no class is found, an exception is thrown, and no command object is returned.

Summary

In this chapter, you learned about the various flexible data structures that are part of the BetterMUD. By now, these concepts should be familiar to you, since I've explained how they work before.

Using a scripting language is a nice and powerful way to enhance the flexibility of your game, as I hope you'll see in the upcoming chapters.

> **TIP**
>
> If you really insist on adding lots of C++ commands to the game, you should note that the chained if-else method is inefficient once you get a large number of commands. You would be better off creating a map of some sort, to map names to classes. Or even better, just use Python for your commands.

> **NOTE**
>
> The `Command` objects returned by the database are always new, and it is up to the character who requested the objects to delete them when he's finished.

In the next chapter, I show you the overall game logic and how to actually use these classes to start putting together a solid MUD.

CHAPTER 15

GAME LOGIC

T o this point, you've learned about the basic structure of the BetterMUD, the entities, accessor classes, databases, actions, and the extensible scripting modules.

All these components must be managed by something, however, and this chapter shows you how to do that.

In this chapter, you will learn to:

- Use the game module to control the physical aspects of the game
- Use action events to tell the game module what is happening
- Understand how the timer system works
- Understand how the physical transaction system works

Game Module

In the SimpleMUD, the game logic was mainly stashed into a Telnet handler for each connection. I know I've mentioned this before, but it needs to be said again: That was not a very flexible design.

There's really no reason why a class that is designed to handle events inside the game should also handle getting input from a player. In a proper design, the core of the game should be abstracted away from the mechanism that handles connections, so that the design can be applied to many different situations. I've also mentioned that I would eventually like to add the ability to use protocols other than Telnet with the BetterMUD.

So, because of the need for flexibility, it makes sense to abstract the core physics engine into a module of its own. Therefore, the Game class controls everything that happens in the BetterMUD.

As you saw in the last chapter, many types of game actions can occur. When logic modules want the game to perform an action, such as moving a player, they notify the game engine by using an action.

The game engine checks to make sure that it can do what was requested, and then notifies all entities involved.

Characters don't know how to move around, pick things up, or perform other actions. Instead, all the physical logic is contained in one central location, the Game class.

Figure 15.1 should give you an overall sense of how the game data flows. The shaded square in the Logics section represents a Reporter object, which I cover when I go over the network stuff in Chapter 16.

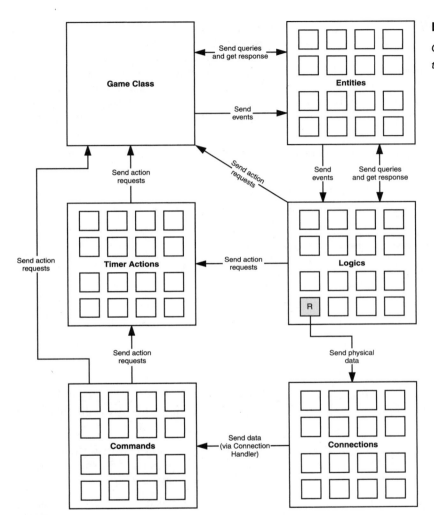

Figure 15.1

General data flow within the BetterMUD.

At the core of the BetterMUD is the game module. This is a "controller" object. It essentially manages the physical part of the game, which consists of entities. Whenever the logical part of the game needs to perform actions on the physical world, it must send an action object to the game module. Or, if you prefer, the game module can instead say "This action is going to happen at time X," and add the action to the global collection of timer objects, which the game module also manages.

Action Queries

Due to the flexible nature of the engine, the game module not only tells entities what happened to them, but asks them if certain things can happen to them as well.

For example, you may want to have a huge gargoyle statue object in a room. On the one hand, you could simply say, "There is a statue in this room" in the description, but that can get boring. Besides, if you wanted the gargoyle to come to life, it would seem more realistic if the gargoyle were an item. So there is an item, and a player comes into the room. He decides to be cute, and tries picking up the gargoyle, which is too heavy to lift and is also solidly implanted into the ground. Obviously, you want to make absolutely certain that *no-one* can pick it up, even if someone manages to cheat and give himself more than enough strength to pick it up.

So for specified, attempted actions, the game queries the *actors* involved and asks each one if he will allow such an act to happen. This is the process taken to pick up an item, for example:

1. Query whether the item allows the player to take it.
2. Query whether the room allows the player to take it.
3. Query whether the player's current condition allows him to take it.
4. Transfer ownership of the item to the player.
5. Tell the room that the item was taken.
6. Tell the item that it was taken.
7. Tell all the characters in the room that the item was taken.
8. Tell all the items in the room that the item was taken.

Obviously, the first three actions are the queries. The game module first checks that the transaction can be completed, and then starts moving things around. Why do I need all those queries?

I've already outlined reasons for the first query; you'll often have items that you just don't want people to take, ever. The second query might confuse you though; why would a room care if an item is taken?

This is where your job comes in. As the MUD implementer, it's your job to brainstorm all the whacky possibilities that can happen. For example, someone casts a super gravity spell on the entire room, and while the room has super gravity, things are too heavy to be picked up.

Or maybe a part of a dungeon starts to crumble, and a precious item is now blocked by a large pile of rubble, which allows a player to see the item but not to take it. If you ask the room if it will allow players to take items, your game can handle these kinds of interesting scripts.

Of course asking players if they can take the item is a no-brainer; it's an easy way of checking to see if a player is carrying too many things. See the "encumbrance" module in Chapter 18 for implementation details.

Action Events

After an event has been thoroughly queried, and the game module decides it's okay to carry out the event, the game module needs to tell every actor involved in the event that it happened. In the example I showed you previously, when an item is taken, the game notifies the following four groups of actors:

1. The room in which the item was picked up
2. The item that was picked up
3. Every character in that room, including the person who picked up the item
4. Every other item in the room

Again, you may be thinking, "Why does the room or the other items need to know when an item is removed?" If you're saying that, you're not using your thinking cap!

Be creative! Imagine...

You're Indiana Jones in some lost Aztec temple, about to claim the Sacred Statue of Pies for your museum, and as you snatch it, you realize all too late that *it was booby-trapped!* As soon as the room realizes you've taken the item, it sets off a trap that shoots poison darts at you, or maybe sets a huge rolling ball object in motion that will crush you to death if you don't get out of there in time!

Okay, so you can understand why rooms must know about items leaving; but what about all the other items? Why would they possibly want to know? Maybe you can imagine some set of magical items, a group of three or so, which erect a powerful force field in the room when they are all together. If you remove one... oops! The force field collapses, and that opens up the room to all sorts of evil creatures.

With a flexible scripting language such as Python embedded into the game, almost anything is possible. There is absolutely no way I could possibly tell you about all the cool things you can implement on your own; it's your job to find out. In Chapter 18, you'll get a brief glimpse into some of the things that can be done with the BetterMUD, but I assure you, the BetterMUD is designed to be taken far above and beyond what I give you.

> **NOTE**
>
> I have to be honest with you here; I was having quite a bit of fun playing around with the BetterMUD before it was even technically a MUD! What you can accomplish is virtually limitless.

Physical Movement

In Chapter 13, you saw that every entity was given functions to add and remove entities from itself. For example, rooms track the collection of all items, characters, and portals currently within them; characters track all of the items they have, and so on.

The game module manages these collections. When a player moves to a different room, the game removes him from the previous room and then places him in the new room. It's a pretty simple process overall.

There are a few things you need to keep in mind when performing actions, however.

The first is that in a highly flexible world, data corruption is very easy. You might have a script written by a new builder for the MUD, and he makes certain assumptions. For example, he may mistakenly assume that a certain character will always exist. So when the script runs, and it tries to get a pointer to the nonexistent character, it's obviously going to crash the script, and possibly cause something bad to happen.

To keep the data corruption to an absolute minimum, the game module always tries to perform the crashable parts of an action before it does any actual moving around.

For example, before *anything* is moved around as part of an action, the game module performs all the database lookups, and then performs all the queries to see if the action can be performed.

Once the lookups and queries are completed, the entity being moved around in the action is moved from one place to another, and the final act is to inform all the entities that are interested in what happened.

If any database lookup causes a crash, or if the queries cause a crash, nothing happens; the action fails, and whoever called the action should try to catch the exception.

The part of the code that performs the physical work should never cause a crash, simply because by the time the function gets to that part of the code, all the entities involved have been confirmed to exist.

Once the entity has been acted on, the function starts notifying everyone about the action, and each one of these calls may cause a crash.

Of course, if the calls *do* cause a crash, you're just going to have to live with it; at that point, the action has already occurred, and you're just informing players.

> **NOTE**
>
> Once an item has been moved, you can handle logic crashes in a few different ways. You're going to be telling many items about the occurrence of an event, and each time you do so, the event may throw an exception at you. A really sturdy approach would be to catch every time an exception is thrown, log it, and then continue telling everyone else about it. However, I didn't take this approach; instead, the first time anything throws an exception, the entire function exits. The action still physically happens, but some entities may not be told about it. While this could destabilize things, you should realize that scripts should only fail during testing. Once you release a logic module to everyone in your realm, exceptions like this shouldn't happen anymore. Testing your scripts is a very important phase of building a MUD.

Rogue Scripts

When you have a rogue script that crashes, what is the worst-case scenario? Maybe the script crashes every time it's run, and the only way to fix it is to delete the script's data and reload it from scratch. This can be a big problem, especially when that script was holding a lot of data. For example, the crashed script was holding data important to a quest.

It's just one of the things you have to deal with though. The great thing about a flexible MUD is that it's relatively painless to test; if a script screws up, you can simply reload it, and start testing again.

Because of this, I highly recommend that whenever you build new areas in the game, you restrict the new area and all its scripts to a certain group of test characters (don't use any real characters, because you may blow away your favorite character by accident). Once you've tested an area thoroughly, you should then be able to integrate it into the rest of the game safely.

> **NOTE**
>
> When I was testing some scripts for the BetterMUD, I really couldn't stop saying to myself, "Wow! This is so cool!" every time I found a tiny little syntax error in a script file. Instead of stopping the whole program, fixing it, recompiling it, reloading the game, and setting everything up again, I could just type `/load <script>` **and it worked!**

Overall Module Design

The game module for the BetterMUD is more complex but still resembles certain aspects of the game module from the SimpleMUD.

Comparing the SimpleMUD Game to the BetterMUD Game

The first item of note is the name. Since I use namespaces for everything, I'm not really concerned about calling the class Game, because it's unlikely that the BetterMUD is going to have a different class with the same name inside it.

Another similarity is that the module keeps a timer (what would a MUD be without a timer, so that you can brag about how long you've been online?), and the module also loads and saves the databases to disk.

That's where the similarities end, however. In addition to the functions in the SimpleMUD that I've just mentioned, the Game class was responsible for the following:

- Translating connection input into game commands
- Performing the game commands
- Responding to user commands
- Sending data back directly to connections

Within the BetterMUD, all these topics are handled in other areas. For example, the BetterMUD now has a specific class called the *TelnetGame* class (see Chapter 16) that is designed *only* to translate connection input into game commands. You'll see this in use in the networking chapter, and understand how the design allows all the protocols you want to add.

Once the SimpleMUD knew what command a player wanted to execute, it figured out how to execute the command and did whatever was necessary to carry out the player's wishes. The BetterMUD's more flexible approach makes it irrelevant for the game module to know how user commands are implemented. Instead, as you learned in Chapter 14, there are command objects that take care of finding out how to do those things. This way, the game module doesn't need to know about player commands at all.

Sending back responses is an indirect process in the BetterMUD. The only thing the game module does is send event notifications back to entities, and it's up to the entities to consult their logic modules and figure out how they're going to send the data back to the player's connection. This is called the *reporter* concept, which is explained in detail within Chapter 16.

Game Module Functions

The BetterMUD game module is in charge of many new things, such as a timer registry, and keeping track of which players and characters are in the game. You can also use the game module to search for characters that are currently logged in or offline.

By and large, the biggest part of the game module is the physical entity management and action management. Let me go over the simple parts first.

So Little Time

As I've mentioned before, the game module keeps a timer, which you may access to get the number of milliseconds that the MUD has been running. The game module also has an elaborate timer system, which enables you to add actions, and run them at a later time. I've mentioned this concept before a few times, but now I'm finally showing it to you.

Timer

The timer functions are very simple:

```
BasicLib::sint64 GetTime();
void ResetTime();
```

You're allowed to reset the timer if you wish, but I don't really recommend doing that because if your game is running, and it has a few hundred timer actions set to go off at time X, and you reset the time to 0, all those actions are going to execute sometime way in the future, quite possibly when they shouldn't be executed.

Timer Actions

In the previous chapter, I introduced you to the idea of actions, which are the primary methods of communication between the game and modules. The Action class is simple, yet very flexible, since it allows for a string data argument. The string data argument can contain almost anything you want, as long as whoever is receiving the action knows how to decode it.

When I showed you the HasLogic mixin class in Chapter 12, you saw that this class has a function called DoAction, which, when an action is passed in, tries to act based on that action.

While this method may not *seem* limiting, it is. Let's think about the actual game play for a moment. Imagine, once again, that you're a famous adventuring archeologist, breaking into a booby-trapped tomb to steal a priceless treasure; the moment you grab the treasure, the game starts a bunch of traps in motion.

Rather than going with the "instant death by dart-in-the-neck" route, you might want to toy with the hapless adventurer first; let him have the illusion that he can get out, instead of just killing him off right away. So this tomb could be a maze of sorts, with only one exit, and the moment the adventurer grabs the treasure, it sets off a trap that would cause the exit to close, but not right away. Instead, you want it to close after about 30 seconds or so, to give the adventurer a chance to actually get out.

This is where the timer actions come in. Instead of telling the game, "Do this now!" you can tell it, "Do this in 30 seconds!" instead. This adds a great deal of flexibility to your game.

Think about it in terms of illness and disease too; perhaps a player is poisoned by weak venom that disperses in an hour. You'd like the script that poisoned the player to also remove the poison, right? So the script executes two actions:

- Tell the game to poison the character now
- Tell the game to remove poison from the character in 60 minutes

To accomplish this, I've created the TimedAction structure (located within BetterMUD/ entites/Action.h):

```
struct TimedAction {
    BasicLib::sint64 executiontime;
    Action actionevent;
    bool valid;

    void Hook();
    void Unhook();
    void Save( std::ofstream& p_stream );
    void Load( std::ifstream& p_stream );
};
```

I've removed the constructors to make it look neater. For now, just look at the three pieces of data; I'll get to the functions in the next section.

The structure essentially maintains a time at which it should be executed, an `Action` structure, and a Boolean that determines if the timer action is still valid. You can simply think of these as actions that are executed at a given time.

Problems with Timer Actions

At this point, I'm going to discuss a concept that I haven't covered fully before, and it's rather difficult to understand at first. Let me explain by using an example—let's go back to the poisoning example.

Example of Poisoning

Let us assume that your character is fighting an evil mutant python snake, and the snake bites the character, injecting a venom into his bloodstream. The character quickly kills the snake, but, alas, he's poisoned and is weakening by the minute.

Since being poisoned is unappealing (at least to most of us), your character wants to be cured as fast as possible. To do this, he'll seek out the local Medicine Man and purchase a venom cure. Congratulations! The character's now cured.

> **NOTE**
> Pythons aren't actually venomous. And now you know.

That whole process took maybe 45 minutes, and the character is eager to get back to fighting those evil snakes, so he goes deep into the forest, takes out his sword, and begins looking for another evil python to kill! OUCH!

It isn't his fault, but the character is not a very good warrior, and he's practicing and trying to improve, but those damn pythons are just too tough for him. While he was searching for another python, one slithered up behind him and poisoned him, again! Argh!

Now the character has to go *all the way back to town*, since, in a fit of impatience, he neglected to buy another venom cure. Or maybe he didn't have enough money; it doesn't matter. The point is that he's walking back to town, and halfway there the effects of the poison suddenly, and quite unexpectedly, disappear. He's cured!

Aftermath

The character is thinking, "What the heck?" The poison is supposed to last 60 minutes, yet he was poisoned only 10 minutes ago! While this isn't something you would normally complain about (Look Ma! Free cure!), as a programmer, it should be tingling that little sense in the back of your mind that keeps repeating, "This is wrong, it's not working the way it should!"

Oh boy. Why would something like this happen? The answer has to do with the timer system. First look at Figure 15.2, in which timer events are shaded. The original "remove poison" timer event was never removed when the poison was mitigated.

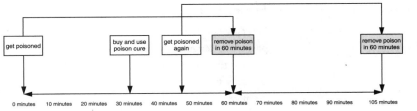

Figure 15.2

The process of being poisoned, cured, and then poisoned again.

Can you see the problem? When a character is first poisoned, the snake poison script automatically sets a timer event for removing the poison 60 minutes from the time of poisoning. In the meantime, the character goes to buy a poison cure, is cured, is poisoned again, but then the poison unexpectedly disappears, since the original timer event still exists. In addition, if your character finally gives up trying to kill those damned pythons, within 45 minutes or so, the game is going to try removing the poison again, but this time, the player isn't poisoned, so the game will be trying to remove a logic script that doesn't exist.

D'oh!

When Things Go from Bad to Worse

Guess what! It gets even worse. Imagine a script that tells a computer character to perform a specific action at a specific time; but before he has the chance to do so, another character comes by and rudely interrupts his life with a sword to the gut. The poor guy dies, but the game still wants to tell him to do something later on.

What can happen? The best-case scenario is that your game, when getting the character from the database, notices that he doesn't exist anymore. This causes your database to throw an exception at you, but that's a good thing. When an exception is thrown, the game catches it, and gives up trying; it says, "Yeah, you know what, this ain't gonna work," and it tosses the action event away, doing no harm at all.

What's the problem then? The problem is that the game re-assigns ID numbers to entities. Imagine, that somewhere else in the game, a random new character receives the previous character's ID. When the game reaches the action, it performs the action *on the new character!* That's a major "OOPS!" right there. Figure 15.3 demonstrates this.

Actions should *never ever ever ever ever* accidentally switch ownership. As far as the game is concerned, when that poor guy dies, every action he's attached to should die as well.

Hooks

So, now what? How do we make a system that links an entity to a timer action? It turns out that this system is actually pretty simple. The timer actions already know which entities they rely on by their values. For example, an "attemptgiveitem" action relies on three volatile entities: the person giving an item, the person getting an item, and the actual item.

For this to work, all three entities must exist; if any of them stops existing, that's it—the timer action cannot possibly work in a meaningful way, so it should be invalidated.

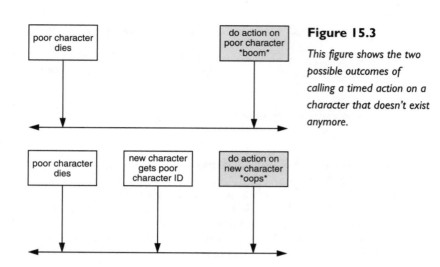

Figure 15.3

This figure shows the two possible outcomes of calling a timed action on a character that doesn't exist anymore.

Since timer actions already know who their actors are, half the work is already done. The other part, of course, is making sure that entities know which timer objects they are attached to. This is where the term *hook* comes from. Essentially the entities are hooked onto the timer action, and when they die, they tell the timer action, "Hey! I died! You're no longer valid!" Then, of course, the timer object has to go to every entity it's attached to and remove itself.

Figure 15.4 shows an example of three entities linked with three timed actions in various ways. All entities have hooks into timed actions that they control.

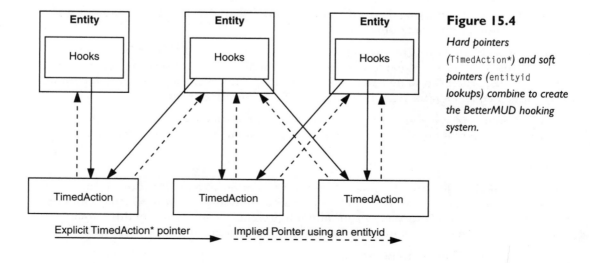

Figure 15.4

Hard pointers (`TimedAction*`) and soft pointers (`entityid` lookups) combine to create the BetterMUD hooking system.

When I showed you the `LogicEntity` mixin class in Chapter 12, I briefly told you about the hook functions it contained, but I didn't elaborate. Here is a listing of them:

```
typedef std::set<TimedAction*> actionhooks;
typedef actionhooks::iterator hookitr;
void AddHook( TimedAction* p_hook );
void DelHook( TimedAction* p_hook );
hookitr HooksBegin();
hookitr HooksEnd();
size_t Hooks();
void ClearHooks();
void ClearLogicHooks( const std::string& p_logic );
void KillHook( const std::string& p_act, const std::string& p_stringdata );
```

Remember, these functions are automatically included in any entity class that inherits from the `LogicEntity` mixin class, so you can give your entities hook capabilities quite easily.

The first two lines define typedefs that make your life easier; `actionhooks` is simply a set of `TimedAction` pointers.

The next two lines are the `AddHook` and `DelHook` functions. Whenever a new timed action is added to the game, it automatically contacts every entity that it interacts with, and tells it to add a pointer to the action to its hooks. When the timed action is removed from the game, it contacts each of its entities and removes itself from the entity's set of hooks. Since these two functions simply wrap around the `std::set::insert` and `erase` functions, there's no point in pasting in the code here.

The other two functions of interest are the `ClearHooks` and `ClearLogicHooks` functions.

Clearing All Hooks

Whenever the game destroys an entity, it calls its `ClearHooks` function, which basically goes through every timed action hook in the entity, and tells it to unhook itself. It's just a simple loop:

```
void ClearHooks() {
    hookitr itr = HooksBegin();
```

NOTE

Figure 15.4 should illustrate why I generally like to stay away from pointers; they can become a huge mess very quickly. There are better ways of going about a hooking system, such as using smart reference classes. Indeed, if I had made the entire timer system in Python, I could have used the built-in `weakref` class to do such a thing. You should look into using weak references if you plan on doing more with Python.

TIP

Heaps, which I also use in this chapter (hooray!), are my favorite data structure. Sets are my second favorite. As I've told you many times already, a set is a cool structure to use when you want fast insertions, lookups, and deletions. The coolest thing about sets is that they work just fine with pointers too.

```
while( itr != HooksEnd() ) {
    hookitr current = itr++;
    (*current)->Unhook();
}
}
```

There's one little catch, however. You need to maintain two iterators at all times, since the timed action's Unhook function actually deletes the object that the current iterator points to. So if you do this

```
(*itr)->Unhook()
++itr
```

your code is likely to crash, since the object the iterator points to doesn't exist anymore.

Clearing Logic Hooks

Whenever the game removes a logic module from an entity, any timed events that were specifically intended to go to that logic module must be deleted. You learned in the previous chapter that there are three events associated with logic modules: addlogic, dellogic, and messagelogic. As it turns out, only two of these actions must be hooked: dellogic and messagelogic.

The adding of logic modules doesn't need to be hooked, because it is assumed that the logic module doesn't already exist, and you can't hook to a nonexistent object, now can you?

On the other hand, messages or logic deletion actions must be told if the logic module suddenly disappears (for example when a character gets a venom cure from a shaman). The player hasn't disappeared at all, but the logic module that the timer needs has disappeared.

You could let the logic modules themselves hold containers of hooks, but as you saw from the previous chapter, I don't do that. There are a bunch of issues to consider, such as needing entities *and* their logic modules to keep pointers to the timer. While this doesn't produce substantial overhead, it does involve extra management and additional code. Another issue is creation time; you will often want to delay the installation of a logic module onto a character by a few minutes, but also set the removal time (give a character the logic in 10 minutes, and remove it in 20). There's a slight problem, however. If you do that, when you put the closing time into the game, the logic module you want closed *doesn't even exist yet!* Obviously there's no way to hook that, now is there?

So, instead of hooking the action to a logic module, I hook it to the entity in question instead, and whenever a logic module disappears, I call the ClearLogicHooks function. This function is rather tricky, because you need to search through all the entity's hooks, and find any that are directed toward the module you just deleted:

```
void ClearLogicHooks( const std::string& p_logic ) {
    hookitr itr = m_hooks.begin();
    while( itr != m_hooks.end() ) {
        hookitr current = itr++;
        if( (*current)->actionevent.actiontype == "messagelogic" ||
```

```
            (*current)->actionevent.actiontype == "dellogic"  ) {
            if( ParseWord( (*current)->actionevent.stringdata, 0 )
                == p_logic )
                (*current)->Unhook();
        }
    }
}
```

The code loops through (keeping track of the next iterator, just like the ClearHooks function), and if you find any messagelogic or dellogic actions, you know they're hooked to the current entity, but you don't know if they point the logic module you're deleting. So you need to call the BasicLib::ParseWord function and extract the name of the target module from the action's stringdata field.

If you determine that the action was intended for the module you're unhooking, you can tell the timer action to unhook itself.

Killing Arbitrary Hooks

At times, you'll need a way to kill a hook manually. For example, you're probably going to want to kill actions like "repeating poison damage" for players when they log off, so that they don't die while they're not even logged in.

> **NOTE**
>
> Remember from the last chapter that when sending messages to modules using the "messagelogic" action, the name of the module is stored in stringdata, but you can also store more string data after the name. This means that the name of the target module is the first word of the string, and that anything after that is just extra data to be interpreted by the module, so the ClearHooks function doesn't need it.

To do this, you need to be able to find a hook to an action and kill it manually. For this purpose, I've created the KillHook function, which searches for an action based on its type and its data string, and then kills it:

```
void KillHook( const std::string& p_act, const std::string& p_stringdata ) {
    using BasicLib::ParseWord;
    hookitr itr = HooksBegin();
    while( itr != HooksEnd() ) {
        hookitr current = itr++;

        // unhook the event if it matches the parameters
        if( (*current)->actionevent.actiontype == p_act &&
            ParseWord( (*current)->actionevent.stringdata, 0 ) ==
            p_stringdata )
            (*current)->Unhook();
    }
}
```

This functions loops through all the hooks and makes sure the action name and the first word of the data string match. For example, in a poison script, you might have a timed action with the action name do and the action string repeatpoison, so to kill that action you merely call the function like this:

```
KillHook( "do", "repeatpoison" );
```

The reason it compares only the first word of the data string is because you can add extra string parameters to the data string; say for example you want to tell the script how much to poison someone (for example, a damage level of 10), you could create the action using "repeatpoison 10" as the data string. Whoever is killing the action probably won't care about the extra parameter, so it doesn't bother comparing anything past the first word.

Hooking and Unhooking Timer Actions

From the previous section, you saw that making an entity unhook itself was a relatively painless process—all you need to do is call the Unhook function of timed action objects. Of course, before you begin to do any unhooking of the timed actions, you need to first hook them to their entities.

Hook Function

When you first create a new timed action object, you need to make it find every entity it is attached to and connect them together. This is accomplished with the TimedAction::Hook function, which I will show you only part of:

```
void TimedAction::Hook() {
    if( actionevent.actiontype == "attemptsay" ||
        actionevent.actiontype == "command" ||
        actionevent.actiontype == "attemptenterportal" ||
        actionevent.actiontype == "attempttransport" ||
        actionevent.actiontype == "transport" ||
        actionevent.actiontype == "destroycharacter" ) {
        character( actionevent.data1 ).AddHook( this );
    }
    else if( actionevent.actiontype == "attemptgetitem" ||
             actionevent.actiontype == "attemptdropitem" ) {
        character( actionevent.data1 ).AddHook( this );
        item( actionevent.data2 ).AddHook( this );
    }
```

This shows the function hooking up seven different types of actions; attempting to say something, sending a command, attempting to enter a portal, attempting to transport, forcing a transport, destroying a character, and attempting to get and drop items.

If you compare this code to the tables in the previous chapter, you'll see that those first five actions are the actions that use data1 as a character pointer and don't rely on any other entities.

The next two actions are the two actions that use data1 as a character, and data2 as an item.

From the code, you can see that they just add hooks to the required entities.

There's one other special case in the code: the logic actions. Here's the code for them:

```
else if( actionevent.actiontype == "messagelogic" ||
         actionevent.actiontype == "dellogic" ) {
    switch( actionevent.data1 ) {
    case CHARACTER:
        character( actionevent.data2 ).AddHook( this );
        break;
    case ITEM:
        item( actionevent.data2 ).AddHook( this );
        break;
    case ROOM:
        room( actionevent.data2 ).AddHook( this );
        break;
    case PORTAL:
        portal( actionevent.data2 ).AddHook( this );
        break;
    case REGION:
        region( actionevent.data2 ).AddHook( this );
        break;
    }
}
```

Remember from the last chapter that data1 represents the type of the entity whose logic module you are acting on—0 means a character, 1 an item, and so on. I've made an enumerated type that wraps around those values, so you can read the code more easily (that is, CHARACTER is an enum with a value of 0, and so on). The function determines what kind of entity you want to act on, and then enters a switch statement to add the hooks where needed.

The function has other cases to handle other kinds of actions, but they're all in a similar vein, so I don't show them here.

> **NOTE**
>
> In the code, I used *unnamed temporaries*—objects that are constructed, called, and then immediately discarded. I did this by calling the constructor character(id), and then adding the function call after that. It's just a trick used to make the code look a little cleaner; since I don't need to look the entities up anywhere else, it's acceptable.

Unhook Function

What is hooked must eventually be unhooked, so there is also an Unhook function. It's *very* similar to the hook function, but it works the other way around. Here's a sample:

```
void TimedAction::Unhook() {
    valid = false;

    if( actionevent.actiontype == "attemptsay" ||
        actionevent.actiontype == "command" ||
        actionevent.actiontype == "attemptenterportal" ||
        actionevent.actiontype == "attempttransport" ||
        actionevent.actiontype == "transport" ||
        actionevent.actiontype == "destroycharacter" ) {
        character( actionevent.data1 ).DelHook( this );
    }
```

The first part of the code sets the valid variable to false—once you unhook a timer action, it is assumed to be invalid and shouldn't be executed.

The next part of code looks very similar to the code I showed you before, but instead of hooking the timer action... you guessed it! It's unhooked instead!

Timer Registry

Now that you have timer actions, a timer object, and the ability to hook actions to entities, you need some way of actually storing these timer action events in the game. I have touched on this topic before, and I mentioned using a priority queue to store timer actions, which is by far the best method.

> **NOTE**
>
> Here's a little something to think about for the future. The action format, while somewhat flexible, is ultimately limited to four entity slots, which have variable meanings depending on the type of action. Because of this setup, you end up with the code shown here—it checks the name of every action to determine what kind of actors it has. In the future, you might want to consider an even more flexible format that will allow you to determine what kind of entity a field represents, instead of making the field meanings depend on a pre-coded action. This method allows you to add an infinite number of actions to the game—all with automatic hooking support. Oh well, you can't have everything. I'll probably implement something like this if I ever create a BetterMUD 2.0; or maybe I'll call it BestMUD.

A Queue for You

Let me go over the concept again. At one point in time, the game may have as many as a few dozen to a few thousand timer actions in memory (quite possibly more, if you wish). If you store all these actions in a list, you have to go through the list every time the game loop executes, and ask every single one of them, "Hey, can you execute yet?"

If you're an experienced programmer, there should be a little voice in your head saying, "*No! No! Bad programmer! No cookie for you!*" Going through *every timer action in the game* once per game loop is incredibly dumb and wasteful. This wastes so much time it's not even funny. There are other solutions, of course, such as checking the timers only once every second as the SimpleMUD did. That's a bad idea, too; you don't allow your game much flexibility by forcing actions to occur on one-second boundaries.

Think about something though; if you have an action that occurs an hour from now, why would you check it every loop from now until an hour from now? If you have an action that happens in 10 minutes, you know that the one that happens in 60 minutes happens after it. So you think, "Hey, why don't I check to see if the 10-minute action can be executed yet, and when it finally can, I'll start checking the 60-minute action."

Now here comes the priority queue. A priority queue (the STL implementation of priority_queue uses a special binary tree called a *heap*) is a queue that automatically arranges items by their number, and puts the item with the highest priority at the top. The game module has a priority queue for timer actions:

```
typedef std::priority_queue<
    TimedAction*,                    // datatype
    std::vector<TimedAction*>,       // container type
    TimedActionComp >                // comparison type
    timerqueue;                      // typedef name
timerqueue m_timerregistry;
```

One thing about STL is that it's very flexible. Of course, that flexibility comes at a price—ugly code. I almost laughed when I made the definition for a timer queue... that is one nasty piece of code right there.

Meaning of the Code

Let me break the priority queue code down for you. The first part of the code, std::priority_queue, obviously represents the STL heap data structure. I want this heap to store TimedAction*s, so that's used as the first template parameter.

The next template parameter is std::vector<TimedAction*>, which tells the queue to use a vector of TimedAction* as its underlying container. The priority_queue class is an *adaptor*, meaning that it only defines *how* to work on a container, not the actual container itself. So, inside of the queue, I've told it to use a vector of action pointers. You could theoretically use any random access container you want (STL has one other, the deque), but it's just easier and faster to use a vector.

The final template parameter is a comparison functor object, which sorts the timer actions inside the queue. For this, I needed to create my own custom `TimedActionComp` functor:

```
class TimedActionComp :
    public std::binary_function<TimedAction*, TimedAction*, bool> {
public:
    bool operator()( const first_argument_type& left,
                     const second_argument_type& right ) {
        return left->executiontime > right->executiontime;
    }
};
```

Ack! More ugly code! Unfortunately, you'll have to get used to this when working extensively with the STL. Basically, the function inherits from `std::binary_function`, which is a base class defined by STL that defines a functor that takes two parameters for `operator()`, and returns a specific type. For example, I used parameters `<TimedAction*, TimedAction*, bool>`, meaning that the functor's `operator()` takes two `TimedAction*`s as parameters, and returns a Boolean.

Here's an example of its use:

```
TimedActionComp comparetimes;
TimedAction* action1 = // whatever
TimedAction* action2 = // whatever
bool b = comaparetimes( action1, action2 );
```

The functor object essentially compares the two timed action pointers and returns a Boolean based on the function defined inside the functor.

If you look back at the functor definition, you can see that the function returns `true` whenever the execution time of the left parameter is greater than the execution time of the right parameter; essentially the function returns `true` when the left action occurs at a later time than the right.

If you don't pass in a custom functor comparison object, the `std::priority_queue` class uses, by default, `std::less<TimedAction*>`. The `std::less` functor is an object that returns `true` if the left `TimedAction*` is *less than* the right `TimedAction*`. Of course, this is not what we want to do, since the function will be comparing pointer values, so that anything that is at a higher memory address will end up at the top of the queue.

So the TimedActionComp class compares two pointers of timed action object and makes it look as if any actions that occur at a later time are *less than* objects that occur at an earlier time.

Eventually this means that the action that must be executed next is *always* at the top of the priority queue, and anything else below it is executed at a later time. This means that for any given game loop, you only need to check one timer object, and if it isn't time for that top object to execute yet, you know it's not time for any other objects to execute yet!

Adding Timed Actions

Now whenever you need to add a new timed action to the game, all you need to do is call the `AddTimedAction` class with a pointer to a new timed action, and the game manages that action from now on.

Here's the function:

```
void Game::AddTimedAction( TimedAction* p_action ) {
    m_timerregistry.push( p_action );
    p_action->Hook();
}
```

The function pushes the new action onto the registry, and then hooks the action to all its actors. You should always pass *new* pointers to timed actions into this function; once the game module has control over a timed object, it takes care of the object and deletes it automatically when it's finished with it.

To Be or Not to Be

Earlier I told you all about hooks, and how entities need to tell the timed actions that they are hooked into to kill themselves when the entity itself dies. But there's a problem: you can't remove timers from the timer registry. The `std::priority_queue` class has absolutely no way to remove anything from the queue except the very top item, so deleting the timer action when it gets unhooked is almost impossible. Sure, you might be able to extract everything, discard the deleted action, and then re-insert everything, but that is just an incredible mess, and a waste of time to boot.

This is where the `valid` field of a `TimedAction` becomes useful. Whenever you tell an action to unhook itself, that means it's no longer a valid action, so the `valid` Boolean is set to `false`. Later on, when the game loop gets around to executing that action, it sees that it's no longer valid, so it won't bother executing the action; it deletes it instead.

Executing Timed Actions

The final part of the timer system is actually executing the actions, which is a very simple process:

```
void Game::ExecuteLoop() {
    BasicLib::sint64 t = GetTime();         // get time
    while( m_timerregistry.size() > 0 &&    // loop while there are timers
           m_timerregistry.top()->executiontime <= t ) {  // is it time yet?
        TimedAction* a = m_timerregistry.top();  // get the action
        m_timerregistry.pop();                   // pop off the action
        if( a->valid ) {                         // make sure it's valid
            try {
            a->Unhook();                         // unhook it
            DoAction( a->actionevent );          // perform the action
            }   catch( ... ) {}
        }
```

```
        delete a;                              // delete the action
    }
}
```

The function starts by retrieving the current system time, so that it doesn't have to perform multiple time lookups, which are usually expensive operations (time lookups typically use a hardware device that isn't attached to the CPU directly).

The while-loop loops through the timer registry while there are timers available (it could be empty), and the top timer has an execution time that is less than or equal to the current game time.

If an action needs to be executed, a pointer is retrieved from the top of the queue, and the pointer is popped off the queue. From this point forward, the game assumes that the action has been handled, so the queue no longer needs to keep a reference to it.

Now the action is checked to see if it's valid, and if so, the action is unhooked and executed.

Once the execution is completed, the timer action itself is deleted, and the loop continues.

The ExecuteLoop function will be called once per loop inside the main function, which I'll get to later in this chapter.

> **NOTE**
>
> **Dealing with dynamic memory here is a very risky business. Either the** Unhook **or the** DoAction **functions may throw exceptions, and if they do, you automatically lose a pointer to** a, **meaning you've got a** TimedAction **object floating in memory with nothing pointing to it. This can be a big problem, since the game** *should* **keep running and actions will fail to perform, and thus the game catches exceptions and keeps running. If you have enough thrown exceptions while performing timer actions (through faulty scripts, or whatever), you'll end up with a large memory leak. That's why whenever an exception is thrown, it is caught.**

Timed Action Helpers

You shouldn't really be creating new TimedAction objects on your own and passing them into AddTimedAction. Instead, you should rely on the four helper functions I've provided:

```
void AddActionRelative( BasicLib::sint64 p_time, const Action& p_action );
void AddActionAbsolute( BasicLib::sint64 p_time, const Action& p_action );

void AddActionRelative(
    BasicLib::sint64 p_time,
    const std::string& p_act,
    entityid p_data1 = 0,
    entityid p_data2 = 0,
    entityid p_data3 = 0,
    entityid p_data4 = 0,
    const std::string& p_data = "" );
void AddActionAbsolute(
```

```
    BasicLib::sint64 p_time,
    const std::string& p_act,
    entityid p_data1 = 0,
    entityid p_data2 = 0,
    entityid p_data3 = 0,
    entityid p_data4 = 0,
    const std::string& p_data = "" );
```

The first two functions allow passing in an action object directly, and the second two allow passing in a variable number of parameters, which will be used to create a new action.

Basically, the functions allow you to create an action at an *absolute time* or a *relative time*. An absolute time means that you're going to execute the action at a time relative to 0; if you specify AddActionAbsolute(10000, act), you're telling the game to execute an action at exactly 10 seconds from the time the game first started. As you can imagine, this function is somewhat limiting, due to the fact that you really can't assume things are going to happen at any specific time.

On the other hand, you'll often want to "add an action, which will execute X minutes from now," and this is the purpose of the AddActionRelative functions. I'll show you the functions that take actual Action objects as their parameters:

```
void AddActionRelative( BasicLib::sint64 p_time, const Action& p_action ) {
    AddTimedAction( new TimedAction( p_time + GetTime(), p_action ) );
}
void AddActionAbsolute( BasicLib::sint64 p_time, const Action& p_action ) {
    AddTimedAction( new TimedAction( p_time, p_action ) );
}
```

The relative version takes the time you passed in and adds the current time to it; the absolute version simply passes the time directly into a new TimedAction object.

Database Functions

The game module has a bunch of functions related to database management. They can be separated into a few categories.

Loading Functions

The first of the database management functions are the loading functions:

```
void LoadAll();
void LoadTimers();
void ReloadItemTemplates( const std::string& p_file );
void ReloadCharacterTemplates( const std::string& p_file );
void ReloadRegion( const std::string& p_name );
void ReloadCommandScript(
    const std::string& p_name,
    SCRIPTRELOADMODE p_mode );
```

```
void ReloadLogicScript(
    const std::string& p_name,
    SCRIPTRELOADMODE p_mode );
```

Some of these functions are self explanatory, such as the `LoadAll` and `LoadTimers` functions, which respectively load *everything* from disk, or just the timers. The other functions load specific types of items from a given file; they wrap around the database classes, so I won't show you the function definitions. However, I will show you how to use them:

```
ReloadItemTemplates( "newitems" );
ReloadCharacterTemplates( "newcharacters" );
ReloadRegion( "SomeArea" );
ReloadCommandScript( "newcommands" );
ReloadLogicScript( "characters.newcharacterlogic" );
```

The previous function calls load entities from the following files:

> data/templates/items/newitems.data
>
> data/templates/characters/newcharacters.data
>
> data/regions/SomeArea/
>
> data/commands/newcommands.py
>
> data/logics/characters/newcharacterlogic.py

The first two are simple; they simply load (or reload) all template entities within a specific file. The function automatically assumes it exists within the /data/templates/items or /data/templates/characters directory.

The region function loads all five standard region files (items.data, characters.data, region.data, rooms.data, and portals.data) from the directory /data/regions/SomeArea.

The last two are Python scripts, which you'll learn about in Chapters 17 and 18. Due to the way the logic databases are set up, you must specify what kind of logic you're loading, such as "character.logic" to load a character logic module, or "items.logic" to load an extra item logic.

Saving Functions

There are a few saving functions as well:

```
void SaveAll();
void SavePlayers();
void SaveRegion( entityid p_region );
void SaveTimers();
```

These functions do the following:

> Save the whole game to disk
>
> Save all players to disk
>
> Save a particular region to disk
>
> Save all the timer objects to disk

Other Functions

The other function related to databases is the `Cleanup` function:

```
void Cleanup();
```

This simply tells all the volatile databases (characters and items) to clean up any entities that have been deleted:

```
void Game::Cleanup() {
    ItemDB.Cleanup();
    CharacterDB.Cleanup();
}
```

You should remember database cleanups from Chapter 12.

Timer Disk Functions

When you shut down the MUD, there's a bunch of timed action objects in memory—events that are important to the game, and thus must be written to disk. Otherwise, the next time the game loads, a number of things won't work properly, since you'll start up with no event objects.

The BetterMUD takes care of loading and saving timer objects by using the `Load` and `Save` functions of the `TimedAction` class. Let me show you the loader first:

```
void Game::LoadTimers() {
    std::ifstream timerfile( "data/timers/timers.data", std::ios::binary );
    std::string temp;
    timerfile >> std::ws;
    if( timerfile.good() ) {        // make sure file exists
        timerfile >> temp;
        BasicLib::sint64 t;
        BasicLib::extract( timerfile, t );   // load the time
        m_gametime.Reset( t );               // set the time

        timerfile >> std::ws;
        while( timerfile.good() ) {           // load each timer now
            TimedAction* a = new TimedAction;
            a->Load( timerfile );
            timerfile >> std::ws;
            AddTimedAction( a );
        }
    }
}
```

The function tries to open up the file, and load in a game time, nearly as it did in the SimpleMUD.

Once the function does that, it creates new timed action objects, loads them from the disk, and sends them off to the timer registry.

The opposite of loading is saving, of course:

```
void Game::SaveTimers() {
    std::ofstream timerfile( "data/timers/timers.data", std::ios::binary );

    timerfile << "[GAMETIME]                 ";
    BasicLib::insert( timerfile, GetTime() );
    timerfile << "\n\n";

    timerqueue temp( m_timerregistry );   // copy queue
    while( temp.size() ) {                 // go through each action
        TimedAction* a = temp.top();
        temp.pop();
        a->Save( timerfile );
        timerfile << "\n";
    }
}
```

This time the function saves the game time out to data/timers/timers.data, and then it writes out everything in the timer event queue.

This is the tricky part, however. The only way to get the contents of a priority queue is to pop them all out and write them. This isn't a problem if you're shutting down the server, but eventually, you'll need to save the actions while the game is running. You could pop them all out, write them, and then push them all back into the queue, but that requires a lot of management. Instead of doing that, I create a copy of the queue, named temp, go through the copy, and pop everything out of it. Since I'm dealing with pointers, there's really no problem with abandoning the pointers.

NOTE

It doesn't really matter what superglue does, but if you're interested, I've included the script on the CD. It's a simple Python script that glues a user to a room for 20 seconds, so that he can't move around. It's pretty funny.

So, the file that is used in conjunction with the timer's Load and Save functions would look something like this:

```
[GAMETIME]           205076603
[TIMER]
    [TIME]           205094154
    [NAME]           messagelogic
    [DATA1]          0
    [DATA2]          1
    [DATA3]          0
    [DATA4]          0
    [STRING]         superglue remove
[/TIMER]
```

This depicts a simple timer action trying to message a logic module that I used for testing: superglue!

The Meat of the Game

The final area that the game module involves is controlling the physical side of the game. It moves things around, deletes them, and tells everyone about the events that happened in the game.

In the previous chapter, I showed you all the actions, and in Chapters 12 and 13, I showed you the entity classes and what you can do with them. Now, I can finally show you how to move things around.

Considerations

The Game.cpp file is by far the largest file in the BetterMUD's C++ core, the only one surpassing 1,000 lines of code.

The reason for this is that there are quite a few physical actions that must be taken care of, and every one of them needs to follow a rigorous process.

In retrospect, I wish I could have designed an even more flexible system of entities, in which the type of the entity is variable. This could become quite useful later on if you ever need to transmogrify items from one type into another, like people turning into stone items, or the other way around. Now, the scripting engine can simulate things like that, but a more flexible core system could have that ability built-in. Another benefit of a flexible system like that is less code clutter.

For the BetterMUD, you'll see that there are three functions for moving items around: player to player, player to room, and room to player. The problem is that these functions all have the same basic purpose—to transfer the ownership of an entity from one entity to another. In a system that treated all entities in the same way, you could conceivably turn these three functions into a single function. I want you to be thinking about these ideas for the future; the BetterMUD isn't perfect, but it's much better than the SimpleMUD.

Transaction Processes

Every physical transaction in the game has a certain general process to follow when it is executed. I've mentioned this before, but let me restate the full process so it's easier to see:

1. Retrieve actor entities from databases.
2. Perform an integrity check.
3. Ask permission to perform the transaction.
4. Perform the physical movement of the actors.
5. Notify every actor involved that the transaction occurred.
6. Clean up (optional).

Sample Transaction Process

Let me begin by showing you the transaction process of the "attempttransport" game action, which is simpler than most others, since it doesn't involve portals.

Retrieving the Actors

Here is the process through which the game retrieves the actors:

1. Retrieve the character who is transporting.
2. Retrieve the room the character is leaving.
3. Retrieve the room the character is entering.
4. Retrieve the region the character is leaving.
5. Retrieve the region the character is entering (may be the same as 4).
6. Figure out if the character is changing regions.

This simple process involves looking up five distinct entities: a character, two rooms, and one or two regions, depending on if the character is switching regions or not. If any of these database lookups fail, they throw an exception. Obviously if you can't look them up, something really bad has happened, because one of the entities in the equation just doesn't exist. At this point, you should simply give up.

> **NOTE**
>
> The code is part of the Transport helper function, which is not callable outside the Game class. I'll show you a complete listing of the helper functions after this example.

There's absolutely no way you can possibly try to move the character if any of the actors are missing in action. So the action throws an exception, and whatever is calling the action catches the exception and cleans up the action.

Here's the accompanying code:

```
void Game::Transport(
        entityid p_character,          // character who left
        entityid p_room )              // room id
{
    character c( p_character );
    room oldroom( c.Room() );
    room newroom( p_room );
    region oldreg( oldroom.Region() );
    region newreg( newroom.Region() );
    bool changeregion = oldroom.Region() != newroom.Region();
```

Nothing here is substantially new; all the databases are consulted for their entities, and the region database may be consulted twice, but I'm not terribly concerned about that since I know it's a vector database with almost instant lookups.

Integrity Checking

The transport transaction doesn't need to do any integrity checking, since it is assumed that you can transport any character from one room to another. You'll see integrity checking later on when I show you item movement; those transactions require that the actors be within the same room.

Asking Permission

The next part of the process asks permission of everyone involved to see if the character can be transported. Here's the exact process:

1. Ask the region in which the character is located if he can leave.
2. Ask the new region if the character can enter.
3. Ask the character if he can leave the region he's in.
4. Ask the character if he can enter the new region.
5. Ask the room in which the character is located if the character can leave.
6. Ask in the new room if the character can enter.
7. Ask the character if he can leave the room he's in.
8. Ask the character if he can enter the new room.

Most of the time the character isn't switching regions, so the first four queries aren't executed, and only 5 through 8 are queried. That's still a high number of different permissions to ask, however.

If any of the queries replies negatively, the entire action is abandoned, and the function returns. This means that any one of the actors involved can deny the movement of a character from one room to another. An Elven region may have a magical spell cast on it that doesn't allow Dwarves into the region at all; or perhaps a character is trapped in a special region that won't allow him to be transported out. Maybe your character has a condition that won't allow him to walk. Whatever the reason, the key is that *any* of the actors involved can deny a character the ability to enter or leave.

> **NOTE**
>
> Because of the fact that any entity can deny a built-in action, you should try to keep your denial scripts sparse. If you have too many denial scripts, your players might encounter some unexpected behavior when they try moving from one place to another, yet your scripts just don't allow it, even if they technically should be able to move.

Here's the code to ask permissions:

```
if( changeregion ) {
    if( oldreg.DoAction( "canleaveregion", p_character, oldreg.ID() ) == 1 )
        return;
    if( newreg.DoAction( "canenterregion", p_character, newreg.ID() ) == 1 )
        return;
```

```
    if( c.DoAction( "canleaveregion", p_character, oldreg.ID() ) == 1 )
        return;
    if( c.DoAction( "canenterregion", p_character, newreg.ID() ) == 1 )
        return;
}
if( oldroom.DoAction( "canleaveroom", p_character, oldroom.ID() ) == 1 )
    return;
if( newroom.DoAction( "canenterroom", p_character, newroom.ID() ) == 1 )
    return;
if( c.DoAction( "canleaveroom", p_character, oldroom.ID() ) == 1 )
    return;
if( c.DoAction( "canenterroom", p_character, newroom.ID() ) == 1 )
    return;
```

In the previous chapter, I told you about logic collections, and how they contain 0 or more logic modules. When you type something like c.DoAction( ), you're telling the character to send an action to its logic collection.

The collection then tries sending the action to every logic module it contains, but if any of them returns a non-zero value, it stops executing them and returns the result right away. Almost all the query actions must return one of two values:

> 0—Operation is allowed

> 1—Operation is denied

I say almost, because there is one query that does just the opposite: the custom "query" action.

The physical part of the game is like a country's constitution; it defines all the rights of entities in the game. By default, entities can do anything the game core defines; characters can get, drop, and give items; characters can move around, say things, and so on.

NOTE

The built-in queries are designed to be called only when a character is serious about entering. The query assumes that the character tries to perform the action. In other words, the query assumes that the character does not ask to perform an action and then decide not to perform it. Because of this, when an actor denies an action, such as a force field denying a player entrance to a room, the force-field script must give the player an error message. This is an important element in making your game more variable. Instead of making a command that tries to move a character from room to room and print generic statements such as, You cannot enter this portal, you allow the force field to give a specific message, such as, "You are burned badly by walking into the force field!" Then you take off a few hitpoints if you like.

These rights must be specifically taken away in specific instances. To understand this, think of the fact that shouting "fire" in a crowded theatre is illegal, and yet we still have freedom of speech in the USA.

On the other hand, you can define new actions in the game, but characters don't have the right to perform those actions by default. For example, characters don't have the right to kill another person; they must have scripts that specifically allow them to kill. You'll see how this works in more detail in Chapter 18.

So whenever a character's built-in action queries return 1, that means he must have the right to perform that action removed, and the function should return without doing anything.

Physical Movement

Now you're ready to physically move the character from one room to another. This is a very easy process:

1. Remove the character from the region he's in.
2. Set a new region for the character.
3. Add the character to the new region.
4. Remove the character from the former room.
5. Set the new room of the character.
6. Add the character to the new room.

The process simply uses the modifier functions you can find within the entity classes you learned about in Chapters 12 and 13:

```
if( changeregion ) {
    oldreg.DelCharacter( p_character );
    c.SetRegion( newreg.ID() );
    newreg.AddCharacter( p_character );
}
oldroom.DelCharacter( p_character );
c.SetRoom( newroom.ID() );
newroom.AddCharacter( p_character );
```

At this point, the objects have been physically moved, and no matter what happens from now on, the actual transaction has been completed.

Notifications

Of course, there's still more work. Now that you've physically moved the character, you must inform everyone involved:

1. Tell the region that the character left.
2. Tell the character that he left the region.
3. Tell the room that the character left.
4. Tell the character that he left the room.

5. Tell all characters in the room that the character left.
6. Tell all items in the room that the character left.
7. Tell the new region that the character entered.
8. Tell the character that he entered the new region.
9. Tell the new room that the character has entered.
10. Tell all characters in the new room that the character has entered.
11. Tell all items in the new room that the character has entered.

You should note several items in this listing. The first is that notifications 1, 2, 7, and 8 are optional, and occur only when the user is changing regions. Although you could conceivably want regions to know whenever someone moves between rooms inside the same region, I honestly couldn't find much justification for it.

You may think there's a step missing. "But you never told the character that he entered the new room!" Actually, I did, but it's very subtle. In step 10, when I tell all the characters in the new room that someone entered, that includes the character that was just transported. This is because when the code is executed, the character has already been moved into the new room.

Likewise, when a room the character was in is told about the character leaving, it must assume that the character has already left, and shouldn't go looking for him.

Here's the code to accomplish this:

```
if( changeregion ) {
    oldreg.DoAction( "leaveregion", p_character, oldreg.ID() );
    c.DoAction( "leaveregion", p_character, oldreg.ID() );
}
oldroom.DoAction( "leaveroom", p_character, 0 );
c.DoAction( "leaveroom", p_character, 0 );
ActionRoomCharacters( Action( "leaveroom", p_character, 0 ), c.Room() );
ActionRoomItems( Action( "leaveroom", p_character, 0 ), c.Room() );

if( changeregion ) {
    newreg.DoAction( "enterregion", p_character, newreg.ID() );
    c.DoAction( "enterregion", p_character, newreg.ID() );
}
newroom.DoAction( "enterroom", p_character, 0 );
ActionRoomCharacters( Action( "enterroom", p_character, 0 ), c.Room() );
ActionRoomItems( Action( "enterroom", p_character, 0 ), c.Room() );
```

The lines roughly correspond to the steps I previously outlined. The only special part of this code is the call to ActionRoomCharacters and ActionRoomItems. These are two helper functions that automatically loop through every character or item in a given room, and send them an action. They're simple loops, so I'm sure you'd be bored out of your mind if I showed them to you; I made them helper functions simply because I need to call them often, and I'd prefer a one-line function call over pasting the same 11-line loop code in multiple places.

Cleanup

I mentioned before that the final step in a transaction is cleanup, but there is no cleanup step for transports. Everything that's needed to be done has already been done. The only transactions that need cleanups are the item-movement actions, and I'll show you an example of that later on.

Analysis

The code for the previous transaction is fairly lengthy, but it follows a well-defined process, so it's not that difficult to follow. The only downside is that you need to remember which actions send which notifications, and from which actors the actions need to ask permissions. Otherwise, the code is fairly straightforward.

Earlier in this section, I discussed a more flexible system in which you could simply define an ownership hierarchy between entities of arbitrary types. Instead of saying explicitly "characters can own items, rooms can own characters, regions can own rooms," and so forth, you might want to simply define the concept of general ownership. I mentioned the fact that you could simplify the concepts of "give," "get," and "drop" into one concept: "transfer item from a to b."

Why not take it one step further? Isn't moving a character from one room to the next similar to moving an item from a player to the ground? Couldn't you simply define one function, in which an entity type would automatically know what kinds of entities it notifies, and then you could simply code one function to move an entity's ownership from one place to another? That way, you could end up with just one function to handle characters moving around, items moving around, or even rooms and portals being moved around—a function that the BetterMUD doesn't support. Just some things to ponder when you go off and make TheBestInTheWorldMUD.

Item Transaction Example

I won't show you all the transactions because much of the information would be redundant, but I do want to show you another example of a transaction—an item transaction. This transaction moves an item from a room into a player's inventory.

Database Lookups

Here's the part of the code for an item transaction that performs the database lookups:

```
void Game::GetItem(
    entityid p_character,          // character who wants item
    entityid p_item,               // item
    entityid p_quantity )          // optional quantity
{
    character c( p_character );
    item i( p_item );
    room r( c.Room() );
    region reg( r.Region() );
```

Nothing special here, the character, room, item, and region are all retrieved.

Integrity Checking

This step wasn't needed for transporting a player from one place to another, but it is required for getting an item.

For a character to gain ownership over an item, the item *must* be within the same room. Trying to get an item that is in a different room from the character doesn't really make any physical sense, so we need to check for that first.

In addition, we also need to check to make sure that the character is trying to pick up a valid quantity of a quantity object. This ensures that a character doesn't get 100 gold coins, when there are only 20 in the room, leaving the game to think that the room now has -80 coins. While that may be humorous to some, it's obviously something that you don't want happening *anywhere* in the game.

Here's the code:

```
if( i.Room() != c.Room() || i.Region() == 0 )
    throw Exception(
        "Character " + c.Name() + " tried picking up item " + i.Name() +
        " but they are not in the same room." );

if( i.IsQuantity() && p_quantity < 1 ) {
    c.DoAction( "error", 0, 0, 0, 0,
        "You can't get " + BasicLib::tostring( p_quantity ) +
        " of those, it's just not physically possible! FOOL!" );
    return;
}

if( i.IsQuantity() && p_quantity > i.GetQuantity() ) {
    c.DoAction( "error", 0, 0, 0, 0,
        "You can't get " + BasicLib::tostring( p_quantity ) +
        ", there are only " + BasicLib::tostring( i.GetQuantity() ) + "!" );
    return;
}
```

Usually the command that is making a player pick up items must ensure that the player gets the appropriate quantity, but you can never assume that the scripts will be playing nicely with the game. Someone, through error or malicious intent, may make a script that tries to get too many or too little of a quantity object (such as a negative number), so when this happens, you need to tell the offending character that an error has occurred.

Asking Permission

Asking permission for item movement is a simple process:

```
if( i.DoAction( "cangetitem", p_character, p_item, p_quantity ) == 1 )
    return;
```

```
if( r.DoAction( "cangetitem", p_character, p_item, p_quantity ) == 1 )
    return;
if( reg.DoAction( "cangetitem", p_character, p_item, p_quantity ) == 1 )
    return;
if( c.DoAction( "cangetitem", p_character, p_item, p_quantity ) == 1 )
    return;
```

This code simply asks the item, the room, the region, and the character if the item can be retrieved. Any one of these actors can deny it, and this makes your game pretty flexible.

Physical Movement

The physical movement of item entities is a tad more complex than the movement of characters, because items can be "quantities." One object could be a "pile of 10 coins," of which a player may only want to grab five, and let his buddy get the other five.

In this case, you're going to have to spawn a completely new item to represent one pile of five, and subtract five from the original pile.

Here's the first part of the code that handles quantity objects:

```
entityid newitemid = 0;
if( i.IsQuantity() && p_quantity != i.GetQuantity() ) {
    newitemid = ItemDB.generate( i.TemplateID() );      // generate new item
    item( newitemid ).SetQuantity( p_quantity );        // set quantity
    i.SetQuantity( i.GetQuantity() - p_quantity );       // reset old quantity
}
```

This checks to see if the item is a quantity object, and if so, checks to see if the desired quantity is different from the existing quantity.

If the quantities are the same (meaning the player wants all ten coins), you don't have a problem, and you can simply move the item as normal.

On the other hand, you'll need to generate a brand new object to represent partial quantities, which is precisely what this part of the function does.

A new item is spawned, and its quantity is set to the requested quantity. At the same time, the previous item has its quantity reduced by the requested amount.

On the other hand, if you're transferring a normal object, or a whole quantity object, this code is executed instead:

```
else {
    r.DelItem( p_item );
    reg.DelItem( p_item );
    newitemid = i.ID();
}
```

This simply deletes the item from the room and region, and sets newitemid to the ID of the item being transferred.

The final physical act is now processed:

```
item newitem( newitemid );
newitem.SetRoom( c.ID() );
newitem.SetRegion( 0 );
c.AddItem( newitem.ID() );
```

The `newitem` accessor now points to the item that is being moved (either the normal item, or a new quantity item), sets its room and its ID, and then adds it to the character.

Notifications

Next up is the notification code, whereby everyone is told about the movement:

```
r.DoAction( "getitem", p_character, newitemid, p_quantity );
newitem.DoAction( "getitem", p_character, newitemid, p_quantity );
ActionRoomCharacters( Action( "getitem", p_character, newitemid,
                              p_quantity ), c.Room() );
ActionRoomItems( Action( "getitem", p_character, newitemid,
                         p_quantity ), c.Room() );
```

The room is told an item left, the item is told that it left, all the characters in the room are told that the item was retrieved, and so are all the items.

Cleanup

Unlike moving characters, getting items has a cleanup phase. This is needed whenever you move a quantity object onto a player; the game needs to see if you have any duplicate quantity items (that is, "Pile of ten coins" and "Pile of 20 coins"), and then the game combines them into one quantity object ("Pile of 30 coins").

```
if( newitem.IsQuantity() )
    DoJoinQuantities( CharacterDB.get( c.ID() ), newitemid );
```

The code simply calls the `DoJoinQuantities` function on an entity that holds items, to see if any existing quantity items match the type of the new quantity item.

DoJoinQuantities

The `DoJoinQuantities` function is a templated helper function that searches through any entity that holds items and tries to join together a given quantity item.

```
template< typename entity >
void DoJoinQuantities( entity& p_e, entityid p_id ) {
    item keep( p_id );          // the item that is being kept

    // go through the items, finding any to merge with "keep":
    typename entity::itemitr itr = p_e.ItemsBegin();
    while( itr != p_e.ItemsEnd() ) {
        typename entity::itemitr current = itr++;
        if( *current != keep.ID() ) { // make sure current item is not "keep"
```

```
            item check( *current );
            if( check.TemplateID() == keep.TemplateID() ) { // matching types
                keep.SetQuantity( keep.GetQuantity() + check.GetQuantity() );
                DeleteItem( check.ID() );
            }
        }
    }
}
```

You pass in two values; a reference to an entity that can hold items, and the ID of the item you want others to merge into (keep). The loop begins and goes through every item the entity is holding. The loop must ensure that you don't accidentally merge the keep item with itself, so that's the reason for the *current != keep.ID() check.

If the item is fair game, you need to compare template IDs. Two "Pile of X coins" objects have two different IDs, but their *template* IDs should be the same, since they are both the same type of object. If they are the same, you need to merge them together, by setting the quantity of the item you want to keep and deleting the previous item by calling the DeleteItem helper function.

CAUTION

Entities are *not* told when quantity items are merged or destroyed by merging. Because of this, it's really not a good idea to perform clever or complex operations with scripts on quantity items; they exist mainly to support the need of large amounts of currency-type objects in the game. The bottom line is this: If you have a quantity item with a specific ID at one point in time, you should *never* assume you'll have that same item later on; the quantity item may have been merged with a different object of the same type.

Example of a Transaction Destroying Entities

Before going on to more interesting things, I want to show you the last transaction example—the "destroyitem" transaction in which an item is literally deleted from the game.

In the game, the transaction to destroy an entity is a special case, and the transaction should be called only sparingly. Therefore it is assumed that whenever an item is being destroyed, it is allowable.

In other words, there is no condition-check stage in this transaction; items can't tell the game, "No, please don't delete me! I deserve to LIVE!" because there are many times when a stubborn item that refuses to be destroyed screws up the logic of other actions.

Here's the code, which is pretty simple:

```
void Game::DestroyItem( entityid p_item ) {
    item i( p_item );
    if( i.Region() == 0 ) {
        character c( i.Room() );
        c.DoAction( "destroyitem", p_item );
        i.DoAction( "destroyitem", p_item );
```

```
    }
    else {
        room r( i.Room() );
        region reg( i.Region() );
        reg.DoAction( "destroyitem", p_item );
        r.DoAction( "destroyitem", p_item );
        i.DoAction( "destroyitem", p_item );
    }
    DeleteItem( p_item );
}
```

Remember, whenever an item's region is 0, it is assumed to be carried by a character.

So if the item is being carried by a character or in a room, the function must tell the actors. If it's being carried, the character and the item are both told that the entity has been destroyed; otherwise it is lying on the floor in a room somewhere, and the region, room, and item are told it's been destroyed.

Finally, the DeleteItem helper is called.

DeleteItem

The DeleteItem function is just a simple helper that removes an item from its room and region and notifies the item database to delete the item:

```
void Game::DeleteItem( entityid p_item ) {
    item i( p_item );
    if( i.Region() ) {
        region reg( i.Region() );
        reg.DelItem( p_item );
        room r( i.Room() );
        r.DelItem( p_item );
    }
    else {
        character c( i.Room() );
        c.DelItem( p_item );
    }

    i.SetRoom( 0 );
    i.SetRegion( 0 );
    i.ClearHooks();
    ItemDB.erase( p_item );
}
```

Again, the function must figure out if an item is being carried by a character or lying on the ground in a room, and depending on that information, the function either deletes itself from its character, or its room and region.

The last part of code clears room and region to 0, clears the item's hooks, and finally tells the item database to erase the item (you saw how this worked in Chapter 13).

Deleting Characters

Deleting characters resembles the process of deleting items, with one significant difference: Characters force all their items into the room when they are destroyed. The room won't be consulted on whether it wants the items or not, because that kind of a thing might end up giving you *zombie items*. Zombies are items that exist within the game, aren't part of any room or character, but haven't been deleted. Here's the snippet of code that drops all of the items on a character (within the DeleteCharacter helper function):

```
c.BeginItem();
while( c.IsValidItem() ) {
    item i( c.CurrentItem() );
    r.AddItem( i.ID() );
    reg.AddItem( i.ID() );
    i.SetRoom( r.ID() );
    i.SetRegion( reg.ID() );
    r.DoAction( "dropitem", p_character, i.ID(), i.GetQuantity() );
    reg.DoAction( "dropitem", p_character, i.ID(), i.GetQuantity() );
    c.NextItem();
}
```

The item is added to the room, its positional ID is rearranged, and then the room and the region are told that the item was dropped. This ensures that any items carried by a character when it dies become part of the game, and are not lost.

Other Transactions

There are numerous other transactions included in the game module, most of which are very similar to the code I've already shown you. Here's a listing of the helper functions that execute the transactions:

```
void DoCommand(
    entityid p_player,              // player doing command
    const std::string& p_command ); // command being executed

void Say(
    entityid p_player,              // character saying something
    const std::string& p_text );    // text being said

void Login(
    entityid p_id );                // the ID of the character

void Logout(
```

```
            entityid p_id );                     // the ID of the character

    void EnterPortal(
        entityid p_character,                    // character who entered
        entityid p_portal );                     // portal entered from

    void Transport(
        entityid p_character,                    // character who left
        entityid p_room );                       // room id

    void ForceTransport(
        entityid p_character,                    // character who left
        entityid p_room );                       // room id

    void GetItem(
        entityid p_character,                    // character who wants item
        entityid p_item,                         // item
        entityid p_quantity );                   // optional quantity

    void DropItem(
        entityid p_character,                    // character who drops item
        entityid p_item,                         // item
        entityid p_quantity );                   // optional quantity

    void GiveItem(
        entityid p_giver,                        // character who is giving
        entityid p_receiver,                     // character who is getting
        entityid p_item,                         // item
        entityid p_quantity );                   // optional quantity

    void SpawnItem(
        entityid p_itemtemplate,                 // template of item
        entityid p_location,                     // location to put it
        entityid p_player,                       // player or room?
        entityid p_quantity );                   // optional quantity

    void DestroyItem( entityid p_item );         // item to destroy
    void DestroyCharacter( entityid p_item );    // character to destroy

    void SpawnCharacter(
        entityid p_chartemplate,                 // template of character
        entityid p_location );                   // location to put it

    void LogicAction( const Action& p_act );
    void AddLogic( const Action& p_act );
    void DelLogic( const Action& p_act );
```

You can see that every action maintains the same parameters as those defined by the actions in the previous chapter. For example, the "attemptgetitem" action defines the `data1`, `data2`, and `data3` values of the `Action` object as the character, the item, and the quantity desired. The `GetItem` function takes those same parameters.

Calling the Actions

The last part of this topic is the `DoAction` function, which accepts an `Action` object and figures out which helper function to call. Here's a sample. (I've snipped most of it out for brevity.)

```
void Game::DoAction( const Action& p_action ) {
    if( p_action.actiontype == "chat" ||
        p_action.actiontype == "announce" )
        ActionRealmPlayers( p_action );
    else if( p_action.actiontype == "vision"  )
        ActionRoomCharacters( p_action, p_action.data1 );
    else if( p_action.actiontype == "enterrealm" )
        Login( p_action.data1 );
    else if( p_action.actiontype == "leaverealm" )
        Logout( p_action.data1 );
    else if( p_action.actiontype == "attemptsay" )
        Say( p_action.data1, p_action.stringdata );
    else if( p_action.actiontype == "command" )
        DoCommand( p_action.data1, p_action.stringdata );
    else if( p_action.actiontype == "attemptenterportal" )
        EnterPortal( p_action.data1, p_action.data2 );
... <SNIP> ...
}
```

For each action type, a matching helper function is called to handle the event. Some actions are so simple that they don't even need helpers, such as the "chat" and "announce" actions; they're simply passed on to every player in the realm.

Commands

The final topic I want to brush on in this chapter is the execution of command objects, which is a special kind of action. I briefly introduced you to commands in the previous chapter, and now I'm going to show you the code that executes commands.

The first thing the command handler needs to do is grab the character that executed the command, and parse the command around a little bit:

```
void Game::DoCommand(
    entityid p_player,                   // player doing command
    const std::string& p_command )  // command being executed
{
    Character& c = CharacterDB.get( p_player );
```

```
std::string full = p_command;
if( full == "/" )
    full = c.LastCommand();           // repeat last command
else
    c.SetLastCommand( full );         // set last command
std::string command = BasicLib::ParseWord( full, 0 );
std::string args = BasicLib::RemoveWord( full, 0 );
```

Just as with the SimpleMUD, you can repeat your last command by using the / key; so your last command is loaded if you type /; if you don't type /, your last command is reset to whatever you typed.

After the if/else clause is executed, full contains the string you want to execute. The strings command and args are filled in with the first word of the string you want to execute, and the rest of the string. So if you typed "/go north", command would hold "/go", and args would hold "north".

The next part of the code determines if a player is actually performing a command, or just chatting:

```
if( !c.Quiet() && command[0] != '/' ) {
    DoAction( "attemptsay", p_player, 0, 0, 0, full );
    return;
}
if( command[0] == '/' )
    command.erase( 0, 1 );
```

You saw from Chapter 13 that characters have a quiet mode. With quiet mode, everything a character types is assumed to be a command. If a character is not in quiet mode, anything he types is assumed to be talking, unless it starts with a /.

Table 15.1 lists the behaviors demonstrated on various inputs.

After the command handler determines if a character said anything, it removes the leading / if it exists, so the command string is left with merely the command name, such as go or look, rather than /go or /look.

Table 15.1   Quiet Mode Behavior

Input	Quiet Mode	Loud Mode
go north	execute command go	say go north
/go north	execute command go	execute command go

Here's the next part of the code that searches to see if the character has the requested command:

```
try {
    Character::commands::iterator itr = c.FindCommand( command );
    if( itr == c.CommandsEnd() ) {
        c.DoAction( "error", 0, 0, 0, 0,
                    "Unrecognized Command: " + p_command );
        return;
    }
    (*itr)->Execute( args );        // execute command
}
catch( ... ) {
    c.DoAction( "error", 0, 0, 0, 0,
                "SERIOUS ERROR: Cannot execute " + command +
                ", please tell your administrator" );
}
}
```

The character finds the command by using its `FindCommand` function, which you saw in Chapter 13. If the command isn't found, the character is informed, and the function merely returns.

If the command is found, however, the function tries to execute it by passing in the arguments. Executing a script that may throw an exception could cause the whole thing to crash, which is a bad thing; eventually it will reach the network system, which catches everything and disconnects the connection if it isn't handled by then. So, I catch all errors, and whenever they occur, and I notify the character by telling him about the error.

And that's it for commands!

> **NOTE**
>
> Ironically, just calling the `DoAction` function on an error can also cause an exception to be thrown, but I haven't found this to be a problem at all. If this is the case, something is probably *really* messed up with the character, and you're safer letting the exception travel all the way up to the network level, which disconnects the offending player. This approach minimizes the amount of corruption that a crashed script can cause.

Main Function

The `main` function of the BetterMUD is located within the file /BetterMUD/BetterMUD.cpp on the CD, and it's a very simple function, reminiscent of the SimpleMUD's main module:

```
#include "SocketLib/SocketLib.h"
#include "BetterMUD/network/TelnetLogon.h"
#include "BetterMUD/network/BetterTelnet.h"
```

```
#include "BetterMUD/Game.h"

using namespace SocketLib;
using namespace BetterMUD;

int main() {
    try {

    ListeningManager<BetterTelnet, TelnetLogon> telnetlistener;
    ConnectionManager<BetterTelnet, TelnetLogon>
        telnetconnectionmanager( 128, 60, 65536 );

    telnetlistener.SetConnectionManager( &telnetconnectionmanager );
    telnetlistener.AddPort( 5110 );

    g_game.LoadAll();
    while( g_game.Running() ) {
        telnetlistener.Listen();
        telnetconnectionmanager.Manage();
        g_game.ExecuteLoop();
        ThreadLib::YieldThread();
    }
    }

    catch( BetterMUD::Exception& e ) {
        std::cout << e.GetError();
    }

    g_game.SaveAll();
    CharacterDB.Purge();
    ItemDB.Purge();
    AccountDB.Purge();
    RoomDB.Purge();
    PortalDB.Purge();
    RegionDB.Purge();

    return 0;
}
```

The actual game loop is shown in bold; everything else mainly involves loading and saving the databases. You should be familiar with the networking setup and the game loop, so I'll skip to the last part of the code.

The final section of code saves all the databases and then purges the entity databases. Why do I do this? It turns out that since I used globals for all the databases, I have absolutely no control over their order of destruction. As you'll see in Chapter 17, my Python script module objects need to exist whenever an entity is destroyed, so that the entities can remove references from the Python modules.

Unfortunately, I can't make C++ destroy the entity databases first, so sometimes the game crashes when you shut down. Instead of crashing, I purge the databases to force the databases to destroy all their entities, so that by the time the global Python script databases are destroyed, nothing points to them anymore.

Summary

As you can see from this chapter, the game module is a complex beast. My line counter says that the Game.cpp file itself contains three times as much code as any other file within the BetterMUD, which should give you some idea of how complex it is.

You saw that the game module manages a number of functions in the game, such as loading and saving databases, executing actions, keeping track of time, and executing commands. Overall, the game module supports features similar to those seen in the SimpleMUD's game handler, but this design is better because it doesn't actually directly interface with connections. You'll see how this is done in the next chapter, when I show you the design of the networking system.

I want you to keep thinking about better designs for entity transactions in the future, and realize that I made the simple design presented here to give more time to the flexible logic layer of the game. Believe me, in Chapter 18 you'll be impressed by learning how the game can be enhanced by using Python.

CHAPTER 16

THE NETWORKING SYSTEM

Since more than half of this book is dedicated to networking, you must be completely bored with the topic by now. Nevertheless, networking is an extremely important part of MUD programming, and the job must get done. Networking code doesn't just write itself.

Because I've covered networking so extensively before, I'm not going to delve too deeply into it in this chapter. I would like to give you a brief overview of the major concepts involved in the networking system of the BetterMUD, and then move on to the more interesting topics.

In this chapter, you will learn to:

- Design a more robust and flexible networking layer
- Abstract reporting events to your clients in a non-specific manner
- Create a flexible color coding system that doesn't require a specific protocol
- Convert colors from the flexible system to VT-100 color codes
- Understand how the BetterMUD logon process works
- Understand how the BetterMUD menu system works
- Implement a Telnet reporter

Files

The classes shown in this chapter can be found on the CD in the directory /BetterMUD/ BetterMUD/network. Table 16.1 lists the files and their contents.

Table 16.1   BetterMUD Network Files

File (.h/.cpp)	Contents
BetterTelnet	Better implementation of the `SocketLib::Telnet` class
TelnetReporter	Reporter that reports to `BetterTelnet` connections
TelnetLogon	Logon handler for BetterMUD Telnet connections
TelnetMenu	All five menu handler classes for BetterMUD Telnet connections
TelnetGame	Game handler class for Telnet connections

A Better Design

The design of the SimpleMUD was basic, because it assumed you were going to use Telnet to access the MUD. Telnet is a great protocol in the fact that almost every operating system in the world has built-in clients. This means that you can log into any Telnet MUD anywhere using any client, which is one of the main claims to fame of MUDs. They're *lightweight* clients; you don't need to have certain system specs to play a game; as long as you have a Telnet client. Years ago, I had a simple PDA (Sharp Zaurus, I think) with a built-in modem and a Telnet client. On this little hand-held thing, I could log in to any MUD in my area. You wouldn't believe how cool that was.

Competition from the Big Boys

Unfortunately, ever since the release of *Ultima Online*, the bar has been raised on persistent world games. No, that's not quite correct; *Ultima Online* literally grabbed the bar and *yanked* it as far high as they could. I was playing on a few different MUDs in 1997, and then suddenly, every one disappeared!

Where did they all go? To graphical MUDs, also known as *MMORPG*s. For the past few years, I've seen MUDs practically go the way of the dinosaurs, and that's for a very simple reason; Telnet clients just don't cut it. Sometimes it's much more entertaining to have the client of a full-blown game handed to you, which takes care of everything, and removes the need to type so much.

Sometimes I find myself thinking that Telnet is too limiting. Only 15 colors, very limited text controls, and so on. Modern clients should be able to support more than 15 colors, for crying out loud!

Designing a Flexible System

Unfortunately, I don't have the room or the time to go over creating a new client for use with the BetterMUD (Hey, server development is more fun anyway!), but that's no excuse for assuming we'll be using Telnet!

The key to a good MUD is extensibility and the ability to adapt to future capabilities. Unfortunately, no one can predict every feature that may be needed in the future (I bet people would pay good money for that ability though), so you need to make sure your design is inherently flexible by abstracting out certain things.

In Chapter 11 you learned the concept of abstracting physics and logic. This same concept can be applied to the networking system. Instead of abstracting the physics and logic, I'm going to abstract the physics and the protocol away from each other.

For example, when a player enters a room in the BetterMUD, everyone in that room must be told about the new entry. This can be done in many ways; you could assume the client is text based, and just shoot off a string. Instead of doing that, though, you may want to think about what a future protocol might be like.

The MUDs Return

One gleam of hope is emerging—MUDs are making a comeback, and this is happening for many reasons.

First of all, ever since the MMORPG explosion, there have been dozens of clones, but very few of them actually manage to be good and entertaining. Many are disasters (and a few didn't even work right out of the box... oy!). Even worse are the monthly charges. Back in the mid- to late-80s, most MUDs were run on a per-hour basis, but that was because they used so much power. As computers became faster and cheaper, running a MUD became cheaper, and more people could afford to run them.

By the mid-90s, almost all the MUDs I knew were completely free of charge, and now I can't find a MUD that charges fees! Times are great indeed; I can't believe I'm running not one, but *two* MUDs of my own now. When I first started playing them, I would have never dreamed this was possible.

Another reason why MUDs are making a comeback is because MMORPGs are *too big*. When they first came out, they were novel, and you could play with tens of thousands of people at a time. But in reality, that's a heck of a lot of people in a game. People tend to like the small-knit communities that MUDs offer naturally, instead of the megalopolis approach of MMORPGs. It's easier to get to know people, and you enjoy yourself more.

Consider a graphical client that knows about character graphics and keeps track of all the characters in the game. Instead of notifying that kind of client in text form, you can probably shoot off a packet containing the information "character X entered from portal Y", and then let the client figure out how to display that information, for example by showing a graphical animation of the character coming through a door.

So the main concern here is translating physical MUD events into data that is reported back to a client.

Reporters

For reporting events to a client, I have created the idea of a *reporter*. Figure 16.1 shows the relationship between the game, characters, and reporters (new components are shaded gray) combined with the connection, protocol, and handler objects you should already be familiar with.

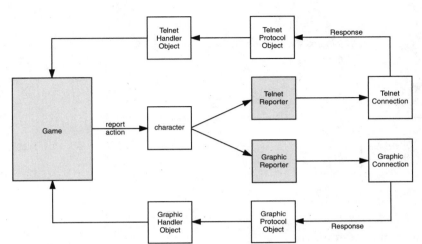

Figure 16.1

The reporter system combined with familiar elements of the connection protocol and handler objects.

If you recall from Part Two of the book, the SimpleMUD implemented most game logic inside of a Telnet handler named Game. In the BetterMUD, the game module is actually completely abstracted from anything dealing with Telnet; it doesn't care what protocol people use.

The game informs characters about actions that happen in the game, such as players entering or leaving the realm, items being dropped, and so on. When the character receives an action, he needs to decide what to do with that action. If the character is a player, the character has a reporter object, and the character passes the command along to the reporter. Figure 16.1 shows a split at this point—an action can go either to a Telnet reporter or a graphic reporter. In the game, every player character has one reporter object; which means that if the character's connected to the game with Telnet, he sends the action to a Telnet reporter.

Once it receives the action event, the reporter figures out how to tell the client what happened. A simple Telnet reporter makes a string out of the action and sends that off. More complex protocols probably require the creation of a complex packet object and its shipping.

That's the design for the reporting system. It allows you to add more protocols in the future, so you can support more complex clients.

Reporter Design

Reporters are basically just special logic modules that are given to players in the game. Every time a player's logic collection is told about a game action, the reporter logic module for that player is told as well. Because of this, they inherit from the Logic class, as shown in Figure 16.2, which shows a simple design, with two possible implementations.

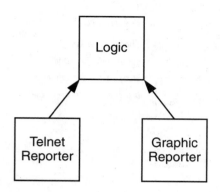

Figure 16.2

Reporter classes inherit from the Logic class.

Telnet Reporters

I only had time to actually implement one reporter class for the BetterMUD, a version that uses Telnet to communicate with players. It's quite simple, but you should feel free to make better versions of your own.

Here's the class definition with most of the helper functions stripped out:

```
class TelnetReporter : public Logic
{
public:
    TelnetReporter(
        entityid p_id,                          // ID of character
        Connection<BetterTelnet>* p_conn )      // address of connection
        : m_id( p_id ),
          m_conn( p_conn )     {}

    std::string Name() { return "telnetreporter"; }
    bool CanSave() { return false; }
    int DoAction( const Action& p_action );

    void SendString( const std::string& p_string );
protected:
    SocketLib::Connection<BetterTelnet>* m_conn;
    entityid m_id;
}; // end class TelnetReporter
```

The class only needs to respond to the DoAction events that it receives, and send messages to its connection (m_conn) when it needs to. As I mentioned earlier, some logic modules shouldn't be saved to disk, and reporter modules are a perfect example of that. They are only valid when players are connected, so there's no reason to write them to disk.

Here's a sample from the DoAction function:

```
int TelnetReporter::DoAction( const Action& p_action ) {
    if( p_action.actiontype == "enterroom" )
```

```
            EnterRoom( p_action.data1, p_action.data2 );

    else if( p_action.actiontype == "leaveroom" )
        LeaveRoom( p_action.data1, p_action.data2 );

    else if( p_action.actiontype == "say" ) {
        character c( p_action.data1 );
        SendString(
            "<$yellow>" + c.Name() +
            " says: <$reset>" + p_action.stringdata );
    }
```

This code snippet takes care of three actions: players entering a room, leaving a room, or speaking. The first two actions simply call the LeaveRoom and EnterRoom helpers (which are helpers that print out information about characters leaving and entering the room), and the third action is simple enough that you can just call the SendString helper function to directly send some text to the connection.

The strings <$yellow> and <$reset> are special additions to my better Telnet protocol, which I go over in the next section.

State Changes

BetterMUD uses a fairly simple state system. This section deals with how the reporter class handles changing between states. The existence of the reporter on a player means that the player's connection is in the "game" state (much like the SimpleMUD). I've also got something new, a "menu" state, in which players can manage their characters.

There are two special actions that deal with changing physical connection states inside the reporter. They deal with the connection being hung up, and the connection leaving the game state. Here they are (these are within the DoAction function I showed you earlier):

```
else if( p_action.actiontype == "hangup" ) {
    m_conn->Close();
    m_conn->ClearHandlers();
}
else if( p_action.actiontype == "leave" ) {
    m_conn->RemoveHandler();
}
```

When a connection is told to hang up, the reporter simply closes the connection and tells the connection to remove all its handlers. This act makes the connection leave the handler it is currently in, so you don't need to perform any other cleanup code, just as long as the game handler logs off correctly (which it does).

On the other hand, the Leave function is called when the player quits the game. Figure 16.3 shows the process of entering and leaving the game, starting from the menu state. When a player enters the game, the menu handler remains on the stack and it isn't removed until the player quits from the menu.

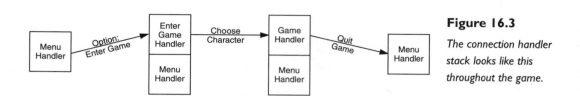

Figure 16.3

The connection handler stack looks like this throughout the game.

When a player enters the game, the function swaps out the `enter game` handler with the `game` handler, and it never removes the menu handler. Therefore, when the player quits the game, the connection handler takes him back to the menu state.

A Better Telnet

I've improved the `SocketLib::Telnet` protocol object from Chapter 6 and integrated it into the BetterMUD. You may remember that I described the idea of making the protocol object automatically translate generic text-color tags into actual VT-100 control codes. This is the main addition to the `BetterTelnet` class (nice original name).

In Chapter 9, I implemented stores and rooms in the SimpleMUD. In some room descriptions, I told you that I had manually inserted VT-100 color codes into the descriptions of some rooms in the actual text datafiles. This was a tricky business; I actually had to use a binary hex-editor program to insert the escape codes.

Another downside of that method is that it assumes everyone is going to be using Telnet, and it's okay to make that assumption for the SimpleMUD, but for the BetterMUD, which should have no idea what Telnet is (outside the networking module, of course), that's just not going to cut it.

BetterMUD Color Codes

Without messing up how the text displays. I created a method to represent color codes inside a piece of text. I've opted to use an HTML-like method of color tags. Here's a sample description of one of the rooms within the BetterMUD:

```
You are in the gardens of Worthington, where you can see much
<#FFFF00>flora<$reset> and <#00FF00>fauna<$reset> all around.
```

The text within the angle brackets is color coded. I've included two different kinds of color codes: hex-numeric, and alphabetic.

Whenever the `BetterTelnet` class is sent a new piece of text to return to the player, it tries to find these tags and replace them with their VT-100 equivalents. So, for example, if this class sees `<$red>`, it removes that from the string and replaces it with the VT-100 code `<esc>[31m`. I've included translation mechanisms for all seven color codes, as well as the dim and bold codes, and a reset code as well:

<$black>

<$red>

<$green>

<$yellow>

<$blue>

<$magenta>

<$cyan>

<$white>

<$bold>

<$dim>

<$reset>

The dollar sign signifies "string", which means that whenever the translator finds <$, it knows a string-based code is going to follow.

Hex-numeric codes are much more versatile and can represent up to 16 million different colors. If you've ever played around with HTML, you should be familiar with the concept. Basically, in <#RRGGBB>, the first two hex-digits represent the red, the next two green, and the last two blue. A code such as <#FFFFFF> represents pure white, whereas <#000000> represents pure black. The two colors shown in the previous description example are pure yellow and pure green.

Converting BetterMUD Codes to VT-100

Unfortunately, there is no magical way to make VT-100 instantly support more than the default 15 colors, so the BetterTelnet protocol module has a bit of work to do. Whenever the protocol class detects a hex-numeric color code, it must translate that color into the puny 15-color palette of VT-100. For this approach, I've used a simple algorithm that splits each color component into the numbers, 0, 1 and 2. For example, the red component of FF (255) translates to the number 2; 00 translates to 0, and 7F (127) translates to 1.

I used an algorithm to downsize the color ranges by splitting up the range 0–255 into three regions. So any component from 0 to 85 is treated as 0, 86 to 171 is treated as 1, and any component from 172 to 255 is treated as 2. Figure 16.4 shows this process for a sample color of <#007FFF>, which is a pretty shade of light blue.

Therefore, <#007FFF> is translated into 012. Inside the BetterTelnet module file, I have a 3×3×3 array of color codes named g_telnetcolors. I use these three numbers as

NOTE

If you have a paint program such as Paint Shop Pro, you can probably open up a color picker tool, and enter the HTML code into it. If your paint program doesn't have an HTML converter, then you'll have to make do with color conversion manually, by converting each hex-color component into a decimal.

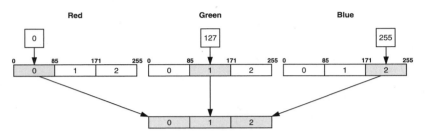

Figure 16.4

The process of converting a hex-decimal color code into a 3-digit based code, which is used to convert into VT-100 color codes.

indexes into that array, like this: g_telnetcolors[0][1][2], and the array at that point holds the Telnet color closest to what I want.

For colors like white, black, blue, and magenta, the translation is exact; VT-100 specifically supports those colors. But VT-100 doesn't support the cool blue color I just converted, so what the heck should I do?

I make an estimate. When I initialized the Telnet color array, the entry 012 looked like this:

```
g_telnetcolors[0][1][2] = blue + bold;
```

So the color that is output is bold blue. This isn't an exact match, since bold blue is a little bit darker than 007FFF, but it's Telnet's closest color match. Most colors are close enough so that you won't notice too much difference, but there are a few colors that VT-100 doesn't come close to supporting:

```
g_telnetcolors[2][1][0] = yellow + dim;
g_telnetcolors[2][1][1] = red + bold;
```

The first color is supposed to be orange, but you'll never get anything orange-looking from VT-100. The closest you'll get is the dim yellow (which, on most clients, ends up looking like a disgusting shade of brownish chartreuse).

The other color is a carnation pink, which the closest you can get to pure bold red.

So you should be aware that the BetterTelnet protocol automatically tries to convert colors as best it can, but sometimes it fails miserably.

BetterTelnet

The BetterTelnet class adds three new functions to the old SocketLib::Telnet class, as well as a hidden class and a hidden array.

Here are the three new functions:

```
static std::string TranslateColors( const std::string& p_str );
static void TranslateStringColor(
    std::string::size_type i,
    std::string::size_type j,
    std::string& p_str );
```

```
static void TranslateNumberColor(
    std::string::size_type i,
    std::string::size_type j,
    std::string& p_str );
```

You shouldn't ever need to specifically call any of these functions yourself, because the protocol class automatically calls them functions for you. For example, when you send text to a BetterTelnet protocol object using the SendString (it has the same parameters as SocketLib::Telnet::SendString), the function automatically calls TranslateColors for you, searches for color tags beginning with <$ or <#, and translates them. The actual translation is done inside the next two functions, which are just helpers. The helpers take the starting index of the color code, the ending index of the color code, and the string to translate as parameters, and it performs the color conversion in place.

I don't want to show you the code, since it is just boring string manipulations, and I'm sure you've had your fill of them.

I also mentioned that I created a hidden class. This class is named INITTELNETCOLORS, and its only purpose is to initialize the g_telnetcolors array with Telnet color codes when the program starts. You don't have to worry about that. If you're interested in seeing how it works though, you can always look at it inside the BetterTelnet.cpp file.

Handler Design

The BetterMUD's account logon process is almost identical to the SimpleMUD's character logon process (the BetterMUD::TelnetLogon and SimpleMUD::Logon classes are almost the same). But once a character is logged on, the similarities end.

Logging On

Logging into the game is a simple task, so I'm not going to spend much time on it. There is one important point to remember, however. In the SimpleMUD, all the text strings printed to the user were hard coded into the executable. The BetterMUD is little more flexible. For example, when you first log into the game, the logon handler consults a text file named /data/logon/logon.data and prints the contents of that file to the connection. For example, my BetterMUD has this logon file:

```
<#FF0000>
        #####   ######  ######  ######  ######  #####
        #    # #          #       #       #      #    #
        #    # #          #       #       #      #    #
        ######  #####     #       #     #####   ######
        #    # #          #       #       #      #   #
        #    # #          #       #       #      #    #
        ######  #######   #       #     ######  #    #
```

```
#    # #    # ######
##   ## #    # #     #
# # # # #    # #     #
# # # # #    # #     #
#     # #    # #     #
#     # #    # #     #
#     # #####  #####
```

<#FFFFFF>
Welcome to BetterMUD v1.0! If you are a new user, type "new" at the prompt
to create a new account. If not, just enter your user name and password to
log in.
<#7F7F7F>
If you have any problems or questions, please email the administrator at
Ron@Ronpenton.net
Please prefix your email titles with <#FF0000>MUD BOOK

<#00FF00>Your Name: <#FFFFFF>

The handler prints out a very basic ASCII text logo (note the usage of the BetterMUD color codes), and short instructions for logging on. It also prints out my contact information, so that people who can't log in can contact me.

You can replace the contents of the file with whatever you want when you run the MUD. I'm going to show you the Enter function of the TelnetLogon class, to show you how this is done:

```
void TelnetLogon::Enter() {
    std::ifstream f( "data/logon/logon.data", std::ios::binary );
    std::string str;
    std::getline( f, str, '\0' );  // read everything from the file
    m_connection->Protocol().SendString( *m_connection, str );
}
```

It's not that difficult. I used the std::getline function to read the entire contents of the file into a single string, and then I print the string out to the player's connection.

Table 16.2 lists the data text files used in the BetterMUD.

Because the data is stored in the files, you can update the news, your logo, or anything else without stopping the MUD and recompiling.

There is one difference in the logon process from the SimpleMUD: accounts can be banned. Whenever an account is banned, the logon process prevents the user from completing a logon, and tells him who to contact about the issue before hanging up on him. This allows you to enforce rules in the game and remove trouble makers.

> **CAUTION**
>
> Whenever you have data like this in a text file, which is meant to be streamed directly out to a connection, you should be cautious. Telnet requires that every line sent terminate in a CRLF pair. ASCII text files on different operating systems use different line endings, however. Windows is okay, because Windows ASCII text files by default end with CRLF on each line. UNIX/Linux is a different beast, however. Those ASCII files have lines that typically end in an LF, which looks messed up when streamed to Telnet. You could easily make a conversion routine that automatically adds CRs before LFs, if you are so inclined. I didn't bother since I do my file editing in the UltraEdit text editor, which has functions to automatically convert LF to CRLF, and vice versa.

Table 16.2 BetterMUD Text Datafiles

File	Contents
data/logon/help.data	A description of the MUD, who runs it, and how to contact him.
data/logon/logon.data	The MUD logo and basic logon information.
data/logon/newaccount.data	Information for people signing up for a new account.
data/logon/news.data	The latest game news.

Menu Process

Figure 16.5 illustrates the entire logon process.

If you recall from Chapter 8, for the SimpleMUD, the player simply entered the player game after logging on. The BetterMUD adds an intermediate step—a game menu. The five game menu handlers can be found in the menu marked with dashed lines. They're all simple little classes, derived from `BetterTelnet::handler`, which is just another name for the `SocketLib::ConnectionHandler<BetterTelnet, std::string>` class. (See Chapters 6 and 8 if you've forgotten what a `ConnectionHandler` is.)

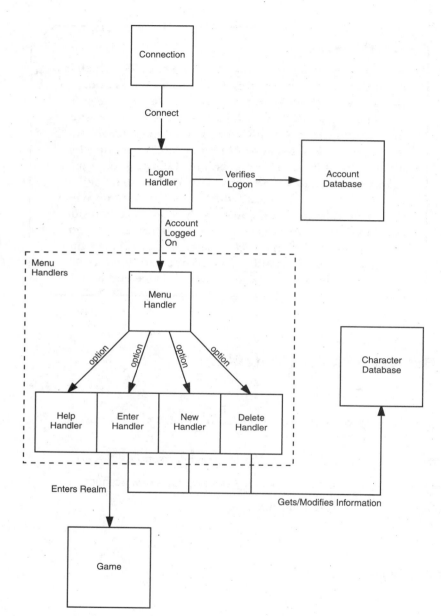

Figure 16.5

All the handlers involved in logging a character onto the game.

Basically, you manage characters through a game menu. Here's a listing of what the Telnet version of the menu looks like:

```
------------------------------------------------------------
BetterMUD v1.0 Main Menu
------------------------------------------------------------
 0 - Quit
 1 - Enter the Game
 2 - Create a new Character
 3 - Delete an existing Character
 4 - View Help
------------------------------------------------------------
 Enter Choice:
```

Option 0 obviously just hangs up your connection, and the other options correspond to the four boxes that "Menu Handler" pointed to from Figure 13.4. Each of these options has its own state class, which can all be found in the TelnetMenu.h and .cpp files.

The simplest of these is the TelnetMenuHelp handler. Its only purpose is to load the help.data file and print it out to the user. Then it waits for user input and goes back to the main menu when it has received input.

The other handlers are a bit more complex, as you can see from Figure 16.6.

It's not really a difficult process to understand. Most of the code deals with interfacing with the various databases to print your available characters, or the available character prototypes to choose from when you enter the game.

Adding Characters

When a player enters the game, he is given a list of prototype characters to choose from. In the SimpleMUD, everyone started out as the same boring character with no individual characteristics.

In most popular game systems, you're allowed to choose a species such as a human, elf, or goblin. In most games, each species has different physical attributes. Elves are usually quicker but weaker than humans, ogres are slower and stronger, and so forth.

Instead of using species, I use *prototypes*. In Chapter 13, I showed you a dual-database that holds templates and instances. A player's "species" is whatever template character his instance character derives from. In the character template database, I have included characters named "Human", "Elf", and "Dwarf", starting at ID 1. So when a player creates a new character, and chooses an ID of 1 as his template, that template also designates his species in the game. The template copies information that makes him unique from other species in the game.

So when a player enters the "new character" state, the game prints out a list of all the characters he can choose to be. The game gets this list by consulting a script, named /data/logon/logon.py. I'll go over the script in more detail in Chapter 18, but for now all you need to know is that it is asked for a string of the character templates that the character can become:

```
void TelnetMenuNew::PrintRaces() {
    std::string str = StringFromPy( m_creationmod.Call( "listchars" ) );
    m_connection->Protocol().SendString( *m_connection, str );
}
```

Don't worry about not knowing exactly what the code in bold does yet; all you need to know is that it returns a string.

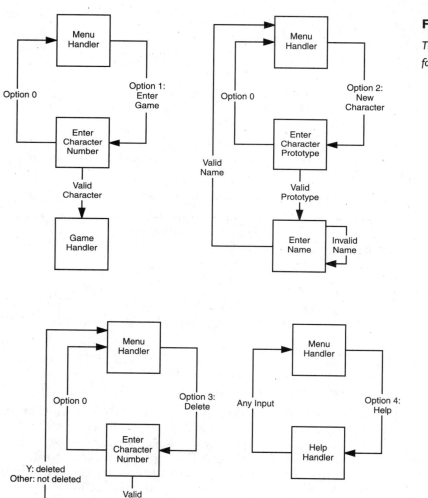

Figure 16.6

The state diagrams of the four menu handlers.

Finally, the handler checks to see if the requested name is taken, and if it isn't, the new-character handler tries to figure out if you've entered a valid character type. Here's a little snippet from that section of code:

```
m_char = EntityFromPy( m_creationmod.Call( "gettemplateid",
                                    EntityToPy( option ) ) );


// check if it was valid
if( m_char == 0 ) {
    m_connection->Protocol().SendString( *m_connection,
        "<#FF0000>Invalid option, please try again: <#FFFFFF>" );
    return;
}

// create character, set its account, and add char to account.
m_char = CharacterDB.generate( m_char );
character( m_char ).SetAccount( m_account.ID() );
m_account.AddCharacter( m_char );

// now perform the inital setup:
m_creationmod.Call( "setup", EntityToPy( m_char ) );
```

This code again heavily relies on the logon.py script. The first thing it does is ask the script to get a character template ID based on the option that the user selected. This should return a number other than 0 if the user entered a valid option, or return 0 if the option was invalid (which can happen; users like to try to break your programs).

Otherwise, the function continues and generates the character. The last line of the function again calls the logon.py script, and this time the script is supposed to set up the new player, by putting him in an appropriate room, giving him commands, and special logic modules or whatever else you want to do.

Deleting Characters

Whenever a character is deleted, the actual character isn't immediately deleted. This is actually a very important security issue. Imagine if someone discovered your password and deleted your character that you spent months creating…argh! To be on the safe side, the character deletion handler removes only the character from the player's account. The administrator can delete the character manually at a later date.

Game Handler

In the SimpleMUD, the Game handler was a very complex piece of code, which managed the game's reaction to every input of the players. I'm not saying it was a great design, emm…it wasn't. But it was okay, simply because it got the job done, and it wasn't designed to handle anything other than Telnet.

For the BetterMUD, however, things are different. In the BetterMUD, the game handler is much simpler; its purpose and flexibility are shown in Figure 16.7.

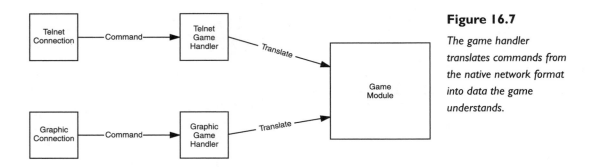

Figure 16.7

The game handler translates commands from the native network format into data the game understands.

The game handlers for the BetterMUD are just simple classes. Their only function is to translate data from the client into data that the game understands. Take a look at the TelnetGame::Handle function, for example:

```
void TelnetGame::Handle( string p_data ) {
    g_game.DoCommand( m_character.ID(), p_data.c_str() );
}
```

The function simply passes the command to the game. You should note that the game handler tracks which character it is currently attached to, much as the SimpleMUD's Game class did. I'll show you how the Game class works in Chapter 15.

Summary

You may have noticed that the SimpleMUD has a "training handler" but the BetterMUD does not. This is because there is no need for a specific handler for modifying statistics. As you'll see later on, the BetterMUD doesn't have such a rigid reward/editing system, and you can use logic modules to edit stats. Instead of going into a trainer and adding points to your strength, you could have a logic module that would be attached to a trainer, and when you pay him, he'll increase your strength through his logic module.

This has been a very quick overview of the networking system for the BetterMUD. I didn't really go over too much code, but that's mostly because so much of the code is based on the same concepts you learned in the SimpleMUD. I find long explanations of code very boring, and you probably do too. So this is enough about networking. It's time to get to the real meat of the BetterMUD!

CHAPTER 17

PYTHON

U ntil now, everything in this book has been done in C++. Until recently, almost
everyone in the game industry used C++; it's been the *only* language that provides the
flexibility and the speed that games need to take advantage of every bit of processing power
available at your fingertips. It's predecessor, C, is perhaps the most popular MUD programming language in the world, and for good reason. When the UNIX operating system hit, it
introduced networking on a wide and flexible scale to everyone in the world, and what better
to do with UNIX than to program MUDs? Consider that when MUDs became popular, C was
by and large the only good language available for UNIX, and it was also the preferred language of MUD builders. C is dying, however. It will never be completely dead (look at CO-
BOL!), but its days in the sunshine are coming to an end. Many would say that C++ is dying
too, but I'm not sure where I stand on that issue yet. Within the past few years, flexible
interpreted languages have hit the mainstream. Among the frontrunners are PERL and Python.

Python is the language that I have chosen to use with the BetterMUD, partly because I don't
understand PERL (it's so UGLY!), and mostly because Python is a very simple, powerful,
and elegant language.

In this chapter, you will learn to:

- Install Python
- Use Python types, functions, classes, exceptions, and packages
- Integrate a Python Interpreter into C++
- Call Python functions from C++
- Call C++ functions from Python
- Integrate Python into the BetterMUD

Python Language

A language is considered *interpreted* if it doesn't create binary files containing machine code.
Keeping your programs in machine code limits you to running them on a single processor
architecture; your Windows programs obviously won't run on a Macintosh, because the
compiled programs don't speak the same machine code.

Interpreted language programs usually have two components: the program and an interpreter. Figure 17.1 shows you how an interpreted language system works.

The major benefit of such a system is that you can run it on *any* system that has an interpreter installed. Even better, you can tell an interpreter to dynamically reload programs
when they change (which is the main argument for implementing a scripting system in the
BetterMUD).

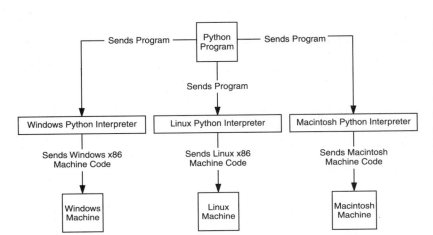

Figure 17.1

With an interpreted language, there is no need to compile the language for different systems, because the interpreter program does the conversion from the language into machine code.

The downside, of course, is the extra layer of abstraction. It takes work to translate the instructions into a native machine format. Processors, however, are so fast these days that the translation of instruction is rarely a concern, which explains why interpreted languages are quickly gaining popularity in the computing world.

Installing Python

If you're on Windows, you probably don't have Python installed. If you're on Linux, you probably have at least version 2.2 installed (at the time of this writing, Python is at version 2.3, which is much faster than Python 2.2). If you don't have Python installed on your Linux machine, please ask your administrator to install it for you, so you can play around with it.

> **NOTE**
>
> For this book, I am using Python 2.2. Even though Python 2.3 is much faster and less buggy, it was released too late for me to switch everything over and test it completely. Feel free to use Python 2.3 if you wish. I've included it on the CD.

I have included the distributions for Python on the CD in the directory /goodies/ python. The Windows version of Python 2.2 is located at /goodies/python/windows/ Python-2.2.3.exe, and the Linux version at /goodies/python/linux/Python-2.2.3.tgz.

Snake Charming

Once you've installed Python on your system, you can jump right into it and start programming right away. The Python distribution comes with an *interactive interpreter* program. This should be named something like `Python2.2` on Linux, and `python.exe` on Windows.

Once you have the interpreter running, you will see something like the output shown in Figure 17.2.

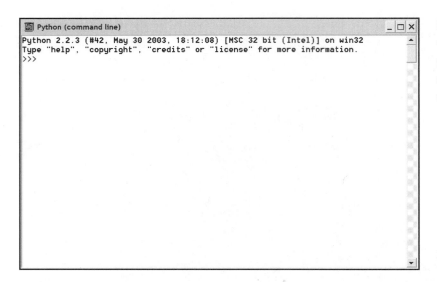

Figure 17.2

The Python interactive interpreter allows you to type Python code that it runs for you on the spot.

Python allows you to type in code, and as soon as you press Enter, the program executes the code you entered. For your first Python program, type in `print "Hello World!"`, and press Enter. The output should look like this:

```
>>> print "Hello World!"
Hello World!
```

Wow! Even BASIC isn't this easy.

Variables

Python has datatypes, but variables are *dynamically bound* to their types. This means that a variable can *change* what type it is, while a program is running! If you're used to *static-typed* languages like C++, this concept may boggle your mind (it sure boggled mine for a few hours!).

Try it out. Type this code into Python:

```
x = 42
x = "YOU'RE SUPPOSED TO BE AN INT!"
```

Here's some sample output that I got from that code:

```
>>> x = 42
>>> x
42
```

CAUTION

Do not show Python to an aged Assembly Code Guru. His mind will either terminally shut down, or promptly explode.

```
>>> x = "YOU'RE SUPPPOSED TO BE AN INT!"
>>> x
"YOU'RE SUPPPOSED TO BE AN INT!"
```

You may experience any of these reactions:

1. Whoa! How cool!
2. THAT'S NOT POSSIBLE!
3. *brain explodes*

I really hope your reaction was #1, because you're going to have to get used to Python if you ever want to do anything interesting in the BetterMUD.

Types

Python has built-in types, but you really don't care much about the types of your data. There's a built-in function to determine the type of something called `type`. Look at the following interpreter interaction:

```
>>> type( 5 )
<type 'int'>
>>> type ("pies" )
<type 'str'>
>>> type( 3.1415926535897932384626433832795 )
<type 'float'>
>>> type( 123456789000000000 )
<type 'long'>
```

Those are the four types you'll be using most often. Python has other built-in types (such as Booleans in 2.3 and complex/imaginary numbers), but you won't be using those as much.

Integers

Python has two types of integers. One is a standard 32-bit type that you're familiar with, and the other is a very cool flexible integer format.

Ints

Python `ints` are standard signed 32 bits, representing numbers from -2,147,483,648 to 2,147,483,647. The really awesome thing, however, is that `ints` never overflow. Look at this code:

```
>>> x = 2147483647
>>> type(x)
<type 'int'>
>>> x = x + 1
>>> type(x)
```

```
<type 'long'>
>>> x
2147483648L
```

Python automatically converts `int`s to `long`s whenever it overflows.

Longs

Python's `long` datatype is *completely* different from the `long` type of C++'s, however. C++ longs are usually 32 bits (depending on the compiler), but Python's longs are special integers that can have *huge* values. Look at this code for a moment, continuing from earlier:

```
>>> x
2147483658L
>>> x = x * x * x * x * x * x
>>> x
98079717355732488831849278277916776199747444886114S121344L
```

That's a long number! Maybe that's where the name came from. Here, try it again:

```
>>> x = x * x * x * x * x * x
>>> x
890174673224950989224344909339850580102383540379533865907262500120651
398303359571312924055596951783353543195046215952854460786132127336962
202329058079176489889535289368883996834478628657762318330221731693433
323501333648123820496784420013400992680124611633700193823222168845171
934806058016485705467286157362404278885621815714812637741056L
```

HOLY CRAP! I love Python. You literally don't have to worry about integer overflows, ever (unless you try passing numbers like this back into C++). I could keep going, but the results could easily be longer than an entire page. I continued playing around, and eventually got a number that overflowed my command window's buffer (11 pages worth, or 25,531 digits), so I can't really say how large the number was, except that it was larger than 25,531 digits.

Floats

Floats in Python are the same as standard 64-bit `double`s in C++. Because of this, you can represent numbers as large as 2.22507×10^{308}, or numbers as small as 4.94066×10^{-324}. Unfortunately, floats *do* over/underflow. Here's an example of overflow:

```
>>> x = 10000000000.0
>>> x = x * x * x * x * x * x * x * x
>>> x
1.0000000000000001e+080
>>> x = x * x * x * x * x * x * x * x
>>> x
1.#INF
```

And underflow:

```
>>> x = 1.0
>>> x /= 1e200
>>> x
9.9999999999999998e-201
>>> x /= 1e200
>>> x
0.0
```

So be careful if you know you're dealing with floats.

Strings

Strings are very easy to use in Python, as shown by the following code:

```
>>> x = "HELLO!"
>>> x[3]
'L'
>>> x[:3]
'HEL'
>>> x[2:]
'LLO!'
>>> x[1:4]
'ELL'
```

As in C++, you can use the square-bracket operator to access individual characters, but you can use it to do more than that. If you put a colon in front of an index, as in x[:3], you're telling it to return the first three characters of the string. On the other hand, x[2:] tells it to return every character after index 2 (assuming indexing starts at 0). Or you could combine the two, and use x[1:4] to return every character from index 1 (inclusive) to index 4 (exclusive). Unfortunately, you can't use this method to change the characters within a string. Instead, you need to re-assign the string.

For example, you can change the character at index 3 like this:

```
>>> x = "HELLO!"
>>> x = x[:3] + "g" + x[4:]
>>> x
'HELgO!'
```

It's a little inefficient, but it gets the job done after all. There's an important reason why inline modification of strings isn't allowed. All Python objects are references. If you run this code

```
x = "Rutabagas"
y = x
```

that means that both x and y are pointing to the same string in memory. Modifying one would cause all references to change, and that is a bad thing™. So, you should modify strings by re-assigning them.

Lists

I'm going to keep this section short, since lists aren't used that much when interfacing with the BetterMUD, but you should be aware that they exist. Look at this example:

```
>>> x = [ 10, 20, 30, 15 ]
>>> x
[10, 20, 30, 15]
>>> type( x )
<type 'list'>
```

In this code snippet x is now a list, which you can use just like a string:

```
>>> x[2]
30
>>> x[:2]
[10, 20]
>>> x[2:]
[30, 15]
>>> x[1:3]
[20, 30]
```

It makes sense, doesn't it? A string is really just a list of characters.

But wait, there's more!

```
>>> x = [10, "pies", 3.14159265358979323846264433832795]
>>> x
[10, 'pies', 3.1415926535897931]
```

Lists can contain many different kinds of items; they don't have to be homogenous like C++ lists. Using this knowledge, you can easily create tree-like structures:

```
>>> x = [ [10,20], [30,40] ]
>>> x
[[10, 20], [30, 40]]
>>> x[0]
[10, 20]
>>> x[1]
[30, 40]
```

Pretty cool, huh? The top list contains two lists!

Libraries

Python has a whole slew of built-in libraries called *modules* that you can use. A module is basically any collection of code within its own .py file.

In order to use a module, you must first import it, like this:

```
import math
```

And once that's in, you can do things with the contents of the module:

```
>>> import math
>>> math
<module 'math' (built-in)>
>>> math.pi
3.1415926535897931
>>> math.e
2.7182818284590451
>>> math.pi + math.e
5.8598744820488378
```

Or call functions:

```
>>> math.cos( 1 )
0.54030230586813977
>>> math.cos( math.pi )
-1.0
```

There are built-in modules for almost any function you would want to do, ranging from threading, to sockets (so you don't have to build a Socket Library that sucks from scratch), strings, checksums, e-mail (send e-mail from Python! How cool!), compression, file access, random numbers, timers... ah, you know what? Python has almost everything—too many modules to list.

Functions

Python supports user-defined functions, and it's really simple syntax. For example, here's a function that computes the Cartesian length of a 3D vector:

```
import math
def length( x, y, z ):
    return math.sqrt( x * x + y * y + z * z )
```

Now you can use it:

```
>>> x = length( 2, 2, 1 )
>>> x
3.0
```

It's that simple.

Python and Coding Standards

You have to be very careful when using Python. Most other languages use brackets of some sort to tell the compiler about the beginning and end of functions and classes. Python doesn't do that. Instead, Python relies on line indentation. This may seem a little weird at first, but you get used to it, and eventually learn to like it, because it enforces a really clean way of displaying your code.

Look at the following code:

```
x = 10
y = 20
if x == 10:
    print x
    print y
x = 30
```

The Python language knows that the if-block starting on line 3 ends after `print y`, because the indenting resets back to the level of the if-statement. If any of the lines inside the block is indented differently, you'll get a syntax error (unless the line is within another nested-block structure).

Try typing this into Python:

```
if x == 10:
    print x
        print y
```

You're going to get something that looks like this:

```
>>> if x == 10:
...     print x
...         print y
  File "<stdin>", line 3
    print y
    ^
SyntaxError: invalid syntax
```

So you need to be very careful about your indenting habits. It works out for the best though. I find myself admiring my Python code for how much better it looks than it would in C++ (blasphemy!). Don't worry, I still love C++. Both languages have their advantages and disadvantages; syntax in C++ just happens to be a downside.

Classes

Python is a *pseudo-object-oriented* language. It supports objects and inheritance, and on the outside, those features look and act like the C++ concepts of the same kind. Classes exist in Python not because of a special effort on the part of the Python developers, but because the overall design of the language happens to support the idea.

Creating a Class

For starters, let me show you a very simple class:

```
class foobar:
    x = 10
```

And now play around with it:

```
>>> y = foobar()
>>> y
<__main__.foobar instance at 0x008E7020>
>>> y.x
10
>>> y.x = 20
>>> y.x
20
```

The first line creates a new *instance* of foobar, and then you toy with its x variable.

Class Variables

What appears to be happening in the preceding code, *isn't actually happening*! I'll explain this in a bit, but first let me show you something (assume you execute this code segment after the previous code):

```
>>> foobar.x
10
>>> foobar.x = 30
>>> foobar.x
30
>>> y.x
20
```

What the heck is going on here?! Isn't foobar a class? How can you access foobar.x, and when you change it, why does y.x remain at 20? This is madness! *Madness I tell you!*

Okay, it's not that difficult, actually. Look at Figure 17.3.

Figure 17.3

The process of creating an instance and changing the x variable for y and foobar.

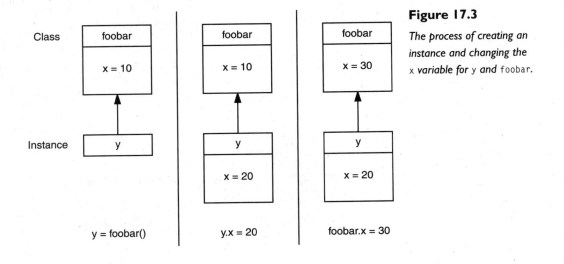

Class   foobar   foobar   foobar

x = 10   x = 10   x = 30

Instance   y   y   y

     x = 20   x = 20

y = foobar()   y.x = 20   foobar.x = 30

When you create a class in Python using the `class` keyword, it actually creates a new *class object*, representing that class. When I typed this line into the class definition:

```
x = 10
```

I was actually saying "this class object, `foobar`, will have x, an integer that is 10". I wasn't saying "all instances of `foobar` will have x". So in the middle panel of Figure 17.3, when you say `y.x = 20`, you are trying to assign 20 to the x variable of y, but y doesn't have that! So, when you execute the statement, the program gives y a new variable named x, and sets it to 20.

This brings up a few questions. When you say `y.x` before you give y an x object, why does it return `foobar.x`? The designers of Python wanted to give Python capabilities that are similar to C++'s `static` variables, so when you do something like this

```
class foobar:
    x = 10
```

you're saying that `foobar` has a static variable named x, which is equal to 10. When you say `y.x` (before you accidentally give y an x object), you're telling y to see if it has x. The instance sees that it doesn't have x , so it determines which class it is an instance of, and if *that class* has an x, it is returned. Look at this code (executed after you accidentally give y an x object):

```
>>> y.x
20
>>> y.__class__.x
30
```

Ah-ha! We found the x variable of `foobar`!

Instance Variables

The question remains, however: "How do I give instances their own variables?" There are many ways to do that, and you've already seen one of them, by accidentally giving an instance a variable. There are other ways though. The most common way is to provide the class with an __init__ function (that's four underscores, by the way—two in front, and two in back):

```
>>> class pie:
...     def __init__( self ):
...         self.kind = "Apple"
...
>>> p = pie()
>>> p.kind
'Apple'
```

What the heck is this business of `self`?

Think of how C++ class functions work internally—they always pass a pointer to the actual class object into the function. For example

```
foo.bar( 10 );
```

is actually interpreted by the compiler as this:

```
bar( &foo, 10 );
```

C++ hides the compiler interpretation from you, but Python doesn't bother. The first parameter passed into any Python class function is a reference to the class on which the function is being used.

In C++, you can do something like this:

```
void init() {
    kind = "Apple";
}
```

And the compiler automatically knows that you're referring this->kind. Python does it a little differently, though. If the initialization function looked like this instead

```
def __init__( self ):
    kind = "Apple"
```

Python would think you're creating a new local variable named kind, which would be discarded the moment the function was finished. Later, when you're trying to determine the class of pie, you get an error:

```
>>> class pie:
...     def __init__(self):
...         kind = "Apple"
...
>>> p = pie()
>>> p.kind
Traceback (most recent call last):
  File "<stdin>", line 1, in ?
AttributeError: pie instance has no attribute 'kind'
```

Inheritance

The fact that Python classes can inherit from other classes makes your life easier in the long run. The syntax for inheritance is relatively simple as well:

```
>>> class superpie( pie ):
...     def isawesome( self ):
...         return "YES!"
...
>>> s = superpie()
>>> s.isawesome()
'YES!'
>>> s.kind
'Apple'
```

This example assumes I'm using the non-broken version of the class pie. See how easy it is?

Exceptions

Python has an effective exception system built-in, much like that of C++. It uses classes as exceptions. Here's a simple example of catching an exception:

```
>>> try:
...     y = thisdoesntexist
... except:
...     print "EXCEPTION!!!"
...
EXCEPTION!!!
```

The `try` block attempts to execute some code, and the `except` block catches all exceptions.

You can also do specific exception catching:

```
>>> try:
...     y = thisdoesntexist
... except OverflowError:
...     print "Overflow Error!"
... except NameError:
...     print "Name Error!"
...
Name Error!
```

Or you can even grab an instance of the exception object that was thrown:

```
>>> try:
...     y = thisdoesntexist
... except Exception, inst:
...     print inst
...
name 'thisdoesntexist' is not defined
```

Whenever you print an exception instance, it prints a description of what was thrown.

You can also raise your own exceptions:

```
>>> try:
...     raise Exception
... except:
...     print "EXCEPTION THROWN!"
...
EXCEPTION THROWN
```

Packages

Python, by default, looks for .py files from within the directory in your global path. This can get annoying, because you may need a hierarchy of Python scripts in order to have your programs organized in an efficient manner. Because of this, Python has introduced the idea of *packages*.

Essentially, to create a package of related files, you need to place a bunch of Python scripts into a subdirectory, and place an empty file named __init__.py into that directory.

For example, if I want to create a package named "data", I create a directory named "data", and put a file named __init__.py into it. Once I do that, I can put other .py files such as characters.py in there, and I'll be able to import that module from within Python like this:

> **NOTE**
>
> Python 2.3 even supports putting packages into .zip files.

```
import data.characters
```

You can recursively apply the same idea to even more subdirectories if you want to, giving you a cool, flexible hierarchy system.

Integrating Python and C++

I hope that my little crash course on Python was enough to give you a general feel for the language. I have to admit, I picked up basics of the language in about two to three days, since the concepts are all very similar to those of C++ (and all other object-oriented imperative languages), so I doubt you'll have any problems.

Now, on to the difficult part—integrating C++ and Python. The good news is that the Python language was originally made in C, so that gives us a nice platform to start with.

The Python-C API is very easy to use, and is well documented as well. As of this writing, you can access the documentation for the Python-C API at this address: http://www.python.org/doc/current/api/api.html.

> **TIP**
>
> If you ever have a question about Python, there is great free documentation available at http://www.python.org. As of this writing, there's a great tutorial to the language here: http://www.python.org/doc/current/tut/tut.html.

Demo 17.1—Making An Interpreter

The first demo I want to show you is an example of how easy it is to integrate the Python interpreter into your C++ program.

You can find this demo on the CD in the directory /Demos/Chapter17/Demo17-01/ on the CD. To compile the demo, set up your compiler as described in Appendix A, which is also on the CD.

I'm going to spit all the code out at you at once, but I don't think you'll mind, since it's really simple:

```
#include <iostream>
#include <string>
#include "Python.h"

int main() {
    std::cout << "Welcome to SIMPLEPYTHON!!" << std::endl;
    std::cout << "Chapter 17, Demo 01 - MUD Game Programming" << std::endl;

    Py_Initialize();                  // initialize python

    std::string str;
    std::getline( std::cin, str );    // get each line
    while( str != "end" ) {           // exit if you got "end"
        PyRun_SimpleString( const_cast<char*>( str.c_str() ) );
        std::getline( std::cin, str );
    }

    Py_Finalize();                    // shut down python
    return 0;
}
```

The three calls to Python functions in the code are marked in bold. The first call initializes the Python interpreter, the second tells it to execute a string, and the final call tells the Python interpreter to shut down.

Figure 17.4 shows the SimplePython interpreter in action.

When I first got this working, I had two thoughts:

1. WOW! THIS IS SO COOL!!
2. Hey, I can't believe I made this in less than two minutes!

See how easy it is to get Python code up and running in your programs?

> **NOTE**
>
> C++ std::strings cannot be converted into char* pointers implicitly, so to accomplish that you must call their c_str function. However, the function returns const char*s, and Python, for some oddball reason, accepts only non-const char*s as parameters to the functions. So in order to properly pass an std::string into the function, I need to cast away its const characteristics first.

Demo 17.2—Python Objects

That first example was quite simple, and really only concerned the execution of Python code from a string. If you want to do anything more complex, you'll have to mess around with the internals of Python.

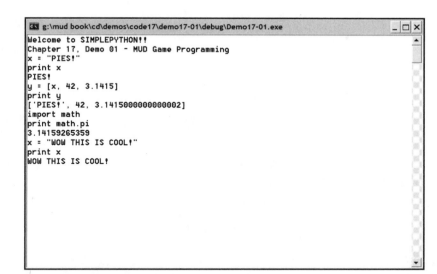

Figure 17.4

SimplePython in action.

Everything in the API is based on the idea of a *Python Object*, which is a structure that points to an object that is being used within Python. This code

```
x = 10
```

creates a new Python object, entitled x, and it holds an integer value of 10. Creating a class creates a new Python object that contains the definition of a class, and creating an instance of that class creates yet another Python object.

Python objects are stored in a simple structure called PyObject. They are large and fairly complex, but luckily, you should never have to deal with them, except to pass them to and from Python-C API functions. Here is a simple example, which loads a file containing Python code:

```
PyObject* mod = PyImport_ImportModule( "pythontest" );
```

After this code has been called, mod should be pointing to a Python object that represents the module pythontest, which was loaded from the file pythontest.py. Python automatically assumes modules end with a .py suffix.

Python Test Module

Now, what can you do with this module? You can actually do anything you want. Let me show you what's in the module first though:

> **NOTE**
>
> Python modules can contain code that is outside functions or classes. This code is executed when the module is first loaded, so the moment you load it up, THIS IS A TEST OF PYTHON!!!! should be enthusiastically printed to your console window. Modules can also have variables, as shown by the x = 10 line.

```
print "THIS IS A TEST OF PYTHON!!!!"
x = 10

def testfunc():
    print "TEST FUNCTION!!"
def printfunc( arg ):
    print arg
def returnstring():
    return "HELLO C++!!"
```

Running the Code from Python

Once you have that loaded, you can execute Python code:

```
PyRun_SimpleString( "import pythontest\n"
                    "pythontest.testfunc()\n" );
```

This imports the module into the namespace of the `PyRun_SimpleString` function, and then calls its `testfunc` function, which should print `TEST FUNCTION!!` to your console.

Running the Code from C++

Now that you can call stuff using a simple string, try the slightly more complex operation of calling it directly from C++:

```
PyObject* result =
    PyObject_CallMethod( mod, "testfunc", null );
```

> **NOTE**
>
> It should be noted that since you're importing the function inside the call to `PyRun_SimpleString`, you don't actually have to import the module in C using `PyImport_ImportModule` first. But since I plan on using the module later on, I load it anyway.

This calls the test function from `mod` with no parameters. Since the function doesn't return anything either, why the heck did I record the result? This is one of the little quirks of Python. Even if you return nothing, the language internally returns the `null` *object*. Of course, if it's a `null` object, you can just ignore it right?

Wrong. Everything in Python is reference counted, which means that the Python-C API tries to track the number of places in the program that are referencing any given Python object. Whenever the reference count drops to 0, the Python-C API knows that it is safe to delete the object. If you accidentally still have it after it has been deleted, you're going to be accessing an invalid object, and you'll be in big trouble.

The `PyObject_` functions always return new references to Python objects, which means that the `null` reference count of the object that was returned from this function increased. It is up to *you* to remove one from its reference count like this:

```
Py_DECREF( result );
result = 0;
```

You're telling Python that you've finished pointing to that object, and that you won't be referencing it anymore. Therefore it's a good idea to clear the pointer as well.

This can get tricky, so later I'll show you my Python wrapper that takes care of this stuff for you.

NOTE

For each function in the API, the Python-C API documentation lists references as *new* or *borrowed*. Whenever you call a function that returns a borrowed reference, you're not supposed to decrease its reference count at all. This can make managing objects somewhat difficult, but luckily, there aren't many functions that return borrowed references. In fact, in my Python wrapper, I never use any of those functions, so I can safely assume that all pointers need to be dereferenced.

Calling Functions with Parameters

Now we can try something more complicated, calling a function with a parameter:

```
result = PyObject_CallMethod( mod, "printfunc", "s", "HELLO PYTHON!" );
Py_DECREF( result );
result = 0;

result = PyObject_CallMethod( mod, "printfunc", "i", 42 );
Py_DECREF( result );
result = 0;
```

This calls the `printfunc` function with a string, and then with an integer, which should print them both.

Getting Results

On the other side of the equation, you're going to need to extract return values from Python objects. This is a relatively painless task to accomplish, because Python contains tons of built-in functions for converting the basic types from objects. This time, we're going to call `returnstring`:

```
result = PyObject_CallMethod( mod, "returnstring", null );
std::string str = PyString_AsString( result );
std::cout << str << std::endl;
Py_DECREF( result );
result = 0;
```

The line in bold is the function that converts a Python object to a C++ char* object, which I then promptly copy into a std::string.

You need to be careful when using the PyString_AsString function. It returns a char*, which is a pointer, but Python still owns the buffer it points to. You shouldn't modify it at all or try to delete it. In fact, the safest, sanest thing to do is to copy the contents of the buffer into a string of your own *right away*, because Python may even modify the buffer later on, or deallocate it without telling you (how rude!).

> **TIP**
>
> The char*s of C are the devil. I have never seen a more evil invention in my life. Well maybe the Oscar Meyer Weeniemobile, but I don't think that counts. Use std::string of C++ instead.

All the code in this section is compiled into Demo 17.2 on the CD, which you compile in the same way as Demo 17.1. When you run it, it should produce output like this:

```
Python Test!
Chapter 17, Demo 02 - MUD Game Programming
THIS IS A TEST OF PYTHON!!!!
TEST FUNCTION!!
TEST FUNCTION!!
HELLO PYTHON!
42
HELLO C++!!
```

That's it for this demo.

BetterMUD's Python Library

I found that all those C-style function calls and the manual reference counting management were extremely annoying parts of the API. Maybe it's just me, but I take routes that make my life easier. I've always said that *programming is the art of avoiding work*. If you think about it, it makes sense. Why would you waste your time coding 800 manual dereferences of Python objects, when you could write a simple wrapper around them to automatically handle it for you?

You can find the code for my Python library in the directory /BetterMUD/BetterMUD/scripts/python.

PythonObject Class

My version of a Python object is called PythonObject. It's a simple wrapper around a PyObject*, but it uses constructors and destructors to automatically increment and decrement reference counts. You can find this class inside the PythonHelpers.h and .cpp files.

Here is the class skeleton:

```
class PythonObject {
public:
    PythonObject( PyObject* p_object = 0 );
    PythonObject( const PythonObject& p_object );
    ~PythonObject();

    PythonObject& operator=( const PythonObject& p_object );
    PythonObject& operator=( PyObject* p_object );

    PyObject* get() const;
    bool Has( const std::string& p_name ) const;

    std::string GetNameOfClass();
    std::string GetName();
protected:
    PyObject* m_object;
};
```

Managing Reference Counts

The constructors are pretty simple; you can construct a PythonObject from either a pointer to a PyObject, or a reference to another PythonObject class.

The first constructor that takes a PyObject* simply assigns the parameter to m_object. It doesn't do anything else. It is designed this way because I am assuming that whenever you pass a PyObject* into the first constructor, it assumes that you're passing in a new reference that is returned from a Python function call.

On the other hand, if you construct an object from another object, the constructor is a little more complex:

```
PythonObject( const PythonObject& p_object ) :
    m_object( p_object.m_object ) {
    Py_XINCREF( m_object );
}
```

The first thing this does is assign p_object's PyObject* to m_object. Once that is done, the function increases its reference count by calling Py_INCREF. Why do I do this? If you're copying something over from another PythonObject, that means you now have two PythonObjects, each with pointers to the same PyObject*, so you need to tell Python that you're now pointing to the object from two places.

On the other hand, the reference count is decremented when the object is destructed:

```
~PythonObject() {
    Py_XDECREF( m_object );
}
```

There are also two `operator=`s, which operate along the same principles:

```
PythonObject& operator=( const PythonObject& p_object ) {
    Py_XDECREF( m_object );
    m_object = p_object.m_object;
    Py_XINCREF( m_object );
    return *this;
}


PythonObject& operator=( PyObject* p_object ) {
    Py_DECREF( m_object );
    m_object = p_object;
    return *this;
}
```

The difference with these functions (as opposed to the previous two) is that when they are called, the `PyObject*` inside the class already exists and owns a reference count, so you can't simply overwrite `m_object` with the new pointer. If you do that, Python thinks that you're using the previous object and never deletes it, even after you've long forgotten it.

Once the outdated objects are dereferenced, you can reassign the pointer, increasing the count if you're copying it over from another `PythonObject`, or doing nothing if it's from a `PyObject*`.

> **TIP**
>
> Forgetting to dereference `PyObject*`s is a great way to introduce huge memory leaks into your program. Amaze your friends, be the life of the party! Leak memory now!

Because of this behavior, you can now rewrite some lines from Demo 17.2:

```
{
PythonObject p;
p = PyObject_CallMethod( mod, "printfunc", "s", "HELLO PYTHON!" );
p = PyObject_CallMethod( mod, "printfunc", "i", 42 );
}
```

Now, when you issue the second call to `PyObject_CallMethod`, the `operator=` of the `PythonObject` class automatically dereferences the return value of the outdated object. Whenever p goes out of scope (which should be after the last curly bracket in the previous code), it automatically dereferences its current object (which is the return value from the second call, in this example).

Not only is the code cleaner, but I shaved off two lines and eliminated a possible source of huge errors—forgetting to dereference the return values. We're human, and we often forget things. So why bother ourselves with remembering every little detail?

See how you can make your life easy? I love avoiding work.

PythonObject Helper Functions

The helper functions assist you in performing specific tasks. For example, I didn't include a *conversion operator* that automatically converts a PythonObject into a PyObject*, because that would wreak havoc with the constructors and produce lots of errors (sometimes C++ can be a pain).

Instead, I provide a get function, which simply returns the pointer it is holding. This way, you can pass the object into Python calls. Here is a modified version of some code from Demo 17.2:

```
PythonObject p = PyObject_CallMethod( mod, "returnstring", null );
std::string str = PyString_AsString( p.get() );
std::cout << str << std::endl;
```

Another helper is the Has function, which determines if a Python object contains an object (could be a class, an instance, a variable; anything!) with a given name. Believe it or not, this is simple to accomplish, because the API has a function like that built right in:

```
bool Has( const std::string& p_name ) const {
    return (bool)PyObject_HasAttrString(
        m_object, const_cast<char*>(p_name.c_str()) );
}
```

This checks to see if an object contains an object with the given name. Again, since Python doesn't use const strings, I need to manually cast away its const characteristics. It's a bit ugly, but it gets the job done.

Every Python object has a name, so it makes sense to design the code to make it easy to extract these names. The two functions that receive names from objects are shown in this code snippet:

```
std::string PythonObject::GetName() {
    PythonObject name = PyObject_GetAttrString( m_object, "__name__" );
    return StringFromPy( name );
}

std::string PythonObject::GetNameOfClass() {
    PythonObject cls = PyObject_GetAttrString( m_object, "__class__" );
    PythonObject name = PyObject_GetAttrString( cls.get(), "__name__" );
    return StringFromPy( name );
}
```

The first function should be fairly straightforward. Every Python object has an attribute called __name__, which is a string representing its name. I extract that object from the current object and call the custom StringFromPy function to convert it into a C++ std::string.

The second function is a little trickier; it's meant to be called on objects that are assumed to be instances of a class. If you call it on an element that isn't an instance of a class, you may crash the program. Two steps are required to get the class name of an instance. The first step is to get an object representing the class, which you can do by grabbing the __class__ attribute. Then, you need to grab the name of the class, by getting its __name__ attribute. Finally, you can return the value as a string.

Data Conversion Helpers

The bunch of helper functions I've included for converting types to and from Python automatically use PythonObjects to manage the reference counting. I'm going to show you the implementation of one extractor, and one inserter, and then just the names of the rest. Here are the implementations:

```
inline PythonObject LongToPy( long p_obj ) {
    return PyInt_FromLong( p_obj );
}
inline long LongFromPy( const PythonObject& p_obj ) {
    return PyInt_AsLong( p_obj.get() );
}
```

They're just simple wrappers, utilizing my object class, so that there are no memory leaks. Here's a listing of all the converters:

```
inline PythonObject IntToPy( int p_obj );
inline PythonObject LongToPy( long p_obj );
inline PythonObject EntityToPy( entityid p_obj );
inline PythonObject LongLongToPy( BasicLib::sint64 p_obj );
inline PythonObject DoubleToPy( double p_obj );
inline PythonObject FloatToPy( float p_obj );
inline PythonObject StringToPy( std::string p_obj );

inline long LongFromPy( const PythonObject& p_obj );
inline entityid EntityFromPy( const PythonObject& p_obj );
inline BasicLib::sint64 LongLongFromPy( const PythonObject& p_obj );
inline double DoubleFromPy( const PythonObject& p_obj );
inline std::string StringFromPy( const PythonObject& p_obj );
```

> **TIP**
>
> I originally implemented these functions as specialized template functions, in which you could write ToPython(blah), and the function would automatically convert whatever type you had into a Python object, or FromPython<double>(obj), which does the opposite. Using templates would have allowed you to write prettier code, but alas, it just wasn't in the cards. VC6 has major problems with template specialization, and absolutely refused to make the template functions work, so I had to resort to creating separate conversion functions for each type. VC6 is a worthless piece of junk, and you should upgrade to VC7 as soon as you can. This has been a public service announcement. Thank you.

Automating Callable Objects

To make calling Python functions and classes easier, I created the concept of a
PythonCallable class, which essentially calls a method inside a Python object. This class is
located within the PythonScript.h and .cpp files.

The Class

Here is a listing of the class:

```
class PythonCallable {
public:
    PythonCallable();
    PythonCallable( PythonObject& p_object );

    PythonObject Call( std::string p_name );
    PythonObject Call( std::string p_name, const PythonObject& p_arg1 );
    // *****SEE EXPLANATION*****

    bool Has( const std::string& p_name ) const;
    PyObject* get() const { return m_module.get(); }
protected:
    PythonObject m_module;
};
```

This class actually has more functions than I've shown you. There are another five versions of
the Call function, each one taking another parameter. There are versions for 0, 1, 2, 3, 4, 5,
and 6 PythonObject arguments. Let me make it extremely clear to you right now: ***this is an ugly
hack***. However, it is necessary. The flexibility of Python allows passing dynamic datatypes and
lists of variable arguments, but when you do this you're obviously going to run into a problem
when you try to interface it with C++, a static language with fixed numbers of arguments.

While it is true that C supports variable argument lists, their support is not standard. There
are tiny little quirks that tend to screw things up at the most inconvenient times. Rather
than mess with all that, I chose to avoid it, and use this hack instead.

The other functions of this class simply wrap around a PythonObject.

Calling Python

Since I basically copy the same function over a few times (Call), I decided to make the
process a little less painful by creating a helper macro:

```
#define PYTHONCALL( CALL )                                      \
    PythonObject r;                                             \
    try{ r = CALL }                                            \
    catch( ... ) {                                              \
        PyErr_Print();                                          \
        throw Exception( "Python Function Call Failed" );       \
```

```
        }                                                \
    if( r.get() == 0 ) {                                 \
        PyErr_Print();                                   \
        throw Exception( "Python Function Call Failed" ); \
    }                                                    \
    return r;
```

This macro is designed to wrap around some Python API function calls that return a new PyObject*. The macro creates a result object named r and then tries calling the function.

In case anything throws, the function catches it, prints out the Python error, and then rethrows the exception inside a BetterMUD::Exception class.

If the function returns 0, it failed, and again, the Python error is printed, and an exception is thrown.

Finally, if all goes well, the result object is returned.

Here's the 1-argument version of Call (which passes 0 arguments into the Python function):

```
PythonObject PythonCallable::Call( std::string p_name ) {
    PYTHONCALL(
        PyObject_CallMethodObjArgs(
            m_module.get(),
            StringToPy( p_name ).get(),
            null ); )
}
```

I use the PyObject_CallMethodObjArgs function, which requires a Python string of the name of the object you are calling, and it has a variable argument list of all the objects you're passing in, which must be terminated with null. Since the PYTHONCALL macro wraps around the call, a result object named r is created and returned (or an exception is thrown if an error occurs).

For comparison, here is the two-argument version, which passes in one argument to the Python function (changes from the original are in bold):

```
PythonObject PythonCallable::Call(
    std::string p_name,
    const PythonObject& p_arg1 ) {
    PYTHONCALL(
        PyObject_CallMethodObjArgs(
            m_module.get(),
            StringToPy( p_name ).get(),
            p_arg1.get(),
            null ); )
}
```

The other five versions are similar, but have more arguments. If you ever need more than six arguments passed into a Python function, you can easily copy and paste more functions into the code.

Finally, here is how you would call a PythonCallable object named obj, with hypothetical function names:

```
obj.Call( "testfunction" );
obj.Call( "needsargument", IntToPy( 42 ) );
std::string str;
str = StringFromPy( obj.Call( "returnsstring" ) );
str = StringFromPy( obj.Call( "returnsstringneedsarg" ), IntToPy( 42 ) );
obj.Call( "needs2args", IntToPy( 42 ), FloatToPy( 3.14159 ) );
```

See how easy that is? If you know the code is not going to return anything, you don't care about return values, because the functions all deal with self-managing PythonObjects.

I love it when everything works out without worrying about all the minor details. Don't you?

Python Modules

I've abstracted Python modules into my own class, named (very originally, I might add) PythonModule. The PythonModule class is somewhat complex, and that's for a very good reason: script reloading.

Problem With Reloading

To gain some experience with the reloading problem, open your Python interpreter again, and start playing around with code like this:

```
>>> class reloaden:
...     def funky(self):
...         print "OLD!!!"
...
>>> a = reloaden()
>>> a.funky()
OLD!!!
```

Now that you've done that, "reload" the class, by redefining it:

```
>>> class reloaden:
...     def funky(self):
...         print "NEW!!!"
...
>>> b = reloaden()
>>> b.funky()
NEW!!!
>>> a.funky()
OLD!!!
```

So what happened here? You created a class named reloaden, and defined a function named funky, which printed out OLD!!! After that, you created an instance of that class, and called its funky function.

Then, you "reloaded" the class, by typing in a new definition, created a new instance named b, and called its funky function, which printed out NEW!!!, just as expected.

The last line, however, calls a.funky() again, which, instead of printing out NEW!!!, still prints out OLD!!!!

Argh! What the heck! Yeah, those were my first reactions too. Well, this behavior actually makes sense. When you loaded the first class object of reloaden (by typing the definition), you created a *class object* called reloaden. When you typed a = reloaden(), you created a new *instance object* that points to the *class object*.

When you redefined reloaden, the old reloaden had not been deleted; it was just hidden because a still references it. But whenever you create new instances of reloaden, the new instances all point to the new version, even though the old version still exists. In fact, the old version of reloaden exists until a stops referencing it. At that point, Python knows that the old reloaden is longer in use, and cleans up after itself.

Figure 17.5 illustrates the process from the code I showed you previously.

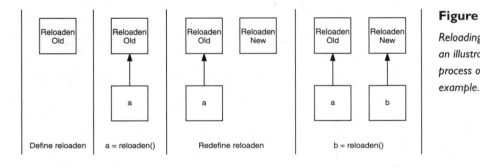

Figure 17.5

Reloading classes— an illustration of the process of the previous example.

Not having automatic reloading can give you a major headache in a game situation. Imagine that you have a bunch of characters using a logic module that has a flaw. You reload the module with a fixed version, but there's a huge problem! Every instance that used the old module still points to the flawed module! Only *new* instances of the module use the correct code. Stupid Python! (BLASPHEMY!)

NOTE

You can still create new instances of the old class, if you're so inclined. Try typing this into the interpreter: c = a.__class__(). That copies the old class, even though you can no longer create it by calling reloaden(). This is an example of one of the many things you can do with the flexibility of Python.

Fixing the Problem

If you still have your interpreter open, you can easily fix a so that it uses the new version of reloaden. Just type this:

```
>>> a.__class__ = reloaden
>>> a.funky()
NEW!!!
```

You just re-assigned the reloaden class object. The reference count of the old version of reloaden is decreased by this operation, and whenever you call functions on a, it references the new version of reloaden, instead of the old one.

You can easily do the same thing from within C++

```
PyObject_SetAttrString( instanceobj, "__class__", classobj );
```

This code assumes that instanceobj is a PyObject* pointing to an instance of the old class, and classobj points to the new version of the class.

Unfortunately, when you reload a module, the module has no idea what instances it created previously, so it must search out all these instances and tell them to reload themselves.

That is a difficult problem, but I've managed to solve it and automate it by using two classes. My PythonModule class generates new PythonInstance objects, and whenever it generates one, it adds a pointer to it into a list. Whenever you tell the module to reload, it goes through the whole list, and tells every instance to reload itself with a new version of its class.

This has disadvantages, however. Whenever an instance is deleted, the instance must tell its module that it no longer exists.

Figure 17.6 shows you how modules and instances form a simple tree, in which modules tell each instance when it must be reloaded, and each instance tells its module when it no longer exists.

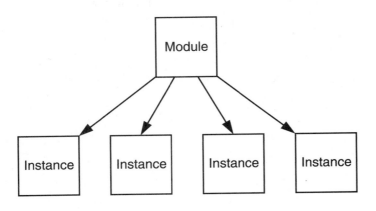

Figure 17.6

The simple layering structure of Python modules and instances.

Module Class Interface

The PythonModule class interface looks like this:

```
class PythonModule : public PythonCallable {
public:
    std::string Name() { return m_module.GetName(); }
    void Load( const std::string& p_module );
    void Reload( PYTHONRELOADMODE p_mode );

    PythonInstance* SpawnNew( const std::string p_str );
    void DeleteChild( PythonInstance* p_instance );

protected:
    typedef std::list<PythonInstance*> spawnlist;
    spawnlist m_spawns;
};
```

PythonModule objects are loaded by passing in a string to the Load function. If you want to load a file named "testpython.py", you call Load("testpython"). In response, the Reload function takes a mode in which you can reload. There may be times (however rare) when you want to reload a module, but allow everyone to temporarily keep the old version of the script, and the function allows you to specify if you want to do that. You can pass in two values: LEAVEEXISTING, and RELOADFUNCTIONS. The first mode simply reloads the module and doesn't touch the instances at all. The second mode goes through all the instances and updates their class objects.

If the module you loaded has a class named "pies", you can create an instance of that class by calling SpawnNew("pies"). You should note that this returns a *brand new* PythonInstance*, and when you finish using it, you should manually delete it (because the module won't).

The final function is the DeleteChild function, which PythonInstances call when they are destructed, so that the module knows that it no longer has to update that instance.

Loading a Module

Loading modules is easy:

```
void PythonModule::Load( const std::string& p_module ) {
    PythonObject p =
        PyImport_ImportModule( const_cast<char*>( p_module.c_str() ) );
    if( p.get() == 0 )
        throw Exception( "Couldn't load python module: " + p_module );

    m_module = p;
}
```

The code simply tries to load the module from disk, and throws an exception if it can't.

Spawning New Instances

Spawning new class instances is a more complex process, since many things can go wrong. Here's the code:

```
PythonInstance* PythonModule::SpawnNew( const std::string p_str ) {
    try {
    PythonObject c =
        PyObject_GetAttrString(
            m_module.get(),
            const_cast<char*>(p_str.c_str()) );
    if( c.get() == 0 )
        throw Exception( "Could not find python class: " + p_str );
```

The previous code chunk tries to load a *class object* from the module (pies from my example previously). Not being able to get that class object means that this module doesn't have a class with that name, and it just throws.

```
    PythonObject i = PyInstance_New( c.get(), null, null );
    if( i.get() == 0 )
        throw Exception( "Could not create python class instance: " + p_str );
```

Now the code tries to create a new instance of that class using `PyInstance_New`. If the instance couldn't be created, then it also throws:

```
    PythonInstance* mod = new PythonInstance( i, this );
    if( !mod )
        throw Exception( "Error allocating memory for python module" );
    m_spawns.push_back( mod );
    return mod;
    }
```

The previous code then creates a new `PythonInstance` object by passing in the `PythonObject` representing the instance (`i`), as well as a pointer to `this`, the module that the instance was spawned from. The new module is added to the list of instances, and the pointer to the brand new `PythonInstance` class is returned.

```
    catch( Exception& e ) { throw; }
    catch( ... )           // catch any extra errors we didn't grab before
    {
        PyErr_Print();
        throw Exception( "Unknown error attempting to create class "
                        "instance: " + p_str );
    }
}
```

Finally, the code catches and rethrows any exceptions (so that the next block of code can work), or catches anything else that happened, prints out a Python error, and throws.

Reloading

Reloading is a simple affair:

```
void PythonModule::Reload( PYTHONRELOADMODE p_mode ) {
    m_module = PyImport_ReloadModule( m_module.get() );
    if( p_mode == LEAVEEXISTING )
        return;
    spawnlist::iterator itr = m_spawns.begin();
    while( itr != m_spawns.end() ) {
        (*itr)->Reload();
        ++itr;
    }
}
```

The module is reloaded using `PyImport_ReloadModule`, and then (if the caller wishes) the function loops through all its instances and reloads them.

Using a Module

You can use the module class quite easily. Since it inherits from `PythonCallable`, you can even use it to call functions inside the module. Here is a hypothetical example of using the class on a module named `pies`, which has a function named `foobar`, and a class named `blarg`:

```
PythonModule mod;
mod.Load( "pies" );
mod.Call( "foobar" );
PythonInstance* inst1 = mod.SpawnNew( "blarg" );
mod.Reload( LEAVEEXISTING );
PythonInstance* inst2 = mod.SpawnNew( "blarg" );
mod.Reload( RELOADFUNCTIONS );
delete inst1;
delete inst2;
```

The code loads a module named `pies`, and then calls its `foobar` function. It then creates a new instance of class `blarg` and stores it in `inst1`. After that, the module is told to reload, but it keeps all the existing instances and does not update them.

Then, the code spawns a new instance, `inst2`. At this point, both instances are pointing to different classes, with `inst1` as the old version of `blarg`, and `inst2` as the new version of `blarg`.

Finally, the code reloads the module again, this time reloading everything, so that both `inst1` and `inst2` are pointing to the very

NOTE

In fact, I've hidden the copy constructor and operator= for both the `PythonInstance` and `PythonModule` class, to make absolutely sure that you *never* copy them to another location, *ever*. Copying them completely messes up the pointer hierarchy that they must have to reload modules properly.

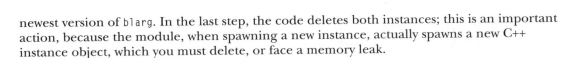

newest version of blarg. In the last step, the code deletes both instances; this is an important action, because the module, when spawning a new instance, actually spawns a new C++ instance object, which you must delete, or face a memory leak.

I chose to do things this way because of the complex relationship between instances and modules. An instance must point to its module, and a module points to its instances, so you can easily reload them when needed. It's a bad idea to copy these objects, since copying them automatically changes their location in memory.

Python Instances

The PythonInstance class also inherits from PythonCallable, so that you can call class functions on it quite easily.

Class Skeleton

Here is the class skeleton:

```
class PythonInstance : public PythonCallable {
public:
    PythonInstance(
        PythonObject p_instance,          // instance object
        PythonModule* p_parent );         // pointer to parent

    ~PythonInstance();
    std::string Name();
    void Reload()
    void Load( std::istream& p_stream );
    void Save( std::ostream& p_stream );
protected:
    PythonModule* m_parent;
};
```

The class is simpler than a module, and represents a class instance. Instances have names, can be reloaded, and can also be loaded and saved to disk. I discussed this idea in Chapter 13. All class instances must have the ability to load and save themselves from streams, because they may have extra data that should be retained (such as a command object that remembers the last time it was executed). When the entity that owns the class is reloaded from disk from the BetterMUD, the data associated with the Python module should be loaded.

Deleting the Instance

Whenever an instance is destructed, it must notify its parent that it no longer exists:

```
PythonInstance::~PythonInstance() {
    if( m_parent )
        m_parent->DeleteChild( this );
}
```

Reloading

Whenever an instance is told to reload from disk, it must overwrite its __class__ attribute. This isn't a difficult task:

```
void PythonInstance::Reload() {
    std::string clsname = m_module.GetNameOfClass();
    PythonObject cls = PyObject_GetAttrString(
        m_parent->get(),
        const_cast<char*>(clsname.c_str()) );

    if( cls.get() == 0 )
        throw Exception( "Could not find python class: " + clsname );

    PyObject_SetAttrString( m_module.get(), "__class__", cls.get() );
}
```

The function first gets the name of the current class object of the instance (assuming it is loaded. PythonInstance objects should not exist unless they have been loaded), and then it retrieves a pointer to the Python class object and stores it into cls.

If cls doesn't exist, that means the class was probably deleted when the module was reloaded, and that's no good. Therefore an exception is thrown.

The final step is to reset the __class__ attribute and make it point to the new class object.

Once this has been completed, the instance object points to a reloaded version of its class.

Disk Operations

As I mentioned earlier, all PythonInstance objects know how to write themselves out to streams. This is required because instances may hold data that must be preserved.

The standard way of representing an instance is like this:

```
instancename
[DATA]
... data goes here ...
[/DATA]
```

Even if there is no data, the tags need to be there. This makes your datafiles look a little ugly, but eventually, you should have a nice editor for the MUD, so that you can't see the ugliness.

> **CAUTION**
>
> The stream format for all script objects in the BetterMUD requires that the [DATA] and [/DATA] tags be on their own separate lines. I did this because of the way I pass streamed data into Python, which is the topic I touch on next.

Loading from Streams

When a `PythonInstance` must be loaded from disk, whatever is loading it first reads its name (usually the entity in charge of the script does this), and that entity creates the instance object. Once the object has been created, the stream is passed into the `PythonInstance` class, so that it can suck out all the data, and load it into itself. Here is the function:

```
void PythonInstance::Load( std::istream& p_stream ) {
    std::string str;
    std::string temp;
    bool done = false;

    // read in the "[DATA] tag:
    std::getline( p_stream, temp );

    // loop until you hit "[/DATA]"
    while( !done ) {
        std::getline( p_stream, temp );
        if( temp == "[/DATA]" )
            done = true;
        else
            str += temp + "\n";
    }

    // send everything in between to the script
    Call( "LoadScript", StringToPy( str ) );
}
```

If you're using just primitive objects such as strings and numbers, interfacing between Python and C++ is very easy. There is no easy way to pass a C++ iostream into Python however, so instead of bothering with that, I've decided to use strings to pass streams.

The loading function plucks out the [DATA] tag from the stream using `std::getline`, which means that the tag must be on a line of its own; everything else on that line is ignored and discarded.

After that, I load things line by line, and store them into `str`, until I find a [/DATA] tag. By the time the loop finishes, everything between (but not including) the data tags is within `str`.

I used the `std::getline` function for a reason. If I just used the `operator>>` stream extractor, it would eat up all the whitespace between every word inside the tags. Look at this hypothetical example file:

```
[DATA]
This            string        has          long          spaces
[/DATA]
```

If I extracted each word until I found [/DATA], I would end up with a string that contains `This string has long spaces`, but there wouldn't actually be any long spaces, because the stream extractor automatically discarded them! There may be times when the whitespace inside a data tag has meaning, and I don't want to destroy that. So the function loads the data line by line, and str holds the appropriate number of spaces between its words.

The final line of the function calls the script's LoadScript function, passing in the string as its parameter. Your scripts should know what to do with this data.

Saving to Streams

Luckily, saving to streams is much easier:

```
void PythonInstance::Save( std::ostream& p_stream ) {
    p_stream << "[DATA]\n";
    p_stream << StringFromPy( Call( "SaveScript" ) );
    p_stream << "[/DATA]\n";
}
```

This simply saves the data tags, as well as the string returned from the Python objects' SaveScript function. It is perfectly legal for the Python script to return ("") if you don't have any data.

> **CAUTION**
>
> **Please remember to return a string. If you don't return anything, the function returns the null object, which can't be converted to a string, and your program crashes.**

Python Databases

In Chapter 12, I told you about the PythonDatabase class, which is a special database class that loads and stores Python scripts. A PythonDatabase is actually a simple class that wraps around a collection of PythonModules. Here is the class skeleton:

```
class PythonDatabase {
public:
    PythonDatabase( const std::string& p_directory );
    ~PythonDatabase();
    void Load();
    void AddModule( const std::string& p_module );
    void Reload( const std::string& p_module, PYTHONRELOADMODE p_mode );
    PythonInstance* SpawnNew( const std::string p_str );

protected:
    void Load( const std::string& p_module );
    typedef std::list<PythonModule*> modules;
    modules m_modules;
    std::string m_directory;
};
```

The functions should immediately remind you of the `PythonModule` class. This class was designed to enable you to separate your related scripts into many files, so that you don't have to shove them all into the same .py file on disk, which can become rapidly disorganized.

Using a managed collection of modules, on the other hand, allows you to do a few things. You can load completely new modules at any time, and you can reload specific modules whenever you want.

I'm not going to show you the `Reload` or the `SpawnNew` functions; they simply loop through every module in `m_modules` until they find a module matching the requested name. Then they call the requested function on the right module. I also won't show the destructor, which simply loops through every module and deletes it.

Loading a Database

Loading the database from a directory is similar to the `Database::LoadDirectory` function I showed you in Chapter 12. The names of all Python modules that you want loaded are stored in a manifest file:

```
void PythonDatabase::Load() {
    std::string filename = m_directory + "manifest";
    std::ifstream manifest( filename.c_str(), std::ios::binary );
    manifest >> std::ws;
    while( manifest.good() ) {
        std::string modulename;
        manifest >> modulename >> std::ws;
        Load( modulename );
    }
}
```

Nothing new here. Each module name is loaded from the manifest, and then the `Load(std::string)` helper is called to add the module to the database.

Adding a Module

Adding a new module while the program is running is also a relatively simple task:

```
void PythonDatabase::AddModule( const std::string& p_module ) {
    Load( p_module );

    std::string filename = m_directory + "manifest";
    std::ofstream manifest(
        filename.c_str(), std::ios::binary | std::ios::app );
    manifest << "\n" << p_module << "\n";
}
```

To load the module, the function invokes the `Load` helper again, and then it opens up the manifest file in append mode, and writes the name of the new module.

Loading Modules

I've written a helper that loads modules by their names. It's a relatively simple process with a few quirks here and there:

```
void PythonDatabase::Load( const std::string& p_module ) {
    std::string modname = m_directory + p_module;

    // convert "/" or "\" to "." for proper module loading
    modname = BasicLib::SearchAndReplace( modname, "/", "." );
    modname = BasicLib::SearchAndReplace( modname, "\\", "." );
```

First I created the name of the module by adding the name of the directory to the name of the module to be loaded. If you created this database with the directory data/logic/characters/, and you wanted to load a module named "defaultplayerlogic", it would create the string data/logic/characters/defaultplayerlogic.

The next step is to convert all slashes into dots, because Python loads modules based on dots. The module name would convert to "data.logic.characters.defaultplayerlogic".

```
PythonModule* mod = new PythonModule();
if( !mod )  throw Exception( "Not enough memory to load python module" );
```

The previous code creates a new module, and throws if it can't be created. Now here's the tricky part:

```
try {
    mod->Load( modname );
    m_modules.push_back( mod );
}
catch( ... ) {
    delete mod;
    throw;
}
}
```

You should try loading the module. Since you created mod using new, if the loading throws an exception, you must be sure to delete the module if something throws, or else you're going to end up with a memory leak.

If the loading goes fine, the new module is added to the list of modules.

BetterMUD Script Databases

The BetterMUD has three database classes that utilize the features of the PythonDatabase class. You've seen them all used before: the CommandDatabase, the ConditionDatabase, and the LogicDatabase. Luckily they inherit most of their functions from PythonDatabase, so you don't have to implement many of the functions in them. In fact, they are so simple, that I'm not even going to waste your time by showing them to you. They're boring and uninteresting, and I want to move on to showing you how to expose C++ classes to Python.

Exposing C++ to Python

As I'm sure you saw with all the examples in this chapter, it's very easy to call Python from C++. It's another thing altogether to expose C++ to Python, however.

Usually, when a programmer wants to expose something to Python from C++, he builds a DLL or SO file that holds the C/C++ code, and then calls it from Python. You can find hundreds of tutorials that describe how to do this.

It is rare, however, to find information on exposing C++ to Python, while at the same time, embedding the Python interpreter into the program. So, here I come, to the rescue.

Trials and Tribulations

There are many ways you can expose C++ to Python. When I first started working on this idea, I had heard about the C++ Boost library (http://www.boost.org), which has a module named boost::python. This is an excellent library, even though it is still under construction.

I spent weeks integrating boost::python into the BetterMUD, making a really stable design that worked perfectly. And then one day I decided to check to make sure it worked in VC6.

It doesn't. I slammed my head on the table a few times over this, believe me. Boost::python uses templates *heavily*, and since VC6 has very awkward and incomplete template support, getting boost::python to work in VC6 proved to be ultimately impossible. I ended up scrapping the entire design, and I had to go back to square one!

Using boost::python on a *real* compiler actually works like a breeze. If you use VC7 or GCC, I urge you to look into boost. It's really cool.

> **TIP**
>
> If there's a moral to learn in this story, it's that VC6 is an evil, horrible, ancient compiler, and you should upgrade to VC7 or the latest version GCC *this very instant!* GO GO GO!

Here, Take a SWIG

When I ultimately had to give up on boost, I had to find a replacement quickly. Luckily, the SWIG library (available free at http://www.swig.org, and you can find it on the CD as well, in /goodies/Libraries/SWIG) is easy to use.

Just install it and add your SWIG directory to your system's path environment variable (for example, in Windows I had to add D:\Programming\SWIG-1.3.19\ to my PATH environment variable, by going to Start->Settings->Control Panel->System->Advanced->Environment Variables).

Demo 17.3—SWIGging It Down

To show you how simple SWIG is, I've created a simple Demo for you, Demo 17.3.

C++ Header

First, create a header containing the code Python is to call. I've put all this code inside SWIGME.h:

```cpp
std::string SWIGFunction() {
    return "This has been brought to you by the letter C";
}


class SWIGClass {
public:
    SWIGClass( int value ) : m_value( value ) {}
    void PrintValue()  { std::cout << "My Value is " << m_value << std::endl; }

protected:
    int m_value;
};
```

I've created a simple function that returns a string, and a simple class that holds and prints an integer value.

SWIG Interface

Now I need to create a SWIG interface file, which I call SWIG.i. Interface files are a simple format that SWIG uses to figure out what you want to call from Python:

```
/* File : SWIGME.i */
%module SWIGME

%include "std_string.i"

/* grab the original header file here */
%include "SWIGME.h"
```

The first part of the file declares that you want to create a Python module named SWIGME.

By default SWIG doesn't support std::string (since SWIG was originally a C tool, it really only supports evil char*s), but recent versions of the library come with a file called std_string.i, which makes SWIG use std::strings properly. Cool!

The final part of the code takes the contents of the SWIGME.h file and includes them into the interface file.

Generating SWIGME

Now that you have a header and interface file, you can generate C++/Python code with SWIG. Open up a console window, go into the Demo 17.3 directory, and type this:

```
swig -c++ -python SWIGME.i
```

Since you're going to be generating C++ code, you must use the -c++ flag, so that SWIG recognizes classes properly. The -python flag means you're going to be interfacing the code with Python, and of course you need to tell it about the interface file too.

Now that you've run the program, it should have generated two files for you: SWIGME.py, and SWIGME_wrap.cxx.

The first file is a Python module that allows Python to know about your C++ code, and the second is a C++ module that contains all the wrapper code for talking with Python.

> **NOTE**
>
> SWIG isn't just a Python tool. You can use SWIG to interface C/C++ with a whole bunch of languages: TCL, Python, Perl, Guile, Java, Ruby, Mzscheme, PHP, Oclaml, C#, Chicken Scheme, and some others. It's a cool utility.

Python Tester

Now I want to create a Python module that calls the C++ functions. I've put this into a file named swiggy.py:

```
import SWIGME

s = SWIGME.SWIGFunction()
print "Result of SWIGME.SWIGFunction: " + s

print "Creating SWIGME.SWIGClass of 10:"
a = SWIGME.SWIGClass( 10 )
a.PrintValue()

print "Creating SWIGME.SWIGClass of 42:"
b = SWIGME.SWIGClass( 42 )
b.PrintValue()
```

This simply calls the C++ functions and classes as if they were Python functions and classes. It should be executed the moment the module is loaded.

C++ Test Frame

The final step is to create the C++ test frame that will import the SWIG-generated Python-C++ module, and run module swiggy. This is file Demo17-03.cpp:

```
#include "SWIGME.h"
#include "SWIGME_wrap.cxx"

int main() {
    std::cout << "Exporting C++!" << std::endl;
    std::cout << "Chapter 17, Demo 03 - MUD Game Programming" << std::endl;

    Py_Initialize();                // initialize python

    // initialize SWIGME module:
    init_SWIGME();

    // Import and run swiggy:
    PyRun_SimpleString( "import swiggy" );

    Py_Finalize();                  // shut down python

    return 0;
}
```

Even though SWIG generated a .cxx module file, I've #included it here like a header file, because the module generated a function named init_SWIGME. I need to call this function to inform the interpreter of the SWIGME module, but I don't know about that function, since it's not in a header. It exists only within the .cxx file.

Now you can compile the demo like all the other Python demos, and run it! You should get output that looks like this:

> **CAUTION**
>
> Since you're treating the **SWIGME_wrap.cxx** file as a header, rather than a module, you need to make sure you don't compile it like a module, but rather, keep treating it like a header file. There are other ways around this limitation of course, but this is the easiest.

```
Exporting C++!
Chapter 17, Demo 03 - MUD Game Programming
Result of SWIGME.SWIGFunction: This has been brought to you by the letter C
Creating SWIGME.SWIGClass of 10:
My Value is 10
Creating SWIGME.SWIGClass of 42:
My Value is 42
```

Ta-da! Isn't that cool?

Exposing the BetterMUD to Python

Now, your Python logic modules, command modules, and condition modules all need to access parts of the BetterMUD. The modules can't do much when they can't access parts of the BetterMUD, so they wouldn't be of much use without this ability.

This is the main reason behind the accessors that I showed you in Chapter 13. The accessor classes are used as an interface between Python and C++.

For example, if you expose accessors to Python, you can do stuff like this:

```
import BetterMUD
c = BetterMUD.character( 20 )
c.SetName( "Ron" )
c.SetAttribute( "intelligence", 500 )   // look! I'm smart!
```

Isn't that cool? You're calling C++ code from Python! You're letting your scripts access any information they need to work better.

Game Wrapper

To give you access to the core game module, I've created a wrapper for the Game class that I showed you in Chapter 15. The wrapper itself is stored in the /BetterMUD/accessors/ GameAccessor.h and .cpp files. I'm not going to bother showing you the implementation, since it's just a simple wrapper around the Game class, and you already know what it can do from Chapter 15.

Here, however, is a sample of Python code that would use the class:

```
import BetterMUD
m = BetterMUD.GameWrap()
m.AddActionAbsolute( 0, "announce", 0, 0, 0, 0, "Python Really Rules" )
```

This code essentially calls the Game module's AddActionAbsolute function, to add an immediate announcement to the game, stating that Python rules, just in case someone forgot that it does.

Taking Another SWIG

All the other wrappers in the game are accessor wrappers. Rather than having my BetterMUD.i SWIG interface file include all the accessor headers, however, I've decided to make your life a little bit more difficult.

I've separated all SWIG-related files into their own directory: /BetterMUD/scripts/python/SWIG.

Within this directory are two files BetterMUD.i, and SWIGHeaders.h. These files exist before you generate any interfaces.

The BetterMUD.i file simply looks like this:

```
/* File : BetterMUD.i */
%module BetterMUD

%include "std_string.i"

/* grab the original header file here */
%include "SWIGHeaders.h"
```

The SWIGHeaders file, on the other hand, contains mainly code that has been copy-and-pasted from the accessor classes. Here's a sample:

```
class character
{
public:
    character( entityid p_id );
    ~character();

    std::string Name();
    entityid ID();
    entityid Room();
    entityid Region();
```

I'm going to stop right there, since you've already seen all this stuff before.

The reason I copied and pasted the interfaces into the SWIGHeaders file is that there will be times when you *don't* want Python accessing some of the features of the accessors. If you don't want Python to access a particular function of an accessor, you need only remove that function from the SWIGHeaders.h file and regenerate it.

Generation Process

To generate the files needed to interface BetterMUD with Python, follow this process:

1. Open a console window.
2. Go into /BetterMUD/scripts/python/SWIG.
3. Type `swig -c++ -python BetterMUD.i`.
4. Copy the file BetterMUD_wrap.cxx into this directory: /BetterMUD/scripts/python.
5. Copy the file BetterMUD.py into the main /BetterMUD directory.

That's almost all you need to do. There's one little quirk, however, which I cover in the next section.

Why the Long Face?

Microsoft's compilers VC6 and VC7.0 don't support the `long long` datatype (VC7.1 does though), as I showed you in Chapter 4. Instead, you need to use the `__int64` type as a replacement.

To prevent confusion, I typedef'ed around it, and created a `BasicLib::sint64` type to use instead. Unfortunately, SWIG doesn't know what a `BasicLib::sint64` is, and it tries to treat it as a new type that needs its own special Python wrapper. Since it's just a normal 64 bit integer, it doesn't need this.

So, in the SWIGHeaders file, whenever I have a `BasicLib::sint64` type, I change it to "long long".

For example, this line

```
BasicLib::sint64 GetTime();
```

becomes

```
long long GetTime();
```

Then, SWIG generates the BetterMUD_wrap.cxx file "properly".

You must take one more step, however. When you try compiling the wrapper module in VC6 or 7.0, you'll get compiler errors (`long` followed by `long` is illegal), so you need to find every place in the BetterMUD_wrap.cxx file that has `long long`, and replace it with `BasicLing::sint64`.

Then you can compile it properly, at last.

Summary

Interfacing two completely different languages is an interesting, fun topic. You can do much more with Python and C combined, especially if you get the boost::python library working. The BetterMUD requires only a small subset of all the things that you can possibly do, however.

I hope I've given you a good introduction to Python, and I doubt you'll have much trouble with it, since it's incredibly simple. If you're ever stuck, the Python website has a great tutorial. Or you can look at all the scripts I'm including with the BetterMUD for examples of how things are done.

And now, we're off the next chapter!

CHAPTER 18

MAKING THE GAME

T he previous seven chapters were concerned with coding the *C++ core* of the BetterMUD. In Chapter 11, I told you about how the C++ core is the *physical* part of the game—how the core manages entities, how entities move around, and how entities are saved to disk.

So far, you've got thousands of lines of code, but no game! The problem with designing a system like the BetterMUD is that you can't put it together in bits and pieces—at least not at first. Once the physical game core is up and running, however, you can go nuts and start adding scripts left and right.

This chapter is designed primarily to show you how to create basic scripts to make your physical engine into an actual game. I'm not going to go bananas with scripts; in fact the version of the BetterMUD that will be on the CD is going to be just a tiny bit more advanced than the SimpleMUD.

However, with all of the flexibility of the BetterMUD at your fingertips, you can immediately start playing around with scripts.

I would like to invite you again to join my own MUD server at http://dune.net and play around (if I change servers, you can find out about it on my website, http://www.ronpenton.net. I'll be continuously adding scripts and updates, so if you're interested in seeing some of the really cool things that can be done, I'll have my own scripts available to download.

In this chapter, you will learn to create:

- A login script to manage new characters
- A base Python script class for your modules to use
- Command scripts
- Logic scripts
- A script to refuse taking dangerous items
- A script to manage encumbrance
- A script to manage arming weapons
- A script to manage currency and merchants
- A script to perform combat between characters
- AI scripts for non-player characters

Login Script

I mentioned in Chapter 16 that the login process accesses a Python script that issued to perform various login tasks, such as printing the races you can choose from and initializing your character whenever you create a new one.

This script is located in the /data/logon/logon.py file.

Listing Available Races

Whenever you want to create a new character, the game's logon module contacts the logon script and asks for a string representing the races your character can participate in.

Here's the function for requesting races:

```python
def listchars():
    s =  "<#FFFFFF>-------------------------------------------------\r\n"
    s += "<#00FF00> Please Choose a Race For Your Character:\r\n"
    s += "<#FFFFFF>-------------------------------------------------\r\n"
    s += "<$reset> 0 - Go Back\r\n"
    s += "<$reset> 1 - Human\r\n"
    s += "<$reset> 2 - Elf\r\n"
    s += "<#FFFFFF>-------------------------------------------------\r\n"
    s += "<#FFFFFF> Enter Choice: <$reset>"
    return s
```

After the options are printed to the user, he can choose one, and the choice is sent to the logon script again, this time to the following function:

```python
def gettemplateid( option ):
    if option == 1: return 1
    if option == 2: return 2
    return 0
```

This function takes an option number and translates it into the template ID of the new player's character. Incidentally, I have the database set up right now so that options 1-2 correspond to template IDs 1–2, but that's a coincidence. Later on, you may want to make an option 3 that creates characters with a template ID of 100 or something like that.

Setting Up the New Character

Once the logon module creates your new character, it sends the ID of that new character into the logon script once more—this time to give the character all the commands he needs, and to put him in the right room. Here's a condensed version of the function:

```python
def setup( id ):
    c = BetterMUD.character( id )
    a = BetterMUD.account( c.GetAccount() )
```

```
        l = a.AccessLevel();

        c.SetRoom( l )
        c.SetRegion( l )
        if( l >= 0 ):
            c.AddCommand( "north" )
...  <SNIP> ...
            c.AddCommand( "say" )

        if( l >= 2 ):
            c.AddCommand( "kick" )
            c.AddCommand( "announce" )

        if( l >= 3 ):
            c.AddCommand( "shutdown" )
...  <SNIP> ...
            c.AddCommand( "destroyitem" )
```

The script sets the room and region of the character and then assigns commands based on your account's access level. You can do whatever else you want here. It's up to you. That's the beauty of scripts.

Python Script Base Class

Almost all Python scripts called from BetterMUD (the command and logic scripts) have similar features. They have names, they can be saved to and from files, and they are always initialized with the ID of the entity they are attached to.

Because all scripts share similar features, it makes a lot of sense to make a base class that you can use for all Python scripts.

This class is stored in the /data/bettermudscript.py file:

```
class bettermudscript:
    # Initialize the script with an ID
    def Init( self, id ):
        self.me = id
        self.mud = BetterMUD.GameWrap()
        self.ScriptInit()

    def ScriptInit( self ):
        pass

    def Name( self ):
        return self.name

    def LoadScript( self, s ):
```

```
        pass

    def SaveScript( self ):
        return ""
```

The `Init` function defines two variables: `me`, the ID of the current entity, and `mud`, a `GameWrap` object that allows you to access the `Game` module of BetterMUD. After that, `Init` calls `ScriptInit`.

When making scripts of your own, you should never create your own `Init` function; instead, you need to do all of your initialization in the `ScriptInit` function, which is actually empty here (the `pass` keyword tells Python that you don't want the function to do anything). So when you create your own script class, you just define a `ScriptInit` function and do your initializing there. The `bettermudscript.Init` function automatically calls your new `init` function. This acts like a pure virtual function in C++.

The `Name` function returns the `name` variable, which hasn't been defined at all. You'll see how this works when I show you an actual script.

Finally, the `LoadScript` and `SaveScript` functions assume that they don't have to load or save any data; they simply ignore what you pass in to them, and return an empty string when you ask it for save-data.

Command Scripts

Now you can join the game, but you can't perform any actions; there are no command scripts! Well, that is remedied easily enough.

Command Class

All commands in the BetterMUD inherit from a base `Command` class, which provides a few functions to make your life a little easier. Here's the class, which can be found in /data/commands/PythonCommand.py:

```
class Command( data.bettermudscript.bettermudscript ):

    # Usage
    def Usage( self ):
        return self.usage

    # description
    def Description( self ):
        return self.description

    # the standard call method.
    def Execute( self, args ):
        try:
            self.Run( args )
```

```
except UsageError:
    me = BetterMUD.character( self.me )
    me.DoAction( "error", 0, 0, 0, 0, "Usage: " + self.Usage() )
except TargetError, e:
    me = BetterMUD.character( self.me )
    me.DoAction( "error", 0, 0, 0, 0, "Cannot find: " + e.value )
```

In addition to names, commands have usage and description strings (as you saw in Chapter 14). So when asked, the Command class returns usage and description strings (they don't exist in this class, but if you inherit from Command class and define strings on your own, the functions still work).

The Execute function is called from C++ whenever you want to execute a command in the game. To make things easier, I've inserted a try/catch block into the code, and it looks for UsageError and TargetError exceptions.

The Execute function tries calling Run with the arguments given, and if that throws a UsageError exception, the command gets an accessor to your character, and prints out an error, telling you how to use the command. This is for cases in which you type go without specifying where you would like to go, or something similar.

Since so many commands depend on finding an item to act on (get <item>, attack <character>, and so on), it's fairly common that the designated targets cannot be found. Rather than hardcode You cannot find: <blah> into each and every command, I've enabled commands to throw a TargetError exception if you try to operate on a target that doesn't exist.

Finding Targets

To make things even easier, I've made a special FindTarget function that attempts to find a target contained by an entity and returns the ID if it's found, or throws a TargetError if it can't be found. Here's the code:

```
def FindTarget( seekf, validf, getf, name ):
    seekf( name )
    if not validf(): raise TargetError( name )
    return getf()
```

The first three parameters are functions; seekf is a function that searches for an entity, validf checks if the result of the seek was valid, and getf returns the ID of the item that seekf found. This might seem confusing at first, so let me show you how to use it:

```
me = BetterMUD.character( 10 )
item = FindTarget( me.SeekItem, me.IsValidItem, me.CurrentItem, "sword" )
```

This code first gets a character accessor, pointing to character 10 (whoever that may be), and then gets the ID of an item with the name sword. If there is no item named sword, an exception is thrown, and this code doesn't bother catching it. Essentially, when passed into FindTarget, the code is transformed into the following snippet:

```
    me.SeekItem( "sword" )
    if not me.IsValidItem(): raise TargetError( "sword" )
    item = me.CurrentItem()
```

You can easily perform the same trick on a room, when searching for either items or characters within that room, or a region, or whatever else you may need!

```
# assume r is a room, reg is a region
i = FindTarget( r.SeekItem, r.IsValidItem, r.CurrentItem, "sword" )
c = FindTarget( r.SeekCharacter, r.IsValidCharacter, r.CurrentCharacter,
                "mithrandir" )
j = FindTarget( reg.SeekItem, reg.IsValidItem, reg.CurrentItem, "pie" )
```

After those lines are successfully executed, i has the ID of the first item that matched sword inside the room, c has the ID of the first person with the name mithrandir, and j has the ID of the first item in the region named pie. If any of those fail, an exception is thrown, and it's up to someone else to handle it.

Movement Commands

Once you enter the game, you really can't do anything but use the built-in C++ commands that I've given you, so it's time to add some Python commands.

At this point, the only movement command available to you is the go command. You type go north or go south if you want to go anywhere, and that can be annoying, so as a simple test of commands, I've made additional directional commands. Here's one of them:

```
class north( PythonCommand.Command ):
    name = "north"
    usage = "\"north\""
    description = "Attempts to move north"
    def Run( self, args ):
        c = BetterMUD.character( self.me )
        self.mud.DoAction( "command", c.ID(), 0, 0, 0, "/go north" )
```

This is the north command, which acts as an alias to go north. You can see that the name, usage, and description are all defined first, and then the Run function grabs an accessor to your character, and commands him to /go north.

Pretty cool, huh? I've included commands for all the common directions: north, south, east, west, up, down, northeast, northwest, southeast, and southwest. I've even included aliases of aliases, which are nw, ne, se, and sw. Here's an example:

```
class ne( northeast ):
    name = "ne"
    usage = "\"ne\""
```

This simply inherits from class northeast, and redefines its name and usage. This class was created so that you can simply type ne instead of northeast to move northeast in the game.

In this particular case, you can't rely on partial matching to match ne with northeast, because the partial string ne doesn't exist in northeast. If you typed no, the game would think you're going north, and not northeast; the smallest string you could type to make the code think you want to go northeast is northe, which isn't exactly a shortcut. So, to fix this, I just created a brand new command named ne.

Simple Commands

Now that you can freely move around, it's a good idea to create commands that modify the physical world. For this, I've implemented the get, drop and give command objects. Here's the get command:

```
class get( PythonCommand.Command ):
    name = "get"
    usage = "\"get <|quantity> <item>\""
    description = "This makes your character attempt to pick up an item"

    def Run( self, args ):
        if not args: raise PythonCommand.UsageError
        me = BetterMUD.character( self.me )
        r = BetterMUD.room( me.Room() )
```

The code if not args checks to see if any arguments were passed into the function; if not, the function raises a UsageError, which causes the command to print out Usage: get <|quantity> <item> to the player. The game doesn't know how to get items if you don't give them a name. The game retrieves accessors to your character (me), and to the room (r).

The usage string for this command is get <|quantity> <item>. The bar in front of quantity means that it's an optional argument; it applies only to quantity items. If there's a sword on the ground, a player could type get sword, or if there is a pile of coins, he could type get 10 coins. If a player wants to get the entire pile (he's greedy!) he would type get coins. The next code segment tries to figure out if a player is trying to get a quantity of items or not:

```
quantity = 0
item = args

if string.digits.find( args[0] ) != -1:
```

The string.digits string is a special built-in string in Python which contains the characters 0123456789. I search that string to see if the first character is a digit.

If a player is getting a quantity, the game extracts that quantity from the arguments using the split function. I've designed the split function so that it splits the string into a list of two strings, one containing the first word, and the other containing the rest of the string:

```
# first letter is a digit, so get quantity
split = args.split( None, 1 )
```

So args was 10 gold coins, split[0] will be 10, and split[1] will be gold coins. The next part converts the quantity into an integer:

```
try:
    quantity = int( split[0] )
    item = split[1]
except:
    # do nothing
    pass
```

This could fail, however. If you try converting something like 1blah into an integer, an exception is thrown. If that happens, the function catches the exception, and just nixes the idea of getting a quantity; quantity is left at 0, and item is left as it was.

If the conversion was successful, the function tries to find the item:

```
i = BetterMUD.item( FindTarget( r.SeekItem, r.IsValidItem,
                    r.CurrentItem, item ) )
```

If the item is valid, an accessor to the item is retrieved; I need to do a little work on it however. If the quantity value is 0, yet the item in question is an actual quantity object, you want the function to get the entire quantity. So that's what it does:

```
if i.IsQuantity() and quantity == 0:
    quantity = i.GetQuantity()
self.mud.DoAction( "attemptgetitem", me.ID(), r.CurrentItem(),
                    quantity, 0, "" )
```

Finally, the item is retrieved, or an error is printed if the item wasn't found.

Dropping an item is almost identical; you need only search the character's inventory for the item to drop (instead of searching the room for an item), and tell the game that you dropped an item.

Giving an item away is slightly more complex, but that's because it must find a player to deliver an item, and then find the item to give to that player. Overall, the code isn't that much different from either getting or dropping an item, so I'm not going to show it here.

All three of these command modules can be found in the /data/commands/ usercommands.py script file.

Logic Scripts

Logic scripts are the real meat behind the game and can be used to accomplish anything you put your mind to.

Can't Get No Satisfaction

There will be times in the game when you want an item to exist, but you want it to be impossible for a character to pick up and carry that item. You could implement some kind of a weight system, and give the item an incredibly large weight value, but that doesn't make it impossible to pick up. There's always a chance someone could gather enough strength to lift it.

For example, a sorcerer could cast a magic "bind" spell on an item, so that it cannot be lifted until someone removes the spell. For casting the spell, you can create a `cantget` logic module.

When I started writing this logic module, I wasn't quite prepared for how simple this would be. Observe:

```
class cantget( data.logics.logic.logic ):
    def Run( self, action, arg1, arg2, arg3, arg4, data ):
        if action == "cangetitem":
            c = BetterMUD.character( arg1 )
            me = BetterMUD.item( arg2 )
            self.mud.AddActionAbsolute( 0, "vision", c.Room(), 0, 0, 0,
                c.Name() + " almost has a hernia, trying to pull " +
                me.Name() + " out of the ground!" )
            return 1
```

Whenever an item with this logic module gets a query `cangetitem`, it simply prints a short error message (to the room, so that everyone sees the character trying to pick up an item that is too big), and returns 1, signifying that it won't allow the action.

That's it! Now, when creating your item templates, all you need to do is this:

```
[ID]                    1
[NAME]                  Fountain
[DESCRIPTION]           This is a large fountain, made of granite and marble.
[ISQUANTITY]            0
[QUANTITY]              1
[DATABANK]
[/DATABANK]
[LOGICS]
cantget
[/LOGICS]
```

Pay attention to the last three lines that state that the fountain item template will have the `cantget` logic module. Now, in the game, whenever someone tries getting a fountain, something like this happens:

```
Mithrandir almost has a hernia, trying to pull Fountain out of the ground!
```

Ta-da! Let's move on to a more complex module.

Receiving Items

Since objects can be given scripts, you're inevitably going to have "malicious" items—items that may injure or attack people when they are picked up. Using your imagination, I'm sure you can think of all kinds of nasty items; hidden bombs that eventually blow up, magical artifacts that drain your health; cursed objects that you can't drop, but weigh you down, and so on.

The BetterMUD allows players to give items to other players, and this is dangerous, since the game by default lets characters accept the items. Any joker can go up to a player and hand him a dangerous object, and that can make for extremely nasty game play—no fun. In fact, if you allow this to happen, I assure you that one of two things will happen: no one will play the game anymore, or you'll end up removing all dangerous items, which entails removing a very interesting part of the game completely.

The "Can't Receive Items" Module

To ensure the game remains fun to play, I've come up with a way to reject receiving items, using the cantreceiveitems logic module. Here's the module:

```
class cantreceiveitems( data.logics.logic.logic ):
    def Run( self, action, arg1, arg2, arg3, arg4, data ):
        if action == "canreceiveitem":
            g = BetterMUD.character( arg1 )
            if not g.IsPlayer(): return 0
            i = BetterMUD.item( arg3 )
            me = BetterMUD.character( self.me )
            g.DoAction( "error", 0, 0, 0, 0, "You can't give " +
                        me.Name() + "" + i.Name() + " but you have
                        item receiving turned off. Type \"/receive on\"
                        to turn receiving back on." )
            me.DoAction( "error", 0, 0, 0, 0, g.Name() +
                        " tried to give you " + i.Name() +
                        " but you have item receiving turned off.
                        Type \"/receive on\" to turn receiving back on." )
        return 1
```

When the game sends an entity an action event, that event is passed into every logic module that entity has. This module for example, responds to the canreceiveitem event, which is an event that the game poses to a character when a character is trying to give another character an item. When this module gets an action event or query, the parameters correspond to those that I defined in Chapter 14. For the canreceiveitem query, action will be canreceiveitem, arg1 will be the ID of the character trying to give the item, arg2 will be the ID of the character receiving the item and arg3 will be the ID of the item being given. The fourth argument and the data parameter are unused.

> **NOTE**
>
> I've made the script automatically accept items given by non-player characters (NPCs). This is a personal taste issue; in the game, I plan on having NPCs give items to players as part of quest scripts, and I don't want scripts being blocked because the player is being cautious. Generally speaking, in my version of the game I don't plan on making NPCs give players evil objects.

If the module sees that the person who is giving an item isn't a player, the module returns 0, allowing the transfer to take place. If the giver *is* a player though, the module sends error messages to both people, saying that the receiver doesn't want to receive items, and then returns 1, signifying failure.

You can find the code for this in the /data/ logics/characters/itemstuff.py script file.

The Receive Command

Of course, you're going to need a command that adds and removes the cantreceiveitems logic from characters, so for this purpose, I've created the receive command. You'll be able to use it in the game to toggle whether you want to receive items or not. Here's the code:

> **TIP**
>
> Don't think that this is the only way to solve the problem. In fact, you may want to make a more complex "opt-in" version of this module, in which you can give the module the names of people who are "trusted" and should be allowed to freely give you items. So if you have friends who you trust, you can make a special command to add them to your "friends" list.

```
class receive( PythonCommand.Command ):
    name = "receive"
    usage = "\"receive <on|off>\""
    description = "Turns your item receiving mode on or off"

    def Run( self, args ):
        if not args: raise PythonCommand.UsageError
        if args != "on" and args != "off": raise PythonCommand.UsageError

        me = BetterMUD.character( self.me )
        if args == "on":
            if me.HasLogic( "cantreceiveitems" ):
                me.DelLogic( "cantreceiveitems" )
                me.DoAction( "announce", 0, 0, 0, 0,
                             "Receiving mode is now ON" )
            else:
                me.DoAction( "error", 0, 0, 0, 0,
                             "You are already in receiving mode!" )
        else:
            if not me.HasLogic( "cantreceiveitems" ):
                me.AddLogic( "cantreceiveitems" )
                me.DoAction( "announce", 0, 0, 0, 0,
                             "Receiving mode is now OFF" )
            else:
                me.DoAction( "error", 0, 0, 0, 0,
                             "You are already in non-receiving mode!" )
```

The first two lines of the Run function check to ensure the arguments are valid; you *must* type on or off after the receive command; everything else isn't recognized, and throws a UsageError exception.

Once you get the mode, the user is retrieved from the database, and the command adds or removes your cantreceiveitems module, or gives you an error if you try setting the same mode that you're already in.

Analysis

Right away, you should be able to see the benefits of having a logical system in BetterMUD. In SimpleMUD, something like this would have been next-to-impossible to implement without first taking down the entire MUD, patching in the code, recompiling, and then hoping it works. Oh, but it gets better. In the SimpleMUD, if you had hardwired this into the game, every character would need a Boolean specifically asking, "Can this player receive items?"

Now, imagine upgrading that system to an "opt-in" system, as I mentioned before. To do this, your characters must be able to store lists of people who are your friends! That means you need to change the physical layout of your files again, and add lists of characters to each item—not a good idea.

But in the BetterMUD, that ability already exists! If the cantreceiveitems module would store a list of your friends, all it needs to do is define its LoadScript and SaveScript functions so that whenever they are invoked, the module simply writes out the list of players in the opt-in list. On disk it would look something like this (this is all hypothetical):

```
cantreceive
[DATA]
10 40 32 86
[/DATA]
```

The numbers in the data block would be the IDs of users from whom the player wants to accept stuff.

I think it's time to move on to something a bit more complex.

Encumbrance

At this point, the BetterMUD allows characters to carry an infinite number of items. Obviously this is not the greatest of ideas, since it would allow your characters to stash as much loot as they wanted, and run around doing whatever they want. An important part of MUD game dynamics is imposing limits on your players and making them work to overcome problems.

In this case, *encumbrance* is a problem. Players should be allowed to carry only a certain number of items, and this number can be increased gradually through the game, as part of a rewards system.

> **NOTE**
>
> I wouldn't recommend establishing the ability to limit the actual number of items carried. Consider this. Quantity objects allow you to carry a whole bunch of a similar kind of item. For example, 100 coins should naturally weigh about 100 times more than 1 coin. But a quantity item is considered just one item. So if you limit the number of items a person can hold to 20, he can hold up to 2 billion coins (a completely unrealistic number in terms of weight), and 19 other items as well. A weight system is far more realistic, however, since it takes into account that you can carry many more small items than large items.

New Attributes

To implement this reward system, you need to add two attributes to your characters—encumbrance and max encumbrance. These values represent the current weight of all the items in your inventory, and the maximum weight that you can carry.

Adding the Attributes

Of course, if you've been running the game for any length of time, and you just decided to add encumbrance to the game, you may run into a snag. Your items don't have weights, and your characters don't have encumbrance values. It's easy enough to add weights to your item templates. Just go into the template files and add the attribute to their databanks. Here's an example of two updated item entries:

```
[ID]                    2
[NAME]                  Pie
[DESCRIPTION]           A BIG <#FFFF00>CUSTARD PIE<$reset>
[ISQUANTITY]            0
[QUANTITY]              1
[DATABANK]
weight                  500
[/DATABANK]
[LOGICS]
[/LOGICS]

[ID]                    5
[NAME]                  Pile of <#> Diamonds
[DESCRIPTION]           A pile of shimmering Diamonds
[ISQUANTITY]            1
[QUANTITY]              1
```

```
[DATABANK]
weight                  1
[/DATABANK]
[LOGICS]
[/LOGICS]
```

So what do these weight values mean? It doesn't matter; it's completely arbitrary in the game—the meanings of the values are up to you. You could use a simple system, in which each number is a pound, or a kilogram, or whatever. Just keep in mind that you can't use fractions, so the smallest positive weight you can use is 1. That means you can't have items that weigh less than 1. I usually try to assign 1 weight point to the weight of a coin, which is usually the lightest object in the game. As you can see from the sample file, the weight of a pie is 500, and the weight of a pile of diamonds is 1.

The weight value for quantity items is *per-quantity*, however. This means that a quantity item with 500 objects weighs as much as 500 times the weight attribute. Since the weight of a pile of 1 diamond is 1, the weight for 500 diamonds is 500.

It's easy enough to give character templates default encumbrance values as well:

```
[ID]                    1
[NAME]                  Human
[DESCRIPTION]           You are a plain old boring human. Deal with it.
[DATABANK]
encumbrance             0
maxencumbrance          2000
[/DATABANK]
[COMMANDS]
[/COMMANDS]
[LOGICS]
cantreceive
[/LOGICS]
```

This shows a human who can hold a maximum weight of 2000, and has a current weight of 0.

Well, that's great, because you can add all this to the templates, reload the templates, and then go into the game, but there's another problem. All existing instances of characters and items *have no idea* what weight and encumbrance are. They were created from templates that didn't have those variables.

To solve this problem, you could make the game go through every item, and load a weight value from its template, and you could do the same with all the characters.

Okay, great! But wait! There's another problem! Characters might have items on them, and if you set all of their encumbrance values to 0, you give all of the characters a bunch of free encumbrance points. When they drop the items they have, their current encumbrance will drop below 0, and that's a bad thing.

So you need to go through all the items that characters have, and add up how much they weigh. Does this sound complex enough yet? How the heck are you going to do all that? If you do it all in C++, your only option is to totally shut down the MUD, and that's just not a good idea.

Initializer Scripts

Instead of adding all this code to C++ to make your updates go smoothly, you can do it all from Python instead. This is the idea of an *initializer script*. It's a simple script that is meant to be run once, and it updates everything in the game that needs updating. More often than not, this involves going through all the item and character instances and giving them the new attributes.

Initializer Command

The first thing you need to do is make a command that executes initializer scripts. This is an easy enough task:

```python
class initialize( PythonCommand.Command ):
    name = "initialize"
    usage = "\"initialize <script>\""
    description = "Performs an initialization using a script"

    def Run( self, args ):
        if not args: raise PythonCommand.UsageError
        exec( "import data.logics.initializers." + args +
            "\nreload( data.logics.initializers." + args +
            " )\ndata.logics.initializers." + args + ".init()" )
```

This code loads a script from /data/logics/initializers, reloads it, and then calls the `init` function in that script file.

The reloading is included because if you run the initializer script once, Python usually doesn't get rid of it. Python keeps the script loaded, and if you import it again, nothing changes, even if you change the initializer script.

The `exec` function essentially allows you to execute the Python code that is in a string. So if you were to execute an `addencumbrance` initializer, the code that would be executed would look like this:

```python
import data.logics.initializers.addencumbrance
reload( data.logics.initializers.addencumbrance )
data.logics.initializers.addencumbrance.init()
```

And the game executes that script for you.

The Add Encumbrance Initializer Script

Now you need to make a script that goes through all the item instances and copies their weights from their templates, and also goes through all the character instances and gives them their encumbrance values, which are also taken from their templates. Figure 18.1 shows this process.

```python
def init():
    mud = BetterMUD.GameWrap()

    # add weight to every item
    mud.BeginItem()
```

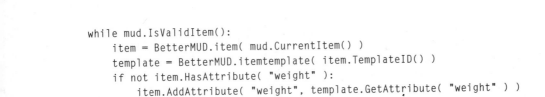

```
while mud.IsValidItem():
    item = BetterMUD.item( mud.CurrentItem() )
    template = BetterMUD.itemtemplate( item.TemplateID() )
    if not item.HasAttribute( "weight" ):
        item.AddAttribute( "weight", template.GetAttribute( "weight" ) )
    mud.NextItem()
```

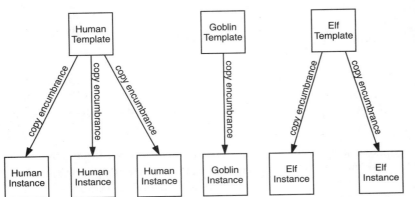

Figure 18.1

An initializer script goes through every instance, and copies an attribute from the templates into the instances.

The previous code chunk goes through every item instance in the game, using the game wrapper accessor as an iterator. It adds one to every item that doesn't have a "weight" attribute.

The next step is to go through all the characters and give them their two encumbrance values:

```
# add encumbrance to every character
mud.BeginCharacter()
while mud.IsValidCharacter():
    character = BetterMUD.character( mud.CurrentCharacter() )
    template = BetterMUD.charactertemplate( character.TemplateID() )
    if not character.HasAttribute( "encumbrance" ):
        character.AddAttribute( "encumbrance",
                        template.GetAttribute( "encumbrance" ) )
    if not character.HasAttribute( "maxencumbrance" ):
        character.AddAttribute( "maxencumbrance",
                        template.GetAttribute( "maxencumbrance" ) )
```

Now that the characters have encumbrance and maxencumbrance variables, you need to calculate the weight of the items currently carried by the character:

```
# now calculate encumbrance of carried items
character.BeginItem()
encumbrance = 0
while character.IsValidItem():
    item = BetterMUD.item( character.CurrentItem() )
```

```
    if item.IsQuantity():
        encumbrance = encumbrance + item.GetAttribute( "weight" ) *
                    item.GetQuantity()
    else:
        encumbrance = encumbrance + item.GetAttribute( "weight" )
    character.NextItem()
character.SetAttribute( "encumbrance", encumbrance )
```

At this point, the encumbrance attribute holds the value of the weights of all the character's items added together. The final step of the initializer gives the characters the "encumbrance" logic module if they don't have it:

```
    if not character.HasLogic( "encumbrance" ):
        character.AddLogic( "encumbrance" )
    mud.NextCharacter()
```

And now your game is initialized to handle encumbrance.

You will probably have to make a script like this for any major update to the game.

Encumbrance Module

Finally, you can program the logic module itself. You must manage two distinct parts of the module: accepting or rejecting items based on weight and modifying encumbrance.

> **TIP**
>
> In case you screw anything up (nobody is perfect!), it's probably a good idea to save the database before and after you run an initialization script.

Calculating Weight

Since it's often necessary to calculate the weight of an item, I've included it as a special helper function inside the encumbrance logic module class:

```
def Weight( self, i, q ):
    item = BetterMUD.item( i )
    if item.IsQuantity():
        return q * item.GetAttribute( "weight" )
    else:
        return item.GetAttribute( "weight" )
```

The parameters are the class itself, the item ID, and the quantity. If the parameter is a quantity item, the weight of the item is multiplied by the quantity and returned, or else the normal weight is returned.

Rejecting Items

Two actions allow the encumbrance module to reject getting items: cangetitem and canreceiveitem. In both cases, the functions must check if the weight of the item will cause a player to carry too much weight, and if so, the player isn't allowed to get it. Here's the code:

```
if action == "cangetitem":
    me = BetterMUD.character( self.me )
    item = BetterMUD.item( arg2 )
    weight = self.Weight( arg2, arg3 )
    if weight + me.GetAttribute( "encumbrance" ) >
        me.GetAttribute( "maxencumbrance" ):
        me.DoAction( "error", 0, 0, 0, 0, "You can't pick up " + item.Name() +
                        " because it's too heavy for you to carry!" )
        return 1
    return 0

if action == "canreceiveitem":
    g = BetterMUD.character( arg1 )
    me = BetterMUD.character( self.me )
    item = BetterMUD.item( arg3 )
    weight = self.Weight( arg3, arg4 )
    if weight + me.GetAttribute( "encumbrance" ) >
        me.GetAttribute( "maxencumbrance" ):
        me.DoAction( "error", 0, 0, 0, 0, g.Name() + " tried to give you " +
                        item.Name() + " but it's too heavy for you to carry!" )
        g.DoAction( "error", 0, 0, 0, 0, "You can't give " + me.Name() +
                        " the " + item.Name() + " because it is too heavy!" )
        return 1
    return 0
```

The code prints error messages appropriate for a character getting an item or for giving an item. In the case of giving, an error is printed to both people involved, so that the giver knows he can't give the item, and the receiver knows that he can't accept the item. Both of these instances return 1, telling the physics layer that the action couldn't be done.

Weight Management

The encumbrance module also needs to manage your weight when you get or drop an item. There are three events that can be triggered when you get a new item, and three events when you lose an item.

Here are two events for getting items:

```
if action == "getitem":
    if arg1 == self.me:
        me = BetterMUD.character( self.me )
        item = BetterMUD.item( arg2 )
        weight = self.Weight( arg2, arg3 )
```

```
        me.SetAttribute( "encumbrance", me.GetAttribute( "encumbrance" ) +
                    weight )
    return 0

if action == "spawnitem":
    me = BetterMUD.character( self.me )
    item = BetterMUD.item( arg1 )
    weight = self.Weight( arg1, item.GetQuantity() )
    me.SetAttribute( "encumbrance", me.GetAttribute( "encumbrance" ) +
                    weight )
    return 0
```

These events are called when a player gets a new item, or a new item is spawned into a player's inventory. Both instances get accessors to the character and the item, calculate the weight, and then add that to the character's encumbrance attribute.

Here are two of the events that occur when you lose an item:

```
if action == "dropitem":
    if arg1 == self.me:
        me = BetterMUD.character( self.me )
        item = BetterMUD.item( arg2 )
        weight = self.Weight( arg2, arg3 )
        me.SetAttribute( "encumbrance", me.GetAttribute( "encumbrance" ) -
                        weight )
    return 0

if action == "destroyitem":
    me = BetterMUD.character( self.me )
    item = BetterMUD.item( arg1 )
```

> **NOTE**
>
> You should note that there may be times in the game when an item is forced into a player's inventory without the player first being asked if he can have it. When this happens, you should still perform the normal duties on the item. Being loaded with an item without being asked could force a player's encumbrance over his max encumbrance, but that's not a huge deal. If you're concerned about this issue, you can add a function to the encumbrance module that keeps a player from moving anywhere if he is over his limit. You would do this by returning 1 whenever you get a `canleaveroom` query.

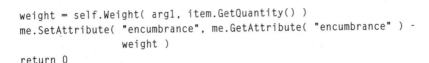

```
weight = self.Weight( arg1, item.GetQuantity() )
me.SetAttribute( "encumbrance", me.GetAttribute( "encumbrance" ) -
                    weight )
return 0
```

These two actions simply remove the weight from a player's encumbrance whenever he loses the item. You should note that the additem and destroyitem actions both check to ensure that the actor (arg1) has the same ID as the character executing the logic script. This is because all characters in a room are told when someone gets or drops an item, so the encumbrance module of everyone in a room is also informed. It would be a major flaw to add or remove weight for an item a player doesn't actually have.

The third event is a "mixed" event and can happen if a player either gives away or is given an item:

```
if action == "giveitem":
    if arg1 == self.me:
        me = BetterMUD.character( self.me )
        item = BetterMUD.item( arg3 )
        weight = self.Weight( arg3, arg4 )
        me.SetAttribute( "encumbrance", me.GetAttribute( "encumbrance" ) -
                            weight )
    if arg2 == self.me:
        me = BetterMUD.character( self.me )
        item = BetterMUD.item( arg3 )
        weight = self.Weight( arg3, arg4 )
        me.SetAttribute( "encumbrance", me.GetAttribute( "encumbrance" ) +
                            weight )
    return 0
```

Whenever this event occurs, arg1 is the ID of the player giving away the item, so if it matches the ID of the character that owns the current logic module, you must remove the weight. On the other hand, arg2 is the recipient of the item, so if the player is the recipient, weight must be added to him.

Analysis

I hope you thought that example was pretty cool. The physical game engine has absolutely no clue about how much items weigh, or how many items a player can carry at any time, but by adding a simple logic module and a few attributes, you've now just added a completely new aspect to the game. Now you can limit what players carry, and force them to perform quests to gain the ability to carry more items. It's little things like this that add immensely to your replay value.

To Arms!

When I first told you about the stuff that will be in BetterMUD's physical layer, you may have been surprised to see that there is no concept of "armed" weapons. How the heck will combat take place if you can't arm weapons?

Well, the physics of BetterMUD isn't involved with "armed" weapons; that's for the logic layer to implement. So you add a new attribute to characters in order to implement "armed" weapons—the weapon attribute. Simply put, the weapon attribute is the ID of the item in your inventory that you are currently using as a weapon.

To make things more interesting, you have another attribute—the defaultweapon attribute. In the SimpleMUD, if a weapon isn't armed, the game assumes that a player is using his fists to attack, and the game calculates a damage range from 1–3. That range is hard-coded into the game, and that very fact should be making you squirm in your seat right now. The appropriate reaction should be "Eeeew, hard-coding! Gross!!"

So the default weapon is the template ID of an item that can be used as a weapon; but these are special items that are never actually created in the game, such as "fists" if the player is human, or maybe "scorpion tail" if the player is some kind of giant mutant scorpion.

Additionally, items are given a new attribute, the arms attribute. This is a simple numeric that determines if an item can be equipped. For now, the value of 0 means no, and the value of 1 means it is a weapon. All other values are reserved for future use, such as adding armor types.

Armaments Module

"Consult the Book of Armaments! And Saint Attila raised the hand grenade up on high, saying, "O Lord, bless this thy hand grenade, that with it thou mayst blow thine enemies to tiny bits, in thy mercy." And the Lord did grin. And the people did feast upon the lambs and sloths, and carp, and anchovies, and orangutans and breakfast cereals, and fruit-bats and-"

All right, enough quoting from Monty Python jokes. The armaments module basically allows characters to arm and disarm weapons. Since the game has no physical sense of "arming" an item, I have to use the query and do actions to ask items if they can be armed, and tell players to arm them.

Here's the armaments module in its entirety:

```
class armaments( data.logics.logic.logic ):

    # helper function to arm an item; only handles weapons for now:
    def Disarm( self, itemtype ):
        if itemtype == 1:
            me = BetterMUD.character( self.me )
            if me.GetAttribute( "weapon" ) != 0:
                weapon = BetterMUD.item( me.GetAttribute( "weapon" ) )
                me.SetAttribute( "weapon", 0 )
                self.mud.AddActionAbsolute( 0, "vision", me.Room(), 0, 0, 0,
                                            me.Name() + " disarms " +
                                            weapon.Name() + "." )

    # helper function to disarm an item; only handles weapons for now:
    def Arm( self, item ):
```

```
me = BetterMUD.character( self.me )
if item.GetAttribute( "arms" ) == 1:
    me.SetAttribute( "weapon", item.ID() )
    self.mud.AddActionAbsolute( 0, "vision", me.Room(), 0, 0, 0,
                                me.Name() + " arms " + item.Name() +
                                "!" )

# handle events:
def Run( self, action, arg1, arg2, arg3, arg4, data ):

    # can only arm weapons (arms = 1) right now:
    if action == "query" and data == "canarm":
        item = BetterMUD.item( arg1 )
        if item.GetAttribute( "arms" ) == 1:
            return 1
        return 0

    # try arming the item:
    if action == "do" and data == "arm":
        item = BetterMUD.item( arg3 )
        self.Disarm( 1 )
        self.Arm( item )

    # try disarming the item:
    if action == "do" and data == "disarm":
        self.Disarm( arg3 )
```

Look at the query function first. If it determines that you can arm an item (if it's a weapon, arms will be 1), it returns 1. Remember that in Chapter 14 I told you about granting rights to entities and that all entities automatically have the right to perform any of the standard physical events, such as moving around. You had to specifically disable an act in order to prevent it.

With custom actions, like canarm, items cannot automatically be armed. The game assumes that a reply of 0 means no. By default, every logic module should return 0, and thus say no whenever a player is asked if he can arm an item. But if the item is a weapon (arms is 1), you know that the item can be used as a weapon, and the function returns 1 for yes.

The other actions, do disarm and do arm simply call the helper functions to disarm and arm weapons.

Table 18.1 defines the event parameters for these actions.

Commands

Like all things in the BetterMUD, you need a way to actually invoke the logic module. This is done via two commands, one that arms an item, and one that disarms an item.

Table 18.1   Event Parameters for disarm and arm

Parameter	arm	disarm
action	do	do
arg1	*entity type	*entity type
arg2	*entity id	*entity id
arg3	item being armed	type of item being disarmed
arg4	not used	not used
data	arm	disarm

*These are optional parameters that are used to route the event to an entity when using timers. See Chapter 14 for more information.

Here's the arm command:

```
class arm( PythonCommand.Command ):
    name = "arm"
    usage = "\"arm <item>\""
    description = "Attempts to arm an item"

    def Run( self, args ):
        if not args: raise PythonCommand.UsageError

        me = BetterMUD.character( self.me )
        item = BetterMUD.item( FindTarget( me.SeekItem, me.IsValidItem,
                            me.CurrentItem, args ) )
        if not me.DoAction( "query", item.ID(), 0, 0, 0, "canarm" ):
            me.DoAction( "error", 0, 0, 0, 0, "Cannot arm item: " +
                        item.Name() + "!" )
            return

        me.DoAction( "do", 0, 0, item.ID(), 0, "arm" )
```

Note that the ID of the item being armed is the third argument while passing the do and query events around. The first two arguments are reserved for routing delayed events in the timer system to a specific entity (see Chapter 14 if you don't remember this). Table 18.2 lists the event parameters for the canarm query.

Table 18.2   Event Parameters for canarm

Parameter	Can Arm
action	query
arg1	item you want to arm
arg2	not used
arg3	not used
arg4	not used
data	canarm

Disarming an item is similar to disarming in theSimpleMUD. A player must type `disarm weapon` to disarm his current weapon:

```
class disarm( PythonCommand.Command ):
    name = "disarm"
    usage = "\"disarm <item>\""
    description = "Attempts to disarm an item"

    def Run( self, args ):
        if not args: raise PythonCommand.UsageError

        me = BetterMUD.character( self.me )
        if args == "weapon":
            me.DoAction( "do", 0, 0, 1, 0, "disarm" )
```

This time, the third argument to the `do` event is the type of armament to be removed. The value 1 signifies a player wants to disarm his weapon.

Initialization Script

There is an initialization script for adding armaments to the game, which is very similar to the encumbrance initialization script. Since the scripts are so similar, I won't show you the code, but you can find it in the /data/logics/initializers/addarmaments.py file.

Analysis

So now a player can add armed weapons to a character, and the physical module isn't involved. Isn't that neat?

For a more complex MUD, you might consider adding more than one weapon slot (you could make it so that a player can hold two small, light weapons), or adding armor slots, or other cool enhancements.

In this example you saw how you could make your own custom event messages that the core BetterMUD physical engine doesn't support. The canarm and arm events are completely new, and can be used to query characters and items about whether they can be armed.

In a similar vein, you could make canread or caneat events, to make the realm even more realistic.

I Put a Spell on You

The next endeavor I want to cover is learning how to "cast a spell". Spell casting requires several elements, as do the other logics.

Basically, I want to create a spell named uberweight, that can be cast on items, and to make them stick to the ground for 20 seconds, so that no one can pick them up.

This spell can only be cast once every 2 minutes, which players learn from reading a magic scroll. Sound complex enough yet?

Designing the Item

The first task is to design the item in question. The actual item template is simple:

```
[ID]                    54
[NAME]                  Scroll of Uberweight
[DESCRIPTION]           This scroll contains the spell of Uberweight on it.
[ISQUANTITY]            0
[QUANTITY]              1
[DATABANK]
weight                  50
arms                    0
[/DATABANK]
[LOGICS]
canread uberweightscroll
[/LOGICS]
```

You can ignore everything but the two logic modules. Each of the two logic modules implements an action: the first says that the item can be read, and the second says that it has the uberweightscroll item logic module attached to it.

Can You Read?

The canread item logic module is really simple; it merely returns 1 whenever someone asks it if it can be read:

```
class canread( data.logics.logic.logic ):
    def Run( self, action, arg1, arg2, arg3, arg4, data ):
        if action == "query" and data == "canread":
            return 1
```

Ta-da! Any item that has this module now returns 1 when asked if it can be read. This class can be found in /data/logics/items/basicitems.py. Table 18.3 lists the event parameters for the canread action event.

Scroll Module

In this particular version of the BetterMUD, I've decided to make it possible for characters to read magical scrolls, and then memorize the spell learned from the scroll. Instead of copying the code for every scroll type, I've made a base spellscroll class that does 95% of the work.

It must return an error if a player is trying to learn a spell that he already knows, or it must give the player the command that controls the spell if he doesn't have it. Here's the code:

> **NOTE**
>
> Here's an idea for future expansion. Perhaps you want to give your characters a sense of "literacy," so that only some characters can read. If you have a big dumb ogre character, for example, he is disadvantaged in the game, because he can't read magic scrolls to learn to cast spells. Maybe you could even expand on this idea, and include the idea of languages for readable objects. Some things could be written in an ancient Elven language, so dwarfs and humans can't read them.

```
class spellscroll( data.logics.logic.logic ):
    def DoRead( self, character, item, name ):

        # look up character and item
        c = BetterMUD.character( character )
        i = BetterMUD.item( item )

        # check if character has spell command already
        if c.HasCommand( name ):
            c.DoAction( "error", 0, 0, 0, 0, "You already know this spell!" )
            return

        # give character new spell command, and tell everyone:
        c.AddCommand( name )
        self.mud.AddActionAbsolute( 0, "vision", c.Room(), 0, 0, 0,
                                    c.Name() + " reads " + i.Name() + "!" )
        self.mud.AddActionAbsolute( 1, "destroyitem", i.ID(), 0, 0, 0, "" )
```

```
c.DoAction( "announce", 0, 0, 0, 0, "You now know the spell " +
        name + "!" )
c.DoAction( "announce", 0, 0, 0, 0, "The " + i.Name() +
        " disappears in a bright flash of flame!" )
```

This code assumes that the command object has the same name as the spell; so if you have a spell named uberweight, the command object is named uberweight as well.

Note that the scroll is destroyed after it is read, and this is just a little quirk I enjoyed inserting into the game. You don't want a single scroll giving everyone in the game a spell (if the owner is generous enough to lend it to other people), so it's simply destroyed.

This class can be found in /data/logics/ items/spellitems.py.

> **NOTE**
>
> Please don't think that this is how you have to implement spells. The beauty of this system is that you can implement spells in *any* way you want. Spells don't have to be commands that you learn by reading scrolls. Instead you could make a "spell book" item that can store all of the spells you know. Maybe you can even have your characters gain specific spells whenever they get to a certain level. The possibilities are limitless.

Uberweightscroll Logic

Now that you have a scroll class, all you need to do is create an item logic that will be attached to the scroll item, and give characters the spell when the item is read:

```
class uberweightscroll( spellscroll ):
    def Run( self, action, arg1, arg2, arg3, arg4, data ):
        if action == "do" and data == "read":
            self.DoRead( arg3, self.me, "uberweight" )
            return
```

Table 18.3   Event Parameters for canread

Parameter	Can Read
action	query
arg1	not used
arg2	not used
arg3	not used
arg4	not used
data	canread

The `uberweightscroll` logic module is meant to be attached to scrolls, and whenever someone sends a `do read` event to it, the base `spellscroll` class is called, adding the spell command `uberweight` to the character.

Table 18.4 lists the parameters for the `read` event.

Uberweight Command

The next step is to create the `uberweight` command. This is the command that actually casts the spell.

This command must do several things. First, it must store data about the last time it was invoked, so that you can limit how often the spell is cast.

Since this spell needs some extra data, I'll need to give it a `ScriptInit` function, so that it initializes the data when the command object is first created:

```
class uberweight( PythonCommand.Command ):
    name = "uberweight"
```

NOTE

If you're inclined, you could limit the "casting time" to a small number such as 5 seconds, and then give the character a "mana" attribute, and have the spell subtract from that variable whenever it is cast. When the mana goes down to 0, the character isn't allowed to cast it anymore, until he gets more energy. This method is used in many MUDs because it allows characters to cast a single spell rapidly, but it sets reasonable limits. I've used a simple system here, to show you that there are many ways to do anything.

Table 18.4   Event Parameters for read

Parameter	Read
action	do
arg1	*entity type
arg2	*entity id
arg3	character performing the reading
arg4	not used
data	read

*These are optional parameters that are used to route the event to an entity when using timers. See Chapter 14 for more information.

```
usage = "\"uberweight <item>\""
description = "puts a magical weight on an item"

def ScriptInit( self ):
    # init the next execution time to 0, so you can execute it right away
    self.executiontime = 0
```

This simply creates an executiontime variable, and sets it to 0. Whenever executiontime is more than the game's current time, you'll be blocked from using the spell. Since the game always starts at 0, you'll be able to cast the spell right away after it's given to you.

Now the actual execution:

```
def Run( self, args ):
    if not args: raise PythonCommand.UsageError

    # grab the character and room
    me = BetterMUD.character( self.me )
    r = BetterMUD.room( me.Room() )

    # check to make sure you can execute it
    time = self.mud.GetTime()
    if time < self.executiontime:
        me.DoAction( "error", 0, 0, 0, 0, "You need to wait " +
                     str( (self.executiontime - time) / 1000 ) +
                     " more seconds to use this again!" )
        return

    # find the name of the item to cast on:
    id = FindTarget( r.SeekItem, r.IsValidItem, r.CurrentItem, args )
    item = BetterMUD.item( id )
    name = item.Name()

    # add 120 seconds; 2 minutes
    self.executiontime = time + 120000

    # tell everyone about it, and add a termination message:
    self.mud.AddActionAbsolute( 0, "addlogic", 1, id, 0, 0, "uberweight" )
    self.mud.AddActionAbsolute( 0, "vision", r.ID(), 0, 0, 0,
                                "<#FF0000>" + me.Name() +
                                " just cast UBERWEIGHT on " + name + "!" )
    self.mud.AddActionRelative( 20000, "messagelogic", 1, id, 0, 0,
                                "uberweight remove" )
```

The function ensures that the character can execute the spell first; if not, he's told how long to wait. If he can execute the spell, the function tries to find the item he wants to cast the spell on. If the item is found, the execution time is reset to two minutes from that time

(120 seconds, or 120,000 milliseconds), and three actions are added. The first adds the `uberweight` logic module to the item, the second tells everyone in the player's room that he cast uberweight on an item, and the last one tells the game to remove `uberweight` in 20 seconds. All of the events use the same parameter conventions I showed you in Chapter 14.

There is a difference between the `uberweight` command object and the `uberweight` item logic module.

Uberweight Item Logic Module

The last component of the system is the logic module that is attached to items when they have `uberweight` cast upon them. This module refuses to let items be picked up, much like the `cantget` script I showed you before.

You should only use special `uberweight` logic for items, rather than re-using `cantget`, to send a customized message to players when they try to get the item, and to tell a room when the spell wears off.

> **NOTE**
>
> It's very difficult for me to intentionally limit the code for the BetterMUD, but if I didn't this book would weigh 50 pounds. You should always be thinking about how you can expand the game. For example, I'm thinking about expanding this spell system later, to give levels of spells. With that system, every time a player reads a new scroll, he advances a level, and the spell becomes more powerful. Or maybe you'll have scrolls with levels built in, so that you need a level 2 uberweight scroll to get to level 2, and so on. The point of all of this is to give you a start, so you can see how a separated logic/physics engine allows essentially limitless expansion.

```
class uberweight( data.logics.logic.logic ):
    def Run( self, action, arg1, arg2, arg3, arg4, data ):
        if action == "cangetitem":
            c = BetterMUD.character( arg1 )
            me = BetterMUD.item( arg2 )
            self.mud.AddActionAbsolute( 0, "vision", c.Room(), 0, 0, 0,
                c.Name() + " struggles like a madman trying to pull " +
                me.Name() + " off the ground, but it's stuck!" )
            return 1

        if action == "messagelogic":
            if data == "uberweight remove":
                self.mud.AddActionAbsolute( 0, "dellogic", 1, self.me, 0, 0,
                                            "uberweight" )
                me = BetterMUD.item( self.me )
                self.mud.AddActionAbsolute( 0, "vision", me.Room(), 0, 0, 0,
                                            "The uberweight on " + me.Name() +
                                            " wears off!" )
```

This object responds to two events: cangetitem and messagelogic. Like the cantget module, the object prints a message to the room, telling everyone that the character can't get the item, and returns 1, telling the physics engine that the action was blocked.

When you first gave the uberweight logic to an item, the uberweight command inserted a message into the timer queue:

```
self.mud.AddActionRelative( 20000, "messagelogic", 1, id, 0, 0,
                            "uberweight remove" )
```

Remember, that code tells the item's uberweight module to remove itself in 20 seconds. When the item's module gets this message, it deletes the actual logic module, and then sends a vision event to the room saying that the uberweight has ended.

That's it!

Example of Item Logic

Here's an example of the game text that appears when using the uberweight item logic module:

```
Avenue
You are on the main Avenue of Betterton. You can see the street stretching
off to the distance in an east-west direction.
Exits: East - Avenue, South - Magicians Door
People: Mithrandir
Items: Mountain Dew
/read scroll
You now know the spell uberweight!
The Scroll of Uberweight disappears in a bright flash of flame!
Mithrandir reads Scroll of Uberweight!
/uberweight mountain dew
Mithrandir just cast UBERWEIGHT on Mountain Dew!
/get mountain dew
Mithrandir struggles like a madman trying to pull Mountain Dew off the ground,
but it's stuck!
The uberweight on Mountain Dew wears off!
/uber moun
You need to wait 94 more seconds to use this again!
/
You need to wait 79 more seconds to use this again!
```

And you've just created your very first spell! Cast away!

Show Me the Money!

The concept of currency is not built into the BetterMUD. If you think about real life, coins and dollars are just physical objects that represent an abstract value. In fact, if you really want to, you can turn the BetterMUD into a *barter system*, in which there is no money at all; you trade items with other people based on how much you think they're worth. If you ever traded in baseball cards as a kid, you know exactly how such a system works.

Simple Systems

It's entirely possible in the BetterMUD to implement bartering, so that a character can, for example, go up to a merchant and trade him two knives for a sword. All you need to do is create a logic module to handle bartering. Heck, if you're really ambitious, you could even make merchant scripts that assign different values to their items based on how much they think the items are worth. An arms merchant might value weapons highly, but a magic merchant wouldn't, so trading him weapons would give you less favorable trades.

Of course, there haven't been barter systems in wide use for hundreds of years in the industrialized world, because barter systems are inconvenient. In such a system, not everyone can trade, because trading requires both parties having something that the other wants. For a barter system to work, the merchant must own a sword that a player wants, and the player must have something that the merchant wants.

Currency Systems

Currency systems work more efficiently than bartering in the world most of us know. Instead of trading in objects, you trade objects for abstract pieces of currency that are worth a particular value. If you want a sword, you pay the merchant for it, and then the merchant can take that money and find someone else who can sell him what he needs, instead of requiring you to give him things.

The entire idea of currency systems is what prompted me to put "quantity items" into the physical engine of the BetterMUD. I've rarely seen a MUD that works without some kind of currency system, so that's just what I'm going to show you how to implement.

You don't need to script any player-to-player transactions involving money. Players basically have to trust each other in transactions—one player gives another money, and that players gives something in return.

Of course, money really isn't worth anything until you can use it to buy things from NPC's in the game, and that's the system you'll be using. The first thing you need to think about is what kind of currency system you want to use. Since quantity objects now have weight, there is an upper limit on the size of piles of cash you can lug around; you can't just pour a few million coins into your pocket (talk about deep pockets!) and skip around as you did in SimpleMUD.

The weight of currency can be inconvenient to wealthy players. How the heck are they going to carry around millions of dollars? How are they even going to accumulate wealth in the first place?

NOTE

Game currencies are not required to be based on a "solid" value. If you've studied economics at all, you know that the value of money changes wherever you go. For example, in Buffalo, NY, you can buy a decent lunch for about $7, but if you go to New York City, it's hard to find lunch for less than $13 or so. Money is worth different amounts in different places. I can't say how useful such a system would be to you, but if you feel like experimenting, feel free. Borrowing an idea from Raymond E. Feists' *Riftwar* books, you could have a region in the game where there is no metal, but tons of diamonds and gems, and therefore metal coins are worth a heck of a lot more than diamonds. I would like to note that managing such a system is an *extremely* difficult task, because there are ways for entrepreneurial players to endlessly convert money between the two systems and gain value with every conversion. I'm just pointing out that if you ever want to make such a system, you can.

Multiple Currencies

An elegant solution to this problem is to have different denominations of money. When you think about coinage systems, you realize that countries press different valued coins. In USA we have pennies (1 cent), nickels (5 cents), dimes (10 cents), quarters (25 cents), and a bunch of less common coins as well. You could create similar equivalents in your game with one kind worth 10 of another kind, and so on.

TIP

When making a currency system with coins using different values, I would always recommend valuing coins as multiples of 10. So the smallest coin would be worth 1, the next up would be worth 10, the next 100, and so on. This makes calculating prices in the game much easier for your players.

Simple Currency Example

For the purposes of this book, I'm not going to go over a complete money system; there are only so many things you can do. But I will show you the general gist of one system, and then you can make changes and additions wherever appropriate.

The key to the basic BetterMUD currency exchange system is the merchant class, which is a character logic module that lists items to sell, and lets you buy them from him.

Currency

The first thing I need is a currency type. That's easy enough to create:

```
[ID]            1
[NAME]              <#> Copper Coins
```

```
[DESCRIPTION]                 These copper coins are small and dirty, they don't
have much value.
[ISQUANTITY]          1
[QUANTITY]            1
[DATABANK]
weight                1
arms                  0
[/DATABANK]
[LOGICS]
[/LOGICS]
```

It's just a standard quantity-type object, with a weight of 1 unit per coin.

Helpers

The next thing you'll need are helper functions, which are functions that perform various money-related tasks, such as checking if a character has enough money to buy something, and removing that money when he does buy something.

> **NOTE**
>
> The great thing about separating transactions into functions like this is that the separation significantly helps later on if you make a multiple currency system. These functions should automatically manage all of that for you, if you make the appropriate changes.

The helpers and the merchant classes I cover in the section after this are located in /data/logics/characters/currency.py

Here's the first helper function:

```python
def HasEnoughCurrency( character, amount ):
    total = 0
    character.BeginItem()
    while character.IsValidItem():
        item = BetterMUD.item( character.CurrentItem() )
        if item.TemplateID() == 1:    # copper pieces
            total = total + item.GetQuantity()
        character.NextItem()

    if total >= amount:
        return 1
    return 0
```

This simply looks through all the items on a player, searching for copper coins. Whenever they are found, their quantity is added to the total. Finally, when the total is added up, if it's enough to pay for the requested amount, 1 is returned, or 0 if not.

The other function removes money from your character and gives it to another character:

```python
def GiveCurrency( character, recipient, amount ):
    character.BeginItem()
    mud = BetterMUD.GameWrap()
```

```
while character.IsValidItem():
    item = BetterMUD.item( character.CurrentItem() )
    if item.TemplateID() == 1:   # copper pieces
        mud.DoAction( "attemptgiveitem", character.ID(), recipient.ID(),
                      item.ID(), amount, "" )
        return
    character.NextItem()
```

CAUTION

Take care to never modify physical attributes such as quantity directly through these functions. Doing so messes up any encumbrance system you have running, since the system is not told that you are losing money. Instead, rely on physical actions. In this example, I give the money from one character to the merchant; keep in mind that you don't have to do that if you don't want to. Instead you could simply tell the character that you're destroying an item.

This finds a bunch of coins, and removes the amount from their quantity. This function assumes you've already checked to see if the character has enough money in the first place.

Merchant Logic

Since merchant characters are frequently found in MUD games, I've decided to create a base Python logic module that acts like a merchant. This is only a simple merchant, however; he'll only list things and sell things.

I would like to note that due to the logic system of the BetterMUD, characters are the merchants, and they don't have to be linked to a specific room, as they were in the SimpleMUD. Of course, this also means that if someone kills a merchant, the merchant can't sell stuff anymore (seems obvious, doesn't it?).

The merchant responds to two different custom events; do list and do buy. Table 18.5 lists the parameters for these events.

Here's the list handler (which is, as usual, executed from within Run, and therefore has the standard event parameters):

```
if action == "do" and data == "list":
    character = BetterMUD.character( arg3 )
    character.DoAction( "announce", 0, 0, 0, 0,
                        "<#7F7F7F>--------------------------------------" )
    character.DoAction( "announce", 0, 0, 0, 0,
                        "<#FFFFFF> Item                            | Cost" )
```

```
character.DoAction( "announce", 0, 0, 0, 0,
                    "<#7F7F7F>----------------------------------------" )
for x in self.iteminventory:
    item = BetterMUD.itemtemplate( x )
    character.DoAction( "announce", 0, 0, 0, 0, "<#7F7F7F> " +
                        item.Name().ljust( 42 ) + "| " +
                        str( item.GetAttribute( "value" ) ) )
character.DoAction( "announce", 0, 0, 0, 0,
                    "<#7F7F7F>----------------------------------------" )

return
```

Table 18.5   Event Parameters for list and buy

Parameter	list	buy
action	do	do
arg1	*entity type	*entity type
arg2	*entity id	*entity id
arg3	character who wants list	character buying
arg4	not used	not used
data	list	buy <item name>

*These are optional parameters used to route the event to an entity when using timers. See Chapter 14 for more information.

Due to width restraints on the page, I've cut the length of the separator bars down a bit; they're actually supposed to be a full 80 characters across.

Basically this prints out a header, and then it goes through every item in self.iteminventory using a Python for loop.

Merchants must have a list of entity IDs named self.iteminventory; this list represents every item the merchant can sell.

The other action that merchants react to is the buy event:

```
if action == "do" and data[:3] == "buy":
    itemname = data.split( None, 1 )
    itemname = itemname[1]
    character = BetterMUD.character( arg3 )
    id = FindName( BetterMUD.itemtemplate, self.iteminventory, itemname )
```

```
if id == 0:
    character.DoAction( "announce", 0, 0, 0, 0, "Sorry, you can't buy " +
                        itemname + "here!" )
    return

t = BetterMUD.itemtemplate( id )
if not HasEnoughCurrency( character, t.GetAttribute( "value" ) ):
    character.DoAction( "announce", 0, 0, 0, 0,
                        "Sorry, you don't have enough money to buy " +
                        t.Name() + "!" )
    return

GiveCurrency( character, me, t.GetAttribute( "value" ) )
self.mud.DoAction( "spawnitem", id, character.ID(), 1, 0, "" )
self.mud.AddActionAbsolute( 0, "vision", character.Room(), 0, 0, 0,
                            character.Name() + " buys " +
                            t.Name() + "." )
```

The format of the data parameter for this event is a bit tricky. Whenever a player wants to buy something, he passes in buy followed by the item name in the data string. So if he wants a sword, data would be buy sword. To get the name of the item, I use the string's split function to chop off buy, and then grab the rest of the string and stash it into itemname.

On the fifth line, I use a function named FindName, which is a Python helper function (I created this for you) that performs the same function as the C++ BetterMUD::match function. The function goes through a list of IDs and tries to make a full or partial match on one of them, and return the ID.

Basically this process searches the inventory for an item that matches the item the user is trying to buy.

> **NOTE**
>
> The IDs in the merchant's inventory represent item templates, rather than item instances. This means that every time a character buys something, a brand new item is spawned and given to the character. You should be aware that this is only one of many ways to do this. In a more highly managed world, merchants might sell only items that they are carrying in their inventory, and when they are sold out, no one can buy anything more. This is a great way of limiting the number of items in a game, and increasing their perceived worth. When items are rare, they generally cost more as well, since demand is larger than supply.

> ## CAUTION
>
> At this point I want to warn you that this is a dangerous system. The function assumes that the transfer of money was completed successfully, even though it may not have been. This is because items can block being transferred, and piles of money are treated as regular items. I would like to point out that it's just not a good idea to either put scripts of *any* kind on quantity objects, or make it so that you can't move quantity objects around. Not allowing scripts to be placed on quantity objects usually works out best for everything in the end. You should probably update the uberweight script so that it can't be cast on quantity objects.

If the merchant doesn't sell the item, an error is returned, and the function quits out. The next step is to make sure the character can pay for the item, so the function calls the HasEnoughCurrency function to figure this out, using the item's "value" attribute as the amount of money he needs to pay.

The final actions include transferring the money from the character to the merchant, spawning the new item into the player's inventory, and then telling everyone that the character made a purchase.

Merchant Character

The last thing I need to do is create an actual merchant character, and his inventory script. Here's the merchant:

```
[ID]                    300
[NAME]                  Magician Keeper
[DESCRIPTION]           A tall fellow dressed in ornate robes.
[DATABANK]
[/DATABANK]
[COMMANDS]
[/COMMANDS]
[LOGICS]
bettertonmagicianshop
[/LOGICS]
```

This can be found in /data/templates/characters/storekeepers.data. The magician merchant has one logic module, betterronmagicshop. Here's the logic module (which can be found in /data/logics/characters/bettertonstores.py):

```
class bettertonmagicianshop( data.logics.characters.currency.merchant ):
    def ScriptInit( self ):
        self.iteminventory = [ 54, 55 ]
```

This simply inherits from the merchant and initializes the merchant script with two items, 54 and 55 (which are a scroll of uberweight and a healing potion, but that's not important).

Now you're *almost* ready to test it out. There are just two more things you need to take care of: the commands to list and buy things.

Listing and Buying

In order for your characters to be able to list and buy items, they must have commands to tell the game to list and buy items.

I'm sure you won't be surprised that these classes are named list and buy. I've put the commands in the /data/commands/usercommands.py script file.

Here's the list command:

```
class list( PythonCommand.Command ):
    name = "list"
    usage = "\"list <merchant>\""
    description = "Gets a list of the merchant's wares"

    def Run( self, args ):
        if not args: raise PythonCommand.UsageError

        me = BetterMUD.character( self.me )
        r = BetterMUD.room( me.Room() )
        m = BetterMUD.character( FindTarget( r.SeekCharacter,
            r.IsValidCharacter, r.CurrentCharacter, args ) )
        m.DoAction( "do", 0, 0, me.ID(), 0, "list" )
```

It finds a character matching the name of the merchant you passed in, and then sends that character a list action event. You should note that if a character tries listing someone who isn't a merchant, he'll kindly ignore the character (since he doesn't have a module that responds to list events).

If a player want to see the magicians list, go into his room and type /list magician. He'll spit out something that looks like this:

```
/list magician
---------------------------------------------------------------
Item                            | Cost
---------------------------------------------------------------
Scroll of Uberweight            | 100
Small Healing Potion            | 10
---------------------------------------------------------------
```

Buying items is a little more complex, because a player needs to find a merchant to buy from, and tell him what kind of item he wants to buy as well.

Here's the command:

```
class buy( PythonCommand.Command ):
    name = "buy"
    usage = "\"buy <merchant> <item>\""
    description = "buys an item from a merchant"

    def Run( self, args ):
        if not args: raise PythonCommand.UsageError
        parms = args.split( None, 1 )
        if len( parms ) < 2: raise PythonCommand.UsageError

        me = BetterMUD.character( self.me )
        r = BetterMUD.room( me.Room() )
        m = BetterMUD.character( FindTarget( r.SeekCharacter,
            r.IsValidCharacter, r.CurrentCharacter, parms[0] ) )
        m.DoAction( "do", 0, 0, me.ID(), 0, "buy " + parms[1] )
```

The first step is to split up the arguments so that the merchant's name is within `parms[0]`, and the item a player wants to purchase is in `parms[1]`.

Then the code finds the merchant and it sends it a buy event with the name of the item added on to the end of the data string.

A player can now use the buy command in the game:

```
/buy magician scroll
You give 100 Copper Coins to Magician
Keeper.
Mithrandir buys Scroll of Uberweight.
```

And now you have a functioning currency system.

> **NOTE**
>
> I didn't implement item buy-backs, but it's a simple task to accomplish if you need it. Using the current merchant system, it would be best if you just destroyed items that were sold, but this can lead to problems if you modify the items in any significant way. Imagine that a player gets a really cool magical effect permanently added to his favorite sword, and then accidentally sells it to the merchant. Oops. Not only would the merchant give a player the normal price, but he'd destroy it as well. In this kind of situation, your best bet is to add a `can't be sold` flag to items that are magically altered.

Cry Havoc and Let Slip the Dogs of War

Can you believe that you've gone through almost eight full chapters about a MUD without having gone over combat yet? There's a reason for this, of course. The SimpleMUD was a really simple *hack and slash* MUD. You run around, slaughtering things, pick up loot, and then kill some more. This was entertaining a few decades ago, but it gets boring after a while. Some major commercial games still use this same old tired format *cough*Diablo*cough*, and there are lots of people who still love playing those kinds of games.

I want more from games than just hacking-and-slashing my way though thousands of orcs and goblins. In the last MUD I played, a full 80% of the people on the MUD actually had programs that would *play the game for them.* It started out simply with players creating simple programs to log in and run around killing monsters for an hour or so while they were away, so that they could gain an edge over anyone else who was playing.

Then people started making these programs more complex and had them executing overnight. Then people made programs to group together with other programs, and wander around, communicating with each other. After a few months, we had characters that were on top of the game, but no one actually ever played them! How ridiculous!

The problem was that it was a typical hack-and-slash MUD. Basically all you could do was run around, kill things, and encounter the occasional quirk here and there. Combat is an essential part of any game like this, but you need to think about what *else* the game should do. That's why I'm not going to spend a heck of a lot of time focusing on combat; it shouldn't be the only thing people do in your game.

Of course, without *some* form of combat, you basically have a game in which players run around, pick up items, and talk to people, which isn't all that interesting.

The combat system I'm implementing as a demonstration is simple. A player can use a weapon that has a specified damage range and accuracy, hit people who have hitpoints, and dodge. This is even simpler than the SimpleMUD's system, but that's not really a big problem because this system is going to be completely flexible and upgradeable.

Combat Data

The first thing I need to do is figure out what kind of data attributes my characters need to participate in combat.

I'll need some kind of an experience attribute to track the progress of characters as they go around killing things. I'll call this experience. I'll also need to know how much experience the character is worth when it dies, so that I can reward the player who killed him. This will be called giveexperience.

Obviously I need some hitpoints, so that's what I'm adding next—the hitpoints attribute. I'll also need a maximum number of hitpoints, covered by maxhitpoints.

The final requirement is a weapon, but you've already seen how I accomplished this, when I showed you how to arm weapons. The weapon attributes are weapon and defaultweapon.

Combat Module

The combat module is easily the most complex logic module I've implemented so far. It's over 150 lines, and that's just for a simple combat module! There are so many things to keep track of.

Module Data

The actual combat module tracks the data of its own, which is temporary data that you won't need to track. There are three attributes within the module, all initialized when the module is created:

```python
class combat( data.logics.logic.logic ):
    def ScriptInit( self ):
        self.attackedlist = []
        self.target = 0
        self.attacktime = 5000
```

The `attackedlist` is simply a Python list of all characters who are currently attacking you (in ID form). This is needed so that you can dole out experience when you die a horrible death. It will happen, trust me. Agony coming up!

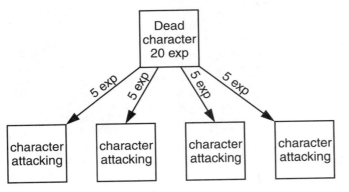

Figure 18.2

The BetterMUD combat module distributes experience equally to all attackers.

The target variable keeps track of the person you are currently attacking; this simple module only supports attacking a single person at a time.

The final attribute is the attacktime attribute, which keeps track of the time it takes to perform one attack round. I've got it hardwired at 5 seconds.

Events

There are a number of events that are related to combat in the game:

- query canattack—asks if a player can be attacked.
- query getaccuracydelta—asks for special accuracy information.
- do attack—a player is performing an attack round.
- do initattack—a player is beginning to attack another player.
- do attacked—a player was attacked by another player.
- do brokeattack—a player stopped attacking another player.
- do breakattack—a player stopped attacking a player's target.
- leaveroom—a player left another player's room (there might be a break in combat.
- do killed—a player killed another player.
- do deathtransport—tells an entity to transport a player somewhere when a player dies.

In addition to these events, there are attributes that you should be concerned with when they are modified:

- modifyattribute maxhitpoints—a player's max hitpoints have changed.
- modifyattribute hitpoints— a player's hitpoints have changed.
- modifyattribute experience— a player's experience has changed.

The basic process goes like this. When a player starts attacking another player, he performs an initattack action. This sets up a timer that causes an attack event to occur immediately. At the same time, a player's target is given an attacked event, telling him that a player started attacking him.

When the attack event occurs, it automatically inserts another attack event to execute in another 5 seconds, and then performs the actual combat logic, which calls the modifyattribute hitpoints event of the target when a player successfully hits it.

> **NOTE**
>
> If you feel ambitious, you can create a multi-attack module that would keep track of groups of people a player is attacking. This would be particularly useful for magic spells that cause hail or fireballs to rain down on everyone in the room.

> **NOTE**
>
> An even better method would be to store the attack time value as an attribute in the character, so that a player can get magic spells and other effects that can make you attack more slowly or faster.

When a player dies, this event is detected by the `modifyattributes hitpoints` event, which performs the death logic. When a player dies, the game sends a `killed` event to all players who were attacking him, so that they know the player died.

This system is an *automatic combat* system. Once a player initializes an attack, he continues attacking until his opponent dies. This is very easy to do using timer event actions. Because of this, however, a player needs a way to stop attacking another player once his opponent dies. This is handled by *breaking combat*, which is handled by the two events `breakattack` and `brokeattack`. The first of these events is triggered when the game wants a character to stop attacking, and the second event is triggered when a character stops attacking another character.

Table 18.6 lists the parameters for the actions.

> **NOTE**
>
> Of the combat events listed in Table 18.6, the most useful event that can be used with the timer system is the `initattack`. If you want, you can make guard logics who demand that you leave the room, and if you don't, they initialize an attack on you in a few seconds or so. Breaking attacks can be useful as timed events as well. The tea-house battle scene from *Matrix: Reloaded* comes to mind—a mentor may stop attacking you after you have proven your worthiness by surviving for a minute or so.

Table 18.6   Parameters for Combat Events

Event	arg1	arg2	arg3	arg4	stringdata
canattack	attacker	target	-	-	-
getaccuracydelta	attacker	target	-	-	-
attack	entitytype*	id*	attacker	-	-
initattack	entitytype*	id*	target	-	-
attacked	entitytype*	id*	attacker	-	-
brokeattack	entitytype*	id*	attacker	-	-
breakattack	entitytype*	id*	-	-	-
killed	entitytype*	id*	victim	-	-
deathtransport	dead player	-	-	-	-

*These are optional parameters that route the event to an entity when timers are used. See Chapter 14 for more information.

Most of those actions can be routed through the timer system, but I don't really have a reason for doing that at this time.

The `getaccuracydelta` query is a special kind of query that asks players being attacked if they have any special accuracy values when being attacked by a certain character. For example, you could have special vampire hunter characters who would get an accuracy bonus when fighting vampires.

May I Attack You, Kind Sir?

The right to attack people isn't a right implicitly granted by BetterMUD's physical engine. As stated previously, the physical engine has no involvement with attacks, nor should it. Attacking is a logical operation in the BetterMUD, and thus you need to ask permission of a character before attacking. By default, characters say, "No," because they don't have any logic modules that say "Yes."

Whenever a character with the combat module is queried about combat, this is the code that is executed:

```
if action == "query" and data == "canattack":
    return 1
```

In this simple module, it is assumed that anyone with the combat module can be attacked. You might think of way to make it more flexible in the future, such as not allowing certain people to attack other people, or whatever you brainstorm.

Experience

Whenever you kill a character and that character gives you experience, the character sends you an event telling you that your experience changed:

```
if action == "modifyattribute" and data == "experience":
    me.DoAction( "announce", 0, 0, 0, 0, "<#00FFFF>You gain " + str( arg4 ) +
                " experience!" )
    return
```

As usual, `me` has already been initialized as a character accessor pointing to yourself.

This simply notifies your character that you've gained some experience. Remember that when you get attribute modification events, `arg3` is the new value of the attribute, and `arg4` is the delta from the old value, so it tells you how much you gained. (`arg4` is optional, but the combat module supports it.)

Modifying Max Hitpoints

The combat module is notified whenever a player's maximum hitpoints change, so that it can ensure that the player never ends up with more hitpoints than his maximum. It's a simple piece of code:

```
if action == "modifyattribute" and data == "maxhitpoints":
    if me.GetAttribute( "hitpoints" ) > me.GetAttribute( "maxhitpoints" ):
```

```
            me.SetAttribute( "hitpoints", me.GetAttribute( "maxhitpoints" ) )
    return
```

Note that I use SetAttribute to directly reset the hitpoints on the character, rather than notifying the Mud's physical engine. This is a matter of personal preference. Telling the physical engine tells everyone that the hitpoints have changed, but that kind of behavior is usually reserved for situations in which a player is being damaged or healed. In this case the player is being neither healed nor damaged, and his physical attributes are changing. If it bothers you, you can change this so that the game tells all the other modules that a player's hitpoints have changed.

Under Fire

Whenever a player is attacked, or a player stops attacking another player, the game announces those events. The messages are relatively easy to handle. The combat module must add characters to its attacked-list when it is attacked, and remove them when they stop attacking.

Here's the attacked event:

```
if action == "do" and data == "attacked":
    try:
        self.attackedlist.index( arg3 )
    except:
        self.attackedlist.append( arg3 )
    return
```

The Python list.index function searches a list for anything matching the argument. In this case I try finding arg3, which is the ID of the character trying to attack the other character. The function returns the index of that item, but I'm not really interested in the index of the item, since it probably doesn't exist in the list anyway. Instead, I am actually counting on it to throw an exception if a match doesn't exist. In the exception block, I add the ID to the list. This just makes sure that you can't put an ID into the list more than once by accident.

Likewise, I need to remove the ID when the character breaks attacking:

```
if action == "do" and data == "brokeattack":
    try:
        self.attackedlist.remove( arg3 )
    except:
        pass
    return
```

This catches any errors and ignores them. remove throws if arg3 isn't in the list.

En Garde!

Whenever you initiate an attack, whether triggered by a command or by some other logic module, the combat module receives an initattack event. This must accomplish several actions, such as adding an attack timer, setting a target, and maybe clearing an old target (if a character was already attacking another character). Here's the code:

```
if action == "do" and data == "initattack":
    if arg3 == self.me: return
    # clear the old target if already attacking someone else
    if self.target != 0:
        t = BetterMUD.character( self.target )
        t.DoAction( "do", 0, 0, self.me, 0, "brokeattack" )
    else:
        self.mud.AddActionRelative( 0, "do", 0, self.me, 0, 0, "attack" )

    # set the new target and tell him he's been attacked
    self.target = arg3
    t = BetterMUD.character( arg3 )
    t.DoAction( "do", 0, 0, self.me, 0, "attacked" )
    self.mud.AddActionAbsolute( 0, "vision", me.Room(), 0, 0, 0, me.Name() +
                                " begins attacking " + t.Name() + "!!" )
    return
```

First you must check to ensure a character isn't attacking himself (no self-hatred in this game). So if a character is trying to attack himself, the function simply returns, and does nothing.

If the module is already attacking another player, you need to break the attack. If a player is already attacking someone else, that means you should already have an attack event in the timer queue, so you don't need to add one. If a player isn't already attacking, however, you need to add an attack event into the global timer queue.

Once that has been done, you set the target, tell him he's been attacked, and tell everyone in the room that the attack has begun.

To the Barricades

On the other hand, you must break an attack when certain events occur. In fact, breaking an attack happens so often that I decided to make it into a helper function:

```
def Break( self, me ):
    if self.target == 0:
        return
    t = BetterMUD.character( self.target )
    me.KillHook( "do", "attack" )
    self.mud.AddActionAbsolute( 0, "vision", me.Room(), 0, 0, 0, me.Name()
                                + " stops attacking " + t.Name() + "!!" )
    t.DoAction( "do", 0, 0, self.me, 0, "brokeattack" )
    self.target = 0
```

The parameter me is supposed to be an accessor pointing to the character who is breaking combat.

It grabs the target, and then tells the current character to kill its attack command that is sitting in the timer queue. There *should* be an attack command in the timer queue, since a character is in attack mode, and there is always an attack command in the queue when a character is in this mode.

The `attack` command tells the room that the attack has stopped, and then tells the former target that the attack has stopped, and finally clears the attacker's target value.

You often need to break combat, for example, when the `breakcombat` event occurs:

```
if action == "do" and data == "breakattack":
    self.Break( me )
    return
```

Or when an attacker or a target leaves the room:

```
if action == "leaveroom":
    if arg1 == self.target or arg1 == self.me:
        self.Break( me )
    return
```

Or when one player tells another that he's killed them (believe me, attacking corpses doesn't improve the world):

```
if action == "do" and data == "killed":
    self.Break( me )
    return
```

There's another instance that calls the `break` function, but I'll get to that later.

The Whites of Their Eyes

The second most complex section of the combat module is the part that carries out the combat rounds. I'll split this up into chunks so it's easier to understand.

```
if action == "do" and data == "attack":
    target = BetterMUD.character( self.target )
    self.mud.AddActionRelative( self.attacktime, "do", 0, self.me, 0, 0,
                                "attack" )
```

First, the combat module gets the target. Then the module adds another attack round to the global timer. Even if a player kills his target in this round, it's not a big deal, because when he breaks off combat, this action is automatically killed.

The next part gets a weapon:

```
    if me.GetAttribute( "weapon" ) == 0:
        weapon = BetterMUD.itemtemplate( me.GetAttribute( "defaultweapon" ) )
    else:
        weapon = BetterMUD.item( me.GetAttribute( "weapon" ) )
```

This is possibly the coolest part of the code. If a character doesn't have a weapon armed, the character uses the default weapon of his character, which is not an actual item, but rather an ID into the item's template database. I showed you this earlier, when I showed you how to arm weapons.

Basically, if you don't have a weapon, an `itemtemplate` accessor is stored in `weapon`; if you do have a weapon, the `item` accessor pointing to your current weapon in stored in `weapon`. Here's the best part: even though they are two totally different accessors, as long as they have the same function names, it doesn't matter! Look at this part of the code and sigh happily:

```
accuracy = weapon.GetAttribute( "accuracy" )
accuracy += target.DoAction( "query", me.ID(), target.ID(), 0, 0,
                             "getaccuracydelta" )
accuracy += me.DoAction( "query", me.ID(), target.ID(), 0, 0,
                         "getaccuracydelta" )
```

The accuracy is grabbed from the weapon and then modified according to the accuracy deltas returned by the target and the player. This allows the player to have special modules that do +5 accuracy versus certain characters, and so on. The next part checks to see if one character hit another:

```
if accuracy <= random.randint( 0, 99 ):
    self.mud.AddActionAbsolute( 0, "vision", me.Room(), 0, 0, 0,
        me.Name() + " attacks " + target.Name() + " with " +
        weapon.Name() + ", but misses!" )
    return
```

This uses the same 0–99 scale that I showed you in the SimpleMUD. If a character misses, the room is informed of the miss, and then the function returns.

The next task is to calculate the damage done, tell everyone about the hit, and then modify the `hitpoints` attribute:

```
damage = random.randint( weapon.GetAttribute( "mindamage" ),
                         weapon.GetAttribute( "maxdamage" ) )
self.mud.DoAction( "vision", me.Room(), 0, 0, 0, "<#FF0000>" +
                   me.Name() + " hits " + target.Name() + " with " +
                   weapon.Name() + " for " + str( damage ) + " damage!" )
self.mud.DoAction( "modifyattribute", 0, target.ID(),
                   target.GetAttribute( "hitpoints" ) - damage,
                   damage, "hitpoints" )
```

And then the combat round is over! Catch your breath.

Note that the hitpoints aren't actually modified. Instead the function sends an action to the game module telling it that the hitpoints have been modified. This is done so that the game can continue and tell every logic module that the character's hitpoints have been changed.

Et Tu, Brute!

There comes a time when all things must die. In a dangerous digital world such as a MUD, the end occurs often. The combat module is naturally the module that detects the ending of a character's mortal coil, which it does by monitoring changes to a character's `hitpoints` attribute:

```
if action == "modifyattribute" and data == "hitpoints":
    if arg3 <= 0:
        me.DoAction( "do", 0, 0, 0, 0, "died" )
```

If a character's hitpoints ever reach 0 or below, he dies! Kerplunk.

The final thing the combat module must manage is handling when characters die. Again, this is a rather large function, so I'm going to break it up into several sections:

```
if action == "do" and data == "died":
    self.Break( me )
    self.mud.AddActionAbsolute( 0, "vision", me.Room(), 0, 0, 0, me.Name() +
                        " dies!!!" )
```

So now the character is dead, and most likely he was engaged in combat when he died (trying to fight off his slayer), so the game tells the character to break off combat (no ghost fighters allowed). After that, characters in the room are told of the untimely demise.

Then the character's experience is calculated and divided up among his attackers:

```
experience = me.GetAttribute( "giveexperience" )
if len( self.attackedlist ) > 0:
    experience = experience / len( self.attackedlist )
```

This grabs a character's giveexperience attribute, and divides it by the number of attackers. You should note that it's perfectly acceptable to have no attackers and still die (from a trap, for example), and the code makes sure the length of the attack list is more than 0 before it performs division.

Now you need to go through the character's attack list, tell everyone he died, and then give them a share of his experience:

```
for x in self.attackedlist[:]:
    c = BetterMUD.character( x )
    c.DoAction( "do", 0, 0, self.me, 0, "killed" )
    self.mud.DoAction( "modifyattribute", 0, x,
                    c.GetAttribute( "experience" ) + experience,
                    experience, "experience" )
```

This uses a standard Python for-loop, with a twist. The [:] notation at the end of self.attackedlist makes a copy of self.attackedlist. This is important, because as you go through the list, telling everyone that the character died, they remove themselves from the list, and you can't iterate through Python lists that change while you're iterating through them.

The next step is to make sure the attack list is clear, and then drop all of the character's items:

```
self.attackedlist = []
me.BeginItem()
```

NOTE

The combat module can only detect changes in hitpoints if you send modifyattribute messages to the game itself. Sending those messages directly to characters isn't a good idea because they don't actually implement the attribute modification. This is also why directly modifying the hitpoints is a bad idea; other modules that might need to know about changes in hitpoints might not be told.

```
while me.IsValidItem():
    self.mud.DoAction( "dropitem", me.ID(), me.CurrentItem(), 0, 0, "" )
    me.NextItem()
```

Any items that refuse to be dropped stay on the character. This is done because it is assumed that items that refuse to be dropped are probably cursed, and should stick to a character until the curse is removed. Since this is in a script, you can easily change it so that it calls the forcedropitem action instead, if you don't want this functionality.

The section of code tries to figure out how to kill a character, based on whether the character is a player or not:

> **NOTE**
>
> As I mentioned in Chapter 15, it is important to force items into the room when a character is destroyed. If they aren't forced, the game thinks that the items are still on the non-existent character, and you'll have a bunch of items that are just floating around in your memory, not able to be used.

```
if not me.IsPlayer():
    self.mud.AddActionAbsolute( 0, "destroycharacter", self.me, 0, 0, 0,
                    "" )
```

If the character isn't a player, the function just destroys him. This means that any items that weren't dropped previously are now forced into the room.

The final part of the code is executed when a player dies; his hitpoints are set to 70% of the maximum, and then the game tries to figure out where to transport him:

```
else:
    me.SetAttribute( "hitpoints", (me.GetAttribute( "maxhitpoints" )
                    / 10) * 7 )

    r = BetterMUD.room( me.Room() )
    if r.DoAction( "do", me.ID(), 0, 0, 0, "deathtransport" ):
        return
    r = BetterMUD.region( me.Region() )
    if r.DoAction( "do", me.ID(), 0, 0, 0, "deathtransport" ):
        return
    if me.DoAction( "do", me.ID(), 0, 0, 0, "deathtransport" ):
        return
    self.mud.DoAction( "forcetransport", me.ID(), 1, 0, 0, "" )
return
```

The respawn system is hierarchical. Whenever a character dies, he is transported somewhere, but the ethereal destination varies depending on where the character is. The room, region, and player are all asked to perform a death transport event. If they don't perform any transporting, 0 is returned, and the function goes on to the next entity. When the deathtransport action is invoked, it should return non-zero to signify that it has accomplished the transportation.

If none of the three—the room, region, and player— transport the player, the function finally gives up and transports the player to room 1 as illustrated in Figure 18.3.

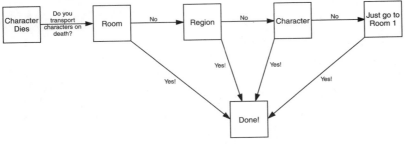

Figure 18.3

The game uses this process to figure out how a player should die.

This kind of a system is useful on a few levels. If you ever implement some kind of honor/reputation system, you can have good players respawn in a pleasant area, or bad players respawn in a dismal area. It's also helpful to have regions respawn players in a local area, so that a player doesn't have to wander around the entire game trying to get back to where he was. Or even more elaborate, you can have a room that serves as an altar to some obscure death-cult, and if a player dies in that room, the game sends you to a special area of the game. The point is that with this scripting system, you can do almost anything you want.

Add-On Modules for the Combat of Nonplayer Characters

Once you have a combat module, you can give it to anyone who you want to be able to attack or be attacked, but that's not quite good enough. This module can be given to *anyone* who will perform combat, but it doesn't actually make anyone attack anyone else. It doesn't send any `initattack` or `breakattack` messages on its own. It just responds to them. To make NPCs in the game attack, you need to give them additional modules that react to certain events.

For example, I could create an `evil` combat AI module, which would attack people the moment it saw them, and wouldn't break until either a character left or died. The `evilmonster` logic module can also be found in /data/logics/characters/combat.py.

The first thing the module must do is attack anyone who enters the room:

```
if action == "enterroom":
    if arg1 != self.me:
        self.mud.AddActionAbsolute( 0, "do", 0, me.ID(), arg1, 0,
                                    "initattack" )

    return
```

Since characters are notified when they themselves enter the room, you need to make sure that the character doesn't start attacking himself. As long as he's not attacking himself, he can start an attack initialization immediately.

Then you must ensure that once the enemy has dispatched his prey, he begins attacking someone else in the room (in case there are other people). This is triggered whenever the enemy receives a "killed" event, telling him that he just killed someone:

```
if action == "do" and data == "killed":
    r = BetterMUD.room( me.Room() )
    r.BeginCharacter()
    while r.IsValidCharacter():
        if r.CurrentCharacter() != arg3:
            self.mud.AddActionAbsolute( 0, "do", 0, me.ID(),
                r.CurrentCharacter(), 0, "initattack" )
            return
        r.NextCharacter()
    return
```

This simply goes through every character in the room and finds a new victim to attack. There is just one thing to watch for, however; this code is called before the old victim has been removed from the room, so you need to make sure you don't try to re-attack him. This is done in the line in bold; arg3 holds the ID of the character who just died.

Of course, the great thing about these kinds of scripts is that you can make different AIs. I've included another AI script called "defender" in the same file, but the AI shown here attacks only when attacked and breaks off when you break off combat.

Once More into the Breach

The final topic dealing with combat involves the attack commands, which allow a character to attack someone else. These two commands can be found in /data/commands/ usercommands.py. The first one handles attacking:

```
class attack( PythonCommand.Command ):
    name = "attack"
    usage = "\"attack <character>\""
    description = "initiates attack mode on a character"

    def Run( self, args ):
        if not args: raise PythonCommand.UsageError
        me = BetterMUD.character( self.me )
        r = BetterMUD.room( me.Room() )
        t = FindTarget( r.SeekCharacter, r.IsValidCharacter,
                        r.CurrentCharacter, args )
        target = BetterMUD.character( t )
        if not target.DoAction( "query", me.ID(), 0, 0, 0, "canattack" ):
            return

        me.DoAction( "do", 0, 0, t, 0, "initattack" )
```

> **NOTE**
>
> The `canattack` query assumes that there's some module attached to the character in question that tells the character why he cannot be attacked. This is useful for many situations. For example, if a player tries to attack a demon god in your game, the god smites him immediately and says to him, "How dare you attack me?!" Or you could have a moral system in place that prevents a character from striking down elderly women. The point is that you can do anything with these script modules.

The code is similar to what you've seen before. The function tries to find a character to attack using the `FindTarget` function, and then the command asks the character if he can be attacked. If not, the function just returns. If the character can attack, the command sends an `initattack` event to the character.

Breaking attacks is even easier than attacking:

```
class breakattack( PythonCommand.Command ):
    name = "breakattack"
    usage = "\"breakattack\""
    description = "Stops attacking your target"

    def Run( self, args ):
        me = BetterMUD.character( self.me )
        me.DoAction( "do", 0, 0, 0, 0, "breakattack" )
```

All you do is send a `breakattack` event to yourself. That's it!

Summary

That's as much as I want to show you about the BetterMUD. I hope that you've gotten a good look at how the whole system is put together, so that you can see how a *dynamic data/ dynamic logic* MUD works.

I hope that now you have a clear sense of the power available to you with this system. I don't want you to go away thinking that the BetterMUD is a complete MUD. It's far from being a complete MUD, but the basic framework is there for you to play around with.

Clearly the most powerful part of the MUD is its flexibility. By abstracting the controls of the logical away from the physical, you're essentially allowing yourself to change the game whenever you want.

I tried not to restrict you to any one paradigm of game, but that's difficult. Obviously, I set most of my items and characters into a pseudo-medieval hack-and-slash style game, but you don't have to accept that setting.

Heck, if you really want to, you can just use the BetterMUD core as a fancy chat program, but that would be like driving a Lamborghini 20 mph to go to the grocery store on Sundays.

I would again like to extend an invitation to you to come and play on my BetterMUD server. It is running on dune.net, port 5110. I can't guarantee that I'll always be there, but when you catch me, if you have any questions, I'll be glad to answer them. I plan on adding tons of scripts and making it a large community, and I'll have scripts available for you to download on my website. Check out http://www.ronpenton.net/MUDBook/ for downloads, add-ons, code updates, and so forth.

I regret that I simply didn't have the time to make a full featured datafile editor for the BetterMUD, but I'll work on one and post it to the website if you're interested.

I want you to think of what I've shown you as a guideline. You should now know enough about network programming, threading, and general MUD design to tackle your own project from scratch. Personally, after the experience I had writing the BetterMUD, I would recommend writing a MUD entirely from scratch in Python. Python has so many built-in libraries that it makes everything incredibly easy to code, and it's not as if you're going to be sucking up too much processor power, since MUDs don't really need that much processing. Good luck, I hope to see you on my server!

Conclusion

"**P**arting is such sweet sorrow," as they say. You have reached the conclusion of the book, and I hope it has been a good experience for you. Throughout the book, I focused on MUD design and had little chance to discuss ideas about what you should put in your games.

I think that was a sound approach, however. As I keep saying, MUDs are such a broad genre of games, that if I tried pushing a single approach, mobs would throng at my door with torches and pitchforks.

The problem is that there are so many different ways to make MUDs. I've seen MUDs with no combat at all, in which players merely run around and dynamically create objects and rooms. I've seen MUDs with nothing but combat. I've even seen MUDs that the inhabitants swear aren't MUDs, even though they have monsters and items; in these, guys stand around and chat all day as if they're in a chat room.

Picking Features

There's really no solid definition of features that a MUD must have, but I've tried to go over the most common features. For example, a room-based system is almost always included in MUDs. Items and characters are also main staples. Beyond that, however, things get a bit hazy.

Feudalism or Capitalism

What kind of economy are you going to have? Both the SimpleMUD and the merchant module of the BetterMUD have *open economies*. Items and money are created on demand, and destroyed as well. This is clearly not how the real world works, but that's okay; you're creating a virtual world! The problem with open economies is that they tend to get unmanageable after a while. Think about this for a moment.

Open Economies

Enemy characters are spawned out of nowhere, appearing by "magic" at certain intervals producing an essentially unlimited supply of people. If every one of these characters is killed, you have a major problem on your hands, because they drop things that are worth money. Eventually the economy of your realm inflates, and there is so much money lying around that new players logging in are instant millionaires. Think I'm kidding? In my copy of the SimpleMUD, I had 10 millionaires after one month. Granted, I didn't actually spend a lot of time balancing the game more evenly, but balancing only goes so far. Eventually the fact that there is an infinite supply of wealth catches up with you.

To counter such a situation, you could implement a system of *sinks* that suck the money out of the game without returning anything. One very common way to implement this is to use *toll roads*. Essentially, you can make your players pay to move around the game. Of course, if you make too many toll roads with excessive fees, your players are likely to revolt against you. But at least toll roads are a start in the right monetary direction.

A proven way of putting sinks into your game is to use the concept of *durability*. In the real world, things are designed to break. Anything you buy is probably designed to stop working after a certain period of time, to make sure you buy a new one. While built in obsolescence sounds evil, it's necessary in a MUD. It ensures that items disappear eventually, and that people cannot accumulate massive amounts of wealth, because they'll have to keep buying replacements.

Another popular option is a *cleanup*. Lots of MUDs have a specific time every day when the MUD goes through every room, and deletes every ordinary item that is lying on the floor (as opposed to special magical or rare items). Although this is one solution to the problem, it's not very elegant. Items shouldn't disappear randomly. What if a player puts something down for a moment, runs off to kill an ogre, and comes back an hour later to find the item has disappeared? That's probably going to anger your players, so it's not a great idea.

An absolutely great idea for a sink would be *charging rent*. Your characters are going to accumulate wealth, and they need to stash it somewhere, so you could have an entire area of a town filled with apartments. The characters can buy keys and be charged by the week for storing stuff. If you're particularly evil, you can write an *eviction script*, one that automatically throws the renter's items on the sidewalk when he doesn't pay the rent.

Closed Economies

On the other hand, you could opt for a *closed economy* that would work like this: when the game starts, there are only a certain number of objects and wealth in the game, and there can never be more. This takes a lot of careful management, and some fudging here and there. I almost never see this kind of a system implemented in a MUD because you eventually run out of items and cash to go around. The entry of new characters into the game does not alter the number of items in the MUD. In this situation, the early players usually gain a stranglehold on all the wealth, and newer players get nothing, because the higher-ups have hoarded it all.

I wouldn't recommend going for a closed system unless you're a "reality" freak, and the very thought of spawning items and wealth out of absolutely nowhere gives you nightmares.

Combat

It is difficult to write about combat in a general sense, simply because combat is different in every kind of MUD out there. Medieval MUDs all seem to have coalesced into similar systems, usually inheriting many features from *Dungeons and Dragons* rules, but those systems only go so far. Honestly the whole "arm weapon and attack" system can get boring quickly, and doesn't work particularly well with anything that is *modern*. For example, games in which you can shoot people with guns rarely work out well, because guns almost always cause immediately incapacitating wounds; and that's just not fun.

I particularly appreciate how Frank Herbert's *Dune* book solved this problem. It takes place tens of thousands of years in the future, and weapons and defense technology have become so advanced that using laser weapons on a shield would cause an intense nuclear fusion reaction, killing everyone involved in the combat. Because of this, everyone in the future ends up fighting with knives versus shields, putting the "art" and the "skill" back into combat. If you're making a combat-oriented MUD, you should definitely think about these kinds of things.

Another important topic is player versus player combat, also known as PvP. This is an intensely contested feature of MUDs. It's one thing to be killed by a computer enemy—you just suck in your chest, accept your loss, and see if you can get your stuff back. But it's completely different when another player kills you. The fact that another human being controlled the character that killed you completely changes the dynamics of the attack. Instead of a numbskull computer character whose only job is to try to kill you, some other player decided that he hated your guts enough to attack you! The nerve!

Things such as PvP inevitably lead to tensions and fierce competition. This can either be really good or really bad. I've seen it turn out both ways. It's good because some people take this as simply another form of sport, and they want to play your game even more. It's bad because there are always people who take it too far. Verbal drubbings and swearing are common when people get too caught up in the game, and when this happens over global chatter, it might seriously annoy other players.

I'll leave the PvP question in your hands. There really is no optimal solution to the problem. There are a number of things you may want to try, however. For example, it's often a great idea to implement levels of penalties. It's just not fair to have a level 70 swordmaster walk into town and slaughter every level 5 character, now is it? One solution is to reward such an action with only 1 or 2 experience points or none at all. Of course, this doesn't solve the issue of psychotic players who delight in killing newbies for absolutely no reason.

> **NOTE**
> Running a **MUD** is an interesting sociological experiment, and it can teach you a good deal about human psychology.

To control psychotic behavior, I suggest making it impossible for characters to attack other characters whose experience range is outside the range of the attacker's experience by a specified amount—maybe 5 levels in each direction. That way, level 70 people can only attack people in the range 65–75. It all depends on how you implement your ranking system. Again, it's your MUD, and you should do what you want.

Administration

Administering your MUD takes a good deal of effort. MUDs don't just run themselves; you have to take care of lots of details.

Hosting

First you need to figure out where you want to run your MUD. You can probably run a MUD over a broadband Internet connection on your home computer, but I really wouldn't recommend that, for many reasons.

First and foremost, your home computer is probably not a server. You probably program on it and play games and music. Therefore, it's not a dedicated environment for a game server. That's acceptable if you're just running a small MUD at your leisure, but for anything more serious, you should look into a professional server solution.

I've only recently started dabbling in Linux, and I'm impressed with what I see. If you know anything about Linux, it shouldn't be difficult for you to find someone who will sell you access to a *Linux shell* that you can run your MUD on. In fact, the site that I use, http://dune.net offers this very service, and for reasonable prices as well. There are many other hosting companies as well, in case http://dune.net doesn't fit your needs, or you don't feel like messing around in Linux.

> ### CAUTION
>
> You should be aware that most broadband connections explicitly disallow the running of servers on your connection. This is mainly due to the way they calculate bandwidth usage, and they assume you'll be downloading far more content than you upload, but a server changes all of this. If you *do* want to run a MUD on your home connection, look at your *end user license agreement* to make sure it's okay first. Some ISPs even cancel your account if you run servers on it.

Here are some sites you may want to check out:

- http://www.silverden.com/   (Linux)
- http://www.genesismuds.com/   (Linux)
- http://dune.net/   (Linux)
- http://www.mudhost.com/   (Linux)
- http://www.gryphonmud.com/   (Linux)
- http://www.mudshell.com/   (Linux)
- http://www.ancientrealms.org/   (Linux or Windows NT available)
- http://www.wolfpaw.net/   (Linux)

As you can see, almost all of the sites offer just Linux shells. This should tell you how important Linux is as a server platform for MUDs. If you're not familiar with Linux at all, I urge you to learn about it. I was hesitant at first, but it didn't take me long to figure out what I was doing. What's the best thing about Linux? It comes with *GCC*, a full (almost standard) C++ compiler, completely for free. How can you beat that?

Another great alternative is running a MUD on a university server, provided you have permission to do so. Considering that most of the original MUDs were created in universities across the world, this is sort of a tradition, and you shouldn't have much trouble gaining permission to run one.

Management

Will you be a benevolent dictator? Will you run a democracy, or will you let your realm be a complete anarchy? These are some of the questions you need to think about when running a MUD. You are taking on the role of a god; you created the realm, you can do anything you want in it, and the players are at your mercy.

But how much control should you exert? Sometimes it's a good idea to impose a legal system such as this: no killing when people are away from the keyboard, or no stealing. These kinds of things can be enforced by the game, but at some point, actual management needs to come into play.

You're going to need people to manually enforce the rules, whether it be yourself, or people you can trust. This is a very difficult thing to manage though. I'm sure you've heard the adage, *power corrupts*. Who can resist the temptation of playing around with power? If all goes well, the people you recruit to have extra police powers will behave, and your realm will live in peace. If they don't, your realm will live in pieces.

Don't hesitate to be strict on frequent offenders. Generally offenders cause everyone else to have a miserable time, so making an example out of one person usually pleases other players.

Security

Security is another topic that I haven't discussed much. When going over the Socket Library, I showed you how to protect against single connections streaming tons of data to you to prevent being flooded with information.

But that's only one way you can be attacked. The SocketLib's connection manager doesn't handle *denial of service* attacks at all. These are the kinds of attacks that occur when one person connects to your server with dozens or maybe even hundreds of connections, thus eating up your resources and denying connections to other people trying to log on. In its current form, the SocketLib can't detect these attacks, because it doesn't detect the number of connections that it has from the same IP address. Therefore, you can have 50 connections all from the same person, all slowly flooding you below the individual connection flood rate, but collectively lagging your server to death.

This could be fixed in the connection manager easily enough, by limiting the number of connections per IP address.

On the other hand, you're going to come across an even trickier attack at times—the *distributed denial of service* attack. These attacks are usually caused by dozens or even hundreds of different computers all attacking your server at once. The best way to block this kind of an attack is to simply disconnect connections that sit in the login state for too long. But if people are really intent on attacking your server, they'll just log in anyway. The best defense in that case is to have a corps of administrators that you trust, and make sure that at all times, at least one of them is online to kick off troublemakers.

Of course, you'll encounter problems besides network attacks, and many will be problems of your own design. Your players *will* find flaws in the game that will give them gains that they should not have. I can recall an instance when a certain NPC in a MUD I played on offered high experience points for killing him, but gave the players evil points when they attacked him. If you accumulated too many evil points, town guardsmen would hunt you down, so people tried to avoid being evil.

> **NOTE**
>
> The term *farming* refers to people staying in an area and killing the same monsters over and over again.

Of course, it got to a point at which the characters became more powerful than the guards, and started *farming* that NPC to death, racking up tons of evil points, and tons of experience, without any drawbacks.

So what happens when your players inevitably find your flaws? Do you punish them? If you do, you're sure to receive complaints such as this, "Hey! I wasn't cheating! Your crappy game allowed me to do that!" It's best to punish only cases in which people take excessive advantage of a bug. Chances are, when a bug is discovered, there will be little doubt that it's not supposed to be there. Your players will probably know that they are exploiting a bug, but people are people. Who can resist the temptation of getting a permanent character boost?

If anything, this should help highlight the importance of *testing*. You must test your game before you unleash it on the world, or else you should *expect* people to take advantage of your mistakes.

The Future

This book isn't the be-all and end-all of MUDs. I've only scratched the surface of what you can do, and you should consider a number of things when thinking about the future.

Databases

I mentioned a few times before that the databases for the SimpleMUD and the BetterMUD aren't real databases, but rather simple classes that store objects in system memory. After running a MUD long enough, you'll have enough objects in memory to be a major drain on the system. In most systems, most of these items sit around and are not used by anything for most of the time. So why should you waste resources keeping them around?

Another reason to use a database is that databases are abstractable, and therefore you can keep them on a separate computer and gain a slight processing advantage, especially for very large systems. If you decide to look into databases, both Python and C++ have APIs that you can use with SQL databases, which are the most common kind.

Online Editing

A concept I've always been fond of has been online editing of games. The basic idea is that you'll be able to log into the game, and modify or add new entities to the game through a remote client. The easiest way to implement this is to use simple clients that upload the new datafiles, and then tell the game to reload them.

A slightly more advanced system would allow direct modification of entities while they are in memory, but this can get to be difficult to manage at times, especially if the entity in question is being used within the game. Imagine loading up a sword, and then modifying it in an editor. While you're doing that, the sword can be modified by anything in the game, and its characteristics may have changed once you reinserted the entity.

To solve this, think about making a system of "locks" for your entities. When editing a room, make sure no one can enter it. When editing a player, make sure he can't log on, and so on. Either do that, or do your editing late at night when very few people are playing.

MMORPGs

When you think about how a MUD works, you realize that it's basically just a messaging system. People log on, and perform different kinds of actions; the game engine figures out what data these actions change, and thens tell every client who cares about the action.

Advanced Connection Systems

Typically MUDs never see more than a few dozen people at a time, a hundred or so at most; but there's absolutely no reason why MUD technologies can't be extended infinitely. Theoretically, the BetterMUD on Linux should support up to 1,024 people, but I don't know 1,024 people who are willing to test it at the same time.

The only reason it's limited to 1,024 connections, however, is because the connection manager is limited to the size of one socket set, which is typically (but not always) 1,024 on Linux. It's not a very difficult task to upgrade the networking system to handle more than that, but at that point, you're going to need a new strategy.

Once you need to handle a lot of connections, you'll discover that multithreading is your best friend. The best strategy is to create multiple threads, so that each thread manages a collection of connections.

In fact, the best way you can do this is by separating the game and connection stuff into completely different threads. The network threads would continuously monitor for any network activity and cache the input somewhere for the game thread to get later.

Adapting a MUD to a MMORPG

When you think about a modern MMORPG, you can see that it's basically a MUD with a graphical client attached. The major difference between the two is the way that maps are usually represented. Instead of having one room that contains many people, you'll have a large area composed of many tiles, which you can conceptualize as miniature rooms.

The notification system is going to be a little different, because you'll have to go to every tile that can see where an action is occurring, and tell everyone within that radius about what happened. So instead of telling one room about an event, you'll find yourself searching for everything within a 32 tile radius (or whatever) and telling them that something happened.

At the very bottom core, a MUD/MMORPG is just a system that figures out *what* happens, *where* it happened, and *who* it happened to, while at the same time sending the messages about what happened to all the network connections.

In modern MMORPGs almost all of the fancy graphic stuff is handled by the clients, letting the server take a precious break from the rendering graphics.

Data Transmission

Of course, since you're handling so much more data, and probably have graphical sprites or models representing everyone, you're going to have to send much more data out to clients. Every time a character changes its state (for example changing from walking to resting or running or talking), you should probably send out a state change notification. Of course since rooms in MMORPGS are smaller objects now, characters are going to be moving in and out of them at a much faster rate. Obviously this means that you're going to need a *lot* of bandwidth, which gets quite expensive.

This makes it really important that you send data only to clients that need to be informed. A client in one area that can't see something happening 40 tiles away shouldn't know about it at all, so there's absolutely no reason to inform him.

MMORPGs use another trick for faster data transmission—*binary packed data*. For everything in this book, I used *ASCII* for the data transmission, so that information is sent as text strings. For binary packed data, the only thing you would send as strings would be actual strings; everything else would be sent as its numerical binary representation instead.

For example, sending the number 128 in ASCII mode takes three bytes of data, one for each digit. On the other hand, you should know that a single byte of data can represent numbers from 0–255, so you could easily pack the number into a single byte, thereby reducing the amount of data you sent by 3 times.

Of course, to make things more flexible, you're probably going to want to use 16-bit (2 bytes) or 32-bit (4 bytes) numbers, because 0–255 is a very small range. Using 16-bit numbers, every number larger than 99 saves you at least a byte, and at most 3 bytes (since the largest number that you can send is 65,535, which is 5 characters). The downside is that any number below 10 wastes a byte, since 0–9 only take up 1 byte in ASCII, but 2 bytes when packed into binary as 16-bit integers. Start here

Using 32-bit numbers offers a potentially higher data compression savings, because you can store numbers up to 10 digits in size in just 4 bytes. The downside is the fact that you very rarely need to send 10-digit numbers, and instead will probably be sending numbers much smaller than that far more often. When sending 32-bit integers, you waste 3 bytes when sending numbers 0-9, 2 bytes when sending 10-99, and 1 byte when sending 100–999. It's only when sending numbers 1000–9999 that you break even, and when you use numbers larger than 9999, you get a compression savings.

Another big problem with binary data transmission is the *endianness* of the data. Some machines like to store the byte with the least significant data in the first byte; others store it in the last byte. So the number 128 could be represented in binary form as 0xF0000000 on a *little-endian* machine, and 0x000000F0 on a *big-endian* machine (remember 0xF0 is 128 in hexadecimal).

Ultimately this means that for every piece of binary data that you send, you need to make sure it's in the proper form for your machine. This can end up giving you a lot of extra work to do, but luckily you don't need to make the server do any of that extra work. Instead, you can make your clients do all the data translation and assume that the server only transfers binary data in one particular way. This has the net effect of distributing all of this extra processing among everyone who is connected, and freeing your server from that work.

Distributed Computing

Once you get past a certain number of connections, one computer just isn't going to be able to handle the load, no matter how powerful it is. A very popular way of making an MMORPG or MUD work with thousands of connections is to use *distributed computing*, so that the game runs on multiple computers. The easiest way to do this is to split up your realm into two or three regions, and have each computer control everything within one given region, and switch connections between the different servers when the characters move between the regions.

Pretty much the only thing you have to worry about in this situation is *load balancing*. Your servers can become unbalanced quite easily if one region is more popular than another. There's little point in having three or four distributed servers if everyone is going to be on just one of them.

With good planning, you can solve this kind of a problem. You should make it so that people want to go to all areas of the game, and that one region doesn't have one huge benefit over another.

Some MMORPGs solve this problem by literally forcing you out of an area by teleportation if there are too many people, but your players won't like this. It's unnatural, first of all, and it's annoying as well. Nothing will anger your players more than being sucked out of an area while they're in the middle of doing something.

Another option would be to prevent people from entering a new area if the server is full, but that can also get annoying. In the end it all comes down to good level design.

The best part of a distributed setup is that it meshes into the database design very well, if you have a professional database stored on a specific database server. You could have three machines, two running the game and one storing the database, and the two game machines never worry about synching data up with each other.

Show Me the Money!

You're going to have to decide early on whether you want to charge people to play your MUD. Back in the bad old days of computing, charging for playing a MUD was not only common, but expected.

Nowadays, servers are so cheap that almost all MUDs you can find are free to play, which makes pay-per-play a somewhat obsolete model. If you were to add on a graphical client, I guarantee that people would be more inclined to play, but the bottom line is that people just don't like dishing out money every month for a game.

The good news is that running a MUD is cheap. Both the SimpleMUD and the BetterMUD are costing me about $16 a month to run, which is cheaper than most ISPs cost. If you can't afford that, it's pretty easy to collect donations, or charge a one-time fee for playing the game. If you charge $20 for someone to join the game, and you have 40 people pay it, you've just collected enough money to run your MUD for four years.

You can also fund your adventures by having a donation system, whereby people can donate through Paypal.com, personal check, or whatever. To make people want to donate money, you might consider offering *incentives*, but you must be *very careful* about these.

When people give you money, you might want to give them something special in return. Initially, this seems like a great idea. It's a great way to reward people for supporting your server. But this can lead to major problems if you're not careful.

Say you decide to bestow a special sword on someone who donated a hefty sum and that sword gives that character a nice boost over other players. This will probably raise resentment against him. What happens when someone steals that sword? Does the thief have the right to keep it? If stealing is allowed in the game, the thief will definitely love to keep the sword, and the donator will have lost *real money* in the game, since he essentially paid for the sword. Either way, you're going to have at least one angry player.

What makes things even worse is the fact that stealing the bonus item is almost indistinguishable from theft in real life. The fact that the donator spent real money obtaining the item means that the thief essentially stole real money from the donator. This may even get you into some legal troubles. My recommendation is to stay away from this kind of thing.

What about players who use donations as a way of not playing? Someone can log on, donate lots of money, and get lots of bonus stuff, and completely skip playing on the lower levels of the game. Someone who played for a few weeks to get past those levels is going to be angry that someone else can just come into the realm and pay real money to advance.

Another downside is figuring out what kind of bonuses to give to players when they donate money. If you *do* give them some kind of super weapon, it may not be so super a few weeks later when they've outgrown it. In a virtual world, things are *constantly* changing, and any bonus you give to someone one week may not be worth anything later on. This also has a tendency to anger people.

The bottom line is that you really shouldn't give tangible things to people as bonuses. It would probably be a better idea to give donators special abilities that no one else can have, or give them special ranks, letting everyone in the realm know that they are important.

Real money tends to bring out the worst in people.

Resources

There are tons of resources out there dealing with MUDs. One of the most popular is the website http://www.mudconnector.com, which lists most active MUDs. You can go there and log into anything you want.

There are also books available on the topic.

Designing Virtual Worlds
By Dr. Richard Bartle (ISBN 0-1310-1816-7)

This is a fairly new book about MUDs and their predecessors, written by Richard Bartle, who helped make the original MUD game. It doesn't have any code in it at all and is mainly focused on overall design and gameplay issues, things that you should think about. Bartle gets into a fair amount of player psychology analysis as well—a very interesting topic.

Overall, the book is written with professional developers in mind, people who charge money to play on their servers. This doesn't prevent it from applying to MUDs though.

Developing Online Games
By Jessica Mulligan and Bridgette Patrovsky (ISBN 1-5927-3000-0)

This book is also new, but is less related to MUDs than *Designing Virtual Worlds*. This book is instead focused on the planning and business sides of making massively multiplayer online games. It's an interesting read nonetheless, due to the inclusion of several *post-mortems* of popular MMORPGs, such as *Anarchy Online* and *Dark Age of Camelot*. You can see the mistakes those and other games made even before a single line of code was written. This book doesn't have any code in it either.

Massively Multiplayer Game Development
By Thor Alexander, et al. (ISBN 1-58450-243-6)

This book is published by Charles River Media, and if you know anything about their books, they usually put out collections of short articles in one hard covered book. This is no exception.

The book contains some good chapters. The chapter dealing with calculation of items in a MMOG is especially good. There's also a good chapter about implementing a *sandbox* for your scripting engine, an idea I talked about earlier. The basic idea is to isolate your scripts in a testing area of the game until you know they work. You can test your scripts in what is termed a sandbox without worrying about spreading "sand" over the rest of your game.

I won't go out on a limb and recommend this book to you if you're just a casual game programmer, however. There are a few chapters in this book that don't really have *anything* to do with MMOG game development, which is disappointing for a $60 book.

Game Scripting Mastery
By Alex Varanese (ISBN 1-931841-57-8)

This is a very good book. It's *huge*, and contains *everything* you might ever want to know about putting a scripting engine into your game, or even making your very own scripting engine. I hope you learned from the BetterMUD how important a scripting engine is.

The book covers several languages, such as LUA, TCL, and Python, and covers creating a completely new scripting language and interpreter as well.

Programming Role Playing Games With DirectX
By Jim Adams (ISBN 1-931841-09-8)

This book isn't very closely related to MUDs and MMORPGs, but it's still a great reference. Along with the networking and socket chapters of *MUD Game Programming*, this book should teach you everything you might ever need to know about making a really good game client for your servers.

Linux Game Programming
By Mark Collins (ISBN 0-7615-3255-2)

Linux and MUDs go together like peanut butter and jelly. You might not want to believe it at first, but eventually you'll catch on. Unfortunately, Linux is just so darned hard to get into, because it has a steep learning curve. Luckily, there are a bunch of books out there that take a game programming approach to Linux. This book teaches you all the basics about programming games in Linux, such as using the SDL graphic library, the OpenGL 3D library, and other things.

Programming Linux Games
By John R. Hall (ISBN 1-886411-49-2)

This is another good Linux book, and the best part about it is that it's *free*! No strings attached. You can download it online at many places. At the time of writing this, it is available at http://www.overcode.net/~overcode/writing/plg/, but that may change. If the site doesn't exist, just google Programming Linux Games, and I'm sure you'll pick up a few dozen links.

I picked up a dead-tree version of this book anyway, because I still prefer to read books on paper.

Network Programming for Microsoft Windows
By Anthony Jones and Jim Ohlund (ISBN 0-7356-1579-9)

This book is the Winsock Bible—anything you ever needed to know about Winsock is in this book. The best part about it is that it goes into the more advanced Winsock features that you can't find in the standard Berkeley Sockets API, such as overlapped sockets. For any network programmer, this book is a must-have.

Unix Network Programming
By W. Richard Stevens (ISBN 0-134900-12-X)

If the previous book is the bible on network programming in Windows, this book is the bible of network programming in UNIX. The book goes over the entire Berkeley Sockets API with a fine-toothed comb, and it's virtually a requirement when working with network programming.

Data Structures for Game Programmers
By Ron Penton (ISBN 1-931841-94-2)

I may be a bit biased when recommending this book, but I feel that to understand any of the more advanced topics in game programming, you *absolutely must* have a solid foundation in data structures and algorithms. This book goes over almost all the basic data structures, as well as a bunch of advanced structures and algorithms, and will help you understand *why* using a priority queue for the BetterMUD timer system was a great idea, and why using sets instead of lists makes the BetterMUD more efficient.

Concluding the Conclusion

You've reached the end of the book. I hope you found it interesting and entertaining. If you have any questions at all, feel free to contact me at MUDBook@RonPenton.net, or log into the BetterMUD or the SimpleMUD, which I have running on Dune.net:

- SimpleMUD: telnet://dune.net:5100
- BetterMUD: telnet://dune.net:5110

I can't promise that I'll always be there, of course, but I'll be running the servers as long as I possibly can (at least two years if interest holds up). Don't be scared if my version of the BetterMUD doesn't look like the version of the BetterMUD on the CD; I'll be slowly improving on it and adding scripts for all occasions. I'll always have the script source code for my version available at my website, http://ronpenton.net/MUDBook/. Also, if I *do* change the MUDs from dune.net (if http://dune.net goes out of business or something), I'll be sure to tell you where I've moved them on my website as well.

I look forward to meeting you there!

What's on the CD?

The CD contains all kinds of goodies dealing with MUDs and MUD programming.

Libraries

The three libraries, BasicLib, SocketLib, and ThreadLib, are stored in the directory /Libraries on the CD. Feel free to use the code in them for whatever you want.

The MUDs

The two MUDs—SimpleMUD and BetterMUD—are stored within the /SimpleMUD and /BetterMUD directories on the CD, respectively. You're free to take them and modify them however you wish, and run them on your own.

The Goodies

I've included a bunch of goodies on the CD, including a few popular free Telnet programs, so you can start playing MUDs on your own if you don't already have a Telnet program.

The distributions for the Python programming language, as well as the SWIG wrapper generator program (both used in Chapter 17) are in the /Goodies directory as well.

Appendixes

The appendixes contain all the auxiliary information you might need to know. They are on the CD but not printed in the book.

Appendix A—Setting Up Your Compilers

Setting up the compilers for the code in the book was a difficult task for me, since I had to make sure the code ran on three different compilers at the same time. Because of the complexity of this task, compilation information and instructions are gathered into this appendix instead of being covered in separate chapters.

Appendix B—Socket Error Codes

There are so many things that can go wrong when you're dealing with socket programming, and there are a ton of error codes detailing what went wrong. This appendix lists all the common error codes and what they mean in plain English.

Appendix C—C++ Primer

C++ and STL are requirements for this book, but no one can possibly be required to remember every little quirk and detail about them. Because of this, I've included this simple primer that enables you to refresh your memory on the features you may have forgotten.

Appendix D—Template Primer

This is a bonus appendix from my *Data Structures* book on how to use templates.

Glossary

This is a glossary of all the fancy terms and acronyms used throughout the book.

Let's Get Ready to Rumble

This book focuses mainly on *how* to implement a MUD, but not so much on the various gameplay issues that will confront you. The basic reason behind this is that people don't like to be told how they should make their gameplay work. The great thing about MUDs is that no two MUDs are the same—every single one is customized to the likings of the person running it.

Because of this, I don't really want to tell you what kind of features and issues you need to have in your game. Chances are you already know what you want, and it's probably not what I have in mind.

Don't forget to drop me a line at MUDBook@ronpenton.net if you have any questions about the book. I'll try to respond to your mail as soon as possible.

With this in mind, you can start *MUD Game Programming!* Enjoy!

Index

W-Z

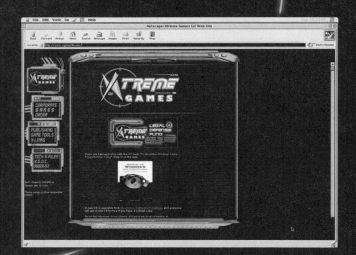

Gamedev.net

The most comprehensive game development resource

- ✦ The latest news in game development
- ✦ The most active forums and chatrooms anywhere, with insights and tips from experienced game developers
- ✦ Links to thousands of additional game development resources
- ✦ Thorough book and product reviews
- ✦ Over 1000 game development articles!
  Game design
  Graphics
  DirectX
  OpenGL
  AI
  Art
  Music
  Physics
  Source Code
  Sound
  Assembly
  And More!

Gamedev.net

License Agreement/Notice of Limited Warranty